# THE WORLD
## STORMRIDER GUIDE
### VOLUME TWO

LOW PRESSURE

# THE WORLD
## STORMRIDER GUIDE
### VOLUME TWO

**First published in 2004 by LOW PRESSURE LTD**

**Production Office**
Unit 11 Efford Farm Business Park, Bude, Cornwall, EX23 8LT

**General Enquiries**
Tel/Fax +33 (0)5 58 77 76 85    enquiries@lowpressure.co.uk

Worldwide Surfspots 2.0 database, YEP©
Compilation of all weather and swell data YEP 2003©
using Visual Passage Planner software©

Creation of all zone maps YEP/Low Pressure Ltd 2003©

Creation of all other maps, graphic arrangement,
pictograms, text and index Low Pressure Ltd 2003©

A catalogue reference for this book can be obtained from
the British Library. ISBN Softback: 0-9539840-2-8

Reproduction and Printing by Hong Kong Graphics and Printing

# THE WORLD
## STORMRIDER GUIDE

# Foreword

When we took the drop on this project to produce *The World Stormrider Guides*, we knew it would be a long paddle. Our co-conspirator, Antony 'YEP' Colas had come up with a concept to map the globe by breaking it into zones, to which we would add the finer points of a continental Stormrider Guide. Seven years and 160 zones later sees us over the crest of the second wave and stroking towards a cultural ride in Volume Three. This book follows in the wake of the first *World Stormrider Guide*, cruising some well-known coastlines, plus some more off the beaten track zones, across the nine established chapters.

The defining difference of *The World Stormrider Guide Volume Two* is the ocean environment text that runs throughout the book. We've always included environmental notes in the Europe and North America continental guides, but to dig up the dirt on the entire world was a daunting task. Volume Two peers through the scum floating on the surface of our Ocean Environment to give you a deeper insight into the pollution, erosion and access issues that might affect your next surfari. Hazards are looked at as well, just to cheer the text up a bit, because there are some truly depressing environmental factoids.

The information is by no means all encompassing, but it should raise your awareness of some of the burning issues that face our oceans. We don't have the answers to many of the problems that are afflicting our line-ups, although it seems that human greed for money is often behind the worst environmental outrages. Pointing the finger at governments, water companies or big business is too simple considering surfers contribute to the destruction of our planet with our chemical cocktail boards and increasingly excessive fuel burning surfaris. Each and every one of us has to carefully consider how we can minimize any adverse impact on our surroundings and ride as lightly as possible through this mortal coil.

We have only listed a few of the surfer environmental activism groups that are out there, campaigning on our behalf. These organisations are a good place to begin looking for answers and where you can become part of the solution. It's not all doom and gloom, because there are plenty of pristine pointbreaks around this wet Earth that remain unridden and unadulterated, cajoling those willing to go the extra mile. As surfers, we are notoriously individualistic, yet we all share one thing in common that is priceless and irreplaceable – the ocean environment.

Keep paddling – Bruce Sutherland

1% of sales of this book will be donated to surfing related environmental organisations.

EDITOR'S NOTE: *I would like to dedicate this volume to the memory of my father, James McDonald Sutherland. His refined bodysurfing skills graced Sydney's beaches for over 60 years where he taught me the importance of the glide through life.*

Tuamotu, French Polynesia

BILL MORRIS

THE 80 ZONES

Conception, Research, Compilation
and Photo Collection Antony 'YEP' Colas

Co-production by Olivier 'YEP' Servaire

Map Origination Julia Ratsimandresy

THE WORLD STORMRIDER GUIDE VOLUME TWO

**Publishing Directors**
Bruce Sutherland   Dan Haylock   Ollie Fitzjones

**Editor** Bruce Sutherland

**Map and Photo Editor**
**Design and Production** Dan Haylock

**Editorial Assistance** Tim Nunn

**Sub-Editor/Proof Reader** Vik Sell

This page – Uluwatu, Bali, Indonesia

Cover – Puerto Escondido PHOTO: SCOTT AICHNER

**Photographic Contributors**
Kirk Lee Aeder  Scott Aichner  Javier Amezaga
Jakue Andikoetxea  Don Balch  Gonzalo Barandiaran
Isabelle Beigbeder  Ricardo Bravo  Dan Burton  Stuart Butler
John Callahan  Gilles Calvet  Patrick Castagnet
Sylvain Cazenave  Francisco Chagas  Christian Corradin
Clemente Coutinho  Mike Cufer  Emmanuel Daubrée
Sean Davey  Philippe Demarsan  Alfredo Escobar
Paul Farraris  Marc Fénies  Javier Fernandez  Luciano Ferrero
Jake Fitzjones  Steve Fitzpatrick  Tony Fleury  Thierry Gibaud
Sean Griffin  Quinn Haber  Warren Hawke  Dan Haylock
William Henry  Phil Holden  Stuart Horstman
Dustin Humphrey  Stéphane Ibarboure  Bryan Jackson
Valery Joncheray  Paul Kennedy  GJ de Konig  Tom Körber
Benjamin Kromayer  Olivier Labat  Alex Laurel
Fred Le Leannec  Phil Le Leannec  John Matthews
Raymond Max  Boots Mcgee  Joe Mcgovern  Tim McKenna
Ross McIntyre  Olivier Michaud  Max Mills  Fabio Minduim
Moonwalker  Bill Morris  Will Newitt  Vangie Palacios
Kristen Pelou  Photo Mobile  David Pu'u  John Respondek
Lee Robertson  Garth Robinson  Steve Ryan  Pedro Salinas
Cory Scott  Olivier Servaire  Roger Sharp  Bruce Sutherland
Wilbur Tilley  Pierre Tostee  Bill Tover  Barry Tuck  Tungsten
Willy Uribe  Alex Williams  Peter Wilson  YEP

Photo contributor Vangie Palacios (www.travelswithjuliana.com) died on May 2nd 2003.
Much loved in the windsurfing community she actively promoted surfing in the Philippines.

**Editorial Contributors**
**EUROPE** 81 Mike Steadman  Stella  82 Tommy Olsen
Erik Jansen  Kristian Breivik  83 Richard/PublicBeach
84 Paul Couderc  85 Costasurf  86 Pedro Almendra
87 Sergio VM  Amadeus  Ziggy  **AFRICA** 88 Hicham El Ouarga
Eric Gamez  89 Sean Griffin  Arthur Moreno  Sylvain
90 Charles Norman  91 Jean-Luc Bourroullec  Artur Nunes
da Silva  Gian Marcio Gey  Richard Norris  92-94 Craig Jarvis
Steve Pike  Tertius Strydom  Garth Robinson  David Malherbe
95 Des Pollock  Garth Robinson  Stuart Butler
**INDIAN OCEAN** 96  Fred Ralaimihoatra  Tony Bafana
Greg Bertish  Jérôme Blanco  97 Rémi Paya  Marc D'Offay
Olivier Bonnefon  98 Shayne McIntyre  Rob Beishuizen
Arthur Moreno  Vincent Stuhlen  Tilbur Kattelbach
99 Haroon Pirzada  Hamid Hamza  Mr Chaundry
100 Simon James  Ian Lyon  Tony Hussein  101 John Callahan
Daniel Ballian  Adam Frost  **EAST ASIA** 102 Mark Flint
Stuart Butler  103 Andy Watson  Stuart Horstman  Mr Zen
104 Paul Edmiston  Philippe Le Leannec  105 Michael Hill
Reddog  Colin Ross  Benny Risanto  106 Sean Murphy
107 Andrew Abel  John Rei  Nick Blanche  108 Vangie Palacios
Todd Mazur  Jacob  109 Quinn Haber  Todd Mazur
Ron & Fraser Kirwan  Sam Bleakley  110 Benoît Rozé
Pascal Lefebvre  SF-J Mercer  Kevin Johns  111 Jack Heckerman
Scott Ellison  112 Mochizuki Noriyuki  Dan Lodge
**AUSTRALIA** 113 Steve Hoson  Sea Surf  114 Glen Duncan

118 Peter Neely  **PACIFIC OCEAN** 119 Warren Hawke
David Robinson  120 Tony & Jude Harbott  Wayne Spence
121 Jérôme Teigné  Joe Entrikin  122 Ivan Sinel  Gavin McGlurg
123 Harley Jones  Dan Thorn  Ray Guin Jr  124 Bryan Jackson
John Harrison  125 Mike Kew  126 Pension Poetana
Jeff Aniort  Antoine Arutahi  127 Woody Howard  Yvon Vivi
Chris O' Gallagher  Henry Morales  128 Max Mills  Victor Ika
130 Ian Haight  **NORTH AMERICA** 131  Mike Kew
132 Lloyd Pollock  133  Mike Durand  134 Fred White
135  Christian Münz  136  Yassine Ouhilal  Jeff Norman
**CENTRAL AMERICA & THE CARIBBEAN** 137 Kevin Warren
John Gibbons  138 Alicia & Richard Lippincott  Ian Hodge
Magnus  139 John Murphy  Leonel Perez Yznez  Bill Cooksey
Brendan Smith  Glen Novey  140 Michael/TuboLoco
Adolfo Cruz  Pedro Pablo  Vergara B  141 Dale Dagger
Lance Moss  142 Kiki Commarieu  143 Kurt Van Duke
Tor Johnson  144 Philippe Demarsan  145 Alan Barnes
146 Jeff Barksdale  147 Jérôme Blanco  Alexis Deforges
148 Alex Dick-Read  Andy Morrell  149 Tiki Yates
150 Nicolas Labat  **SOUTH AMERICA** 152 Nicolas Nowak
Gastón Lagrange  153 Eddie Salazar  Ricardo Nunez
Paul Kennedy  154 Gonzalo Barandiaran  Karin Sierralta
Gustavo  155 AJ Whilar  Gonzalo Barandiaran
156 Diego Sotomayor  Alejandro Sanchez  157 Mickey Arandia
158 Marcos Conde  Rémi Quique  159 Benjamin Kromayer
Lawrence Scafield  160 Lima Junior

**Special Thanks**
Hugues Gosselin  Mary Alegoet  Gibus de Soultrait
Laurent Masurel  Philippe Lauga  Nicolas Dejean  Benoit Duthu
Mireille Lahiholle  Joël de Rosnay  Latif Benhaddad  Fabrice Colas
Tiki Yates  Kore Antonson  Marc Hare
David Sims  Camilo Gallardo  Ryall Mills
Andrea Dillon Ty Ryder Sheila Jake Shani and Marla Fitzjones
Louise Aedan Anna Ella and Jamie Millais
Sue John Mathew and Adam Haylock and Millie

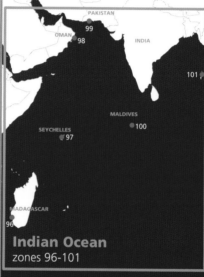
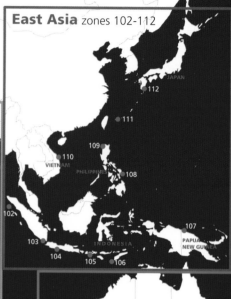

**Europe** zones 81-87

**East Asia** zones 102-112

**Africa** zones 88-95

**Indian Ocean** zones 96-101

**Australia** zones 113-118

# Contents
## Volume Two

**THE OCEAN ENVIRONMENT**

I   The Environmental Factors
II  Pollution
III Erosion
IV Access
V  Hazards

**EUROPE**

The Ocean Environment
81  Gower, WALES
82  Lofoten Islands, NORWAY
83  West Kust, NETHERLANDS
84  Finistère, FRANCE
85  Asturias, SPAIN
86  Lisbon, PORTUGAL
87  Fuerteventura, CANARY ISL.

**AFRICA**

The Ocean Environment
88  Rabat to Casablanca, MOROCCO
89  Gold Coast, GHANA
90  GABON
91  ANGOLA
92  Western Cape, SOUTH AFRICA
93  Garden Route, SOUTH AFRICA
94  Wild Coast, SOUTH AFRICA
95  Inhambane, MOZAMBIQUE

**INDIAN OCEAN ISLANDS**

The Ocean Environment
96  Vezo Reefs, MADAGASCAR
97  SEYCHELLES
98  OMAN
99  West Makran, PAKISTAN
100 Huvadhoo Atoll, MALDIVES
101 Andaman Islands, INDIA

**EAST ASIA**

The Ocean Environment
102 Simelue and Banyak, INDONESIA
103 Lampung, Sumatra INDONESIA
104 Java Tengah, INDONESIA
105 Lombok, INDONESIA
106 West Timor, INDONESIA
107 Sandaun and East Sepik, PNG
108 Eastern Samar, PHILIPPINES
109 North West Luzon, PHILIPPINES
110 Da Nang, VIETNAM
111 Okinawa, JAPAN
112 Kyu Shu, JAPAN

**The World Stormrider Guide Volume Two**

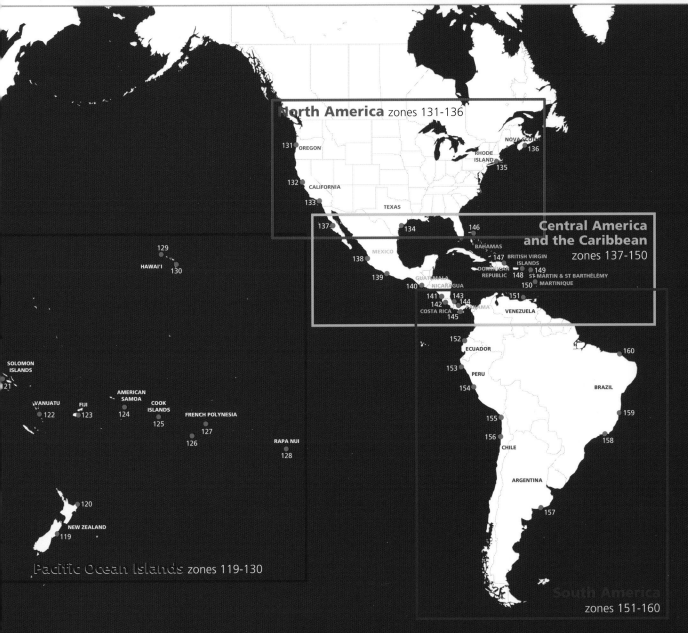

**North America** zones 131-136

131 OREGON
132 CALIFORNIA
133
137
134
138
139
140

**Central America and the Caribbean** zones 137-150

146
BAHAMAS
147 BRITISH VIRGIN ISLANDS
DOMINICAN REPUBLIC 149
148 ST MARTIN & ST BARTHÉLÉMY
150 MARTINIQUE
GUATEMALA
NICARAGUA
141 143
142 144
COSTA RICA PANAMA
145
151
VENEZUELA

129
HAWAI'I 130

152
ECUADOR
153
PERU
154
155
156
CHILE
160
BRAZIL
159
158
ARGENTINA
157

SOLOMON ISLANDS
121
VANUATU FIJI
122 123
AMERICAN SAMOA
124
COOK ISLANDS
125
FRENCH POLYNESIA
127
126
RAPA NUI
128

120
NEW ZEALAND
119

Pacific Ocean Islands zones 119-130

**South America** zones 151-160

## AUSTRALIA

**The Ocean Environment**
113 Perth, WESTERN AUSTRALIA
114 Adelaide, SOUTH AUSTRALIA
115 Phillip Island, VICTORIA
116 Hobart, TASMANIA
117 Byron Bay, NEW SOUTH WALES
118 Sunshine Coast, QUEENSLAND

## PACIFIC OCEAN ISLANDS

**The Ocean Environment**
119 Kaikoura, NEW ZEALAND
120 Gisborne, NEW ZEALAND
121 New Georgia, SOLOMON ISLANDS
122 Efate, VANUATU
123 Kadavu Passage, FIJI
124 Tutuila, AMERICAN SAMOA
125 Raratonga, COOK ISLANDS
126 Huahiné & Raiatea, POLYNESIA
127 Tuamotu, FRENCH POLYNESIA
128 RAPA NUI
129 Kauai, HAWAII
130 Big Island, HAWAII

## NORTH AMERICA

**The Ocean Environment**
131 Northern OREGON
132 San Fransisco and
     San Mateo, CA – USA
133 Santa Monica Bay, CA – USA
134 TEXAS – USA
135 RHODE ISLAND – USA
136 NOVA SCOTIA – CANADA

## CENTRAL AMERICA AND THE CARIBBEAN

**The Ocean Environment**
137 Central Baja, MEXICO
138 Nayarit, MEXICO
139 West Guerrero, MEXICO
140 GUATEMALA
141 Rivas Province, NICARAGUA
142 Golfo de Nicoya, COSTA RICA
143 Limón, COSTA RICA
144 Bocas del Toro, PANAMA
145 West Panamá Province, PANAMA
146 Eleuthera & Gt Abaco, BAHAMAS

147 Amber Coast, DOM. REPUBLIC
148 BRITISH VIRGIN ISLANDS
149 ST MARTIN AND ST BARTHÉLÉMY
150 MARTINIQUE

## SOUTH AMERICA

**The Ocean Environment**
151 Margarita, VENEZUELA
152 Esmereldas, ECUADOR
153 Southern Piura, PERU
154 Costa Verde, PERU
155 Tarapaca, CHILE
156 Antofagasta, CHILE
157 Mar del Plata, ARGENTINA
158 Rio de Janeiro, BRAZIL
159 South Bahia, BRAZIL
160 West Ceara, BRAZIL

POLLUTION

EROSION

NO
SURFING
10AM TO 5PM

ACCESS

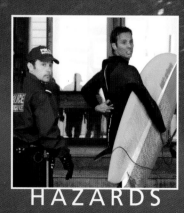

HAZARDS

# The Ocean Environment

# I. The Environmental Factors

An estimated 400,000km (250,000mi) of coastline separates the "Earth" from its defining feature – water. This thin frontier is where most human interaction takes place with the ocean environment and is the principle setting for the act of surfing. Many natural and human factors affect the ocean environment, altering conditions in the coastal zone and ultimately shaping the surfing experience. The central subjects that crucially influence the quality of surfing in the ocean environment include pollution, erosion, access and hazards. The following chapters investigate the burning issues in these four categories and illuminate current trouble spots where heightened environmental awareness is necessary.

## Pollution

This defines a wide range of harmful or poisonous substances introduced into an environment. Mankind dumps millions of gallons of effluent into the sea every day and yet expects the sea to continue to provide millions of tons of safe, edible food for harvest. Highly toxic industrial waste, heavy metals and radioactive by-products of the nuclear age are being deposited in the oceans at the same time as growing numbers of people are regularly entering the sea for recreational purposes. Cities concentrate and add pollution as vast areas of concrete are washed down by rain but the sea picks up the cleaning bill. Inland impurities are carried to the coast via aquatic arteries, which are choked and hardened on a centuries' old diet of sewage and fertilizer. These pollution problems are all surmountable with modern treatment technologies and all that is required to effect change is money.

**Environmental activism groups are campaigning to preserve the pristine ocean environment we all take for granted.**

GILLES CALVET

## Erosion

Paradoxically, large amounts of money have been spent on the construction of sea defences in a vain attempt to halt the oceans' inexorable march inland. Erosion is unavoidable, driven by the primeval forces that have shaped the continents and is an integral part of nature. Resisting such powerful forces usually focuses the erosional process on adjacent coastlines and often increases damage whenever seawalls, jetties, breakwalls and harbours are constructed.

## Access

These issues often take a back seat on the environmental front line, but are arguably the most crucial. Without access to the ocean environment, there is no interaction and apathy quickly ensues. Once again, financial gain is often at the heart of the matter as individuals, corporations and governments annexe coastal land resources and endeavour to restrict access or promote exclusivity.

## Hazards

Coming in many shapes and guises, hazards encompasses a healthy number of natural examples that are elements of or exist in the ocean environment. Supporting the emerging pattern, natural elements like dangerous sea creatures are not the biggest threat to surfers, but in fact, the man-made perils such as the humble surfboard are far more likely to inflict injury.

## Activism

Human activity is inevitably altering the surrounding land and seascape, unbalancing natural ecosystems through pollution and over-exploitation of resources. Preventing the continued rape and pillage of the environment must centre on raising awareness, education and funding for research that will break the visious circle of government sanctioned greed that permits mankind to desecrate the oceans. Mainstream organisations such as Greenpeace have the resources and membership to provide international monitoring and response to a wide range of global issues. Surfing orientated environmental activism is still in its infancy and has yet to develop a cohesive, worldwide organisation, relying instead on small localised groups, concentrating on local issues. The Surfrider Foundation represents the highest profile, largest membership environmental group focused on conservation, activism, research and education, providing an invaluable resource for surfers in North America, Australia, Japan, France and Brazil. Some of the challenges facing Surfrider and other groups include raising awareness at local, grassroots level, lobbying or advising governments, challenging inappropriate coastal developments, promoting low impact beach access, databasing coastal resources and monitoring pollution, not just for surfers but all water-users. Legislation on water quality has been introduced in most developed countries, although implementation and enforcement will prove to be both expensive and difficult unless full public support is forthcoming. Without a future plan for sustainable, environmentally sound waste management, erosion control policy, and adequate coastal access, surfers will continue to be denied the right to enjoy a clean, natural ocean environment.

| SURFERS ENVIRONMENTAL ORGANISATIONS | |
| --- | --- |
| **Surfrider Foundation** | www.surfrider.org |
| **Europe; Japan; Australia; USA; Canada; Brazil** | |
| **Surfers Against Sewage, UK** | www.sas.org.uk |
| **Wild Coast, USA** | www.wildcoast.net |
| **Save The Waves, USA** | www.savethewaves.org |
| **Surfers Environmental Alliance, USA** | www.damoon.net/sea |
| **Save Ningaloo, AUS** | www.save-ningaloo.org |

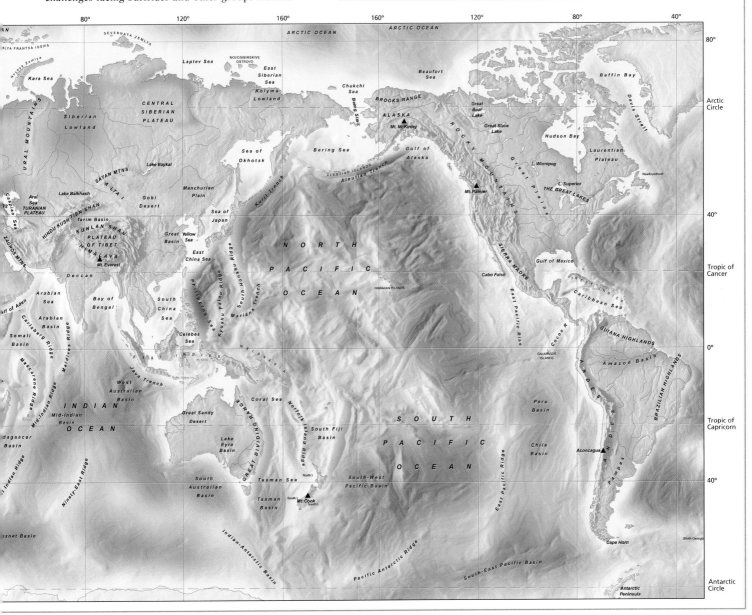

# II. Pollution

For several thousand years, the ocean has proved to be a convenient and seemingly bottomless receptacle for human waste, yet pollution is not solely generated by mankind. Eons before man ever set foot on the Earth, naturally occurring elements would make impacts on the environment through oil seepage, dissolved metals in runoff and dangerous chemical emissions from volcanic eruptions. The Earth's environment has the ability to adapt to these pollutants that are relatively harmless in relation to geological time. Compare this time scale to the brief evolutionary curve of the human race and their ability to quickly damage the environment. Short-sighted, resource exploitation and contamination of the eco-systems only threatens the survival of evolved life on earth, but not the earth itself. All references to pollution in this volume pertain to man-made substances that have a bearing on the ocean environment.

DAVID PU'U

**Global legislation on industrial effluent is patchy and difficult to enforce. Industry often receives government permits to pollute and quotas are easily exceeded without detection.**

Pollution takes many forms but the most obvious and universal is domestic human waste or raw sewage. On its own, this organic matter is easily dealt with, but add to this the increased use of slowly degrading materials in sanitary towels, nappies, condoms, toilet tissues, in fact anything modern society can fit down a drain and treatment becomes more problematic. Mix in all household and commercial waste-water, detergents, bleach and cleaning compounds plus a myriad of potentially dangerous industrial chemicals, and you have a nasty sewage soup to clean up. In this soup, bacteria and viruses survive for surprisingly long lengths of time and if released into the ocean without adequate treatment, intensive year round water-users such as surfers are highly prone to exposure. Sewage is generally dealt with in four ways. Preliminary treatment consists of a long sea outfall with a grid on the end to remove solid particles like plastics and paper. The raw sewage enters the sea untreated, containing around 10 million faecal coliform bacteria per 100ml.

Primary treatment removes some of the solids from the effluent, which has the effect of reducing the oxygen demand when it enters the sea. Primary treated effluent contains about one million faecal coliform bacteria per 100ml.

Secondary treatment allows the effluent to settle in holding tanks, bacteria are added to feed on the sludge, then the sludge and liquid are separated. The solid matter is typically disposed of on landfill sites, whilst the remaining, now almost clear, liquid is discharged into rivers or the ocean or further treated. Secondary treated effluent contains ten thousand faecal coliform bacteria per 100ml. Tertiary treatment involves the disinfection of the remaining liquid. Ultra-violet (UV) rays are passed over the liquid, destroying the DNA of the bacteria and viruses, rendering them incapable of reproduction. Beyond these methods, micro-filtration is also used to remove all bacteria. Tertiary treatment is the standard advocated by all the environmental groups, as it is the only way of safely discharging the effluent, however it is still rare for water companies worldwide to be using it. Technology is improving and new tertiary treatment plants often use the recycled water for irrigation or commercial purposes.

Stormwater, polluted runoff or non-specific point pollution causes many beach closures and brings a whole new assortment of debris and pollution to near shore waters. After rain, all the detritus of urban living gets washed into the gutters along with oil, petrol, detergents and trash before arriving at the beach on mass. Illegally dumped commercial waste, pesticides, herbicides, silage and agricultural products all contribute and the stormwater system often utilises natural watercourses and rivers which absorb contaminants into the watershed.

Pesticides and fertilizers have an alarming affect on the eco-system and along with poorly treated sewage can be the main cause of eutrophication. Eutrophication occurs when waters become overly rich in nutrients and minerals, causing the rapid growth of cyanobacteria and algae, resulting in a huge reduction in oxygen levels. In extreme cases, the amount of algae becomes toxic and beaches and coastal waters are closed, however this usually happens under low energy conditions (no waves). Eutrophication can devastate coral reefs, because the algae smothers the coral polyps and the reef dies, leaving a weakened structure prone to erosion. Pesticides kill marine plants like sea-grass and aid in the destruction of mangrove forests, which physically filter pollutants through the anaerobic, wetland environment.

Oil pollution is probably the highest profile pollutant on the planet. Every time a tanker goes down or runs aground, shedding its viscous load, the incident is guaranteed to make headline news. Most surfers have encountered some kind of oil contamination from minor slicks to high tide tar balls. It is estimated that about 6.4

KORE ANTONSEN

**Where does it come from?**
1. Atmospheric pollutants including heavy metals and hydrocarbons
2. Traffic exhausts
3. Agricultural fertilizers and pesticides
4. Sewage effluent
5. Primary treatment ocean outfall
6. Stormwater and urban runoff
7. Industrial waste
8. Oil Spills
9. Ship waste and plastic
10. Ballast water
11. Oil-rig waste
12. Lost or dumped vessels, their cargoes and power plants
13. Dumped nuclear and industrial waste

million tons of oil and petrochemical related products spill into the sea every year. Major spills have immediate, catastrophic affects on the environment, infiltrating the eco-system on many different levels. Crude and fuel oils are a mixture of hydrocarbons, an organic compound that contains hydrogen and four or more carbon molecules. They range from light petroleum with only three or four carbon molecules up to heavy fuel oils with in excess of twenty. Heavy fuel oil is more damaging, destroying habitat, killing wildlife such as birds, fish and mammals and it can also have toxic effects on humans. Cleaning up these spills is not an exact science and the use of detergent often compounds the damage to the environment. Prevention is the best cure and while double hulled tankers are now the minimum standard for new construction, ageing single hulled ships still ply the ocean and are only slowly being replaced. A source of further oil pollution is the discharging of ballast tanks in coastal waters. After an oil tanker has unloaded its cargo, sea water is pumped into the vessels cargo tank as ballast to balance the ship at sea. Sludge and oil residue in these tanks mixes with the sea water ballast and is later flushed out when the tanker approaches port. Ballast water is also blamed for the introduction of invasive species to new environments like the red tide toxic algae blooms or foreign invertebrates and fish that have been unwittingly repatriated to the other side of the world. Hundreds of ships dump dirty ballast water everyday, adding to the leaks from pipelines and oil fields that are all part of a growing problem. International laws are slowly being implemented but guidelines are constantly flouted and few harbours provide the facilities to treat ships ballast. So whilst big spills like the *Prestige* off Galicia in Spain

get the media scrutiny, it is in fact the every day minor discharges that continually put strain on the ocean.

Sea water has natural radiation readings from potassium 40, but since the 1940s, governments have been contributing to ocean radioactivity. Above ground weapons testing created uncontrolled fallout across large areas of the Pacific, although this practice is no longer tolerated. Today, most radioactive pollution is a result of nuclear power stations and waste from the reprocessing of spent fuel. Nuclear particles can travel great distances and arrive on the shores of countries that have anti-nuclear legislation, while fallout from a nuclear explosion can quickly circumnavigate the globe. Nuclear authorities dismiss any leaked waste as being insignificant, but coming into contact with a single particle could prove terminal.

TIM NUNN

**Uninhabited, isolated beaches also suffer from rubbish, fishing debris and plastic.**

Other forms of pollution we take for granted include all kinds of plastic packaging, cigarette butts, aluminium or steel cans, fishing nets, ropes, floats and lines and are commonplace on high tide marks across the globe. Well distributed far from civilisation, they are not only unsightly, but also potentially fatal to any bird or animal that tries to ingest them. To highlight the problem, Jean-Michel Cousteau headed to Midway Island, miles from any significant population, where his team collected 60 tons of plastic related debris.

# III. Erosion

Erosion describes the group of natural processes, including weathering, dissolution, abrasion, corrosion and transportation, by which material is worn away from the earth's surface. It is one of the shaping forces in geomorphology: the study of the evolution and configuration of landforms. Coastlines are one of these landforms that are in a constant state of change, largely due to the eroding action of the sea.

The world's coastline is a dynamic interface between land and sea, governed by inputs and outputs of energy that modify in three major ways – marine erosion, transportation of sediment and deposition of sediment. Headlands, bays and wave cut platforms are all signs of active marine erosion, while a beach or a sandbar results from sediment transportation and deposition. Typically, a coastline is a balance of erosional and depositional landforms, dependant on geological and hydrological circumstances.

There are four fundamental coastal erosion processes:
1. Corrasion/abrasion occurs when a wave picks up suspended material and hurls it at cliffs and other rocks.
2. Hydraulic action defines water forcing its way into cracks in rocks, constantly compressing and releasing the air pressure, which stresses the rock, especially in heavily bedded or faulted areas.
3. Attrition is where rocks, sand and other material collide with each other and erode.
4. Corrosion/solution affects certain types of rock, whereby weak acids in the sea dissolve them.

The rate at which a coastline naturally erodes is down to three major factors. Coastal geology is paramount so slowly eroding metamorphic and igneous rocks such as granite and volcanic basalt forms are far more resistant to the sea. The softer sedimentary rocks including sandstone, limestone, shales, slate and conglomerates erode at a much faster rate. The second factor concerns the amount of energy generated by the adjoining ocean. A high-energy coastline is one which faces into a long fetch and regularly encounters powerful wave action which speeds up erosion. The third factor is sediment input from inland, deposited via rivers and streams, plus some direct runoff. Equilibrium remains the key, achieved on a hard, high-energy coast by deeper bays at weak spots in the geology such as river valleys, which in turn supply fresh sediment. A sedimentary rock coast will erode quickly but deposit the erosional spoil in sandbanks that diffuse ocean energy and retard the wave action on the softer rocks. A water column's ability to carry sediment is enhanced in high-energy periods, transporting greater volumes of sand and silt over longer distances, offsetting the erosive forces off the heightened wave activity.

This balance and symmetry is upset when humans interfere with these natural processes and attempt to manipulate or challenge the awesome power of the ocean. Until recently, ignorance of these inter-connected coastal processes facilitated the construction of rudimentary structures, designed to protect harbours, shipping lanes, roads, beach widths or privately owned coastal properties against the ravages of the sea. Coastal armouring includes the building of seawalls, revetments, ripraps or offshore reefs, all methods of absorbing and redirecting energy away from the threatened coast. Another approach is to use groynes or jetties to trap sediment and build up a natural protective barrier of beach material. Both methods are expensive, unsightly, and ultimately impact on an adjacent coastal area. Seawalls absorb some of the waves energy and reflect the rest. The reflection causes backwash, which has the ability to pick up sediment from the shoreline and take it back seawards. Seawalls tend to exacerbate the problem they were designed to prevent and ultimately cause beach narrowing and the eventual undermining of their own foundations. As the predicted benefits of the construction disappear

**Coral wall**
BRUCE SUTHERLAND

JOHN CALLAHAN
**Threatened by global warming**

**Dropping anchor onto a coral reef**
BRUCE SUTHERLAND

**Jetty**
PAUL KENNEDY

**Dredging ship**

desperate engineers usually implement beach nourishing, a technique using imported, beach quality sand to replace the local reserves lost due to the seawall. This is a common practice in many countries and often employs supporting structures, but is completely reliant on vast volumes of sand and periodical re-nourishment. Being a finite resource coveted by the cement industry, sand supplies are often pilfered from coastal or inland dune systems, or alternatively dredged from offshore sources, but if the sand is too fine for the high energy beach environment, it won't last long. Revetments and ripraps are slightly more effective as they absorb more energy by allowing water to pass through the gaps integrated into their design, reducing the impact of sediment-laden backwash. These loose assemblages of rock and wooden or concrete angled constructions are transient structures, requiring constant maintenance and re-installation.

Groynes and jetties are built to protect an eroding coastline, or to stabilize a rivermouth or shipping channel. Groynes trap sediment moving along the coastline, carried in a current called the longshore drift. Slowed by the obstructions, the drift can no longer carry its sediment

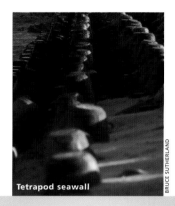
**Tetrapod seawall**
BRUCE SUTHERLAND

buffer zone between the sea and the vegetation line. Allowing coastlines to be shaped by the natural processes of erosion and sedimentation without disturbing the equilibrium is becoming the enlightened way to deal with the problem. Obviously, the coastal set back zone is already heavily built up in most developed countries and property owners expect their governments to protect their existing houses. Where legislation can help is the areas about to be exploited by property developers or ill-planned constructions too close to a coast in recession.

On a positive note for surfers and sea defences is the growing trend towards artificial reefs as dual-purpose structures. By dropping sand-filled bags onto the ocean floor in a specific formation, the waves become a surfing asset as well as dissipating energy offshore and providing erosion protection. At present, there are only a small number, but many more are planned around the globe.

Erosion and the surrounding issues have a significant effect on the surfing

**Harbour entrance protection**

**ty construction**

load, which gets deposited around the groyne and the beach grows. This unfairly redistributes the coastal wealth, starving the neighbouring littoral region of sediment and encouraging erosion at a faster rate. The stabilisation of rivermouths and shipping channels has the same affect, denying the down-drift stretch of coastline of beach building sediment and causing a constant requirement for harbour entrance dredging.

Coastal urbanisation is also playing a significant role by changing the way in which water runs off the land and the amount of sediment it carries with it. Vast concrete plains form an impenetrable barrier between the precipitation and the earth, preventing runoff from picking up sediment and flowing to the coastline in streams and rivers. Many urban watercourses become cement stormwater drains, delivering pollution instead of particles, while upstream dams and reservoirs strangle any rural sediment from the supply chain.

As more data becomes available and scientific studies shed more light on the effects of erosion, environmentalists advocate the concept of managed retreat from the coastline and introducing a no build

**Sandbag seawall**
PAUL KENNEDY

EROSION CONTROL PROJECT IN PROGRESS
PAUL KENNEDY

world. Seawalls remove beaches and cause backwash, groynes trap sand, starving other breaks, while harbour and marina breakwalls simply destroy surfbreaks. Many awesome breaks have been lost due to coastal modification and the list of waves under threat is even more worrying. Classic, seminal surf spots are constantly endangered by seawall and marina developments, along with average, low profile breaks that few would consider as a surfing resource worth saving. Tempering all this destruction is the fact that quite often, these expensive, badly planned sea defences, create a quality wave that brings pure stoke to the local surfers. On some coastlines, jetties and groynes are an integral and indispensable part of the surfing landscape and beach nourishment projects bring the promise of the perfect sandbar. Creator and destroyer in one, coastal defences will be irrelevant if predictions of sea-level rise due to global warming are correct. The entire world's coastlines will be changed irrevocably as miles of beaches will be lost and the pessimists predict it could all take place in as little as one hundred years.

# IV. Access

One aspect of the surfing experience that is often taken for granted is access. Defined as the ability or right to approach, enter, exit, communicate with, or make use of, access is almost as indispensable as a surfboard. Without the act of approaching, there is no surfing, so being aware of any physical or legal barriers to the coast is imperative. Twenty years ago, there were more surfing frontiers than surfers knew what to do with and simply getting to the surf was more than half of the mission. Off-roading down rutted tracks, trailblazing through tropical, malaria infested jungles, navigating open ocean and coral reef passes in fishing boats or scouting round the wilderness areas above and below 40° has illuminated the innumerable surfing locations that grace the planet. Challenges and virgin coastlines still exist, but the world is shrinking as modern travel and communication systems have opened up a huge proportion of the world's surfable coastline to a capacious population of wealthy surf tourists. This spontaneous expansion of the surfable world increasingly brings surfers into conflict with man-made restrictions rather than natural inaccessibility factors.

Private land is the main barrier between surfers and the waves and while it rarely includes the actual beach and water either side of the high tide line, it does prevent getting sand between the toes. Landowners vary from private house owners, farmers and ranch managers to operators of factory and industrial complexes, but the biggest coastal landowner of all is the military. Private, often wealthy coastal home owners can effectively privatise their beachfront by making access and parking as difficult as possible. Camouflaging or even gating public access pathways or preventing all non-resident parking are just some of the depths plumbed by selfish individuals. On the next level are agreements made behind closed doors between local governments and property developers to effectively exclude public access to the beach in front of exclusive gated communities. Local governments often circumnavigate federal laws in many countries that guarantee public ownership of the foreshore and that adequate access points must be provided. By exploiting legal grey areas, developers often arrive at the desired result that virtually excludes the public and almost amounts to localism by a non-surfing community. This ideal of an élite community sometimes attracts surfers to larger ranch style reservations, where a coastal lifestyle and emptier line-ups can be bought at a premium and enjoyed by surfing patricians. While members of the public are legally permitted to enter these ranch zones by boat, the landowners often discourage and rarely welcome visitors to what they consider as their waves. Farmers are also custodians of hundreds of miles of coastline and generally permit coastal access across their land. The surfer farmer relationship is often strained by abuse of landowner's generosity and assuming access has been granted without first asking permission.

INDIAN RIVER INLET JETTY
THE JETTY IS OWNED AND MAINTAINED BY THE US ARMY CORPS OF ENGINEERS TO STABILIZE THE INLET. IF YOU CHOOSE TO GO ON THE JETTY, BE ALERT FOR UNPREDICTABLE CONDITIONS SUCH AS LARGE WAVES, STRONG CURRENTS, AND SLIPPERY FOOTING.
DELAWARE DIVISION OF PARKS & RECREATION

PAUL KENNEDY

WARNING
THIS BEACH IS PRIVATE PROPERTY CLOSED TO PUBLIC
• Entrance Only By • Owners Permission
Violators Will Be Prosecuted

Indo ferry, Timor

Charter boat

JOLI

Steep Madeiran access

WILL HENRY

Industry presents a major restriction to attaining coastal passage. Mining companies often control protracted coastlines, vetting all activities via a permit system and often excluding surfers from the acceptable visitor list. Power stations needing to be situated near sources of water often end up dominating prime surfing locations such as rivermouths. Nuclear power stations and reprocessing plants bring a sinister twist to the access issue by denying entry to a coastline that is highly likely to have health implications for surfers.

By far the largest, most widespread impediment to surfers wishing to get to the maritime margins is the world's military. Strictly controlled coastal access is the international standard and by some cruel twist of fate, military installations seem to occupy some of the finest surfing real estate in

Difficult desert access

the world. Comprehensive restrictions are prevalent, however military personnel are often permitted to use these areas recreationally, which is essentially seen as a free pass to uncrowded surf.

The recent, rapid expansion of the surf travel industry has both solved and created many issues centred around access. Surf exploration has historically employed the method of long arduous journeys via dilapidated local transport to a destination that no one was even sure had any

decent surf. This has now been supplanted by modern, rapid transport and transfers that have been co-ordinated to seamlessly deposit surfers in remote locations in as short a period as possible. Time is money, so by avoiding sluggish, traditional methods of transport and utilising modern swell prediction technology, surf travel operators can virtually guarantee surf, at a price. Convenience costs, but many of these new travel services cater in areas where access was either non-existent or sketchy and provided a new waveriding resource for the burgeoning numbers of affluent surf tourists. Operating costs for maintaining a charter boat are high, but staffing costs are often minimized by employing local labour at third world, labour market prices. While expanding some horizons, these same travel operators have restricted access in

4WD only

Luxury surf travel

some other cases. In the past decade, surfing resorts have sprung up around the world, providing safe, easy access to remote waves in the immediate vicinity. Not satisfied with prime positioning, some resorts have paid for exclusive rights to ride the waves that break over the nearby reefs. Exploiting local laws and traditional entitlements, segregated surf zones have been created where the dollar is king and resourceful travellers are excluded. Attempts at justification are often based on safety grounds and the number of surf camps claiming ownership of waves is continually increasing.

Beach closures are responsible for keeping surfers on terra firma, but this is a direct pollution issue. A tiny proportion of the global coastline is protected by marine sanctuaries and a few surfing bans exist for political reasons.

# v. Hazards

Many hazards exist in the surf line-up, which marries the open ocean with the inter-tidal zone. Surfing forces humans into an unnatural habitat, bringing them into contact and conflict with creatures that are right at home in the ocean environment. Most feared (and hyped) of these potentially hazardous creatures is the apex predator, the shark. These numerous species of elasmobranch fishes are grouped because they

**Hazardous Reef Shark**

have a cartilaginous skeleton, 5 to 7 gills on each side of the head, an oil filled liver and tough skin covered in small tooth-like scales. Many sharks possess rows of sharp, serrated, flesh tearing teeth, but only a small proportion are considered dangerous to man. The man-eating sharks mostly belong to the genera *Carcharhinus*, *Carcharodon*, and related genera. The great white shark (*Carcharodon carcharias*), tiger shark (*Galeocerdo cuvier*) bull shark (*Carcharhinus leucas*) and other assorted requiem sharks from the *Carcharhinidae* family account for almost all the 456 fatalities recorded from 1909 attacks registered on the International Shark Attack File. As the global human population rises, more people are using the near-shore waters for recreational purposes and although shark populations are dwindling thanks to over-fishing, shark attack figures are gradually rising. Surfers are at the top of the table when it comes to attacks but many feel that bites are often a case of mistaken identity as the silhouette of a board bears similarities with a seal or turtle from below. North America

registers the most attacks, but dogs, snakes, mountain lions, alligators and bee stings account for more animal deaths than sharks while drowning and cardiac arrest claim far more lives at the beach. Probability of fatal attack is extremely remote, considering you are 30 times more likely to die after being struck by lightning in the United States, where electrical storms create another serious surfing hazard. To minimize the risk of shark attack, never enter the water if sharks are obviously present, avoid dawn and dusk, murky water, rivermouths and don't surf alone. First aid treatment centres around controlling loss of blood by applying pressure to arteries or

**Sea snake**

**Non hazardous dolphins**

a tourniquet while waiting for emergency medical help who should be notified of the nature of the injury. Lie patient with head down to increase blood flow to the brain and minimize movement to reduce shock. Carry out CPR where necessary and continue to prevent bleeding.

Stinging jellyfish called Portuguese man-o-war or bluebottles (*Physalia physalis*) have colonised the oceans by growing either left sided or right sided sails, ensuring differing direction of travel for half the swarm. With tentacles up to 50m (165ft), delivering a very painful sting, causing possible fever, shock and interference with heart and lung function, these cnidaria are extremely dangerous. Even when apparently dead or detached tentacles meet human skin, they have the ability to fire or discharge the complex venom that is almost as powerful as that of a cobra. If stung, remove visible tentacles without touching them, irrigate area with copious quantities of sea or fresh water, use ice to reduce pain and for persistent itching or rash, apply hydrocortisone cream. Treatments like vinegar, methylated spirits, alcohol, urinating or rubbing sand on the sting will do more damage than good. Even more deadly is the sting of the box jellyfish (*Chironex fleckeri*), but fortunately, it is only prevalent in the surfless zones of Northern Australia and surrounding Indo Pacific waters. An agonizingly painful death is almost guaranteed unless antivenom can be administered immediately. Confusingly, Hawaiian box jellyfish (*Carybdea alata*) arrive on

| Total Shark Attacks and significant country stats (>10) | | |
|---|---|---|
| | **Total** | **Fatal** |
| **Europe** | **39** | **18** |
| Italy | 14 | 4 |
| **Africa** | **255** | **67** |
| South Africa | 208 | 41 |
| Mozambique | 11 | 3 |
| **Indian Ocean** | **62** | **27** |
| Mascarene Islands | 21 | 12 |
| Iran | 23 | 8 |
| India | 10 | 4 |
| **East Asia** | **89** | **38** |
| Papua New Guinea | 36 | 15 |
| Philippines | 15 | 6 |
| Japan | 19 | 12 |
| **Australia & NZ** | **326** | **141** |
| Western Australia | 28 | 9 |
| Southern Australia | 30 | 16 |
| Victoria | 20 | 8 |
| Tasmania | 16 | 6 |
| New South Wales | 123 | 62 |
| Queensland | 101 | 47 |
| **Pacific** | **211** | **62** |
| Marshall Islands | 12 | 0 |
| Soloman Islands | 17 | 8 |
| Fiji | 25 | 10 |
| Hawaii | 104 | 19 |
| **North America** | **720** | **38** |
| Oregon | 17 | 1 |
| California | 111 | 8 |
| Texas | 30 | 3 |
| Florida | 187 | 13 |
| South Carolina | 43 | 3 |
| North Carolina | 24 | 3 |
| New Jersey | 16 | 5 |
| **Central America** | **118** | **50** |
| Mexico | 39 | 21 |
| Panama | 16 | 9 |
| **South America** | **89** | **21** |
| Brazil | 81 | 20 |
| | | |
| **TOTAL** | **1909** | **456** |

Courtesy of The International Shark Attack File, Florida Museum of Natural History, University of Florida. www.flmnh.ufl.edu/fish/Sharks/ISAF/ISAF.htm.

windward shores but pose less of a threat to life. Treatment of sea wasp stings is to neutralise the stinging nematocysts with household vinegar before removing the tentacles. Other jellyfish can sting including the larval form of thimble jellyfish, better known as sea-lice. Pressure triggers the microscopic organism to fire poison into its victim, usually leaving a rash underneath swimming costumes. Treatment for sea-lice and most other common jellyfish stings is to wash area with seawater (not fresh water) remove any tentacles and applying various hydrocortisone or calamine creams will help.

Further poisonous sea creatures worth keeping an eye out for include sea snakes stonefish, lionfish, blue-ringed octopus, stingrays and cone shells.

One of the most dangerous elements associated with surfing is the damaging affect of long-term exposure to the sun. The well-documented loss of ozone from the upper atmosphere is linked to the rapid global increase of the occurrence of skin

**Non poisonous jellyfish**

ROSS MCINTYRE

**Poisonous bluebottle jellyfish**

JOLI

but over-exposure to cold conditions invites hypothermia. Drysuit surfers can be vulnerable to drowning if the seals, zip or fabric fails, flooding the suit with icy water and dragging the hapless wearer under. Impacting rocks, boulders, reefs and coral can lead to cuts, abrasions, broken bones or even unconsciousness and drowning. The most common cause of injury to surfers is inflicted either by their own board, or in a collision with another water-user, so crowded spots are therefore more likely to be the scene of a surfing injury.

The popularity and population growth of surfing has skyrocketed in recent years and it is no longer seen as a fringe activity enjoyed by the enlightened few. With so many more converts in the water, it is inevitable that the pressure on surf spots is growing and increasing incidences of localism. The transient, fleeting nature of ocean waves and the deeply personal nature of waveriding cultivates a highly selfish pursuit. Each wave is unique, a never to be repeated offering of ocean energy that could provide the rider with unparalleled euphoria and is definitely a covetable resource. Desire and greed have always bred conflict and so we find the early days of surfing history when riders rode four abreast is a dim memory in these modern times of drop-ins and intimidation.

Violent clashes have been observed for over three decades and as the advent of modern surf forecasting technology puts more people in the right place at the right time,

cancers. Damage by various short wavelengths of ultra-violet (UV) radiation is what causes skin cancers but they may take 20 years to manifest themselves after the initial sunburn. Although the reported holes in the ozone layer are above the poles, UV intensity increases at low latitude around the Equator and also at high altitude. Reduction in natural, upper atmosphere protection increases surfers high risk demographic, compounding the long periods of sun exposure in the surf, where re-application of sun cream in the water is impractical. Most people will have received 80% of their lifetime exposure to the sun by the time they are 18 years old. High factor, waterproof sun screens, long-sleeved UV protection lycra rash vests and surf hats are highly recommended summer surfing accessories. At the other end of the temperature spectrum, cold water surfing has expanded along with improved modern wetsuit technology,

**Gnarly coral**

HUMP

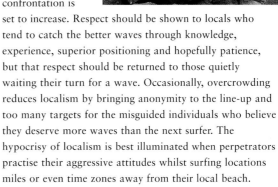

PAUL KENNEDY

**Gnarly locals**

confrontation is set to increase. Respect should be shown to locals who tend to catch the better waves through knowledge, experience, superior positioning and hopefully patience, but that respect should be returned to those quietly waiting their turn for a wave. Occasionally, overcrowding reduces localism by bringing anonymity to the line-up and too many targets for the misguided individuals who believe they deserve more waves than the next surfer. The hypocrisy of localism is best illuminated when perpetrators practise their aggressive attitudes whilst surfing locations miles or even time zones away from their local beach.

Just getting to the surf can take a lot of effort, especially in isolated areas like Lofoten, Norway.

# Europe

# The Ocean Environment

Modern industrial society was born in Europe, creating a centuries old tradition of simultaneous creation and destruction. Driven by rampant consumerism, the industrial revolution has left a long-term legacy of multi-layered pollution that successive governments have failed to address. Europe's dynamic aquatic systems have been under pressure from pollution for far longer than any other continent and not only coastal waterways are affected but also many rivers, lakes and streams. Realisation that this natural resource is threatened has forced Europe into becoming the world leader in pioneering technologies and promoting a new environmental awareness to help prevent the existing situation from worsening.

## Pollution

Ireland's west coast is one of the few areas of Europe where pristine coastline and good water quality exist. Exceptions include holiday towns like Bundoran, where rapid, EU funded, tourism building projects have lead to the local sewage systems being unable to cope with the influx of summer visitors, resulting in near shore pollution. This is not a long-term problem as secondary sewage treatment is planned. Northern Ireland is not as fortunate, as under-investment in sewage treatment means that coastal water quality, especially around main towns is actually deteriorating. Unlike the rest of the United Kingdom, Northern Irish residents do not pay separate water rates, so other essential services have diluted the amount of funding available for drainage and sewage treatment, often resulting in raw discharges. There are well-founded concerns that the Irish Sea suffers from radioactive contamination, courtesy of the re-processing plant at Sellafield on the English coast, but the exact extent of the problem is not certain.

Like Ireland, Scotland's isolation means much of its Atlantic coastline is unspoiled, particularly the Outer Hebrides where water quality and clarity are excellent. The same should apply to the north coast, but currents can bring radioactivity from the Irish Sea to mix with roaming isotopes from the toxic white elephant that is the Dounreay Nuclear Power and Reprocessing Plant. With a legacy of accidents, poor disposal of radioactive material and general mismanagement, the area around the power station has been confirmed as hazardous. Radioactive particles have been found on nearby Sandside Beach on three occasions, which British Nuclear Fuels dismissed as only being the size of a grain of sand. These particles represent a significant health risk to surfers who are obviously in contact with many grains of sand during an average session. The whole plant is currently being decommissioned and in the next fifty years, all signs of its existence will hopefully be removed.

England has long had the reputation as the dirty man of Europe and whilst pressure group Surfers Against Sewage continue to campaign tirelessly for clean seas, the country's water quality remains unacceptably poor in places. One major problem is sewage related debris, which refers to anything that can be put down a domestic drain. Only two English water companies (Wessex and Yorkshire) have taken up full tertiary treatment, guaranteeing the removal of all harmful bacteria and viruses. Levels of treatment vary wildly, depending on location and time of year, with water companies being permitted to increase untreated outfall in winter months when there are supposedly no water-users. SAS have proved there is a large winter surfing population, many of whom have contracted illnesses from the surf, but South West Water, the controlling body for the principle surf areas in England, continues to be the poorest performing UK water company per capita. Summer 2003 saw several cases of raw discharge onto crowded beaches due to equipment failure, resulting in illness for some beach-goers. Ridiculously small fines do little to deter a company that regularly increases local water bills. Busy, near-shore shipping lanes add to pollution problems and it is common in winter months for several ships to shed thier loads or run aground. Oil and plastic debris are a feature on many English beaches.

WARNING
RADIOACTIVE PARTICLES ARE BEING FOUND ON THE BEACHES AT SANDSIDE

TIM NUNN

Top – **The sign says it all. Sandside Bay, Scotland.** Bottom – **The shallow, radioactive, toxic North Sea is becoming more heavily surfed, despite the uninviting water characteristics.**

Wales has a history of heavy industry, mining and a dense coastal population sited on the already polluted Bristol Channel coast. Self imposed, tertiary treatment of all sewage, exceeding EU law, is one of the bold steps taken leading to a marked improvement in water quality, especially around popular tourist towns. The heavy industrial polluters of twenty years ago have declined and areas of severe contamination such as Swansea Bay and Cardiff Bay are slowly seeing an improvement in the surrounding environment. Being bordered by the Irish Sea and the Bristol Channel, means Wales will continue to be affected by effluent from domestic, industrial and radioactive sources in England. In Pembrokeshire, Milford Haven is home to three oil terminals and was the scene of a major spill in 1996 when *Sea Empress* hit Saint Anne's head at the entrance to the Haven. The resultant spill of 72,000 tonnes of crude oil covered 1300km (813mi) of coastline, closing miles of surfable beaches and damaging a coastal national park. When entering the Haven the largest tankers have only five meters (15ft) leeway on each side of the channel.

Beside the spectre of nuclear waste, the Norwegian coast also lives under the shadow of Europe's largest oil fields and although no major incident has occurred, statistics would suggest it is just a matter of time. Illegal washing of ballast tanks continues to add oil to the northern European coastline.

The North Sea nations encircle the most diversely used and abused body of water on the planet. Surrounded by a near coastal population of 35 million both industrial and domestic effluent has been gushing into the North Sea for decades. Add seven major rivers draining some of Europe's principle industrial and agricultural regions and the result is a serious build up of pollutants. To make matters worse, the southern North Sea is a shallow bottleneck

GJ DE KONING

Top – **Of the 77,000 tonnes the *Prestige* was carrying it is estimated that a further 20,000 tonnes are yet to surface.** Bottom – **Massive clean-up programmes have been implemented across the Spanish north coast but fresh black tides reappear in onshore conditions.**

EFE/MARINA ESPANOLA

with limited water circulation and it is also one of the busiest shipping lanes in the world. Surfers in SE England, Belgium, Holland, Germany and Denmark bear the worst water quality and although changing agricultural and industrial practices are reducing the ultra-toxic discharges, sediments remain which show traces of DDT and heavy metals. Shipping lane depths prevent truly huge tankers from plying the English Channel, but after a few large spills and ships constantly discharging oil-laden ballast, there are significant volumes of oil in a relatively small body of water. The northern reaches of the North Sea fare slightly better and the heavily surfed Yorkshire coast in England is one of only three counties enjoying tertiary sewage treatment, however heavy local industry more than compensates. Eutrophication is an issue amongst the North Sea nations that are causing excessive agricultural runoff and the resulting algal blooms create hazardous toxic slicks in summer months, particularly on Norwegian, Danish and German coastlines.

The coast of France has a bit of everything when it comes to pollution, suffering from nuclear, agricultural, industrial and domestic outfall. Like SAS in the UK, the French based Surfrider Foundation Europe has increased pollution awareness and is forcing the improvement of coastal water quality through regional initiatives and political lobbying. Convincing local authorities that year-round ocean water-users were getting ill more often than non-users has led to improving water quality although not to a level beyond that required by European law. The French coastline has also been the scene of two major oil spills in the last four years. The Erika shed its load of 14,000 tonnes affecting French beaches from Brittany to Gironde with Brittany being particularly heavily hit.

KIRSTEN PELOU

More recently, the Prestige sinking off Galicia in Spain has devastated coastal environments as far away as Normandy, causing beach closures and severe pollution throughout the Bay of Biscay. The rusting hull still contains a huge amount of thick fuel oil, which will continue to rise up from the depths and coat surfers' bodies and equipment for years to come. Authorities are enforcing beach closures and a blanket ban on entering the water when the deposits are thickest or the media are focused on the insidious problem.

Recent history has shown the Basque coast of Spain has been blighted by heavy industrial and domestic pollution, verified by the unnatural water colour surrounding San Sebastian. However the decline of heavy industry, most notably steel, has led local government to adopt the service sector and tourism to fuel its economy and a realisation that clean coastal water is an important resource. Although vastly cleaner than before, beaches around San Sebastian and Bilbao still suffer from big city related polluted run-off and under-treated domestic discharges. The steep coastal topography brings further agricultural and decaying factory output from upstream, but out of urban areas water quality is generally good. That is if you ignore the seemingly constant list of oil related pollution courtesy of shipping disasters. In 1992, the Aegean Sea spilled its cargo in storms off Galicia polluting miles of Galician coastline around la Coruña. The most recent spill involved the Prestige in the winter of 2002/03, again off Galicia. It was carrying 77,000 tonnes of fuel oil which devastated the coastline from Galicia all the way across to Pais Vasco and beyond into France, bringing catastrophic, long-term damage to the environment and local economy.

Portugal is one of the poorer countries of Europe and as is often the case, when money is tight the environment suffers. Rapidly expanding tourist resorts are overloading the creaking sewage treatment facilities, which are suffering from decades of under-investment. Industrial pollution is a major issue around Lisbon and especially Porto where effluent rich water regularly closes city beaches. With lax controls on commercial waste disposal accidents affecting watercourses are not uncommon and early 2003 saw 30,000m³ of pig slurry enter the Tigris near Lisbon, resulting in the closure of all the city's beaches.

The Canaries are fairly pollution free, sewage is strictly controlled around resorts so as not to wreck the resource people visit to enjoy.

Extending over 2.5 million square kilometres the Mediterranean is the world's largest enclosed sea. Environmentally it is under huge pressure from industry, oil and the ever-expanding tourist industry. Tourism brings a staggering 250 million visitors per year to the Med coastline, predicted to rise to 350 million by 2020. The affect is coastal degradation on a grand scale including polluted run off, sedimentation, habitat destruction and some pretty serious near coastal pollution, including everything from oil to sewage. The Mediterranean represents less than 1% of the earth's total marine surface, but it's oil tanker traffic accounts for more than 20% of global movement. 635,000 tonnes of oil are spilled in the Mediterranean each year, equivalent to 45 Erika's. Fortunately, it's a very deep sea, and the huge volume helps to deal with the pollutants. Numerous large rivers also drain into the Med carrying industrial and agricultural effluent. Eutrophication is a major issue, especially in the more enclosed areas such as the Adriatic, where algal blooms seriously damage the eco system and pose a toxic risk to water-users.

## Erosion

Marina development in Bundoran threatens its reef and the scale of sea defences necessary to protect boats from the North Atlantic means irreversible damage to the world famous Peak. A fierce campaign has been fought against the development, as the reef is not only important for surfing, but is also a unique habitat. Thanks to seven years of campaigning and an increasing awareness of surfing the local authority were convinced that having such an invaluable asset in the middle of town was much more important than a marina.

Coastal protection has long been affecting waves around the English coastline; harbour expansion and seawalls affecting breaks are common along the coast. More recently, coastal defence strategies have taken on a more environmentally sound approach by allowing the coastline to recede to protect the natural environment

sandbars. There is legitimate concern over the amount of waste and chemicals in the silt. The stabilisation of the Adour rivermouth in the late '60s and then further groyne building has changed the world-class Le Bar beachbreak into a rarely breaking, backwashy set of peaks.

Coastal modifications built under the guise of sea defences have destroyed many waves, especially around tourist spots in the Canaries. A prime example of this is Los Christianos in Tenerife where artificial reefs and sand pumped beaches have swallowed natural reef and waves in the name of tourism.

Madeira's finest wave, Jardim do Mar, has an uncertain future as a road and seawall are currently under construction. Ill effects are already apparent as backwash compounded by errant tetrapods that have strayed into the line-up have made high tide, medium swell sessions impossible. The full extent of the damage will not be

Coastal hardening and seawall constructions like this one on Madeira are often the death knell for many breaks across Europe. Jardim do Mar groaning under a concrete straightjacket.

IAN BATTERICK

and the long-term stability of the coastline as a whole. Most significant for surfers are the current feasibility studies looking into the viability of two artificial reefs, which if built will serve a dual role of coastal protection and surfing reefs in Bournemouth and Newquay.

The Netherlands exists courtesy of a huge complex of sea defences built to prevent the North Sea from inundating much of the country that lies below sea level. In such an unnatural scenario, the dykes are protected by a bristling army of seawalls and jetties, which provide surfers with better waves and wind protection. However, constant intervention has destroyed the notable peaks of Maasexpress with an all too familiar harbour development.

Dredging of the entrance to the Capbreton harbour in France damaged La Gravière, once renowned as the best beach-break in the world. Dredging spoils deposited outside, starved the inside sandbanks of swell but it has slowly recovered. More recent marina dredging has led to the sludge being dumped on La Piste, south of the river, and it is unclear how this may affect the world-class

known until the project is finished but the prognosis is bad. Road modification at Paul do Mar has seen a steepening of the beach, creating a high tide backwash. Lugar de Baxio was saved from a destructive marina project but a seawall has again caused backwash problems. Elsewhere another five waves are under threat from total destruction or wave alteration. Local action groups have filed a court action against the developments, which, if Portuguese law is upheld, appear to be illegal, as any new construction within 150ft (50m) of the sea is against the law.

Coastal development on the Azores has had a big impact on the local surfing topography. Terceira has been hardest hit where a stretch of pristine beaches and reefs at Praia Vittoria, has been swallowed by a huge US Navy funded harbour, oil terminal and sewage treatment plant. Numerous waves were lost and it galvanised the small surfing population to protect what they have got. A similar project has destroyed waves on San Miguel when a harbour extension went wrong dumping rocks onto a quality reef.

JAKUE ANDIKOETXEA

### Access

Access across the majority of Europe is good, where well developed transport systems and a large coastal population means little of the mainland is hard to get to. In general, most countries legislate for public access to the bulk of the coastline around the mean high water mark and exceptions are generally limited to military ranges or large industrial complexes.

Irish surfers are currently battling for the right to continue to surf the bay at Doughmore as an exclusive golf course is making access via the public right of way difficult. Irresponsible behaviour from surfers during the recent Foot and Mouth cattle disease crisis has irked rural coastal landowners. British surfers failed to heed warnings about crossing agricultural land, increasing the risk of spreading the disease and now all surfers are deterred from quick field runs by farmers. The remote north of Norway is a true surfing frontier, but few roads, long hikes in shortened daylight hours and treacherous, cold conditions, present unique problems for those searching for waves inside the Arctic Circle.

French nuclear submarine bases occupy a large, out of bounds area of the Crozon Peninsula in Brittany. Poor, un-surfaced roads in Portugal and the Canaries can make getting to the surf interesting, especially after rain. The Azores has access issues and going in on foot to many breaks, especially on the outer islands can be a mission. Madeira's steep topography makes for some tricky situations, where vertiginous climbs, rock falls and thunderous shorebreaks are all part of the access story.

### Hazards

Europe is short on dangerous sea life and while sharks do exist, attacks on surfers are unheard of. England, France and Spain have seen 9 attacks since records began and only 1 fatality. Italy is far more likely to host an attack but the last fatality was in 1962. Sea urchins are commonplace in Morocco and Portugal, which lends its name to the globally distributed stinging jellyfish or man-o-war. These *Physalia physalis* can wash up just about anywhere on Atlantic coasts as far north as southern Britain. Another summer scourge of the Atlantic, usually referred to by its misnomer, is sealice or seabathers eruption. Recent clinical research has shown that the rash and intense itching that occurs is caused by the larval form of thimble jellyfish, not some biting mini-beast. Trapped in the net-like fabric of a bathing suit, pressure triggers the microscopic organism to fire poison into its victim. The less material worn (including lycra) the less stings occur although trapping them between chest and board causes "firing". Treatment for most jellyfish stings is to wash area with sea water (not fresh water) remove any tentacles visible and various hydrocortisone or calamine creams will help. In northern latitudes, water temperatures can be brain numbingly cold in the winter and hyperthermia is a distinct possibility. Strong currents are also an issue, and the waters around the British Isles and Brittany have some of the biggest tidal ranges on the planet. Coastal rescue services are widespread throughout the continent, but more care should be taken in remote locations.

With a rapidly expanding surf population, high coastal population and generally good coastal access, localism is inevitable. Unlike the traditional surfing continents, it is less severe, so line-ups are competitive but violence is uncommon. Hot spots exist where travellers must show respect. Certain spots in Ireland, the Basque coast of France into Pais Vasco, Asturias, Portugal, the Canary Islands and the Azores all suffer from isolated localism. Often only an issue at the extremely competitive, hyper-crowded spots like Mundaka, or at big wave spots where visitors are inexperienced and a possible liability in the more dangerous line-ups. Searching for less ridden reefs and beaches, keeping a low profile and showing a lot of respect should ensure a trouble free, travel experience.

Top – **Respect for the indigenous surfers is of paramount importance in many regions. Asturias local crew.**
Right – **Rocky coastlines and shallow reefs are a hazard to consider across much of Europe.**

ROGER SHARP

# Surf Travel Resources

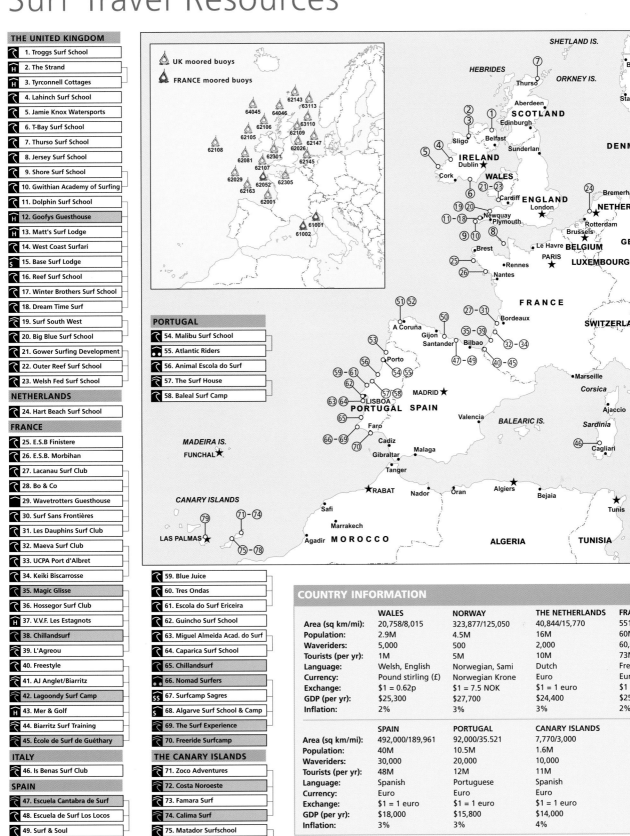

## THE UNITED KINGDOM
1. Troggs Surf School
2. The Strand
3. Tyrconnell Cottages
4. Lahinch Surf School
5. Jamie Knox Watersports
6. T-Bay Surf School
7. Thurso Surf School
8. Jersey Surf School
9. Shore Surf School
10. Gwithian Academy of Surfing
11. Dolphin Surf School
12. Goofys Guesthouse
13. Matt's Surf Lodge
14. West Coast Surfari
15. Base Surf Lodge
16. Reef Surf School
17. Winter Brothers Surf School
18. Dream Time Surf
19. Surf South West
20. Big Blue Surf School
21. Gower Surfing Development
22. Outer Reef Surf School
23. Welsh Fed Surf School

## NETHERLANDS
24. Hart Beach Surf School

## FRANCE
25. E.S.B Finistere
26. E.S.B. Morbihan
27. Lacanau Surf Club
28. Bo & Co
29. Wavetrotters Guesthouse
30. Surf Sans Frontières
31. Les Dauphins Surf Club
32. Maeva Surf Club
33. UCPA Port d'Albret
34. Keiki Biscarrosse
35. Magic Glisse
36. Hossegor Surf Club
37. V.V.F. Les Estagnots
38. Chillandsurf
39. L'Agreou
40. Freestyle
41. AJ Anglet/Biarritz
42. Lagoondy Surf Camp
43. Mer & Golf
44. Biarritz Surf Training
45. École de Surf de Guéthary

## ITALY
46. Is Benas Surf Club

## SPAIN
47. Escuela Cantabra de Surf
48. Escuela de Surf Los Locos
49. Surf & Soul
50. Surf House Tapia
51. RAZ Surf Camp
52. Surf & Rock
53. ES Clube de Viana

## PORTUGAL
54. Malibu Surf School
55. Atlantic Riders
56. Animal Escola do Surf
57. The Surf House
58. Baleal Surf Camp
59. Blue Juice
60. Tres Ondas
61. Escola do Surf Ericeira
62. Guincho Surf School
63. Miguel Almeida Acad. do Surf
64. Caparica Surf School
65. Chillandsurf
66. Nomad Surfers
67. Surfcamp Sagres
68. Algarve Surf School & Camp
69. The Surf Experience
70. Freeride Surfcamp

## THE CANARY ISLANDS
71. Zoco Adventures
72. Costa Noroeste
73. Famara Surf
74. Calima Surf
75. Matador Surfschool
76. Cowabunga
77. Ineika
78. Homegrown
79. Pura Vida Cat 42

## COUNTRY INFORMATION

|  | WALES | NORWAY | THE NETHERLANDS | FRANCE |
|---|---|---|---|---|
| Area (sq km/mi): | 20,758/8,015 | 323,877/125,050 | 40,844/15,770 | 551,500/212,935 |
| Population: | 2.9M | 4.5M | 16M | 60M |
| Waveriders: | 5,000 | 500 | 2,000 | 60,000 |
| Tourists (per yr): | 1M | 5M | 10M | 73M |
| Language: | Welsh, English | Norwegian, Sami | Dutch | French |
| Currency: | Pound stirling (£) | Norwegian Krone | Euro | Euro |
| Exchange: | $1 = 0.62p | $1 = 7.5 NOK | $1 = 1 euro | $1 = 1 euro |
| GDP (per yr): | $25,300 | $27,700 | $24,400 | $25,000 |
| Inflation: | 2% | 3% | 3% | 2% |

|  | SPAIN | PORTUGAL | CANARY ISLANDS |
|---|---|---|---|
| Area (sq km/mi): | 492,000/189,961 | 92,000/35.521 | 7,770/3,000 |
| Population: | 40M | 10.5M | 1.6M |
| Waveriders: | 30,000 | 20,000 | 10,000 |
| Tourists (per yr): | 48M | 12M | 11M |
| Language: | Spanish | Portuguese | Spanish |
| Currency: | Euro | Euro | Euro |
| Exchange: | $1 = 1 euro | $1 = 1 euro | $1 = 1 euro |
| GDP (per yr): | $18,000 | $15,800 | $14,000 |
| Inflation: | 3% | 3% | 4% |

# 81. Gower

Gower Reefs

ALL PHOTOS PHIL HOLDEN

## Summary

+ DIVERSITY OF REEFS AND BEACHES
+ MANY EASY WAVES
+ ALWAYS OFFSHORE SOMEWHERE
+ SCENIC AND CULTURALLY RICH AREA

− COLD WATER AND AIR
− TIGHT SWELL WINDOW
− MANY INCONSISTENT SPOTS
− WINDY
− ALWAYS CROWDED

Well preserved despite being surrounded by heavy industry, Gower was the first area in the UK to be officially recognised an "area of outstanding natural beauty". This 16x7 mi (25x12km) peninsula projecting into the Bristol Channel has over 20 bays and sheltered coves along its rugged coastline. From long, expansive strands to tiny inlets, this stretch of coast provides a wide variety of breaks, combining endless wind options with good swell exposure. Surfing started in Wales in the early 1960s and took-off at spots such as Langland and Llangennith, which remain the focal points of Welsh surf today.

**Broughton Bay** may well be the longest left in South Wales and a real longboarder's delight during heavy SW storms. Strong rips are always a factor and can easily ruin a session for the less experienced surfer. The most

## TRAVEL INFORMATION

**Population:** 2.9M Wales
**Coastline:** 988km (617mi)
**Contests:** Local
BPSA Welsh Open (Oct)
**Other Resources:**
gowersurfing.com
dark-tides.com
enjoygower.com
explore-gower.co.uk
a1surf.com
surfsup-mag.co.uk

**Getting There** – Swansea is the closest city to the Gower Peninsula. Airwales fly there (SWS) from London City (LCY), but there is a stopover and driving doesn't take much more than 3h. Cardiff and its international airport are only 50mn away from Swansea Bay by road or rail. Express coaches travel to Swansea from most parts of Britain but may not take boards.

**Getting Around** – This is a rural area but communications networks are quite good. An extensive bus service covers the Swansea Bay area and reaches Llangennith 15mi (24km). Traversing the peninsula takes around 30mn, allowing for surf checks. Car rentals average $250/week.

**Lodging and Food** – B&B's are the local flavour and there are many to choose from. Right behind the dunes of Llangennith, Hillend campsite is fine before it gets too cold. For maximum

comfort try the Oxwich Bay Hotel ($110/dble), the Worm's Head Hotel in Rhossili ($100/dble) or the Carlton Hotel in Mumbles ($95/dble).

**Weather** – Regular SW onshores blow across the Bristol Channel and hills to block some of the cold N winds and give the Gower a real oceanic climate. This allows the peninsula to avoid experiencing the temperature extremes recorded in other parts of the UK, but freezing temperatures are still a regular occurrence in winter. The same moderation applies in summer and it rarely gets over 20°C (68°F), even in the warmest months of July and August. Rain is another major issue and locals often crack the joke: "if you can see the Mumbles Head clearly, it is going to rain; if you can't, it is raining". It rains every other day, more during the peak precipitation months between October and January. Even when it doesn't rain, the peninsula will suffer from days of total cloud cover. May and June will see the most sunshine. Since most of the surf happens in the cold season Gower is definitely a fullsuit destination. Hood, gloves, boots and a 5/4/3 wetsuit are needed to combat water temperatures which dip below 10°C (50°F), unless you opt for a dry suit, which some locals do.

**Nature and Culture** – Touring the Gower coastline, be it by foot, cycle or car, reveals why it was designated as 'an area of outstanding natural beauty'. In addition to beautiful beaches there are medieval castles and churches, megalithic burial tombs and other visual treats set among a natural landscape. Mumbles is widely reputed for partying, centred on the Mumbles Mile, an endless procession of pubs.

**Hazards and Hassles** – Welsh surfers are friendly but travellers should keep a low profile around spots where localism remains present. Water quality is improving despite neighbouring heavy industries. Breaks such as Llangennith suffer from strong rip-tide currents and flotillas of every type of surfcraft in summer.

**Handy Hints** – A shortboard is all you really need for these waves but longboarding fits in as well. There are several shops including Gower Boardriders in Swansea and PJ's in Llangennith. This one is owned by local legend Pete Jones and can handle surfboard hire and repairs. Lessons are available in Llangennith with the Welsh Surfing Federation and in Caswell Bay with GSD.

| WEATHER STATISTICS | J/F | M/A | M/J | J/A | S/O | N/D |
|---|---|---|---|---|---|---|
| total rainfall (mm) | 100 | 70 | 75 | 100 | 115 | 135 |
| consistency (days/mth) | 16 | 13 | 13 | 15 | 16 | 18 |
| min temp (°C/°F) | 3/37 | 7/45 | 12/54 | 15/59 | 11/52 | 6/43 |
| max temp (°C/°F) | 6/43 | 9/48 | 15/59 | 18/64 | 14/57 | 11/52 |

consistent place on the Gower
Peninsula is the oversized beach of
**Llangennith**. Its northern end
will pick up all available
swell, shared amongst a
handful of peaks that are usually best
around mid to high tide.
Paddle outs on bigger
swells are gruelling, but it's
always possible to find shelter
from S winds around **Rhossili**. It's a
really long walk from Rhossili to
**Fall Bay**, another big swell option.
**Pete's Reef** remains consistent
throughout summer thanks to a deep-
water trench which funnels swell into the
reef. However, this little barrelling A-frame

Broughton Bay ①
Llangennith Beach ②
Rhossili Bay ③
Fall Bay ④
Pete's Reef ⑤
Boiler Reef ⑥
Sumpters ⑦
Port Eynon Point ⑧
⑨ Horton Beach
⑩ Slade Bay
⑪ Oxwich Bay
⑫ Threecliff Bay
⑬ Hunts Bay
⑭ Caswell Bay
⑮ Langland Bay

*Bristol Channel*

Llangennith

tends to break in ankle-deep water and the spot suffers
from rips on incoming tides as well as a tricky entry and
exit. These same conditions affect **Boiler Reef** so many
locals go to **Sumpters** rights, where a deep-water gully
eases the paddle-out. All the reefs suffer from dodgy
access, little available parking and treks across farmland
to get to the water. **Port Eynon Point** starts breaking in
shallow water for the initial, intense section before the
wave flattens off in deeper water. **Horton Beach** needs
much more swell to start breaking, but it then offers
shorebreak barrels protected from SW winds. From the
east part of Horton, you can walk below the cliffs and
along the coast to reach **Slade Bay**, where a right and left
reef breaks with a solid swell. **Oxwich Bay** is so protected
it's usually flat or breaking really small, but major swells
can get the right point to fire. The word spreads fast on

such days and parking issues aren't enough to
keep the crowds away. **Threecliff Bay** gets nice
peaks next to a rivermouth, requiring a large swell
and higher tides, but the currents can be a pain.
**Hunt's Bay** can offer the possibility to score an
uncrowded session, but the reef only breaks on a
solid 6ft (2m) swell. Because it is so sheltered,
**Caswell Bay**'s beachbreak will appeal to those
looking for waves a little smaller than what's on
offer at Langland. Concentrating a huge variety of
waves in a single location, **Langland Bay** is the
alpha spot in SW Wales, so it sometimes cultivates
a bit of localism. Nevertheless, one can't imagine
surfing Gower without having a go at the
Rotherslade lefts, the middle reef or the
righthander that peels off Crab Island on the larger
swells. The beachbreak can be sluggish but with
constantly changing wind and tide conditions a constant
vigil will reap short windows of decent waves.

Welsh surfers regularly wish that Ireland could be
towed away so that NW swells generated south
of Iceland could hit their shores. Since Gower is
on the south side of the country even that would not be
enough and the area would still rely on SW-W swells.
Summers are usually quite lame since lows don't sit south
enough in the Atlantic. Year round onshore south-
westerlies are the dominant pattern, but autumn and
winter swells awaken spots where onshore becomes
offshore conditions. The Gower handles NW winds, the
bane of the West Cornwall coast. All in all, winters are
best, but way too cold for most,
which leaves spring and autumn
as the exceptional seasons. With
33ft (10m) tides in the Bristol
Channel, tide tables are almost
as important as thick rubber.

Crab Island, Langland Bay

| SPOT DESCRIPTION | | | |
|---|---|---|---|
| | Spot Size | Btm | Type |
| ① | 8/2 | | |
| ② | 8/1 | | |
| ③ | 8/2 | | |
| ④ | 8/2 | | |
| ⑤ | 8/2 | | |
| ⑥ | 10/2 | | |
| ⑦ | 10/2 | | |
| ⑧ | 6/2 | | |
| ⑨ | 6/2 | | |
| ⑩ | 8/3 | | |
| ⑪ | 6/2 | | |
| ⑫ | 10/2 | | |
| ⑬ | 8/2 | | |
| ⑭ | 6/2 | | |
| ⑮ | 8/2 | | |

| SURF STATISTICS | J F | M A | M J | J A | S O | N D |
|---|---|---|---|---|---|---|
| dominant swell | SW-W | SW-W | SW-W | SW-W | SW-W | SW-W |
| swell size (ft) | 6 | 5 | 3 | 1-2 | 4-5 | 5-6 |
| consistency (%) | 50 | 60 | 60 | 30 | 70 | 60 |
| dominant wind | S-SW | S-SW | S-SW | S-SW | S-SW | S-W |
| average force | F5 | F4 | F3-F4 | F4 | F4-F5 | F5 |
| consistency (%) | 38 | 34 | 38 | 45 | 35 | 53 |
| water temp (°C/°F) | 9/48 | 10/50 | 12/54 | 16/61 | 14/57 | 11/52 |
| wetsuit | | | | | | |

# 82. Lofoten

Unstadt Left

JORGEN MICHAELSON

## Summary

+ LONG, EMPTY POINTBREAKS
+ MIDNIGHT SUN
+ UNRIVALLED ARCTIC SCENERY
+ FRIENDLY VIBE

− COLD SUMMER CONDITIONS
− SHORT SURFING SEASON
− DIFFICULT COASTAL ACCESS
− SUPER EXPENSIVE

Until recently, Norway's surf potential has been mostly ignored, leaving it to a small core crew to enjoy the waves around Stavanger, in the south. This area has easy access via the coast road stretching from Stavanger to Egersund, which has a relatively straight shoreline not seen elsewhere in Norway, boasting a gentle slope into the sea, strewn with cobblestone and sand. A good exposure to the inconsistent swell patterns of the North Atlantic, supplies a handful of fun, reliable spots. However, way up north, above the Arctic Circle, the spotlight has fallen on Lofoten as a primo surfing destination, highlighted by projects such as The Arctic Challenge, created by noted Norwegian boarder, Terje Haakonsen and

MICHAEL KEW

Unstadt Left

MICHAEL KEW

an article in *Surfer* mag called 'Valhalla'. The Lofoten are a cluster of mountainous islands extending 100km (62mi) out to see off the north Norwegian coastline, stretching for more than 160km (100mi) around the 68th degree parallel. Between the mainland and the "Lofoten Wall" lies the wild and dangerous stretch of water known as Vestfjorden. Lofoten is mountainous, with

## TRAVEL INFORMATION

**Population:**
24,500 Lofoten
**Coastline:**
3,419km (2,136mi)
**Contests:** None
**Other Resources:**
Video: E2K; Back 9
lofot-ferie.com
surfsentrum.no
lofoten-tourist.no
visitnorway.com

**Getting There** – Most int'l flights go to Oslo. Flying to Bodø costs 500$ o/w with Braathens Airlines. It takes 3 days to drive from Oslo. Daily departures from Bodø to Lofoten airfields. The Coastal Express calls daily at Stamsund and Svolvær. Bodø and Vesterålen are served by express boatsExpress boats serve Bodø and Vesterålen from Svolvær. In addition, there are express Bus-boat services to/from Narvik.

**Getting Around** – The road distance is 170km (106mi) from Vesterålen to Å, in the south, where the E10 ends in Bodø. The air distance is more than 60km to Skomvær. Bridges and tunnels have replaced the ferries between the largest islands in Lofoten. Use ferries to get to the southern Lofoten from Bodø. Rental cars cost 800$/wk, rent a wreck is cheaper. Unleaded is $1.20/litre.

**Lodging and Food** – Lofoten is more expensive than the rest of Norway, which is already very expensive, especially alcohol! Favour "rorbu" camping or self-catering units for cheaper stays, budget at least $40/day. If surviving on a budget, cod and potatoes are cheap and shop in large supermarkets (Leknes or Svolvær), it is possible to get by with $15 /meal.

**Weather** – Due to the warm Gulf Stream, Lofoten has a much milder climate than other parts of the world at the same latitude, such as Alaska. The coastal climate makes mild winters and cool summers. January and February are the coldest months, with an average temperature of −1°C (30°F). July and August are warmest with an average of 12°C (54°F). May and June are the driest months, with an average 40mm of rainfall. In areas to the west and north of the Lofoten islands, the midnight sun is visible from 27 May – 17 July. The coastline is vegetation free for the first few hundred metres. Optimum timing is mid-September to mid-October, wear a full 5/4mm with booties, gloves and hood for the worst conditions. On a balmy day, gloves and hood may not be necessary.

**Nature and Culture** – "Skrei" (spawning cod from the Barents Sea) are caught in the Lofoten area during the winter, which means boats could be available for chartering the coast in autumn. Fishing is the main industry. The white-tailed eagle flourishes. Besides dramatic landscapes, don't miss the Aquarium in Kabelvåg.

**Hazards and Hassles** – Seals and killer whales are often observed offshore Lofoten and Vesterålen. Norway is the land of Vikings, but also the land of a handful of hardcore waveriders. However, the surfer's main adversary is the cold. Come prepared! Just getting wax for the cold conditions is a problem, not mentioning staying warm and being able to move in 7mm wetsuits.

**Handy Hints** – Nearest shop is Surfsentrum in Stavanger, 2000km (1,273mi) away! Bring a pointbreak fast gunny board, but not necessarily a full gun. Get the full winter set with gloves, hood and heavy booties. The locals prefer to drink deadly homebrew (illegally) rather than hassle around for other warmer clime substances so don't ask!

| WEATHER STATISTICS | J/F | M/A | M/J | J/A | S/O | N/D |
|---|---|---|---|---|---|---|
| total rainfall (mm) | 61 | 51 | 41 | 59 | 101 | 89 |
| consistency (days/mth) | 15 | 16 | 17 | 18 | 20 | 16 |
| min temp (°C/°F) | -4/25 | -3/27 | 5/41 | 11/52 | 4/39 | -1/30 |
| max temp (°C/°F) | 2/35 | 4/39 | 12/54 | 15/59 | 9/48 | 3/37 |

Unstadt Right

MICHAEL KEW

| SPOT DESCRIPTION | | | |
|---|---|---|---|
| Spot | Size | Btm | Type |
| ① | • | • | • |
| ② | 6/2 | ◑ | ◿ |
| ③ | 8/3 | ◐ | ◿ |
| ④ | 4/1 | ◐ | ◿ |
| ⑤ | 10/3 | ◐ | ◿ |
| ⑥ | 12/3 | ◕ | ◿ |
| ⑦ | • | • | • |
| ⑧ | • | • | • |
| ⑨ | • | • | • |

peaks plunging down into wide-open ocean, pocked with sheltered inlets and a general vibe of virgin wilderness. Transformed rock, which is over 3 billion years old, is predominant, meaning these islands are some of the oldest rocks on the planet. The mountains of Lofoten were not formed until in the last Ice Age, which only ended 10,000 years ago. Surfing began in Norway in the late '60's to early '70s when Thor Frantzen and Hans Egil Krane made their own boards after being exposed to surfing in Australia while in the merchant navy. Their crude construction methods included using foam from a refrigerator and using plans cribbed from a Beach Boys album cover!

Missing the flight or ferry from Bodø, means a 13h drive via Narvik's ski resorts to access Lofoten via bridges and the peninsular that joins to the mainland. The most northerly spot to check on Vestvågøy is **Kvalnes**, which is close to the coast road. It's rarely surfed, like the nearby break of Vinje which picks up most SW to N swells. Further down is **Eggum**'s beautiful pebble beach, which needs a big swell, S wind and is pretty sectiony. **Unstadt**'s three waves only became easily accessibe in 1995 when the tunnel to the village (pop 30) opened. If one of the predominant SW swells is firing, there are awesome lefts reeling in front of an impressive 800m mountain. It's top drawer over the shallow, sketchy ledge but inconsistent and a fairly technical ride, plus getting in and out is tricky, so experienced surfers only. The right pointbreak has more consistency and works on most tides, tubular sections are numerous but it's almost unmakeably fast. The mountains can funnel the variable winds, producing strong offshores that are less of a problem at the boulder and sand beachbreak. Little is

known of other spots, so there's still much to explore. On Vestvågøy check **Utakleiv**, which is fairly easily accessible. On Flakstadøy, have a go at **Vikten**, which is right by the road. The main road on Moskenesøy heads to the east side but checking promising exposed spots like **Sand** or **Skiva** probably requires a boat. Å is the last fishing village going south, intriguingly named and well-preserved. It boasts a shoreline of red rorbu and plenty of cod drying on racks. Nearby is Moskenesstraumen, a maelström with a mighty whirlpool, which inspired tales by Jules Verne and Edgar Allen Poe.

The Lofoten lie on the eastern edge of the Norwegian Sea, bordered by Svalbard to the north, Greenland to the west and Iceland to the south. Some North Atlantic depressions do get as far as Norway, but many of them die en route. Being so high in the Arctic Circle, it's mostly a venue for windswells from SW to N. SW winds are best for Lofoten. In summer, high pressure dominates above the Hotlands. Swells are short but powerful and can produce 6-8ft (2-2.5m) waves. Lofoten breaks are pretty consistent because of the wide swell window. Unlike the Stavanger area where there are virtually no tides, most Lofoten islands are surrounded by strong tidal currents. The maelström whirls are a direct consequence of major tidal action. Spring tidal range can reach 10ft.

Unstadt Beach

JØRGEN MICHAELSON

| SURF STATISTICS | J F | M A | M J | J A | S O | N D |
|---|---|---|---|---|---|---|
| dominant swell | SW-N | SW-N | SW-N | SW-N | SW-N | SW-N |
| swell size (ft) | 5-6 | 4-5 | 3-4 | 3 | 4-5 | 5-6 |
| consistency (%) | 0 | 10 | 40 | 60 | 30 | 10 |
| dominant wind | S-SW | S-SW | N-NE | N-NE | S-SW | SE-SW |
| average force | F5 | F5 | F4 | F4 | F4-F5 | F5 |
| consistency (%) | 34 | 34 | 39 | 41 | 31 | 53 |
| water temp (°C/°F) | 5/41 | 6/43 | 7/45 | 10/50 | 9/48 | 7/45 |
| wetsuit | 🏄 | 🏄 | 🏄 | 🏄 | 🏄 | 🏄 |

# 83. West Kust

DENMARK
GERMANY
ENGLAND
NETHERLANDS

**Summary**
+ Mellow beachbreaks
+ Excellent beach facilities
+ Good transport links
+ Close to Amsterdam

− Lack of groundswells
− Flat, crowded summers
− Freezing winters
− Expensive
− Beach access restrictions

Scheveningen Overview

RAYMAX

G.J. DE KONING

Nearly a quarter of The Netherlands sits below sea level, so the population, who rely on dykes to defend the country from the worst North Sea swells, may not consider waves a blessing. Much of the seabed is shallow, continental shelf, bordered by a predominantly soft coastline of sand dunes, saltmarsh and the world's largest stretch of uninterrupted mudflats at Waddensea. The surf favours the in-between seasons of autumn and spring when strong lows send NNW swells to endless flat beaches, where conditions improve in the vicinity of huge boulder jetties. The Netherlands is certainly not a prime surfing destination, but it's rumoured that Jan Nederveen started surfing in the '30s, making him one of the first surfers in Europe! During the '80s trend for windsurfing, the first wave of regular surfers hit the waves and it has been growing in popularity ever since. There are three surfing regions: the Wadden Islands; Westkust and

G.J. DE KONING

Zeeland to the south. Scheveningen is by far the most popular surf area as well as the major seaside resort.

Like Tershelling further north, **Texel** is one of the best Wadden Islands for catching NNW groundswells. Whilst the swell is larger than further south, it lacks jetties and other wave shapers, so unless it's directly offshore or the sandbanks are lined up, it will be messy. If clean, it's worth the drive and ferry journey; Kogerstrand by De Koog holds

## TRAVEL INFORMATION

**Population:** 3.5M
**Coastline:** 451km (280mi)
**Contests:** May, Oct, Nov
**Other Resources:**
surfholland.nl
mousemotel.com
publicbeach.nl
hotelsscheveningen.nl
holland.com

**Getting There** – Amsterdam Schiphol airport offers connection to 200+ worldwide destinations. KLM Royal Dutch Airlines is the national carrier. Distance to the beach is close but it all depends on traffic and parking availability, as population density is high.

**Getting Around** – Holland has a very compact and modern railway network. Every village in Holland can be reached by public transport. All roads are well signposted. The green ëEí indicates int'l motorways, the red ëAí nat'l motorways and other main roads are marked by yellow ëNí. Rental cars start from $20/day. No hills means loads of bicycles.

**Lodging and Food** – Expensive by European standards as it's a wealthy area. Scheveningen has the widest range of accommodation from deluxe Kurhaus Hotel sea view rooms to the campsite in the woods near Scheveningen. Hotel Lunamare costs $50/d (dble). $15 should buy a decent meal.

**Weather** – There is a moderate coastal climate with cool summers and mild winters. The average temperature in January is 2°C (35°F) and 21°C (70°F) in August. Feb to May are the driest months. June and October are typically wet months and the coast enjoys more sunny hours than inland. In the land of windmills, the SW-W wind can add a chill factor coming off the cold North Sea. Hardcore waveriders will have to handle 5°C (41°F) water or less and freezing air temps. Winter is the best season but it's said to be late autumn-early winter for a good combo of frequent swells and 4/3mm

wetsuit. The heart of the winter requires 6/5/4mm and all the other bits of rubber.

**Nature and Culture** – Festivals include the North Sea Jazz Festival and the National Sea Life. Beach cafés and coffee shops are central to the vibe. There is a Flowrider at De Eemhof.

**Hazards and Hassles** – Hazards include surfing bans, jetties, jellyfish, lifeguards tickets, cold winter water and pollution (every rivermouth hosts a harbour). There is no unpaid parking and expensive wheel clamping is enforced.

**Handy Hints** – Dutch, Belgian and German surfers mostly frequent this surf zone, as it isn't really on the main European surf trail. Surfboards are available for rent ($10/d) at the Hart Beach Shop. Go Klap runs a long established surf school.

| WEATHER STATISTICS | J/F | M/A | M/J | J/A | S/O | N/D |
|---|---|---|---|---|---|---|
| total rainfall (mm) | 54 | 41 | 46 | 68 | 72 | 65 |
| consistency (days/mth) | 19 | 16 | 13 | 15 | 17 | 20 |
| min temp (°C/°F) | 1/34 | 4/39 | 11/52 | 14/59 | 11/52 | 4/39 |
| max temp (°C/°F) | 5/41 | 11/52 | 18/64 | 21/70 | 17/63 | 8/46 |

an outside sandbank which can be truly hollow. Closer to Zandvoort (and Amsterdam) it becomes more crowded but also gains swell focusing jetties. Bigger, messy swells will clean up thanks to dykes and jetties like **Hargen**. The resort towns of **Petten** or **Bergen aan Zee** favour clean swells and Petten in particular can have fast hollow peelers, dependent on tide. **Egmond aan Zee** handles the biggest swells (8ft/2.5m), but they have to be from the N and the wind from the E. The **Noordpier** at Wijk am Zee is one of the best beachbreaks, protected by a long harbour wall, but it suffers from rips and lots of windsurfers. South of Noordpier, past the 20km of open beach at **Zandvoort**,

Zud

which only works in SW swells, is **Pier**, sitting at the entrance of the North Sea Canal, linking the Port of Amsterdam to the North Sea. These piers extend 3km (2mi) into the North Sea, offering good fishing options and a vantage point of the shifting peaks and dodgy currents. Visit the lighthouse (36m high and 162 stairs to the top) for a commanding view. Scheveningen is a 4km (2.75mi) long strand with beach cafés lining the promenade. The **Noorderstrand** has shifting sandbars holding longer lefts, best on NW swells with SW winds but is also likely to be crowded. The southern end, **Zud**, needs more swell, holds more size, has better shape, is protected from N winds and is less crowded. Before reaching Maasvlakte's well known spots, **Kijkduin** and **Ter Heijde** offer low tide alternatives off rock jetties which can break better than Scheveningen. Massvlakte's reputation was forged on powerful peaks at Maasexpress, but unfortunately these waves disappeared with a harbour development. It takes a drive through Rotterdam to get this the isolated stretch, sandwiched between waterways. Pass Maasexpress and exit for

Ter Heijde

Kijkduin

**Blokken** or **Slufter** but only go when the swell is over 4ft (1.2m) – mostly on disorganised storm swells. Blokken works on any bigger swell and sits close to a power plant so the water is considerably warmer, especially in winter. Slufter can get surprisingly hollow, but beware of rips during side-shore winds.

| SURF STATISTICS | J F | M A | M J | J A | S O | N D |
|---|---|---|---|---|---|---|
| dominant swell | NW-N | NW-N | NW-N | NW-N | NW-N | NW-N |
| swell size (ft) | 3 | 2-3 | 1-2 | 1 | 2-3 | 3 |
| consistency (%) | 50 | 40 | 30 | 10 | 30 | 50 |
| dominant wind | S-W | SW-W | SW-W | SW-W | SW-W | SW-NW |
| average force | F4 | F4 | F4 | F4 | F4-F5 | F5 |
| consistency (%) | 52 | 39 | 32 | 41 | 33 | 56 |
| water temp (°C/°F) | 5/41 | 6/43 | 12/54 | 16/62 | 15/60 | 9/48 |
| wetsuit | | | | | | |

Once North Atlantic low pressure cells have crossed the ocean, they traverse the UK within 12 hours and resume their wave generation process in the North Sea. Summer is usually pretty flat but winter brings regular 1-2 day swells. Most spots on the Dutch coast are best with NW swells and to a lesser degree W, N and sometimes SW short period windswell. Thus, Holland mostly receives 2-8ft (0.6-2.5m) windswell and occasionally a clean 2-5ft (0.6-1.5m) N swell kicks in. In the land of windmills, winds are pretty steady, though rarely very strong with SW dominance, tending S in winter and W in summer. There is a brief N-NE wind quadrant before summer in May-June. Beware, in summer beach crowds hit the coast and many beaches have surfing bans. Spring tidal range can reach 7ft (2.2m), affecting the flat slope on these coastal lowlands (polders), so pick up a tide chart for variation. Breaks usually favour low to mid-tide although some high tide spots can deliver shorebreak power.

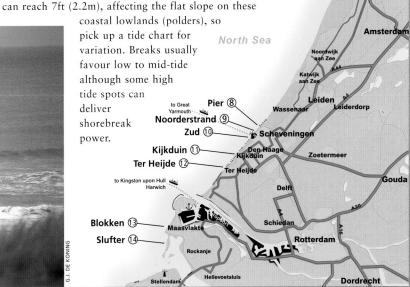

**SPOT DESCRIPTION**

| Spot | Size | Btm | Type |
|---|---|---|---|
| ① | 6/1 | | |
| ② | 6/1 | | |
| ③ | 6/1 | | |
| ④ | 6/1 | | |
| ⑤ | 8/1 | | |
| ⑥ | 6/1 | | |
| ⑦ | 6/1 | | |
| ⑧ | 6/1 | | |
| ⑨ | 6/1 | | |
| ⑩ | 8/1 | | |
| ⑪ | 6/1 | | |
| ⑫ | 6/1 | | |
| ⑬ | 8/1 | | |
| ⑭ | 6/1 | | |

Texel ①

Hargen ②

Petten ③

Bergen aan Zee ④

Egmond aan Zee ⑤

Noordpier ⑥

to Göteborg, Kristiansand, Stavanger, Bergen

Zandvoort ⑦

*North Sea*

to Great Yarmouth

Pier ⑧

Noorderstrand ⑨

Zud ⑩

Kijkduin ⑪

Ter Heijde ⑫

to Kingston upon Hull Harwich

Blokken ⑬

Slufter ⑭

FRANCE

SPAIN

# 84. Finistère

Pointe Leydé

FRED LE LEANNEC

## Summary

+ WIDE SWELL WINDOW
+ UNSPOILT CROZON PENINSULAR
+ INDENTED COASTLINE
+ SPLENDID CELTIC EVIDENCE
+ FESTIVALS AND FEST-NOZE

– WIND SWEPT REGION
– COLD AND RAINY
– LACK OF EPIC POINTBREAKS
– SUMMER CROWDS
– EXTREME TIDAL RANGES

France is well known for its blend of waves and culture with most surftrippers heading for Hossegor and the Côte Basque in the southwest. However, en route, some of those travelling from the UK will stop in Brittany for a taste of France's Celtic tradition. With 1500km (930mi) of coastline, Brittany juts out to sea and provides variety in its coastal structure. The south facing Atlantic shoreline has large bays, long peninsulas and low lying land; while the north shore is characterised by high cliffs and deep, narrow, indented estuaries. Finistère, the most westerly of Brittany's four 'départements', combines these features, and provides the ideal snapshot of this varied surfing area. Unlike southwest France, the

Le Conquet

FRED LE LEANNEC

Le Minou

KIRSTEN PELOU

northwest is dotted with many fair-sized cities which produce more demographic pressure on its coastline, but due to the dramatic tidal range, fierce storms and strict construction laws concerning coastal development, there are still long stretches of untouched coast. Most of the accessible spots will be crowded in small and clean conditions but there remains ample space for the average surfrider who avoids the rare pointbreaks.

## TRAVEL INFORMATION

**Population:** 852,000
**Coastline:** 795km (497mi)
**Contests:** Regional
**Other Resources:**
surfinistere.fr.st
longboardspirit.com
brittanytourism.com
finisteretourisme.com

**Getting There** – From Paris it's a 4h drive to Brest or Quimper. It takes 3h by TGV (bullet train). Boards charged at $30. Ferries go from Roscoff to both Plymouth (UK) and Cork (Eire). It's 6h to Plymouth – service varies from 1/day to 1/week. Costs $260/car with 2p o/w.

**Getting Around** – Motorways are toll-free in Brittany but fuel costs almost $1/litre. Lots of driving between spots. Roads can be very narrow in villages. The exposed coastline doesn't have many access points or car parks so be prepared to walk through the heaths. July-August is jammed.

**Lodging and Food** – La Torche is lacking in facilities with no accommodation apart from a

summertime campsite, 2 or 3 surf shops and a couple of crêperies. If you don't have a campervan, the guest houses cost ($40/dble) or hotels ($50/dble) in the cities – Crozon is a good bet. Typical foods are crêpes (sweet or savoury pancakes). Pay $15 for a meal with cider.

**Weather** – Brittany has a typical maritime climate with cool summers and mild, wet winters but is also extremely exposed to the Atlantic winds. In fact, these winds are what keep the temperature above 0°C in winter and have, over millennia, helped create Brittany's rugged coastline. Rain is a frequent occurrence but rarely gets too intense – the total rainfall is actually lower than in most French regions. The quick, radical weather changes are a regular feature of Brittany's weather. Water temperature remains cold year round and even in the height of summer, days without a full suit on will be rare. In winter a 4/3mil fullsuit, hood, booties and gloves will be on the cards.

**Nature and Culture** – Brittany is the 3rd most visited region in France. Evidence of its Celtic past is scattered throughout the countryside and villages (Locronan). Crozon's untouched scenery, often veiled in mist patches, has its charms. Visit Oceanopolis in Brest or the Rade. There are lots of festivals in the summer and locals party hard at the biggest one known as Fest-Noze.

**Hazards and Hassles** – Besides being very cold and rainy, there is not much to fear apart from hypothermia. Some spots have strong riptides but trying to get to the right spot before its optimum tidal phase is crucial. Surfing started here in the early '70s, and surfers are mellow but numerous.

**Handy Hints** – ESB is a chain of surf schools and Brittany is home to Bic surfboards (Vannes). Surf shops can be found at major spots and cities but gear is expensive – $450/board. Best shapers are in Quiberon, South Brittany, where surfing has developed more than in the north. Home of Kana Beach surfwear.

| WEATHER STATISTICS | J/F | M/A | M/J | J/A | S/O | N/D |
|---|---|---|---|---|---|---|
| total rainfall (mm) | 115 | 83 | 63 | 70 | 98 | 145 |
| consistency (days/mth) | 16 | 12 | 9 | 11 | 13 | 18 |
| min temp (°C/°F) | 4/39 | 6/43 | 9/48 | 13/55 | 10/50 | 6/43 |
| max temp (°C/°F) | 9/48 | 12/54 | 17/63 | 20/68 | 17/63 | 11/52 |

La Torche

*KRISTEN PELOU*

There are still waves to be discovered on the rocky north coast, between **Dossen** and **Penfoul**, when SW winds bring enough swell, but easy access is scarce. Avoid the due W facing coast, which is tucked behind offshore islands, receives little swell and sees plenty of huge ships, plying the Ouessant Rail. The S facing beaches, like **Porsmilin** and **Petit Minou**, west of Brest are usually crowded but there are other breaks to choose from. The Crozon Peninsula is blessed with long, consistent, quality beachbreaks like **La Palue** and occasional right pointbreaks such as **Anse de Dinan** and **Cap de la Chèvre**. This area is the most consistent part of Brittany, holding decent surf if there is any swell and providing shelter from many wind directions. No access north of Crozon, where the nuclear submarines are based. The huge Douarnenez Bay usually filters so much swell that only storms produce poor quality, high tide surf, perfect for beginners. The exception is **Pointe Leydé**, a machine-like left wrapping in over shallow rocks when huge swells and SW winds batter the coast outside the bay. The spectacular **Baie des Trépassés**, ('Bay of Death'), is a narrow W facing beach, which produces average beachbreaks. **St-Tugen** on Cap Sizun is a quality S facing low tide barelling beachbeach. **Lervily** is home to what is probably the region's best right pointbreak and there are other peaks nearby. South from Audierne towards La Torche is a long beach with only a few known access points and Plozevet probably hides a multitude of spots. **La Torche** made its name in the early '80s due to amazing conditions for national and international wavesailing competitions. Crowded beachbreaks next to a right

pointbreak plus some nearby SW wind protected lefts. Further south are low tide rights at **Porzcarn** and the intriguing stretch of Les Etocs, rumoured to hold big, outside waves although the surf world awaits photographic evidence. **Lesconil** is popular with windsurfers because it is often cross onshore on the due S facing coast.

**B**rittany enjoys good exposure to the North Atlantic swells, only sheltered by Cornwall on its northern shores. Swells average 4-15ft (1.2-5m) in winter and 2-10ft (0.6-3m) in summer when they tend to be from a more northerly direction. Up to 200 swells hit the coast on an annual basis but are usually messy. However, the rugged coastline will allow for some good swell/wind combinations, unless the wind is directly from the W. Predominant winds are from the SW-NW, with W winds prevalent in summer. During high pressures, winds will generally be easterly in the morning before a moderate sea breeze picks up later in the day. Apart from swell and wind combinations, tidal range is a significant factor. Spring tides reach to 9m (27ft), increasing their range as you head north inside the Channel. This usually means hitting most breaks before optimum tide and accounting for the vast changes between an incoming or outgoing flow.

| SURF STATISTICS | J F | M A | M J | J A | S O | N D |
|---|---|---|---|---|---|---|
| dominant swell | SW-NW | SW-NW | SW-NW | SW-NW | SW-NW | SW-NW |
| swell size (ft) | 7 | 6 | 4 | 2 | 5-6 | 6-7 |
| consistency (%) | 60 | 70 | 70 | 60 | 80 | 70 |
| dominant wind | SW-NW | SW-NW | SW-NW | SW-NW | SW-NW | SW-NW |
| average force | F5 | F4-F5 | F4 | F4 | F4 | F5 |
| consistency (%) | 55 | 56 | 47 | 56 | 63 | 59 |
| water temp (°C) | 10/50 | 10/50 | 13/55 | 16/61 | 15/59 | 12/54 |
| wetsuit | | | | | | |

**SPOT DESCRIPTION**

Map labels:
Dossen ①
Roscoff
Ile de Batz
St Pol de Léon
Plouescat
Brignogan Plage
Goulven
Penfoul ②
Lannilis
Landivisiau
Ile Vierge
Plouguerneau
Lesneven
Ploudalmézeau
Argenton
Ile d'Ouessant
St Renan
Landerneau
Plouarzel
Pte de Corsen
Plouzané
Brest
Ile de Molène
Ile de Béniguet
Le Conquet
Pte de St-Mathieu
Plougastel Daoulas
Pte du Pit Minou
Pte des Espagnols
Le Faou
Porsmilin ③
Petit Minou ④
Pte de Pen-Hir
Crozon
Anse de Dinan ⑤
Pte de Dinan
Chateaulin
La Palue ⑥
Baie de Douarnenez
Cap de la Chèvre ⑦
Pointe Leydé ⑧
Douarnenez
Locronan
Baie des Trépassés ⑨
Pte du Van
Ile de Sein
Pte du Raz
Lescoff
Audierne
Quimper
St-Tugen ⑩
Plozevet
Lervily ⑪
Pouldreuzic
Baie d'Audierne
Plonéour-Lanvern
Fouesnant
Bénodet
Pont-l'Abbé
La Torche ⑫
Penmarc'h
Loctudy
Porzcarn ⑬
Pte de Penmarc'h
Guilvinec
Lesconil ⑭
Iles des Glénans

Crozon Peninsula

*KRISTEN PELOU*

PORTUGAL
SPAIN

# 85. Asturias

Rodiles

WILLY URIBE

**Summary**

+ Epic left rivermouth
+ Exploration potential
+ Consistent in winter
+ Many exposed beachbreaks

− Wet and windy
− Cold winter water
− Needs bigger swells
− Flat, crowded summers.

When most surfers think about Spain, Mundaka instantly comes to mind, but what about the rest of that north facing coastline?

Divided into two regions, namely Galicia and El Cantabrico, it's the Cantabrican coastline that extends westwards from the French Basque border, for 867km (542mi). Encompassing the 3 provinces of Pais Vasco, Cantabria and Asturias, the coast is shadowed by the Cordillera Cantabrica and Picos de Europa mountain ranges, reaching up to almost 10,000ft (3000m). These wet, verdant mountains meet the sea as high cliffs, cut by deep valleys leading to both narrow and wide rivermouths called rias. The unspoiled landscapes are regularly interspersed with dense pockets of urbanisation and heavy industry.

JAKUE ANDIKOETXEA

Salinas

JAKUE ANDIKOETXEA

Much of northern Spain's coast was targeted by Franco for industrial development alongside the traditional local economy of agriculture and fishing, resulting in some stark visual contrasts.

Centrally located in Asturias, a triangular promontory adjacent to the busy centres of Gijon, Aviles and Oviedo,

## TRAVEL INFORMATION

**Population:** 1M
**Coastline:** 334km (208mi)
**Contests:** WQS, National
**Other Resources:**
costasurf.com
vivirasturias.com

**Getting There** – Madrid is Spain's main gateway. From Madrid, it takes 5h to drive to Oviedo-Gijón by autopistas. Beware of surfer unfriendly national airline Iberia who charge heavily for boards. For public transport, favour buses which are cheap and board-friendly. Most surfers do the Europe tour with a van bought in London or Amsterdam.

**Getting Around** – Coastal N634 is efficient with breathtaking views of the surf but it diverts inland on the Asturias central coast. There's plenty of slow traffic on the N632, as it twists and winds between the main coastal towns and cities, quite a way from the coast. Best empty waves may be found down the many side tracks or at the bottom of cliffs. Be prepared to walk. Rental car: $200/ week.

**Lodging and Food** – Almost every Spanish beach has a campground with amenities: Rodiles has 3! They are cheap and very lively in summer. If you want to stay dry, look for pensions (P), hostels (Hs), or hotels (H) depending on budget. Beach hotels tend to be expensive. Meals cost $10. Stay in Villaviciosa for Rodiles.

**Weather** – The climate is humid, with mild, year round temps, however weather patterns are unstable. Summer days are temperate, hovering around 25°C (77°F), but often cloudy. Winters are very mild and rainy, even though the mountains may be cloaked in snow. Spring remains overcast but heats up quickly. A 4/3mm winter suit will cover the coldest months, along with booties and a helmet for the rocks. During summer, a light steamer/ springsuit combo will be needed as it gets colder further west.

**Nature and Culture** – Asturias offers a rich artistic patrimony, highlighting 9th century "pre26mánica" architecture, in the old part of the Principado capital, Oviedo (with its Gothic

cathedral) and Avilés. Check the high Picos de Europa (Covadonga), enjoy local musical folklore and apple cider fiestas in fall.

**Hazards and Hassles** – Since the disastarous sinking of the *Prestige*, there is a constant threat of fuel oil slicks being blown ashore as the tanker continues to leak. This environmental devastation has affected all ocean-users and will continue to do so for some time. With so many rivermouths and numerous heavy industries, polluted line-ups are unavoidable, exacerbated by summer tourist invasions. Hazards include summer jellyfish, rocks and jetties in rough seas, strong riptides and fishing lines. Localism can be heavy at urban spots and Rodiles.

**Handy Hints** – Avoid temporada alta (high season, summer), hotel prices double up and driving is crazy. In winter, you'll need a gun for serious spots (Mongol, Cabo Lastres). Tablas surf shop in Gijón sells boards from $290 to $385. Local tapas are tasty, but they can leave an empty stomach and wallet!

| WEATHER STATISTICS | J/F | M/A | M/J | J/A | S/O | N/D |
|---|---|---|---|---|---|---|
| total rainfall (mm) | 105 | 83 | 78 | 75 | 125 | 143 |
| consistency (days/mth) | 4 | 4 | 6 | 7 | 5 | 3 |
| min temp (°C/°F) | 7/45 | 9/48 | 13/56 | 16/62 | 14/57 | 9/48 |
| max temp (°C/°F) | 12/54 | 15/59 | 19/66 | 22/72 | 20/68 | 14/58 |

provides a flexible area for the cities' surfers. The indented coastline offers sporadic protection from the NE winds that blow throughout the summer months, grooming the small windswells at the more westerly facing beaches like **Los Quebrantos**, **Playon de Bayas**, **El Espartal**, **Playa de Xago** and **Tenrero**. The cliffs leading around to Gijón have recently been found to hide a few tidally sensitive reefs at their base but farmland treks and short working windows will ensure that very few surfers will score in this area. In big swells and W winds, it is worth a look round Luanco. The Gijon city beaches like **Xivares** and **San Lorenzo** are predictably crowded along with **El Mongol**, a larger swell, right pointbreak, breaking over shallow rocks at high tide. **Peñarrubia**'s rocky beach peaks also handle size. Further east are the popular, dependable mid-tide beachbreaks of **Playa España**, flanked by the average waves at the nudist pocket-beaches of **La Nora** and **Cala de Meron**. Of the many left rivermouths in Northern Spain, **Rodiles** is the most outstanding example in Asturias. Although it is slightly shorter than Mundaka and the barrels are not as intense, it's an easier tube to negotiate. Underestimating the size from the beach and the strength of an outgoing tide is an easy trap to fall into, so longer boards are the go. The lower the tide, the better it gets. Although Rodiles itself is mainly comprised

Rodiles Beach

WILLY URIBE

Typically, 6-20ft (2-6m) swells first come from the W and then shift to the NW and even due N while the low pressures track eastwards. Statistics prove that swell frequency increases as you head west towards Galicia, because the United Kingdom blocks some NW-N swells, that originate in higher latitudes. Summers (June-Sept) suffer long flat spells, resulting in overcrowding at the few W-NW exposed spots. Avoiding this period also increases the likelihood of scoring the standout reefs and rivermouths that need size to go off. Autumn is the best season but Dec-March can be a consistent period, with cool weather and potential for perfect surf. When a low pressure crosses the region, it first blows SW, sometimes at gale-force, which is offshore or sideshore on N-NW facing beaches. Then it clocks W and NW as the front goes by, ruining most breaks for a short time. The summer afternoon seabreeze is NE-NW, usually light with hopefully more east in it for the west facing beaches. High pressure means constant S-SE in winter and morning offshores. River valleys focus the wind and offshores can be really strong at rivermouths. Few spots are good for more than several hours at a time, irrespective of swell or wind conditions since the tidal variation is huge (up to 4m (12ft), so it's essential to get a tide table. Rivermouth tidal rips can be extreme and are generally at their weakest from low to mid-tide, incoming.

| SPOT DESCRIPTION | | | |
|---|---|---|---|
| Spot | Size | Btm | Type |
| ① | 8/1 | | |
| ② | 6/1 | | |
| ③ | 6/1 | | |
| ④ | 6/1 | | |
| ⑤ | 6/1 | | |
| ⑥ | 6/1 | | |
| ⑦ | 6/1 | | |
| ⑧ | 10/4 | | |
| ⑨ | 10/4 | | |
| ⑩ | 6/3 | | |
| ⑪ | 6/2 | | |
| ⑫ | 6/2 | | |
| ⑬ | 8/1 | | |
| ⑭ | 12/3 | | |

Salinas

JAKUE ANDIKOETXEA

of summer campsites, there is always a crowd of surfers from Gijón, who can be quite aggressive. Further east, past the A-grade big swell pointbreak of **Cabo Lastres**, the Ribadesella area is dotted with decent beachbreaks. The western part of Asturias is probably the most ignored coastline except for Tapia, which has hosted surfing contests for decades, including an Easter WQS event.

| SURF STATISTICS | J F | M A | M J | J A | S O | N D |
|---|---|---|---|---|---|---|
| dominant swell | W-N | W-N | W-N | W-N | W-N | W-N |
| swell size (ft) | 5-6 | 4-5 | 3-4 | 2-3 | 4-5 | 5-6 |
| consistency (%) | 80 | 70 | 60 | 50 | 70 | 80 |
| dominant wind | SW-NW | SW-NW | NW-NE | NW-NE | NW-NE | SW-NW |
| average force | F4-F5 | F4-F5 | F4 | F3-F4 | F4 | F4-F5 |
| consistency (%) | 69 | 76 | 58 | 62 | 46 | 72 |
| water temp (°C/°F) | 12/54 | 13/55 | 15/59 | 19/66 | 17/63 | 14/57 |
| wetsuit | | | | | | |

Playa Tenrero ⑤
Playa de Xago ④
El Espartal ③
Playon de Bayas ②
Los Quebrantos ①
Cabo de Peñas
Cabo Negro
Ferrero
Verdicio
Granda
El Campo
Luanco
Nievo
Isla La Deva
Pta Vidrias
Ensenada de Sta Marta del Mar
Nayalón
Piedras Blancas
Avilés
Candás
Cabo Torres
⑥ Xivares
⑦ San Lorenzo
⑧ El Mongol
⑨ Peñarrubia
⑩ La Ñora
⑪ Playa España
⑫ Cala de Meron
⑬ Rodiles
Cabo Lastres ⑭
Gijón
San Esteban de Pravia
La Arena
Muros del Nalon
Soto del Barco
Quinueles
Quintes
Carehes
Tazones
Rodiles
Luces
Lastres
Cabo Lastres
to Oviedo
to Villaviciosa

PORTUGAL

SPAIN

# 86. Lisbon

Carcavelos

ALL PHOTOS RICHARDO BRAVO

## Summary
+ LARGE SWELL WINDOW
+ VERY CONSISTENT SWELLS
+ VARIETY OF BREAKS
+ EASY CITY ACCESS

− URBAN CROWDS
− NO EPIC POINTBREAKS
− COOL WATER YEAR ROUND
− SOME LOCALISM AND RIP-OFFS

Much like Ireland, Portugal receives most North Atlantic swells and while its lower latitude makes it a far warmer destination, the water remains cold year-round. Most of the coast is wide open to the consistent W-NW swells, except for 20km (12.5mi) of SE facing coastline from Caiscais to Oeiras, producing perfect conditions when a big swell pounds the coast. Although there are several good set-ups along this stretch, peaks are competitive 24/7, year round. Driving alongside this beach boulevard (or taking the Linha de Estoril train) in classic winter conditions will give idyllic views of Carcavelos or the peeling rights of Bica or Bolina. Being so close to the city of Lisbon brings some pollution issues as the flow from the mouth of the Rio Tejo and Lisbon's huge, busy harbour, swing right past these breaks. It's not enough to deter the crowds, which have been swelling since the first Portugese pioneers took to the water on Hawaiian koa imports in the 1950s.

Military Museum

YEP

Caparica

If the swell is under 8ft (2.5m), the W facing beaches north of Guincho will be the only reliable spots. **Praia das Maças** is a small swell option at low to mid-tide. **Praia Grande** is the regular contest spot thanks to its barrelling beachbreak and shelter from the frequent N winds. Aggressive crowds get as thick as the heaving shorebreak so check further north at Pequena. **Guincho**'s two beaches, although known as wavesailing spots, also

## TRAVEL INFORMATION

**Population:** 2M
**Coastline:**
1,793km (1,120mi)
**Contests:**
WQS (May & July)
**Other Resources:**
surftotal.tv/praias.asp
beachcam.pt
caparica-online.com
portugalmania.com

**Getting There** – Lisbon is the main int'l airport, well serviced from Europe and America. This is the only hub to the Azores (Sata), Madeira and ex-Portuguese territories (Cabo Verde, Angola, Sao Tome). Nat'l airline TAP is cheap and relatively surfer-friendly. Dep Tax: $10. Lisbon is 12h drive from the French border.

**Getting Around** – The road network is good and the new Vasco de Gama 12km (7mi) bridge eases the congestion on the 25 April bridge crossing to Caparica. The road casualty rate is still one of Europe's highest; 3-lane roads are the main reason. Nat'l car rentals (Auto Jardim) are $220/wk. Don't get stuck in the sand south of Caparica.

**Lodging and Food** – Caparica is a pretty busy seaside resort with many cheap 'parques de campismo' to the south. Guincho is a good hub for the north side but it gets more crowds. Pensao Mar y Sol charges $30/dble while Hotel Maia is $60/dble. A decent meal costs $10. Avoid June-Sept.

**Weather** – Although Portugal is relatively high in latitude, it still manages to enjoy the best maritime climate in Western Europe. Lisbon in the middle is stuck between the dry Algarve and the soggy regions north of Porto. The wettest season starts in November and lasts till March-April. There is even snow in the Serra da Estrela but the snow resorts are only reliable in February. The best climate occurs in the mid-seasons even if the dead of summer rarely gets too hot. The fact is Nortada winds always cool down the coast and create upwelling currents in summer, keeping the water unseasonably cold. However, it's stable year-round and a 3/2 steamer will do most of the time.

**Nature and Culture** – Great services, seaview restaurants (Europa Mar, Café do Mar) and bars in Caparica (Waikiki, Kontiki). The Arriba Fossil zone shelters thick pine forests facing 30km (19mi) of virgin beaches. Lisbon contrasts greatly with the Albufeira lake area. Get a view from the Capuchos mirador.

**Hazards and Hassles** – Avoid the tourist season, and the Caparica zone will be cool. The northern part with the best waves is very urban and thievery is common at Carcavelos and Praia Grande. The Tagus rivermouth spits out some effluent and bordering beaches can be filthy. Traffic jams can be really bad around Lisbon!

**Handy Hints** – Plenty of shapers: Matta, Luffi, Y, Josafa F. Boards are cheap $300+: expect some bargaining. Try the Twister Surfshop in Caparica. Only take a gun for winter west coast spots. Take surfing lessons with the Clube or Bulldog surf school. There is a summer coastal train running along 11km (17mi) of Caparica's beaches.

| WEATHER STATISTICS | J/F | M/A | M/J | J/A | S/O | N/D |
|---|---|---|---|---|---|---|
| total rainfall (mm) | 93 | 83 | 31 | 4 | 32 | 100 |
| consistency (days/mth) | 10 | 9 | 5 | 1 | 6 | 10 |
| min temp (°C/°F) | 8/46 | 11/52 | 14/58 | 17/63 | 15/59 | 10/50 |
| max temp (°C/°F) | 15/59 | 19/66 | 23/74 | 28/82 | 25/77 | 16/62 |

host medium consistency beachbreaks, which work better in the lighter wind conditions of winter. Mid-tide on a decent swell will hold some large outside lefts. Heading down the coast and around the corner, **Praia do Tamariz**'s breaks work on high tide but lack consistency and shape whereas **Bolina**'s intense but unfortunately rare righthand pointbreak is worth checking from the road when conditions are favourable. Other spots are reefbreaks varying from the short tubing lefts of **Azarujinha** or the long, fat right pointbreaks like **Bica**. Since surfing's beginnings in the '60s to the World Surfing Games in '98, **Carcavelos** has been host to thousands of surfers keen to ride the hollow beachbreak at the edge of town. It needs offshore winds for barrelling lefts and rights, depending on swell direction, and works best at mid-tide. **Santo Amaro**'s rare, sewage-polluted pointbreak only fires in winter with huge swells and is currently threatened by coastal development. South of the river, more jetties and high tide surf can be found around Cova do Vapor at **São João** and very occasionally at Rio's, a

lower tides. Places like **Bicas** get the occasional pounding lefthand shorebreak. Towards super scenic Cabo Espichel are small coves and a few secret spots, without anyone around despite being only 50 km (32mi) from an international airport.

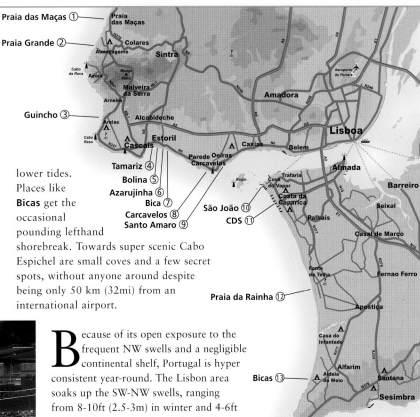

Praia das Maças ①
Praia Grande ②
Guincho ③
Tamariz ④
Bolina ⑤
Azarujinha ⑥
Bica ⑦
Carcavelos ⑧
Santo Amaro ⑨
São João ⑩
CDS ⑪
Praia da Rainha ⑫
Bicas ⑬

**B**ecause of its open exposure to the frequent NW swells and a negligible continental shelf, Portugal is hyper consistent year-round. The Lisbon area soaks up the SW-NW swells, ranging from 8-10ft (2.5-3m) in winter and 4-6ft (1.2-2m) in summer, decreasing in size to the south. Linha de Estoril surf spots get more swell to the west. Storms washing ashore are frequent but Lisbon offers the perfect shelter to filter swells and get offshore winds. Dominant winds are moderate N-NW, named la Nortada, which often blow from April to September. Autumn and winter are best for winds, when E-NE'ers blow. Beware of the tidal variation up to 12ft (4m) – the vast majority of spots favour low tide.

Santo Amaro

long rivermouth left. Slow rolling waves between 7 jetties along Costa da Caparica, known as **CDS**, often produce ideal conditions for longboarders and beginners. The drive south from Caparica goes past heaps of 'parques de campismo', eventually reaching **Praia da Rainha** at the neat fishing village of Fonte da Telha, flanked by 2km of average but consistent beachbreaks. The countryside in this area is unreal. The Arriba Fossil zone enjoys protection laws since 1984, meaning that access to uncrowded beaches is via a walk through pine forests and dunes. The beach contour gets steep and as such favours

| SURF STATISTICS | J F | M A | M J | J A | S O | N D |
|---|---|---|---|---|---|---|
| dominant swell | SW-NW | SW-NW | W-NW | W-NW | SW-NW | SW-NW |
| swell size (ft) | 6-7 | 6 | 4-5 | 3 | 5 | 6 |
| consistency (%) | 80 | 80 | 70 | 50 | 70 | 80 |
| dominant wind | W-E | W-N | W-N | NW-N | W-N | W-E |
| average force | F4 | F4 | F3-F4 | F3-F4 | F3-F4 | F4 |
| consistency (%) | 71 | 54 | 65 | 55 | 51 | 73 |
| water temp (°C/°F) | 13/56 | 14/57 | 16/61 | 18/64 | 17/63 | 15/60 |
| wetsuit | | | | | | |

| SPOT DESCRIPTION | | |
|---|---|---|
| Spot | Size | Btm Type |
| ① | 6/1 | |
| ② | 10/1 | |
| ③ | 8/1 | |
| ④ | 10/1 | |
| ⑤ | 6/2 | |
| ⑥ | 6/1 | |
| ⑦ | 8/2 | |
| ⑧ | 10/2 | |
| ⑨ | 8/2 | |
| ⑩ | 6/1 | |
| ⑪ | 8/1 | |
| ⑫ | 4/1 | |
| ⑬ | 8/2 | |

Guincho

Caparica

# 87. Fuerteventura

AZORES

MADEIRA

La Palma
Gomera  Tenerife
Hierro            Lanzarote
CANARY ISLANDS  Gran  Fuerteventura
Canaria

**Summary**
+ POWERFUL LAVA REEFBREAKS
+ NORTH TRACK SPOT DENSITY
+ GREAT WEATHER AND WATER TEMPS
+ GOOD RESTAURANTS AND NIGHTLIFE

– SHARP, SHALLOW REEFS
– STRONG WINDS
– DANGEROUS ROADS
– WAVESAILING CROWDS

Derecha

ALL PHOTOS ALEX WILLIAMS

The Canary Islands consist of seven large islands and six smaller ones, stretching 500km (313mi) east to west and 200km (125mi) north to south. While Lanzarote is undoubtedly the best bet for world-class conditions, Fuerteventura conceals many short, sucky lava reefs alongside the long, sandy beaches that attract so many windsurfers. The island's name comes from fuerte (strong) and viento (wind). Every year in August, the world speed windsurfing championships are held while the biggest surf contest was the 1998 longboard world championship. This volcanic island only recently emerged from the Atlantic, is the second largest of the Canary Islands and the least developed island accessible by plane. Tenerife and Gran Canaria were first surfed by US servicemen in 1970 and word quickly spread, leading explorers to the easterly islands and their powerful, Pacificesque reefbreaks.

Spew Pits

There are 152 beaches including those on Isla los Lobos, 50km (31mi) of white sand and 25km (16mi) of black sand and shingle, but this accounts for a mere 22% of the total coastline of Fuerteventura. The best surfing spots in the north are between Corralejo and Cotillo, around a dirt road known as the 'North Track'. Most surfers stay in Corralejo because of the plentiful amenities.

Cotillo

## TRAVEL INFORMATION

**Population:** 42,000
**Coastline:** 340km (210mi)
**Contests:** WQS (Oct)
**Other Resources:**
Video: The Pulse
surfcanarias.com
radikalboard.com/
surfcanarias
fuerteventura.info
fuerteventuraturismo.com

**Getting There** – From London or Germany you can find charter flight and accommodation packages from $130. Apart from peak times, it's very cheap to fly from Europe. Beware Iberia, who enforce severe board charges! No dep tax. A taxi to Corralejo costs $27.

**Getting Around** – Car hire is a mere $140/week. Because the North Track is a beat-up road, a 4WD Wrangler jeep can be a plus ($100 for 3 days). Ineika Surf arrange surf transfers to 'North Track' spots ($6), You can't ferry rental cars around islands. It's 1h to Lanzarote and 1h½ - 3h to Gran Canaria.

**Lodging and Food** – Avoid all-inclusive deals in east coast resorts. Most new apartments in Corralejo are built on the eastern outskirts of the town, 3kms (2mi) away from the North Track, camping there is illegal. Favour Dunas Club, Sol y Mar or Bristol Playa Apartments (4p/$60). Hotel Corralejo is $25. The seafood is good, imported food is costly ($12 for meal)

**Weather** – Fuerteventura enjoys a semi-arid subtropical climate, temps rarely dip below 20°C (68°F) and it hardly ever rains. Fuerte has the best sunshine of all the Canary Islands with an average of 2,938 hours/yr. Being only 84km (53mi) from the African coast, most of the east coast of the island is covered by white sand, blown in on Saharan winds. The worst phenomenon is 'La Calima', a strong E wind bringing downpours and red dust. The high wind factor raises the wind chill probability, in and out of the water. Combined with the coldish Canaries current, this means most winter

days require a light fullsuit with occasional springsuit sessions in windless periods.

**Nature and Culture** – Enjoy the semi-desert environment, and quiet holiday vibe. Try the Glass Bottom Boat to Lobos, the Camel Safari based at Jandia or visit Fortaleza del Toston. Great pubs and clubs: Corkys Surf Bar, Waikiki Club and Oink surfbar show latest surf vids.

**Hazards and Hassles** – Shallow reefs, urchins, razor sharp lava are the main threats. Driving on the North Track is sketchy. Break-ins have been reported in Cotillo. Localism is the lowest in the Canaries, but Lobos can get aggressive. Beware the wavesailors jumping and surfing.

**Handy Hints** – Plenty of surf shops to buy boards, or rent and take lessons with Ineika, Matador, and Home Grown. You need a gun at some spots if you can handle the juice. Despite Morocco's proximity, there is no easy transport to Tarfaya.

| WEATHER STATISTICS | J/F | M/A | M/J | J/A | S/O | N/D |
|---|---|---|---|---|---|---|
| total rainfall (mm) | 37 | 22 | 3 | 0 | 18 | 55 |
| consistency (days/mth) | 5 | 3 | 1 | 0 | 2 | 6 |
| min temp (°C/°F) | 14/57 | 15/59 | 17/63 | 20/68 | 19/66 | 16/61 |
| max temp (°C/°F) | 21/70 | 24/75 | 26/79 | 28/82 | 28/82 | 23/74 |

There are several spots within walking distance from the town like **El Muelle** (Harbour Wall) or **Shooting Gallery**. These lefts break over lava reefs and get crowded for their obvious accessibility. The pothole ridden North Track runs alongside dozens of quality spots, like **Generosa**, a hollow left or **Suicides**, an aptly named shallow right which remains critical even at high tide. The swell magnet for the area is **Mejillones**, where peaky rights and lefts break in deeper water over an urchin covered reef. Acid Drops at **Majanicho** gets lots of lookers but few takers for the radical drops over super-shallow, uneven reef. **Izquierda** (Yarro) is a nice left with a steep take-off. Across the channel is **Derecha** (The Bubble), the islands favourite righthand barrel and most popular contest venue. Travelling further west along the track will mean less crowds and many of the reefs break close to shore, helping to minimize the NE trades, that gain strength in the channel between Lanzarote and Fuerte. **Cotillo** is usually offshore, along with **Spew Pits**, a mutant right that catches plenty of swell but gets packed when the North Track spots are too small or windy. The beach south of town is interesting as it always breaks the same distance from the shore regardless of swell and tides. The entire west coast picks up a lot of swell but there is no easy access. Head to **La Pared** or **Cofete** for scenic crowd-free rides when the swell is small but watch out for heavy rips. Check **Punta del Tigre** if there is a rare S swell running. The east coast up to Puerto del Rosario doesn't get waves unless a S windswell is pushing something in. Unlike Lanzarote, the NE coast rarely has decent pumping waves but there are a couple of lefthanders tucked into bays that work in the NE trades. **Glass Beach** is the official beginner's spot. If there's a significant swell with the right wind, take the ferry to **Los Lobos** island and join the crowd waiting to sample one of the longest, top quality pointbreaks in the Canaries.

Lobos

disorganised and wind-blown. Rare south swells are pushed in by strong winds in the late summer. The best conditions occur when the NE trades activity is low (Nov-Jan). In the early surf season, winds tend to blow more E-NE than N-NE until the trades get strong and regular from March. April to September gets very windy and the surf is usually small and erratic, so look hard for the right wind/swell combination. The 15km (9mi) channel between both islands focuses the wind on the North Track spots. Tides matter over sharp, shallow reefs with spring tides up to 6ft (2m), so get a chart from one of the many shops in Corralejo.

| SURF STATISTICS | J F | M A | M J | J A | S O | N D |
|---|---|---|---|---|---|---|
| dominant swell | W-N | W-N | N | N | W-N | W-N |
| swell size (ft) | 5-6 | 5 | 4 | 2 | 4-5 | 5-6 |
| consistency (%) | 80 | 70 | 40 | 20 | 80 | 70 |
| dominant wind | N-E | N-NE | N-NE | N-NE | N-NE | N-E |
| average force | F4 | F4 | F4 | F4 | F3-F4 | F4 |
| consistency (%) | 73 | 68 | 81 | 91 | 72 | 74 |
| water temp (°C/°F) | 18/64 | 18/64 | 19/66 | 22/72 | 22/72 | 20/68 |
| wetsuit | | | | | | |

La Pared

Fuerteventura and Lanzarote claim the best consistency in the Canaries due to their superior exposure to the N-NW swells that churn the North Atlantic from October to March. Most exposed reefbreaks will average 4-12ft (1.2-4m), the major waves being produced by the deepest lows slamming into Western Europe. Even small systems off of the US East Coast can send some swell across the Atlantic. Summer trades can produce surprisingly big east coast surf but it is usually very

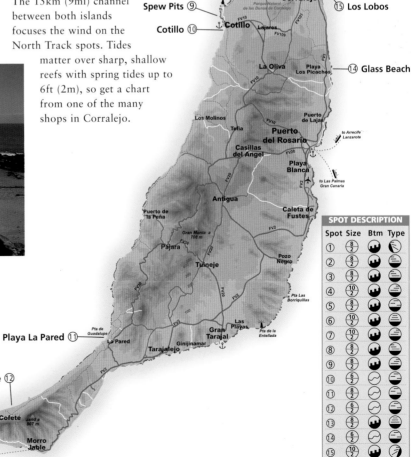

Estrecho de la Bocaina

③ Generosa
Suicides ④ ② Shooting Gallery
Mejillones ⑤ ① El Muelle
Majanicho ⑥
Derecha ⑦
Izquierda ⑧
Majanicho
Corralejo
⑮ Los Lobos
Spew Pits ⑨
Cotillo ⑩ Cotillo
Lajares

La Oliva
Playa Los Picachos
⑭ Glass Beach

Los Molinos
Tefia
Puerto de Lajas
to Arrecife Lanzarote
Puerto del Rosario
Casillas del Angel
Playa Blanca
to Las Palmas Gran Canaria

Antigua
Caleta de Fustes

Puerto de la Peña
Gran Montaña 708 m
Pájara
Pozo Negro
Tuineje

Las Playas
Gran Tarajal
Pta la Entallada

Playa La Pared ⑪
Pta de Guadalupe
La Pared
Tarajalejo
Giniginamar

Playa de Cofete ⑫

Punta del Tigre ⑬
Cofete
Jandía 807 m
Puerto de la Cruz
Morro Jable
to Las Palmas Gran Canaria

| SPOT DESCRIPTION | | | |
|---|---|---|---|
| Spot | Size | Btm | Type |
| ① | 8/2 | | |
| ② | 8/2 | | |
| ③ | 8/2 | | |
| ④ | 10/2 | | |
| ⑤ | 8/2 | | |
| ⑥ | 10/2 | | |
| ⑦ | 10/2 | | |
| ⑧ | 8/2 | | |
| ⑨ | 8/2 | | |
| ⑩ | 6/2 | | |
| ⑪ | 8/2 | | |
| ⑫ | 8/2 | | |
| ⑬ | 6/2 | | |
| ⑭ | 6/2 | | |
| ⑮ | 10/2 | | |

"Don't destroy what you came to enjoy"

QUIKSILVER INITIATIVE

# Africa

Benguela beauties bend into another un-named bay south of Luanda, Angola. Typifying African village problems, the dry ravine in the foreground is a rubbish dump and the beach may be used as a latrine.

# The Ocean Environment

Africa spans 68° degrees of latitude, is bordered by three separate bodies of water and encompasses various environments ranging from arid desert through to snow capped mountain ranges with everything else in between. Its human population mirrors this diversity by including impoverished, Third World nations alongside well developed First World cultures. Africa's huge littoral span sees a varied coastal environment that is relatively untouched by man. With most of the continent labelled as Third World, environmental legislation is at best poorly implemented and more commonly non-existent.

## Pollution

Population centres are the hub of all problems, discharging both industrial and sewage related pollution. It should be taken as read that effluent from all sources is only basically treated and in a lot of cases not treated at all. Long stretches of Morocco's coastline is under-populated and hence unpolluted, however, major towns and cities suffer from poor water quality. Rabat, Casablanca and Agadir experience sewage problems from rapid growth of tourism, oil and shipping related pollution around ports, plus there are some large, under-regulated coastal industries including large phosphate factories. Of more concern to surfers is polluted runoff, which can occur anywhere along the coast. Heavy rains flush stagnant waters from the arid interior and rubbish dumped in dry riverbeds out into the line-ups, bringing conditions conducive to infections like hepatitis. Right through West Africa, the same developing country rules apply; water around centres of population and rivermouths can be of horrendous quality, while undeveloped areas like the Cape Verde Islands are likely to be pristine. Gabon, Angola, Namibia and the western cape of South Africa are all so sparsely populated that pollution is almost non-existent, aided by the cleansing effect of the Benguela Current. There is, however, plenty of oil in the area so spills and illegal pumping out of ballast tanks is a likely cause of occasional, but persistent oil pollution.

Durban based SEA (Surfers Environmental Association) have been putting pressure on government bodies over existing environmental pollution problems, plus monitoring the state of the beaches on a daily basis. This watchdog project is unique to Africa's vast coastline, as is Durban's cutting edge tertiary water treatment infrastructure. Waste water is treated to the point where it becomes drinkable again, to counter the growing water shortages in the burgeoning city. The recycled water is used by industry and discharges have been greatly reduced. Unfortunately, Durban is the exception to the rule and across the rest of South Africa, there are numerous outfalls. Oil spills have also been a feature of this coastline, most notably around Cape Town's busy shipping lanes. The largest spill was in 1983 when the *Castillo de Bellver* shed 257,000 tonnes into Cape waters, some of which was burnt to try to minimize the impact. Since then, there have been numerous spills from tankers running aground or hull failures in heavy seas. The only pluses to oil spills in such latitudes is the high energy sea environment tends to disperse oil quickly.

## Erosion

Coastal protection initiatives are virtually unheard of for the African continent. Morocco has built a number of long breakwalls and harbours along the north to central coast, some of which provide waves while others have destroyed them. The main beach at Agadir has offshore artificial barrier reefs to halt erosion at what is an unsurfed, poor beachbreak. Far more serious is the proposed development of the coastline around Tarhazoute. If plans go ahead then a multi-complex resort incorporating three marinas will be built along the point. The point is home to three excellent waves; Anchor Point, Hash Point and Panoramas, all of which would be threatened. Currently the World Bank has granted a loan for the development and it awaits the next step. Gabon has some decrepit steel jetties around the big harbour at Port-Gentil, which services the oil and timber industries. Unsurprisingly, South Africa has the most coastal protection schemes, all sited around its cities, but vast stretches of coast are totally untouched. Durban's surf scene is synonymous with jetty waves inside the Bay of Plenty. Occasional harbour breakwalls and rivermouth stabilization projects can be found along the east coast.

Right – **Morocco is one of the few African nations that have large sea defences and man made harbours. Hicham el Ouarga benefits.**
Bottom – **There is plenty of coastal industry in Morocco, but no information exists on its regulation.**

WILBUR TILLEY

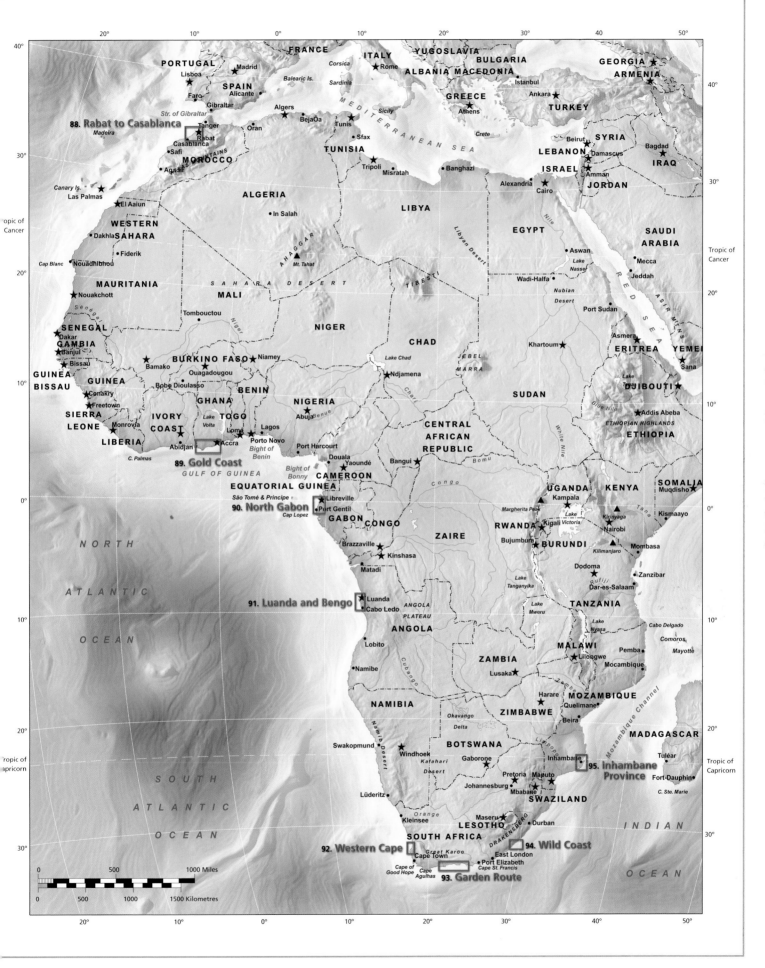

**88. Rabat to Casablanca**

**89. Gold Coast**

**90. North Gabon**

**91. Luanda and Bengo**

**92. Western Cape**

**93. Garden Route**

**94. Wild Coast**

**95. Inhambane Province**

### Access

The African continent is a land of extremes, graphically illustrated when natural disasters like cyclones, floods, droughts, famine and disease epidemics regularly sweep through a region. Compounded by seemingly incessant wars and despotism, getting around Africa is very tricky. Morocco has a decent road network but getting to the more out of the way breaks can require a bit more effort and a 4WD. The disputed southern border region is restricted and negotiating the correct paperwork is as difficult as getting through the minefields that pepper the brutal Saharan coast into Mauritania. Senegal has an excellent transport system with easy access to the surf, but southern areas become impassable in the wet season. This becomes the rule for West Africa but by no means the only access problems. Many countries are heavily mined, regularly war torn, and simply not safe to travel through. The Ivory Coast and Ghana's flat coastal plain benefits from colonial infrastructure and maintains a great road system by African standards. Gabon's coastal road system is haphazard at best, so boats are the best way to move around. The Angolan main coastal highway is sealed, but there are regular checkpoints, which can frustratingly delay journeys, and these are especially lengthy when entering National Parks. A 4WD is absolutely essential in Namibia's shifting desert, unless you remain in a big, coastal town. Further restrictions exist as large mining companies control vast tracts of coastline, mainly searching for diamonds. Permits are required and strict guidelines have to be followed, including a veto on "finders keepers" since gems can be found lying on the beach. South Africa has the best transport system, with most major roads being paved, promoting personal transport over the poor public transport system. Away from major population centres things deteriorate, although compared with the rest of Africa, it's good. Access to the spots varies from unsealed tracks accessible by all vehicles to serious 4WD tracks, which in times of heavy rain can become totally impassable. Mozambique has a poor network of roads away from all but the biggest of settlements, so 4WD would be wise.

Top – **Cape Cross, Namibia.**
Bottom – **Much of Africa's undeveloped coast is best accessed by boat. YEP expeditions, Gabon.**

TOM KOIBER

### Hazards

The most obvious hazards in Africa are the land and water based wildlife. Surfers probably fear shark attack above all else and Africa has its fair share of which about 1 in 4 attacks prove fatal. Senegal, Cape Verde, Sierra Leone and Liberia all have seen the odd attack in the last century but otherwise, the west coast is relatively safe. Attacks are most common in South Africa, and reflect the population most likely to use the ocean for recreation purposes. Mozambique has a large shark population and the rest of the east coast countries have all seen attacks with a high fatality ratio. At least one of the big three (great white, tiger or bull sharks) are to be found in all African waters while SA entertains all three. Since surfers have become the largest attack demographic, certain precautions can be taken to minimize the risk. Surfing early morning or late evening, in muddied waters or rivermouths and near seal colonies should all be avoided. There's plenty more dangers lurking underwater like crocodiles and hippopotamuses, which are responsible for more human deaths than any other African animal. Hippos have been spotted in the surf as far north as Guinea Bissau and as far south as Gabon. Rivermouths also present easy access to the surf for crocodiles. Disease is probably of greater concern, with Africa experiencing epidemics like Aids and cholera, which is incubated by poor sanitary conditions in areas that lack basic clean water supplies. Malaria is endemic in much of West and Central Africa. Robberies and hijackings are commonplace in the politically unstable countries (i.e. just about everywhere) and travelling should always be undertaken in daylight.

Morocco has a growing population of second generation surfers and hierarchies are well established. With so many spots going un-surfed, hassles are very rare, except at the name breaks. Across the rest of the continent localism is very isolated. Namibia, Mozambique, Angola and Ghana all have low surfing populations and with the exception of over zealous ex pats it's unlikely you'll be running into trouble. South Africa's Jeffery's Bay is considered as one of the greatest waves on the planet, a label that has been attracting a growing international crowd of transplants for decades. Rapid expansion in a small coastal community has resulted in friction with local surfers who have formed the J-Bay Underground. Easily distinguished in their white rashies with a water buffalo on the back they have brought order to the line-up by demanding and enforcing respect for proper surfing etiquette. While this is unlikely to promote equality, many condone this syndicated localism as a fair way of controlling a dysfunctional line-up where respect and patience will be rewarded with a share of the waves. The JBU are also concentrating on preserving the surrounding beach environment and promoting the growth of the sport amongst the local community.

ISABELLE BEIGBEDER

# Surf Travel Resources

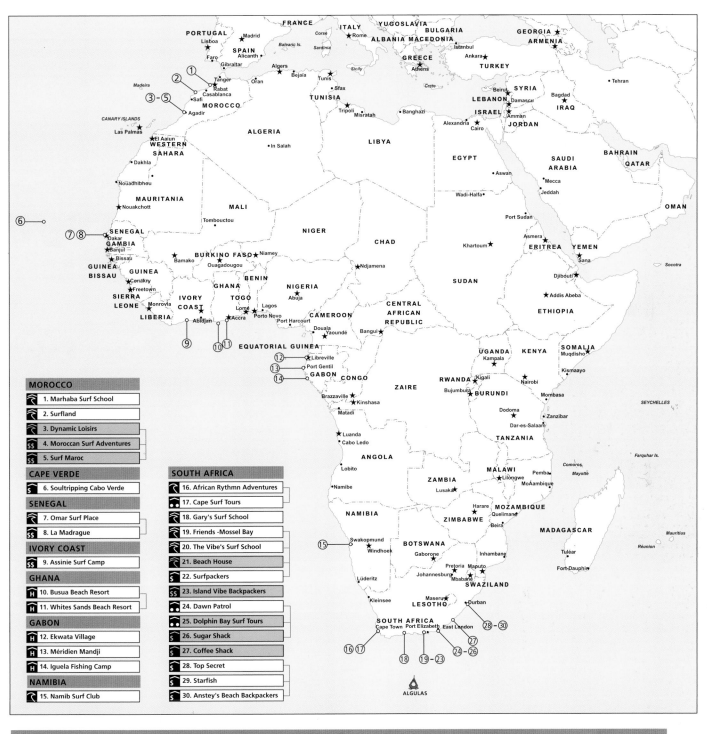

**MOROCCO**
1. Marhaba Surf School
2. Surfland
3. Dynamic Loisirs
4. Moroccan Surf Adventures
5. Surf Maroc

**CAPE VERDE**
6. Soultripping Cabo Verde

**SENEGAL**
7. Omar Surf Place
8. La Madrague

**IVORY COAST**
9. Assinie Surf Camp

**GHANA**
10. Busua Beach Resort
11. Whites Sands Beach Resort

**GABON**
12. Ekwata Village
13. Méridien Mandji
14. Iguela Fishing Camp

**NAMIBIA**
15. Namib Surf Club

**SOUTH AFRICA**
16. African Rythmn Adventures
17. Cape Surf Tours
18. Gary's Surf School
19. Friends -Mossel Bay
20. The Vibe's Surf School
21. Beach House
22. Surfpackers
23. Island Vibe Backpackers
24. Dawn Patrol
25. Dolphin Bay Surf Tours
26. Sugar Shack
27. Coffee Shack
28. Top Secret
29. Starfish
30. Anstey's Beach Backpackers

## COUNTRY INFORMATION

| | MOROCCO | GHANA | GABON | ANGOLA | SOUTH AFRICA | MOZAMBIQUE |
|---|---|---|---|---|---|---|
| Area (sq km/mi): | 446,500/172,414 | 238,533/92,098 | 267,668/103,347 | 1,246,700/481,354 | 1,221,000/471,000 | 801,590/318,261 |
| Population: | 28M | 18.5M | 1.2M | 12.3M | 44M | 18M |
| Waveriders: | 2,000 | 5 | 50 | 15 | 40,000 | 10 |
| Tourists (per yr): | 3M | 335,000 | 194,000 | 45,000 | 6M | 250,000 |
| Language: | Arabic, French, Berber, Spanish | English, Ewé | French, Fang, Bantu languages | Portuguese, Bantu | Afrikaans, English | Portuguese, Tsongo & Chope dialects |
| Currency: | Dirham | Cedi | CFA | Kwanza | Rand | Metical |
| Exchange: | $1 = 10 DH | $1 = 8,000 GHC | $1 = 670 XAF | $1 = 44 AOA | $1 = 10.9 ZAR | $1 = 12,500 MZM |
| GDP (per yr): | $3,100 | $1,310 | $6,300 | $1,000 | $8,500 | $1,000 |
| Inflation: | 6% | 9% | 2% | 106% | 5% | 13% |

MOROCCO

# 88. Rabat to Casablanca

WILL NEWITT

**Doura**

**Summary**

+ SWELL CONSISTENCY
+ PROTECTED JETTY BREAKS
+ EASY ACCESS
+ FASCINATING CULTURE

– NO WORLDCLASS SPOTS
– COOL WINTER WATER
– URBAN HASSLES
– NO ALCOHOL

Despite being in Africa, Morocco has always been an extension of the European surf trail. With 2900km (1813mi) of coastline (the southern 1100km (688mi) of coastline has been disputed since the 1975 Moroccan occupation of Western Sahara) located at the ideal latitude, and a perfect NW exposure, travellers have been hitting the Agadir area for decades, soaking up the desert sun and riding clean pointbreaks. However, when driving south from Europe, there's plenty of epic breaks to check out on the way, like Dar Bouazza, Oued Cherrat or inside Rabat's jetties when the swell is firing. Despite the proximity of major cities, the north coast waves rarely get crowded. Local waveriders are the happy few who can afford a board; French expats or those who benefit from the support of King Mohammed VI. Morocco fires in the

PHOTO MOBILE

**Doura**

WILL NEWITT

northern hemisphere winter, but the rest of the year favours the north coast, as it's more consistent and less windy than the Agadir area. The construction of a major highway between Tangier and Rabat gives more options to check less known spots in between although much of it is a straight sandy beach.

## TRAVEL INFORMATION

**Population:** 3.5M Grand Casablanca
**Coastline:** 1,835km (1,150mi)
**Contests:** National (Aug), ETB in Casa (June)
**Other Resources:** surfaumaroc.com marhaba-surf-school.com maroc1.com tourisme-marocain.com

**Getting There** – Most charter flights hit Agadir or Marrakech. Casablanca and Rabat might be more pricey, but there are plenty of flights from Europe, Africa and the Middle East. National Airline is RAM, charging little for boards. Many surfers drive campervans down taking the ferry from Algeciras to Ceuta or Tangier. Dep tax: $20.

**Getting Around** – Be prepared for intuitive driving: erratic locals, French/Arabic signs, random crossroads, narrow roads, unpainted surfaces and high beams left on at night. This coast has the best main roads in the country. Weekly rates for a type A hire car costs $210, Fiat Uno have replaced Renault 4 as the norm!

**Lodging and Food** – Budgeteers can pay from $5 for quite good quality hotel beds. Eating is cheap ($4 for a 3 course meal). If you can afford it, luxury is available at European prices. Tagines and couscous make for tasty local cuisine: no pork or alcohol. Marhaba surf school in Les Sablettes offer training and lodging.

**Weather** – Although it crosses the Tropic of Cancer in the south, Morocco's central surf zone barely rates as a semi-tropical venue. The climate is warm but desert nights get chilly. The coast gets some moisture but tends to be quite arid. In Rabat, winter rainfall peaks at 70mm (3in) per month. Beware of pollution at rivermouths (oued) after strong rains. Summer gets extremely hot with virtually no rain. Water gets down to 16°C (61°F) which requires a 2mm fullsuit. You might get away with a shorty on a balmy autumn day but a short-sleeve fullsuit is definitely the all-round wettie.

**Nature and Culture** – Spectacular architecture abounds eg. Rabat's Kasbah des Oudayas, Salé's

mosque and Gnaoua's kasbah and the world's tallest mosque (Hassan II Mosque) in Casablanca. Enjoy Sidi Bouknadel's exotic gardens, Rabat Surf club and open-air markets in medinas. Snow resorts are 6h away in winter.

**Hazards and Hassles** – The ocean is pretty safe if you ignore sharp barnacles, lots of urchins and rocks. Keep a close eye on personal possesions because robberies do occur. With a smile, even the worst hustlers won't do you any harm. Avoid carpet shops. Smoking hash is an illegal temptation; don't get caught with it! Morocco suffers from industrial and residential pollution issues plus rain can bring some nasty diseases to rivermouth line-ups!

**Handy Hints** – Marhaba Surf School. Surf shops in Rabat (Ocean & Beaches) and many in Casa'. Avoid Ramadan month when everything slows down (Autumn for 2003-2010). Remember that small restaurants don't have toilet paper in the bathrooms. It's a muslim country (99% are Sunni), so dress respectfully.

| WEATHER STATISTICS | J/F | M/A | M/J | J/A | S/O | N/D |
|---|---|---|---|---|---|---|
| total rainfall (mm) | 60 | 48 | 11 | 1 | 24 | 70 |
| consistency (days/mth) | 7 | 6 | 3 | 0 | 3 | 8 |
| min temp (°C/°F) | 9/48 | 12/54 | 16/61 | 20/68 | 17/63 | 11/52 |
| max temp (°C/°F) | 18/64 | 20/68 | 23/74 | 26/79 | 25/77 | 19/66 |

Les Sablattes

MARHABA SURF SCHOOL

**Medihya Plage**, near the Kenitra army base, was first surfed in the late 1950s. There is a sheltered right on a big swell and higher tides, breaking beside the major jetty running south of Oued Sebou. On the way to Salé is **Plage des Nations**, a wealthy resort with fast breaking, powerful beachbreaks and strong currents, which is best when it's small. Rabat-Salé has a great combination of sensitive, small swell reefs, like **Kbeir**, a short, shallow and sucky left, and stormy condition spots inside the jetties, like **Doura** which had a Kirra-esque reputation before the rivermouth was dredged.There are 8 spots around Rabat-Salé and the highest density of local surfers, resulting in what is probably Morocco's surfing capital. Don't miss the Oudayas Surf Club; the biggest on earth with 20 employees and 400m². This great looking

WILL NEWITT

PHOTO MOBILE

Kbeir

building, close to the kasbah, is the result of King Mohammed VI's passion for surfing, allowing many youngsters to learn to surf and borrow gear. The King has been President of the club since 1999. There are several exits off the main highway south, leading to quality surf. Near Tamara, there's a fabled right called Smuggler's Point, but it's pretty fickle. **Skhirat** is a small swell left off a jetty prefering low tides while the adjacent beachbreak provides overflow for the crowds. **Oued Cherrat** is the most consistent year round spot because it is sheltered from westerlies. Regularly overrun by bodyboarders and there's a parking charge in summer. The neat fishing village at **Bouznika**, sits in a sheltered bay, hiding from the NW winds. At low tide there are chunky, long rights by the point; beware of the "table" rock section and urchins. Despite Mohammedia's many oil refineries, it is a good option. **Pont Blondin** occasionally holds hollow but risky rights over shallow rocks and across the bay at **Les Sablettes**, the lefts work far more regularly. Casablanca, the financial capital, has plenty of beaches like **Zeneta** or Monica, an intense but short right, ideal for bodyboarders. Many prefer **No. 23** beach in Aïn Diab for its consistency. It held a European bodyboarding contests in May 2002 and June 2003. Further

south is **Dar Bouazza**, the best left pointbreak in Morocco. It's a long, wrapping, cutback wave with two main sections working fairly regularly. Avoid zillions of urchins and the rusty remains of the *La Bobine* wreck on shore. When it's too small, go to **Jack Beach**, a good, punchy beachbreak, and regular contest site.

Morocco's coastline has the straightest NW swell exposure in Europe, meaning most of the numerous lows out in the northern Atlantic will produce waves from 3-15ft (1-5m) on the NW exposed beachbreaks. Many beaches max out in winter but that's when pointbreaks and sheltered spots come into their own. North Morocco is more consistent than the south in summer, despite NW winds on the exposed beaches and reefbreaks. In winter, NE trades will make light to medium cross-shores. Mid-April is the landmark for the strong NW Chergui blowing out much harder to the South. Conditions will be rideable throughout the summer. During this period, straight N winds blow 40% of the time. Tides vary from 2-6ft (0.6-2m), but no tide tables are available!

| SPOT DESCRIPTION | | | |
|---|---|---|---|
| Spot | Size | Btm | Type |
| ① | 8/2 | ◐ | ◗ |
| | 8/2 | ◐ | ◑ |
| ② | 6/1 | ◇ | ◑ |
| ③ | 6/1 | ◇ | ◑ |
| ④ | 6/2 | ● | ◑ |
| ⑤ | 6/2 | ● | ⌀ |
| | 6/2 | ● | ⌀ |
| ⑥ | 6/2 | ◐ | ◑ |
| ⑦ | 8/2 | ◐ | ◗ |
| ⑧ | 6/2 | ◐ | ◗ |
| ⑨ | 6/1 | ◐ | ◑ |
| ⑩ | 6/1 | ◐ | ◑ |
| ⑪ | 6/1 | ◇ | ◑ |
| ⑫ | 10/2 | ● | ◐ |
| ⑬ | 6/1 | ◇ | ◑ |

| SURF STATISTICS | J F | M A | M J | J A | S O | N D |
|---|---|---|---|---|---|---|
| dominant swell | NW-N | NW-N | NW-N | NW-N | NW-N | NW-N |
| swell size (ft) | 5-6 | 5 | 3-4 | 2 | 4 | 5-6 |
| consistency (%) | 70 | 60 | 60 | 50 | 60 | 70 |
| dominant wind | N-NE | NW-NE | NW-NE | NW-NE | NW-NE | N-NE |
| average force | F2-F3 | F2-F3 | F2-F3 | F2-F3 | F2-F3 | F2-F3 |
| consistency (%) | 35 | 56 | 70 | 82 | 63 | 36 |
| water temp (°C/°F) | 16/61 | 18/64 | 20/68 | 22/72 | 21/70 | 18/64 |
| wetsuit | | | | | | |

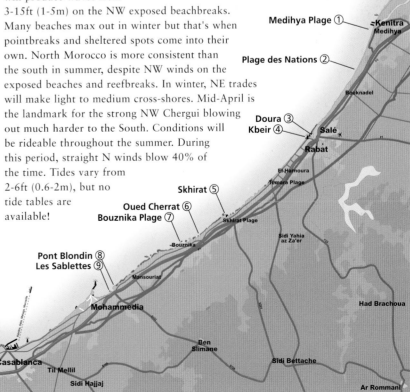

Medihya Plage ①  Kenitra  Medihya

Plage des Nations ②

Bouknadel

Doura ③
Kbeir ④  Salé
Rabat

El Harnoura
Temara Plage

Skhirat ⑤

Oued Cherrat ⑥
Bouznika Plage ⑦  Skhirat Plage

Bouznika

Sidi Yahia az Za'er

Pont Blondin ⑧
Les Sablettes ⑨  Mansouriat

Mohammedia

Had Brachoua

Zeneta ⑩
No. 23 ⑪

Ben Slimane

Dar Bouazza ⑫
Jack Beach ⑬  Casablanca  Til Mellil  Sidi Bettache

Dar Bouazza  Sidi Hajjaj  Ar Rommani

GHANA TOGO
IVORY COAST

# 89. Gold Coast

Dixcove

SEAN GRIFFIN

## Summary
+ MELLOW RIGHT POINTBREAKS
+ CONSISTENTLY HEAD HIGH
+ RELATIVELY CHEAP AND SAFE
+ VIRGIN, WARM WATER SURF
+ TROPICAL AFRICAN SCENERY

– LACK OF POWERFUL WAVES
– FLAT DRY SEASON
– BEACH POLLUTION
– HOT, HUMID AND MALARIAL
– EXPENSIVE FLIGHTS

Busua

EMMANUEL

Most surfers would know little about surfing in Ghana, apart from the backwash waves that were surfed out to sea on *The Endless Summer*. Ghana was the first country in Africa (1957) to claim independence from Britain, basing its economic growth on gold and cocoa. It's densely populated and despite sitting amidst the shadows of turbulent neighbours, has evolved in a democratic way. For years, intrepid travellers raved about the coastal area west of Accra, a 250km (156mi) stretch of sand and rocky patches, interspersed with 15 old slave-trading forts and castles, many dating from the 17th Century. The coastal area is relatively flat, consisting of plains and numerous lagoons near river estuaries. Few have taken advantage of the easy surf conditions – in fact, local surfers can be counted on the fingers of one hand.

Elmina Slave Fort

EMMANUEL DAUBRÉE

The only obvious left point in Ghana discovered so far is **Mutrakni Point** by Ajemra. It is well regarded and breaks over sand covered reef. Further west lies Axim's hefty beachbreak by the beach resort with a fun reef nearby. The SW facing coastline at **Cape Three Points** picks up maximum available swell and the right pointbreak boasts a very promising set-up but it's hard to reach. Prince's Town also has a great rivermouth to the east, and a fast hollow left reefbreak to the west, within sight of the port. **Akwaadi** is an exposed rivermouth that

## TRAVEL INFORMATION

**Population:** 3.5M West & Central districts
**Coastline:** 539km (336mi)
**Contests:** None
**Other Resources:**
*Video:* The Endless Summer
gbhghana.com/busua.html
whitesandsbc.com
ghana.co.uk
ghanaweb.com

**Getting There** – Visa: $20. Kotoka Airport in Accra is mostly served from London, Frankfurt, Milan, Amsterdam and New York. Ghana Airways fly in almost every country in West Africa. Dep tax: $20. Use STC buses to Takoradi (4h away, $4) then take a tro-tro (minibus) until Agona junction and take a taxi for Busua: about 1h.

**Getting Around** – The road network is in decent shape, but secondary roads are unsealed. Car rental is very costly ($450/week with Sputnik), only available in Accra. Better options for getting around include taxis, tro-tros and mammy wagons. Favour State Transport Corporation buses for long distance journeys, as they are more comfortable and safer.

**Lodging and Food** – The ideal location is Busua Beach Hotel costing $50 for a double room right on the beach. They have facilities like a swimming pool. Budget rooms in Guest Houses are $3-10. Street food is dirt-cheap; expect $3 for a meal. Soups, jollof rice, fufu and lobsters ($6/kilo) are the mainstay of menus.

**Weather** – Ghana has an equatorial climate with temps varying between 21-32°C (70-90°F). There are two rainy seasons, from March to July and from Sept to Oct, separated by a short cool dry season in August and a relatively long dry season in the south from mid-October to March. Annual rainfall in the south averages 2,030mm (79in) but varies greatly throughout the country, with the heaviest rainfall in the south western part. Along the coast (including Accra), the rainfall is light and the rainy season lasts from April until June with a short spell in October. The water is warm year round and cooler rainy season water is a plus as it gives some light relief from the oppressive heat. No rubber necessary.

**Nature and Culture** – Besides palm-fringed beaches and slave forts, try national parks. Ghana's best known, the Mole Game Reserve, is way inland, but Ankasa is only 2h away. Lots of festivals like Fetu Afahye in Cape Coast during September. Fish markets are unavoidable! Laid-back atmosphere in Busua.

**Hazards and Hassles** – Yellow fever inoculation is necessary. Malaria is common, so are other tropical diseases. Take along a good supply of mosquito repellent and suntan lotion! Night walks along beaches invite muggings. Drink bottled water only. Trash and beach sanitation can be worrying. Snakes and scorpions.

**Handy Hints** – Bring all gear, longboards and mini-mals are ideal. The nearest shop is in Assinie or Abidjan, in Ivory Coast. Crossing the border overland is not a major hassle. Change currency at Forex Bureaux. No civil war, no locals, no hustlers! Ghana is one of the last land-based surf trips with empty line-ups!

| WEATHER STATISTICS | J/F | M/A | M/J | J/A | S/O | N/D |
|---|---|---|---|---|---|---|
| total rainfall (mm) | 33 | 145 | 487 | 117 | 140 | 150 |
| consistency (days/mth) | 4 | 8 | 18 | 8 | 10 | 10 |
| min temp (°C/°F) | 23/74 | 24/75 | 24/75 | 23/74 | 23/74 | 23/74 |
| max temp (°C/°F) | 32/90 | 32/90 | 30/86 | 28/82 | 28/82 | 31/88 |

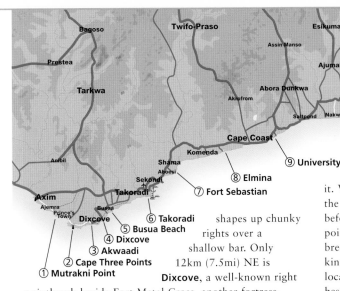

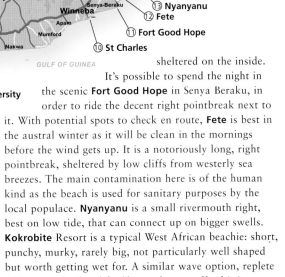

**SPOT DESCRIPTION**

| | Spot | Size | Btm | Type |
|---|---|---|---|---|
| ① | | 6/2 | | |
| ② | | 8/2 | | |
| ③ | | 8/2 | | |
| ④ | | 8/2 | | |
| ⑤ | | 8/1 | | |
| ⑥ | | 6/2 | | |
| ⑦ | | 6/2 | | |
| ⑧ | | 8/2 | | |
| ⑨ | | 6/1 | | |
| ⑩ | | 6/2 | | |
| ⑪ | | 8/2 | | |
| ⑫ | | 6/1 | | |
| ⑬ | | 8/2 | | |
| ⑭ | | 6/1 | | |
| ⑮ | | 6/1 | | |

① Mutrakni Point
② Cape Three Points
③ Akwaadi
④ Dixcove
⑤ Busua Beach
⑥ Takoradi
⑦ Fort Sebastian
⑧ Elmina
⑨ University
⑩ St Charles
⑪ Fort Good Hope
⑫ Fete
⑬ Nyanyanu
⑭ Kokrobite
⑮ Labadi Beach

shapes up chunky rights over a shallow bar. Only 12km (7.5mi) NE is **Dixcove**, a well-known right pointbreak beside Fort Metal Cross, another fortress-turned-slave storage barn built in 1691. There are long waves to be had but the water by the rivermouth is murky and polluted. Regarded as Ghana's best beach, **Busua Beach** with Abokwa Island offers ideal scenery to hang out as well as an offshore break. The beachbreak is fast and hollow, plus there is a right point, but many surfers walk to the west and paddle 20min to a good quality reef right. While it is not as good as Busua, the rights at **Takoradi**, Western District's capital, can be ridden on the western side of the harbour. Along the Slave Fort Line, check **Fort Sebastian** in Aboesi which hosts another right point that is protected from westerly sea breezes. **Elmina**'s exotic beaches are fringed with palms, the obligatory fort and a slow breaking, right pointbreak. In the early morning and evening, canoes paddle out through the surf and return, surfing on the crests of the waves, laden with fish for immediate sale at the local market. Cape Coast is the Central Region's capital, where below average beachbreaks appear in front of the **University** and the castle. Further east, there is only one spot known at Winneba called **St Charles**, an outside righthand reef come pointbreak, which is nicely

sheltered on the inside. It's possible to spend the night in the scenic **Fort Good Hope** in Senya Beraku, in order to ride the decent right pointbreak next to it. With potential spots to check en route, **Fete** is best in the austral winter as it will be clean in the mornings before the wind gets up. It is a notoriously long, right pointbreak, sheltered by low cliffs from westerly sea breezes. The main contamination here is of the human kind as the beach is used for sanitary purposes by the local populace. **Nyanyanu** is a small rivermouth right, best on low tide, that can connect up on bigger swells. **Kokrobite** Resort is a typical West African beachie: short, punchy, murky, rarely big, not particularly well shaped but worth getting wet for. A similar wave option, replete with expensive hotel for those who can afford it is **Labadi Beach** on the other side of Accra.

Fete

Akwaadi

Groundswells come from the southern hemisphere, about 10,000km (6250mi) away, which means a lot of size decay, but organised, long period lines. Swells never exceed 8ft (2.5m) and typically range from 2-6ft (0.6-2m) producing fun 2-4ft (0.6-1.2m) surf. The best swell season is April - September but that's also the rainy season. The Harmattan is a cool and dry northerly wind that blows offshore from Dec - May (10-20%). During this time, beachbreaks can be awesome but unfortunately it's flat most of the time. The straight offshores occur from 7am to noon, then a gentle westerly sea breeze ruins the beachbreaks. In summer, the SW monsoon blows a mild onshore most of the time. Wind patterns are pretty calm and at this equatorial latitude, tidal ranges are very low, 1m (3ft) max, which only matter on the shallowest sections of the rights, thus practically negating the tidal factor.

Elmina Beach

| SURF STATISTICS | J F | M A | M J | J A | S O | N D |
|---|---|---|---|---|---|---|
| dominant swell | S | S-SW | S-SW | S-SW | S | S |
| swell size (ft) | 1-2 | 2-3 | 3-4 | 4 | 2-3 | 1-2 |
| consistency (%) | 30 | 50 | 60 | 80 | 60 | 30 |
| dominant wind | S-W | S-W | S-W | S-W | S-W | S-W |
| average force | F2 | F3 | F3 | F3 | F3 | F3 |
| consistency (%) | 65 | 73 | 75 | 82 | 74 | 72 |
| water temp (°C/°F) | 27/80 | 28/82 | 27/80 | 25/77 | 24/75 | 26/79 |
| wetsuit | | | | | | |

# 90. North Gabon

Cap Lopez Peninsula

ALEX LAUREL

**Summary**

+ MELLOW WAVES
+ NO CROWDS
+ SANDY LEFT POINTBREAKS
+ CALM WINDS, WARM WATER
+ FISHING PARADISE

− INCONSISTENT SWELLS
− MALARIA AND DISEASES
− SMALL, MUSHY WAVES
− FEW FLIGHT CONNECTIONS
− EXPENSIVE LOCAL PRICES

As a surf destination, Gabon remains a mystery to most waveriders. Nestled below the "Armpit of Africa", few foreigners make the journey, while the sparse local surfing population rarely travel beyond France. Most of the known spots are located close to Port-Gentil and the capital, Libreville, where expatriates provide the greatest number of potential surfers among the city's 300,000 population. West Africans have long harboured a distinct fear and mistrust of the ocean, leaving the bulk of the population firmly on dry land with limited swimming skills.

To escape the virtually waveless estuary of Libreville, drive north on one of the few paved roads to Cape Esterias, or get a boat to Ekwata. **Ferme aux Crocos** (Crocodile Farm) is a private beach resort reached by 4x4 with a wide beach and sloppy

MARC DE TIENDA

Cap Lopez

ALEX LAUREL

shorebreak waves. There is a rideable wave in Libreville at **Gueque** but it is very poor quality. On the west side of the Gabon Estuary are the ten neat beach bungalows, which make up Ekwata village. From here, it is a 15 minute walk up to **Ngombé** lighthouse where an occasional long, wrapping left breaks over the shiny black stones that line the coast. When it is on, it's a very long wave, so head for the beach and walk back to the peak under the shade of

## TRAVEL INFORMATION

**Population:** 165,000 Port-Gentil
**Coastline:** 885km (553mi)
**Contests:** Local
**Other Resources:** tourisme-gabon.com

**Getting There** – While it is easy to fly from West Africa to Libreville, access from Europe is slightly more difficult; Paris has the widest choice of flights (Air France is the best). No departure tax but a visa is $50. National carrier, Air Gabon is good by African standards. Locally the Cessna planes don't take boards so use the Mandji Express (4h, $70) to get to Port-Gentil.

**Getting Around** – With so many rivers and lagoons travelling overland is a nightmare. Use a boat to get from Libreville to Port-Gentil, as there are too few paved roads to drive it. Outboard canoes leave from Port Môle to Ekwata. Cheap taxis can be hired in Port-Gentil to get to Cap Lopez (20km, $10 r/t). Speedboats are rented from Olendé for $400/d.

**Lodging and Food** – Apart from the bungalows at Ekwata Village, stay in Port-Gentil. Novotel is $50/d. L'Hirondelle is the cheapest at $35/dble. If you stay in Ozuri or Iguela fishing camps it is $1200/wk. Expect to pay $20 for a Western meal, $5 for a local one. Regab beer is $0.6 Extras are costly.

**Weather** – Being equatorial, Gabon is very hot and humid. Temps vary from 23-33°C (72-92°F) and during the seven month long rainy season, humidity wavers between 90-100%. From mid-September to May rainfall is about 300mm/month (12in) although this will increase the further north you go. The main rainy season is from mid-January to mid-May, with another smaller one from mid-October to mid-December. Fortunately the remainder of the year is less rainy. Only June-September is dry, luckily coinciding the main swell season. Water temps rarely get below 25°C (77°F) but take a light neoprene rashvest for wind protection.

**Nature and Culture** – Besides the plentiful African wildlife (chimps, birds, elephants), visit Elf Museum, Cap Lopez oil terminals or platforms. Port-Gentil has more restaurants, nightclubs and shops per capita than any other African city and also a casino. The fishing is excellent.

**Hazards and Hassles** – Yellow Fever immunisation is a must, providing all other injections are up to date. Malaria is rife with lots of Nivaquine-resistant mosquitoes. Port-Gentil has a decent hospital if you are unlucky enough to need one. Gabon is politically stable having been led by Omar Bongo since 1967. Water dangers include sharks, hippos and the strong equatorial sun.

**Handy Hints** – Bring all your gear with you as local surfers may buy it for a fair price. You won't need a gun as longboards/hybrids are ideal. The *Solmar II* sails between Libreville and São Tomè on a regular basis; a one way ticket is under $100US.

| WEATHER STATISTICS | J/F | M/A | M/J | J/A | S/O | N/D |
|---|---|---|---|---|---|---|
| total rainfall (mm) | 248 | 330 | 143 | 6 | 233 | 338 |
| consistency (days/mth) | 15 | 18 | 9 | 3 | 18 | 19 |
| min temp (°C/°F) | 24/75 | 23/74 | 24/75 | 22/72 | 23/74 | 24/75 |
| max temp (°C/°F) | 31/88 | 31/88 | 30/86 | 28/82 | 29/84 | 30/86 |

Cap Lopez

ALEX LAUREL

ALEX LAUREL

Olendé

the trees. The main problem with this estuarine area is that even at a full 20km (12mi) out to sea, the water depth remains a mere 40m (130ft) deep, draining the power from the swell. The beach skirts a swampy savannah full of birds, monkeys and elephants, while to the south surfing opportunities diminish in the shadow of Port-Gentil and heavy silting in the Baie de Nazaré.

From Libreville, the Mandji Express catamaran ferry crosses the Equator to Port-Gentil, Gabon's economic capital, which trades in oil and timber. Off the tip of the peninsula, Mandji Island rises out of deep water, unlike anywhere else in West Africa. This undoubtedly makes it

Palplanche

ISABELLE BEIGBEDER

the most consistent area to surf, plus it is home to a classy left, **Palplanche**, which breaks about 25-30 days a year. Opposite the rusty steel jetties of an old erosion prevention programme, the wave wraps around the NW of the island for up to 200m (650ft) with some tube sections. If Palplanche isn't working, check **Cap Lopez**, the most reliable spot, on the other side of Village des Togolais, just below the lighthouse. Open to all swells, these beachbreaks break predominately left, jack up close to shore and produce hollow barrels with some shape. The water quality, like everywhere in this area, is a little murky but at least there is some power. When it's glassy there are good beachbreaks, like **Ferme aux Cochons** (Pig Farm). This spot probably gets some of the biggest surf but the fast beachbreak cannot handle any wind. Closer to Port-Gentil are **PG2**, near the wharf where the transit ships for the oil platforms dock and **Plage du Dahu**, facing the Novotel. Heading southwards from here there is a vast 600km (370mi), SW facing stretch of coastline down to Congo. Little is known but it's a fairly straight sandy shore with lagoons creating sandspits, which potentially could hold some insane lefts. **Olendé** is host to one of these with a 1km long, wrapping left, skirting the Barre des Portugais shore. It has only been surfed a handful of times. Unfortunately, the fishing camp at Olendé was closed in 2000 but there are two camps at Ozuri and Iguela, south of Omboué. Be warned that local surfcasters catch plenty of sharks and barracudas in this area. Either use a speed boat (very expensive) from Port-

Gentil or fly to Omboué, the nearest main village. One of the last surf checks on this area was in December 2000 when the *National Geographic* Congotrek expedition hit the coast at **Petit Loango** and found hippos swimming in the waves.

South Atlantic lows deliver swell between April and September but only the biggest swells make it to the Gabon coastline some 5000km (3050mi) north. These swells tend to be slowed by the extended continental shelf and then hit a predominately W facing coast, producing an average wave height of 2ft (0.6m) and rarely getting bigger than 5ft (1.5m). Being right on the Equator and lacking straight exposure to S swells, the main surf spots lack consistency. However, the unsurfed SW facing coastline may be bigger. Don't count on windswell or tidal range to help as 90% of all wind is less than Force 2, usually on a SE-SW quadrant and the biggest tide is a mere 7ft (2.1m). There is a constant south to north sideshore drift, getting stronger the further south you go.

| SURF STATISTICS | J F | M A | M J | J A | S O | N D |
|---|---|---|---|---|---|---|
| dominant swell | S-SW | S-SW | S-SW | S-SW | S-SW | S-SW |
| swell size (ft) | 1 | 1-2 | 2-3 | 3 | 2 | 1 |
| consistency (%) | 20 | 40 | 50 | 60 | 40 | 20 |
| dominant wind | S-SW | S-SW | SE-SW | SE-SW | S-SW | S-SW |
| average force | F3 | F3 | F3 | F3 | F3 | F3 |
| consistency (%) | 69 | 67 | 88 | 90 | 88 | 76 |
| water temp (°C/°F) | 27/80 | 28/82 | 25/77 | 23/74 | 24/75 | 26/79 |
| wetsuit | | | | | | |

| SPOT DESCRIPTION | | | |
|---|---|---|---|
| Spot | Size | Btm | Type |
| ① | 6/1 | | |
| ② | 4/1 | | |
| ③ | 6/2 | | |
| ④ | 6/1 | | |
| ⑤ | 8/1 | | |
| ⑥ | 8/1 | | |
| ⑦ | 6/1 | | |
| ⑧ | 6/1 | | |
| ⑨ | 6/1 | | |
| ⑩ | 6/1 | | |

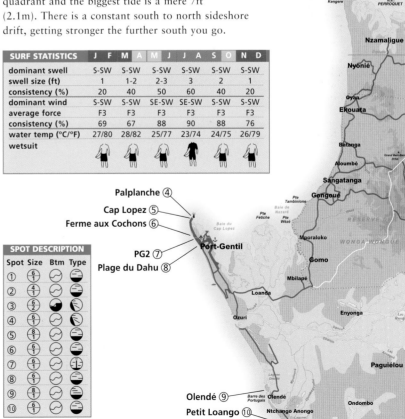

Ferme aux Crocos ①
Gueque ②
Ngombé ③
Libreville
Cap Santa Clara
Pte Pongara
Port Mole
Pointe Denis
Ekwata Village
Owendo
ILE CONNIQUET
Pte Kengere
ILE PERROQUET
Nzamaligue
Nyónié
Oyan
Ekouata
Batanga
Grand Ban-Ban
Aloumbé
Sangatanga
Gongoué
Palplanche ④
Cap Lopez ⑤
Ferme aux Cochons ⑥
PG2 ⑦
Plage du Dahu ⑧
Pte Tamblione
Baie de Nazaré
Pte Fétiche
Pte Wèze
Baie du Cap Lopez
RESERVE D
WONGA-WONGUE
Port-Gentil
Mporaloko
Gomo
Mbilapé
Loanda
Enyonga
Lac Mandji
Ozuri
Olendé ⑨
Barre des Portugais
Olendé
Ondombo
Petit Loango ⑩
Ntchango Anongo
Paguiélou

ZAIRE

ANGOLA

NAMIBIA

# 91. Luanda and Bengo

JOHN CALLAHAN

**Summary**
+ EASY, LONG LEFT POINTBREAKS
+ CONSISTENT SWELLS
+ WARMISH WATER
+ UNDISCOVERED WAVES

− WINDY, EXPOSED SPOTS
− COSTLY FLIGHTS AND VISAS
− NO TOURISM INFRASTRUCTURE
− WAR ZONE, LAND MINES
− SHARKS AND CROCS

JEAN-LUC BOURROULEC

JOHN CALLAHAN

It's impossible to talk about Angola without looking at the dismal political situation. Since its independence from Portugal in 1975, there have been nearly 30 years of civil war wreaking havoc all over the country. The political power resides with MPLA-PT, whose president is M. Dos Santos but since 1976, UNITA has waged devastating insurgency from bases in the SE. About 100,000 people have been killed, lowering average life expectancy to 38 years, in this western backed war for oil and diamonds. Angola probably rates as the worst mine affected country in the world, with 31 land mines per square mile, totalling 15 million. Fortunately, the surfing areas in Luanda and Bengo, are free of significant mine contamination and Angola is thought to be an African Peru, with a long coastline of unknown surf spots. Randy Rarick's 1974 article "A day in the Past, a place for the Future", showed no surf pictures ('74 was the heyday of secret locations) despite having some good surfing shots. At this time, probably less than 100

## TRAVEL INFORMATION

**Population:** 500,000 Luanda
**Coastline:** 1,600km (1000mi)
**Contests:** None
**Other Resources:**
wannasurf.com/ spot/Africa/Angola/ index.html
pensador.com
angonet.org

**Getting There** – Pay $60 for a 30 day visa once you have obtained a "Guest Letter". Luanda has direct flights from Libreville (Air Gabon, good value), Jo-burg (SAA), Lisboa (TAP, best deals), Paris (Air France, costly), New York or Rio. Nat'l TAAG is expensive. Being mostly business flights, it's very expensive to get to Luanda.

**Getting Around** – Since 1975, many bridges have been blown up and many roads have been subject to attack by UNITA guerrillas, necessitating military convoys for road transportation. However, the 130km (80mi) stretch down to Cabo Ledo is ok. Overloaded transport will get stuck in the sand. A 4WD is a must that costs $100+ per day (Wapo). The tourism infrastructure is practically non-existent.

**Lodging and Food** – Costs a fortune. Int'l Hotels (Meridien, Continental) range from $180/night. Cheapest hotels would be $50 per night. There is a camp at the mouth of the Cuanza River with basic facilities ($100/d).

**Weather** – The cold N flowing Benguela current substantially reduces rain along the coast, making the region relatively arid further south towards the Namib Desert. In Luanda, the average annual rainfall is as low as 50cm (20in), supporting little more than dry scrub. The rainy season is from November to March/April. The dry season (cacimbo) is often characterised by a heavy morning mist and holds the region to only 2341 hours of sunshine per year (200 days). Rain is higher in the north, but at any latitude it's greater in the interior than along the coast and increases with altitude. The coolest months are July and August 18-25°C (64-77°F). Springsuits are probably only necessary on a windy day in June-September when water temps drop beneath 22°C (72°F).

**Nature and Culture** – The Quissama National Park, 120km (75mi) alongside the Atlantic, sits south of the perennial Cuanza River. Apart from world-class fishing with huge river tarpon there is a golf course and some nightlife in town. Good place to buy diamonds.

**Hazards and Hassles** – Being constantly on the travel advisory list, Angola sits in the top 5 most dangerous countries in the world, although for land mines or rebel attacks, this zone is safer than most. Police checks can be hassley and expensive. Besides road dangers, there are regular shark sightings. Except for rips, the sandy points are pretty harmless!

**Handy Hints** – Take everything. The waves aren't suitable for a gun; a longboard would be ideal. Local currency is not exportable and dollars in cash are a must for the visitor. Contact WTA (World Travel Agency) in Paris or Jo-Burg, who specialize in this part of the world.

| WEATHER STATISTICS | J/F | M/A | M/J | J/A | S/O | N/D |
|---|---|---|---|---|---|---|
| total rainfall (mm) | 30 | 113 | 10 | 1 | 4 | 30 |
| consistency (days/mth) | 3 | 8 | 1 | 0 | 1 | 3 |
| min temp (°C/°F) | 24/75 | 24/75 | 22/72 | 18/64 | 21/70 | 23/74 |
| max temp (°C/°F) | 30/86 | 31/88 | 28/82 | 25/77 | 28/82 | 29/84 |

Cabo Ledo

OLIVIER MICHAUD

sandbank with mechanical precision and it actually works best with a small swell making it ideal for less experienced surfers. The first outside section facing the rocks has the most power and as the swell increases, the rips get pretty horrendous. Towards the Namibian border is a long stretch of coast with colder water but many more unsurfed, quality, left pointbreaks.

Most South Atlantic swells reach Angolan shores, although at this latitude, some power has been lost along the way. Long distance 4-8ft (1.2-2.5m) swells with 15+ second intervals usually occur between April and September while some windswell waves can be observed whenever SE trades off

waveriders had the privilege of enjoying these long mellow left pointbreaks in the Luanda South coastal lowlands.

The closest spots to the capital city Luanda, are **Chicala** and **Mussolo**, but they're not worth considering for foreign visitors. These mushy beachbreaks are more suited to kids playing in the waves while their family picnic on the beach. It's a 40km (25mi) drive to get to the entrance of the Mussolo sandspit, then 8km (5mi) north to reach **Buraco**. This left is a gem, breaking close to shore down a sandy point with excellent shape and length. Without a booming swell it will be flat but the local fishermen will be happy to supply beers and lobsters. Palmeirinhas hosts **Shipwreck**, unimaginatively named as the sandbar faces a sunken freighter. It picks up a lot of swell but is also very exposed to the wind. This tubular spot needs to be hit early as it gets blown out by 10am. Drive to a more sheltered spot if the swell exceeds 6ft. The Cuanza River marks the entrance of the Quissama National Park. To the north is **Miradouro**, a short left pointbreak breaking in murky water with the major danger coming from falling cliffs. It needs a 4x4 at the best of times and is impassable with rain. South of the river is **Barra da Cuanza** with several spots that are hardly ever ridden because of tough access. One of the three reefs is the only right in Angola, nestled under multi-coloured cliffs. Just remember not to paddle across the river because of sharks and crocs! There is also a nearby military installation. The view from the road at **Cabo Ledo** reveals the unique set-up of this world class pointbreak. Really long lefthanders reel down the

Namibia blow with strength for a long period of time. These swells only reach the S facing spots. Winds are thermally driven, picking up quite consistently after 10am, as the sun heats up the white coastal plain. Dominant wind direction is S-SW, getting stronger towards the end of the year. As far as tides go, the range never exceeds 5ft (1.5m) max while the type is semi-diurnal with a slight diurnal inequality.

| SURF STATISTICS | J F | M A M | J J A | S O N | D |
|---|---|---|---|---|---|
| dominant swell | S-SW | S-SW | S-SW | S-SW | S-SW | S-SW |
| swell size (ft) | 1-2 | 2-3 | 4 | 4-5 | 3-4 | 1-2 |
| consistency (%) | 40 | 60 | 80 | 90 | 70 | 50 |
| dominant wind | S-SW | S-SW | S-SW | S-SW | S-SW | S-SW |
| average force | F3 | F3 | F2-F3 | F2 | F2-F3 | F3 |
| consistency (%) | 59 | 57 | 58 | 51 | 70 | 70 |
| water temp (°C/°F) | 26/79 | 26/79 | 24/75 | 21/70 | 23/74 | 25/77 |
| wetsuit | | | | | | |

Shipwreck

JEAN-LUC BOURROULEC

NAMIBIA

SOUTH AFRICA   LSOTA

# 92. Western Cape

## Summary

+ VARIETY OF LEFT POINTBREAKS
+ SOME EASY MELLOW WAVES
+ CHEAP AND UNCROWDED
+ SCENERY AND WILDLIFE

− FEW CONSISTENT SPOTS
− COLD WATER YEAR ROUND
− KELP AND MUSSELS
− LACK OF TOURISM INFRASTRUCTURE

Elands Bay

BARRY TUCK

BARRY TUCK

Divided between the Atlantic and the Indian Oceans, South Africa's 2800km (1750mi) of time eroded coastline creates an underrated surf destination of quality, consistent waves. While there is a tremendous proliferation of right pointbreaks on the East Coast, don't forget about the Atlantic West Coast north of Cape Town. The shivering cold Benguela Current, which brings colder water temperatures in summer than winter, also acts as a highway for swells to arrive at several kelp-covered, north facing, left pointbreaks tucked behind headlands. The late John Whitmore, considered the father of South African surfing

Lambert's Bay

JOHN HENWOOD/ALAMY

discovered Eland's Bay in 1957 and retired there. It has become a popular exit for Capetonian waveriders, whenever there is some significant swell action and there are plenty of other possibilities south of the mountainous Namaqualand area.

A natural harbour has been created at Lambert's Bay by building a breakwater out to Bird Island, a massive

## TRAVEL INFORMATION

**Population:** 4.4M
**Coastline:** 2,800km (1,750mi)
**Contests:** Regional
**Other Resources:**
*Video:* African Sensemilla; Pits & Pieces
wavescape.co.za
capesurftours.com
elandsbay.co.za
http://tourism.org.za

**Getting There** – South Africa is not exactly an int'l travel hub so flying there is not cheap except from London. Most of the 50+ airlines fly into Jo-Burg (sometimes Cape Town). SAA usual boardtax: $US93! E-Bay is 2h1/2 from CT: 1h1/2 N7 West Coast Hwy + 1h dirt road.

**Getting Around** – The road network gets wild once you leave Cape Town. Most spots can be reached by gravel road but some Vredenburg Peninsula secrets require a 4WD and a lot of intuition. Expect $150/w and gas is cheap. Consider buying a car if you spend ± 3 months. Traffic keeps to the left.

**Lodging and Food** – E-Bay is tiny: stay in the beach caravan park ($3 per tent) but if you

think it's too windy, stay in the green Hotel Eland. Bed and breakfast is $15/day. Eat as much red gold (crayfish) as you can. Seafood is cheap including anchovies, pilchards and long, thin, silvery snoek. Avoid Lambert's Bay, 27km (17mi) north.

**Weather** – Weather patterns are very unstable but rainfall is low. Winters (May-Sept) bring many cold fronts over the peninsula. Once the coastal low has passed, winds and clouds move in from the NW. Rain starts falling and the ocean gets rough. Summers are usually warm and dry but very windy in the afternoon. Because of the cold Benguela Current, water hardly ever gets over 15°C (59°F) and sometimes gets down to 9°C (48°F) on west facing spots with summer upwelling. 4/3 fullsuit + booties required year round.

**Nature and Culture** – Plenty of birds like flamingos, pelicans and herons at E-Bay river or at the National Park. Do your best to enjoy

the barren landscape filled with short scrubs and dotted with lonely farmhouses. Don't expect city action, E-Bay has two pool tables and two cafes. Visit the Bobbejaanberg Cave in Baboon Point.

**Hazards and Hassles** – Most visitors are Capetonian weekenders so most of the crowd disappear on weekdays. Have enough neoprene to protect your feet from the mussels. Frequent winds and a strong smell of fish can be a hassle as well as the thick kelp, which can hamper your board speed. Country towns are breeding grounds for the endemic racism that blights South Africa. On a positive note, sharks are not a problem in this area of SA.

**Handy Hints** – Buy your gear in Cape Town since there are no shops or shapers around E-Bay. Get a new board (Geraghty: $230, $300 for a LB) or a wettie (Reef: $80) at Ocean II Ocean shop. You don't need a gun. Living costs in SA are low.

| total rainfall (mm) | 10 | 33 | 83 | 78 | 38 | 14 |
| consistency (days/mth) | 2 | 5 | 9 | 10 | 11 | 3 |
| min temp (°C/°F) | 16/61 | 13/55 | 9/48 | 8/46 | 10/50 | 14/57 |
| max temp (°C/°F) | 26/79 | 24/75 | 19/66 | 18/64 | 20/68 | 24/75 |

BARRY TUCK

slab of rock colonised by thousands of penguins, cormorants and cape gannets. In front of the rivermouth, at the north end is the **Caravan Park** with a tide dependant, mushy beachbreak, favouring lefts. **Garbage Dump** has a wrapping left, far out in the kelp and a right pointbreak in rare, calm wind conditions. Check 10km (6mi) south in similar, no wind conditions and **Farmer Burger's** powerful right reefbreak should be good in small swells. Eland's Bay hamlet sits on a sandy riverbank, waiting for a swell to hit **The Point**. Steep drops into fast tubular walls, spinning across a kelp covered, low tide reef before bending into a sandy end section at the rivermouth. Besides a consistent beachbreak up north and some possible rights on a nearby reef, **Baboon Point** is worth checking if the swell is not big enough for E-Bay. The black cliffs offer some shelter for the lefts, but SW winds will blow out this

spot. The long stretch of Santa Helena Bay would only suit beginners, lacking shape and shelter. **Stompneus** is the first break on the north side of the Vredenburg Peninsula. Not as epic as E-Bay and needs similar big swell conditions, but it combines an outside, low tide reef with an inside, high tide set-up that handles any swell size and even W winds. This wild area hides many secret spots (like Pastures, Heaven and Hell) but access is the main problem without a 4WD and a local guide. Another fun left is to be found at **Cape St Martin** after a tricky network of farm gravel roads. **Trekostraal** is an inconsistent right point in a deepwater bay full of crayfish. Around Paternoster is a fun, triangular reef called **Perlemoen Bay**. When small and clean, check the swell at Swartriet Beach Resort if you feel like paying a fee for the small, fun beachbreak at **Jacob's Bay**.

Antarctica's SW-S swells are pretty active and powerful from March to September, providing lots of 6-15ft (2-5m) swells. Although potentially being year round, N-exposed reefs like E-Bay definitely need these strong, winter, SW swells to break. Common SW winds will be offshore and the day after a cold front passes is usually the classic day. Then, summer starts in October with strong SE winds (The Cape Doctor), bringing upwelling cold currents ashore and blown-out conditions after 10am. When a rare high pressure protects the West Coast, winds and swell diminish and warm NE Berg winds fan the SW-exposed spots, bringing small and perfect conditions. Tidal range can reach 10ft (3m), most reefs and pointbreaks favour low tides, further reducing surf time, so get a tide table in Cape Town.

The Point

TOSTEE.COM

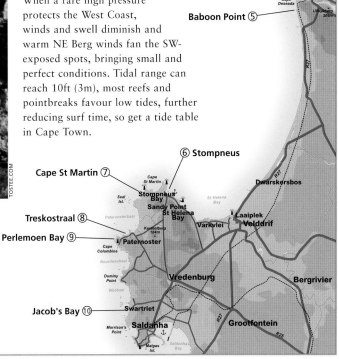

| SURF STATISTICS | J F | M A | M J | J A | S O | N D |
|-----------------|-----|-----|-----|-----|-----|-----|
| dominant swell | SW-W | SW-W | SW-W | SW-W | SW-W | SW-W |
| swell size (ft) | 1-2 | 3-4 | 5 | 6 | 4 | 2 |
| consistency (%) | 50 | 60 | 80 | 70 | 60 | 50 |
| dominant wind | SE-S | E-S | E-NW | SE-NW | SE-SW | SE-S |
| average force | F4 | F4 | F4 | F4 | F4 | F4 |
| consistency (%) | 61 | 55 | 75 | 78 | 66 | 60 |
| water temp (°C/°F) | 16/61 | 15/59 | 14/57 | 13/56 | 14/57 | 16/61 |
| wetsuit | | | | | | |

NAMIBIA

SOUTH AFRICA

LESOTHO

# 93. Garden Route

Secret Spot

GARTH ROBINSON

## Summary
+ HIGH SWELL CONSISTENCY
+ VARIETY OF RIGHT POINTBREAKS
+ CHEAP AND UNCROWDED
+ FABULOUS NATURE ACTIVITIES

- COOL WATER YEAR ROUND
- VIRTUALLY NO LEFTS
- NO MAJOR AIRPORT NEARBY
- PACKED TOURIST SEASON
- GREAT WHITE SHARKS

H alf way between Cape Town and J-Bay are clusters of right pointbreaks, condensed in a popular area known as the Garden Route. This 250km (156mi) stretch of coastal towns with exposed beachbreaks or sheltered bays, usually produce fine pointbreak set-ups. Amongst the more obvious are Mossel Bay, Knysna and Plettenberg while the likes of Stillbay or Victoria Bay stay out of the limelight. Renowned for its unique flora, the Southern Cape is rugged country, backed by mountains and river filled valleys, providing habitat for many wild animals. The water teems with life as whales and dolphins frequent the wild ocean off South Africa's tip.

Victoria Bay

ALAN VAN GYSEN

Buffelsbaai

GARTH ROBINSON

To the west of Mossel Bay is **Jongensfontein**, a small SE swell reefbreak for when it's too wee for the likes of **Stillbay**'s sharky but epic righthand pointbreak. Huge SW swells will halve in size by the time they have wrapped into the bay, but it is rocky, sectiony and a gruelling rip pushes down the point. A huge SE swell is

## TRAVEL INFORMATION

**Population:** 15,000 Plettenberg
**Coastline:** 2,798km (1,750mi)
**Contests:** Vic Bay (Jun)
**Other Resources:**
*Video:* African Sensemilla; Pits & Pieces
wavescape.co.za
friendzsurf.com
gardenroute.co.za
http:tourism.org.za

**Getting There** – South Africa is not exactly an int'l travel hub so flying there is not cheap except from London. The majority of airlines fly to Jo-Burg, R/T flights to George Airport: $185. Plettenberg is 6h from Cape Town and 2h from Port Elizabeth. Plett is 18h by bus from Jo-Burg with Translux. SAA boardtax: $93! Dep Tax: $5

**Getting Around** – It takes 2h to drive from Mossel Bay to Plett, with ample spot checking opportunities. Rental car (from $150/wk), or inter city transport by bus or minibus is excellent and cheap. ($12 o/w to CT with Mainliner). Traffic keeps to the left. Gas is cheap ($0.40/l)

**Lodging and Food** – Plett seaside resort offers accommodation and services; avoid the high tourist season Dec-Feb when prices hit the roof.

Stay in Robberg resort ($14/n), prestigious Beacon Island Hotel ($70/dble) or in one of the cheap B&B (Little Sanctuary: $28/dble). Expect $7 for a meal at the Boardwalk Cafe.

**Weather** – The Garden Route has a mediterranean/maritime climate, with semi-hot summers and mild to chilly winters. It is one of the richest rainfall areas, most of it in the winter, supplied by the moisture laden ocean winds. Any time of the year is good for visiting, but there are massive variations between the quiet winters and bustling summers. Rainfall is year round but not torrential. Summers are usually warm and it's the only time the water feels bearable enough to wear springsuits. The rest of the year is not that cold although mid-winter, cloudy mornings are chilly while the SW winds require adequate clothing and fullsuits all the time (boots and even hoods), despite the warm Agulhas Current. Sometimes, before a cold frontal system moves onto the coast, the hot Berg winds come from the mountains and make a real nice day before a sudden temp drop.

**Nature and Culture** – Dive in cages to see white sharks. Whale and dolphin watching spots are plentiful. On either sides of the Route are two bungee jumping sites. Visit Tsitsikamma Park forests, Robberg in Plett has a reserve. Mossel Bay is scenic despite Mossgas' huge oil refinery.

**Hazards and Hassles** – The shark factor can be a problem, recent fatal attacks have occurred in Keurbooms, Buffel and Mossel Bay. Avoid sardine runs (well noticed by the media), sunset sessions and murky waters and all should be fine. Summer bluebottle flies can be much more of a hassle. Some localism at Mossel Bay.

**Handy Hints** – Buy gear in Mossel Bay (Billeon Surfboards), Knysna (Nirvana Trading, Surf Culture) or Plett (Ocean Life). Get a new board ($230, $300 for a mal) or a wettie (Reef: $80). Use Friends Tours out of Mossel Bay. A semi-gun in winter might be necessary. Living costs in SA are low, which is a bonus in a well-developed country.

| WEATHER STATISTICS | J/F | M/A | M/J | J/A | S/O | N/D |
|---|---|---|---|---|---|---|
| total rainfall (mm) | 53 | 60 | 64 | 65 | 70 | 58 |
| consistency (days/mth) | 5 | 6 | 6 | 6 | 8 | 6 |
| min temp (°C/°F) | 17/63 | 15/59 | 9/48 | 8/46 | 11/52 | 15/59 |
| max temp (°C/°F) | 25/77 | 24/75 | 21/70 | 20/68 | 21/70 | 23/74 |

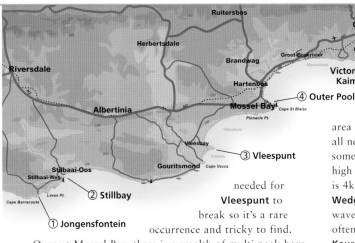

Map locations: Ruitersbos, Herbertsdale, Brandwag, Groot-Brakrivier, George, Wilderness, Paalaltsdorp, Sedgefield, Knysna, Keurboomstrand, Plettenberg Bay, Keurbooms ⑬, Lookout Beach ⑫, Victoria Bay ⑤, Groenvlei ⑦, Kaimansriver ⑥, Gericke Point ⑧, Goukamma ⑨, Murphys ⑩, The Wedge ⑪, Outer Pool ④, Mossel Bay, Hartenbos, Albertinia, Riversdale, Cape St Blaize, Pinnacle Pt., Vleesbaai, Vleesbay, Visbaai, Vleespunt ③, Gouritsmond, Cape Vacca, Stilbaai-Oos, Stilbaai-Wes, Stillbay ②, Leven Pt., Cape Barracouta, Jongensfontein ①, Buffelsbaai, Walker Pt., Cape Seal, Nature's Valley

| SPOT DESCRIPTION | | | |
|---|---|---|---|
| Spot | Size | Btm | Type |
| ① | 6/2 | | |
| ② | 10/4 | | |
| ③ | 8/3 | | |
| ④ | 8/2 | | |
| ⑤ | 10/3 | | |
| ⑥ | 6/2 | | |
| ⑦ | 4/2 | | |
| ⑧ | 6/1 | | |
| ⑨ | 6/1 | | |
| ⑩ | 6/1 | | |
| ⑪ | 4/3 | | |
| ⑫ | 6/1 | | |
| ⑬ | 6/1 | | |

...needed for **Vleespunt** to break so it's a rare occurrence and tricky to find. Once at Mossel Bay, there is a wealth of multi-peak bays lined up along the north facing coast of Cape St Blaize. **Outer Pool** is the pick, throwing up long, speedy walls with cavernous tubes at low tide, washed by a tiring drift

The Wedge

area with services and accommodation to suit all needs. With eight spots in the area, there should be something for everyone, outside of the summer tourist high season. From the rivermouth to Beacon Island, there is 4km (1,3mi) of spots, the most spectacular being the **Wedge** lefts, only breaking on a rare easterly swell. Most wave-riders in Plettenberg surf **Lookout Beach**, but this often breaks too fast to be any good. Last but not least is **Keurbooms**. It's an exposed beachbreak, getting epic on small, clean swell with no wind. Share the lefts and rights with a school of local dolphins in stunning scenery.

The Roaring Forties SW-S swells are always active and powerful from March to September, providing lots of 6-15ft (2-5m) swells. When the swell machine is on, it can last for weeks. Lows travel quickly from west to east, spinning clockwise. SW facing spots will be onshore, so the best coastal orientation is SE. Swells march against the W flowing warm Agulhas current, building sandbanks in the SE facing bays. From November to March, winds shift from W to E, blowing out most spots with the ENE winds, produced by high pressures. Note that occasional strong E winds or

Plettenberg Bay

| SURF STATISTICS | J F | M A | M J | J A | S O | N D |
|---|---|---|---|---|---|---|
| dominant swell | E-SW | SE-SW | SE-SW | SE-SW | SE-SW | E-SW |
| swell size (ft) | 2-3 | 4-5 | 5 | 5-6 | 4-5 | 3 |
| consistency (%) | 50 | 60 | 80 | 70 | 70 | 60 |
| dominant wind | E-W | SW-NW | SW-NW | SW-NW | SW-NW | E-W |
| average force | F4 | F4 | F4 | F4 | F4 | F4 |
| consistency (%) | 88 | 61 | 70 | 73 | 67 | 86 |
| water temp (°C/°F) | 22/72 | 22/72 | 19/66 | 18/64 | 19/66 | 20/68 |
| wetsuit | | | | | | |

tropical cyclones from January to March can provide short E swells. The best period is from April to October with dominant W winds, usually NW (the beloved Berg Winds) in the morning turning SW (sideshore) after noon. Any time a cold front passes, there will be E winds. Fortunately, the heart of the swell is gone by then. Tides only vary between 1-2m (3-6ft), but get a chart if you can.

down the point. Inner Pool prefers higher tides and is far slower and fatter. Around George are a couple of quality breaks like **Victoria Bay**, a popular right pointbreak zipping over the rocky headland beneath steep cliffs in a pocket bay. Further east is **Kaimansriver**, a small swell, light winds option whose lefts and rights featured in the *Endless Summer*. Dolphin Point Lookout is a great place to check the swell. Checkout **Groenvlei** for uncrowded beachbreak fun. On an easterly wind, there's the novelty of a left pointbreak at **Gericke Point**, but only in small summer conditions. **Goukamma**'s beautiful rivermouth peaks are totally sand dependant and the red alluvial soil in the outflow gives cover to the ever-present sharks. Close to Knysna is Buffelsbaai, where many different spots can be checked. There's an inconsistent point that fires in SE swells, plus some fun beachbreaks but the pick of the pack is **Murphys** reef and sand peak. Only an hour's drive from J-Bay, Plettenberg Bay is a convenient

Mossel Bay

NAMIBIA
SOUTH AFRICA  SOTH

# 94. Wild Coast

Ntlonyane (Breezy Point)

ALL PHOTOS GARTH ROBINSON

## Summary

+ TOP CLASS RIGHT POINTBREAKS
+ CROWD FREE
+ WARM WATER
+ CHEAP LIVING COSTS

– SHARKS
– POOR ROAD NETWORK
– LACK OF FACILITIES
– POVERTY AND PETTY CRIME

The Wild Coast, once known as the Transkei homeland, is a 280km (175mi) stretch of cliff faces, perfect beaches and rich tidal estuaries, running from Great Kei River (East London) to Mtamvuna River (Port Edward) on the border with KwaZulu Natal Province. Inland, lie the Stromberg and Drakensberg mountain ranges, ascending to 7200ft (2400m), before great ridges descend down to the ocean, resulting in a narrow continental shelf. The NE flowing Agulhas Current, only 100km (62mi) wide off the Transkei coast, is one of the fastest flowing currents in the world (5 knots). Long distances between towns, the poor condition of the roads, a lack of facilities and some strenuous access to breaks; this region suits the more experienced searcher

Ntylonyane

with some pioneering spirit. There is a balanced equilibrium between exposed, quality beachbreaks and protected right pointbreaks and many bays have both. The imbalance comes with the inordinately high population of large, dangerous sharks including the

Kubornvu Rivermouth

## TRAVEL INFORMATION

**Population:** 100,000 Umtata
**Coastline:** 280km (175mi)
**Contests:** None
**Other Resources:**
Video: African Sensemilla; Pits & Pieces; Sarge video
wavescape.co.za
dawnpatrol.co.za
coastingafrica.com
http://tourism.org.za

**Getting There** – Flying to South Africa is not cheap except from London. Most of the 50+ airlines fly to Jo-Burg, R/T flights (daily) to Umtata: $160. Umtata is 6h from Durban + 1h to Coffee Bay and Port St Johns or 3h from East London. SAA boardtax: US$93! Dep Tax: $5.

**Getting Around** – Dirt roads are in poor condition and road signs are unreliable. If heading for a bay, make sure you know which side you want, as there won't be any bridge over the numerous rivermouths. Rent a car ($150/ week) or a 4WD/Camper van for the wildest access at Wildcoastrentals. Don't speed on the roads: lots of cattle and many people hitchhiking. Left driving.

**Lodging and Food** – Tourism facilities are low but the coast is dotted with small lodges (from

hotels to whitewashed and thatched rondavel huts). In Coffee Bay, Backpackers are fine: Coffee Shack ($8/day in dorms, $20/double in huts; or Bomvu. Ocean View Hotel: from $22/day. Try Amapondo in PSJ or the Kraal in Mpande. A meal will cost $5.

**Weather** – The climate along the Wild Coast is nearly always warm to hot, with humidity levels rising from Dec to March. Thunderstorms are frequent in summer. Inland the climate is temperate with warm summers and cool winters although colder spells may occur. The Wild Coast lies in a summer-rainfall region, swelling many rivers that flow into the ocean. The drier, winter climate is most favourable during the months of May and June. Sea temperatures usually exceed 17°C (63°F) and can go as high as 23°C (73°F) when the warm Agulhas (or Mozambique) Current flows close to shore.

**Nature and Culture** – Xhosa rural people live by tribal tradition and beliefs. Brightly coloured examples of the beadwork, together with

traditional pottery and basketwork can be bought from roadside vendors and at some trading posts. Backpacker's activities: horse-riding, hiking, music, yoga and parties!

**Hazards and Hassles** – On remote beaches, beware of muggings and car break-ins. Reduce shark risks: don't surf too early or too late; don't surf near flooded rivermouth; don't piss in the sea (even if wearing a wetsuit) and avoid the sardine runs. Winter is less sharky as the rivers subside and don't flood the ocean with brown, debris-strewn water. Beware the strong weed.

**Handy Hints** – Gear can be bought in East London (Sunset Surf, Screeming Blue) or in Margate (Surf Action), as shops/shapers are non-existent in this zone. Old boards can be rented in Coffee Bay. A semi-gun might be needed for rare big days. With the scrapping of Apartheid, the Transkei became part of SA but blacks make up 90% of the Wild Coast's population, 15% above the national average.

| WEATHER STATISTICS | J/F | M/A | M/J | J/A | S/O | N/D |
|---|---|---|---|---|---|---|
| total rainfall (mm) | 127 | 115 | 48 | 47 | 94 | 121 |
| consistency (days/mth) | 10 | 8 | 4 | 3 | 7 | 9 |
| min temp (°C/°F) | 20/68 | 18/64 | 15/59 | 13/55 | 16/61 | 18/64 |
| max temp (°C/°F) | 25/77 | 24/75 | 23/74 | 21/70 | 22/72 | 23/74 |

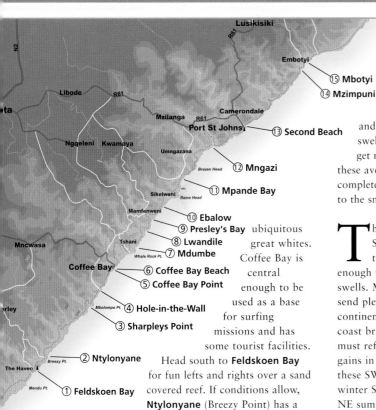

Map labels:
- Lusikisiki
- Embotyi
- ⑮ Mbotyi
- ⑭ Mzimpuni
- Libode R61
- Mzilanga R61 Camerondale
- Port St Johns
- ⑬ Second Beach
- Ngqeleni Kwamaya
- Umngazana
- Brazen Head
- ⑫ Mngazi
- Sikelweni
- ⑪ Mpande Bay
- Rame Head
- Mamfenweni
- ⑩ Ebalow
- ⑨ Presley's Bay
- Tshani ⑧ Lwandile
- ⑦ Mdumbe
- Whale Rock Pt.
- Coffee Bay ⑥ Coffee Bay Beach
- ⑤ Coffee Bay Point
- Mbolompo Pt. ④ Hole-in-the-Wall
- ③ Sharpleys Point
- Breezy Pt. ② Ntylonyane
- The Haven
- Mendu Pt. ① Feldskoen Bay
- Mncwasa
- N2

**Ebalow**. These rare but epic lefts are deep in 4WD country along with Sharks Point's long, hollow rights. **Mpande Bay** throws up some nice beachies in small swell, light offshore conditions. Port St Johns is the main coastal town, exuding a strange melange of styles and cultures with several beaches close-by. On a small swell, beachbreaks like **Mngazi** and **Second Beach** will get most of the crowds, not that there are many at these average spots. Further north, **Mzimpuni**'s large bay complete with big S-SE swell righthand pointbreak, is close to the small swell, beachbreaks peaks of **Mbotyi**.

The Wild Coast occupies an enviable location on SA's coastline by being just removed enough from the path of the big winter depressions but close enough to receive a good deal of the winter 6-15ft (2-5m) swells. Most of the spinning lows travel eastwards and send plenty of SW-SE swells back towards the African continent, although occasionally one will parallel the coast bringing more E to the swells. Because the swell must refract around headlands, it loses some size but gains in quality. Spots like Mdumbi or Lwandile rely on these SW-S swells, but truly epic conditions occur on winter SE swells or rare E cyclonic swells in late summer. NE summer winds from highs sitting in the Mozambique

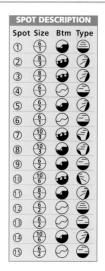

| SPOT DESCRIPTION | | | |
|---|---|---|---|
| Spot | Size | Btm | Type |
| ① | 6/1 | | |
| ② | 8/3 | | |
| ③ | 8/2 | | |
| ④ | 6/1 | | |
| ⑤ | 6/2 | | |
| ⑥ | 6/1 | | |
| ⑦ | 10/3 | | |
| ⑧ | 10/2 | | |
| ⑨ | 6/2 | | |
| ⑩ | 10/2 | | |
| ⑪ | 8/2 | | |
| ⑫ | 6/2 | | |
| ⑬ | 6/2 | | |
| ⑭ | 10/6 | | |
| ⑮ | 6/2 | | |

ubiquitous great whites. Coffee Bay is central enough to be used as a base for surfing missions and has some tourist facilities. Head south to **Feldskoen Bay** for fun lefts and rights over a sand covered reef. If conditions allow, **Ntylonyane** (Breezy Point) has a J-Bay-like right point that is super-consistent but is more notorious for its ominous fatal shark attack record. **Sharpleys Point** needs S-SE swells to wrap in properly. Heading north to Coffee Bay, check **Hole-in-the-Wall**, a scenic sandstone hole and a beachbreak if small. **Coffee Bay Point** breaks right off the southern headland of the arcing Coffee Bay, needing smaller E swells or bigger S swells to reform over the rock shelf and sand bottom. Most wave-riders walk to **Coffee Bay**'s main beach, which can produce classic waves especially in summer. Within 15 minutes walk is White Clay, a scenic beach with average conditions most of the time but picking up most of the available swell. To the north, both **Mdumbe**'s freight train waves and **Lwandile** are 4x4 access only, both are righthand pointbreaks with inside sandbanks fed by a rivermouth and they are both definitely epic waves. Be warned getting in and out of Mdumbi can be problematic. Beachbreak peaks can be found at **Presley's Bay**, but a better choice would be

Mtentu Rivermouth

Channel bring some choppy 2-5ft (0.6-1.6m) swell. Dominant SW-W winds varying from 32% (Mar) to 45% (Sept), are interspersed by NE-E winds from 38%(Mar) to 22% (Jun), which increase in the summer. The water is cleaned by the offshore westerly winds, which also flatten it to a degree, while the NE brings cold, dirty and choppy waters. Tides vary little but incoming or outgoing phases might create different current conditions at rivermouth spots.

Tshani Reef

| SURF STATISTICS | J | F | M | A | M | J | J | A | S | O | N | D |
|---|---|---|---|---|---|---|---|---|---|---|---|---|
| dominant swell | N-E | | SE-S | | SE-S | | SE-S | | SE-S | | N-E | |
| swell size (ft) | 2-3 | | 4-5 | | 5 | | 5-6 | | 4-5 | | 3 | |
| consistency (%) | 60 | | 70 | | 90 | | 90 | | 80 | | 70 | |
| dominant wind | SW-W | | SW-W | | SW-W | | SW-W | | SW-W | | SW-W | |
| average force | F4 | | F4-F5 | | F5 | | F5 | | F5 | | F5 | |
| consistency (%) | 36 | | 38 | | 45 | | 43 | | 43 | | 38 | |
| water temp (ºC/ºF) | 22/72 | | 21/70 | | 19/66 | | 18/64 | | 19/66 | | 21/70 | |
| wetsuit | | | | | | | | | | | | |

MOZAMBIQUE

MADAGASCAR

SOUTH AFRICA

# 95. Inhambane Province

Tofinho

GARTH ROBINSON

## Summary

+ Fast, hollow waves
+ Warm water
+ No crowds
+ Friendly people
+ Cheap

− Frequent onshores
− Lack of spot density
− Inconsistent
− Malaria and AIDS

Thanks to images of war, floods, disease, land mines and a population wracked by Aids, Mozambique probably doesn't rate on most surfers' wish lists. Times have changed and the war is a fading memory, the land mines have been cleared from the main tourist zones and despite their tragic past, the inspirational people of Mozambique have come through it all smiling. As for the waves, there's roughly 2,500km (1,560mi) of coastline, most of which receives ample, seasonal swell and almost no crowds. If you're after a surf explorer's paradise then Mozambique could fit the bill perfectly. Famous breaks like Ponta D'Ouro, a fabulous right point nestled up against the South African border, or Ilha de Inhaca, an island right near the capital, Maputo, both suffer from

Back Beach

EMI MAZZONI

EMI MAZZONI

inconsistency and isolation. For the travelling surfer after quality and consistency, the best area to focus on is probably Inhambane province, a 6hr drive from Maputo.

Inhambane town is situated at the end of a long peninsula. On one side is a sheltered lagoon with many mangroves and traditional wooden dhows ferrying people and goods to and from Inhambane's little port.

## TRAVEL INFORMATION

**Population:** 1.3M Inhambane
**Coastline:** 2,470km (1,643mi)
**Contests:** None
**Other Resources:** africansoulsurfer.com oceansurfpublications.co.uk mozambique.mz

**Getting There** – All foreigners need a visa. 30-day tourist visas are available for $20. Inhambane is a long 480km (300mi) drive from Maputo. It's possible to fly directly to Maputo from outside of Africa (Lisbon, Asia) but it's cheaper to travel via Jo-burg or Durban and cross overland or take a cheap connecting flight. Flights to Inhambane from Jo-burg and Nelspruit.

**Getting Around** – Main coastal road from Maputo to Inhambane is good. Roads in the far north of the country are bad. A family sized car in SA can be hired for $240/week and taken across the border. Beach access is limited, even with a 4WD (up to double in price, with a very high deposit). Always carry all required papers. Walk from any of the Tofo beach lodges to Tofinho.

**Lodging and Food** – There's a wide range of accommodation in Tofo, most surfers and backpackers choose to stay at Fatimas ($4/d) or Bamboozi Beach Lodge; the owner Des is an avid surfer. For other accommodation try Casa Barry ($30). Seafood is the big thing all along the coast. General living costs are similar to South Africa. Expect $3 for a meal.

**Weather** – Mozambique is a big country and its climate varies from sub-tropical to tropical. The rainy season coincides with the hot months between Nov and March. Most areas of the country have at least some rainfall every month. The south is generally drier than the north. Winter lasts from July to September but the coast remains hot and sticky year round and even on winter mornings, a shorty will suffice.

**Nature and Culture** – The diving around Tofo is superb. At the right time of year whale sharks can be seen while manta rays and dolphins are common year round. The decaying old town of

Inhambane is one of the highlights of Mozambique. Check out the markets and nightlife of Maputo. Tofo beach bars are the travellers' hangout.

**Hazards and Hassles** – There are still millions of landmines, mostly in the central and northern parts but the coast around Tofo is mine free. Petty crime is growing in Maputo; avoid walking along beaches at night. Malaria is a very serious risk. The Aids rate is terrifyingly high. Droughts and floods occur with depressing regularity. The shark factor is overrated.

**Handy Hints** – Bring absolutely everything, as nothing is available inside Mozambique. Most waves are surfable with a fish and bring something suitable for fast, hollow and ledgy waves. A gun won't be necessary. Don't count on renting a dhow to explore new waves; they only suits calm bays. Summer sun protection is a must.

| WEATHER STATISTICS | J/F | M/A | M/J | J/A | S/O | N/D |
|---|---|---|---|---|---|---|
| total rainfall (mm) | 128 | 83 | 28 | 13 | 43 | 138 |
| consistency (days/mth) | 9 | 8 | 3 | 2 | 5 | 8 |
| min temp (°C/°F) | 22/72 | 20/68 | 15/59 | 15/59 | 17/63 | 21/70 |
| max temp (°C/°F) | 30/86 | 30/86 | 26/79 | 26/79 | 28/82 | 29/84 |

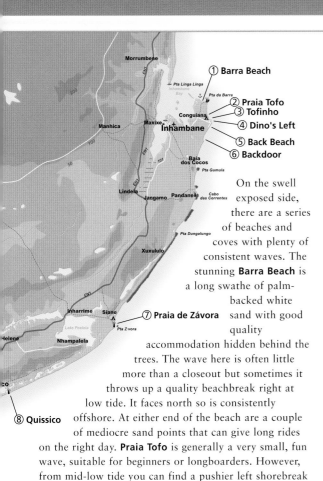

Map labels:
Morrumbene
① Barra Beach
Pta Linga Linga
Inhambane Bay
Pta da Barra
② Praia Tofo
③ Tofinho
Conguiana
Maxixe
④ Dino's Left
Manhica
Inhambane
⑤ Back Beach
⑥ Backdoor
Baia dos Cocos
Pta Gumula
Lindela
Jangamo Pandane
Cabo das Correntes
Pta Dungalungo
Xuxululo
Inharrime  Siane
⑦ Praia de Závora
Pta Z-vora
Lake Poelela
Nhampalela
⑧ Quissico

On the swell exposed side, there are a series of beaches and coves with plenty of consistent waves. The stunning **Barra Beach** is a long swathe of palm-backed white sand with good quality accommodation hidden behind the trees. The wave here is often little more than a closeout but sometimes it throws up a quality beachbreak right at low tide. It faces north so is consistently offshore. At either end of the beach are a couple of mediocre sand points that can give long rides on the right day. **Praia Tofo** is generally a very small, fun wave, suitable for beginners or longboarders. However, from mid-low tide you can find a pushier left shorebreak about halfway down the beach near a rock groyne. After the NE onshore has blown for a few days, there are also good lefts further north in front of Bamboozi beach lodge.

The main attraction around here is **Tofinho** point, a high quality right that gathers plenty of swell. The take-off can be quite critical with a ledgy drop over a very shallow and sharp reef. After this initial section the wave peels quickly along the edge of the reef and offers good tube sections. On the opposite side of the headland is **Dino's Left**. This needs an easterly swell combined with rare berg wind conditions to produce Indo-style lefts. Further south over the headland is **Back Beach** which has an extremely intense left reef that gathers up the most swell in the area. It's a short and hollow ride more suitable for bodyboarders with a freefall drop over a barely submerged razor sharp reef, and offers good snorkelling on small days. Back Beach also offers a reasonable righthand beachbreak. It gets hollow, but shuts down a lot and there are some shallow patches of coral that can come as a nasty surprise. In the far right corner of the bay is **Backdoor**, a super-shallow, right tube that slams onto almost dry reef. The more adventurous might like to check out the potential of the Bazaruto Archipelago to the north and **Praia de Závora**'s right pointbreak to the south. There is also some potential around **Quissico**, but getting over the lagoon is tricky.

The main source of swell is from S-SE swell pulses tracking in a west-east direction below South Africa. Like most east coasts though, Mozambique's swell exposure is not ideal and it tends to be only the heart of the swell that makes it to shore, so be prepared to wait around. The best season is April to September when there are two or three solid swells a month, each lasting a couple of days and producing waves between 3-8ft (1-2.5m). The rest of the year is likely to be flat on the points and small, mushy and onshore on the beaches. The summer does see the occasional cyclone generating heavy E-NE swells that will produce perfect lefts or widespread destruction depending on how close to land it comes. Wind patterns in the summer are predominately moderate NE trades, whilst in the winter swell season, NE winds will be mixed S-SW winds. Tidal variations increase further up the Mozambique Channel and can have a big affect on the shallow reefs.

### SPOT DESCRIPTION

| Spot | Size | Btm | Type |
|------|------|-----|------|
| ① | 6/1 | | |
| ② | 4/1 | | |
| ③ | 8/2 | | |
| ④ | 4/2 | | |
| ⑤ | 4/2 | | |
| ⑥ | 6/2 | | |
| ⑦ | 8/2 | | |
| ⑧ | 6/1 | | |

Dino's Left
EMI MAZZONI

Backdoor
EMI MAZZONI

GARTH ROBINSON

| SURF STATISTICS | J F | M A | M J | J A | S O | N D |
|---|---|---|---|---|---|---|
| dominant swell | SE-NE | SE-NE | S-SE | S-SE | S-SE | SE-NE |
| swell size (ft) | 1-2 | 2-3 | 3 | 3-4 | 2 | 1-2 |
| consistency (%) | 30 | 50 | 60 | 70 | 60 | 20 |
| dominant wind | NE-S | NE-S | N-NE | N-NE | NE-S | NE-S |
| average force | F3-F4 | F3-F4 | F4 | F4 | F4-F5 | F4 |
| consistency (%) | 78 | 70 | 38 | 42 | 69 | 75 |
| water temp (ºC/ºF) | 25/77 | 25/77 | 23/74 | 21/70 | 22/72 | 24/75 |
| wetsuit | | | | | | |

www.atolltravel.com

The Andaman Islands are a true surfing frontier, relatively untouched by the surf travel juggernaut. Access to these rights at Kumari Point is difficult and expensive.

# Indian Ocean

JOHN CALLAHAN

# The Ocean Environment

With the Indian subcontinent to the north, strings of atolls across the Equator, volcanic islands to the southwest, plus the world's fourth biggest island, the Indian Ocean presents a varied surfing environment. It is the planet's third largest body of water, and is dominated by a regular pattern of wind oscillations called the monsoon.

## Pollution

The atolls and islands are not without problems, thanks to tourism and growing populations continually putting pressure on sewage and waste disposal. Tourist areas have taken on sensitive disposal of waste realising that destruction of the local environment is detrimental to business, however, only the regions with upscale resorts

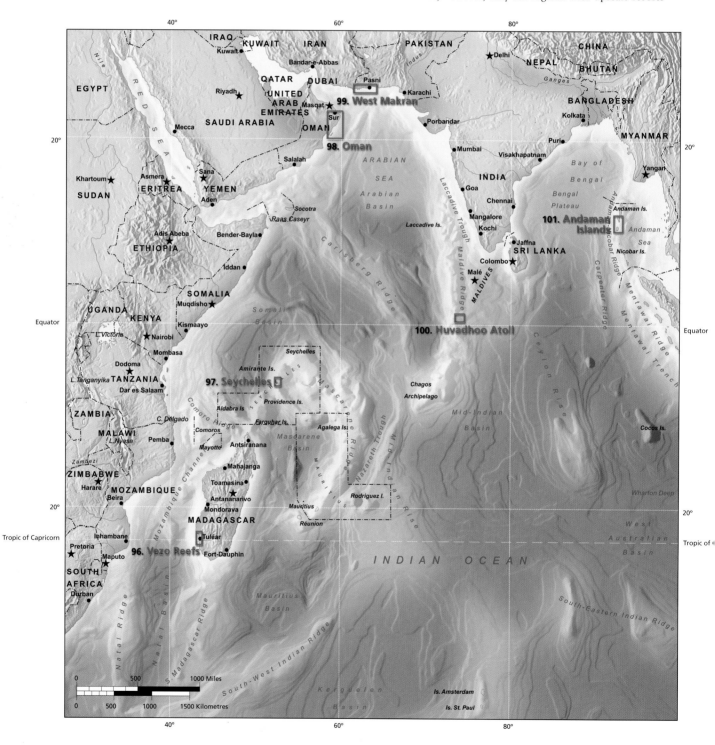

and enough money can afford to implement proper treatment. This translates to no waste treatment infrastructure in Madagascar, where unsanitary conditions in villages often leads to outbreaks of serious disease like cholera when faecal matter permeates the water supply. The better off governments of The Maldives and the Seychelles insist on sustainable development principles when a new resort license is granted, yet landfill and disposal of rubbish at sea is a regular practice. Local communities have always used the sea as a dumping ground but all their waste was naturally biodegradable. Now, modern plastic packaging is enemy number one, particularly drinking water bottles, which pervade the dwindling landfill sites. Agricultural pollution is a problem on Mauritius where runoff from the sugar plantations is causing eutrophication on the surrounding reefs, where the algal blooms smother the coral. Oman sees a lot of shipping plying its waters, much of it oil related, but the surfing areas are remote and fairly clean. The same can be said for Pakistan's coast until reaching the major cities where untreated sewage and polluted runoff is a certainty. In August 2003, a Greek owned vessel chartered by The Pakistan Oil Corporation ran aground off Karachi. It broke up two weeks later in monsoonal swells spilling 12,000 metric tonnes of crude oil onto Karachi's beaches, rendering them wastelands.

Throughout the subcontinent, the huge population pressures result in rushed coastal development and poor land usage, leading to serious water quality issues and beaches becoming open toilets. Sri Lanka means resplendent land, yet two thirds of Hikkaduwa's coral reefs are dead, choked by sewage and sediment from coastal development. Local groups have joined forces to try to clean the reef and the situation is improving, however, with continued sewage discharge and increasing tourism development its future is in the balance. Collecting coral for the tourist market plus over-fishing are also threatening the future existence of the reef, which actually lies within a government declared nature reserve. This situation is sadly repeated across the environmentally unlegislated subcontinent.

100 million tonnes of oil moves through Sri Lankan waters every year, the vessels are unregulated and communities have no way of getting compensation in the event of a spill. The last major spill was from a poorly maintained Spanish vessel in 1999 carrying oil and fertilizer that decimated a stretch of coastline ten miles long killing reef and associated ecosystems just east of Hikaduwa.

### Erosion

Loss of land and reefs due to erosion is the big issue for Indian Ocean Islands especially the low-lying atolls. Deforestation and the removal of mangroves on Madagascar has allowed increased sediment and agricultural chemicals to infiltrate the reefs, smothering growth and increasing erosion rates. Mauritius allows 500,000 tonnes of coral sand to be mined a year, seriously depleting the resource. Perhaps the most alarming and avoidable threat to the reefs is collection of coral for sale to tourists and aquariums. It is estimated that there is more coral from the reefs of Mauritius and Réunion on coffee tables and in aquariums in the West than in the sea around the islands! Seychelles and The Maldives are much stricter on coral mining, having seen islands disappear in a matter of years due to the removal of their reefs for building material. The traditional coral houses have given way to modern breeze block examples, which are less aesthetically but more environmentally pleasing. The big threat to all of the atolls and their fringing coral reefs is global warming and the possible sea level rise. A rise above 30°C (87°F) leads to bleaching as the polyps die, leaving weakened structures which rapidly erode. This has been going on for thousands of years due to El Niño events and the coral recovers quickly, however a permanent temperature rise would signal an end for the reefs. Recent rises in $CO_2$ levels in the surface water increases acidity, meaning shallow water corals cannot build their calcium based skeletons and so erosion continues at a faster pace. Even a small sea level rise could be terminal for The Maldives where a maximum elevation of just 1.5m (5ft) is all that prevents a nation and its waves from slipping under. Recent sea defences built to protect the capital Malé, have had an adverse effect on the surfbreaks and will undoubtedly cause increased erosion at adjacent, undefended areas. Similar low lying islands of the Seychelles have experienced a 2°C (6°F) average local temperature increase since 1998, severely bleaching the coral and softening defences in the face of rising sea levels. Coral mining on the subcontinent is illegal, however poor enforcement encourages the poachers. Eutrophication and algae blooms also kill coral, weakening the reef structure and contributing to erosion.

Top – **Global warming and a sea level rise spells the end for atoll nations like the Maldives.**
Bottom – **Increased sea surface temperatures kill polyps, leaving a calcium skeleton that quickly erodes . This coral bleaching is compounded by coral mining and collection for western fish tanks.**

Above – **Boat access is common across the Indian Ocean. Flame Balls, Madagascar.**
Bottom – **An armed guard is essential at access this remote Makran surf spot.**

## Access

The virtually non-existent Madagascan coastal road network dictates that going by 4WD, on foot or by boat are the only reliable means of getting to those out of the way places. The Fort Dauphin area is more developed than elsewhere while the west coast is boat access only. The Seychelles is an expensive destination where privately owned land and exclusive resorts can prevent access to the beach, or in some cases, the entire island. Coral atoll exploration presents some difficult access problems, so without a boat the best waves in The Maldives may as well not exist. Around the capital Malé and the adjacent atolls, water taxis (dhonis) provide reliable, expensive transport to all of the public breaks. The remote southern atolls are a different story, where tourism is yet to be established and there is no accommodation available. The only access is on government approved, chartered surfari boats, complete with travel permits. Entering under your own steam on private vessels is difficult, as permits only allow for a stay of five days and the atolls are poorly charted and a navigational nightmare. Travel along the Makran Coast of Pakistan requires permits, local guides and a masochistic penchant for digging jeeps out of soft sand. Sri Lanka's east coast is in Tamil Tiger territory, where the long running civil war is in ceasefire, however access to some areas is still not advised and mines litter areas of the east coast. The Andamans are extremely remote, and like the southern atolls of The Maldives, are only accessible with government permits and sanctioned tour operators. Some islands are out of bounds to protect the unique indigenous tribes that have lived in isolation for millennia.

## Hazards

Sharks are abundant in the Indian Ocean, and attacks on surfers are a major problem. Madagascar has a bad reputation for sharks, however statistics show it is unfounded, especially on the most surfed southeast coast. The west coast is definitely sharky, but bears no resemblance to the high attack figures across the Mozambique Channel. In the Mascarene Islands, the west coast of Réunion is rarely surfed as rivermouth breaks and reef passes are collecting grounds for feeding sharks. With a fatality rate of 2 out of every 3 attacks, this is some of the most dangerous water on the planet. There are sharks across all of the other zones but attacks are extremely rare with Pakistan, the Maldives and Sri Lanka yet to report a fatality while India's last death was 125 years ago.

In the atolls of The Maldives and Seychelles, currents should be taken very seriously. Whole atolls empty and fill with the tide through the same reef passes that hold the best waves.

Civil unrest in Pakistan is an issue especially towards Westerners and a low profile should be maintained at all times. Armed smugglers frequent the Makran coast, so travelling without a guide, an armed escort and a government permit is not possible.

Localism is not a widespread problem, however it does occur in the more densely populated areas, and where it does occur it is serious. Réunion has a large population of surfers and only a few breaks, so crowd pressure is common and St Leu suffers from heavy localism, which occasionally boils over into violence. On the island of Mauritius, the "White Shorts" rule the world-class lefts of Tamarin Bay with an iron fist and use all forms of intimidation to get their waves, often preventing visitors from getting a single ride. Fortunately Tamarin is inconsistent and the island's other breaks are not localized in the same way, although respect is always needed. Hikkaduwa on Sri Lanka has been the scene of occasional severe violence, although generally a good attitude and respect in the water will meet with nothing but friendly exchanges.

# Surf Travel Resources

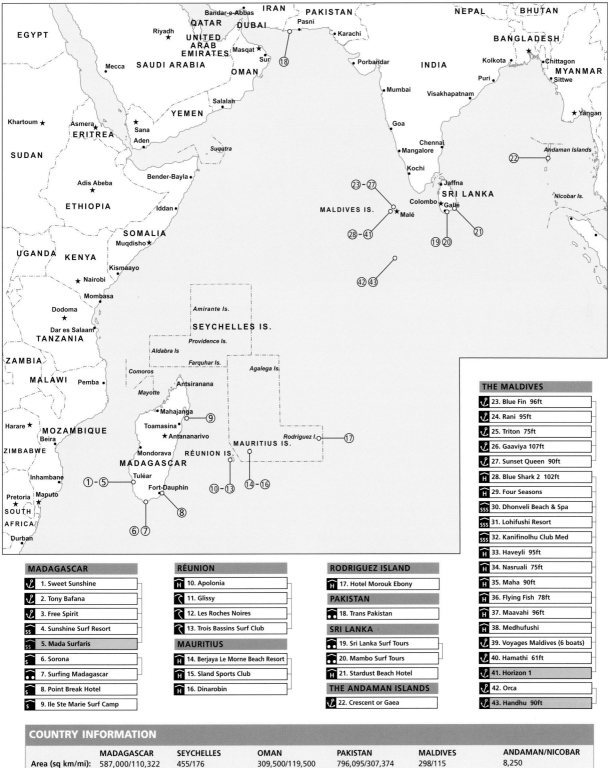

## THE MALDIVES

| | |
|---|---|
| 23. Blue Fin 96ft |
| 24. Rani 95ft |
| 25. Triton 75ft |
| 26. Gaaviya 107ft |
| 27. Sunset Queen 90ft |
| 28. Blue Shark 2 102ft |
| 29. Four Seasons |
| 30. Dhonveli Beach & Spa |
| 31. Lohifushi Resort |
| 32. Kanifinolhu Club Med |
| 33. Haveyli 95ft |
| 34. Nasruali 75ft |
| 35. Maha 90ft |
| 36. Flying Fish 78ft |
| 37. Maavahi 96ft |
| 38. Medhufushi |
| 39. Voyages Maldives (6 boats) |
| 40. Hamathi 61ft |
| 41. Horizon 1 |
| 42. Orca |
| 43. Handhu 90ft |

## MADAGASCAR

1. Sweet Sunshine
2. Tony Bafana
3. Free Spirit
4. Sunshine Surf Resort
5. Mada Surfaris
6. Sorona
7. Surfing Madagascar
8. Point Break Hotel
9. Ile Ste Marie Surf Camp

## RÉUNION

10. Apolonia
11. Glissy
12. Les Roches Noires
13. Trois Bassins Surf Club

## MAURITIUS

14. Berjaya Le Morne Beach Resort
15. Sland Sports Club
16. Dinarobin

## RODRIGUEZ ISLAND

17. Hotel Morouk Ebony

## PAKISTAN

18. Trans Pakistan

## SRI LANKA

19. Sri Lanka Surf Tours
20. Mambo Surf Tours
21. Stardust Beach Hotel

## THE ANDAMAN ISLANDS

22. Crescent or Gaea

## COUNTRY INFORMATION

| | MADAGASCAR | SEYCHELLES | OMAN | PAKISTAN | MALDIVES | ANDAMAN/NICOBAR |
|---|---|---|---|---|---|---|
| Area (sq km/mi): | 587,000/110,322 | 455/176 | 309,500/119,500 | 796,095/307,374 | 298/115 | 8,250 |
| Population: | 16M | 80,000 | 2.4M | 145M | 300,000 | 360,000 |
| Waveriders: | 30 | 120 | 10 | 5 | 200 | 0 |
| Tourists (per yr): | 138,000 | 125,000 | 502,000 | 450,000 | 467,000 | – |
| Language: | Malagasy, French | English, French, Creole | Arabic, Baluchi, English | Urdu, Baluchi, Punjabi, English | Dhivehi, Sinhalese, English | Hindi, Nicobarese Malayalam, Tamil |
| Currency: | Malagasy Franc | Seychelles Rupee | Omani Rial | Pakistani Rupee | Rufiyaa | Indian Rupee |
| Exchange: | $1=6,600 MGF | $1 = 5.7 SCR | $1 = 0.38 OMR | $1 = 60 PKR | $1=12 MVR | $1 = 48 INR |
| GDP ($ per yr): | $800 | $7,700 | $7,700 | $2,000 | $2,000 | $2,200 |
| Inflation (%): | 10% | 6% | -1% | 5% | 3% | 3% |

MADAGASCAR   MAURITIUS
              RÉUNION

# 96. Vezo Reefs

GILLES CALVET

## Summary
+ WORLD CLASS CORAL REEFS
+ CONSISTENT SWELLS
+ DESERTED SPOTS
+ DIRT CHEAP LOCAL COSTS

− ERRATIC TRADEWINDS
− LACK OF BEACHBREAKS
− UNDEVELOPED INFRASTRUCTURE
− EXPENSIVE FLIGHTS AND TRANSPORT

Measuring 1600km (1000mi) in length and 650km (406mi) across at its widest, Madagascar is the world's 4th largest island. A mountainous central 'spine' separates the permanently damp east from the drier west and sub-desert south. Omitted as a surfing location due to its reputation for sharks (mainly on the east coast), it has only recently hit the surfing world's consciousness. With nearly 5000km (3125mi) of coastline, there is huge potential, especially along the 1,000km (625mi) strip between Fort-Dauphin and Morombe. This stretch has a 270° swell window, facing directly into the SW swells with mainly offshore conditions. Thanks to the harbour at

MADA-SURFARI.COM

Tuléar, the 700km (438mi) of varied coral reef has become accessible by charter boat. This region of the island consists of two barrier reefs, two coral banks, three lagoon reefs and a fringing reef.

Only 22km (14mi) north of Tuléar's sand and mangroves, Ifaty boasts several hotels and a couple of

GILLES CALVET

## TRAVEL INFORMATION

**Population:** 60,000 Tuléar
**Coastline:** 4,828km (3,015mi)
**Contests:** None
**Other Resources:**
Video: Chocolate Barrels
mada-surfari.com
madagascar-travel.net

**Getting There** – Antananarivo is one of the most difficult and expensive capitals to fly to. First fly to Mauritius, Réunion or South Africa. Air Madí is reliable and don't charge much for boards. Flights to Tuléar are $350r/t and get full, book early. It's a 1h ride by Snipper Euro boat (8h overland by 4x4) from Tuléar to Anakao ($40, r/t) and 1h15 to Ifaty. Dep tax: $15

**Getting Around** – Land transport (rickshaws, zebu cart, Taxi Brousse) is extra slow. A 4WD with driver is the way to speed up but is expensive ($100+/d). It's hard to rent motorised dugouts, most are beam pirogues, highly dependant on wind and tide. There are 3 boats: *Hoonos*, *Sweet Sunshine* and *Free Spirit* (Jubilation Charters: $150/day).

**Lodging and Food** – True Blue operates *Sweet Sunshine* for $1000/9days inc. flights, 12 nights in Ifaty or Anakao cost $900 inc. flights. For 2-3p groups, contact Tony (Bafana shop) in Tulear (facing Plaza Hotel) for a 33ft wharram cat Hoonos for $60/ day. Stay in Safari Vezo in Anakao, Bamboo in Ifaty, Plaza in Tulear. Local food costs are ridiculously low.

**Weather** – This is the driest region of Madagascar. Tuléar with an average of 36cm (14in) rainfall makes it the junction between a tropical west coast and the desert south. The southern regions (Vezo, Antandroy) show a bushy kind of vegetation, with spiny desert and unique flora varieties: baobab-like plants, thickets, euphorbias, didiereaceas, aloes and bottle trees. The dry season lasts 9 months from March to Nov and even during summer. Ifaty is rather shrubby with grassy savannahs, palm trees and tamarind trees fed by muddy rivers in the estuaries, deltas and mangroves. During winter, air temps hover around 28°C (82°F), while the water temps rarely dip below 23°C (75°F), but take a shorty for windy days.

**Nature and Culture** – Wild ringtail lemurs live near St Augustin Bay, where a visit to the Sarodrano Cave is a must. Active travellers spending a night in Tuléar have to check the 'Zaza Club' and dance the Minotsobe. Bird watching in Anakao and awesome forest hikes around Ifaty. Good diving facilities.

**Hazards and Hassles** – Despite the heavy presence of zambezi sharks in the Mozambique Channel, threats are relatively low considering the amount of food in the water. Getting severely burned by the sun is an issue as well as being stuck in transit. Take plenty of water and always have an emergency kit. Beware the strong currents and shallow sections.

**Handy Hints** – A gun could be useful for 10-12ft (3-3.6m) conditions. Bring everything. Don't get confused with other Nosy Ves, which translates as small island. It's a very poor country but the people don't starve. Be patient, this is one of the last true surfing frontiers. Check with mada-surfari.com; the main surf operator all around the island.

| WEATHER STATISTICS | J/F | M/A | M/J | J/A | S/O | N/D |
|---|---|---|---|---|---|---|
| total rainfall (mm) | 70 | 24 | 15 | 4 | 12 | 45 |
| consistency (days/mth) | 5 | 2 | 2 | 1 | 1 | 3 |
| min temp (°C/°F) | 23/74 | 21/70 | 16/61 | 15/59 | 17/63 | 21/70 |
| max temp (°C/°F) | 32/90 | 32/90 | 28/82 | 27/80 | 29/84 | 31/88 |

GILLES CALVET

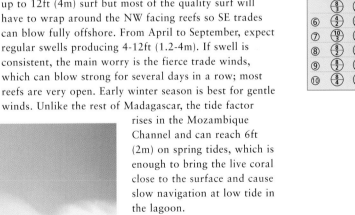

only works on big swells. Near the Safari Vezo Resort are two islands, Nosy Ve and Nosy Satrana. Only 10min away, by motorised dugout, Nosy Ve is a reserve, being the only breeding ground in Madagascar for the red-tailed tropic bird. An area of the coral reef around Nosy Ve, named the Aquarium, has been declared a protected area by the local communities and is hence off-limits for fishing. There are the sites for some of the stupendous surf spots shown in *Chocolate Barrels*. First, **Flame Bowls** is one of those long spitting lefts with plenty of barrelling sections near Nosy Ve. It's a semi-heavy wave, not for beginners. Not far off is the fun and ultra-consistent, left and right peak, **Jelly Babies**. Another left, next to Jelly Babies, requires medium/large swell and is a great spot for beginners or longboarders. When it's small, check **Puss-Puss**, a speedy, hollow righthander that picks up heaps of swell. When the surf is big, head straight to **Chefs**, a long lefthand pointbreak. Unless a sailing yacht like the *Sweet Sunshine* is available, Flame Bowls is 10min by motorized dugout from Anakao. Be aware the surfing potential also extends south towards Androka.

GILLES CALVET

breaks. Getting to **Behakio**'s (meaning large sharks!) consistent righthand reefbreaks, lying 3kms (2mi) offshore, requires a boat. Finding one with a reliable engine can be problematic, but it's a long wave and can hold up to 12ft (4m) surf. Get there before the trades pick up. A lucky few may find **La Gauche**'s pointbreak working but don't count on it. Tuléar itself is sheltered by offshore reefs and feels more like a huge, dusty harbour town than a resort. However, it's a 10min drive north by taxi to a long sandy beach and a left at the rivermouth called **La Batterie**, but it's only worth checking on a big swell. South from Tuléar is Sarodrano, site of a short-lived, 17th century European colony, established by shipwrecked sailors. There are 2 inconsistent spots around: **TTs** (which stands for ton and Tavarua) and **Nosy Andrea**. A 3h boat ride from Tulear is Anakao, home of the Vezo, migratory fishermen relying on traditional dugouts. Out in front of the **Resort** north of Anakao, there is a fun little right and left reef that

Low pressure systems moving east, away from South Africa, will spray swell up and along the Mozambique Channel. SW facing reefs will receive up to 12ft (4m) surf but most of the quality surf will have to wrap around the NW facing reefs so SE trades can blow fully offshore. From April to September, expect regular swells producing 4-12ft (1.2-4m). If swell is consistent, the main worry is the fierce trade winds, which can blow strong for several days in a row; most reefs are very open. Early winter season is best for gentle winds. Unlike the rest of Madagascar, the tide factor rises in the Mozambique Channel and can reach 6ft (2m) on spring tides, which is enough to bring the live coral close to the surface and cause slow navigation at low tide in the lagoon.

**Map labels:**
Pointe Tony
Ambolomailaka
Passe Fanambosa
Behakio ①
La Gauche ②
Ifaty
La Batterie ③
Tuléar
Pte Anosy
Pte Befotaka
Pte Sarodrano
TTs ④
Nosy Andrea ⑤
St Augustin
Baie de Saint Augustin
Resorts ⑥
Flame Bowls ⑦
Soalary
Jelly Babies ⑧
Nosy Ve
Puss-Puss ⑨
Anakao
Chefs ⑩
Nosy Satrana

Jelly Babies

TRUEBLUE.CO.ZA

| SPOT DESCRIPTION | | |
|---|---|---|
| Spot | Size | Btm | Type |
| ① | 15/3 | | |
| ② | 8/3 | | |
| ③ | 6/2 | | |
| ④ | 8/3 | | |
| ⑤ | 8/3 | | |
| ⑥ | 6/2 | | |
| ⑦ | 10/2 | | |
| ⑧ | 6/2 | | |
| ⑨ | 8/2 | | |
| ⑩ | 8/4 | | |

| SURF STATISTICS | J F | M A | M J | J A | S O | N D |
|---|---|---|---|---|---|---|
| dominant swell | S-SE | S-SE | S-SE | S-SE | S-SE | S-SE |
| swell size (ft) | 2 | 3-4 | 4-5 | 5-6 | 4 | 3-2 |
| consistency (%) | 30 | 70 | 80 | 70 | 60 | 40 |
| dominant wind | SE-S | SE-S | SE-S | E-S | E-S | SE-S |
| average force | F4 | F4 | F4 | F4 | F4 | F4 |
| consistency (%) | 51 | 63 | 54 | 73 | 72 | 54 |
| water temp (°C/°F) | 27/80 | 27/80 | 25/77 | 23/74 | 24/75 | 26/79 |
| wetsuit | | | | | | |

# 97. Seychelles

**Summary**

+ SMALL FUN WAVES
+ FEW CROWDS
+ WARM WATER
+ UNREAL ISLAND SCENERY

– VERY INCONSISTENT
– EXTREMELY EXPENSIVE
– LOTS OF WINDCHOP
– FLAT SUMMERS

The Seychelles were put on the '60s surfing map when hot-dogging small clean waves on heavy longboards was the go. Aussie surf travel legend Ron Perrott, described it as a surfing paradise, influencing many surfers to make the trip, but they usually came back disappointed. Small, clean, relatively uncrowded surf does exist, but these islands suffer from shallow offshore waters and extremely inconsistent swells that struggle to produce more than a dozen good days a year. Because of poor exposure to the predominant Indian Ocean SW swells, the central group relies on a major S-SE swell to hit, or for consistent onshore winds to create surf on the few exposed beaches. Rarely big enough to wrap around to the west coast for offshore conditions, it's either onshore slop or flat. However, it's an isolated archipelago of outstanding natural beauty comprising of 115 islands; about 35 islands of the Inner Islands Group are granite

rock and mountainous with narrow coastal strips. The other remote island groups (Amirante, Farquhar, Aldabra) are coralline and flat with elevated reefs. The Inner Islands Group mainly consists of Mahé, Praslin and La Digue. The large boulder-strewn, granite islands offer diverse marine landscapes with underwater tunnels and

## TRAVEL INFORMATION

**Population:** 72,000 Mahé
**Coastline:** 491km (306mi)
**Contests:** None
**Other Resources:**
sey.net
pps.gov.sc/meteo/
seychelles.com

**Getting There** – SEZ airport is located 10km (6mi) south of Victoria on Mahé. Air Seychelles, British Airways, Air Mauritius, Kenya Airways, Aeroflot and Air Austral. Air Seychelles operates 20 seat Twin Otters from Mahé to and from 4 islands but boards can be a problem. Dep Tax: $40. 1h high speed crossing between Mahé and Praslin ($80 r/t) or 3h by ferry ($18 r/t). 5 times daily ferry between Praslin and La Digue ($20 r/t). Only Mahé and Praslin have paved roads and a good system of buses. Drive on the left. Rental cars (mostly Mini Mokes) are plentiful on Mahé, less so on Praslin. Rates are high: from $65 daily. Bikes are rare, buses may refuse surfboards.

**Getting Around** – Hotels and resorts have special honeymoon offers. In the high season, book early. Everything, including accommodation is expensive: in Mahé, Anse

Soleil Beachcomber from $145/dble or Lazare Picault Chalets in Baie Lazare for the same price. Anse Boileau/Chez Plumís ($70/dble). La Digue/Chez Marston $120/dble half board. Camping is not permitted anywhere. Expect $25 for a meal; try the millionaire's salad, fresh tuna steaks and marinated kingfish. Visitors must pay their expenses in foreign currency, such as dollars or euros, not in the local currency, the Seychelles rupee.

**Weather** – The tropical climate is warm and humid, evidenced by high annual sunshine and rainfall figures. From May to Oct, temps average 27°C (80°F) and 8hrs sunshine per day. The SE trade winds waft pleasantly during this period of low humidity and rainfall. From Oct to Dec, a calm period results in light variable breezes, calm seas but higher temps and humidity. From Dec to Mar, the period of fluctuating NW-NE winds brings frequent tropical rain, high humidity, average temps of 28°C (82°F) and 6hrs sunshine per day. March to May is similar to the Oct to Dec period, generally calm seas, light breezes and average humidity.

**Nature and Culture** – Coral reef diving is the main sporting attraction in the islands. There is also world-class sailing, cruising, snorkelling and game fishing. Despite being a playground for the rich, the nightlife is limited to the entertainment at hotels and discos. There are many species of flora and fauna unique to the Seychelles, so there are two World Heritage sites: the Vallée de Mai on Praslin, and Aldabra Island. Praslin is the only home of the unique Coco de Mer, the largest seed in the world.

**Hazards and Hassles** – The best pointbreaks have shallow coral bottoms so there's a risk of hitting the reef. Never mind sharks or stonefish but be very careful with the equatorial sun and possible thievery, carried out by determined and possibly armed groups of 4 or 5 individuals.

**Handy Hints** – A shortboard should be fine but don't expect to find any gear. Because it is rarely good, crowds are increasing at the name breaks when it is on. Tight take-off zones and a lack of surfing etiquette result in hassling and drop-ins. British style 3-pin plugs are used.

| WEATHER STATISTICS | J/F | M/A | M/J | J/A | S/O | N/D |
|---|---|---|---|---|---|---|
| total rainfall (mm) | 334 | 180 | 121 | 103 | 172 | 245 |
| consistency (days/mth) | 9 | 8 | 5 | 4 | 6 | 10 |
| min temp (°C/°F) | 25/77 | 28/82 | 28/82 | 26/79 | 26/79 | 25/77 |
| max temp (°C/°F) | 30/86 | 31/88 | 30/86 | 28/82 | 29/84 | 30/86 |

wrecks. The coral islands have dramatic wall dives, caverns and chimneys plus the offshore banks host an array of large pelagic fish. Mahé supports 90% of the Seychelles' population, along with the package tourists. Victoria, with 24,000 souls is said to be the world's smallest capital.

Most waves in Mahé are reefbreaks, between 150-800m away from the beach. **Grande Anse** is a right reef at the north end of one of the islands two beachbreaks. Poor shape and few defined sandbanks are offset by decent southerly exposure. There is accommodation nearby but Baie Lazare would be a more central base. Down the coast are a few quality but rare reefbreaks, favoured by the locals. **Anse Poules Bleues**, close to Anse la Mouche, is a wrapping left that breaks close to shore and the SE trades blow directly offshore. This attracts an instant crowd on one of the five or so days it will break in a good winter. With some S groundswell, Baie Lazare has several spots like **Anse Gaulette**, a fairly consistent coral pass covered with sand. The "Plantation Club Hotel" at Val Mer, holds headhigh plus walls, but is very shallow so it needs a high spring tide of 1.8m (±6ft) and a proper offshore to truly work. On regular 1-2ft SE windswells, **Police Bay** is probably the most exposed beach on the island, but is inaccessible by car so a boat is required to get there. Consistent but not necessarily quality waves can be found at **Anse Bougainville**. Best with summer NW winds, it can be surfed pretty much year round. A little further along, **La Passe**'s infrequent beauty occasionally shows when S swell and NW winds combine. Northeast Point holds a short but fun left. On rare N summer swell, some north facing beaches at **Carana** may produce some dumping shorebreak for bodyboarders and bodysurfers. Most of the hotels are located in the NW facing part of Mahé where surf is extremely unlikely. Being practically encircled by shallow waters, Praslin is a rare venue for waveriders but Anse Volbert and **Anse Georgette** can surprise with some turquoise peelers. Nearby on La Digue **Pointe Camille** is the main place to be checked but like Anse Georgette, access is difficult through private property. **Grande Anse** again is the spot to surf, where

GILLES CALVET

several reefs have a window on SE wind and groundswells. Any S swell around **Frégate Island** makes the most of the privately owned harbour jetties and its reefs have the potential for small, clean perfection, exclusively reserved for guests who can afford the $2000 per night!

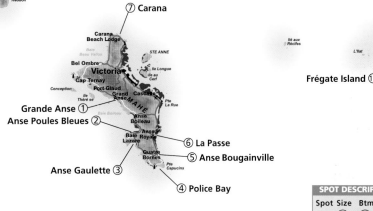

Being in the middle of a wide and shallow shelf, the Seychelles location in the Indian Ocean is not ideal for receiving SW swells. During the winter SE trade wind period, the wind comes in at the same direction as the swell, causing sloppy conditions, and during the summer N wind period, there is little swell source. Occasional S to SE groundswells hit the islands in winter and produce quality reefbreak surf if they wrap around to the west coast, where SE trades are offshore. The SE trades produce consistent 2-4ft (0.6-1.2m) slop on the east coast, but it is mostly unsurfable. There can be N windswell, but it's a long shot. No cyclones have ever reached the Seychelles. The equatorial waters of the Indian Ocean are clear and warm in summer, but winter trades stir up windward shores, bringing in cooler water that can dip below the average to 20°C (68°F). A shorty should suffice against the windchill and average winter temps of 24°C (75°F). In the summer the water averages around 27°C (80°F) to 30°C (85°F). There are two different tides a day, with a range of 5-6ft (1.5-2m) at high water springs.

| SPOT DESCRIPTION | | | |
|---|---|---|---|
| Spot | Size | Btm | Type |
| ① | 4/1 | 〰 | ◔ |
| | 4/1 | 〰 | ◔ |
| ② | 8/2 | ◑ | ◔ |
| ③ | 6/2 | ◑ | ◔ |
| ④ | 6/1 | ◕ | ◔ |
| ⑤ | 6/2 | ◑ | ◔ |
| ⑥ | 6/2 | ◑ | ◔ |
| ⑦ | 4/1 | 〰 | ◔ |
| ⑧ | 4/1 | 〰 | ◔ |
| ⑨ | 4/1 | ◑ | ◔ |
| ⑩ | 6/2 | ◑ | ◔ |
| ⑪ | 6/2 | ◑ | ◔ |

| SURF STATISTICS | J F | M A | M J | J A | S O | N D |
|---|---|---|---|---|---|---|
| dominant swell | N-NE | S-SE | S-SE | S-SE | S-SE | N-NE |
| swell size (ft) | 0-1 | 1-2 | 2 | 2-3 | 1-2 | 0-1 |
| consistency (%) | 20 | 40 | 50 | 60 | 40 | 20 |
| dominant wind | NW-NE | NW-NE | SE-SW | SE-SW | SE-SW | W-NW |
| average force | F2-F3 | F2-F3 | F3 | F4 | F4 | F3 |
| consistency (%) | 79 | 44 | 79 | 91 | 71 | 43 |
| water temp (°C/°F) | 28/82 | 28/82 | 27/80 | 25/77 | 26/79 | 27/80 |
| wetsuit | 🩳 | 🩳 | 🩳 | 🩳 | 🩳 | 🩳 |

Map labels:
- Anse Georgette ⑧
- ⑩ Grande Anse
- ⑨ Pointe Camille
- ⑦ Carana
- Frégate Island ⑪
- Grande Anse ①
- Anse Poules Bleues ②
- ⑥ La Passe
- ⑤ Anse Bougainville
- Anse Gaulette ③
- ④ Police Bay

# 98. Oman

JEFF DIVINE

## Summary
+ CONSTANT SEASONAL WINDSWELL
+ FUN SIZE, VIRGIN WAVES
+ HOLLOW RIGHT POINTBREAKS
+ TROUBLE-FREE ENVIRONMENT
+ NATURAL ISLAND IDYLL ON MASIRAH

− MONSOON SEASON ONLY
− ONSHORE WIND EXPOSED SPOTS
− NO FACILITIES, NO ENTERTAINMENT
− LACK OF QUALITY CONDITIONS
− INLAND HEAT, GUSTY WINDS

The Middle East is not exactly a renowned surfing zone and is undoubtedly the least surfed area of the Indian Ocean. Recent expeditions to discover its potential include the *Surfer Mag* trip to the 'Empty Quarter' in 2000. While this milestone expose awakened the surfing world to the area's possibilities, it's highly likely that ex pats from Dubai and Muscat have been riding some spots for years. The Sultanate of Oman, third largest country on the Arabian Peninsula, occupies its SE corner and is 82% desert. The coastline extends from the Strait of Hormuz in the north, to the Republic of Yemen in the south and overlooks three seas – the Arabian Gulf, Gulf of Oman and the Arabian Sea. Although the surfers of Dubai get some surf in the Gulfs, headhigh, clean surf is more likely to be found in the Arabian Sea. Oman has strong seafaring connections and the

JEFF DIVINE

JEFF DIVINE

legendary sailor, Sinbad, is thought to have originated in Sur, where 'Sea Songs' have developed over centuries of close association with the water.

Southeast of the city of Muscat, **Sur** in the Sharqiya region, works with a strong NE onshore wind. There's the odd rideable wave on the beach but don't expect any quality. The odds are better at **Ra's Al Hadd**, which still has evidence of its life as a military base during WWII. The cove is known for the hundreds of green turtles that

## TRAVEL INFORMATION

**Population:** 9,000 Hilf
**Coastline:** 2,092km (1,307mi)
**Contests:** None
**Other Resources:**
surfersofdubai.com
omanet.com
desert-discovery.com

**Getting There** – A visa is necessary: it's valid for 6 months but only allows a stay of 3 weeks from the date of entry and can be extended once for a period not exceeding 1 week. The cost is $13. Most flights to Seeb int'l airport at Muscat come from Europe via Dubai with BA, KLM, Swiss Air, Kuwait, and Emirates. Dep tax: $8.

**Getting Around** – Although Oman Air flies daily to Masirah, it's better to drive with boards - 7h journey, skirting the Wahibah Sands. At the Shanna ferry terminal, dhows leave 4 times daily for a 1h trip. Most roads are gravel roads. Because of sands and wadis (riverbeds), a 4WD is recommended.

**Lodging and Food** – There is no middle ground between top rate hotels and free, basic shacks.

In Muscat, try the Matrah hotels in the harbour ($35). In Masirah, there is a 5 room hotel in Hilf: $40-70. Book early! Camping is the only option to stay in front of Jazirah. Fish is dirt cheap and plentiful, there are small food stores in Hilf. Dates and tea!

**Weather** – Masirah is hot and dry with short periods of very heavy rain in Oct-Dec and March-April. Average rainfall in Muscat is 75mm (3"in) while the Monsoon season in Dhofar (Salalah) can bring rainfall between 100 and 400mm (4-16"in). The weather is hot for most of the year with temps peaking at around 35°C (96°F) during May-June. In the months of June to August, the island is affected by the strong winds of the SW monsoon, known as the Khareef or Harif. No rain falls at this time but the air is quite humid. Remember day/night temps vary a lot in the desert; bring a warm sleeping bag. Water temps are warmish during the surf season but use a shorty for the high wind chill.

**Nature and Culture** – Gathering rare shells (like eloise) on the soft, golden sand beaches, gazing at wild camels or huge green turtles in the water is about as fun as it gets. No beer or other addictive substances! Because Masirah is barren, it's got a low population wearing local keffieh and djellabah, mostly based around Hilf. Go fishing or wavesailing!

**Hazards and Hassles** – Despite the raw nature of the country, it's trouble free with regard to diseases, thefts or muggings. It is however, a desert with myriads of flies! Avoid sharp shells on rocks at pointbreaks. Plenty of stingray and jellyfish. Avoid Ramadan. Don't expect any locals, crowds, hustlers etc.

**Handy Hints** – Take everything, including a longboard and a funboard/kitesurf for the numerous windy days. Don't forget books, cd player, games etc for killing some time. This is an extremely peaceful set-up, relax and go slowly in the heat! Boats with 80hp outboards can be rented to explore the coastline.

| WEATHER STATISTICS | J/F | M/A | M/J | J/A | S/O | N/D |
|---|---|---|---|---|---|---|
| total rainfall (mm) | 3 | 3 | 3 | 3 | 2 | 7 |
| consistency (days/mth) | 0 | 1 | 0 | 0 | 0 | 1 |
| min temp (°C/°F) | 24/75 | 26/79 | 29/84 | 30/86 | 28/82 | 25/77 |
| max temp (°C/°F) | 26/79 | 31/88 | 35/95 | 31/88 | 31/88 | 28/82 |

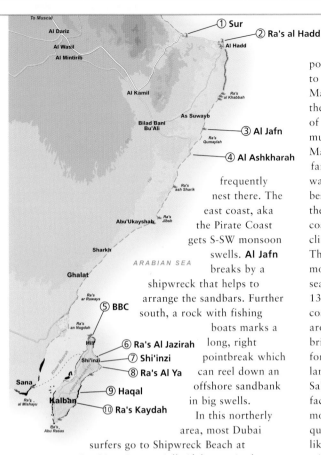

Map labels:
To Muscat
Al Dariz
Al Wasil
Al Mintirib
Al Kamil
Bilad Bani Bu'Ali
As Suwayb
Ra's al Khabbah
Ra's Qumaylah
Ra's ash Sharik
Abu'Ukayshah
Ra's Jibsh
Sharkh
ARABIAN SEA
Ghalat
Ra's ar Ruways
Ra's an Nugdah
Hilf
Shi'inzi
Sana
Ra's al Mishayu
Kalban
Ra's Abu Rasas

① Sur
② Ra's al Hadd
Al Hadd
③ Al Jafn
④ Al Ashkharah
⑤ BBC
⑥ Ra's Al Jazirah
⑦ Shi'inzi
⑧ Ra's Al Ya
⑨ Haqal
⑩ Ra's Kaydah

frequently nest there. The east coast, aka the Pirate Coast gets S-SW monsoon swells. **Al Jafn** breaks by a shipwreck that helps to arrange the sandbars. Further south, a rock with fishing boats marks a long, right pointbreak which can reel down an offshore sandbank in big swells.

In this northerly area, most Dubai surfers go to Shipwreck Beach at **Al Ashkarah**, especially if decent sized, powerful surf is on the cards. The reef extends out a fair way, so at low tide long, mellow righthanders break 100-200m (300-600ft) off the beach. If it's small, there's a surfable shoredump at high tide and Al Ashkharah Hotel is handily situated. Driving through the desert from Muscat towards Sana is a different world. From Sana a ferry can be caught to Masirah Island. Masirah is Oman's largest island (65km/41mi) where Alexander the Great made his base, referring to it as 'Serepsis'. Nowadays, dates, olives, pomegranates and mangos are grown and the islanders' main occupations are weaving and making fishing nets. Masirah's hills are mainly barren limestone rock. A quality righthander can allegedly be found close to the **BBC** telecom towers on a big swell but permission from the Jazirah military is needed to gain access. Further down, **Shi'inzi**'s powerful beachbreak usually closes out on the days when it is big enough to work. The closest spot to Hilf is **Ra's Al Jazirah**, a sectioney, semi-long, righthand point breaking over rocks near a fishing camp.

Getting in and out is fairly easy but bear in mind, there are usually strong cross-shore winds and possibly some windsurfers. Similar wind conditions apply to **Ras Al Ya**'s long rights, which break close to the cliffs. Masirah has at least eight potential righthand points on the east coast and the Jazirah area is usually half the size of the more SE facing breaks. To the south is **Haqal**, much better at high tide, like most of the spots on Masirah. It's a pretty juicy reefbreak with long rights and fares better than **Ra's Kaydah**'s frequently blown-out wave. There is still much potential for discoveries. The best surf potential in Oman is probably located close to the Yemen border. The 560km (350mi) long Dhofari coastline offers a variety of features from mountainous cliffs to large bays. The summer SW monsoon or Harif season affects about 130km (81mi) of the coastline, mainly around Salalah, bringing rain, which forms the varied landscape. South of Salalah, the beaches facing the SW monsoon produce quality beachbreaks like Rakhyut. Less wind, bigger waves, better surf!

Haqual

Masirah

The SW monsoon winds between June and September are the strongest winds in the tropical zone. During that period, there is a constant 8-12ft (2.5-3.6m) windswell. The waves are generally from a SE-SW direction with 6-12 sec periods. Swells don't have much power but the messy 5ft (1.5m) beachbreaks can be fun. The rest of the year might get long distance remnants of Southern Ocean swells but it would be 1-2ft (0.3-0.6m) maximum at exposed spots. The dominant monsoon winds are SW (Jun-Aug) and NE (Nov-Jan) monsoons. Gusty winds blow for several days in a row, then seem to calm down for a while. Cyclones are mainly produced in the Indian Ocean when sea surface temperature exceeds 29°C (84°F). Watch out as 75% of these cyclones end up on the Oman coast! Oman has semidiurnal tides with diurnal inequality, reaching 5ft (1.6m) max; high tides are often the best time to surf.

| SURF STATISTICS | J F | M A | M J | J A | S O | N D |
|---|---|---|---|---|---|---|
| dominant swell | S-SW | S-SW | S-SW | S-SW | S-SW | S-SW |
| swell size (ft) | 1 | 1-2 | 3-4 | 4-5 | 2-3 | 1 |
| consistency (%) | 10 | 20 | 80 | 90 | 70 | 10 |
| dominant wind | NW-NW | S-SW | S-SW | SE-SW | SE-SW | NW-NE |
| average force | F3 | F3 | F4 | F3-F4 | F3-F4 | F3 |
| consistency (%) | 41 | 31 | 49 | 70 | 55 | 47 |
| water temp (°C/°F) | 22/72 | 23/74 | 25/77 | 24/75 | 23/74 | 23/74 |
| wetsuit | | | | | | |

# 99. West Makran

Mirages

DAN HAYLOCK

## Summary
+ CONSTANT MONSOON SWELL
+ MELLOW RIGHT POINTBREAKS
+ DISCOVERY POTENTIAL
+ NO DISEASE OR BUGS
+ GUARANTEED SUN

– SHORT SURF SEASON
– ONSHORE WINDS
– TOUGH ACCESS
– MILITARY RESTRICTIONS
– VERY HOT, WINDY AND DUSTY

YEP

Ganz

YEP

Pakistan is a relatively new country, having formed in 1947, before East Pakistan became Bangladesh in 1971. Withdrawn and insular for decades, the events of September 11th 2001, placed the country firmly in the international spotlight, due to its location as Afghanistan's neighbour. Earlier that year, a crew of 12 people including four surfers explored the Makran Desert's coast looking for rideable surfspots in the Baluchistan province. In 325BC, Alexander the Great and his army marched through its harsh desert wastes and suffered heavy loss of life from shortages of food and water. Until 1809, no other Europeans visited the Makran. In terms of physical geography, Baluchistan has more in common with Western Asia than with the subcontinent. Its wild and mysterious desert vistas contain formidable mountain ranges of amazing rock formations, dramatically contoured and twisted by the Earth's violent geological movements. The Makran Coast's deserted sandy beaches stretch 700km (438mi)

## TRAVEL INFORMATION

**Population:**
20,000 Gwadar
**Coastline:** 300km (187mi)
**Contests:** None
**Other Resources:**
surftrip.net
transpakistan.com.pk

**Getting There** – Karachi is the main int'l airport reached by increasingly less airlines but it is the hub for PIA, the national airline. Domestic flights are busy Fokker 70s, which can't carry boards over 7'6". Gwadar can be reached from Mosqat with larger airplanes (Oman Air). Flying over the Makran Coast will offer the best views.

**Getting Around** – Apart from a few tar roads around towns, there are mostly beat up dirt tracks and huge potholes. Average speed is 20km/h (12mph) under extremely hot and dusty conditions, providing you have your NOC. A coastal road is being built in the next few years. A 4WD rental in Gwadar costs 4000 Rps ($65US) daily. A 'No Objection Certificate' (NOC) is required by the Deputy Commissioner

to travel around and will entitle the holder to an armed guard escort, as protection from potential smugglers.

**Lodging and Food** – Some foreigners have access to the Marjan Resort up on the Gwadar Hammerhead providing A/C rooms (40$/dble w breakfast), excellent food (800 Rps/meal) ($12US) but a cheaper option is the Rest House, facing West Bay but very basic (600 Rps /dble) ($10US). Dhal, Nan, fish and dates (300 varieties) will be your food.

**Weather** – The Makran Coast lies outside the monsoon system of weather, therefore, the climate is extremely dry. The annual rainfall is less than 15cm, which combined with the natural geographical features makes it a most daunting environment for the small local population. Many observers think that the region resembles the surface of the moon. Temps never drop below 30°C (86°F) and hover around 38°C (101°F) after noon. Airborne dust reduces visibility and gets into every nook and cranny. Sea surface temperature of the

Arabian Sea varies between 24°C (75°F) and 30°C (86°F) from NE to SW monsoon.

**Nature and Culture** – Gwadar is a huge chunk of rock 10km (6.5mi) long, 2km (1.5mi) wide and 200m (600ft) high, linked by a narrow stretch of sand of 20km (12mi) long. The white clay cliffs are unreal. Don't miss the shipyards, the harbour, mud volcanoes and the lively Bazaar at night. It's incredibly cheap. Islamic beliefs are strong but more liberal than neighbouring countries.

**Hazards and Hassles** – Apart from dozens of coastguard checks, the intense heat and dust, occasional sea and land snakes (garr) and rare sharks, it's pretty cool.

**Handy Hints** – The Makran was closed to foreigners until recently so most trips are of an exploratory nature as tourist infrastructure is non-existent. Hire TRANSPAKISTAN services to organise transport, food, translation and guidance. Bring everything you need and let them take you to the surf spots.

| WEATHER STATISTICS | J/F | M/A | M/J | J/A | S/O | N/D |
|---|---|---|---|---|---|---|
| total rainfall (mm) | 9 | 4 | 4 | 73 | 9 | 4 |
| consistency (days/mth) | 1 | 0 | 1 | 3 | 1 | 1 |
| min temp (°C/°F) | 16/61 | 23/74 | 29/84 | 29/84 | 26/79 | 18/64 |
| max temp (°C/°F) | 27/80 | 31/88 | 35/95 | 33/92 | 33/92 | 30/86 |

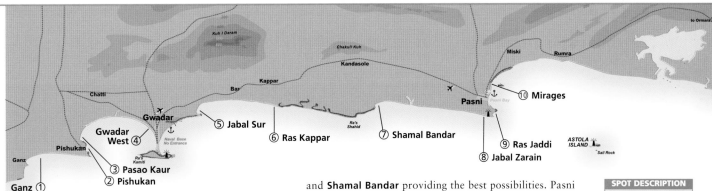

along the Arabian Sea. Around Karachi there are several spots surfed by expats and travellers fresh off the plane, like the Paradise Cove beachbreak and the best pointbreak, Goth Munjar on the Hub rivermouth. The main problem with the Makran Coast is simple: it's too shallow! Most of the white clay cliffs erode into the sea, building huge, shallow banks, especially around reefs and capes, dissipating rather than focusing the swell power. The best coastal feature for finding surf are the hammer-shaped headlands found in Gwadar and Ormara. Once islands they became joined to the mainland by a thin sand or shingle bar (tombolos). This region is located on very active tectonic plates, which constantly shake up to three on the Richter Scale.

During the monsoon season, June to August, SW exposed beaches produce consistent but messy 4-8ft (1.2-2.5m) beachbreaks and 1-2ft (0.3-0.6m) clean right pointbreaks on the SE-E facing set-ups. During the transition months, exposed beaches like **Ganz** could go off if the SW winds weren't blowing. Ras Pishukan should be better but uneven water depths makes the line-up shifty and unpredictable, although further inside the point, **Pishukan** has the potential for perfect head high rights. Even deeper in the bay, **Pasao Kaur** is perfectly offshore but won't get bigger than waist high peelers.

**Gwadar West** is mushy, exposed beachbreak in boiling hot water trapped in the bay. The best set-up in Gwadar, Ras Nuh, is off-limits as it's located in the naval base – undoubtably quality but no way of surfing it. Fortunately to the east is **Jabal Sur**, producing long 4-6ft (1.2-2m) mellow rights with monsoon swell. The fishing village is pretty active and the bluff sheltering the spot is spectacular. Between Gwadar and Pasni, most of the coastal access points are very shallow, with **Ras Kappar**

and **Shamal Bandar** providing the best possibilities. Pasni itself offers three types of breaks in a short stretch. **Jabal Zarain** would only be worth trying in the transition months, being too big and messy during the SW monsoon. The best bet for decent organised waves is **Ras Jaddi**, a rocky ledge filled with sand that throws up cross shore lefts at high tide. Don't miss **Mirages**, 45mins drive away, a symmetrically perfect peeling right, which unfortunately rarely exceeds 3-4ft (1-1.2m) on the biggest swells.

The SW monsoon winds between June and August are the strongest winds on earth in the tropical zone. During that period, there is a constant 8-12ft (2.5-3.6m) open sea windswell. The waves are generally from a 240° direction and have a 6-15 second period. Swells lack power and don't refract much around the capes. The dominant monsoon seasons are June-August (SW) and November-January (NE). In summer, the SW wind, although it frequently picks up during the day, is calm in the morning. There is no offshore but it's rarely blown out, at least around Gwadar. During SW monsoon sea water circulation is

Pishukan

clockwise while during NE monsoon it is anticlockwise. Cyclones are mainly produced in the Indian Ocean when sea surface temperature exceeds 29°C (84°F). 75% of these cyclones end up at the Oman coast and the remaining 25% cross the coast of Runn of Kutch.

Pakistan has semidiurnal tides with diurnal inequality, reaching 9ft (2.8m) max, high tides often being the best time to help the swell get into the beaches and points.

| SPOT DESCRIPTION | | | |
|---|---|---|---|
| Spot | Size | Btm | Type |
| ① | 6/1 | ∼ | ⌒ |
| ② | 8/2 | ∼ | ◣ |
| ③ | 6/1 | ∼ | ◣ |
| ④ | 4/1 | ∼ | ● |
| ⑤ | 6/2 | ∼ | ◣ |
| ⑥ | 6/1 | ∼ | ● |
| ⑦ | 6/1 | ∼ | ● |
| ⑧ | 8/2 | ∼ | ● |
| ⑨ | 6/2 | ● | ● |
| ⑩ | 4/1 | ∼ | ◣ |

DH, Ras Jaddi

| SURF STATISTICS | J F | M A | M J | J A | S O | N D |
|---|---|---|---|---|---|---|
| dominant swell | S-SW | S-SW | S-SW | S-SW | S-SW | S-SW |
| swell size (ft) | 1 | 1-2 | 3-4 | 4-5 | 2-3 | 1 |
| consistency (%) | 10 | 20 | 80 | 90 | 70 | 10 |
| dominant wind | NW-NE | W-SW | S-SW | S-SW | S-SW | NW-NE |
| average force | • | • | • | • | • | • |
| consistency (%) | | | | | | |
| water temp (°C/°F) | 24/75 | 26/79 | 29/84 | 29/84 | 28/82 | 25/77 |
| wetsuit | 🏄 | 🏄 | 🏄 | 🏄 | 🏄 | 🏄 |

LACCADIVE ISL.
INDIA
SRI LANKA
● Malé
**MALDIVES**

□

CHAGOS
ARCHIPELAGO

# 100. Huvadhoo Atoll

Beacons

DAN HAYLOCK

## Summary

+ ATOLL PASS PERFECTION
+ ONLY A FEW CHARTER BOATS
+ CALM WATER CRUISING
+ AWESOME FISHING AND SCENERY

– STORMY WINTER SEAS
– NO LAND CAMP OPTION
– LONG TRANSFERS
– EXPENSIVE CHARTERS

The 26 pancake-flat atolls of The Maldives are coralline formations that formed around the edges of volcanic peaks, thrusting up from diverging plates in the Earth's crust. These peaks then subsided, leaving the characteristic ring shaped atolls to continue to grow around the original coastline. This pattern has created a surfing playground rife with reef passes amongst the 1,200 islands, which are part of the 2000km (1,280mi) ridge extending from Lakshadweep to Chagos Islands. Southern hemisphere swells cross the Equator bringing lined up, smaller swell to the shallow fringing reefs, while predictable monsoonal winds govern the seasons. The southern atolls, namely Gaafu Dhaalu (South Huvadhoo) has an exposed SE facing coast, boasting a dozen good passes, in a 2hr cruising zone. Charter boats are the only form of access, making this an expensive, luxury type surf trip,

Blue Bowls

TIM NUNN

TIM NUNN

but unlike the Mentawais, only a few boats operate in the area. Three southern atolls tried to break away from the Maldivian government as recently as 1962, keeping this area well outside the "Tourist Zone" and government permits are required for foreigners to travel here. Maldivian pioneer Tony Hussein, discovered the area's potential in 1973, keeping it to himself until the first charters began in 1993, but it remains a secluded destination on the world surf atlas.

## TRAVEL INFORMATION

**Population:** 20,000 Huvadhoo
**Coastline:** 644km (400mi)
**Contests:** None
**Other Resources:**
*Video:*
Tripping the Planet;
atolltravel.com
maldivesurf.org.mv
visitmaldives.com
voyagesmaldives.com
maldivesurf.com

**Getting There** – 30 day visa on arrival. Malé is a medium-priced ticket from Europe and SE Asia. Connections at the airport for inter-atoll flights or board vessel for long voyage south. Island Aviation 26 seaters fly from Malé to Kaadedhdhoo, 5 times per week (1h10min, $188 r/t), no charge for boards but 20kg limit applies. Superb, scenic flight!

**Getting Around** – From Kaadedhdhoo, there are 2 main boats complete with experienced Aussie surf guides. The new *Handu* is one of the few surf charter boats to provide A/C twin cabins, a reliable dingy, plus a 30ft dhoni, allowing 2 surfing groups, and flexible fishing

trips ($1950/10d) – Atoll Adventures). Other regular boat is 85ft *Orca* ($1400/12d), or travel down with Voyages Maldives ($85/d).

**Lodging and Food** – All mod cons aboard *Handu*, staffed by extremely helpful crew. Food is varied as long as it is fish! Go snorkelling for lobster.

**Weather** – It's a typical tropical monsoon climate with 2 definite seasons and high yearly rainfall. NE monsoon is the driest period with lighter winds from NW to E. During that period (Dec-March), temps get very hot, sunshine is plentiful, accompanied by high humidity. The SW monsoon brings many storms, so May-Oct is characterised by gusty SW winds and regular rainfall. Consider these points when booking a non A/C boat. A shorty is rarely required as water temps remain around 28-30ºC (82-86ºF), which is boardies, long sleeved lycra and sunhat!

**Nature and Culture** – Typical boat trip culture of insane fishing, great snorkelling (no tanks available), surf vids and board games. Vaadhoo and Gadhdhoo offer telecom services and village scenery while Vaadhoo is renowned for its kunaa (fine hand-woven mats).

**Hazards and Hassles** – At 0º latitude, your worst enemy is the sun. Serious high factor sunscreen is crucial. Keep well hydrated and treat coral cuts carefully. The horrendous tidal rips rule. No alcohol, pornography, drugs, or spear guns are allowed at customs. Few mosquitoes, even on islands, where there is some dengue fever and leprosy.

**Handy Hints** – Bring your best 2 shortboards and reef equipment. Surfshops in Malé are expensive with little gear. Names are confusing – Gaafu Dhaalu is South Huvadhoo or Suvadiva and many atolls share identical names but slightly different spellings.

| WEATHER STATISTICS | J/F | M/A | M/J | J/A | S/O | N/D |
|---|---|---|---|---|---|---|
| total rainfall (mm) | 17 | 16 | 22 | 14 | 27 | 19 |
| consistency (days/mth) | 2 | 8 | 10 | 8 | 10 | 9 |
| min temp (ºC/ºF) | 25/77 | 25/77 | 25/77 | 25/77 | 24/75 | 24/75 |
| max temp (ºC/ºF) | 30/86 | 31/88 | 31/88 | 31/88 | 30/86 | 30/86 |

The two options are to fly to Gaafu Dhaalu (silent 'u's) and meet the charter boat, avoiding the two days motoring (in good weather) that it takes to cruise from Malé to the surf zone. There is no tourist accommodation on any of the inhabited islands like Thinadhoo, Gadhdhoo or Vaadhoo, so no land camps exist yet. Lucky punters will score good lefts at **Airport's** with a strong S-SW swell and NE wind, but the boat usually heads direct to **Beacons**, 2hrs away, at the first southern reef pass. Touted as the Maldives' gutsiest wave, Beacons' powerful rights tube onto a shallow, unforgiving reef. SW swells will break down the reef, but a SE swell will create peaks slamming straight onto close-out sections of coral. Less intense is **Castaways**, exposed on an outside reef which is predictable but shallow on the end section, especially at low tide. Anything N is offshore and the deserted island backdrop is idyllic. Both Beacons and Castaways are flanked by unnamed lefts across the channels, which have their days in big swells but tend to go unridden. **Blue Bowls** is the most flexible right, tucked inside the pass and protected from SW-W winds. More of a point style wave, it has good length of ride and nice bowly sections for performance moves. All swells, all tides and all sizes. 30 minutes motoring east, **Five Islands** is another righthander that breaks hard and hollow on the shallow inside reef. The outside section encourages deep take-offs into racy walls and handles the biggest swells at all tides. **Two Ways** does just that and the right is generally better but it needs a big swell to hit its protected position, making it a favourite with intermediates. Fun, peeling, long walls with a bit of depth to the water. Directly next-door are the reliable lefts of **Love Charms**, which can handle E winds and any size swell. Low tide is best when it is small, soft and broken into two distinct sections. Bigger swells morph it into a long, hollow wall, with powerful pockets. The next pass to the east is a narrow inlet between the islands of Gan and Gadhdhoo, where the first local surfers are starting to ride the lefts and reforms at **Tiger Stripes**. **Antiques** are the rights, which are always a couple of feet smaller and way more forgiving than the lefts. Named after the narrow gouges in the reef that give a striped effect, Tigers has some real growling lefts in a strong swell. Tricky take-offs into a long speed wall before committing to an inside tube section that wraps and peters out in the channel. Unimpressive when small, it always seems to be bigger than everywhere else. All tides, all variations of S swells and any N wind. **KH** is almost east coast and the two distinct take-off spots link together in bigger swell and tide conditions. There's scattered, quality surf like **Koodhoo** and **Viligili**, located in Gaafu Alifu (North Huvadhoo Atoll), surfed by boats on their

AC, Love Charms

way to/from Malé. Despite its idyllic location in the doldrums, the sea can be pretty rough, especially crossing the one and half degree channel.

Swell comes from the usual Indian Ocean culprits of the Roaring Forties storms, the occasional cyclone, and localised windswells. Due its size and location, Gaafu Dhaalu is the only atoll with SW-SE exposure. March-Oct is the most consistent swell season with usual 2-6ft (0.6-2m) waves on the most exposed breaks, plus some 6-10ft (2-3m) swells in the depths of the southern hemisphere winter. However, this coincides with the SW monsoon (Hulhangu) and the boats don't operate during the stormy, windy conditions from May-August. The best period is the NE monsoon (Iruvai) for clean and sunny conditions during Feb to April and Sept-Oct. Winds will generally have a NW-NE direction but the monsoon can be early or late, bringing unwelcome SW winds to the transition periods. Any wind from the S to E quadrant kills off all the breaks, especially when it's small. Dec-Jan suffers flat spells but exposure is better than Malé Atolls. This time of year the charter boats are fully booked by the diving operators around Malé, who have yet to start diving trips in the South. Semi-diurnal odd tides bring an unpredictability to the reef passes, where intense rips drain in and out of the atoll, so check with the boat captain before jumping over the side!

### SPOT DESCRIPTION

| Spot | Size | Btm | Type |
|---|---|---|---|
| 1 | 6/3 | | |
| 2 | 10/2 | | |
| 3 | 8/3 | | |
| 4 | 8/3 | | |
| 5 | 8/2 | | |
| 6 | 6/3 | | |
| 7 | 10/2 | | |
| 8 | 8/2 | | |
| 9 | 8/2 | | |
| 10 | 6/2 | | |
| 11 | 8/2 | | |
| 12 | 8/2 | | |

### SURF STATISTICS

| | J F | M A | M J | J A | S O | N D |
|---|---|---|---|---|---|---|
| dominant swell | SW-SE | SW-SE | SW-SE | SW-SE | SW-SE | SW-SE |
| swell size (ft) | 2-3 | 4 | 5 | 6 | 4 | 2-3 |
| consistency (%) | 60 | 80 | 40 | 40 | 80 | 60 |
| dominant wind | N-E | W-N | SW-W | SW-NW | SW-NW | W-N |
| average force | F3 | F2-F3 | F3 | F3 | F3-F4 | F3 |
| consistency (%) | 76 | 48 | 71 | 68 | 83 | 47 |
| water temp (°C/°F) | 28/82 | 29/84 | 29/84 | 28/82 | 28/82 | 28/82 |
| wetsuit | | | | | | |

*ONE AND HALF DEGREE CHANNEL*

Map labels:
Kolamaafushi
NORTH HUVADHOO ATOLL
Viligili
Koodhoo
Maamendhoo
⑫ Viligili
⑪ Koodhoo
Nilandhoo
Dhaandhoo
Dhevvadhoo
Funadhoo
Thinadhoo
Kodey
Kaadedhdhoo
Dhiyadhoo
Airports ①
Madaveli
Hoadedhdhoo
Gemanafushi
SOUTH HUVADHOO ATOLL
Kaduhulhudhoo
Nadallaa
Vashavehaa
Boduhuta
Gazeera
Gadhoo
⑩ KH
Gan
⑨ Tiger Stripes
Vaadhoo
⑧ Antiques
Fiyoari
Faruko
⑦ Love Charms
Beacons ②
⑥ Two Ways
Castaways ③
⑤ Five Islands
④ Blue Bowls
EQUATORIAL CHANNEL

AC, Love Charms

# 101. Andaman Islands

Kumari Point

## Summary
+ VIRGIN CORAL REEFBREAKS
+ EPIC KUMARI POINT
+ ONLY ONE BOAT OPERATOR
+ UNTOUCHED PARADISE
  WITH WILD TRIBES

– UNFAVORABLE WINTER SEASON
– SHORT IDEAL SEASON WINDOW
– EXPENSIVE BOAT OPTION ONLY
– OPPRESIVE HUMIDITY

D ubbed "The land of the head-hunters" by Marco Polo, who was the first Western visitor to this chain of 572 islands, islets and rocks, they are now commonly referred to as the Andaman and Nicobar Islands. They were annexed by the British as part of India in the 19th Century and then used to dump Indian convicts sentenced to life imprisonment. Geographic isolation, heavily restricted travel, mysterious Stone Age culture and totally uncharted waters characterise this zone. Geographically more 'Indo' than India, the Andaman's have been on many surfers' travel wish lists but the first surf trip to this area, organised by surf photographer John Callahan, only took place in 1998. Whilst foreign tourists are permitted to visit the Andaman Islands, the Nicobars are only accessible to Indians. The Ten Degree Channel

Kumari Point

separates the two chains and the surrounding waters quickly plummet to 3km (2mi). The bulk of the 239 Andaman Islands are known as the North, Middle, and South Andaman, which along with Baratang and Rut-Land forms one land mass known as the Great Andamans. With only 36 inhabited islands, this region is

## TRAVEL INFORMATION

**Population:**
360,000 Andaman & Nicobar Islands
**Coastline:**
2,000km (1,250mi)
**Contests:** None
**Other Resources:**
*Video:* Thicker Than Water
seal-asia.com/surfing/index.htm

**Getting There** – Foreigners need an Indian tourist visa and a 30-day tourist permit, both easily obtained on arrival at Port Blair from the immigration authorities. Port Blair is served weekly by Indian Airlines flights from Calcutta (5) and Madras (3). Jet and East-West private airlines have 4 flights from Chennai. Book very early. Ferries are slow, taking 56h from Calcutta!

**Getting Around** – Port Blair has buses, taxis and a few auto rickshaws. Boats from the mainland moor at Haddo Jetty, 1km (0.6mi) north of Phoenix Jetty; arrival point for inter-island ferries and live aboard surfing charters from Phuket, 50h+ away. SEAL is the most experienced operator. Get around Port Blair by moped, on hire for $3/day.

**Lodging and Food** – In PB, it varies from posh guesthouses (Hotel Bay Island, 5 star) and tourist resorts (Peerless Resort at Corbyn's Cove) to budget lodges (Sinclair's Bay View). Taste samosas and saris. Boat charters are the only way to get to the best spots - *Crescent*: $1973/day for 8 people, *Gaea*: $1400.

**Weather** – The climate remains tropical throughout the year with temperatures varying between 24°C (78°F) and 35°C (94°F). Due to the incessant sea breeze, the Andaman's has very humid weather. The SW monsoon first touches Indian soil in the Andaman's and then proceeds towards the mainland. From mid-May to October, heavy rains flush the islands, often bringing violent cyclones that leave the west coast beaches strewn with fallen trees. In November and December, less severe rains arrive with the NE monsoon. The best time to visit these islands is between mid November and April. Annual rainfall can reach 3180mm (127in). Water temps remain warm year round; take 2 pairs of boardies at least!

**Nature and Culture** – In Port Blair, the Cellular Jail is worth a visit and Ross Island will give a lasting impression of British imperial rule. A natural trail leads to Mt Harriet (1095ft/365m). To the north is a national park where elephants are trained to carry logs. This is a world-class diving zone with large pelagics and amazing visibility. Great fishing.

**Hazards and Hassles** – Due to its remoteness, any emergency would take days to repatriate. Coral cuts would be the main threat. Sharks are abundant but well fed. Locals are non-existent. Be patient on the boat as spot density is not like the Maldives or Mentawai. These islands are wild: mind the sea crocs and potentially hostile tribes.

**Handy Hints** – Take everything including 2 regular boards, reef boots and repair kit. Entry permits are issued to foreigners from the counter in the corner of the arrivals hall while the baggage is being transferred. There are no beggars in the street like in Calcutta.

| WEATHER STATISTICS | J/F | M/A | M/J | J/A | S/O | N/D |
|---|---|---|---|---|---|---|
| total rainfall (mm) | 30 | 40 | 420 | 400 | 380 | 190 |
| consistency (days/mth) | 1 | 4 | 8 | 3 | 3 | 2 |
| min temp (°C/°F) | 23/74 | 25/77 | 26/79 | 25/77 | 25/77 | 25/77 |
| max temp (°C/°F) | 28/82 | 30/86 | 29/84 | 27/80 | 28/82 | 28/82 |

Jarawa Point

a mass of dense forests with endless varieties of exotic flowers and birds. Thick, tropical forests cloak the hilly terrain and the meandering, sandy beaches are fringed with coconut palms, swaying to the rhythm of the monsoon. South Andaman is by far the most densely populated island, especially around its capital city, Port Blair (80,000). The islands have a fragile ecosystem and in order to preserve the tranquillity and protect the diverse and unique array of flora and fauna, there are 96 sanctuaries and nine national parks.

Port Blair, a characterless cluster of tin-roofed buildings tumbling towards the sea only merits a short stay. Close to Port Blair are some decent overland spots like **Butler's Bay**; a beautiful beach with a reef and tourist huts right on the seashore flanked by the coconut plantation. **Corbyn's Cove**, 4km (6.5mi) north of Ramshackle airport, is another palm fringed beach with some surf. Foreign tourists are permitted to explore only a fraction of the southern region at Wandor, 35mi (56km) southwest of Port Blair. However, these breaks are not the reason for coming to the Andamans. The first quality spot is **Jarawa Point** (also called Totem's Reef), a long wrapping left with good hollow sections. Small island groupings seem to host Andaman's best surf spots. Jarawa is located on the Cinque Islands and there are breaks on the tiny **Twin Islands** off Rutland plus a right on the NW coast of the **Sentinel** Islands. On Little Andaman, **Jackson Creek** and **Tochangeou** are more options to check while sailing around the west coast. However, the real focus lies just inside Sandy Point on the SW tip of the island, usually referred to as **Kumari Point**. It's the fastest and longest right pointbreak in the country and if there's enough size and no SW winds, you'll be telling your grandchildren about this awesome coral pass. Most Andaman waves are fairly easy with good shape and fantastic colours on the reef below. Further south across the 10° Channel, the Nicobar Islands are off limits, protecting their surf potential and their unique indigenous population from outside interference. Home to Stone Age, pigmy tribes (Onge,

Jarawa, Sentinelese...) these reclusive aboriginal people live in impenetrable jungles, hunting wild boar and deer, and still practising age old rituals including some cannibalism.

Few charter boats operate – Thaiwave's SEAL sailing yachts: *Crescent*, a 65ft (19.5m) fibreglass Ketch suitable for eight passengers or *Gaea*, a wooden ketch-rigged tri-maran, 51ft (15.3m) long. It's a bit slower but more comfy and cheaper than *Crescent*.

The same SW monsoon swells hitting Sumatra travel as far as the Andamans, 10° or so above the Equator, albeit arriving with less power and consistency. Unfortunately, most of the breaks are directly onshore in the SW winds, so therefore, the season is a short spell from Mid-March to Mid-May. The best conditions occur when there is an early season swell with perfect NE winds, before it switches when the SW monsoon arrives, sometimes as early as April. Choose your time very carefully; April seems to be most reliable month. Once the SW monsoon is on, the sea gets rough with constant 15-25 knot winds, blowing out spots, but creating a small windswell for Phuket beaches. Tidal phases are minimal, check with the captain for water depths.

### SPOT DESCRIPTION

| | | | |
|---|---|---|---|
| ① | 6/2 | ◐ | ⊜ |
| ② | 6/2 | ◐ | ⊜ |
| ③ | 8/3 | ◑ | ⊜ |
| ④ | 8/3 | ◐ | ⊜ |
| ⑤ | 8/3 | ◑ | ⊜ |
| ⑥ | 8/3 | ◑ | ⊜ |
| ⑦ | 8/3 | ◑ | ⊜ |
| ⑧ | 8/3 | ◑ | ⊜ |

### SURF STATISTICS

| SURF STATISTICS | J F | M A | M J | J A | S O | N D |
|---|---|---|---|---|---|---|
| dominant swell | S-SW | S-SW | S-SW | S-SW | S-SW | S-SW |
| swell size (ft) | 2 | 3-4 | 4-5 | 5 | 4-5 | 1-2 |
| consistency (%) | 40 | 70 | 10 | 10 | 20 | 30 |
| dominant wind | N-NE | NW-NE | SW-W | SW-W | SW-W | NE-E |
| average force | F3 | F2-F3 | F3-F4 | F4-F5 | F3-F4 | F3-F4 |
| consistency (%) | 76 | 60 | 73 | 83 | 51 | 66 |
| water temp (°C/°F) | 27/80 | 28/82 | 29/84 | 28/82 | 27/80 | 27/80 |
| wetsuit | 🩳 | 🩳 | 🩳 | 🩳 | 🩳 | 🩳 |

Kumari Point

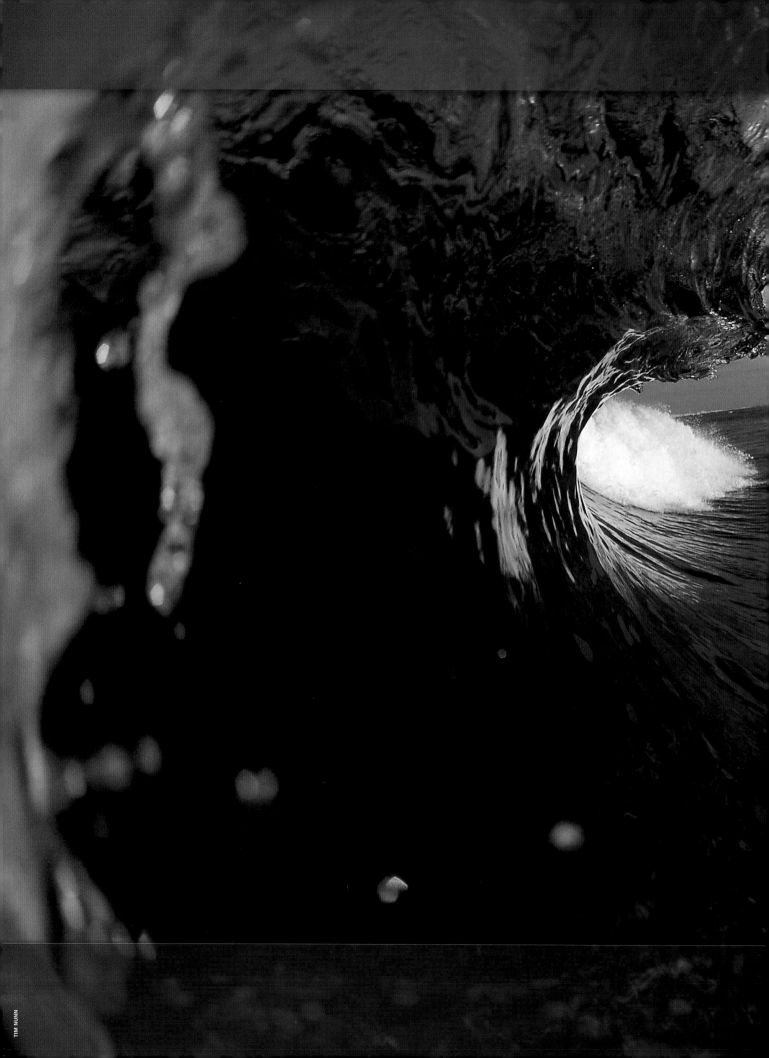

The Bukit Peninsula, Bali, Indonesia has seen a rapid increase in coastal development yet waste management remains crude.

# East Asia

HIJMP

# The Ocean Environment

Straddling two oceans and incorporating literally dozens of seas, Eastern Asia is an aquatic wonderland. Dominated by the great archipelagos of Indonesia and the Philippines, East Asia presents itself as one of the richest areas for surf in the world. With high population densities and a near coastal population of around 1.2 billion, the ocean is under enormous pressure to provide food and resources for the inhabitants of this dynamic region.

## Pollution

By removing vast areas of tropical forest and coastal mangrove swamps, local populations have eliminated a natural filter that prevents pollution reaching the ocean. Over fishing has contributed by depleting stocks that are able to cope with and absorb a certain amount of pollutants. Without these filters, the system collapses, evidenced by figures estimating that 90% of reefs in South East Asia are in a critical state. If they disappear, so will 80% of all the top quality surf breaks. Sumatra, Java and Bali have all been heavily deforested and their fisheries harvested to the point of commercial extinction. Around coastal villages with rivermouths, surf camps and holiday resorts, it is not uncommon to find untreated sewage floating in the line-up. Rampant consumerism has added huge amounts of plastic packaging to the environment and local landfills are ill equipped to cope with the increase in non-degrading waste. A legacy of dumping rubbish at sea is coming back to haunt Indonesian shorelines. A snorkel at Uluwatu will reveal coral heads wrapped in plastic bags, while a surf at Kuta Beach won't be without floating debris. New Guinea has pristine water quality and the coral reefs are amongst the best in the world. Isolated incidences of untreated human waste around settlements should be expected as with any other under-developed country. Increasing logging and agriculture threaten the mainland's coastal waters and the fledgling tourist industry is sure to bring its associated problems as it expands in the years to come. The principle surfing areas on the east coast of the Philippines are the cleanest in the archipelago, pollution is restricted to areas around settlements and agriculture is light. Continued heavy demand for hardwood is increasing logging activity in the east where the isolation makes it easy to exploit a valuable resource. Over-fishing is also a problem right across the Philippines, including blast and cyanide fishing methods, which decimate the otherwise healthy reefs. The number of endangered marine species off Vietnam skyrocketed from 15 in 1989 to 135 in 2000, while healthy coral reefs plummeted from 35% to only 5-7% due to pollution and over-fishing. Around coastal communities, sanitation is generally poor with raw sewage emptying directly into the ocean. Deforestation of the coastal strip is also resulting in increased sediment and agricultural runoff in coastal waters. China's potential to pollute is as large as the growth in manufacturing that is sweeping through this vast population as it steers towards western, capitalistic values which will undoubtedly bring some environmental disasters.

Despite being a first world nation Japan has severe pollution problems. High density of population, heavy industry and an intensively farmed coastal strip, coupled with poor treatment of waste has lead to some serious water quality issues. Surfing near major cities conditions can be intolerable. Once out into the countryside, pollution is less noticeable but agricultural runoff is still very damaging to the local ecosystem. Japan's high shark fatality rate may be karmic considering their insatiable appetite for shark fin soup, which creates a market for the most barbaric and wasteful fishing techniques around.

TIM NUNN

## Access

Indonesia is made up of 13,677 islands whilst the Philippines sports a mere 7107. Obviously, this means that access is troublesome and island-hopping by local transport can be time consuming and unpredictable. Indo has developed to a point that this is only of concern to the budget or hardcore traveller who refuses to pay a premium and hop on A/C buses to the nearest surf camp or boat charter. Only the fringes of the Indonesian archipelago are a real mission for surfers to get to and even charter boats are available to those with enough money. A solo mission to Papua New Guinea attracts extra expense to get out to the waves; however with about 90% of visiting surfers arriving to stay in surf camps with all wave transfers included, access becomes less of an issue. The fledgling surf tour infrastructure in the Philippines suffers because it is a couple of days journey time from Manila to get to the main surfing areas where surfers must then rely on local boats to access the major spots.

Japan has an excellent public transport system, so getting to the beach can be easy using the train, however, like everything in Japan, it is pricey and often crowded. The road network is also excellent and access easy so long as you can read the signposts!

Landfill sites are sources of contamination to the water table and rubbish is often swept to the coast after tropical rains.

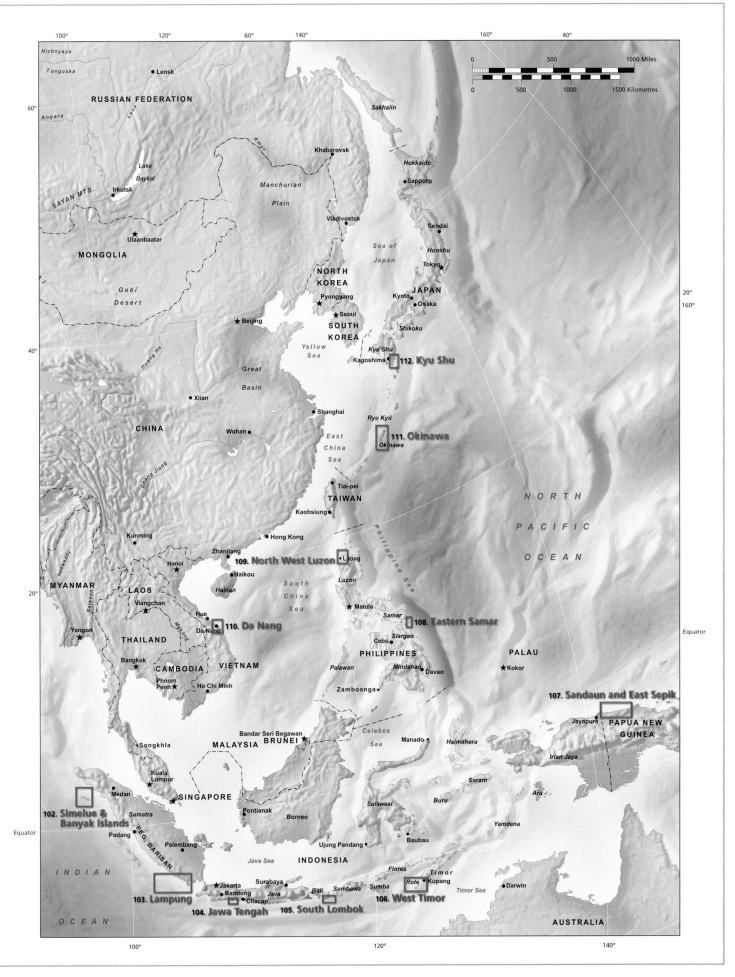

### Erosion

The whole of South East Asia has a potentially major problem with erosion and any significant sea level rise due to global warming could be catastrophic. Even a small rise would decimate miles of Indonesian, Filipino, Vietnamese and New Guinean coastline. It doesn't take much imagination to realise that a rise as little as ten centimetres, besides harming reefs and increasing erosion could alter the characteristics of most surf breaks. Imagine Speedies as a fat wall instead of a screaming barrel or Kuta destroyed by high tide backwash. These speculative scenarios, whilst difficult to accurately predict are undoubtedly distinct possibilities if sea levels rise, and encourages re-evaluation of our greenhouse gas emissions. Vietnam would lose 36% of its coastline due to inundation, if sea levels rise as predicted over the century. Vietnam practises illegal coral mining and whole villages are nomadically moving up the coast blast mining reefs for building materials. Once a reef is exhausted, they simply move on totally uncontrolled. Indonesia and the Philippines certainly cause damage to the environment with coral mining, although it tends to take place on coastlines without surf. Japan has legalised coral mining for pharmaceutical purposes, threatening the stability of the fragile ecosystem of the southern islands.

Japan's coastal hardening projects reflect its geographical position. Lying in one of the most active earthquake zones and at risk of tsunamis, there are also regular, strong typhoons for the high coastal population to worry about, so coastal defences have long been seen as essential. Considering 55% of the Japanese coastline is armoured with seawalls, tetrapods and offshore reefs many surf spots have been lost, although a few have been inadvertently created by the building projects. Surfrider Japan states that this massive armouring process is more political than environmentally driven. There is no cohesive, coastal protection plan or department, leaving local and regional bodies to initiate projects, which protect their interests or enhance their popularity in front of a disaster-paranoid, coastal population. This has resulted in some serious damage to the natural coastline and surfing resources. Surfrider Japan was formed as a direct result of a coastal modification project that destroyed a pointbreak in Chiba Prefecture and it has since fought hard against coastal hardening.

**Top – Kuta Karnival Rememberance ceremony for the victims of the Bali bombings.**

**Traditional fishing techniques are being superceded by environmentally un-friendly blast and cyanide methods.**

### Hazards

Sharks are found right across East Asia, although with heavy fishing they are becoming a less common sight and rarely pose a threat to surfers. Small reef sharks are often close by and occasional sightings of big tiger sharks cannot be discounted. Japan has the highest attack figures and a surprisingly high fatality ratio of 2 out of every 3 attacks. An even higher percentage of deaths occurs in Hong Kong, but heading south, reported attacks diminish leaving Indonesia barely registering with a couple of fatalities more than 50 years ago. However, Papua New Guinea is a different kettle of fish and has seen 28 fatalities from 58 reported attacks. Jellyfish are common in Japan (some species are actually eaten) and apart from the man-o-war, the occasional leviathan stomolophus nomurai (which reaches 200kg in weight) may be encountered.

The risk of malaria varies greatly across the region and surfing epicentres of Bali and West Java present a low risk while Catanduanes in the Philippines presents no risk. The rest of Indo remains a variable risk with some chloroquine resistance while Lombok, Timor and Irian Jaya are substantially more risky for falciparum malaria. Chloroquine-resistant plasmodium vivax strains of malaria are becoming prevalent in parts of South East Asia.

The current world political situation with regard to terrorism should be taken seriously. Both Indonesia and The Philippines have extremist groups within their countries and in the aftermath of the Bali attack the utmost care should be taken. Keep updated on the country travel warnings and stay abreast of political developments in areas that are known as hot spots. Be aware that kidnappings in the Philippines are on the increase.

Natural disasters are a regular, Asian occurrence where seismic activity brings earthquakes and the odd tsunami to the shores of Japan, Papua New Guinea and even the hallowed surfing shores of Grajagan in Java.

Sailors in the region should also be aware that piracy is still an issue, especially in Filipino and Indonesian waters bordering the South China Sea and in the more remote corners of the archipelagos.

Surfing across South East Asia has exploded, with young men in Indonesia and the Philippines mimicking their western counterparts and taking to the water in numbers. Bali has the largest, established local crew and a crowded day at Uluwatu is not without stress. Talented locals will often make it hard for a visitor but violence is uncommon, particularly since most locals earn their living from travelling surfers. Visiting surfers in Japan are welcomed with open arms, but be aware that intense weekend crowds can often number in the hundreds.

# Surf Travel Resources

## COUNTRY INFORMATION

|  | VIETNAM | JAPAN | PHILIPPINES |
|---|---|---|---|
| Area (sq km/mi): | 331,689/128,066 | 377,801/145,870 | 300,000/115,800 |
| Population: | 80M | 127M | 83M |
| Waveriders: | 300 | 200,000 | 1000 |
| Tourists (per yr): | 2.2M | 4.8M | 2.2M |
| Language: | Vietnamese, English | Japanese | Filipino (Tagalog), English, Visayan |
| Currency: | Dong | Yen (¥) | Philippine Peso |
| Exchange: | $1 = 15,000 VND | $1 = 120 JPY | $1 = 50 PHP |
| GDP ($ per yr): | $1,950 | $24,900 | $3,800 |
| Inflation (%): | -1% | -1% | 5% |

## INDONESIA

1. Bohemian
2. KM Nauli
3. Baneng Simeulue Resort
4. Wisma Jendela
5. Gangsta's Paradise
6. Nusantara
7. Mangalui
8. Navistar
9. Nagalaut
10. Bintang
11. Wavepark Losmen
12. Ombak Indah
13. Karang Nyimbor Losmen
14. Hotel Mutiara
15. Nomad
16. Just Dreaming
17. Cimaja Surfing Association
18. Pondok Kencana Lodge
19. Cimaja Point Resort
20. Batu Besar Losmen
21. Casuarina Indo
22. Insearch Travel
23. Bobby's Camp
24. Jungle Camp
25. Choko Bay Resort
26. Wanasari Wisata
27. Puri Dajuma
28. Oceana Biru Bali
29. Island Wave Tours
30. Mick's Place, Bingin
31. Uluwatu Resort
32. Bali Cliff Hotel
33. Jungutbatu Bungalows
34. Surf Maniac Camp
35. Bali Learn to Surf
36. Cheyne Horan SS
37. Sri Noa Noa

38. Moggy
39. Heaven on the Planet
40. Kuta Indah
41. Anne Judith II
42. Queen of the Sea
43. Purnama Indah
44. Dreamwaver
45. Eka Wisata II
46. Ria Wasata
47. Kapal
48. Bali Waves
49. Aman Gati
50. Nihiwatu Resort
51. East Sumba, Kelala
52. East Sumba 2
53. Nemberala Beach Resort
54. Sri Noa Noa
55. Indo Jiwa
56. Mahalo II

## PAPUA NEW GUINEA
57. Lido Village
58. Vanimo Resort

## PHILIPPINES
59. Jungle Reef
60. Tuason Point
61. Pansukian Tropical Resort
62. Sagana Resort
63. King of Sports III
64. MIA Surf & Sports Resort
65. Bay's Inn - Sabang Beach
66. Crystal Beach Resort
67. San Juan Surf Resort
68. Yokohama Surf School
69. Sunset German Beach Resort
70. Badoc Island Resort

## VIETNAM
71. Furama Resort

## JAPAN
72. OM Tour
73. Yesco Girl Surf School

## COUNTRY INFORMATION

|  | INDONESIA | PAPUA NEW GUINEA |
|---|---|---|
| Area (sq km/mi): | 1,904,569/760,000 | 462,840/178,704 |
| Population: | 228M | 5M |
| Waveriders: | 8,000 | 1,200 |
| Tourists (per yr): | 5M | 70,000 |
| Language: | Bahasa Indonesian English | English (Pidgin), 800 local languages |
| Currency: | Indonesian Rupiah | Kina |
| Exchange: | $1 = 9,000 IDR | $1 = 4 PGK |
| GDP ($ per yr): | $2,900 | $2,500 |
| Inflation (%): | 9% | 17% |

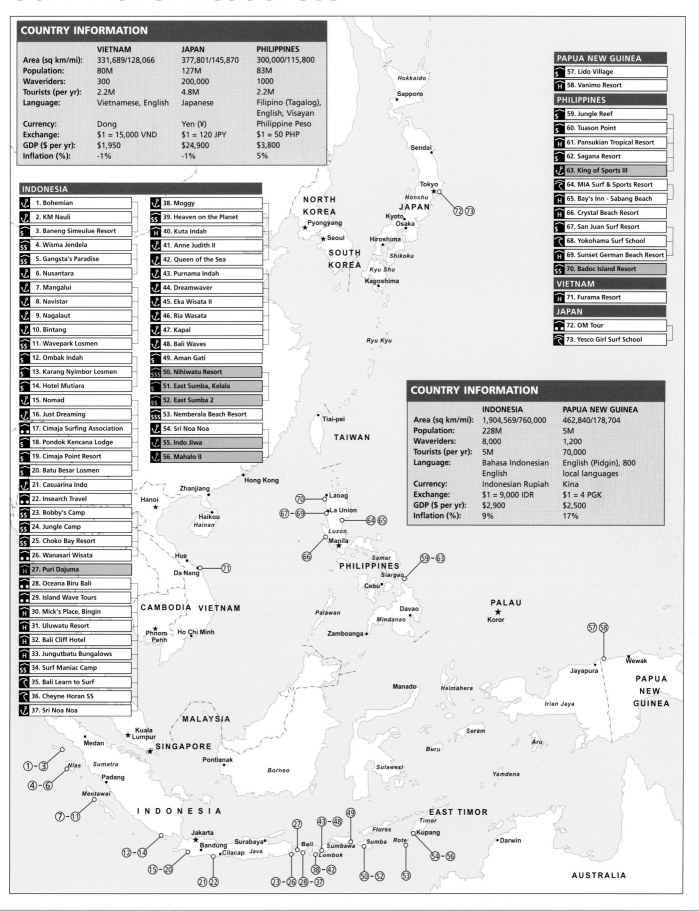

# 102. Simeulue and Banyak Islands

ALL PHOTOS JOHN CALLAHAN

## Summary

+ REEF QUALITY
+ CONSISTENT SWELLS
+ NO CROWDS
+ UNTOUCHED SCENERY

– NO BUDGET OPTIONS
– LACK OF INFORMATION
– DANGEROUS NAVIGATION
– MALARIA INFESTED

The offshore islands of Sumatra are no secret to surfers: the Mentawai are the new craze among pros and photographers looking for pictures of perfect tropical barrels, Nias has drawn surf adventurers to its shore for over 25 years, but head further north and you step into the unknown. The remote island of Simeulue is located 120km (75mi) from the Sumatran west coast, where the surprisingly busy town of Sinabang thrives on trading cloves. To the east, the Banyak Island group is in the South Aceh Regency, supporting small populations on seven of the bigger islands, while the majority of the others remain uninhabited. A centum of islands was reduced to 99 after a large storm swept one clean off the face of the earth. Besides clove, local resources come from copra and lolak, a kind of seashell. Many spots remain nameless, but there's a wide choice of lefts and rights, ranging from shallow barrelling waves to deeper, long, cruisey walls as well as some good off-season beaches.

There are a couple of waves on the SW facing coast of Simeulue: **Tea Bags**, a solid right that freight trains down a reef when the swell is up, and a good left reefbreak called **Thailand**. Banyak Islands' spots are extremely remote and most of them are very dangerous because of their shallowness. **Turtle Island** (Pulau Bangkaru) is,

## TRAVEL INFORMATION

**Population:** 4.3M
**Coastline:** 382km (239mi) Simeulue
**Contests:** None
**Other Resources:**
sailbohemian.com
surfingsumatra.com
simeulue.com
acehtourism.com

**Getting There** – 60d visa-free from most countries (not Portugal). Flights and ferries from Jakarta and Penang (Malaysia) to Medan. Sibolga is an 8h bus ride from Medan. For Simeulue, occasional boats from Meulaboh and flights from Medan via Meulaboh. There is no airport on Banyak and rough weather often makes crossings impossible. Cross from Tapaktuan (12h), Bakongan (6h) or Singkil (3h) to Desa Balai on Pulau Balai.

**Getting Around** – The lack of regular transportation makes it difficult to visit the Banyak Islands and the good waves are only accessible by boat. Boat owners on Pulau Palambak take people to snorkel, but many are scared of the west coast of Tuangku. Booking a trip with a reliable surf trip operator is best.

**Lodging and Food** – Only the eastern islands of Banyak offer accommodation, they're mainly located on Palambak Besar. 11 nights surfing charter onboard the *Bohemian* are $2,220/person. 11 nights on the *Nauli* cost $1,920. The Baneng Simeulue Island Resort is $1,800 for 14 days or $2,110 for the land/boat combo.

**Weather** – The climate in these islands is typically equatorial with very high temperatures interspersed by a few months of rain. Temperatures vary little across the year. Western Indonesia's dry season is May-Sept but 1-2h late afternoon showers can still be expected. During the October to April rainy season, it's rare to see more than half a day pass without any precipitation. Water is as warm as it gets, neoprene would only serve as reef protection. Lack of winds is good for glassy surf but does not help to dry clothes or feel cool — it takes a few days to adapt.

**Nature and Culture** – This is one of the remotest areas on earth, forget about raging

nightlife and think eco-activities: trek and dive on Pulau Palambak or Pulau Balai. Green turtles and occasionally leatherback turtles can be seen laying eggs on Pulau Bangkaru. The untouched jungles offer unique flora and fauna and are best explored by boat.

**Hazards and Hassles** – With few surf-related charters and one camp, crowds should not be a problem, even when other boats from the Mentawai area cruise over. Chloroquine-resistant malaria cases have been reported- take the appropriate medication. These shallow and treacherous reefs are several days away from medical attention; take a helmet and serious medical equipment.

**Handy Hints** – Take everything, there are no exchange facilities and surfing equipment is unheard of. Pulau Balai (Banyak) is one of the only places with electricity in the evening. The Banyak Islands are getting increasingly popular with travellers and may not remain off the beaten path for long.

| WEATHER STATISTICS | J/F | M/A | M/J | J/A | S/O | N/D |
|---|---|---|---|---|---|---|
| total rainfall (mm) | 120 | 110 | 130 | 130 | 200 | 220 |
| consistency (days/mth) | 6 | 8 | 7 | 7 | 10 | 10 |
| min temp (°C/°F) | 23/74 | 23/74 | 23/74 | 24/75 | 23/74 | 23/74 |
| max temp (°C/°F) | 30/86 | 31/88 | 31/88 | 31/88 | 30/86 | 29/84 |

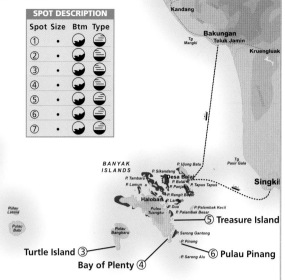

unsurprisingly, known for the many turtles that come and lay their eggs here, but a short left is rumoured to break at the southern end of the island. A wide bay on the SW shore of Pulau Tuangku, the largest island in the Banyak group, is known as **Bay of Plenty** since it's very consistent and hosts several breaks. The left is an excellent wave for those with sufficient tube-riding skills and lust for speed. This spot is truly dangerous and simply too

| SPOT DESCRIPTION | | | |
|---|---|---|---|
| Spot | Size | Btm | Type |
| ① | • | | |
| ② | • | | |
| ③ | • | | |
| ④ | • | | |
| ⑤ | • | | |
| ⑥ | • | | |
| ⑦ | • | | |

Tea Bags ①
Thailand ②

Turtle Island ③

Bay of Plenty ④

⑤ Treasure Island

⑥ Pulau Pinang

shallow to be surfed under 3-4ft (1-1.2m). The right on the other side of the bay is shorter and comparatively playful although it has a hollow section and ends in shallow waters. The other advantage to this is that if the left is onshore, the right will be offshore and clean – and vice versa. Another long and hollow left breaks in the middle of the bay if the swell picks up. On the east side of the island, the **Treasure Island** righthander is almost 1km (0.6mi) long. It breaks in several sections, with some being quite long and hollow, but it needs a fair swell to get going. Other little islands offer more breaks, but many are just close-outs like the shallow righthander located on the beautiful island of **Pulau Pinang**. As these spots are so remote and little-known, it's best to rely on an established operator to guide an expedition there. This area is developing into a boat trip destination, but for the moment only two vessels, the *Bohemian* and *Nauli* operate out of Sibolga. Other boats sporadically take the 480-640km (300-400mi) trip from Padang, but it may take them a couple of days to get there. The *Bohemian* is a 47ft (14m) aluminum catamaran built in Australia for the specific purpose of surf chartering by owner/operator Steve Bridge. The 75ft (22m) *Nauli* is operated by Mark "Rock" Flint, the previous manager of the Sorake Beach Resort in Nias. The Baneng Simeulue Island Resort operated by Brian Williams, located on the SW tip of the island, is the only land option. A 28ft (9m) speedboat takes guests surfing at the surrounding spots and now they offer a one week on land/one week Banyak boat trip deal.

Equatorial shores generally suffer from a lack of exposure to swells, but the Southern Indian Ocean is the most efficient swell machine on the planet. Expect numerous 6-10ft (2-3m) SW swells per month between April and October, as well as occasional 3-6ft (1-2m) swells during off-season, with various 2-6ft (0.6-2m) cyclonic swells and some 1-2ft (0.3-0.6m) underlying windswell. This area receives the same swells as the Mentawais between April and October, the optimal season being June-August. It still receives less swell than Nias which can be used as a back-up option if it's really too small. Due to the doldrums latitude, wind patterns are pretty calm, allegedly producing glassy conditions 15% of the time. There are no real dominant winds. January to May tends to be NW, June to Sept is rather SE, and October to Dec is more NE. Tide ranges are only 0.6-1m (2-3ft) but matter plenty at shallow spots, where sharp reefs pose a real threat.

| SURF STATISTICS | J F | M A | M J | J A | S O | N D |
|---|---|---|---|---|---|---|
| dominant swell | S-SW | S-SW | S-SW | S-SW | S-SW | S-SW |
| swell size (ft) | 3 | 4 | 4-5 | 5-6 | 5 | 3-4 |
| consistency (%) | 55 | 65 | 75 | 85 | 70 | 60 |
| dominant wind | W-NE | SE-N | E-SW | E-SW | SW-N | SW-N |
| average force | F2 | F2 | F2 | F2 | F3 | F3 |
| consistency (%) | 55 | 56 | 45 | 56 | 63 | 59 |
| water temp (°C/°F) | 29/84 | 28/82 | 28/82 | 27/80 | 27/80 | 28/82 |
| wetsuit | | | | | | |

*NB: With the war that started against the Free Aceh Movement (GAM) in June 2003, the government has made Aceh 'off limits' to foreigners until further notice. Simeulue, Banyak and Banda Aceh (the capital) are unaffected by fighting but as they are officially a part of the Aceh Province, tourists are not allowed in without a police permit and sponsorship by a local.*

# 103. Lampung

Karang Nyimbor

**Summary**
+ Consistent, sizable surf
+ Uncrowded for Indo
+ Exploration potential
+ Cheap surfcamps

− Cross-shore winds
− Few services, no night-life
− Tedious access
− Isolated

The offshore islands of Nias and the Mentawais have been under the surf media spotlight for years, while Sumatra's mainland has remained off the radar of most travelling surfers. Despite an ideal orientation to Indian Ocean swell hitting the contoured coastline of the fifth biggest island in the world, Sumatra remains a quiet surfing backwater off the beaten Indonesian track. Sumatra has a reputation for being wild, riddled with malaria and the west coast of Lampung lies uncomfortably close to Krakatau, responsible for the most violent volcanic eruption ever recorded (1883) accompanied by 120ft (40m) high waves. Today the area remains scarcely populated and is rarely visited by tourists, despite the Bali bombing highlighting the fact that remote areas may be safer than tourist hotspots. The fishing town of Krui, is the centre of the

Jimmy's Point

region's coastal districts, being the first village accessed from the interior road network and providing the most services for locals and travellers alike.

Furthest north from Krui, **Jimmy's Point** enjoys the best reputation among the northern breaks. The left is long with an intense barrel from take-off, while the similarly intense right offers a hollow wall, but is plagued by a

## TRAVEL INFORMATION

**Population:** 7M Lampung
**Coastline:** 4,870km (3,043mi)
**Contests:** None
**Other Resources:**
Video: Rubber Time
freelinesurf.com.au
visit-lampung.com

**Getting There** – 60d visa-free from most countries (not Portugal). Cheap flights land in Jakarta (CGK), several companies let you take boards. Fly from Jakarta to Bandar Lampung, then 7hr in the small Krui Putra bus or take the morning express bus from the Pulo Gadung terminal in JKT (14h instead of 21h for regular ones).

**Getting Around** – Dirt cheap taxi-trucks cruise the coastal road, but get rare after 4pm. 'Becaks' are only found in town; these bike powered carts are a nice and environmentally friendly way to cover short distances. Motorbikes are rented for $5 a day. Surf camps can organise a driver for a full day's expedition for under $25.

**Lodging and Food** – Surfers spread between 3 surf camps providing a room and 3 meals a day for less than $15 in basic comfort. Mr Zen's Hotel Mutiara is the closest to town and face Ujung Walur's right. Karang Nyimbor Losmen run by Andy Watson and his wife, face the point. Next door, Ombak Indah (Big Rock 5) organises all inclusive tours through Freeline Indonesian Surf Adventures.

**Weather** – This is a wet, tropical climate. The dry season, May-Oct is the best time to visit, with SE trades, clear skies nearly everyday and the occasional evening thunderstorm. The rainy season is a worry for inland travellers since the mountains are shrouded in clouds and rainfall in the highlands can dampen travel plans. On the coast, mornings can have drizzle whereas afternoons get intense rains or alternatively it can just tip down all day. Strong equatorial sunshine, intense humidity and loads of insects are a given. As for the water temperature, booties will be the only neoprene you need year round.

**Nature and Culture** – Although Lampung has been inhabited since prehistoric times, don't expect many cultural sights. It's all about nature being surrounded by the Bukit Barisan National Park. Walk the beautiful beaches, bike from one village to another, cruise the local market in Krui or go fishing or snorkelling.

**Hazards and Hassles** – Close reef inspections are unavoidable, especially at low tides and at the treacherous Way Jambu. Check out the garbage thrown in Krui's river, explaining why rivermouths are off limits after the rain. Chloroquine-resistant malaria is a risk throughout Sumatra, take appropriate prophylaxis.

**Handy Hints** – This is not a tourist area, take everything with you! There's no bank to change money, no internet access and no surfshop. You'll find wax and leashes at Ombak Indah. Water is warm but a shorty provides protection against reef cuts and wind chill. English isn't widely spoken, get a Lonely Planet Indonesian phrasebook and start learning.

| WEATHER STATISTICS | J/F | M/A | M/J | J/A | S/O | N/D |
|---|---|---|---|---|---|---|
| total rainfall (mm) | 320 | 300 | 230 | 220 | 310 | 430 |
| consistency (days/mth) | 8 | 10 | 10 | 6 | 9 | 9 |
| min temp (°C/°F) | 23/74 | 23/74 | 23/74 | 23/74 | 23/74 | 23/74 |
| max temp (°C/°F) | 30/86 | 30/86 | 31/88 | 30/86 | 30/86 | 30/86 |

tricky shallow exit. **Pulau Pisang** translates as 'Banana Island' where a choice of waves, break along both sides of the island, reachable by boat from Tambakak. Definitely a rainy season spot, since its orientation favours the off-season winds. **Krui** itself hosts two good reefs, right on its main beach. These are hollow, quality breaks and the left compares to Bingin on Bali, but they'll only break on the largest swells, since the beach is protected by a large southern point. On the outskirts of the city, **Ujung Walur** picks up more swell while still enjoying offshore winds, the ride is real short but barrel technicians able to

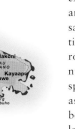

Enggano ⑫

backdoor the hollow peak will be rewarded. The beachbreak of **Mandiri** can be worth a look on small, windless mornings and allows surfing without booties. The point at **Karang Nyimbor** (Flying Coral), is the main attraction and most travelling surfers stay there to enjoy this consistent left somehow sheltered from the trades. On smaller swells, it's a pretty mellow wave by Indo standards, 200m plus (650ft) rides are not uncommon and it will handle some size. A big wave gun can come in handy for these bigger days. Remember it has to be more than double-overhead here for the reefs in town to start breaking. 15 minutes south is the answer for those looking for a more challenging wave. The set-up at **Way Jambu** (Pear River) is far more challenging than Karang Nyimbor, few surfers will actually dare to tackle these hollow and powerful waves breaking dangerously close to sharp reef. Nicknamed the Sumatran Pipeline, it goes

without saying this spot is for experts only and will be safer on a high tide. The coastal road leads to numerous other spots seldom surfed as most surfers don't bother checking out these less documented, wind sensitive breaks. An expedition south will pass by **Bali Village**, a set of rights and lefts facing a Balinese settlement. Despite being a promising set-up, **Siging** seldom delivers the goods and on a huge swell, a better bet would be **Benkunqut**, where the SE winds blow offshore. More spots hide between headlands all the way to **Balimbing** on the tip of the Benkulen Peninsula, which is rumoured to have a good wave, but no roads lead there. Surfing **Enggano** is a whole different story, requiring a charter boat to explore the promising shores of this remote, almost desert island.

R oaring Forties lows send plenty of 6-12ft (2-4m) swells April-October. The SSW direction is perfect for this SW facing area. Off-season is rarely flat because of the Southern Ocean's ability to produce constant swells in the 2-6ft (0.6-2m) range. Cross-shore winds are the rule as Lampung means "place of the southerly winds". The SE trade-season starts in May with mild winds getting stronger towards the end of the season in October. NW winds dominate the rest of the year. Tides affect the way some spots break and how hard you'll hit the reef if you fall. There is a big tide and a small tide every day (mixed) so a tide table comes in handy, but don't expect to find one locally. Christmas Island (Aus) tidal charts can be found on the net and are relatively accurate.

STUART HORSTMAN

RESPONDEK

**Karang Nyimbor**

**Jimmy's Point**

ANDERS

| SPOT DESCRIPTION | | | |
|---|---|---|---|
| | Spot Size | Btm | Type |
| ① | • | 🌀 | ⬖ |
| ② | • | 🌀 | ⬖ |
| ③ | • | 🌀 | ⬖ |
| ④ | • | 🌀 | ⬖ |
| ⑤ | • | 🌊 | ⬖ |
| ⑥ | • | 🌀 | ⬖ |
| ⑦ | • | 🌀 | ⬖ |
| ⑧ | • | 🌀 | ⬖ |
| ⑨ | • | 🌀 | ⬖ |
| ⑩ | • | 🌀 | ⬖ |
| ⑪ | • | 🌀 | ⬖ |

| SURF STATISTICS | J F | M A | M J | J A | S O | N D |
|---|---|---|---|---|---|---|
| dominant swell | S-SW | S-SW | S-W | S-W | S-SW | S-SW |
| swell size (ft) | 5 | 6 | 7 | 8 | 6-7 | 5 |
| consistency (%) | 60 | 80 | 90 | 90 | 80 | 70 |
| dominant wind | NW-N | NW-N | SE-S | SE-S | SE-S | NW-N |
| average force | F3 | F3 | F2-F3 | F3-F4 | F3 | F3-F4 |
| consistency (%) | 42 | 38 | 32 | 44 | 42 | 44 |
| water temp (°C/°F) | 28/82 | 28/82 | 28/82 | 27/80 | 28/82 | 28/82 |
| wetsuit | 🩳 | 🩳 | 🩳 | 🩳 | 🩳 | 🩳 |

MALAYSIA
Sumatra
INDONESIA
Java Bali Sumbawa

# 104. Jawa Tengah

**Summary**

+ MELLOW WAVES
+ NO CROWDS
+ WARM WATER
+ LAIDBACK ATMOSPHERE
+ JAVA CULTURAL CENTRES

– LACK OF HIGH-CLASS WAVES
– POOR BEACHBREAKS
– REGULAR ONSHORE WINDS
– NO FLIGHTS TO PANGANDARAN

**Batu Karas**

STÉPHANE IBARBOURE

STÉPHANE IBARBOURE

With excellent surf at both ends of Java (G-Land to the east and the Cimaja area to the west), one could reasonably expect the remaining 1,000km (625mi) of south-facing coastline to conceal many more gems. Unfortunately, this is not the case and central Java has never been highlighted as a prime surf destination for a few good reasons. A spine of volcanoes dominate the south of the island, so consequently most of the coast is lined with dangerous black sand shorebreaks with few points where the swell can wrap and be groomed by the SE trades. Many breaks rely on shifty sandbanks and unusual swell directions to produce quality waves. Unlike Sumatra, isolation and tricky access aren't problems here, since Java's 110 million inhabitants often travel to the island's

STÉPHANE IBARBOURE

many coastal resorts. Fortunately, the laidback atmosphere and beautiful scenery make up for the lack of epic waves. Surfers consider Pangandaran as the place to be located on the isthmus of a teardrop-shaped peninsula near the west Java/central Java border, Pangandaran is a popular beach resort for both domestic tourists from the city of Bandung and backpackers

## TRAVEL INFORMATION

**Population:**
38M Jawa Barat
**Coastline:**
2,885km (1,803mi)
**Contests:** None
**Other Resources:**
insearchtravel.com
indo.com/java/
 pangandaran.htm

**Getting There** – Visa requested for Portuguese. Many cheap flights land in Jakarta, Garuda's hub. No flights to Pangandaran. Direct buses from Jakarta start from Bekasi or Tangerang terminals, away from the city centre ($3, 10h). Train lovers will ride to Bandung, then Banjar thus limiting the bus to the last 50km (31mi) totalling 9h (3h+4h+2h).

**Getting Around** – Public transport including the traditional becaks (pedal cabs) is reliable but renting a small motorbike is another option ($3/d). iNSEARCH travel.com organises a complete JavaSoul tour ($899/10d). A scenic three-hour ferry ride links Pangandaran to Cilacap. Boards are often refused on trains.

**Lodging and Food** – Modest accommodation is available around Pananjung beach. Pantai Sari

Hotel is very close to the beach and the best rooms have A/C ($10). Bamboo House is a little more inland but a bamboo bungalow is only $8. A more luxurious option is the Sunrise Beach Hotel and its pool for around $30. Pick a fish for dinner and watch it being cooked in one of the many warungs.

**Weather** – The west part of Java has a wet tropical climate throughout the year. The dry season, May-Oct is the best time to visit, the SE trades clear the skies everyday, producing rare thunderstorms in the evening. The rainy season is always warm and humid which is more of a worry for inland travellers as the mountains are shrouded in clouds and rainfall in the highlands can dampen travel plans. On the coast, mornings can have drizzle whereas afternoons get intense rains. Be prepared for wet season changeability as it can rain all day or be mostly sunny. This brings intense humidity and insects abound. The further east, the dry and wet seasons become more distinct. As for the water, booties are the only neoprene needed year round.

**Nature and Culture** – Watch the wildlife and rare flora of the Pangandaran recreational park and Pananjung nature reserve. Travelling by boat along the Cijulang River offers dramatic views of the Green Canyon. Visit to the village of Rajapolan to purchase many different types of bamboo handicraft unique to the area.

**Hazards and Hassles** – The surf here is mellow by Indonesian standards but the beachbreaks get heavy and strong rips are common. There are an increasing number of local surfers but hardcore surf-trippers don't come here, so crowds are not a problem. This is one of Indonesia's most devout Muslim provinces, but don't expect extremist mentalities.

**Handy Hints** – No need for a full Indonesian quiver, a shortboard or Malibu will suffice. No surf shops around, but boards can be rented on the beach for $5/d. Pangandaran is packed on Indonesian holidays and weekends, prices explode and it gets difficult to find a room. There's a little fee to pay upon entrance of the Pangandaran beach resort area.

| WEATHER STATISTICS | J/F | M/A | M/J | J/A | S/O | N/D |
|---|---|---|---|---|---|---|
| total rainfall (mm) | 340 | 260 | 100 | 30 | 60 | 280 |
| consistency (days/mth) | 12 | 10 | 5 | 2 | 4 | 12 |
| min temp (°C/°F) | 22/72 | 22/72 | 21/70 | 20/68 | 21/70 | 22/72 |
| max temp (°C/°F) | 28/82 | 30/86 | 30/86 | 30/86 | 31/88 | 30/86 |

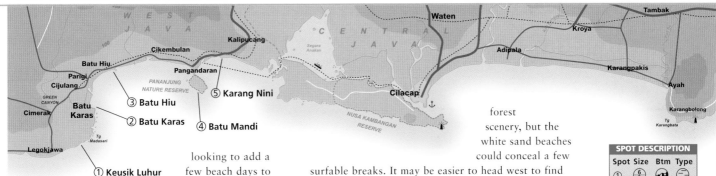

looking to add a few beach days to their cultural tour of the island. The traditional fishing village has long understood the profit it could gain from its long black-sand beach lined with coconut palms and is slowly turning into one of the largest Javanese beach resorts.

While better waves are known of further west, just 30km (19mi) southwest of Pangandaran, **Keusik Luhur** and Mandasari Beach are two rarely surfed beachbreaks with rocky outcrops in the water. Further to the northeast, **Batu Karas** is a fishing village that is gearing-up to cater for and accommodate the increasing number of tourists. When a large S swell is able to wrap around the point into this north-facing bay, the best wave in the area starts to line up. A fun right starts breaking over a sandy bottom, peeling nicely down the pointbreak type set-up that keeps the SE trades blowing cross/offshore. The beauty of Batu Karas is that it's adaptable to any level of surfing, from beginners to advanced, although the latter may find it a little fat and slow. The length of the ride increases exponentially with the size of the swell but wave faces remain half the size of exposed breaks. Between Batu Karas and Pangandaran, the road passes a string of beachbreaks such as **Batu Hiu**. This area is plagued by really strong currents and the waves generally close-out too much to bother getting wet, however the sandbanks tend to improve in the wet season.
**Batu Mandi** is a short and punchy lefthand reefbreak about a half hour walk from Pangandaran. It breaks hard and hollow on a sharp rock ledge and is best left to advanced riders as hitting the reef is a serious possibility. It's extremely shallow at low tide but even on high tide it is vital to exit the wave early, before the tricky shut down end section. 12km (7.5mi) east of Pangandaran, **Karang Nini** is easily recognisable by the huge rock on the beach. Access to these average beachbreaks is from the top of the cliffs where a recreational park is located. Nusa Kambangan Island is now a nature reserve, but due to its prison past it's been nicknamed Indonesia's Alcatraz. Visitors mostly go there to enjoy its caves and pleasant

forest scenery, but the white sand beaches could conceal a few surfable breaks. It may be easier to head west to find more spots; a motorbike ride from Batu Karas will lead to spots that pick much more swell than Batu Karas itself. The problem is that they're more exposed to the wind as well, so they should be surfed early in the morning or even during the rainy season.

Roaring Forties lows send numerous 6-12ft (2-4m) swells between April and October. The SSW direction is perfect for the S facing Java beachbreaks. Off season is rarely flat because these southern latitudes' have constant swells in the 2-6ft (0.6-2m) range. The beachbreaks actually handle the swell better in the wet season as runoff from the rains add some much needed shape to the usually straight sandbanks. Winds are like a clockwork: the SE trade-season starts in April with mild E-SE winds, SE is the major direction, up to October with more S winds towards the end of the season. November is a transition month with winds oscillating around S, shifting W-NW till March. Offshore winds typically become onshore by the afternoon as land temperatures increase, messing up the conditions. The mixed tides should be watched closely as some spots only work at certain stages of tide. Tidal range reaches 6ft (2m), alternating between a big and a small tide every day.

**SPOT DESCRIPTION**

| Spot | Size | Btm | Type |
|------|------|-----|------|
| ① | 6/2 | | |
| ② | 10/3 | | |
| ③ | 8/2 | | |
| ④ | 10/3 | | |
| ⑤ | 6/2 | | |

Batu Karas

| SURF STATISTICS | J F | M A | M J | J A | S O | N D |
|---|---|---|---|---|---|---|
| dominant swell | S-SW | S-SW | S-W | S-W | S-SW | S-SW |
| swell size (ft) | 3-4 | 4 | 4-5 | 5-6 | 4-5 | 4 |
| consistency (%) | 40 | 55 | 65 | 70 | 60 | 50 |
| dominant wind | W-NW | E-SE | E-SE | E-SE | E-SE | SE-W |
| average force | F3 | F3 | F3-F4 | F4 | F4 | F3 |
| consistency (%) | 55 | 32 | 62 | 73 | 66 | 65 |
| water temp (°C/°F) | 28/82 | 28/82 | 28/82 | 27/80 | 27/80 | 28/82 |
| wetsuit | | | | | | |

# 105. South Lombok

Desert Point

PAUL KENNEDY

## Summary

+ VOTED WORLDS BEST WAVE
+ CONSISTENT, YEAR-ROUND SURF
+ GREAT SCENERY
+ NO MASS TOURISM
+ CHEAP LODGING AND FOOD

− OVERCROWDED DESERT POINT
− ONLY ONE OUTSTANDING BREAK
− HARD ACCESS TO EASTERN SPOTS
− LACK OF ACCOMMODATION
  OUTSIDE KUTA

Only 35km (22mi) east of Bali at its closest point, Lombok is inevitably compared to its famous westernised neighbour, although major physical, cultural, linguistic and religious differences exist. It also contrasts quite markedly for the visitor, with less widespread tourist facilities, sparser public transport and simpler accommodation. The deep strait separating Bali from Lombok marks part of the "Wallace Line", an established physical division between Asia and Australia. Bali is green with lush, tropical vegetation, while equatorial Lombok is drier, more rugged, with completely different flora and fauna. While the mountainous north rises to 12,224ft (3726m) at the top of Mount Rinjani, the south is a range of low inland

Desert Point

MARK

hills spread behind the sweeping bays and pure white sands of the southern beaches. In terms of location, most surf breaks are truly breathtaking, but are generally regarded as of lower quality or intensity than Bali's, with the notable exception of Desert Point, elected "Best Wave in the World" by *Tracks* magazine's readers.

## TRAVEL INFORMATION

**Population:** 2.4M Lombok
**Coastline:** 464km (290mi)
**Contests:** None
**Other Resources:**
surfpartama.com
surfdesertstorm.com
lombok-isle.com
lombok-network.com

**Getting There** – Merpati has daily flights from Denpasar (Bali) to Mataram ($27 o/w). Standard ferries run between Padangai (Bali) and Lembar ($6, 4h). The Mabua Express' speed and comfort comes at a price ($30, 2h, from Benoa). Drive to Kuta (1h) or ride public bemos from Mandalika terminal in Mataram. Oceanea Biru Bali runs all-inclusive tours.

**Getting Around** – The road network is good although minor roads can be tricky; expect roadblocks during wet season. Rent a Suzuki Jimny for $31/d (insurance included) or a motorbike for $10/d. Charter a boat for around $12/d. Week-long boat trips leave from Bali to Desert Point and West Sumbawa, sometimes stopping in Grupuk and Ekas.

**Lodging and Food** – Basic rooms in Kuta cost under $5, for more comfort head to the Kutah Inda Hotel ($30 including beach transfers) or the luxurious Novotel ($160). Basic accommodation is available at Bangko-Bangko and Laut Surga (Ekas). Lombok food revolves around poultry, meat and fish cooked with tropical veggies in spices & coconut milk sauce.

**Weather** – Lombok lies less than 400km (250mi) south of the Equator and as such the weather is tropical. Days are almost universally 12 hours long with sunrise at around 6.20am and sunset at 6.30pm. The daytime temperature averages 30°C (86°F) all year long, but take warm clothing if planning a trek of Mt. Rinjani. Lombok's tropical monsoon climate has two distinct seasons; dry (May to September) and wet (October to April). Monsoon refers to the wind, not the rain. However even in the wet monsoon the rain tends to be short lived and localised. May, June and July are generally considered the best for visiting but spring and autumn are ok despite the humidity. Jan-Feb suffer heavy rains and stifling hot temps and can be considered a time to avoid. Water remains around an ideal 28°C (82°F), a shorty would only be used for protection against bouncing along the reef or wet season windchill.

**Nature and Culture** – Trekking at least part of the way up Rinjani is the reason many tourists come to Lombok, take a packaged tour to join them. Activities are few in the south, bike along the coastal road to appreciate the breathtaking scenery or ask boat owners for a ride to the best diving spots. Witness traditional culture in Relbitan and Sade, north of Kuta.

**Hazards and Hassles** – Desert Point is a gnarly wave; rips, shallow reef and other surfers all contribute to the danger; wear a helmet. Other spots break softer but medical attention is far away. Bring some reefboots. Theft stories are common. Whilst surfing, it's worthwhile tipping someone to be a security guard. Unlike Bali, malaria is a serious threat.

**Handy Hints** – Boards can be fixed or rented from the Ocean Blue surf shop in Kuta. It's common practice to hire a local surfing guide. Unlike in Hindu Bali, Islamic Sasaks make up 90% of Lombok's population. Many speak English, but appreciate any efforts to speak Bahasa Indonesian. Bring a regular shortboard and a semi-gun, especially for Desert Point.

| WEATHER STATISTICS | J/F | M/A | M/J | J/A | S/O | N/D |
|---|---|---|---|---|---|---|
| total rainfall (mm) | 310 | 150 | 70 | 35 | 65 | 220 |
| consistency (days/mth) | 4 | 2 | 1 | 0 | 1 | 4 |
| min temp (°C/°F) | 25/77 | 25/77 | 25/77 | 24/75 | 25/77 | 25/77 |
| max temp (°C/°F) | 30/86 | 30/86 | 29/84 | 28/82 | 29/84 | 30/86 |

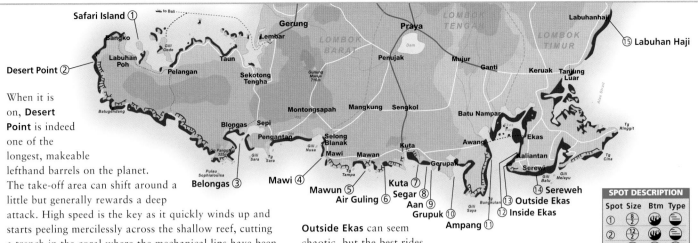

Safari Island ①
Gerung
Praya
Labuhanhaji
⑮ Labuhan Haji
Desert Point ②
Bangko
Labuhan Poh
Pelangan
Taun
Lembar
Penujak
Mujur
Ganti
Keruak
Tanjung Luar
Batugendang
Blongas
Sepi
Pengantan
Montongsapah
Mangkung
Sengkol
Batu Nampar
Ekas
Awang
Kaliantan
Sereweh
Belongas ③
Mawi ④
Selong Blanak
Mawi
Mawan
Kuta
Gerupak
⑭ Sereweh
Mawun ⑤
Kuta ⑦
Air Guling ⑥
Segar ⑧
Aan ⑨
Grupuk ⑩
Ampang ⑪
⑬ Outside Ekas
⑫ Inside Ekas

When it is on, **Desert Point** is indeed one of the longest, makeable lefthand barrels on the planet. The take-off area can shift around a little but generally rewards a deep attack. High speed is the key as it quickly winds up and starts peeling mercilessly across the shallow reef, cutting a trench in the coral where the mechanical lips have been slamming for centuries. The caverns get larger and faster as the inside section commits the tube-rider to a lock-in that usually ends on dry reef. Only surfers good enough to deal with that tricky exit, the shallow reef, evil out-going currents and plenty of wave-starved rippers should apply. Deserts has a reputation for inconsistency, with only the biggest groundswells igniting it and high tides making it disappear as fast as it came. Surf charters keep flocking from Bali and dedicated hardcore surfers wait for weeks in basic beach shacks. Boats have access to **Safari Island**, which also enjoys offshore trade winds, but needs an even bigger size to break. It's only worth checking on a high tide when Desert gets huge. The south coast is where the majority of breaks are found, and boat access is easier than the 2km (1.25mi) walk to the long (and sharky) bay of **Belongas**. There's a left on the E side and a right on the W side, both usually working best during wet season. Another left at the centre of the bay can be surfed on windless days. **Mawi** is a typical dry season break; it takes a bit of swell for the long left to reveal itself and peel in a beautiful set-up. A faster, hollower right can be had on smaller days. **Mawun** is an even nicer bay, with left and right points on each side of the beach. Cliffs bring protection from the wind. **Air Guling** is a short boat ride from Kuta, with short, mid to high tide lefts and a fast inside barrel on the low tide rights. **Kuta** is the surfing hub of Lombok, not because of the fickle right or the average, sectiony left there, but because that's where rooms, restaurants and cold Bintangs are available. 2km (1.25mi) east, **Pantai Segar**, is a small swell, wind sensitive, fun righthander, plus occasional left. If it gets big, get to **Tanjung Aan**, whose two peaks can be seen from the roadside. The left enjoys W winds, while the right will be better on N winds or glassy days. With so many peaks spread across its bay, **Grupuk** is often the main attraction. It's a short walk from the village to the tip of the bay, where the outside right can be ridden up to 15ft (4.5m). For smaller, fun surf and barrel hunting, jump in a boat to the inside reform peak. The rights are usually the best but often crowded. Fortunately other shifting peaks grace the E side of the bay and split the pack. The road coming from Kuta stops in **Ampang**, an east facing village thus requiring a rare combination of S-SE swell and W wind. On such conditions, long bowling rights break south of the village. The spots of Ekas Bay are best reached by boat from Awang. The **Inside Ekas** rights lack power, but can peel perfectly with the offshore tradewinds.

**Outside Ekas** can seem chaotic, but the best rides are long with fast hollow walls. The area east from Ekas is barely accessible from land, and is considered a wet season surf zone. In **Sereweh**, there are two righthanders; one is adapted to performance surfing while the other further to the west is more of a barrel. Access can be difficult. **Labuhan Haji** also needs some specific wet season conditions to deliver fun waves on the different reefs south of the village.

More than any other island in Indo, Lombok is a year round surfing destination. The peak season is obviously from April until early November, when classic 6-12ft (2-4m) waves come rolling-in. These swells originate in the Southern Indian Ocean's Roaring Forties and arrive from a SW direction. Wet season tropical cyclone positions can vary greatly, thus sending swell from the east as well as from the west. They prove to pack in as much power as winter depressions but are usually shorter lived. Winds blow like

BILL MORRIS
Desert Point

clockwork: the SE trades start in April with mild E-SE winds, SE being the major direction, up to October with more S winds towards the end of the season. November is a transition month with oscillating winds around S. Then, it shifts to W-NW with W first and then NW until end of March. Get a tide table in Bali and pay attention: there is a big and a small tide every day, some spots working only at certain stages of the tide.

SPOT DESCRIPTION

| Spot | Size | Btm | Type |
|---|---|---|---|
| ① | 8/3 | | |
| ② | 12/4 | | |
| ③ | 10/3 | | |
| | 10/3 | | |
| ④ | 6/2 | | |
| ⑤ | 10/3 | | |
| | 10/3 | | |
| ⑥ | 8/2 | | |
| | 8/2 | | |
| ⑦ | 6/2 | | |
| | 6/2 | | |
| ⑧ | 6/2 | | |
| ⑨ | 6/2 | | |
| | 6/2 | | |
| ⑩ | 10/3 | | |
| | 8/2 | | |
| ⑪ | 6/2 | | |
| ⑫ | 6/2 | | |
| ⑬ | 10/3 | | |
| ⑭ | 8/3 | | |
| ⑮ | 4/1 | | |

| SURF STATISTICS | J F | M A M | J J A | S O N D |
|---|---|---|---|---|
| dominant swell | S-SW | S-SW | S-SW | S-SW | S-SW | S-SW |
| swell size (ft) | 4-5 | 5-6 | 6-7 | 7-8 | 6 | 4-5 |
| consistency (%) | 60 | 80 | 90 | 90 | 80 | 70 |
| dominant wind | W-NW | E-NW | S-SE | S-SE | E-S | SE-NW |
| average force | F3 | F2 | F3 | F3 | F3 | F3 |
| consistency (%) | 65 | 88 | 74 | 80 | 79 | 72 |
| water temp (°C/°F) | 29/84 | 28/82 | 28/82 | 27/80 | 27/80 | 28/82 |
| wetsuit | | | | | | |

# 106. West Timor

**Summary**

+ MELLOW, ACCESSIBLE WAVES
+ CHEAP LOSMEN OPTION
+ NO BOAT CHARTER CROWDS
+ PERFECT DRY SEASON WEATHER

− SMALL SWELL WINDOW
− STRONG MID-MORNING TRADES
− LACK OF NIGHTLIFE & BEER
− ISOLATED SPOTS WITH NO
  LAND ACCESS

Pulau Dana

Pulau Rote

Shaped by the chain of powerful volcanoes that stretch right across Sumatra and Java, the 550 islands of East Nusa Tenggara differ greatly from western Indonesia. Hot, dry trade winds blowing from Australia make for an arid landscape in direct contrast to typical Indonesian tropical rainforests. Flora and fauna have links to Australia as opposed to Asia, a fact duly noted by the eminent naturalist Charles Darwin. Timor has a long colonial history polarised by recent political upheaval, which has wreaked decades of terror on the islands' population, before East Timor Independence became a reality in May 2002. Coupled with geographical isolation from the main Indonesian surf hubs, West Timor has remained a bit of a frontier, with most surfers looking to escape the Bali crowds heading to Nusa Tenggara's more accessible Lombok and Sumbawa. Tucked in above Australia with only its SW corner facing the Indian Ocean swells, Timor seems to lack potential compared to the rest of the Indonesian archipelago. But in typical Indo fashion, minor islands can hide major surf breaks and Rote, Savu and the surrounding outcrops are no exception.

More than a 100km west of Rote lies **Pulau Dana**, which has remained uninhabited since, according to the legend, all its inhabitants were murdered in the 17th

## TRAVEL INFORMATION

**Population:** 60,000 Savu
**Coastline:**
291km (180mi) Rote
**Contests:** Local (Oct)
**Other Resources:**
*Video*: Momentum 3:
 Under the Influence
waterwaystravel.com/
 timor.html
nusa-tenggara.com

**Getting There** – 60d visa-free from most countries (not Portugal). Fly to Bali (DPS), then Kupang (KOE) with Merpati ($180). They also fly from Darwin. Garuda doesn't fly to Kupang, other Indonesian airlines do, but from Jakarta or Surabaya. Daily morning ferries link Bolok to Pantai Baru ($1, 4h), then it's a 3h drive to Nemberala.

**Getting Around** – To get around the island, rent a bike, a motorbike or go to Busalangga or Baa to charter a bemo for a day (around $12). Charter a boat to reach the offshore islands. To go to Savu ride the ferry from Kupang (twice a week, 9hrs, $2). Some boat trips offer the full crossing to Sumbawa, others just cruise around Rote.

**Lodging and Food** – Rooms can cost under $3, the losmen at Anugurah is close to T-Land. For more comfort, head to the Nemberala Beach Resort ($15 double). Get onboard the 62ft (20m) *Mahalo II* (11 nights, $2,500), the 100ft (33m) *Indo Jiwa* (12 nights, $2,000) or the 57ft (18m) *Queeyai Kaye* (7nights, West Timor only, $850). There are only a few places to stay on Savu. Nightlife and supplies of beer are limited for the landbased traveller.

**Weather** – Central highlands and closeness to Australia make for irregular seasons in the area but the long dry season (May-Oct) makes the islands semi-arid. The dry season is warm but rarely too hot, tempered by gentle sea breezes and some overnight rains. Average air temp is 30°C (86°F) and the water remains ideal at around 27°C (80°F). Nov-April is rainier and cloudier, with Jan-Feb suffering from heavy rains and can be considered a time to avoid. Cyclones are rare in Indonesia but this area of Nusa Tenggara seems to be more prone to receiving them.

**Nature and Culture** – Nemberala's reef supports varied marine life – go snorkelling. Check out the Ikats (woven textiles), Rote's unique palm hats and dance to the sound of the Sasando, the 20 stringed local guitars made of palm leaves. Animist rituals still take place on Savu.

**Hazards and Hassles** – T-Land is a mellow wave, until it gets big. Most other spots break harder and closer to the reef. A boat trip in this area guaranties less crowds. Chloroquine resistant malaria has been reported, ask your doctor about prevention pills. East Timor's independence in May 2002 has helped to decrease tensions in the area.

**Handy Hints** – Pick up any surf accessories in Bali. Bring your shortboard, a semi-gun for the hollow reefbreaks and an Indo gun if you want to charge huge T-Land. Learning a little Indonesian will help you get around an area of many obscure dialects. Respect local beliefs in Savu, no matter how strange!

| WEATHER STATISTICS | J/F | M/A | M/J | J/A | S/O | N/D |
|---|---|---|---|---|---|---|
| total rainfall (mm) | 340 | 140 | 20 | 5 | 10 | 150 |
| consistency (days/mth) | 8 | 5 | 1 | 0 | 1 | 13 |
| min temp (°C/°F) | 24/75 | 24/75 | 24/75 | 23/74 | 24/75 | 25/77 |
| max temp (°C/°F) | 28/82 | 30/86 | 31/88 | 30/86 | 32/90 | 31/88 |

century. Its long, barrelling left pointbreak and attendant right pick up all available swell and the only locals are turtles. Closer to Savu, Raijua's **Wedge** is a classic left on the island's SW tip. Midway between Rote and Sumba, Savu is definitely off the beaten path and local people haven't been exposed to much Western culture. On a very large swell **Savu Right**, reputedly the best right in the region, will be a perfect 4-6ft (1.3-2m) barrel.

**Savu Left**, on the eastern end of the same dead coral reef holds 'Sunset like' heavy walls with hollow sections. Lying just off the southwestern tip of Timor, Rote is the southernmost island in Indonesia. Some surf spots are located on offshore islands and require chartering a boat. **Ndao** is only 10km (6mi) away, but the people are very different and have their own language. The waves are fast and steep but are known to be fickle and plagued by cross-currents. In the land of lefts, a long right like **Do'o** is welcomed, but facing almost north, it mainly works before or after the standard surf season. Baa is the main city on Rote, but Nemberala Beach, with its reefbreak and white sandy beach, is the place to be for surfers and tourists alike. The local spot, **T-Land**, is a consistent left with three sections that can connect for a 200m (600ft) long ride. The name may sound like G-Land, but this is a much more accessible wave, slower and not so hollow, encouraging cutbacks. This fun wave handles up to 15ft (5m)! If the swell is breaking up, a 30min bike ride will take you to the reefs of **Peanuts** and **Boa**. Breaking on shallow reef, these spots are hollower

and faster than T-Land. **Ndana** has year round flexibility, because the left and right face each other, so one is always offshore. Needs decent swell size and a 20m (60ft) channel is the only access point on the western side of the island.

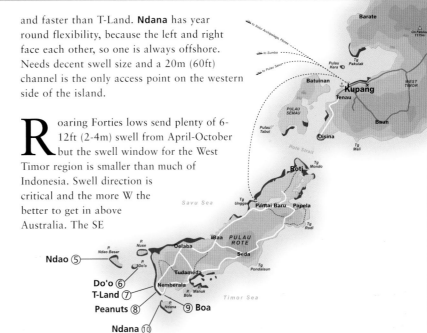

Roaring Forties lows send plenty of 6-12ft (2-4m) swell from April-October but the swell window for the West Timor region is smaller than much of Indonesia. Swell direction is critical and the more W the better to get in above Australia. The SE trade winds start in April, E-SE being the major direction through August, then shifting to more S winds until October, which is still offshore for the west-facing coastline, but other spots should be surfed before 10am. The off season sees more SW-NW winds which benefit the rare east-facing locations. This, combined with inconsistent swell, makes for a less obvious surf season reserved for explorers looking for a rare, hidden gem. Early season should be the best time for a boat trip, before the trades strengthen, making navigation and anchorage more difficult. There is a big tide and a small tide every day and some spots only work on certain stages, but charts are hard to find.

Pulau Rote

| SPOT DESCRIPTION | | | |
|---|---|---|---|
| Spot | Size | Btm | Type |
| ① | • | | |
| ② | • | | |
| ③ | • | | |
| ④ | • | | |
| ⑤ | • | | |
| ⑥ | • | | |
| ⑦ | 15/2 | | |
| ⑧ | • | | |
| ⑨ | • | | |
| ⑩ | • | | |

| SURF STATISTICS | J F | M A M | J J | A S | O N | D |
|---|---|---|---|---|---|---|
| dominant swell | SW-W | SW-W | SW-W | SW-W | SW | SW-W |
| swell size (ft) | 3 | 4 | 5 | 5-6 | 4-5 | 3 |
| consistency (%) | 50 | 70 | 75 | 80 | 75 | 60 |
| dominant wind | SW-NW | E-SE | E-SE | E-SE | E-SW | S-W |
| average force | F3-F4 | F3 | F3-F4 | F3-F4 | F3 | F2-F3 |
| consistency (%) | 72 | 41 | 74 | 73 | 79 | 56 |
| water temp (°C/°F) | 29/84 | 29/84 | 27/80 | 26/79 | 27/80 | 29/84 |
| wetsuit | | | | | | |

PAPAU NEW GUINEA

New Ireland
INDONESIA
New England
AUSTRALIA

# 107. Sandaun and East Sepik

## Summary

+ CONSISTENT MONSOON SWELL
+ FUN SIZED UNCROWDED WAVES
+ LOW TOURIST NUMBERS
+ CHEAP SURF CAMP OPTION

− NO OUTSTANDING BREAKS
− TRICKY ACCESS AND TRANSPORT
− HOT AND STICKY WEATHER
− STREET CRIME AND DISEASES

ALL PHOTOS MICHAEL KEW

Vanimo

COURTESY AIR NIUGINI

Papua New Guinea is known as 'the land of the unexpected' with its enormous diversity of cultures, peoples and landscapes. It is one of only three tropical areas in the world that also supports a glacier, high up on Mount Jaya's 16,404ft (5,000m) peak. PNG is 2,400km (1,500mi) long and 720km (450mi) wide and is exposed to three seas. Port Moresby is the mainland capital city, facing the Coral Sea, which produces erratic surf, and the town of Hula is the most consistent area. The Solomon Sea is similarly unreliable, leaving the Bismarck Sea (backed by the Pacific Ocean) as the major swell producer. This NW-N swell affects many different provinces including Madang and the Bismarck Archipelago, home to Kavieng, PNG's best known surf area. Sandaun (the

tok pisin word for sundown) was formerly West Sepik Province, an undeveloped region bordering Irian Jaya, with 260km (163mi) of mostly grey sand coastline. Expats based in Vanimo working in the logging industry soon discovered good surf on this mountainous coast during the NW monsoon season.

## TRAVEL INFORMATION

**Population:**
165,000 Sandaun
**Coastline:** 260km (162mi)
**Contests:** Local
**Other Resources:**
surftheearth.com.au/
pngtourism.org.pg
niugini.com
surfingpapuanewguinea.
org.pg

**Getting There** – A 60-day visa is available on arrival in Port Moresby for $4.50, or only $2.50 prior to arrival. Fly to Port Moresby (POM) with Qantas or Air Niugini, then Air Niugini or Airlink to Wewak (WWK)-Vanimo (VAI). Daily flights via Madang - Wewak. POM-VAI: $95 o/w. Air Niugini flies a fleet of Fokker 28; boards over 8ft could be a problem. $7.50 dep. tax.

**Getting Around** – Transport is very limited because of poor roads. Most travel is by PMV (Passenger Motor Vehicle): a bus, a truck or even a motorboat. Buses are cheap but dirty and crowded. Hertz car rental for a Toyota Corolla is $67/day. Local boats can be hired cheaply. *Katani2*, a 58ft (18m) sailing catamaran can be chartered with PNG expert Surf the Earth (STE).

**Lodging and Food** – For A/C rooms, stay in Vanimo at the Resort Hotel ($12/dble) by the beach, or the Sandaun Motel ($25/dble). Lido Village guesthouse next to the surf ($7.50). Dirt-cheap accommodation in Aitape. Try the noisy Windjammer Hotel in Wewak. An average meal is $5. STE Brisbane package: air + 4 nights + surf transfers from $525. Add $35 from Sydney, extra nights are $60, all meals $35 per day, upgrade to deluxe room $20 per night. Katani 2 boat trip: $120/d from Madang.

**Weather** – Like the rest of PNG, Sandaun has a hot wet climate all year round. However, rainfall is less than most South Pacific islands. With 2.7m (9ft) of annual rainfall, Vanimo is the wettest part of Sepik Provinces, getting drier between May to November with the SE trades, corresponding to the flat season. Bear in mind that rains here mean reduced visibility, 100% humidity, frenzied insects and washed out roads. On the other hand, Wewak with half a metre less rainfall/year is blessed by relatively dry weather during the surf season from Dec to March, experiencing its highest

rainfall when SE trades bring tropical downpours. Water remains super warm year round, requiring a rashie as the sun is fierce.

**Nature and Culture** – Vanimo is a pretty little seaside town with a free trade zone. Take a trip to Narimo Island and over the Irian Jaya border to the bustling city of Jayapura. Wewak is way busier but don't expect nightlife or shopping. Visit the Japanese war memorial, WWII bomb craters, one of the five markets to buy sacred masks and carvings or play golf.

**Hazards and Hassles** – Street crime stories are plentiful but PNG is big and Sepik is safe. Steer clear of pickpockets and scammers. Everyone suffers a few nicks and scratches from the reef, so to prevent skin wounds from becoming infected, apply an antibiotic cream immediately. Transport and hygiene are hassley.

**Handy Hints** – There are surfboards for rent at Lido Village but a favourite board is unlikely to snap in these conditions. Vanimo Surf Club, the oldest in PNG, was established in 1987.

| WEATHER STATISTICS | J/F | M/A | M/J | J/A | S/O | N/D |
|---|---|---|---|---|---|---|
| total rainfall (mm) | 130 | 170 | 210 | 170 | 210 | 160 |
| consistency (days/mth) | 8 | 8 | 4 | 2 | 6 | 11 |
| min temp (°C/°F) | 23/74 | 23/74 | 23/74 | 22/72 | 23/74 | 23/74 |
| max temp (°C/°F) | 29/84 | 30/86 | 30/86 | 30/86 | 30/86 | 30/86 |

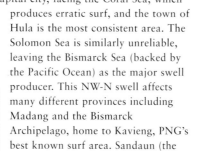

A 10min drive west of Vanimo lie the classic pointbreaks off Lido Village. **Lido's Right** can get really hollow and are often surfed between 3-8ft (1-2.5m). **Lido's Left** is one of PNG's most consistent waves and can be surfed every afternoon even when the NW wind picks up. In Vanimo, the province's only natural harbour, there is **Logs**, a right near the jetty or **Jailbreak** a left, unsurprisingly, in front of the jail. The coastal plain widens to the east and swamps occur inland from **Sissano Lagoon**, where sandbanks are rumoured to form off the rivermouth and offer up a few waves. It was off this stretch of coast that the epicentre of a 7.1 on the Richter Scale earthquake hit in 1998. The accompanying 33ft (10m) tsunami trashed this area, leaving 700 people dead and thousands homeless. **Aitape** is Saudaun's largest settlement with 25,000 people and a major catholic mission station. Off the point protecting the town's harbour, a superb left spins for 75m (225ft) over a reef, working better on a medium to low tide and so far, the only crowd to deal with is one Aussie local. Aitape is connected by a rough coastal road to the large East Sepik Province. Sacred masks, carvings and pottery from East Sepik are in museums around the world, while Robusta coffee and cocoa are other cash earners. The Sepik River is the heart of the province, but regular flooding limits the use of nearby flat land. Offshore islands including **Tarawai** and Muschu can create a swell shadow, but are rumoured to have boat only surf spots along their coasts, like **Cape Barabar**. Back on land, follow the **Karawop** Plantation signs, which lead to fun wrapping lefts, breaking on boulders. Once in Wewak (pop. 63,000) some swell consistency and size might be lost but access and services help make it an enjoyable experience. **Wewak Point** is a reliable lefthand reefbreak, easy to check from town, tubular at low tide whilst at high tide, the harbour channel produces a soft left. **The Wharf**, aka Mission Point, is difficult to get to because the shallow outside reefs breaking 1km (0.6mi) from shore face the private

property of the Sepik International Hotel. Travelling east, take Moem Barracks turn-off and check **Moem Point**, a mellow right reefbreak. If flat, drive further to **Forok Point**, a very consistent, all tides, right pointbreak with the occasional left, considered the best wave in East Sepik. Also called Dabiar Beach, the 7km (4.5mi) of dirt access road is prone to flooding.

Despite being located in a western Pacific corner where most groundswells travel eastwards, the Sepik Provinces enjoy relative consistency from NW monsoon winds, producing regular 3-6ft (1-2m) windswell waves with rare 8-10ft (2.5-3m) from November to April. These mellow waves are better suited to longboarders and lighter shortboarders. El Niño years are very inconsistent and worth avoiding, even though rainfall is lower. Offshore islands in East Sepik definitely create some swell shadow, so Sandaun, especially around Vanimo is the most consistent area. The most exposed reefs need to be surfed in the morning, as they are blown out by W-NW seabreezes. Nearby mountains like the Ocenake Range behind Vanimo, funnel morning offshores before the moderate NW breeze picks up. November is the least windy month while the dry season features SE winds and months of long flat spells. Tides are an issue and the Flinders University release data for Lombrum on Manus Islands, quite a distance offshore. Maximum tidal range is 2ft (0.6m) with unusual tide cycles combining diurnal and semi-diurnal phases.

| SPOT DESCRIPTION | | | |
|---|---|---|---|
| Spot | Size | Btm | Type |
| ① | • | | |
| ② | • | | |
| ③ | • | | |
| ④ | • | | |
| ⑤ | • | | |
| ⑥ | 5/2 | | |
| ⑦ | • | | |
| ⑧ | 8/2 | | |
| ⑨ | • | | |
| ⑩ | 8/2 | | |
| ⑪ | 5/2 | | |
| ⑫ | 8/2 | | |
| ⑬ | 12/2 | | |

| SURF STATISTICS | J F | M A | M J | J A | S O | N D |
|---|---|---|---|---|---|---|
| dominant swell | N-NW | N-NW | N-NW | N-NW | N-NW | N-NW |
| swell size (ft) | 3-4 | 3 | 0-1 | 0-1 | 0-1 | 3 |
| consistency (%) | 80 | 60 | 10 | 5 | 10 | 50 |
| dominant wind | W-NW | W-NW | E-SE | E-SE | E-SE | W-NW |
| average force | F3-F4 | F3 | F2-F3 | F3 | F2-F3 | F3 |
| consistency (%) | 61 | 48 | 42 | 50 | 48 | 49 |
| water temp (°C/°F) | 28/82 | 28/82 | 29/84 | 28/82 | 28/82 | 28/82 |
| wetsuit | | | | | | |

Map legend:
- ① Lido's Right
- ② Lido's Left
- ③ Logs
- ④ Jailbreak
- ⑤ Sissano Lagoon
- ⑥ Aitape
- ⑦ Tarawai
- ⑧ Karawop
- ⑨ Cape Barabar
- ⑩ Wewak Point
- ⑪ The Wharf
- ⑫ Moem Point
- ⑬ Forok Point

Map labels: Utung, Musu, Yako, Waromo, Vanimo, Waterstone, Ningera, Bapa, Rawo, Leitre, Puari, OCENAKE RANGE, Mt Asowa 2200m, Kilipau, Bewani, Imonda, Amanab, PAPUA NEW GUINEA, SANDAUN PROVINCE, Lumi, Yankok, Dreikikir, Balit, Nuku, Maprik, Yangoru, Sassuia, Passam, EAST SEPIK PROVINCE, Bismarck Sea, EARTHQUAKE July 17th 1998, Onei, Serai, Prittwitz Pt., Baudissan Pt., Sissano, Arop, Yalingi, Aitape, Drome, Waui, Lemieng, Paup, Tameio Isl., Ali Isl., Seleo Isl., EARTHQUAKE September 8th 2002, Ulau1, Babiang, Suain2, Abau, Cape Djeruen, Balam, But, Dagua, Mt Sapau 4698m, PRINCE ALEXANDER MTNS, Mt Baum 4111m, Mt Wesagumini 3646m, Walis Isl., Tarawai Isl., Kairiru Isl., Yuo Isl., Muschu Isl., Cape Pus, Cape Worn, Wewak

# 108. Eastern Samar

PHILIPPINES

INDONESIA

## Summary

+ TYPHOONS AND WINDSWELLS
+ UNDISCOVERED QUALITY BREAKS
+ WARM AND TROPICAL
+ CHEAP AND LIVELY

− ERRATIC TYPHOON SWELLS
− MESSY WINDSWELLS
− HEAVY RAINS
− NO TOURIST INFRASTRUCTURE
− TIME CONSUMING TRAVEL

Philippine Dream

ALL PHOTOS JOHN CALLAHAN

Out of the 7,107 islands of the Philippines, Samar is the 3rd largest volcanic island. It was once the largest province in the Visayas until it was divided into three provinces: Western, Eastern and Northern Samar. Amongst these provinces of Region VIII, Northern and Eastern Samar boasts some undiscovered surf potential. Eastern Samar itself is 150km (94mi) long and only 40km (25mi) wide. The province has a rough and hilly terrain covered by lush tropical vegetation, with some 200-300m (600-900ft) mountains and a few narrow strips of lowland. Borongan, the provincial capital with 50,000 people, lies some 550km (360mi) east of Manila and 65km (40mi) north-west of Tacloban City, the capital of Eastern Visayas. Predominantly a pristine area, as a local Borogan surfer said during the Eastern Samar Inaugural Surfing Crown in September 2000, "we haven't even explored 30% of Samar waves". Photographer John Callahan has led many boat expeditions from Siargao and made discoveries like the "Philippine Dream."

## TRAVEL INFORMATION

**Population:** 59,000
**Coastline:** 800km (500mi)
**Contests:** Local
**Other Resources:**
surf.com.ph
typhoon2000.com
flyphilippines.net
wowphilippines.com.ph

**Getting There** – Visas: none for less than 21 days, $35 valid for 3 months. Plenty of charter flights from Asian cities, Australia, Europe and USA. There is a 24h bus trip from Manila all the way to Borongan. Or fly from Manila to Tacloban City, then by road from Tacloban City, Leyte to Borongan (4h). Tacloban City is on the island of Leyte. Dep tax: $20

**Getting Around** – Domestic flights (PAL) are cheap. Local transport includes jeepneys (rebuilt jeeps), metered taxis, sidecar motorbikes, PU-cabs (small taxis, no meters) and trishaws. Favour local town rental cars for day trips. From Leyte to Samar, you cross the picturesque San Juanico Bridge, the longest in Southeast Asia. The King of Sport 3 provides boat access.

**Lodging and Food** – In Borongan, try Pension Alang-Alang, in front of Provincial Capital building ($4-8/d), or Domsowir Hotel in the same range. In Guiuan, try the Tanghay Lodge ($3-14/d), on the W-facing beach (flat). Expect to pay $3 for a decent meal.

**Weather** – Samar's climate provides heavy rainfall year round, with all months having a minimum of 160mm. Despite this tropical wet climate, it has two distinct seasons: rainy from Nov-Feb with NE monsoon providing the prevailing wind and 'dry' from July- Sept when the westerly winds locally called 'Habagat' become dominant. Average yearly rainfall: 10ft (3m). Number of rainy days: 192. Mean temp is a balmy 27°C (80°F). Different weather in Northern Samar due to the San Bernardino Strait, means rainy season here is from Dec-Feb with a long dry season from Mar-Nov. The province is often visited by typhoons; the last one that hit land was in Dec '95. It's very humid throughout the year. Maximum rainfall is from November to March. Occasional dry spells occur in May and June. Water temps don't get super warm, bring a light shorty and booties.

**Nature and Culture** – Samar has the 2nd largest virgin forest in the Philippines. 40mins by boat are secluded waterfalls, caves and jungle treks. Try 'river tubing' which involves lazily drifting down river and enjoying cool waters and the tropical scenes of the riverbanks. Local sailboats are called 'siling'. Borongan Fiesta in September. Cross Sohoton Natural Bridge!

**Hazards and Hassles** – Be ready to face buckets of rain especially in the NE monsoon season. There is low risk of malaria in Northern Samar, but Eastern Samar should be fine, look for updates! Take chloroquine plus proguanil in case. A Yellow Fever certificate is required if arriving from infected areas. Coral reefbreaks can be very shallow.

**Handy Hints** – There is allegedly a Green Earth Shop and Surfing Cafe in Borongan but don't count on it. Take two all-round boards especially if staying for a while; the locals should be stoked to buy old gear upon departure. Carlos Aga and Rodel Aboy are the best locals in Borongan. English is widely spoken.

| WEATHER STATISTICS | J/F | M/A | M/J | J/A | S/O | N/D |
|---|---|---|---|---|---|---|
| total rainfall (mm) | 550 | 290 | 240 | 160 | 260 | 590 |
| consistency (days/mth) | 20 | 12 | 10 | 8 | 12 | 20 |
| min temp (°C/°F) | 22/72 | 23/74 | 23/74 | 23/74 | 23/74 | 22/72 |
| max temp (°C/°F) | 28/82 | 30/86 | 32/90 | 32/90 | 31/88 | 30/86 |

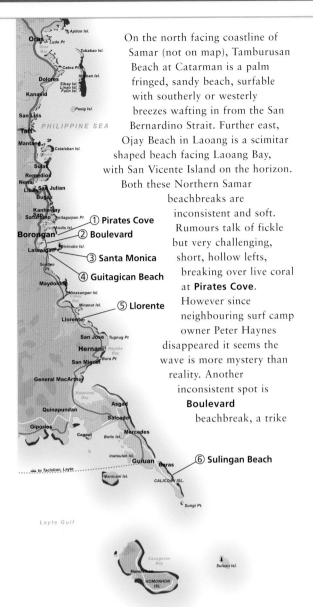

On the north facing coastline of Samar (not on map), Tamburusan Beach at Catarman is a palm fringed, sandy beach, surfable with southerly or westerly breezes wafting in from the San Bernardino Strait. Further east, Ojay Beach in Laoang is a scimitar shaped beach facing Laoang Bay, with San Vicente Island on the horizon. Both these Northern Samar beachbreaks are inconsistent and soft. Rumours talk of fickle but very challenging, short, hollow lefts, breaking over live coral at **Pirates Cove**. However since neighbouring surf camp owner Peter Haynes disappeared it seems the wave is more mystery than reality. Another inconsistent spot is **Boulevard** beachbreak, a trike

- ① Pirates Cove
- ② Boulevard
- ③ Santa Monica
- ④ Guitagican Beach
- ⑤ Llorente
- ⑥ Sulingan Beach

**Jurassic Point**

2 hours travel on good asphalt roads, followed by 45 minutes of dodgy road. Guiuan is a fishing town situated on a long, low, narrow coralline peninsula jutting out of Samar. Guiuan was once the biggest US Military base in the Philippines. The road to **Sulingan Beach** is 15 minutes by jeep from Guiuan, along a 3km (2mi) military runway. The sand of Sulingan is very white and coralline. There is no habitation, just coconut trees on a low hill overlooking the beach. At both ends of the 2km (1.3mi) beach, the land protrudes a bit, allowing the best waves to break. Beginners favour the centre part of the beach, sometimes referred to as ABC. There is a left and a right break on both sides of a narrow channel. The wave works well up to 5ft (1.6m), but closes out after that. Incoming tides bring better waves. The reef bottom of Sulingan has a gradual slope, devoid of the crevices of Siargao's Cloud 9, but the live coral is covered with sea urchins. Paddling out is fairly easy, though at low tide, expect a fair walk over coral in booties.

| SPOT DESCRIPTION | | | |
|---|---|---|---|
| Spot | Size | Btm | Type |
| ① | • | 🌀 | ⊖ |
| ② | • | ∿ | ⊖ |
| ③ | • | 🌀 | ⊖ |
| ④ | • | ∿ | ⊖ |
| ⑤ | • | 🌀 | ⊖ |
| ⑥ | • | 🌀 | ⊖ |

Surfing in Samar presents a choice between the rainy season with dominant offshores and erratic typhoon swells or else a very rainy season with dominant onshores and consistent windswell. Usually, travellers aim for a lucky break between August-October hoping for the perfect ideal typhoon swell but many have been badly skunked, even on a month long trip. If it's possible to stay for a month, choose November as the E-NE typhoon season switches to the NE monsoon season lasting up to February, sometimes March. Those onshores will bring a constant supply of 2-4ft (0.6-1.2m) waves with occasional clean conditions. Winds are then offshore S-W during the typhoon season also referred as the SW monsoon. Then, winds shift NE but rarely reach gale force. As far as tides go, they have a diurnal inequality so expect different tidal ranges during the day; they reach 3ft (1m) on spring tides, which is significant enough on shallow reefs.

ride north of town, near the discos. It only works with a big swell due to the protection of the cove. Close to Borongan are the **Santa Monica** Caves, with splendid views catering for fishermen, scuba divers and surfers. **Guitagican Beach**, in Barangay, Santa Maria, is a 2km (1.3mi) long beautiful white beach with occasional rideable waves. Further south, 1h from Borongan, is **Llorente**, where good waves have been seen, surfed and photographed. Guiuan, 118km (73mi) from Borongan is

**Philippine Dream**

| SURF STATISTICS | J F | M A | M J | J A | S O | N D |
|---|---|---|---|---|---|---|
| dominant swell | N-NE | N-NE | E-NE | E-NE | E-NE | N-NE |
| swell size (ft) | 3-4 | 2 | 0-1 | 1-2 | 3 | 4 |
| consistency (%) | 60 | 30 | 10 | 20 | 40 | 70 |
| dominant wind | NE-E | NE-E | E-S | S-W | S-W | NE-E |
| average force | F4 | F4 | F3 | F3-F4 | F4 | F4 |
| consistency (%) | 85 | 80 | 67 | 59 | 43 | 65 |
| water temp (°C/°F) | 23/74 | 23/74 | 24/75 | 25/77 | 24/75 | 23/74 |
| wetsuit | 🧍 | 🧍 | 🧍 | 🧍 | 🧍 | 🧍 |

PHILIPPINES

INDONESIA

# 109. North West Luzon

Car-rile Point

JOHN CALLAHAN

## Summary
+ CONSISTENT **NE** MONSOON SWELL
+ OCCASIONAL **SW** TYPHOON SWELL
+ MANY UNCROWDED BREAKS
+ CHEAP LIVING COSTS

− SMALL SIZE WAVES
− SOME MANILA CROWDS
− NATURAL AND SOCIAL DISASTERS
− SEX TOURISM

I t's commonly thought that surfing in the Philippines started in 1976 after Francis-Ford Coppola shot *Apocalypse Now* in Baler, Aurora province and left a couple of boards behind for the local Pinoys. However, it's more likely that US airmen started surfing Mona Liza Point in La Union in the early '70s. Relying mainly on NE monsoon wind-driven waves, the focus of east coast surfing in the South China Sea has shifted further north around a trendy surf resort called Badoc Island. Badoc is a true surf paradise with four quality uncrowded reefbreaks nearby and a reliable beachbreak. Being an exclusive private property, it might not appeal to those who believe in public access to the beach.

Mona Liza Point

JOHN CALLAHAN

Carabou

JOHN CALLAHAN

The island breaks are exclusive but anyone can surf the mainland breaks. Jetskis or outrigger boats can be hired to ease access. Since the resort can only accommodate 12 guests and there is only one local surfer, line-up hassles are unlikely. It's a 10min paddle

## TRAVEL INFORMATION

**Population:**
650,000 La Union
**Coastline:**
3,250km (2,030mi)
**Contests:** La Union
Longboard Open (Jan)
**Other Resources:**
surf.ph
typhoon2000.com
flyphilippines.net
wowphilippines.com.ph

**Getting There** – Visas: None for less than 21 days, $35 valid for 3 months. Plenty of charter flights from Asian cities, Australia, Europe and USA. Manila-La Union is 6-8h by bus. Take the Swagman Hotel bus if arriving late and spend the night in Angeles. By bus (Partas Bus in Cubao) San Juan-7h; Badoc-10h. Flights to Laoag: $38o/w. Dep tax is $20.

**Getting Around** – Domestic flights (PAL) are cheap but crash records are heavy. Nat'l Highway is busy but fairly good and very coastal. Local town rentals ($160/week in San Juan) beat Manila airport rates. Local transport includes 'jeepneys' (re-built jeeps), metered taxis, sidecars motorbikes, PU-Cabs (small taxis, no meters) and trishaws.

**Lodging and Food** – Stay (±$10/dble) in Urbutzondo, San Juan: La Union Surf Resort,

Mona Liza Cottages, S-E Bay Resort or Blue Heaven. For better standards, go to San Fernando or book Badoc Resort: $65/day, exclusive access, 2 jetskis + outrigger, airport pick up. Contact Surf The Earth. Filipino cuisine has Chinese, Malay and Spanish influences.

**Weather** – The Philippines has a tropical climate with gentle winds but abundant rainfall. Expect three pronounced seasons: the extremely wet season June-October, the dry season November-February and the hot/dry season from March to May. Being on Luzon's west side, La Union is perfectly clear, warm and dry November-April and wet from May to October. The SW monsoon brings stupid amounts of rains but no surf. The dry season is caused by the NE monsoon passing over the Cordillera Mountains. Annual rainfall is 2,067mm (72in) compared to twice that in the mountains. Average temp is 27°C (82°F): avoid March-June for excessive heat. Situated amid pine-covered hills, with its cool climate, Baguio is the Philippines 'summer capital'. The Philippines are visited every year by 20 or so typhoons known as 'Baguiosi' during the SW monsoon season and Luzon is top of the list. Boardshorts only.

**Nature and Culture** – Don't miss Vigan - oldest surviving Spanish colonial city, Hundred Islands National Park, the epic journey from Baguio to Banaue across Central Cordillera. Avoid Poro Point sex tourist traps. High Altitude in San Fernando is a cool disco. Many Karaoke bars!

**Hazards and Hassles** – It's a land of natural disasters! Typhoons pass periodically; nearly half of the Philippine's 25 major earthquake faults are in Luzon (the Pinatubo eruption in June 1991 killed 900 people and left 1 million homeless). Beware flash floods and transport failures. Some coral reefs can be treacherous and there's some foul smelling kelp! Minimal localism.

**Handy Hints** – For beginners, it is possible to rent boards from San Juan Resorts or get stuff in Yokohama surf shop in Metro Manila. Yokohama is also a well-organised surf school in La Union. A gun won't be necessary but a wide board for slow waves in La Union will be. San Fernando population is 90,000. English is widely spoken.

| WEATHER STATISTICS | J/F | M/A | M/J | J/A | S/O | N/D |
|---|---|---|---|---|---|---|
| total rainfall (mm) | 10 | 45 | 270 | 450 | 250 | 45 |
| consistency (days/mth) | 1 | 3 | 12 | 11 | 8 | 1 |
| min temp (°C/°F) | 22/72 | 24/75 | 26/79 | 25/77 | 25/77 | 23/74 |
| max temp (°C/°F) | 30/86 | 33/92 | 32/90 | 31/88 | 31/88 | 30/86 |

Turtle Head

Star Tubes

working on most swells, opposite the German Sunset Beach resort, home of the Baguio surf club, which rents boards for $1/hour. **Urbitzondo** holds long lefts over sand and is the site of the La Union Longboard Open. NW Luzon's Malibu-esque break, **Mona Liza Point** faces the resort of the same name. The Point favours rights but anything will break gently over dead coral both ways until maxing out at above 6ft (2m). The Point gets busy at times but longboard rules are the go so be prepared to share. When there is a 6ft (2m) SW typhoon swell, the fabled spot is **Car-rille**, a 1km (0.6mi) long right point, with some comparisons to Rincon. Now, the US soldiers are gone and the Filipino army runs the army base, access to **Poro Point** might be banned. It's inconsistent, but there are some good rights to be had over the rocky shoreline. If venturing to **Bauang**, near the cemetery and an abandoned beach resort, there's some consistent beachbreak.

across the bay to **Star Tubes** where fast, walling rights fold over a very shallow bottom covered by thick seaweed. **Badoc Point**, right in front of the grass-roofed main house breaks very close but is rare. It can be intense on a typhoon swell and the beachbreak can also get pretty good. It is vital to get the resort jetski out to **Badoc Island Lefts**; the most consistent wave with some nice pockets to get covered or throw some moves. Next is **Turtle Head**, marked by a spectacular rock that shelters this twisting, short right with its gaping tube section. There are more virgin spots up north like Bangui or Bacarra, but south at Pinget Island, which is actually a peninsula, there's good potential for both SW and NE swells. **Puro Pinget** is the best spot in this area with its mix of beach and reefbreaks. In Vigan, there is a small and friendly surfing community, patient enough to wait for the right swells. Head for **Manangat** and stay in the Don Juan Resort facing the beach. Since Manangat faces south, it's better suited for summer waves and rides can be very long! North of Santa, lefts break off a huge seawall at **Parada Santa**, making the most of weak SW swells. **Nalvo**, near Santa Maria has reef and beachbreak with options for most surfers. South of Darigayos Point is the occasionally crowded, winter surf region of San Juan. Waves are mellow and easy unlike the shallow reefbreaks dotting most of this coast. There are about 15 identified spots on a 40km (25mi) stretch of brownish sand down to San Fernando. **Darigayos** itself catches both SW and NE swells, so if it's flat there, it's flat everywhere. **German Sunset Break** is a beachbreak

| SURF STATISTICS | J F | M A | M J | J A | S O | N D |
|---|---|---|---|---|---|---|
| dominant swell | N-NE | N-NE | S-SW | S-SW | SW-NE | N-NE |
| swell size (ft) | 2-3 | 1 | 0-1 | 2-3 | 3-4 | 3 |
| consistency (%) | 70 | 20 | 10 | 50 | 70 | 80 |
| dominant wind | N-E | NE-SE | SE-SW | S-SW | NE-E | N-E |
| average force | F4-F5 | F4 | F3-F4 | F4 | F4-F5 | F4-F5 |
| consistency (%) | 73 | 66 | 54 | 44 | 50 | 85 |
| water temp (°C/°F) | 24/75 | 26/79 | 26/79 | 27/80 | 26/79 | 25/77 |
| wetsuit | | | | | | |

Despite sources of swell in the South China Sea being weak, there are two windswell seasons plus an option for powerful typhoons. The main season goes from October to March, November to February being the most reliable months. NE monsoon driven waves break in the 1-5ft (0.3-1.5m) range, with constant offshore winds favouring rights. The near constant wind during that period almost guarantees daily surf, however the smallest days will only be safe on sand or flat bottoms. Spring is the worst season with mostly flat days. A gentle SW monsoon starts pushing occasional swells and tropical storms and typhoons hit Luzon from July to November. Resulting 6-8ft+ (2-2.5m+) conditions will also bring torrential rains and wreak havoc if they hit the coast. SW winds will mostly bring onshores, favouring lefts. However, if waves are generated in close proximity, local winds are pretty weak courtesy of the Cordillera Mountains. Wind patterns might be a bit stronger in Ilocos Norte than La Union. As for tides, don't worry! Barometric tides will be more significant than astronomic ones.

Badoc Island Lefts

SPOT DESCRIPTION

| Spot | Size | Btm | Type |
|---|---|---|---|
| ① | 8/3 | | |
| ② | 8/2 | | |
| ③ | 10/3 | | |
| ④ | 10/4 | | |
| ⑤ | 6/1 | | |
| ⑥ | 6/1 | | |
| ⑦ | 4/1 | | |
| ⑧ | 8/2 | | |
| ⑨ | 8/2 | | |
| ⑩ | 6/1 | | |
| ⑪ | 6/1 | | |
| ⑫ | 6/2 | | |
| ⑬ | 6/2 | | |
| ⑭ | 6/1 | | |
| ⑮ | 6/1 | | |

Star Tubes ①
Badoc Point ②
Badoc Island Lefts ③
Turtle Head ④
Puro Pinget ⑤
Manangat ⑥
Parada Santa ⑦
Nalvo ⑧
Darigayos ⑨
German Sunset Break ⑩
Urbitzondo ⑪
Mona Liza Point ⑫
Car-rille ⑬
Poro Point ⑭
Bauang ⑮

# 110. Da Nang

**Summary**
+ RELIABLE SEASONAL WINDSWELL
+ SOFT, EMPTY BEACHBREAKS
+ DISCOVERY POTENTIAL
+ EXOTIC, WARM AND FRIENDLY
+ CULTURAL SMORGASBORD

– SMALL DISORGANISED WAVES
– NO KNOWN REEFBREAKS
– SHORT SURF SEASON
– EXPENSIVE VISA AND FLIGHTS
– HEAVY RAIN AND HUMIDITY

Non Nuoc Beach

JOHN CALLAHAN

Thung Chai Boats

JOHN CALLAHAN

TUNGSTEN

Anyone who's seen the movie *Apocalypse Now*, will already know that there is surf in Vietnam. Although the surfing scenes were shot in the Philippines, the reality is that US soldiers have probably surfed China Beach since the '60s. Da Nang was the home to 20% of all US servicemen based in Vietnam; it was an R&R destination for American soldiers during the war and it eventually fell to the North Vietnamese in 1975 with hardly a bullet fired. US soldiers were definitely surfing Da Nang beaches on Sept 13th, 1970 when Private Wyatt Miller drowned while boardriding, which was probably the consequence of typhoon waves. Then China Beach hosted Vietnam's first (and last) International Surfing Competition in 1992. While competitors from all over the world were competing, kids were taught to surf and 15 boards were left behind to create the Da Nang surf club. When the *Endless Summer* film crew visited Da Nang in July 2002, the club was still there but there were only 6 boards among 20 members. Now, nothing is left and it would be easy to blame poverty and board availability, but the main problem is

## TRAVEL INFORMATION

**Population:**
700,000 Da Nang
**Coastline:**
120km (75mi) QN
**Contests:** None
**Other Resources:**
windsurf-vietnam.com
vietnamtourism.com
vnn.vn/province/
  quangnam/tourism.html

**Getting There** – Visa: 30d/1 entry ($65) and 3-month multi-entry ($150). Don't do it last minute! Ho Chi Minh (Saigon) is the main int'l airport but Hanoi can be fine. 12 flights weekly from Hanoi to Da Nang with Vietnam Air ($70 o/w). Fly direct to Da Nang from Bangkok, HK, Manila or Kuala Lumpur. Dep tax is $14

**Getting Around** – Da Nang is 108km (68mi) from Hue, 759km (474mi) from Hanoi, and 965km (603mi) from Ho Chi Minh. The 'express train' from Ho Chi Minh to Da Nang takes 24 hours. Buses travel slowly at 50kph (30mph). Vietnamese law does not allow foreigners to drive cars. Rent a minivan with driver for a group or a 110-125cc motorbike from street vendors ($8-$10/day).

**Lodging and Food** – Eliminating the Soviet dormitory-style lodging at Non Nuoc leaves exactly two options: My Khe, a funky little budget place (from $10) and the 5-star Furama Resort (from $150). Food is varied and very cheap ($3 /meal). Best soups (pho) in the world.

**Weather** – The country is located in both a tropical and a temperate zone but Da Nang climate, south of Hai Van path, is rather tropical, characterised by strong monsoon influences with two distinct rainy and dry seasons. There is a massive amount of sun, a high rate of rainfall and high humidity. The second half of the year is way more rainy. The most noticeable variations are found in the Northern provinces where differences of 12°C (54°F) between summer and winter have been observed. The average annual temp in Da Nang is 25°C (77°F), cooler during the swell season. Storms hit the area every year in September and October. Annual rainfall is even higher in the hills, especially those facing the sea, in the 2000-2500mm (72-88in) range. The N winds sometimes cool the water down

to 23°C (74°F) – springsuits aren't really necessary but may come in handy.

**Nature and Culture** – Since Vietnam can't be a full-on surf trip, enjoy the scenery and the culture. Pay a visit to the Cham Museum, climb the Marble Mountains for awesome views of China Beach from Linh Ung Pagoda. Don't miss Hoi An and My Son. Vietnam's former capital city of Hue lies 4h north via scenic Hai Van pass.

**Hazards and Hassles** – Beware of rips, Vietnamese drown here every year. During the surfing season, excessive heat can be a problem. There is no malaria around Da Nang but it is still a problem in rural areas. Because of drugs and prostitution, AIDS is common. Driving a motorbike is fun but hazardous.

**Handy Hints** – The Da Nang surf club does not exist any more. Bring your everyday gear and maybe an old board to leave behind. The New Year Festival (late Jan, early Feb) can be fully booked. US dollars are still part of the economy. Laos is less than 100km (62mi) away.

| WEATHER STATISTICS | J/F | M/A | M/J | J/A | S/O | N/D |
|---|---|---|---|---|---|---|
| total rainfall (mm) | 65 | 15 | 45 | 110 | 490 | 215 |
| consistency (days/mth) | 11 | 4 | 8 | 12 | 19 | 21 |
| min temp (°C/°F) | 20/68 | 22/72 | 25/77 | 25/77 | 24/75 | 21/70 |
| max temp (°C/°F) | 25/77 | 29/82 | 34/94 | 34/94 | 30/86 | 26/79 |

**Marble Mountains**

JOHN CALLAHAN

| Spot | Size | Btm | Type |
|------|------|-----|------|
| ① | ④ | ⌣ | ◖ |
| ② | ④ | ⌣ | ◖ |
| ③ | ④ | ⌣ | ▤ |
| ④ | ⑥ | ⌣ | ◖ |
| ⑤ | ④ | ⌣ | ◖ |
| ⑥ | ④ | ⌣ | ◖ |
| ⑦ | ④ | ⌣ | ▬ |

good reform next to the bridge. There are also some less exposed jetty breaks to the north. To get to My Khe, cross the Han River via the Nguyen Van Troi Bridge and travel about 6km (4mi) out of town. Beware, there is another **My Khe** Beach located on Highway 24B, 15km (9mi) from the town of Quang Ngai in the Son Tinh District! Actually, My Khe, **Non Nuoc** and **China Beach** are the same stretch of below average, shallow beachbreak, part of a stunning coastline backed by verdant mountains. The Marble Mountains are made up of five limestone outcrops in isolation from the surrounding plains, each riddled with caves and grottoes, with some made into pagodas and shrines. Surprisingly this beach area has seen relatively little development. One exception is the 5-star Furama Resort, which opened in March 1997. Try to get down to **Cue Dai Beach** near Hoi An, which feels like a tourist haven, with an artistic atmosphere and friendly local people. Famed for cheap tailor-made clothes and seafood, it is small enough to get around on foot, but a set of wheels will be necessary to get out to Cue Dai Beach, which has a steeper slope than China Beach and picks up more swell.

that South China Sea surf only breaks four months of the year and when it does, it's not very good.

Nha Trang, Phan Thiet and China Beach are amongst Vietnam's most well-known beaches, scattered along the central coast. Because it is so inconsistent, detailed spot knowledge is virtually non-existent, but there are pretty good odds of finding decent pointbreak waves, especially around rivermouths. Most of the surf is beachbreaks with an outside sandbank, trough in the middle and a reform on the inside. The outside waves are the biggest, up to 8ft (2.5m) on the strongest NE wind push, which creates a choppy, disorganised line-up. The outside mushburgers quickly die in the trough before reforming into the shorey, which is where the power is. More rights than lefts, these shoreys can often be quite hollow. Although southern E facing locations should pick up a bit more swell, the best bet for a Vietnamese surf search is Da Nang because that's where other surfers congregate and unlike most surfing zones, crowds are never a nuisance.

Da Nang is a busy, dusty, colourless city, the fourth largest in Vietnam, with a large business community. To the north **Binh An** is hardly worth checking but scenic **Lang Co** is well exposed and becoming popular with kitesurfers. **Nam O Point** is probably the highest quality wave with some protection from NE winds and a

① Binh An
② Lang Co
③ Nam O Point
④ My Khe
⑤ Non Nuoc
⑥ China Beach
⑦ Cue Dai Beach

Da Nang

Binh An

Hon Son Cha

Nui Hoi 1192m

Lien Chieu

Vinh Da Nang

Ban Dao Son Tra

Mui Da Nang

Ap Huong

Hon La

Cu Lao Cham

Hon Giai

Dien Ban

Hoi An

Cue Dai Pt

Mui An Luong

Hon Tai

My Khe

Dong Son

Thanh Binh

Hon Ong

Tan An

Binh Tinh

Thang Binh

Khuong Nam

An Tuyen

*South China Sea*

Phu Binh

Phu Qui

Tam Ky

*QUANG NAM*

Mui Ag Hoa

Phu Xuan

Vung Dung Quat

Mui Vian Ka

Mui Nam Tram

Cu Lao Bo Bai

Cu Lao Re

Hai Ninh

Son Tra

Vung Viet Thanh

Tri Binh

Phuoc Thien

Go Nhan Pt.

Tra Mi

Hon Gioc 1119m

An Cuong

*QUANG NGAI*

Long Vinh

An Thinh

Mui Ba Lang An

to Quang Ngai

TUNGSTEN

The N-NE monsoon is a strong seasonal trend in the South China Sea starting in November until February-March. 8-14ft (2.5-4.5m) seas happen quite often, so expect messy 3-6ft (1-2m) on the most exposed beachbreaks and 1-2ft (0.3-0.6m) on the sheltered pointbreaks. There is 1500km (938mi) between the Luzon Straight and Vietnam Central coast; the fetch is probably better between Nha Trang and Phan Thiet but wind exposure is higher. Local winds in Da Nang are fairly calm with windless spells and moderate E-NE onshore winds. The reform waves should be less choppy than outside banks and are ideally suited to beginners and longboarders. During the June-October typhoon season, some major swell might hit with clean conditions but this is rare and short. During the SW monsoon, it's offshore everyday but mostly flat. Diurnal tides predominate in the South China Sea and won't exceed 3ft (1m) in range.

| SURF STATISTICS | J F | M A | M J | J A | S O | N D |
|---|---|---|---|---|---|---|
| dominant swell | N-NE | N-NE | N-E | N-E | N-E | N-NE |
| swell size (ft) | 3-4 | 1 | 0 | 0-1 | 1-2 | 3-4 |
| consistency (%) | 70 | 30 | 0 | 10 | 30 | 80 |
| dominant wind | N-SE | E-SE | SE-S | SE-SW | N-SE | N-E |
| average force | F4 | F4 | F4 | F4 | F3-F4 | F4 |
| consistency (%) | 77 | 46 | 57 | 64 | 69 | 74 |
| water temp (°C/°F) | 23/74 | 24/75 | 28/82 | 29/84 | 28/82 | 25/77 |
| wetsuit | 🏄 | 🏄 | 🏄 | 🏄 | 🏄 | 🏄 |

# 111. Okinawa

ALL PHOTOS JOHN CALLAHAN

Blue Corner, Kudaka-jima

**Summary**

+ EPIC TYPHOON SWELLS
+ SUBTROPICAL REEFBREAKS
+ SECRET SPOTS AND ISLANDS
+ LOW CRIME RATE
+ ENGLISH SPEAKING JAPAN

− FLAT SPRING, MOSTLY WINDSWELL
− SHALLOW REEFS, NO BEACHBREAK
− MAINLY HIGH TIDE SPOTS
− CROWDED PREMIERE SPOTS
− EXPENSIVE

Fisherman's memorial

Okinawa Prefecture consists of 161 islands, of which only 44 are inhabited. Scattered over 1,000km (600mi), Yonagoni, the southernmost island, lies a mere 100km (60mi) from Taiwan. Although once an independent state, the Ryukyu Islands are now the most popular Japanese beach resort destination, thanks to its mild climate and fringing coral reefs. Okinawa is smack dab in the middle of Typhoon Alley, sandwiched between the Pacific Ocean on its east side and the East China Sea to the west. This positioning allows for a wealth of spots facing in all directions to pick up virtually any swell going. They break over very shallow shelves of reef and/or basaltic rock, which is why 90% of the spots are mid-to-high tide breaks, but experienced surfers not scared of the odd bounce will find plenty of low tide waves. Most spots are

Fukuchi Takayuki

covered by only 2-5ft (0.6-1.6m) of water at high tide. There are only two sandy beachbreaks. Crowds are heavy at the main spots, but some breaks remain unpopulated. Most of the outer reefs and islands are still uncharted.

## TRAVEL INFORMATION

**Population:**
1.3M Okinawa district
**Coastline:** 400km (250mi) Okinawa Is
**Contests:** Nirai Kanai – Suicide Cliffs (Mar)
**Other Resources:**
*Video:* Tsunami Calling 1 & 2
mensoresurfing.com
ocvb.or.jp/english/index.html
okinawa.com

**Getting There** – No visa, 90 days. You can fly to Naha (AHA) from Hong Kong, or Taiwan. Daily flights from Tokyo, Osaka, Nagoya and Fukuoka. Companies: JAL, ANA, JAS, ANK, JTA. Tokyo to Okinawa is $290o/w. Board tax: $60 to $165! Inter-island flights are big Boeing 737's: plenty of room for boards. Naha-Miyako: $105. Tokyo Narita Dep tax: $17.

**Getting Around** – A rental car is a must but costs $80 daily. Traffic is often heavy with Japanese road signs. Route 58 is congested during rush hour from Naha to Nago; take the express toll road ($8). If you're a non-Japanese speaking 'gaijin', use buses and taxis. Taxi fees start at $3.50 then $0.50 for each 407m unit: a 20km ride costs $28. Left side driving.

**Lodging and Food** – There are three types of accommodation: 1. City hotels in Naha, Sunabe,

Chatan-cho area on the west side for $50-60 a night. 2. Beach resorts in the central and northern parts like the Big Time on Ikei. 3. Island resorts. Facilities are very good. Expect to pay between $60 and $300 for 1 night B&B for 2) Expect $15-20 for a meal, drink Awamori!

**Weather** – Okinawa enjoys Japan's only subtropical oceanic climate, with an annual mean temp of 22.5°C (73°F) and 75%+ humidity year round, allowing lots of pineapple and sugar cane to be grown. Being an island, Okinawa is highly influenced by seasonal winds: S winds in summer and N winds in winter. In the summer, July-Sept, there are many days when temps exceed 30°C (86°F) but squalls can also occur. This is in 'Typhoon Alley', Okinawa has 7-8 per year. Even in the winter months from December to February, temps rarely drop below 10°C (50°F) but bear in mind that North Korean windchill! Water temps range from 20°C (68°F) to 30°C (86°F). In winter, the west side cools down so bring a springsuit. Then, warm water migrates north with the Kuroshio (the 'Black Current'), bringing 6 months of boardshort surfing.

**Nature and Culture** – The longevity of Okinawans ranks #1 in the world: healthy diet, mild climate and a peaceful society. With beautiful white sand beaches, 40 golf courses, good diving or Togyu Bull fighting, every minute can be filled. Best are the Festival of Sun, Ocean & Joggers and Dragon boat races. It's the land of Karate and the Iriomote wildcat, a 'living fossil'.

**Hazards and Hassles** – Coral reefs are alive, sharp and shallow; reef cuts are frequent. Because of steep and hollow take-offs, many locals wear booties and helmets. There are shark sightings and shark attacks have occurred on Miyako (300km/188mi SW of Okinawa) a surfer died there on Sept 2000. Very low crime and hassles. Traffic and crowds will be the main problems.

**Handy Hints** – Surf supplies at the Source Surf Shop or the Ryukyu Glass Factory but prices are heavy. Prices start from: longboard ($800), shortboard ($500), bodyboard ($230), springsuit ($200).Board Rental is $25/day. Take your best shortboard. 'Mensore' means welcome, most locals speak some English.

| WEATHER STATISTICS | J/F | M/A | M/J | J/A | S/O | N/D |
|---|---|---|---|---|---|---|
| total rainfall (mm) | 130 | 165 | 290 | 240 | 160 | 130 |
| consistency (days/mth) | 4 | 5 | 6 | 9 | 7 | 5 |
| min temp (°C/°F) | 13/55 | 17/63 | 22/72 | 25/77 | 23/74 | 16/61 |
| max temp (°C/°F) | 18/64 | 22/72 | 27/80 | 30/86 | 28/82 | 22/72 |

Samurai Reef

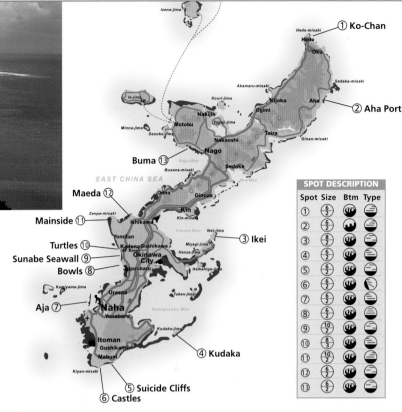

Ko-Chan
Aha Port
Buma
Maeda
Mainside
Turtles
Sunabe Seawall
Bowls
Aja
Suicide Cliffs
Castles
Ikei
Kudaka

| SPOT DESCRIPTION | | | |
|---|---|---|---|
| Spot | Size | Btm | Type |
| ① | 6/2 | | |
| ② | 6/2 | | |
| ③ | 8/2 | | |
| ④ | 6/2 | | |
| ⑤ | 6/2 | | |
| ⑥ | 6/2 | | |
| ⑦ | 6/2 | | |
| ⑧ | 6/2 | | |
| ⑨ | 10/2 | | |
| ⑩ | 8/3 | | |
| ⑪ | 10/2 | | |
| ⑫ | 6/2 | | |
| ⑬ | 6/2 | | |

The north side is less crowded at spots like **Ko-Chan**, aka Hedo Point, a summer right that is best with an E swell and S-SE winds. The take-off is steep, into a hollow barrel, followed by a 30m (90ft) smooth, workable section. Despite its remote position, **Aha Port** suffers from crowding, as it is one of the few known low-tide spots. The rights are worth the priority game but a better spot allegedly lurks in the vicinity. For those not interested in braving the roads, head to **Ikei** Island, stay at the Big Time Hotel and wait for the right conditions. The reefs facing the hotel enjoy a wide swell window and are fun at head high. If it gets bigger, the west side of Ikei produces Sunset Beach-like rights but care should be taken avoiding sea urchins and strong currents. Another island worth the 1h ferry trip from Baten Harbour is **Kudaka**, which has a very long left pointbreak next to the seawall and small island marina. Lots of sections but when they all link up, with the biggest NE swells, it's a beauty! Stay a full day; the local 'soba' house is one of the best places for a hot meal. **Suicide Cliffs** is the most consistent summer spot but due to its proximity to Naha, it's also the most crowded spot. Named after WWII events, the place is fairly wild with tricky cliff access when it's wet. Don't go if the swell is above 5ft (1.6m) and N winds blow into the scattered, punchy peaks. Walk a bit further to **Castles**, which is just as consistent, much less crowded and offers a left point with two long sections. The west side has the greatest surf spot and population density, so even winter breaks like **Aja** or **Bowls** can get crowded. Unfortunately, these good quality reefs rely on the combination of meagre N windswells and SE winds which is very infrequent. Bowls can be an incredible A-frame and the outside reefs can, occasionally provide cooking surf. Without doubt, **Sunabe Seawall** is the main surfing arena with half a dozen reefbreaks including Typhoon Break's long lefts, Hotels' sectiony rights, 5-Rocks short peaks, Californias and Hawaiians, Bowls rights or Sunabe Marina which is threatened by harbour development. Further north, **Turtles** can produce massive lefts, among the biggest waves rideable on Okinawa but crazy currents have been known to drag unwary surfers to the seawall. Kamikaze bodyboarders head to scenic Cape Zanpa to ride one of the three breaks at **Mainside**. Consistent, tubey rights are common but the Outside reef is definitely the island's most radical wave! There's a left for the goofies as well. Check **Maeda** down the 300ft (100m) cliffs, for spinning lefts and rights plus good fishing and diving. Nago City's closest spot is **Buma**; two fun right and left pointbreaks of poor consistency.

Okinawa gets two types of swells, which apart from a flat spring, produces year round waves, with a mixture of S and N windswells. Summer swells are created by tropical disturbances and typhoons, usually accompanied by S winds and July is often the start

Mainside

of consistent swells on S and E facing shores. The summer climaxes in August-October with several monthly typhoons and occasional super-typhoons, which deliver up to 12ft (4m) surf on all corners of the island. They normally begin on the same latitude as the South China Sea before moving north. The west coast gets three to four typhoons and the east about double that. The west coast is calm during summer, but gets lively Nov-March when lows move quickly down from Korea, delivering choppy 3-8ft (1-2.5m) short period windswell. The lows usually bring the wind from the NW with the approach of the storm and end up from the NE-E, which means clean surf on the west side but size drops quickly. A typical winter sees the west coast with 10-15 days of good surf and another 5-10 days of mediocre surf a month. The east coast is reasonably consistent during the winter, but mostly onshore due to predominant NE winds. Tidal range can reach 7ft (2.2m) on spring tides: surf 2h before and after high tide for safety.

| SURF STATISTICS | J F | M A | M J | J A | S O | N D |
|---|---|---|---|---|---|---|
| dominant swell | N-NE | N-NE | E-SW | E-SW | E-SW | N-NE |
| swell size (ft) | 3-4 | 2 | 1 | 2-3 | 3 | 3-4 |
| consistency (%) | 70 | 40 | 10 | 40 | 50 | 70 |
| dominant wind | NW-NE | N-E | E-SW | E-SW | N-E | N-NE |
| average force | F4-F5 | F4 | F4 | F4 | F4 | F4-F5 |
| consistency (%) | 72 | 54 | 63 | 74 | 68 | 65 |
| water temp (°C/°F) | 19/66 | 21/70 | 25/77 | 28/82 | 26/79 | 22/72 |
| wetsuit | | | | | | |

# 112. Kyu Shu

ALL PHOTOS BY JOHN CALLAHAN

## Summary
+ WARM WATER TYPHOON SWELLS
+ LESS CROWDED POINTBREAKS
+ SEAGAIA OCEAN DOME
+ JAPANESE CULTURE

– INCONSISTENT SWELLS
– COLD WINTER DAYS
– VERY EXPENSIVE LIVING COSTS
– COMMUNICATION DIFFICULTIES

While not generally thought to be among Japan's top surfing destinations, it is worth remembering that the Miyazaki SE facing shoreline is ideally located to catch the typhoon swells. This coast is also extensive enough to escape the hordes from Honshu and while the best waves do get crowded at times, there are plenty of less accessible spots with good potential. Before visiting the Miyazaki Prefecture, bear in mind that winter produces decent surf in the Sea of Japan. Also, Tanega Shima island has optimum swell exposure and can be accessed from Kagoshima for less than $100. The 397km (250mi) long Nichinan Coast has impressive sea-stacks up to 210ft (70m) high, including the renowned Umagase at the tip of Cape Hyuga.

Matthew Pitts

Much of this area's surfing is based around the reliable beachbreaks at **Okuragahama** or **Kanegahama**. Neither are particularly good quality waves but work on small swell with NW winds and have accommodation to hand.

## TRAVEL INFORMATION

**Population:**
1.2M Myazaki ken
**Coastline:** 1,950km
(1,220mi) Kyu Shu
**Contests:** None
**Other Resources:**
miyazaki.surf.to
mnet.ne.jp/~kimiaki/
home.html
pref.miyazaki.jp
jnto.go.jp

**Getting There** – No visa, 90 days. Most likely access is through Tokyo, then Fukuoka, then drive or fly Miyazaki direct. Miyazaki is $225 o/w to Tokyo. Fukuoka is well serviced from East Asian cities, Oz and NZ. Fly Skymark for cut-price deals. Using rail is fine, Shikansen trains are fast, buy a pass before arrival to get discounts. Dep tax: $17.

**Getting Around** – The Nippon Honsen coastal drive is great. There is a good public bus system. Lots of people in Miyazaki City ride bicycles. Renting a 1300cc car costs $75/day! Road signs are in Japanese, so driving can be an ugly experience. Use taxis if car hire too dear. For a small taxi, the capacity is 4 people and the taxi fare is $4.50 for the first 1.5km (1mi) plus $2 per km thereafter.

**Lodging and Food** – Most flats in the city are Japanese style: straw tatami mats on the floor, sliding shoji doors and a deep Ofuro (bathtub). A cheap Youth Hostel or Minshuku costs $30. A hotel like Kanko costs $90 (double). Seagaia resort's Kitago Hotel is $55-70 per person (dble). Expect $20 for a meal at izakayas, udon, ramen and sushi shops.

**Weather** – Because of the warm Black Current, Kyu-Shu experiences very different climate in winter and summer. Summers in Miyazaki are hot and humid with strong sunshine. Temps easily get above 30°C (86°F), even at night. May to August are really wet and prone to localised flooding. Then, autumn is warm and pleasant, the very best time to visit unless a typhoon hits the coast (rare). Winter can be cold; temps don't often drop below freezing and snow is rare, but the lack of heating in many buildings can make an apparently mild day seem unpleasantly cold. Apart from the rainy season and autumn typhoons, Miyazaki often enjoys fine weather with 57 days of sunshine or 2,103 hours on a yearly basis. Annual rainfall is 2400mm (95in) while the average temp is 17°C (63°F). Water feels tropical from July to October and doesn't drop much below 18°C (64°F) despite coldish winter days; take a light steamer and springsuit.

**Nature and Culture** – Don't miss the Miyazaki shrine, Heiwadai Peace Park (107ft/37m) tower built with stones collected from all over the world. The Beat Clap is Miyazaki biggest dance floor, $8 entry, 'all-you-can-drink' for gaijin (foreigners). The Cannabis is a reggae bar: no cover, but no cannabis either! Seagaia Ocean Dome: open April-Sept. $17 day fee.

**Hazards and Hassles** – Apart being completely lost due to communication problems, there is not much to be feared. Crime is low to nil, locals will be very helpful with foreigners. Some spots are localised but not to foreigners. Typhoon swells can be intense and some shallow breaks can be dangerous.

**Handy Hints** – There are good supplies at the Blast surf shop in Huyga or PWS Surf Design but prices start from: longboard ($800), shortboard ($500), bodyboard ($230), springsuit ($200). Board rental is $25/ day. Most surf is in the 2-5ft (0.6-1.5m) range and shortboardable.

| WEATHER STATISTICS | J/F | M/A | M/J | J/A | S/O | N/D |
|---|---|---|---|---|---|---|
| total rainfall (mm) | 80 | 190 | 320 | 290 | 250 | 90 |
| consistency (days/mth) | 7 | 9 | 12 | 12 | 11 | 8 |
| min temp (°C/°F) | 3/37 | 10/50 | 18/64 | 23/74 | 18/64 | 7/45 |
| max temp (°C/°F) | 12/54 | 18/64 | 25/77 | 30/86 | 25/77 | 16/61 |

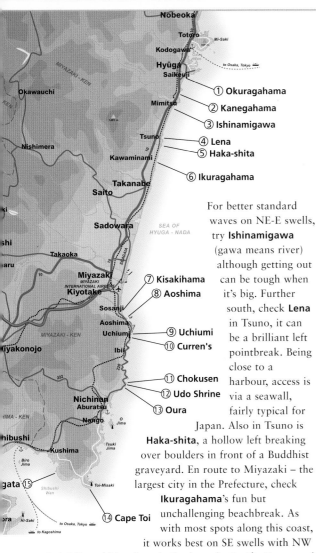

① Okuragahama
② Kanegahama
③ Ishinamigawa
④ Lena
⑤ Haka-shita
⑥ Ikuragahama
⑦ Kisakihama
⑧ Aoshima
⑨ Uchiumi
⑩ Curren's
⑪ Chokusen
⑫ Udo Shrine
⑬ Oura
⑭ Cape Toi

For better standard waves on NE-E swells, try **Ishinamigawa** (gawa means river) although getting out can be tough when it's big. Further south, check **Lena** in Tsuno, it can be a brilliant left pointbreak. Being close to a harbour, access is via a seawall, fairly typical for Japan. Also in Tsuno is **Haka-shita**, a hollow left breaking over boulders in front of a Buddhist graveyard. En route to Miyazaki – the largest city in the Prefecture, check **Ikuragahama**'s fun but unchallenging beachbreak. As with most spots along this coast, it works best on SE swells with NW wind. Miyazaki has been built along the Pacific Ocean and the banks of the Oyodo River, backed by low mountains. It is not an industrial or high-rise city, so the air is clean and palm trees and flowers line the main streets. 10km (6mi) north of Miyazaki is Seagaia, a 700ha resort, located amidst lush greenery of the Hitotsuba coastline home to Ocean Dome, the world's largest indoor water park (300 x 100m/900 x 300ft). It had a breaking wave with an 8ft (2.5m) chlorine barrel. Twice a day, there was a 15 minutes surfing show when Matthew Pitts was paid to get barrelled. However operating costs meant the attraction closed in 2002. The main wave-riding area is Sosanji, where **Kisakihama** beach is plagued by intense crowds but localism is low, especially towards western surfers.

Typhoon 21, 1991

**Aoshima** resort area is nice and while the beachbreak is less consistent than Sosanji, the harbour reefbreak is great for longboarding. Uchiumi is a zone filled with punchy reefbreaks. **Uchiumi** itself has a pass with rights and lefts on either side; north swells favour the lefts and vice-versa. Very close is **Curren's**, named after Tom's epic ride on the long right pointbreak during 1991's classic conditions. It needs a typhoon to get the spot working but paddling out and catching a wave requires some experience and confidence. This is even truer of **Chokusen**'s powerful reefbreak, which is experts only. The same goes for **Udo Shrine**, a nice-looking right peak on NE swells and W-S winds although there will be crowds when it's classic. **Oura** is one those magic spots which can be perfect when everywhere else is messy, because the shallow lefts hold N winds. If feeling energetic, scout **Cape Toi** where hundreds of wild horses roam around and there are different reefbreaks with varied exposures. On a big SE typhoon swell, hit **Nagata** for a truly outstanding left pointbreak up to double-overhead.

SPOT DESCRIPTION

| Spot | Size | Btm | Type |
|---|---|---|---|
| ① | 6/1 | | |
| ② | 6/1 | | |
| ③ | 6/1 | | |
| ④ | 8/2 | | |
| ⑤ | 6/2 | | |
| ⑥ | 6/1 | | |
| ⑦ | 6/1 | | |
| ⑧ | 6/1 | | |
| ⑨ | 8/2 | | |
| ⑩ | 10/4 | | |
| ⑪ | 8/2 | | |
| ⑫ | 6/2 | | |
| ⑬ | 10/2 | | |
| ⑭ | 6/2 | | |
| ⑮ | 12/2 | | |

J uly sees the first summer swells on S-E facing shores but wait until August as the summer climaxes in August-October with several monthly typhoons and occasional super-typhoons, which deliver up to 12ft (4m) surf. They normally approach from the South China Sea before moving north. Summer swells, more often in the 4-6ft (1.2-2m) range, are created by tropical disturbances and typhoons, usually with S winds. Then, North Pacific lows as well as monsoonal NE winds produce some waves from November to February. Even if the water remains warm enough, good surf is rare despite dominant offshore winds. Winter waves are often better on the north coast of Kyushu facing the Japan Sea side. Spots like Karatsu near Fukuoka show that an active small sea is more reliable than a passive ocean. Winds often blow from the W-NE. Tidal range can reach 8ft (2.5m) on spring tides and even more within deep bays, so get a tide table in a shop, and practise basic Japanese.

| SURF STATISTICS | J F | M A | M J | J A | S O | N D |
|---|---|---|---|---|---|---|
| dominant swell | E-NE | E-NE | E-NE | SW-SE | SW-SE | SW-SE |
| swell size (ft) | 2-3 | 2 | 1-2 | 2-3 | 3-4 | 3 |
| consistency (%) | 40 | 30 | 20 | 40 | 70 | 60 |
| dominant wind | W-NE | W-NE | E-SW | E-SW | N-E | W-NE |
| average force | F4 | F4 | F3-F4 | F3 | F4 | F4 |
| consistency (%) | 80 | 61 | 57 | 62 | 56 | 76 |
| water temp (°C/°F) | 18/64 | 17/63 | 22/72 | 27/80 | 25/77 | 21/70 |
| wetsuit | | | | | | |

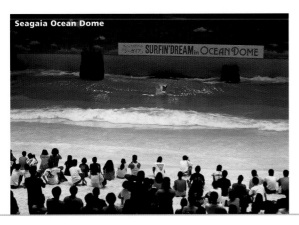
Seagaia Ocean Dome

A rugged, inaccessible coastline beckons
the more adventurous to some heavy,
cold water action in Tasmania.

# Australia

# The Ocean Environment

Three oceans, four seas, climates ranging from tropical to cool maritime, three swell drenched coastlines and it's not hard to see why Australia is dubbed "the lucky country". With a population of only 19 million residing on almost 3 million square miles, the environment of the island continent should be in good shape. This is broadly correct, however, 90% of the population live in the narrow coastal zone, bringing concentrated areas of pollution around urban centres.

### Pollution

The Australian coastline is approximately 36,700km (22,800mi) long. Water quality around major cities is the biggest issue facing Australian coastal waters. Western Australia's coastline is pristine, but sewage treatment is still on the poor side in many key surfing areas like Perth and Margaret River. A high profile, proposed development overlooking Smiths Beach, just outside Yallingup in WA, would see a new village and holiday development being built on the bluff. Sandwiched between Leuwin National Park

Left – **Deserted desert waves characterise the south and west. Cylindrical South Australian shorey.** Right – **Massive growth of urban developments is a big threat to water quality and encourages coastal armouring. Sunshine Coast, Qld.**

and the sea, it's an area of outstanding natural beauty and a valuable surfing resource as the heavy barrels of Supertubes are located in the middle of the bay. Destruction of the unspoilt natural environment, pollution problems and altering the geomorphology of the beach through urbanisation are the primary fears. Smiths is just one example of increasing coastal development around the coast. Both South Australia and Victoria's coastlines are squeaky clean until you hit town with its sewage, stormwater and industrial pollution. The most heavily populated area stretches down the east coast from Brisbane in Queensland to Wollongong in New South Wales. Sewage, stormdrains full of urban runoff, industrial effluent and ship related pollution are all too common. Sewage facilities are mainly low tech and ageing, often just screening followed by some primary treatment before outfall pipes carry the sewage varying distances away from the coast. As is often the case, onshores quickly return the slick straight back onto the city beaches. A recent extension to the outfall on Sydney's Northern Beaches relieved pollution levels at the beaches close to the outfall but distributed sewage to beaches further up the coast that previously had no problems. Surfrider Australia is targeting Margaret River (WA), Torquay (VIC), Cronulla (south Sydney), Manly (northern Sydney), Byron Bay (northern NSW) and the Gold Coast to clean up their outfalls into some of the world's most heavily surfed areas. After rain, urban runoff is a major problem for Sydney's coastal waters and

many beaches still sport blatant, concrete, stormwater pipes, laid directly across the sand, bringing litter, plastic bags, cigarette butts and an oily film to the line-up. Sydney's harbour and its busy port sees illegal bilge discharges and there have been a number of minor spills in the harbour. The most recent of these was the *Laura D'Amato*, which released an estimated 80,000 litres of light crude oil into Sydney Harbour. Southern Sydney's suburbs also suffer from heavy industry and whilst there are controls on effluent discharges, some breaks suffer from their location at the entrances to Botany Bay and Port Hacking. The same goes for the industrial cities of Wollongong in south New South Wales and Newcastle on the central coast, long associated with coal and steel production. Northern New South Wales and South Eastern Queensland bask in sub-tropical sunshine, while warm water and world-class waves substantiate the Surfers Paradise tag. A massive population boom, growing at a rate of 4% per annum, means an average of 450 acres of virgin land has to be cleared each year and often encroaches onto National Park or unspoilt shoreline. This urban sprawl is over-pressuring outdated sewage treatment systems, which deliver poorly treated sewage to the ocean outfall pipes. As the coastal development mushrooms, so too does the urban run off from the beachside stormwater pipes. The Gold Coast was cloaked in semi-tropical, coastal rainforests, but now all that is left is a 27 hectare plot at Burleigh Heads. In general, Australians are not the most environmentally friendly nation and have the highest per capita $CO_2$ output of any developing country.

### Erosion

The vast majority of the Australian coastline is completely unadulterated, and coastal populations are usually centred around natural harbours like Sydney. Cable Station Reef in Perth, WA was the first artificial reef project in Australia and the city beaches feature the odd groyne. Typically, rivermouths are most likely to attract coastal modification and a couple of these have had big impacts on the surfing environment. Numerous waves have been created and destroyed by groynes, built to stabilise river channel entrances. In New South Wales, Port Macquarie is a good example, where two rock

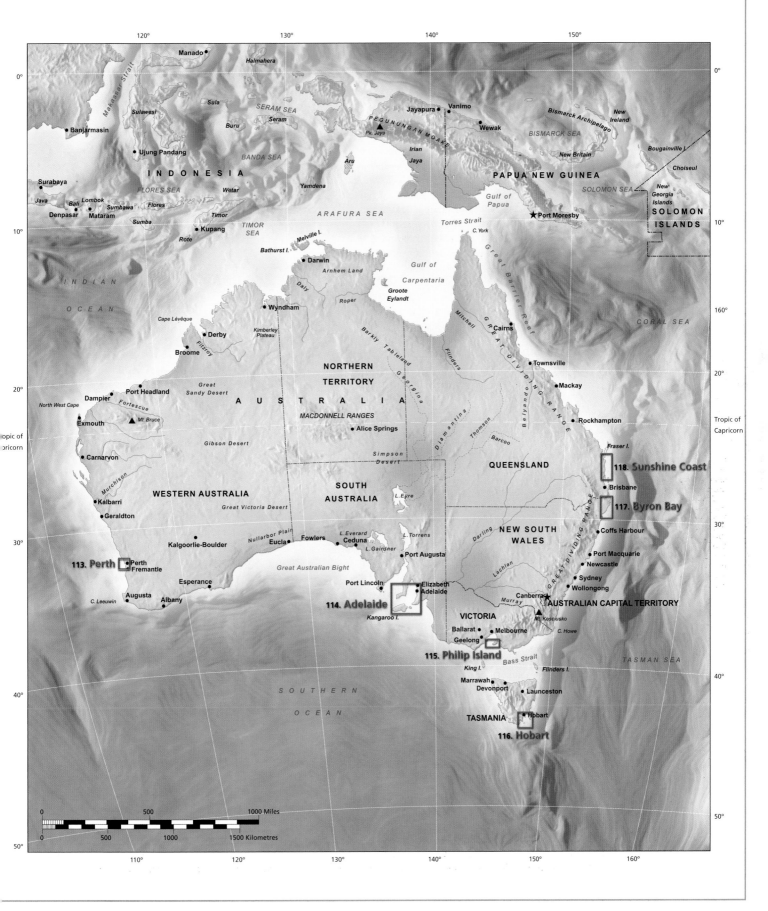

Manado
Halmahera
Sula
SERAM SEA
Seram
Banjarmasin
Buru
BANDA SEA
Ujung Pandang
INDONESIA
FLORES SEA
Wetar
Surabaya
Java
Bali
Lombok
Sumbawa
Flores
Denpasar
Mataram
Sumba
Timor
Kupang
Rote
TIMOR
SEA
Melville I.
Bathurst I.
Darwin
Arnhem Land
Daly
Wyndham
Roper
Cape Lévêque
Derby
Kimberley
Plateau
Broome
Fitzroy
NORTHERN
TERRITORY
AUSTRALIA
Great
Sandy Desert
Dampier
Port Headland
North West Cape
MACDONNELL RANGES
Exmouth
Mt. Bruce
Alice Springs
WESTERN AUSTRALIA
Gibson Desert
Carnarvon
Simpson
Desert
SOUTH
AUSTRALIA
L. Eyre
Kalbarri
Great Victoria Desert
Geraldton
Nullarbor Plain
L.Everard
Kalgoorlie-Boulder
Eucla
Fowlers
Ceduna
L. Gairdner
L.Torrens
Port Augusta
113. Perth
Perth
Fremantle
Esperance
Great Australian Bight
Port Lincoln
Elizabeth
Adelaide
Augusta
C. Leeuwin
Albany
114. Adelaide
Kangaroo I.

Pk. Jaya
PEGUNUNGAN MOAKE
Jayapura
Vanimo
Wewak
Irian
Jaya
Aru
PAPUA NEW GUINEA
Yamdena
ARAFURA SEA
Gulf of
Papua
Bismarck Archipelago
New
Ireland
BISMARCK SEA
New Britain
Bougainville I.
Choiseul
SOLOMON SEA
New
Georgia
Islands
SOLOMON
ISLANDS
Port Moresby
Torres Strait
C. York
Gulf of
Carpentaria
Groote
Eylandt
Great Barrier Reef
CORAL SEA
Cairns
Mitchell
Flinders
Townsville
GREAT DIVIDING RANGE
Mackay
Georgina
Barkly Tableland
Belyando
Rockhampton
Diamantina
Thomson
Barcoo
QUEENSLAND
Fraser I.
118. Sunshine Coast
Brisbane
117. Byron Bay
Darling
Coffs Harbour
NEW SOUTH
WALES
Port Macquarie
Lachlan
Newcastle
Sydney
Canberra
Wollongong
AUSTRALIAN CAPITAL TERRITORY
Murray
VICTORIA
Mt. Kosciusko
C. Howe
Ballarat
Melbourne
Geelong
115. Philip Island
Bass Strait
King I.
Flinders I.
TASMAN SEA
Marrawah
Devonport
Launceston
SOUTHERN
OCEAN
TASMANIA
Hobart
116. Hobart

INDIAN
OCEAN
Tropic of
Capricorn
ropic of
pricorn

0°
10°
20°
30°
40°
50°

120°
130°
140°
150°
160°

110°
120°
130°
140°
150°
160°

0°
10°
20°
30°
40°
50°

0        500        1000 Miles
0     500     1000     1500 Kilometres

groynes destroyed waves at the rivermouth but created new ones. North Wall is now an excellent peaky wedge popular with bodyboarders. The most famous coastal modification occurred on the New South Wales/ Queensland border when the mouth of the Tweed River was stabilised by constructing two rock groynes. These groynes greatly reduced the amount of sand moving northward into Queensland by longshore drift, starving the points of Snapper Rocks, Rainbow Bay and Kirra of barrel forming sand. The construction created a more stable beach, just north of the river at Duranbah (D-Bar), resulting in excellent, A-framing beachbreaks. Further damage occurred when a groyne was added at the top of Kirra Point to stop erosion of the beach at Coolangatta, but this further starved Kirra of sand and the wave virtually disappeared for a couple of years. In 1999, state governments, having consulted with residents, harbour-users and surfers began plans for pumping sand from the shoals forming at the mouth of the Tweed River back onto the points. The sand is now pumped to several points at Snapper Rocks and Rainbow Bay and the result is the Superbank, an epic sand pointbreak that connects all the way from Snapper Rocks to Kirra. Further north is the highly successful artificial reef at Narrowneck. The triangular reef constructed using sand-filled bags acts as coastal protection and as a surf spot.

Left – **Redistributing the wealth after man-made structures strangled the flow of sand to Queenslands legendary points. The Superbank.**
Right – **Many bush tracks are negotiable by car, but 4WD is often essential, especially in Tasmania's wetter climate.**

### Access

With so many thousands of miles of coast, access varies greatly and no more so than in WA. The southwest of the state has a decent highway system and tarmac roads to the major spots but there are a lot of lesser known spots, which require a good 4WD or the use of someone else's Holden! North of Perth and desert conditions prevail, so safety precautions should include food, water, first aid and a communication device. Well known spots now have graded dirt roads to them but a 4WD is essential for even the simplest exploration off the beaten track. Same applies to the South Australian coast west of Adelaide and getting to the coast is a mission, except at seaside towns. Victoria's beach access is reasonably straightforward, unlike its southern neighbour, Tasmania. Vast tracts of coastline are only accessible by hiking in and with a wet climate, dirt roads rapidly become rutted, mud-filled nightmares for all but the best 4WDs. The east coast from

Sydney up to the Gold Coast has an excellent road network. Coastal towns are regular and give easy access to the beach. Between towns, tracks through the bush to the beach are common and a decent car can make the trek in dry conditions. Further north, beach driving in 4x4s is the only way to get to some breaks.

### Hazards

Sharks encircle the continent and Australian surfers are often the targets for unprovoked attacks. South Australia has the worst reputation, being home to a significant number of the world's dwindling great white population, yet NSW and Queensland have hosted far more attacks. What is clear is that all the states have a consistent trend that shows around half of all attacks will be fatal. Other deadly marine creatures include the blue ringed octopus found in rock pools and the box jellyfish, which can kill in minutes but thankfully is only found in the surfless far north. Way more prevalent is the Portuguese man-of-war or bluebottle as it is referred to in Australia, which can turn summer sessions into a stingfest. Perhaps the most dangerous aspect of surfing in Australia is the sun. Proximity to the well documented hole in the ozone layer in the Antarctic's upper atmosphere means the sun strength and the potential for skin cancer are very high. Australia has about a quarter of a million regular surfers, and up to four times as many part-timers that head to the beach in summer on all types of watercraft. This results in some serious crowding issues at the best waves and occasional outbreaks of violence. Western Australia has problems in Perth because the wave resources are limited and Triggs can be a hotspot. Elsewhere is a little mellower with the waves sorting out the men from the boys. Up north, travellers should be respectful of the hardy locals, who are more protective of the less hyped, semi-secret reefs. South Australia has the worst reputation for localism at many of the more remote surfing outposts. Cactus is probably the most notorious and locals guard its line-up zealously. Victoria's harsh winter conditions are not enough for a warm welcome to the line-up and some of the more challenging reefs are best left to the cold local crew. This goes double in Tasmania where new faces are easy to spot. Sydney's surf is often absolutely mobbed which makes it hard to discern the locals from the blow-ins. Bad vibes are more of a factor at the point and reefbreaks, where luck and good positioning prevail. Queensland's epic righthand pointbreaks get ridiculously zooed out, but skill and paddling power are often just as important as postcode.

# Surf Travel Resources

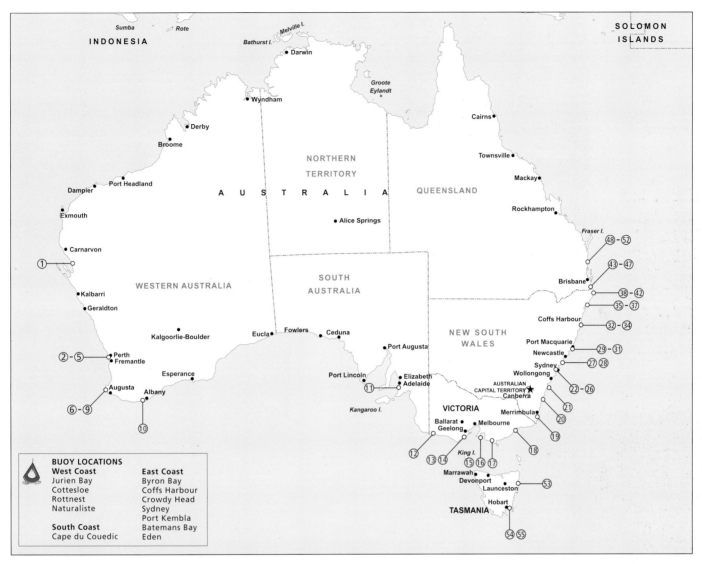

**BUOY LOCATIONS**

**West Coast**
Jurien Bay
Cottesloe
Rottnest
Naturaliste

**South Coast**
Cape du Couedic

**East Coast**
Byron Bay
Coffs Harbour
Crowdy Head
Sydney
Port Kembla
Batemans Bay
Eden

## WESTERN AUSTRALIA

1. Gnaraloo Surf Safari
2. Heron Charters
3. Insearch Travel
4. Surfing WA
5. Big Wave Surf School
6. Margaret Beach Resort
7. Yallingup Surfschool
8. Josh Palmateers Surf Academy
9. Margaret River Surf Safari
10. Pines Surf Academy

## SOUTH AUSTRALIA

11. Surf Culture

## VICTORIA

12. Easyrider Surf School
13. Go Ride a Wave
14. Gally's Surf Coaching
15. Mornington Pen. Surf School
16. Island Surfboards, Phillip Isl.
17. Offshore Surfschool
18. Surf Shack Surf School

## VICTORIA

19. Sapphire Surfschool
20. Soulrider Batemans Bay
21. U can Surf
22. Manly Surfschool
23. Lets Go Surfing
24. Surfing Cronulla
25. Sydney Surf Experience
26. Waves Surf School
27. Terry McDermott Surf Coaching
28. Central Coast Surfschool
29. Dawn Light
30. Saltwater Surf School
31. Anna Bay Surf School
32. Surfing Coffs Coast
33. Bullet Bodyboarding Academy
34. Sun & Surf Tours
35. Summerland
36. Rusty Miller Surf Instructing
37. Nats Place

38. True Blue Longboarding
39. Byron Bay Surf School
40. Surfaris
41. Style
42. Go Surfing

## QUEENSLAND

43. Australian School of Surfing
44. Global Surf Lessons
45. Surfing Qld Coaching Ac.
46. SIC Surfschool
47. Exscreeme Day Tours
48. Learn to Surf
49. Wavesense Surfschool
50. Coolum Surfing School
51. North Caloundra Surfschool
52. Surfing Qld Coaching Ac.

## TASMANIA

53. 42 South Surfschool
54. Tasmania Surfing Adv.
55. Tasmania Surfing Adventures

## COUNTRY INFORMATION

**AUSTRALIA**

| | |
|---|---|
| Area (sq km/mi): | 7.7M/2.99M |
| Population: | 19M |
| Waveriders: | 1M |
| Tourists (per yr): | 5M |
| Language: | English |
| Currency: | Australian Dollar |
| Exchange: | $1 = 1.8 AUD |
| GDP ($ per yr): | $23,200 |
| Inflation (%): | 1% |

# 113. Perth

WESTERN
AUSTRALIA

Perth

Strickland Bay

### Summary
+ Year round southern swells
+ Rottnest Island A-grade spots
+ Functional city – great climate
+ Cable's artificial reef
+ Access to epic surf areas

– Perth's inconsistent spots
– Intense crowds
– Unpredictable Rottnest surf
– Fremantle Doctor's onshores
– Sharks

Quokka

Despite its ideal location, Perth can't be taken seriously as a city for surfers due to a shallow offshore seafloor, known as the Five Fathom Bank (approx 10m/33ft), which absorbs most of the swell. Surf is usually mushy and summers are mainly flat, maxing out at 4ft. It's ironic that the entry point for wave-rich Western Australia is so deprived of good surf. However, this means Perth is an ideal place to learn, plus there is the added bonus of Rottnest Island, where some serious waves can be had, a short ferry ride from the city. Prior to two significant changes in sea level over 7,000 years ago, Rottnest was initially attached to the mainland. Local Aboriginal people knew the Island as 'Wadjemup', which has been suggested

Scarborough

to have the meaning "land across the water". The island was named in 1696 by the Dutch explorer Willem de Vlamingh, who called it 'Rottnest' (meaning 'rats nest'), mistaking the marsupial quokkas for huge rats.

**Trigg Point** is Perth's most consistent and crowded wave, producing a decent length, peeling righthander,

## TRAVEL INFORMATION

**Population:** 1.4M Perth
**Coastline:** 40km (25mi) Rottnest
**Contests:**
Gromsearch (May),
Sunsmart WA (Nov)
**Other Resources:**
srosurf.com
heroncharters.com.au
rottnest.wa.gov.au
perthwesternaustralia.net

**Getting There** – Visas for all except NZ. Perth (1,2M hab) sees fewer flights than Sydney but many connections to Asia (Qantas, Singapore...). Rottnest Island can be reached by a short ferry ride or 15min Air Taxi (from $35 r/t, ask for boards). The numerous ferries take 25min from Fremantle ($17/p r/t), 45min from Hillary's or 1h from Perth.

**Getting Around** – Perth traffic is fine for a city. A special permit is required to hire or drive a vehicle on Rottnest. Vehicle hire is subject to availability. Local speed limits and 'no go' areas apply. Rent a bike with board racks, prices are low (helmets and lock inc.). Some spots require a boat. Check Heron surf charters for day access or week trips.

**Lodging and Food** – Favour Cottesloe to stay around Perth. Most of the 500,000 visitors to

Rottnest every year come for the day. The Rottnest Lodge is costly ($75/day), renting one of the 250 villas/cottages are cheap ($225/week for 4p). Renting a tent only costs $7/2people! At Thomson Bay, it's possible to get food but bring as much as possible from the mainland.

**Weather** – Call it Californian or Mediterranean: expect mild winters and hot dry summers. Perth is the sunniest state capital with 8h of sunshine a day on average, the average yearly rainfall being around 880mm (24in). The skies are often bright blue and cloudless. The summer months are hot with temps between 17-29°C (63-84°F). The warm summer days are cooled down in the afternoon with the Fremantle Doctor, a strong SW sea breeze. Perth experiences a very low rate of humidity. Due to the warm weather, there may be water restrictions during the summer. Winter months (June to August) are mild and rainy, with average temps 9-18°C (48-64°F). Water is stable year round at 18-20°C (64-68°F), a light steamer with short arms being the most convenient neoprene. Booties are necessary for the reefs.

**Nature and Culture** – The Sorrento Quay and Hillary's Boat Harbour, 5km (3mi) north of Trigg, house major attractions for tourists including Underwater World. Rottnest Island is an A Class Reserve, has a record of 97 species of tropical fish and is popular for migrating humpback whales, bottlenose dolphins and sea lions.

**Hazards and Hassles** – On Perth metro beaches, beware of robberies, crowds and visiting hungry sharks. Rottnest surf conditions are often uncrowded but strong rips, razor-sharp reefs and sea urchins are prevalent. Surfers should take care and use designated pathways when accessing surf spots, to help protect fragile dune vegetation.

**Handy Hints** – Plenty of surf shops to get good gear: Murray Smith Surf Centre (Cottesloe, Scarborough), Fluid Surf shop (Fremantle), Surf, Dive n' Ski (Perth)...Expect $400 for a shortboard and $600 for a longboard. A couple of guns would be useful for a stay on Rotto. Add a couple of inches to your normal boards. Ask for the Rottnest Island Surf Map at the Tourist Information Centre.

| WEATHER STATISTICS | J/F | M/A | M/J | J/A | S/O | N/D |
|---|---|---|---|---|---|---|
| total rainfall (mm) | 10 | 33 | 154 | 137 | 68 | 18 |
| consistency (days/mth) | 3 | 7 | 16 | 19 | 14 | 6 |
| min temp (°C/°F) | 19/66 | 15/59 | 11/52 | 9/48 | 11/52 | 15/59 |
| max temp (°C/°F) | 30/86 | 26/79 | 20/68 | 18/64 | 21/70 | 26/79 |

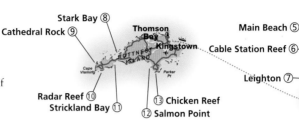

over a sand-covered reef by the groyne. The adjacent beachbreak can get some well shaped banks but it all depends on how much sand has collected over summer, when surfing restrictions apply. The popular beaches of Scarborough are just 2km (1.2mi) south, where the rich and backpackers are catered for with accommodation near the beach at **Observation City**. The surf won't be good unless there is a rare combo of huge swell, E winds and well formed sandbanks. Check one of the webcams located on the beach patrol tower. **Floreat Groyne** offers good shelter from dominant SW winds, where the lefts can wrap decently, but rarely get above head high. The **City Beach Groyne** is a similar set-up, plus the very real option of night surfing on a clear night, but beware of sharks. Perth's city beaches have seen a spate of great white shark attacks in recent years, including a fatality. There are several spots in Cottesloe besides **Main Beach** like Cove, Seconds, Isolator, Dutch Inn or Deep 6. Because of the lack of waves and density of surfers, Cottesloe City Council voted in 2000, to build the first artificial surfing reef at **Cable Station** in Mosman Park, 500m offshore. An underwater canyon funnels more swell energy towards "Artos", but it is still a low frequency spot, needing a big NW swell to get going. When it's on, the peak can be damn good, but it will be

Rottnest Island

super-crowded. For fewer crowds, drive through the industrial area before Fremantle and check **Leighton**, which will work on any major W swell. A visit to the 11km (7mi) long Rottnest Island is essential and it's only a 30min ferry ride from Perth. Rotto is a popular trip with experienced surfers, because it's often 2-3ft (+/-1m) larger than Perth's beaches. Best times are during autumn and winter with prevailing northerly winds. However, surfers can catch the early morning surf on the south side during the summer months (Oct to Feb). The north side of the island is home to **Stark Bay**, a growling, hollow, mid-

Strickland Bay

high tide left at all sizes of SW-NW swell. A boat would help as it breaks way out there and snapping boards can be a reality. Hellmen (and women) only. **Cathedral Reef** is just out of the brunt of the onshore SW'ers but the lefts are still hollow and punchy. **Radar Reef** is

totally exposed to SW swells and winds and requires a long paddle out through strong currents, in order to ride an isolated scary righthand bommie at higher tides. Bicycles are the only way to get around Rottnest and swarms of surfers pedal straight to **Strickland Bay**, the most consistent break. Superb lefts up to 12ft (4m) over a shallow reef ledge that has a lock-in end tube section. There are decent rights on smaller swells. The reefs at **Salmon Point** are powerful and hollow on mid-sized SW swells and **Chicken Reef** is an insane tube over a sharp coral reef up to 10ft (3m). Mid tides and N winds are best. There are many other potentially awesome surf spots on the island.

Plenty of SW swells from the Roaring Forties make their way to Perth area but remember that it needs at least 6ft (2m) of swell before Trigg or the Artos reef start pushing a decent sized wave. When there is a big swell, straight E winds and clean conditions are rare. Autumn and winter mid-to-big swells will pound 6-12ft (2-4m) on Rottnest breaks. Cyclone swells very rarely produce N swells that make it so far south. Offshore winds occur once the storm has passed, with rain and wind as well. Although S winds are predominant, especially in summer, there can be plenty of N winds in winter, which are the best for Rotto south shore. Glassy days are very rare. In summer, wake up early as the SW "Fremantle Doctor" will ruin most of the spots by 11am. A major factor influencing Rotto is the path of the warm Leeuwin Current, adding a couple of centigrade to the water. Tides are minimal (often less than 2ft/0.6m) and diurnal/semi-diurnal (once or twice a day) but manage to affect the very shallow reefs.

| SPOT DESCRIPTION | | |
|---|---|---|
| Spot | Size | Btm | Type |
| ① | 8/1 | | |
| ② | 6/1 | | |
| ③ | 6/1 | | |
| ④ | 6/1 | | |
| | 6/1 | | |
| ⑤ | 6/1 | | |
| ⑥ | 10/2 | | |
| ⑦ | 6/1 | | |
| ⑧ | 15/3 | | |
| ⑨ | 8/2 | | |
| ⑩ | 12/3 | | |
| ⑪ | 12/3 | | |
| | 10/2 | | |
| ⑫ | 8/2 | | |
| ⑬ | 10/2 | | |

| SURF STATISTICS | J F | M A | M J | J A | S O | N D |
|---|---|---|---|---|---|---|
| dominant swell | SW-W | SW-W | SW-W | SW-W | SW-W | SW-W |
| swell size (ft) | 3-4 | 4-5 | 5-6 | 6-7 | 5 | 3-4 |
| consistency (%) | 40 | 60 | 70 | 80 | 70 | 40 |
| dominant wind | SE-SW | SE-SW | SW-NW | SW-NW | S-W | SE-SW |
| average force | F4 | F4 | F4-F5 | F5 | F4 | F4 |
| consistency (%) | 77 | 61 | 48 | 60 | 66 | 69 |
| water temp (°C/°F) | 20/68 | 20/68 | 19/66 | 18/64 | 16/61 | 19/66 |
| wetsuit | | | | | | |

Map labels:
Marmion
Trigg Point ① — Northbeach
Observation City ② — Scarborough — Coolbinia
Floreat Groyne ③ — City Beach — Perth
City Beach Groyne ④ — Swanbourne
Stark Bay ⑧ — Thomson Bay — Main Beach ⑤ — Cottesloe
Cathedral Rock ⑨ — Kingstown — Cable Station Reef ⑥
ROTTNEST ISLAND — Leighton ⑦
Cape Vlaming — Parker Pt — Fremantle
Radar Reef ⑩ — ⑬ Chicken Reef
Strickland Bay ⑪ — ⑫ Salmon Point
CARNAC ISL. — Jandakot Airport
Woodman Point
Entrance Point — GARDEN ISLAND — Cockburn Sound
Collie Head — Medina
Cape Peron — Kwinana
PENGUIN ISL. — Safety Bay — Rockingham — Swan River

SOUTHERN AUSTRALIA

# 114. Adelaide

ALL PHOTOS JOLI

**Summary**

+ SOUTHERN OCEAN SWELLS
+ WIDE VARIETY OF SPOTS
+ DESERT-LIKE SURROUNDINGS
+ CHOICE OF COASTLINES
+ RARE CROWD HASSLES

- COLD WATER, HOT AIR TEMPS
- MAINLY FOR EXPERIENCED SURFERS
- WHITE POINTERS, BRONZE WHALERS
- SNAKES, FLIES AND BEES
- POTHOLES AND ROUGH ROADS

Adelaide is South Australia's capital city of one million plus people situated on the Adelaide plains, a flat, fertile corridor of land between Gulf St Vincent and the arc of the Mount Lofty Ranges. It's a quick drive to the closest surf spots but it's crowded and inconsistent because of a very narrow swell window. Yorke Peninsula is a 4h drive west of Adelaide, and this crooked finger of rock presents some incredibly good waves at its tip, which is part of the Innes National Park. On a 40km (25mi) stretch, there are 15 known quality breaks, usually short and powerful reefbreaks down sheer cliffs. This amazing concentration of quality waves suit experienced surfers with no fear of air drops and Australia's dangerous wildlife like sharks and snakes. To top it off, Kangaroo Island is Australia's third biggest island,

**Yorke Peninsula**

measuring 150km (96mi) long, and featuring many remote and spooky surf spots, exposed to the full force of the swell coming out of the Great Southern Ocean.

With out a doubt, **Chinamans** is the classic South Australian spot for advanced surfers. The take-off zone is small and crowded, the drops are vertical, the reef is shallow and sharp, getting in and out is tricky but the

---

## TRAVEL INFORMATION

**Population:**
1.1M Adelaide
**Coastline:**
3,700km (2,310mi)
**Contests:**
Roxy Surf Jam,
Yorkes Classic (Oct)
**Other Resources:**
surfsouthoz.com
swellnet.com.au
southaustralia.com
yorke.sa.gov.au

**Getting There** – Visa: all nationalities apart from NZ. Adelaide is a rare int'l flight but Singapore and MAS fly direct from SE Asia main cities. There are 20 flights (Virgin Blue, Qantas) from Melbourne and Sydney daily; Melbourne ($150o/w). Driving from Melbourne would take 10h. Cabs cost $9 from City to Airport. It's 4h to Yorke's tip, 1h30 to Victor Harbor.

**Getting Around** – Cruising along the Esplanade on the mid-coast is a treat, driving around Victor Habor is fine unless it's summer high season. Most of the beat-up, unsealed roads are on Yorke's. Thrifty rental cars: $215/w. Kangaroo Island is a 30min flight or a 40min crossing from Cape Jervis.

**Lodging and Food** – On Yorke, use cheap Caravan Parks close to the surf. Marion Bay Seaside Apartments for groups: $9/p. Don't miss the Rhinos Tavern! Around Mid and South Coasts, try the backpackers for reasonable rates. The Beachport is $9, the Grosvenor Hotel in Victor Harbor is good. On Kangaroo, be prepared to camp, or use the Ozone Hotel in Kingscote.

**Weather** – The climate is mostly dry with hot summers and cool winters. Sometimes, there are oppressive hot spells of 35°C (97°F). The nearby Southern Ocean ensures cool & mild winters. Average summer temps are 16-27°C (61-80°F) while winter can go from 8-16°C (46-61°F). The windchill factor can be harsh. Long periods of continuous rainfall around Adelaide are rare: average rainfall is 585mm (23in), mostly between May and August. Keep out of the fierce Aussie summer sun. Water temps are low compared to air temps. Winter surf requires a 3/2 steamer and booties will be necessary. Summer will allow springsuits but most surfers remain covered.

**Nature and Culture** – Apart from Adelaide, wild bush is the landscape! Main wildlife parks are Urimbirra Wildlife Park, Victor Harbor and Gorge Wildlife. Churches are outnumbered by pubs and nightclubs. Don't miss Rodney Fox (the man with 462 stitches from a bite) Shark Museum. Fishing is amazing. SA produces 50% of Australian wines. Kangaroos galore!

**Hazards and Hassles** – Bronze whalers and white pointers often patrol the area, be aware of when to avoid the water. Strong rips often happen with winds and tides. When on land, take care while scrambling down cliffs on Yorke and avoid the prodigious brown snakes. Crowd pressure is much less than other parts of Australia.

**Handy Hints** – All kinds of waves so take a full quiver. Check out Cutloose or MidCoast Shop&Board in Lonsdale or Nasty Boards in Beverly. Check Surf Power in Victor Harbor. No shops or shapers on Yorke. Expect $400 for a shortboard and $600 for a longboard. Beginners need to look for Surfbreak Surf School.

| WEATHER STATISTICS | J/F | M/A | M/J | J/A | S/O | N/D |
|---|---|---|---|---|---|---|
| total rainfall (mm) | 20 | 35 | 70 | 65 | 50 | 25 |
| consistency (days/mth) | 5 | 8 | 14 | 16 | 12 | 7 |
| min temp (°C/°F) | 17/63 | 14/57 | 9/48 | 8/46 | 10/50 | 14/57 |
| max temp (°C/°F) | 30/86 | 25/77 | 18/64 | 16/61 | 21/70 | 27/80 |

barrels are excellent. Baby Chinamans is a softer version, east of the main break which also works on lower tides and N winds. In summer, when everywhere is flat, **Ethel Wreck** can produce small intense waves next to a shipwreck. It's often too rippy and disorganised but when it's on, it's a crowd magnet! **Pondie** (Pondalowie Bay) is a safe bet when strong S winds and sizeable surf hit the sand covered reefs at low-mid tides, opposite an all-facilities campsite. It's a long walk over private property to get to **Trespassers**, a right with a heavy take-off and good workable wall, that doesn't like high tide so much. **Salmon Hole** is a scenic right pointbreak, when N winds are blowing it's fast, hollow and long, but avoid the suck rock in the middle. If it's a S wind, check around the other side at Daly Heads which is very consistent and can have big, challenging walls. Long, occasionally spitting lefts give **Spits** its name in a rippy, sharky area that has some other breaks worth finding.

The Adelaide spots inside the St Vincent Gulf are very tide reliant, working best on mid-high tide, on the push. Big swells from the right direction are needed and summers are mainly flat, so don't expect waves over 5ft (1.6m). The Esplanade makes coastal access easy, with lots of car parks. If there is a major storm with gusty SW winds, try **Y-Steps** or the Hump at Christies Beach, where refraction can make A-frames which should have a bit of power. In an E wind and large W-SW swell, **Seaford** rights offer the longest walls around, despite the sections and crowds. **Trigs Beach** needs the same conditions to get the average rights and lefts working near the observation tower. Goofies should check **The Trough**; the first section delivers some punch before fattening out in the channel. The south coast on the Fleurieu Peninsula picks up more swell and is offshore when N winds are blowing. Encounter Bay's epicentre is Victor Harbor, SA's most popular summer holiday area, although it is sometimes referred to as "shark alley"! Expect some brilliant sandbanks, mellow points and a few big wave locations, best surfed before the summer S winds get up. For mal-riders/beginners, **Middleton Point** is the place. Even with 50 guys out, this right point, rated in the top 10 gutless waves by *Tracks* in 2002, has room for everyone. It's useful to stay in Middleton where a handful of surf spots can be checked in 10 minutes. Drive west to **The Dump** for powerful reef rights, next to Granite Island. If swell action is close to zero, the final option is **Waitpinga**, which means "windy place" in Aboriginal. The beach can be seriously hollow but beware of rips and white pointers. The adventurous can take the ferry to Kangaroo Island, with countless turn-offs to rugged deserted spots. **Pennington Bay**'s shallow beachies can be fun on a medium swell with NE winds and, if swell and confidence get big, try **Cape Kersaint**'s left pointbreak, it's awesome!

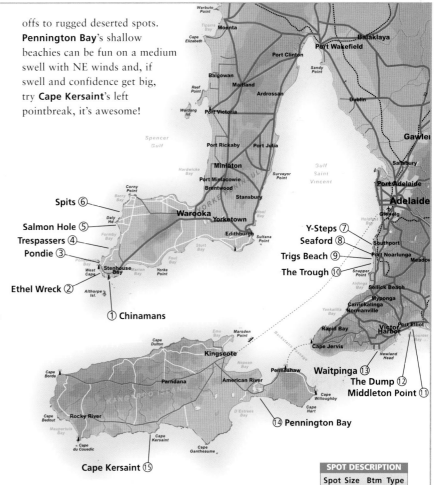

Spits ⑥
Salmon Hole ⑤
Trespassers ④
Pondie ③
Ethel Wreck ②
① Chinamans

Y-Steps ⑦
Seaford ⑧
Trigs Beach ⑨
The Trough ⑩

Waitpinga ⑬
The Dump ⑫
Middleton Point ⑪

⑭ Pennington Bay

Cape Kersaint ⑮

A lthough the Southern Ocean swells lash the coast with plentiful surf, only the most exposed parts get the full brunt of the 3-20ft (1-6m) swells with less seasonal changes than elsewhere. The profusion of islands and peninsulas has to be taken into account to know about Adelaide's local zones. Kangaroo blocks most of the S swells for Yorke and the mid-coast so favour the south coast in summer S swells. Only strong SW-W swells hit the mid-coast, preferably with high tides, so winter is usually better. Yorke's is definitely the best bet around Innes National park but not as many spots work at high tide. Surfing low tides on Yorke and high tides on the mid-coast is unrealistic but can help to decide itineraries depending on tidal timing. Because of straights and deep bays, tidal phases can be significant, over 8ft (2.5m). This is one of the country's few regions with tidal restrictions. As for winds, it's pretty much S-SW year round apart from winter when N-NE winds groom up the best surf conditions.

| SPOT DESCRIPTION | | | |
|---|---|---|---|
| Spot | Size | Btm | Type |
| ① | 12/3 | | |
| ② | 8/2 | | |
| ③ | 10/2 | | |
| ④ | 12/2 | | |
| ⑤ | 8/3 | | |
| ⑥ | 8/2 | | |
| ⑦ | 6/2 | | |
| ⑧ | 6/2 | | |
| ⑨ | 6/1 | | |
| ⑩ | 6/2 | | |
| ⑪ | 6/2 | | |
| ⑫ | 6/2 | | |
| ⑬ | 8/2 | | |
| ⑭ | 6/1 | | |
| ⑮ | 6/2 | | |

| SURF STATISTICS | J F | M A | M J | J A | S O | N D |
|---|---|---|---|---|---|---|
| dominant swell | S-SW | S-SW | S-SW | S-SW | S-SW | S-SW |
| swell size (ft) | 2 | 3-4 | 5-6 | 6 | 5 | 2-3 |
| consistency (%) | 30 | 50 | 70 | 80 | 60 | 40 |
| dominant wind | SE-SW | SE-SW | N-NE | SW-N | S-W | S-SW |
| average force | F3-F4 | F3 | F3-F4 | F3-F4 | F3-F4 | F4 |
| consistency (%) | 69 | 62 | 31 | 67 | 53 | 57 |
| water temp (°C/°F) | 19/66 | 18/64 | 15/59 | 13/55 | 14/57 | 17/63 |
| wetsuit | | | | | | |

Chinamans

# 115. Phillip Island

Corsair

ALL PHOTOS STEVE RYAN

**Summary**
+ CONSISTENT SUMMER SWELL
+ RIGHT POINTBREAKS
+ EASY ACCESS
+ QUALITY, POWERFUL BEACHES
+ GREAT OCEAN ROAD PROXIMITY

− COOL/COLD WATER
− COMPETITIVE CROWDS
− RIPS AND ONSHORES
− UNPREDICTABLE WEATHER

While the Great Ocean Road draws most surfers' attention, there is much more to the Victorian surf scene than meets the eye. If waveriders from Melbourne usually go west, it's because dominant SW winds are offshore there. What the East Coast lacks in quality, it gains in quantity with spots like Gunnamatta on the Mornington Peninsula or Woolamai on Phillip Island, rarely going flat. The indented coastline allows for a few offshore spots when the SW'ers are blowing, producing some quality rights in stormy, winter conditions. Portsea is only 91km (57mi) from the capital and reportedly a surfing venue since the '30s. In December '67, Cheviot Beach near Portsea made

Express Point

Woolamai

national headline news when Prime Minister Harold Holt either drowned or got taken by a shark in the surf.

West of Portsea, out on Point Nepean, **Quarantines** is very unusual, sometimes working when everywhere else is a mess. On a SE wind with a big swell, locals will boat in, otherwise it is a long trek to the unfriendly left line-up. The large expanse of Portsea's **Back Beach** has

## TRAVEL INFORMATION

**Population:**
4.9M Victoria
**Coastline:**
1,800km (1,125mi)
**Contests:**
WQS Woolamai (Jan),
Balin pro Junior
**Other Resources:**
triggerbros.com.au
surfshop.com.au
visitvictoria.com
phillipisland.net.au

**Getting There** – Visas: any country except NZ. Melbourne (3M hab) is Australia's 2nd busiest airport, open 24h a day, servicing all major int'l airlines. Major domestic carriers are Qantas and Virgin Blue. Melbourne is 10h drive from Adelaide and Sydney. A taxi costs $25 to the city centre. Driving time is 1h to Portsea and 2h to Phillip Island. Dep tax: $21

**Getting Around** – Victoria has first class freeways and highways. Roads are classified using M, A, B & C according to their quality and function – M roads are freeways and A roads are highways. Philip Island is connected to the mainland by a 640m long bridge at San Remo. Renting a car costs $30/d.

**Lodging and Food** – On Mornington Peninsula, stay in Portsea (Clifton Lodge: from $30/day), in Sorrento (Rose Caravan Park: cabins from $30 daily / 4 people) or Rye. On Phillip Island, stay in Ventnor (1st class B&B: from $35/day) or Woolamai (Sea Breeze: flats from $35/day). Expect $12 for a good meal.

**Weather** – South Victoria has the coolest weather in mainland Australia but not the rainiest with only 680mm (27in). The heaviest rainfall occurs on the East Coast. The main drag is the weather instability, it changes all the time. Aussies say: 'if you don't like the weather, just wait a minute'. Avoid June-August as it gets quite cold. Between seasons can be pleasant even though there will be cool spells with gusty winds. Summers from Dec to Feb are fairly dry and warm, averaging 22°C (72°F). The water never gets really warm, summers rarely reach 20°C (68°F) and in winter it dips down to 12°C (54°F). A 4/3mm steamer in winter and a light one in summer is the go.

**Nature and Culture** – Phillip Island switches gear for the 500cc Motorcycle Grand Prix in October. Don't miss the Seal Rocks Sea Life Centre, the Nobbies and the blowhole at Point Grant. Watch the Penguin Parade at sunset, when they cross Summerland Beach to return to their sand-dune burrows. Cape Woolamai rocks host a million short-tailed shearwaters.

**Hazards and Hassles** – By Australian standards, this is a trouble-free zone. Apart from reef cuts and intense crowds, there is not much to fear. The shark factor is relatively low although great whites have been witnessed in the area. Big, gnarly waves on the SW coasts, and beware regular, strong rips.

**Handy Hints** – Buy gear in local shops. Famous Trigger Bros surfboards & shops in Sorrento: from $470 up to 6'7" to $780 for a longboard. Try Ozmosis boards in Hastings. East Coast Surf School at Pt Leo, Mornington Peninsula Surf School on St Andrews Beach both give lessons. Mornington is home of the Balin surf brand.

| WEATHER STATISTICS | J/F | M/A | M/J | J/A | S/O | N/D |
|---|---|---|---|---|---|---|
| total rainfall (mm) | 50 | 55 | 55 | 50 | 65 | 60 |
| consistency (days/mth) | 9 | 11 | 15 | 17 | 15 | 12 |
| min temp (°C/°F) | 14/57 | 12/54 | 8/46 | 6/43 | 9/48 | 12/54 |
| max temp (°C/°F) | 26/79 | 22/72 | 16/61 | 14/57 | 18/64 | 21/70 |

variable banks,
none of which
compare to nearby
Spooks for heaviness. The
most consistent spot on
this SW exposed coast is
**Gunnamatta**, home of many contests
for its power and shape. A webcam
looks out from the second car park
(pay in summer), focusing on fast
peaks whose quality is dictated by the equally
fast flowing rips that shape the sandbanks and
channels. Takes a SW swell, NE winds and
anything up to double overhead on the push. Since
November '98, surfers have been demonstrating to get
the sewage outfall closed. The lighthouse at **Cape Shank**
attracts some serious lefts, holding some serious size,
amidst serious scenery. Flinders Beach is dotted with
different reefbreaks, **Meanos** being the nastiest wave,
tucked beneath the West Head cliffs. Even at high tide,
the lefts can be intimidating, but the rights are easier, as
is the inside reform. The main spot at Point Leo,
**Suicides**, is actually a playful right point with long,
workable walls, boosted by the incoming tide on bigger
swells. If it's not big enough for the point, then nearby
breaks like Peak Rock, Crunchies Pt and some other reefs
should have a wave. Philip Island, 26km (16mi) long and
9km (5mi) wide is Victoria's leading tourist destination
attracting 3.5 million visitors each year. There are over
20 spots, ranging from quality beachbreaks to right and
left reefs and world-class right pointbreaks. The western
tip, best known for multitudes of penguins, benefits from
breaks on its north side like **Flynn's Reef**'s epic rights that
zip down the point and stay offshore in winds from NE
to S. **Cat Bay** is the mellow beachie where all beginners
should go, especially on decent swells and southerly
winds. The south side has many good right pointbreaks
like **The Crack**, a section of the point at Summerland Bay.
**Smith's Beach** is a rare, relaxed beachbreak with good
low tide form and some wind protection, close to the
experts-only **Express Point**. EP is the most radical reef on
the island, sporting world-class, ledgy righthand tubes,
only for those who can handle ankle-biting crowds,
elevator drops and reef rash. **Surfies Point** is a bigger
swell spot, needing more S and E in the swell to make the
big drops link through to the inside. The most reliable
beachbreaks are at Woolamai, a series of powerful breaks
facing car parks; walk eastwards to **Magic Lands** to enjoy

a bit more space.
If Woolamai is flat,
there's always **Kilcunda** on
the mid-east coast. This swell magnet is often too
big and dangerous but power is the rule. Another spot
to hold stormy conditions is **Eagle's Nest**, 8km (5mi) from
Inverloch, whose long slow rights can imitate a decent
Torquay right pointbreak in big S swells and W winds.

Reef near Cat Bay

Australia's SW facing coast gets huge conditions,
sometimes up to 15-20ft (5-6m), but it is the SE
facing coast that sees these unruly swells cleaned
up and groomed by the dominant westerly air flow. Come
summertime, exposed SW facing beachbreaks enjoy extra
consistency, even though the W-SW winds will be
cross/onshore. There will be plenty of 2-6ft (0.6-2m)
messy waves or smaller and cleaner waves by the
sheltered right pointbreaks. Because of Tasmania, the low
pressure systems can stall, sending S or even SE swells
back to the coast. Winds tend to be W, more SW in
summer and NW in winter but as cold fronts move in on
the coast, any direction is possible. When storms come,
winds blow S, then E, then N on a cycle that can vary
from a few hours to several
days. Tide amplitude can
reach 8ft (2.5m), so grab a
Port Phillip Bay tide table and
work out the variations for
remote spots.

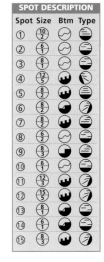

## SPOT DESCRIPTION

| Spot | Size | Btm | Type |
|---|---|---|---|
| ① | 10/2 | | |
| ② | 6/1 | | |
| ③ | 8/1 | | |
| ④ | 12/3 | | |
| ⑤ | 8/2 | | |
| ⑥ | 8/2 | | |
| ⑦ | 6/2 | | |
| ⑧ | 5/1 | | |
| ⑨ | 5/2 | | |
| ⑩ | 6/1 | | |
| ⑪ | 12/4 | | |
| ⑫ | 15/4 | | |
| ⑬ | 8/2 | | |
| ⑭ | 6/1 | | |
| ⑮ | 8/3 | | |

Point Lonsdale to Portsea

## SURF STATISTICS

| | J F | M A | M J | J A | S O | N D |
|---|---|---|---|---|---|---|
| dominant swell | S-SW | S-SW | S-SW | S-SW | S-SW | S-SW |
| swell size (ft) | 4 | 4-5 | 5-6 | 6-7 | 5-6 | 4 |
| consistency (%) | 50 | 70 | 80 | 80 | 70 | 50 |
| dominant wind | SW-W | SW-W | SW-NW | SW-NW | SW-W | SW-W |
| average force | F4 | F4-F5 | F4-F5 | F4 | F4-F5 | F4-F5 |
| consistency (%) | 39 | 44 | 55 | 59 | 44 | 47 |
| water temp (°C/°F) | 17/63 | 17/63 | 14/57 | 12/54 | 13/55 | 15/59 |
| wetsuit | | | | | | |

VICTORIA

TASMANIA

Hobart

# 116. Hobart

Chain of Lagoons

**Summary**

+ ROARING FORTIES EXPOSURE
+ VARIETY OF BEACH AND POINTS
+ PENINSULAS AND INDENTED COAST
+ UNCROWDED AND MOUNTAINOUS

– WINDY AND CHILLY WINTER SURF
– OCCASIONALLY FLAT SE COAST
– SLOW ACCESS
– EXPENSIVE TO GET THERE

ALL PHOTOS SEAN DAVEY

Until April 2001, not much was known about Tasmania's waves. Australia's sixth state, a 300km (188mi) long triangular island was, until around 10,000 years ago, joined to the mainland but it is now about 240km (150mi) away across a shallow sea, the Bass Strait. Tassie was put on the map when Drew Courtney, Mark Matthews and Kieren Perrow scored an horrendous right ledge on the Tasman Peninsula vaguely named VD Land (Tasmania was originally known as Van Dieman's Land). Like Jeff Clark with Mavericks, a tall and quiet guy named Andrew Campbell rode the waves for years before the spot got worldwide exposure. It is a Teahupoo-like right, without the contest and tropical allure, but with awesome triple lips and huge screaming barrels. The majority of surfers will be seeking less life-threatening spots and Hobart makes a good base to explore from.

## TRAVEL INFORMATION

**Population:**
130,000 Hobart
**Coastline:**
3,200km (2,000mi)
**Contests:**
Bruny Southern
Challenge (Feb),
Clifton
**Other Resources:**
*Video:* Taz Zero One
coastview.com.au
discovertasmania.com.au
tourtasmania.com
tasmicup.com

**Getting There** – Visa: all apart from NZ. Qantas, Regional Express and Virgin Blue operate frequent direct flights. Melbourne/Hobart is $250r/t, Sydney is $360 and Brisbane is $500 (rarely direct). Launceston is the main north coast entry: cross the Bass Strait with *Spirit of Tasmania* ship (15h, overnight crossing, $50min/p + $15 car).

**Getting Around** – The road system is dense around Hobart (like the Derwent 5-lane concrete-arch Tasman Bridge) and topography gets wild with islands and peninsulas. Changing coasts, catching ferries (Bruny) & hiking to spots takes time. Car rental starts at $30/d. Consider boat trips with Tassie Surf.

**Lodging and Food** – Staying in Hobart is an option but driving times increase considerably. Favour Taranna (Norfolk Bayview B&B,

$36/dble), or Port Arthur (Sea Change Safety Cove, $78/dble) or Eagleneck (Wunnamurra Waterfront B & B: $67). Enjoy a wide spectrum of berry fruits and apples, world-beating ales and wines or full flavoured cheeses.

**Weather** – With latitudes between 40° and 43.5°, the Apple Isle enjoys a temperate, maritime climate, meaning four seasons in one day! Its location on the north edge of the Roaring Forties westerly airstream, plus its mountainous terrain, produce marked variations of climate and rainfall, including the highest average rainfall of Australia. Annual rainfall can be as high 3600mm (142"in) in the west and as low as 500mm (20"in) in the east. In the western districts, maximum rainfall is received in winter while the eastern coasts have evenly distributed rainfall. In winter, it occasionally snows in Hobart and snow on Mt Wellington's 1270m (3810ft) peak is common. Tassie is the most mountainous of Australian States and small peaks dominate the landscape. Because of gusty winds and winter surfing, be prepared with 5mm wetsuits, thick gloves, hoods and booties. A 3/2mm steamer may just be acceptable in summer.

**Nature and Culture** – 40% of Tassie is National Parks, making an outdoor playground free of pollution. Ski and surf in the same day (Ben Lomond resort). Climb Mt Wellington or visit Port Arthur's penal settlement. Coal used to be mined around Nubeena in convict times: look for barracks, convict quarters and the lime kiln. Keep eyes peeled for Tasmanian devils or the presumed extinct Tasmanian tigers!

**Hazards and Hassles** – Cold conditions might feel freezing to visiting Aussies from warm regions. Although crowds are rare, some spots are very sensitive, be very respectful with locals. Mind the nasty rips when close to rivermouths. Be ready to walk and get wet if camping. Weather is very unstable and unpredictable. Bring lots of clothes.

**Handy Hints** – Buy gear at South Arm Surf Shop and there is a women's surfing school. Book a surf mission with Tassiesurf.com: day package cost $85, camping packages are $100 and boat charters are $260 to be divided by the number of surfers. There are webcams at Clifton Beach and Eagleneck Reef.

| WEATHER STATISTICS | J/F | M/A | M/J | J/A | S/O | N/D |
|---|---|---|---|---|---|---|
| total rainfall (mm) | 45 | 45 | 50 | 50 | 55 | 55 |
| consistency (days/mth) | 12 | 14 | 15 | 18 | 18 | 15 |
| min temp (°C/°F) | 12/54 | 10/50 | 6/43 | 5/41 | 7/45 | 10/50 |
| max temp (°C/°F) | 22/72 | 19/66 | 13/55 | 12/54 | 16/61 | 20/68 |

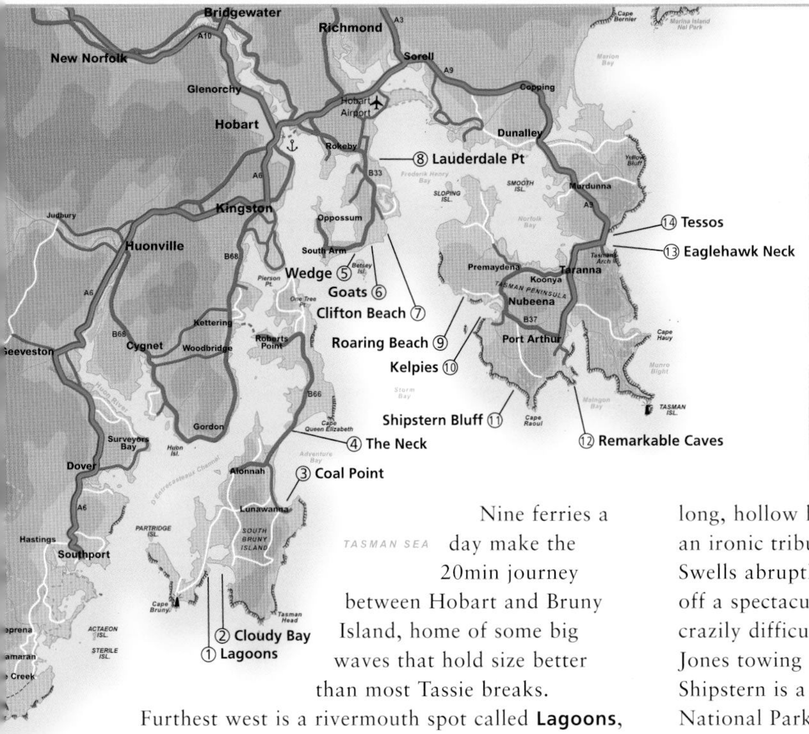


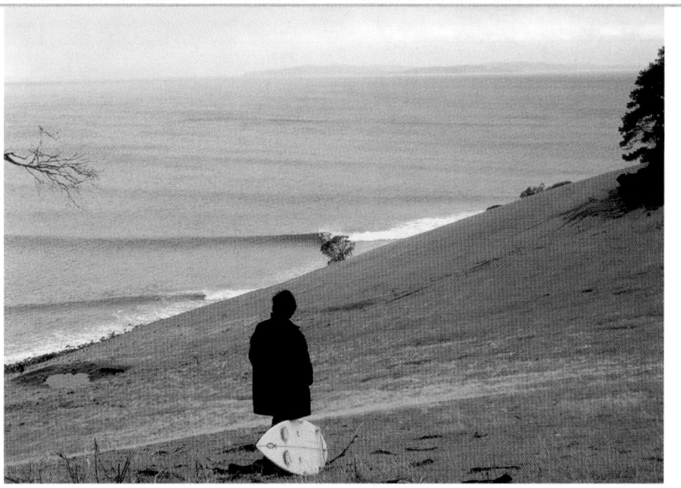

Nine ferries a day make the 20min journey between Hobart and Bruny Island, home of some big waves that hold size better than most Tassie breaks.

Furthest west is a rivermouth spot called **Lagoons**, where there is potential for long rights on a big swell, with the right sandbank, high tides and W-NW winds. On a medium swell, scenic **Cloudy Bay** can produce good beachbreak waves, favouring rights breaking into the rip. Around this area is Labillardire State Reserve, hosting a few fickle reefs and Australia's southernmost lighthouse. Driving back, stop by **Coal Point** if the swell is big, because this is Bruny's best pointbreak. Hairy lefts unload over rock and kelp, the first section being fast with a challenging take-off. Other spots like **The Neck** are less consistent but it's a small island and waves are fairly easy to find. There are quite a few places to stay but many waveriders tend to camp in the surf's backyard. Betsey Island sits 1km (0.6mi) off the South Arm's coastline, forcing large swells to wrap around it and reform into the sucky barrels of the occasionally crowded **Wedge**. Access is through private property. Another fun stretch of exposed beachie is **Goats** but **Clifton Beach** is Hobart's most popular spot, only 30min drive from the city centre. When the swell gets huge, other breaks on the E side get classic, small right points like Seven Mile, Cremorne or **Lauderdale Point**. Out on the Tasman Peninsula, the main town of Nubeena has access to **Roaring Beach**'s often surfed beachbreak and **Kelpies**, a long, hollow left pointbreak. **Shipstern Bluff** or Fluffys, an ironic tribute to its power, is hardly ever ridden. Swells abruptly hit the granite ledge, only a few metres off a spectacular boulder-piled headland, creating a crazily difficult ride that only Campbell, Ross Clarke-Jones towing in and a handful of others have ridden. Shipstern is a 2h or 7km (4.5mi) hike around the Tasman National Park. South of Port Arthur, **Remarkable Caves** is not only a tourist spot but also has low tide peaks, and a scary paddle out past caves. A 1h drive from Hobart is **Eaglehawk Neck**, hosting a powerful left on special conditions that include NE swell, W winds and high tide. **Tessos**, a sucky, demanding, quality right over kelp-covered rock, is just next door. It needs huge SE swells to turn on but can handle any wind and works on high tide.

Roughly the same latitude as New Zealand South Island, Tasmania receives the brunt of Roaring Forties winter swells pounding its western shores. Most of the swell there is big and onshore with very little access apart from Marrawah. Driving the north coast is easy but it faces the Bass Strait, is very inconsistent and should only be checked on major swells. The east coast is also inconsistent but the coastline hides some great spots like Bicheno or Scamander and the weather is drier. That leaves the south coast with the best surf through austral winter, but the water is cold (11°C/52°F) with fresh snow on Mt Wellington. Most spots don't face directly into the swell apart from Bruny's Cloudy Bay where 10ft+ (3m) surf can be had. Normally a 15ft (5m) SW swell will see 4-6ft (1.2-2m) waves along the coast. N-NW winds are the best for S-SE exposed spots, usually during May-June but as with any low latitude destination, instability is the rule. However, the extremely indented coastline is useful for offshores or sideshores.

**SPOT DESCRIPTION**

| Spot | Size | Btm | Type |
|---|---|---|---|
| ① | 8/1 | | |
| ② | 10/1 | | |
| ③ | 10/2 | | |
| ④ | 8/1 | | |
| ⑤ | 6/1 | | |
| ⑥ | 6/1 | | |
| ⑦ | 6/1 | | |
| ⑧ | 6/2 | | |
| ⑨ | 8/1 | | |
| ⑩ | 6/2 | | |
| ⑪ | 18/2 | | |
| ⑫ | 6/2 | | |
| ⑬ | 6/2 | | |
| ⑭ | 6/2 | | |

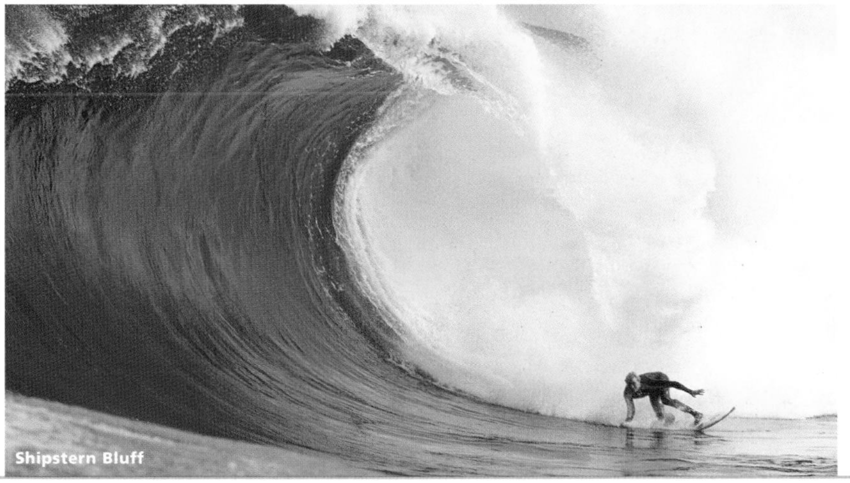
Shipstern Bluff

| SURF STATISTICS | J F | M A | M J | J A | S O | N D |
|---|---|---|---|---|---|---|
| dominant swell | S-SE | S-SE | S-SE | S-SE | S-SE | S-SE |
| swell size (ft) | 2-3 | 4-5 | 5-6 | 6 | 5-6 | 3 |
| consistency (%) | 50 | 60 | 70 | 80 | 70 | 60 |
| dominant wind | W-NW | SW-NW | W-N | SW-NW | W-N | W-NW |
| average force | F3-F5 | F3-F5 | F3-F5 | F5 | F4-F5 | F4-F5 |
| consistency (%) | 34 | 53 | 58 | 59 | 58 | 38 |
| water temp (°C/°F) | 15/59 | 13/55 | 11/52 | 11/52 | 11/52 | 13/55 |
| wetsuit | | | | | | |

# 117. Byron Bay

Lennox Head

DON BALCH

## Summary

+ BEAUTIFUL RIGHT POINTBREAKS
+ N-S SWELL WINDOW
+ BYRON BAY BACKPACKER HEAVEN
+ WARM, CLEAR WATER & DOLPHINS
+ LUSH NATURAL BACKDROP

– RARELY ANY BIG SWELLS
– LACK OF REEFBREAKS
– INTENSE AND CONSTANT CROWDS
– PRICEY ACCOMMODATION

B yron Bay is on mainland Australia's eastern tip, sticking out into the Pacific and attracting a wide range of curious visitors. Dolphins and sharks frequent the veritable array of long golden beaches and rocky headlands that have attracted surfers for almost half a century. From a sleepy coastal hippy town that encompassed the NSW north coast vibe, Byron has mutated into a virtual city, attracting movie stars, property developers and hordes of backpackers. While there are some epic set-ups, a lack of decent sized swell dictates that conditions are fairly inconsistent, relying on summer cyclone swells or big winter south swells to create waves worth remembering. Typically, shoulder high waves snap across the sandbanks in clean, small size swells, while bigger

The Wreck

JOLI

BILL MORRIS

days see short, steep close-outs relying primarily on wind and tide to give rideable waves at the main beaches. It's these bigger days that get the handful of pointbreaks to rumble into life with locals descending from miles around. Byron Bay gained its popularity in the '60s as a

## TRAVEL INFORMATION

**Population:** 6,500 Byron
**Coastline:**
1,900km (1,180mi) NSW
**Contests:** None
**Other Resources:**
*Video:* Five North Swells
coastalwatch.com.au
byronbaynow.com

**Getting There** – 3 months electronic visa except for NZ. Most int'l flights arrive in Sydney (12h away), but Brisbane is only 2h30 drive away. The bus from Sydney to Byron Bay takes about 14h (A$140 r/t). Local airport is Ballina but favour Coolangatta on the Gold Coast (1h) for dirt cheap rental cars (from $18/d). No dep tax.

**Getting Around** – There are very few coastal roads and lots of curves and hills on Pacific Highway 1. Beware of speed traps and random breath testing. Driving around the rivermouth at Ballina takes time; don't paddle across, there are rips and sharks! Byron Car hire costs $175/week. Getting a parking space in downtown Byron can be tricky.

**Lodging and Food** – Despite its success, Byron has not become a high-rise metropolis. Pressure on real estate means finding a place to stay is getting expensive. Backpacker dorms remain around $15 (Nomads, Arts Factory), but a double is $60 and up! Expect $20 for a decent meal, lots of natural, organic food places. Save some budget for a coldie!

**Weather** – The north coast climate is much closer to the Gold Coast subtropical weather than Sydney. The northern rivers provide as much humidity but hills and mountains like Mount Warning (3535ft/1160m) provide more inland breeze at times. Summer temps average 21-28°C (70-82°F) and winter temps 15-21°C (59-70°F), giving Byron Bay an excellent year round climate. The beaches around Byron offer clean, warm water, 26°C/79°F in summer and 21°C/70°F in winter, a springsuit should be enough for most sessions, the need for a light fullsuit only required on cold winter mornings or in cold SW'ers.

**Nature and Culture** – It's a model of mixing nature and development. The coast looks untouched with erosion beating wooden stairways to walk around headlands. Gaze at whales Feb-March and schools of dolphins May-October. Socialising is great in lively bars like the Beach Hotel, which displays big screen surf videos.

**Hazards and Hassles** – A honeymooner diving off Julian Rocks was killed by a shark in 1994. Lots of shark sightings though at Tallows, Suffolk Park and Ballina. Bluebottles (stinging man-o-war) on NE winds are more of a nightmare. Crowds are the thickest ever but respect and competitiveness are the rules.

**Handy Hints** – Don't bother travelling with equipment; shapers like McTavish, Maddog and Bamboo surfboards have showrooms both in town and the industrial estate. Expect $350 for a shortboard and $450 for a longboard. Beginners can have a go with Byron Bay Surf School, Stylesurfing or Kool Katz. Avoid Dec-Jan high season.

| WEATHER STATISTICS | J/F | M/A | M/J | J/A | S/O | N/D |
|---|---|---|---|---|---|---|
| total rainfall (mm) | 178 | 197 | 175 | 97 | 98 | 132 |
| consistency (days/mth) | 15 | 16 | 13 | 9 | 10 | 12 |
| min temp (°C/°F) | 21/70 | 18/64 | 13/55 | 12/54 | 15/59 | 19/66 |
| max temp (°C/°F) | 27/80 | 26/79 | 21/70 | 20/68 | 23/74 | 26/79 |

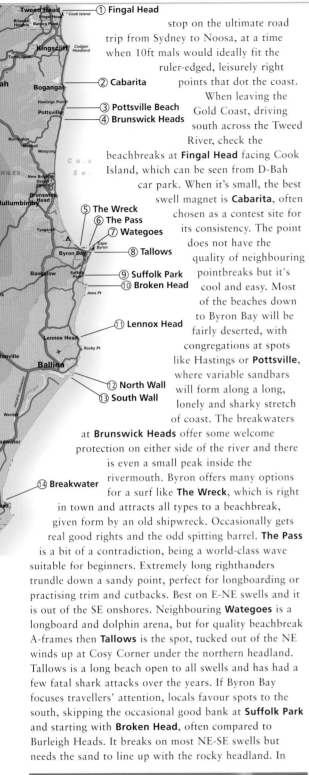

Map labels:
- Tweed Head
- Cook Island
- Bilambil Heights
- Banora Point
- Fingal Head
- ① Fingal Head
- Kingscliff
- Cudgen Headland
- Tumbulgum
- ibah
- Bogangar
- ② Cabarita
- Hastings Point
- ③ Pottsville Beach
- Pottsville
- ④ Brunswick Heads
- Burringbar
- Mooball
- Wooyung
- Coral Sea
- THWALES
- New Brighton
- Ocean Shores
- Brunswick Head
- Mullumbimby
- ⑤ The Wreck
- ⑥ The Pass
- ⑦ Wategoes
- Cape Byron
- Tyagarah
- Byron Bay
- ⑧ Tallows
- Bangalow
- Suffolk Park
- ⑨ Suffolk Park
- ⑩ Broken Head
- Jews Pt
- unes
- ⑪ Lennox Head
- Lennox Head
- Rocky Pt
- Alstonville
- Ballina
- ⑫ North Wall
- ⑬ South Wall
- Warden
- Broadwater
- ⑭ Breakwater
- s Head

stop on the ultimate road trip from Sydney to Noosa, at a time when 10ft mals would ideally fit the ruler-edged, leisurely right points that dot the coast. When leaving the Gold Coast, driving south across the Tweed River, check the beachbreaks at **Fingal Head** facing Cook Island, which can be seen from D-Bah car park. When it's small, the best swell magnet is **Cabarita**, often chosen as a contest site for its consistency. The point does not have the quality of neighbouring pointbreaks but it's cool and easy. Most of the beaches down to Byron Bay will be fairly deserted, with congregations at spots like Hastings or **Pottsville**, where variable sandbars will form along a long, lonely and sharky stretch of coast. The breakwaters at **Brunswick Heads** offer some welcome protection on either side of the river and there is even a small peak inside the rivermouth. Byron offers many options for a surf like **The Wreck**, which is right in town and attracts all types to a beachbreak, given form by an old shipwreck. Occasionally gets real good rights and the odd spitting barrel. **The Pass** is a bit of a contradiction, being a world-class wave suitable for beginners. Extremely long righthanders trundle down a sandy point, perfect for longboarding or practising trim and cutbacks. Best on E-NE swells and it is out of the SE onshores. Neighbouring **Wategoes** is a longboard and dolphin arena, but for quality beachbreak A-frames then **Tallows** is the spot, tucked out of the NE winds up at Cosy Corner under the northern headland. Tallows is a long beach open to all swells and has had a few fatal shark attacks over the years. If Byron Bay focuses travellers' attention, locals favour spots to the south, skipping the occasional good bank at **Suffolk Park** and starting with **Broken Head**, often compared to Burleigh Heads. It breaks on most NE-SE swells but needs the sand to line up with the rocky headland. In

The Pass

MOONWALKER

February 1962, two Kiwis stumbled upon **Lennox Head**, now generally regarded as Australia's finest righthand point. Few compare for speed, barrel sections, length of ride and an ability to handle the biggest NE-S swells. Also outstanding is the current, difficult entry and exit over nasty boulders and the thick crowd of local rippers. The first photos were published in *Surfing World* in 1966, followed by a sealed road in 1972, and since then surfers have flocked to the break, including hardcore riders from the surrounding countryside that keep a long pintail under the house for big Lennox days. There are uncrowded reefs down to Ballina where real wedging peaks hit the **North** and **South Wall** groynes at the Richmond rivermouth. Great wind protection from NE or S winds, but the talented local crew are always on it. Evans Head tends to get by-passed as it is a detour off the Pacific Highway. The **Breakwater** at the rivermouth has its days with some rights protected from the S winds, but the curious will find better beachbreaks and a right point nearby.

The main 2-8ft (0.6-2.5m) winter swells occur April-September from lows stationed in the Tasman Sea producing consistent E-S swells. In summer, December-April, there is the tropical NE cyclone season in the Coral Sea. There are usually about 2-3 per month lasting 3-7 days. However, they're not as predictable and wave-generous as Antarctic lows. If the cyclone is too close, the surf will be choppy and erratic. Wind is crucial, the best being SW, which often blows May to August. Between January and April, winds are sea breezes with dominant NE direction. Occasional hot NW'ers will groom everything on the coast but as temps rise, the NE'ers kick back in. As a general rule, beachies are better at high tides and pointbreaks on the low tides. Tide range can reach 6ft (2m), get a tide table.

**SPOT DESCRIPTION**

| Spot | Size | Btm | Type |
|---|---|---|---|
| ① | 6/1 | | |
| ② | 8/1 | | |
| ③ | 8/1 | | |
| ④ | 8/1 | | |
| ⑤ | 8/1 | | |
| ⑥ | 8/1 | | |
| ⑦ | 6/1 | | |
| ⑧ | 6/1 | | |
| ⑨ | 6/1 | | |
| ⑩ | 8/1 | | |
| ⑪ | 12/3 | | |
| ⑫ | 8/1 | | |
| ⑬ | 8/1 | | |
| ⑭ | 8/1 | | |

| SURF STATISTICS | J F | M A | M J | J A | S O | N D |
|---|---|---|---|---|---|---|
| dominant swell | NE | NE-SE | SE | SE | SE | NE |
| swell size (ft) | 3-4 | 3-4 | 2-3 | 3-4 | 2-3 | 2 |
| consistency (%) | 70 | 80 | 60 | 70 | 60 | 50 |
| dominant wind | E-S | E-S | SE-SW | SE-SW | N-SE | N-SE |
| average force | F4 | F4 | F4 | F4 | F4 | F4 |
| consistency (%) | 62 | 63 | 59 | 49 | 61 | 73 |
| water temp (°C/°F) | 25/77 | 24/75 | 21/70 | 19/66 | 20/68 | 23/74 |
| wetsuit | | | | | | |

Tallow Beach

JOLI

# 118. Sunshine Coast

QUEENSLAND

Brisbane

NEW SOUTH WALES

**Summary**
+ GROUND AND CYCLONE SWELLS
+ LOTS OF SOFT RIGHT POINTBREAKS
+ MANY EASY ACCESS BEACHIES
+ BEGINNERS PARADISE IN NOOSA

− INTENSE CROWDS
− FICKLE POINTBREAKS
− LACK OF POWER AND SIZE
− FAIRLY EXPENSIVE

MOONWALKER

Tea Tree, Noosa

An hour's drive from Brisbane lies a long coastal strip of pristine beaches, tropical landscapes, shimmering waterways and exciting towns. There are dozens of so-called sunshine coasts but this is "The" Sunshine Coast, the northernmost stretch of reliable surf in Australia and home of the fabled right points of Noosa Heads. Noosa has become a ritzy resort village with beachfront boutiques, bars and restaurants, surrounded by lush, tropical vegetation and National Parks. Heading south down to Caloundra are a string of modern tourist towns and miles of golden sand beachbreak, broken only by a couple of headlands. In stark contrast, a trip north in a 4WD over 80km (50mi) of low tide beach, arrives at Double Island Point and the totally wild landscape of Frasier Island.

Wurtulla Beach near Kawana

MOONWALKER

It's a short hop from Rainbow Beach over to Frasier Island, the largest sand island in the world and probably Queensland's biggest surf. There are two right points: Waddy Point and Indian Head, both highly dependent on the constantly shifting sandbanks for any quality shape. The 120km of Seventy-Five Mile Beach is dead straight with few good sandbanks except near the *Maheno* shipwreck.

YEP

## TRAVEL INFORMATION

**Population:**
3.7M Queensland
**Coastline:**
7,400km (4,625mi)
**Contests:**
Noosa Surf Festival (Mar)
**Other Resources:**
learntosurf.com.au
sunshinecoast.com

**Getting There** – Most international flights arrive in Sydney, but Brisbane is only 1hr south of Caloundra. The Sunshine Coast Airport is 30min from Noosa with daily flights from Sydney: $150o/w or Melbourne $220o/w. Suncoast Pacific is the major bus company serving the coast from Brisbane to Noosa: $10 o/w. No departure tax. 3 months electronic visa.

**Getting Around** – The Sunshine motorway is efficient, free and coastal while the Bruce Highway is faster but 15km (9mi) from the coast. Zealous police use laser guns, radar and automatic cameras for catching speedsters. Double Island Point or Fraser Island require a good 4WD. Rent a car in Brisbane ($25/d). You could get by in Noosa biking and walking.

**Lodging and Food** – There are only 2 cheap backpackers in Noosa (Koala: $20 for dble, $10 for a dorm), most other places to stay are deluxe motels and Units ($60p/p) up to Sheraton (from $200/d). Other towns are easier to find deals. Avoid summer high season or book very early. Expect $10 for a decent meal or go to fast food establishments if you need to save money.

**Weather** – The Sunshine Coast enjoys a warm, subtropical climate with rainfall concentrated in short wet seasons. There are about 120 rainy days with an annual rainfall of 1200mm (48in). It has one of the highest sunshine readings in the world, averaging 7h a day. The variation between summer and winter is minimal. Winter varies between 12-21°C (54-70°F) while summers (Dec-Feb) average 17-28°C (63-82°F). Spring (Sep-Nov) and autumn (March to May) temps range from 13-25°C (56-77°F). Temps in the Blackall Range can be a bit cooler while coastal areas enjoy sea breezes. Ocean temps rate up to 26°C (79°F). No wetsuits needed Oct-April while a springsuit or thin steamer is perfect from May-Sept.

**Nature and Culture** – Visit Underwater World in Mooloolaba, the Glasshouse Mountains, Australia Zoo with its amazing saltwater crocodile shows, Aussie World & Ettamogah Pub in Caloundra. Noosa gets lively at The Koalas but there is more wildlife than nightlife in Hasting Street.

**Hazards and Hassles** – Australians suffer the highest skin cancer rates in the world – take precautions. Avoid the deadly blue ring octopus and box jellyfish. Shark attacks, especially near islands, occur more frequently on cloudy, sultry summer days. Noosa hides many urchins in the eroded boulders but the constant, competitive crowd is the main hassle.

**Handy Hints** – Noosa longboards cost a mere $400-450 or try Eternity Surf or Classic Malibu. Take lessons with Learn to Surf or Wavesense. Pick up a Surfing Queensland leaflet, which lists 56 locales (surf spots).

| WEATHER STATISTICS | J/F | M/A | M/J | J/A | S/O | N/D |
|---|---|---|---|---|---|---|
| total rainfall (mm) | 160 | 120 | 70 | 50 | 60 | 110 |
| consistency (days/mth) | 14 | 14 | 9 | 8 | 9 | 11 |
| min temp (°C/°F) | 21/70 | 18/64 | 12/54 | 10/50 | 15/59 | 19/66 |
| max temp (°C/°F) | 29/84 | 27/80 | 22/72 | 21/70 | 26/79 | 29/84 |

Back on the mainland, **Double Island Point** is a safe cyclone swell bet for extremely long rights by the lighthouse and occasional lefts on the beachbreak. Jelly legs and arms dictate walking back, decreasing the chance of meeting the abundant sharks. Not usually crowded thanks to the difficult access. Reliable, local tour operators can provide the necessary 4WD transport. *Cherry Venture* shipwreck can be the exception to the close-out rule along the beach highway beside the Cooloola National Park. Noosa became a surfing Mecca back in the '60s, so expect heavy crowds, especially during cyclones. The five points all differ slightly; First Point is mellow smaller and perfect for beginners. Johnsons is slightly bigger and faster, but still easy. **Boiling Pot** is the outside take-off section of National Park, which diminishes in size as it heads towards Johnsons. **Tea Tree** (Ti or T) is the locals' favourite and a 20 minute walk into the Noosa National Park, but it doesn't deter the crowds. Steeper and hollower than the other points, especially at low tide, when there is more chance of stepping on an urchin. Granite Bay shows the most size, but relies on sand formations and rarely equals the other points for perfection. Drop-ins are inevitable and local longboarders often practise the time-honoured code of wave-sharing. The media rate Noosa as being one of the world's top 4 longboard waves, which is celebrated by the Noosa Surfing Festival in early March. The point set-up is ideal for both beginners and advanced surfers as swell regularly wraps into the north facing bays giving perfect 2-8ft (0.6-2.5m) waves and is offshore in winds from SE-W. Relief from the masses requires a long walk through the National Park to **Alexandria Bay** which is a consistent beachbreak that picks up any swell going. It is also accessible from **Sunshine Beach**, another swell magnet with powerful peaks in the lee of the northern headland. From here the coastline is straight to Coolum, with many access routes leading to numerous beachbreaks like **Peregian Beach**. The playful sandbars at **Coolum Beach** need a bit of size to get into the two NE-facing bays, sheltered from S winds by Point Arkwright. En route to Maroochydore, are the serious waves of **Mudjimba Island**, aka Woman Island. Legend has it that the island is the 'head' of a nearby mountain, which was decapitated. The island provides a rocky base for some chunky lefts and grinding, ledgy rights that wrap around the ends of the

MOONWALKER

**Point Cartwright**

island. Most surfers will hire a boat, as the 30min paddle back is arduous and scary in the sharky waters. Maroochydore is the biggest centre on the Sunshine Coast (pop 125,000), incorporating some walled up beachbreaks and pockets of reef leading down to Alexandra Headland. Avoid the central beach masses by checking places like **Pin Cushion** behind the caravan park. In small swells, Alexandra Headland or **The Bluff** is a fat and forgiving righthand point that gets packed with longboarders in the water and tourists on the beach. **Point Cartwright**'s scenic headland provides S wind shelter for a challenging right point which shuts down on a breakwall. Further out there's an even heavier right ledge for hellmen only. **Kawana** has tons of access to consistent and hollow beachbreaks, sometimes stabilised on the coffee rock bottom. The surf becomes less crowded and more powerful down towards Wurtulla and **Long Track** in the Currimundi Lake Conservation Park. The most southerly surf town, Caloundra, has eight spots facing both north and south. Apart from the Ann Street peaks, The Reef is the premier wave, breaking way offshore with malicious power. Big boards and big balls for the big barrels! **Moffats** is a longboard friendly right point with crumbly sections, more makeable at higher tides. South of town, Kings Beach gets good beachies in NE'ers and **Happys** offers long, full lefts off the Pumicestone Passage.

The main 2-8ft (0.6-2.5m) swells occur December-March during the tropical NE cyclone season in the Coral Sea. There are about 2-3 monthly lasting 3-7 days. However, they're not as predictable and wave-generous as Antarctic lows. If the cyclone is too close, the surf will be choppy and erratic. Southern Hemisphere winter also produces 2-8ft (0.6-2.5m) SE swells on the E-SE exposed breaks. The best winds (SE-SW) often blow May to August, which unfortunately is not the cyclone season. Between January and April, winds are not bad with dominant E-S direction. The most unfavourable period starts in September with lots of N winds on the E-NE facing coastline but it begins to improve in December. The northerly drift of coastal sands is a local phenomenon. As a general rule, beachies are better at high tides and pointbreaks on the low tides. Tidal range can reach 6ft (2m), so get a tide table.

## Map labels

① Double Island Point
② Boiling Pot
③ Tea Tree
④ Alexandria Bay
⑤ Sunshine Beach
⑥ Peregian Creek
⑦ Coolum Beach
⑧ Mudjimba Island
⑨ Pin Cushion
⑩ The Bluff
⑪ Point Cartwright
⑫ Kawana
⑬ Long Track
⑭ Moffats
⑮ Happys

### SPOT DESCRIPTION

| Spot | Size | Btm | Type |
|---|---|---|---|
| ① | 10/2 | | |
| ② | 8/2 | | |
| ③ | 8/2 | | |
| ④ | 8/1 | | |
| ⑤ | 8/1 | | |
| ⑥ | 6/1 | | |
| ⑦ | 6/1 | | |
| ⑧ | 10/2 | | |
| | 10/2 | | |
| ⑨ | 6/1 | | |
| ⑩ | 6/2 | | |
| ⑪ | 8/2 | | |
| ⑫ | 8/1 | | |
| ⑬ | 8/2 | | |
| ⑭ | 8/2 | | |
| | 8/2 | | |
| ⑮ | 6/1 | | |

### SURF STATISTICS

| SURF STATISTICS | J F | M A | M J | J A | S O | N D |
|---|---|---|---|---|---|---|
| dominant swell | NE | NE | NE | SE | NE | NE |
| swell size (ft) | 4 | 4 | 2-3 | 2 | 2-3 | 3 |
| consistency (%) | 60 | 70 | 60 | 50 | 40 | 50 |
| dominant wind | E-S | E-S | SE-SW | SE-SW | N-SE | N-SE |
| average force | F4 | F4 | F4 | F4 | F4 | F4 |
| consistency (%) | 62 | 63 | 59 | 49 | 61 | 73 |
| water temp(°C/°F) | 26/79 | 24/75 | 23/74 | 21/70 | 22/72 | 24/75 |
| wetsuit | | | | | | |

Great surf, clean water and few erosion issues are balanced off with some tough access, numerous hazards and heavy localism. Panoramic of Hanalei Bay, north coast Kauai, Hawaii.

# Pacific Ocean Islands

SYLVAIN CAZENAVE

# The Ocean Environment

Covering roughly a third of the Earth's surface, the Pacific Ocean is the biggest single feature on the planet. Landmasses are small and scattered with small indigenous populations of predominantly Polynesian descent. The Pacific's huge size is a major determining factor when it comes to the ocean environment, accounting for both difficult access and a general lack of pollution problems around the myriad coral reefs.

**Pollution**

The huge volume of the Pacific makes it the cleanest place to surf in the world, as any pollution emitted by the very low population is quickly dispersed. In the most recent surveys, 70% of coral reefs were found to be in good to excellent condition, leaving the other 30% in a fair to poor condition. Following global trends, deforestation, agriculture and construction are

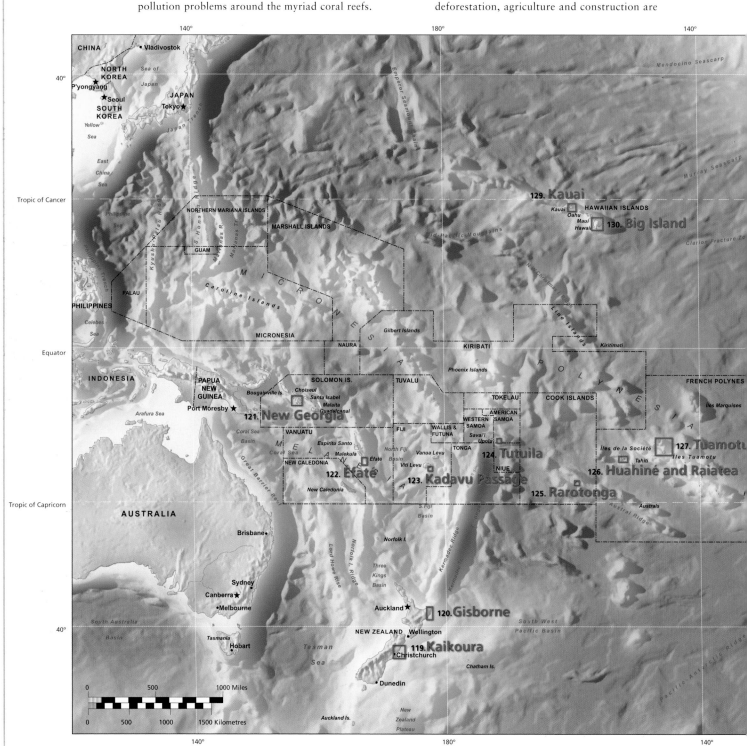

increasingly putting coastal waters and coral reefs under pressure. Tourism development brings unsatisfactory waste disposal and increased runoff and whilst this pollution may not be immediately recognisable on land, it is having a direct impact on the reefs. New Zealand has the largest landmass, population, urban zones and agricultural activity in the Pacific. Auckland has been treating sewage in huge oxidisation ponds but upgrade works are implementing biological nutrient removal, activated sludge technology and UV disinfection tertiary treatment. The city's ageing sewer network regularly leaks and coupled with polluted stormwater, are the main cause of beach closures. Wellington has full tertiary treatment before discharging a short distance offshore, but occasionally untreated effluent is discharged during heavy rain periods when illegal stormwater connections to the sewer system create a volume that exceeds the treatment plants capacity. Agricultural products are constantly being washed down to the coast in the wet climate. Both Fiji and Samoa have a long legacy of clearing native forest to make way for agriculture. Heavy, tropical rainfall means regular leaching of pesticides and fertilizers from the sugar cane fields into the coastal lagoon habitat, particularly along the southern "coral coast" of Viti Levu, which is now more of a "dead coral coast" from the ensuing eutrophication. Grand tourist developments along the south coast and the populous city of Suva combine to add domestic pollution to the most surfed stretch of coastline. All hotels treat their sewage but the nutrient rich water ends up in the ocean. One hotel has constructed a trio of lagoons or artificial wetlands, removing the high nutrient content that attracts reef killers like the crown of thorns starfish. Hawaii's reefs and coastal waters have suffered from years of agricultural runoff and after heavy rain, high bacteria and algal levels can result in the closing of beaches on Oahu. Urbanisation on the south shore of Oahu has increased polluted runoff, and around 115 million gallons of treated sewage is discharged off Honolulu every day. New tertiary treatment will disinfect outfalls with UV but the project is far from finished. New EPA laws require that all large capacity cesspools servicing small communities in Hawaii are to be filled in by 2005 and proper sewage treatment implemented. Shipping in Hawaii brings associated oil discharges and cruise ship access to smaller communities is hotly debated. The building of harbours in the chain has often been at the expense of pollution filtering wetlands. Proposals exist to demonstrate the economic and environmental benefits of utilising natural systems in constructed wetlands to reclaim raw sewage effluent. The Pacific's vast size and diluting properties have made it a target for weapons (of mass destruction) testing and dumping, throughout the French and US territories. The French used Mururoa and Fangataufa Atolls for the detonation of more than 200 nuclear devices exposing the surrounding ocean environment to intense radiation and fallout with unknown consequences. The US have used remote and not so remote parts of the Hawaiian chain for bombing ranges, weapons silos and burying chemical weapons. In 1962, a nuke was deliberately aborted on launch showering Johnston Atoll with plutonium (half life 35,000 years), 800 miles SW of Honolulu. Currents typically pick up and bring together plastic and any rubbish dumped by shipping, leaving a non-degradable legacy on many remote shores.

KIRK LEE AEDER

The damaging effects of decades of nuclear testing in certain corners of the Pacific are as yet undisclosed, putting ocean pilgrims like turtles in the line of fire. While testing is on hold, New Zealand leads the world with encompassing, anti-nuclear legislation.

### Erosion

Coastal erosion in NZ is particularly apparent on the east coast where greywacke (dark, clay ridden sandstone) and other types of splintering rock are prevalent. Houses perched on the coastline are threatened by the fast encroaching coastline and retreat is the only option. Sea defences are limited to the odd breakwall, jetty and pier, around major towns and cities. The National Institute of Water and Atmosphere has cameras installed around the country monitoring the coastal environment. Coral mining is the main issue with erosion and destruction of fringing reefs. The business of mining and coral sand dredging in Fiji is worth $7.6 million a year and hence restrictions have only been imposed slowly. Sedimentation and blast fishing techniques are contributing to the weakening and destruction of reefs, while on Mururoa Atoll, huge cracks and fissures in the rock forewarn of catastrophic subsidence. Global warming and the associated sea level rises threaten outer atolls on the Cook Islands, French Polynesia and Fiji.

Hawaii's coastal defences have seriously compromised the reef at Ma'aleea, Maui, renowned as being the fastest rideable wave in the world. A breakwall extension would destroy the fickle right, affect local fishing areas and possibly disturb the annual visiting humpback population. Harbour and marina construction have also had affects on Oahu's south shore, however the now famous Ala Moana Bowls didn't exist before the channel was widened. On a down side, dredging spoils from this project had a negative affect on other waves.

**Right – While Hawaii has recorded 96 shark attacks, the 14 fatalities reflect the global 1990's average. This 13% figure is dropping in the new millennium, possibly affected by a range factors, including people's use of the ocean patterns and overfishing.**

Cloudbreak and Restaurants and the Hideaway Resort discourages non-clients from riding Namotu. Dormitory accommodation has been withdrawn, leaving only full price rooms, although permission to surf Namotu Lefts and Swimming Pools may be granted to visiting surfers making a polite request at the resort reception.

The growing global surf tourism industry is alleviating the common Pacific access problems, although expect a hefty price tag attached. Military restrictions apply on some of the US islands and the east coast of Oahu has some 'military personnel only' areas.

KIRK LEE AEDER

### Hazards

Fiji and The Solomon Islands have seen a few shark attacks and about a 40% fatality rate, but considering the Solomon Islanders have a long history of ritual interaction with sharks, the figures are low. Hawaii's fatalities are a small percentage of the highest attack incidence in the Pacific. Other ocean nasties include man-o-war and Hawaiian box jellyfish (rarely fatal), stonefish, lionfish, scorpion fish, sea snakes, cone shells, sea urchins and the coral itself. More of a worry to surfers should be the power and ferocity of the ocean currents and waves, which are as serious as it gets.

The Pacific is the birthplace of modern localism, drawing on aspects of ancient Hawaiian surf culture and a need to bring some order to burgeoning crowds at the best reefs. Respect for the power of the waves must also extend to the people who regularly ride them and have paid their dues. Other Polynesians have followed the lead of Hui O He'e Nalu wavesliding club (Da Hui), well known for violent enforcement of surf etiquette in Hawaii, albeit with less intensity. New Zealand line-ups are generally laidback although city or major provincial breaks will be competitive and extra respect is usually demanded by the Maori population. Fiji has enforced a financial form of localism that requires all surfers to stay at the expensive Tavarua resort in exchange for exclusive waves. Samoan religious beliefs preserve Sunday as a day of rest and expect surfers to show the appropriate respect. Popular breaks throughout Tahiti's main islands are heavily surfed and locals can get as heavy as the waves. Nowhere is as intense as the North Shore of Hawaii, when winter brings the pro tour and international travellers to the proving grounds of the surfing world. However, crowds bring anonymity and visitors may find the outer islands of Maui and Kauai even more intimidating.

TIM MCKENNA

**Exclusive rights or ownership of waves is a concept that has been embraced in Fiji and implemented by resort owners. Access is becoming increasingly expensive at Namotu, converging towards the paying guests only policy at neighboring Tavarua.**

### Access

Accessing the surf can be extremely challenging on many of the Pacific islands and varies from long paddles to long boat rides. New Zealand presents fewer problems with many spots just off a main road or highway, however the majority of breaks will require longer drives down gravel or 4WD access roads. Farmers' permission is required for some locations and others will require hiking or a boat. A boat is indispensable in New Caledonia, Vanuatu, Solomon Islands and much of French Polynesia, but Fiji, Tonga, Samoa, Rapa Nui and Hawaii are all accessible from land. Day boat charter costs fluctuate wildly, as does established inter-island transport. Paddles vary from short lagoons and reef walks to long arduous rip busting paddles often out to very serious, lonely waves. In Fiji, only Tavarua Island guests can ride the reefs at

# Surf Travel Resources

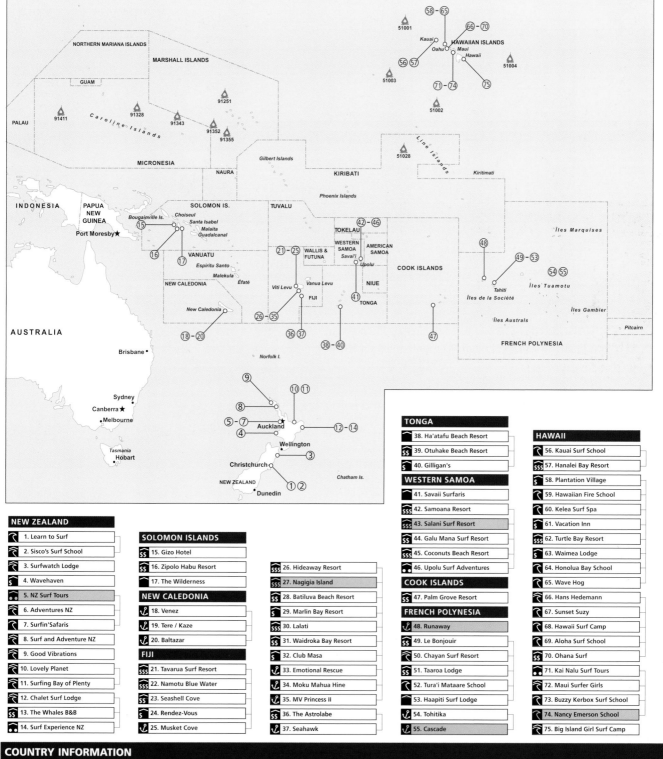

**TONGA**
- 38. Ha'atafu Beach Resort
- 39. Otuhake Beach Resort
- 40. Gilligan's

**WESTERN SAMOA**
- 41. Savaii Surfaris
- 42. Samoana Resort
- 43. Salani Surf Resort
- 44. Galu Mana Surf Resort
- 45. Coconuts Beach Resort
- 46. Upolu Surf Adventures

**COOK ISLANDS**
- 47. Palm Grove Resort

**FRENCH POLYNESIA**
- 48. Runaway
- 49. Le Bonjouir
- 50. Chayan Surf Resort
- 51. Taaroa Lodge
- 52. Tura'i Mataare School
- 53. Haapiti Surf Lodge
- 54. Tohitika
- 55. Cascade

**HAWAII**
- 56. Kauai Surf School
- 57. Hanalei Bay Resort
- 58. Plantation Village
- 59. Hawaiian Fire School
- 60. Kelea Surf Spa
- 61. Vacation Inn
- 62. Turtle Bay Resort
- 63. Waimea Lodge
- 64. Honolua Bay School
- 65. Wave Hog
- 66. Hans Hedemann
- 67. Sunset Suzy
- 68. Hawaii Surf Camp
- 69. Aloha Surf School
- 70. Ohana Surf
- 71. Kai Nalu Surf Tours
- 72. Maui Surfer Girls
- 73. Buzzy Kerbox Surf School
- 74. Nancy Emerson School
- 75. Big Island Girl Surf Camp

**NEW ZEALAND**
- 1. Learn to Surf
- 2. Sisco's Surf School
- 3. Surfwatch Lodge
- 4. Wavehaven
- 5. NZ Surf Tours
- 6. Adventures NZ
- 7. Surfin'Safaris
- 8. Surf and Adventure NZ
- 9. Good Vibrations
- 10. Lovely Planet
- 11. Surfing Bay of Plenty
- 12. Chalet Surf Lodge
- 13. The Whales B&B
- 14. Surf Experience NZ

**SOLOMON ISLANDS**
- 15. Gizo Hotel
- 16. Zipolo Habu Resort
- 17. The Wilderness

**NEW CALEDONIA**
- 18. Venez
- 19. Tere / Kaze
- 20. Baltazar

**FIJI**
- 21. Tavarua Surf Resort
- 22. Namotu Blue Water
- 23. Seashell Cove
- 24. Rendez-Vous
- 25. Musket Cove
- 26. Hideaway Resort
- 27. Nagigia Island
- 28. Batiluva Beach Resort
- 29. Marlin Bay Resort
- 30. Lalati
- 31. Waidroka Bay Resort
- 32. Club Masa
- 33. Emotional Rescue
- 34. Moku Mahua Hine
- 35. MV Princess II
- 36. The Astrolabe
- 37. Seahawk

## COUNTRY INFORMATION

| | NEW ZEALAND | VANUATU | SOLOMON ISLANDS | US SAMOA | FIJI | COOK ISLANDS | FRENCH POLYNESIA |
|---|---|---|---|---|---|---|---|
| Area (sq km/mi): | 270,534/104,454 | 12,189/4,706 | 28,896/11,157 | 199/77 | 18,270/7,054 | 236/91 | 4,200/1,544 |
| Population: | 3.9M | 193,000 | 480,000 | 67,000 | 0.8M | 21,000 | 250,000 |
| Waveriders: | 50,000 | 20 | 50 | 30 | 1,000 | 40 | 2,500 |
| Tourists (per yr): | 1.7M | 50,000 | 5,000 | 20,000 | 0.5M | 60,000 | 211,000 |
| Language: | English, Maori | English, French, Pidgin | English, Pidgin | Samoan, English | English, Fijian dialects | English, Maori | French, Tahitian |
| Currency: | NZ Dollar | Vatu | Solomon Islands Dollar | US Dollar | Fijian Dollar | New Zealand Dollar | Franc Pacifique |
| Exchange: | $1 = 2 NZD | $1 = 135 VUV | $1 = 7 SBD | $1 = $1 USD | $1 = 2.15 FJD | $1 = 2.1 NZD | $1 = 116 FCP |
| GDP ($ per yr): | $17,700 | $1,300 | $2,000 | $8,000 | $7,300 | $5,000 | $14,500 |
| Inflation (%): | 2% | 3% | 10% | 1% | 0% | 2% | 2% |

NEW ZEALAND

North Island

South Island

# 119. Kaikoura

Mangamaunu

ALL PHOTOS: WARREN HAWKE

## Summary

+ CONSISTENT SWELLS
+ QUALITY RIGHT POINTBREAKS
+ UNCROWDED AND FRIENDLY
+ GREAT SURF/SNOWBOARD COMBO

− COLD WATER, STRONG WINDCHILL
− POOR CHRISTCHURCH BEACHIES
− FREQUENT ONSHORES
− LONG FLIGHTS

This zone is the lowest latitude destination in the Southern Hemisphere, so think cold. Cross-over boarders may be more interested in the winter snow capped peaks rather then the white capped ones in the sea. While much of South Island, like the West Coast or Dunedin, rely on quality beachbreaks, here is a zone littered with right pointbreaks, helping hardcore surfers avoid ice-cream headache paddle outs. South Island, aka Te Wai Pounamu meaning Jade Island has 3,200km (2000mi) of coastline and a small population so expect small crowds at the worst. Archaeological remains indicate that Moa hunters inhabited the Kaikoura Peninsula 900 years ago. To the Maori this is a place of great historical significance. The foothills of

the Seaward Kaikoura Range extend down to the Pacific coast leaving a narrow corridor for rail and road access. Fishing settlements, seal and bird colonies cling to rocky shores, from which pods of dolphins and occasionally whales can be spotted.

## TRAVEL INFORMATION

**Population:** 500,000 Canterbury
**Coastline:** 3,200km (2,000mi) South Is
**Contests:** Kaikoura Coldwater Classic
**Other Resources:**
*Video:* Wet Rubber
surf.co.nz
dcbodyboardworld.co.nz
canterburypages.co.nz
kaikouranet.co.nz

**Getting There** – No visa for most visitors. Main entry is Auckland; Air New Zealand is a surfer friendly airline. The full price to fly Auckland-Christchurch is $188 o/w (1h20min). Christchurch (CHC) is South Island's only international airport: BA, Singapore, Qantas, Japan, Air Pacific. Kaikoura is 170km (106mi) from Christchurch, 2h1/2 drive. Dept tax: $13.

**Getting Around** – Excellent InterCity bus network. Catch the Coastal Pacific train. Buy a car if staying more than 3 months. Rental cars start from $27/day with Omega. Renting a motorhome is a great way to see NZ. Fuel costs vary from $0.76-$0.96/litre.

**Lodging and Food** – Ample choice among motels, motor inns, bed & breakfast, home-stays, holiday parks, farm-stays or backpacker hostels. Surfwatch Lodge over Mangamaunu is great:

$53/dble. Topspot Backpacker in town. Expect $20/dble for a budget room. Kaikoura means 'eat crayfish'. A typical meal would be $10

**Weather** – The climate of this zone is greatly dependent on the massive Southern Alps to the west. Weather changes can happen very quickly so it is necessary to be prepared for every possibility. Summer temps are warm, especially when hot, dry, Foehn winds blow over the Alps and plains from the NW. Mean annual rainfall is a low 666mm (26in) and long dry spells can occur. Average sunshine is 2040h per annum. Summer daytime max air temps range from 18-26°C (64-79°F), often moderated by a cool NE sea breeze. Winters are cold with frequent frost. Typical winter daytime max air temps range from 7-14°C (45-58°F). NE winds prevail year round and SW winds are more frequent during winter adding up to 52 days of 63km/h+ gusts. Water is cold and windchill can be intense, bring a 4/3mm, booties, gloves and hood in winter and a 3/2 fullsuit in summer and a springsuit for the warm days.

**Nature and Culture** – Treat yourself to whale watching in Kaikoura; soak in the natural pools

of Hanmer Springs; relax in the French atmosphere of Akaroa; ski in one of Canterbury's 12 ski areas (eg Mount Lyford); go alpine trekking in the Mt Cook region; experience "flightseeing" from Lake Tekapo or enjoy the beauty of Christchurch, the garden city.

**Hazards and Hassles** – Shingle/boulder shorebreaks can be intimidating at high tides with some swell, be patient getting in and out. Seals are common in the water and great whites are rumoured in the Foveaux down south. Be ready for the cold. Crowds, if any, are mellow. If entering farmland, ask owners – especially during lambing time in spring.

**Handy Hints** – Get your gear at Kaikoura Surf Shop where they make Surge Surfboards. Shortboards cost $400. Contact Rarangi Surf Club in Kaikoura if need be. Travel with Surf Experience NZ; they have a 12 day trip to North and South islands for $735 (summer) per surfer (Max 5). Queenstown is the NZ snow capital with world class heli-boarding. Remember Christchurch is only 4h from Kumara on the west coast and the breaks between Westport and Greymouth.

| WEATHER STATISTICS | J/F | M/A | M/J | J/A | S/O | N/D |
|---|---|---|---|---|---|---|
| total rainfall (mm) | 65 | 70 | 90 | 90 | 70 | 70 |
| consistency (days/mth) | 9 | 11 | 15 | 15 | 12 | 11 |
| min temp (°C/°F) | 13/55 | 10/50 | 5/41 | 4/39 | 8/46 | 10/50 |
| max temp (°C/°F) | 21/70 | 18/64 | 13/55 | 11/52 | 16/61 | 19/66 |

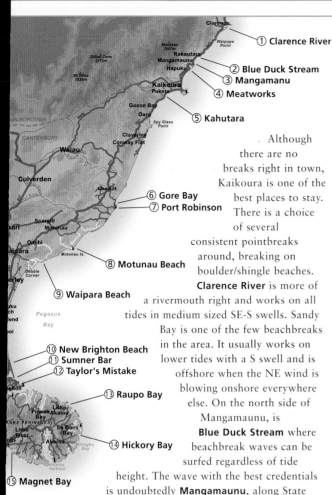

① **Clarence River**
② **Blue Duck Stream**
③ **Mangamanu**
④ **Meatworks**

⑤ **Kahutara**

⑥ **Gore Bay**
⑦ **Port Robinson**

⑧ **Motunau Beach**

⑨ **Waipara Beach**

⑩ **New Brighton Beach**
⑪ **Sumner Bar**
⑫ **Taylor's Mistake**

⑬ **Raupo Bay**

⑭ **Hickory Bay**

⑮ **Magnet Bay**

Clarence River

Although there are no breaks right in town, Kaikoura is one of the best places to stay. There is a choice of several consistent pointbreaks around, breaking on boulder/shingle beaches. **Clarence River** is more of a rivermouth right and works on all tides in medium sized SE-S swells. Sandy Bay is one of the few beachbreaks in the area. It usually works on lower tides with a S swell and is offshore when the NE wind is blowing onshore everywhere else. On the north side of Mangamaunu, is **Blue Duck Stream** where beachbreak waves can be surfed regardless of tide height. The wave with the best credentials is undoubtedly **Mangamaunu**, along State Highway 1. This Rincon-like, right pointbreak is a beauty, aided by its proximity to the snow-covered Kaikoura Range. The cool air blowing off the mountains creates offshores that blow every morning and during the winter, it can blow all day, despite the prevailing NE winds. The walls are hollow but not too powerful and long, cruisey rides are the norm. Big NE-E swells will result in epic conditions, while S-SE swells create more rips. It gets some crowds but nothing worrying as there are other pointbreaks close-by. For those who want more power, try the consistent reef and beach peaks of **Meatworks** at low tide. **Kahutara** could be Mangamaunu's twin, except it's heavier, less consistent and it's also less scenic. It holds waves up to 10ft (3m) and is an excellent righthand rivermouth breaking over a reef of gravel and boulders. To its right is K Reef another great wave that breaks best on an easterly swell. There are over twenty other excellent surf spots given the right conditions – some are secret while others are right beside State Highway One. Pegasus Bay is well sheltered from S swells by the Banks Peninsula, but **Gore Bay** is popular in summer and produces many peaks along its 5km (3mi) stretch. High tide, SW winds and a big SE-S swell awakens the point at **Port Robinson** accessed through farmland. **Motunau Beach** dishes up high tide beachies plus a rare left point inside a wildlife reserve. **Waipara Beach** in Midshore Bay also has a left point but it is difficult access through private farmland and down a cliff. Christchurch city area only offers average beachbreaks like **New Brighton**, the centre of beach culture and also the only webcam. If **Sumner Bar** is on, most waveriders check **Taylor's Mistake**, which is a bit

more exposed to an E-NE swell and gets some juicier lefts and rights near the beach headlands. Banks Peninsula's unreal coastal features make it a tough place to travel, with hellish, winding gravel roads. There are four reliable beaches with different exposures, **Raupo Bay** and **Hickory Bay** being the most consistent. Good lefts in the north corner, heavy, hollow walls and punishing paddle-outs when it is overhead; a common theme on the peninsula. Car can be parked by the farmland gates before making the 15 min walk down. **Magnet Bay** has been surfed since the early '60s by the Midshore Boardriders club. While the lefts don't really wrap, the walls can be pretty juicy and this small scenic cove full of bull kelp holds size and gets crowded.

New Zealand has multiple exposures to swell, with the west coast receiving the lion's share of SW-W groundswells. The east coast picks up SE-SW swells off the back of lows moving east towards South America. The Banks Peninsula blocks straight southerly swell for the Pegasus Bay spots. Between March and October, Canterbury gets 3-10ft (1-3m) surf from the reliable S-SE source, which keeps coming in summer. A recent large storm on Waitangi Day (6 February 2002) caused havoc along eastern coasts and significant wave heights peaked at 7-8m (23-28ft). Check the Banks Peninsula wave buoy for real-time data. Coastal waters are referred to by fishermen as Clarence and Pegasus. Dominant NE winds give light onshores during summer and SW are typical winter winds, perfectly offshore on the rights. The Kaikoura Range creates local offshores. Spring tides are 5ft (1.6m) max; a lower range than the west coast. Mid-eastern coast's biggest tides occur only once a month. These semi-diurnal tides are called perigean tides, because they occur when the Moon is closest to the Earth.

Christchurch area

| SPOT DESCRIPTION | | | |
|---|---|---|---|
| Spot | Size | Btm | Type |
| ① | 8/3 | | |
| ② | 6/3 | | |
| ③ | 8/3 | | |
| ④ | 8/3 | | |
| ⑤ | 12/4 | | |
| ⑥ | 6/3 | | |
| ⑦ | 10/4 | | |
| ⑧ | 6/3 | | |
| ⑨ | 6/3 | | |
| ⑩ | 6/2 | | |
| ⑪ | 6/3 | | |
| ⑫ | 8/3 | | |
| ⑬ | 6/3 | | |
| ⑭ | 8/2 | | |
| ⑮ | 12/3 | | |

| SURF STATISTICS | J F | M A | M J | J A | S O | N D |
|---|---|---|---|---|---|---|
| dominant swell | S-NE | S-E | S-E | S-E | S-E | S-NE |
| swell size (ft) | 2-3 | 3-4 | 4-5 | 5 | 5 | 3 |
| consistency (%) | 40 | 60 | 70 | 70 | 60 | 40 |
| dominant wind | N-NE | N-NE | S-SW | S-SW | NW-N | NW-NE |
| average force | F4 | F4 | F4-F5 | F4-F5 | F4 | F4-F5 |
| consistency (%) | 33 | 32 | 36 | 32 | 33 | 46 |
| water temp (°C/°F) | 16/61 | 14/57 | 13/55 | 12/54 | 11/52 | 13/55 |
| wetsuit | | | | | | |

**NEW ZEALAND**

North Island

South Island

# 120. Gisborne

Makarori Point

CORY SCOTT

**Summary**

+ MANY RIGHT POINTBREAKS
+ CLEAN MID-SEASON SWELLS
+ HOLLOW, POWERFUL BEACHIES
+ UNTOUCHED COASTLINE

− SMALL AND CRAPPY SUMMERS
− SEMI-CROWDED MAIN SPOTS
− CHILLY WINTER TEMPS
− SOME DIFFICULT ACCESS

Gizzy Pipe

CORY SCOTT

PAUL KENNEDY

With nearly 3,500km (2190mi) of coastline, there are many areas to check on the North Island. On the east side, there are up to eight surf regions: Northland, Coromandel, Bay of Plenty, East Coast, Mahia, Hawke's Bay, Wairapapa and Wellington down south. Gisborne can get a bit too busy in summer, but further north towards East Cape, less crowded conditions quickly become apparent. Despite the endless pointbreak lefts of Raglan to practise on, many of New Zealand's best competitive surfers come from the Gisborne area, because what it lacks in primo surf spots, is more than made up for by its consistency. Although the Gisborne zone surf is smaller and generally cleaner than the west coast, don't think that it's any less powerful. Above average surfer density combined with quality spots, conveniently hidden amidst the sunniest and most untouched part of New Zealand, gives rise to Gisborne's reputation as the surf capital.

## TRAVEL INFORMATION

**Population:** 44,000
**Coastline:** 3,436km (2,150mi) North Is
**Contests:** SEP (Nov), Smokefree Woman (Feb)
**Other Resources:**
*Video:*
Coastal Disturbances
gisborne.co.nz
surf.co.nz
gisbornenz.com
purenz.com

**Getting There** – No visa for most visitors. Main entry is Auckland, Air New Zealand being a surfer-friendly airline. Gisborne is equidistant to Wellington and Auckland, 9h drive. Take highway SH38 only for scenery through the Raukumara chain. It looks shorter but it's twice as long as the SH2. Flying to Gisborne (GIS) costs $110o/w. Dep tax: $13.

**Getting Around** – Coastal SH35 is pretty good. From Gisborne, it takes 1h45 min to Tokomaru Bay and 2h to Hick's Bay. Excellent bus network; main operator is InterCity. Buy a car if you stay more than 3 months. Rental cars start from $24/day with Rent a Dent. Renting a motorhome is perfect for NZ. Fuel varies from $0.76-$0.96/l. Right-hand drives, driven on the left.

**Lodging and Food** – The 4 categories are Hotels/Motels, Self-contained Hideaways,

Backpackers, Camping Grounds/Motor Camps. Gisborne Backpackers has doubles for $15. Best is Wainui: Whales B&B for $44/day or Chalet Surf Lodge with sea view rooms for $60/dble and backpacker beds at $20. A typical meal would be $10.

**Weather** – Sheltered by high country to the west, Gisborne enjoys a fairly dry and sunny climate. Warm, dry, settled weather predominates in summer. Frosts may occur in winter. Typical summer daytime max air temps range from 20-28°C (68-82°F), which may be accompanied by strong, dry, Foehn winds from the northwest. Sea breezes often occur in coastal areas on warm summer days. Sunniest months are February and October, followed by Nov-Dec-Jan. Annual hours of sunshine average 2200. Winter is mild and cool, typical daytime max air temps range from 10-16°C (50-61°F). Monthly rainfall varies between 60 and 162mm (2-6in), April being the wettest month. Heavy rainfall comes in from the ESE, but westerly winds prevail. Water temps never get below 13°C (55°F) requiring a 4/3mm fullsuit and boots but never get above 20°C (68°F) either so a 3/2 fullsuit is recommended.

**Nature and Culture** – Besides being an outdoor sports heaven, New Zealand's sunny East Coast has more to offer than waves. Turoa, Whakapapa, or Turino ski resorts are 7h away. Try shark cage dives, horse trekking or winery visits and don't overlook Maori culture. With 30,000 people, Gisborne is traditionally rural, with only a few happening bars like Scotty's Bar & Grill or Fat Cats.

**Hazards and Hassles** – No snakes or poisonous, dangerous creatures can be found in New Zealand. With one of the most laid-back people in the modern world, crime is low and land hazards are virtually non-existent. Localism can be felt at some spots or on classic days because of extra crowd pressure. Beware with rocks and rips...No shark sightings.

**Handy Hints** – Many surf shops to buy cheap quality gear: Action or Blitz, The Boardroom (TOA tribal designs), or the New Wave Surfboard factory sell shortboards for $400, malibus for $620. Rentals and lessons at the Chalet Surf Lodge. For a Surf Tour, Surf Experience NZ 3-day Eastland Explorer costs $145 in summer, $175 in winter, 5 surfers max.

| WEATHER STATISTICS | J/F | M/A | M/J | J/A | S/O | N/D |
|---|---|---|---|---|---|---|
| total rainfall (mm) | 80 | 80 | 110 | 50 | 70 | 50 |
| consistency (days/mth) | 7 | 10 | 11 | 10 | 7 | 6 |
| min temp (°C/°F) | 13/55 | 11/52 | 6/43 | 5/41 | 7/45 | 11/52 |
| max temp (°C/°F) | 24/75 | 21/70 | 15/59 | 14/57 | 17/63 | 22/72 |

Hick's Bay cradles a long and beautiful beach, which needs E-NE swell and is offshore with the dominant SW winds. On a big swell, the adjacent **Horseshoe Bay** beachbreak might be maxed-out but the left and righthand points on either side of the bay won't be. Heading south, there are plenty of waves that go unridden, but with no less than five right pointbreaks, **Waipiro Bay** is the place to be. Take care on the steep gravel road but a significant swell and high tide will make the trek worthwhile. Further down the coast, **Tokomaru Bay**'s exposed beachbreaks need S-SW winds and work on all tides. **Three Points** is a set of right pointbreaks that everyone talks about but are rarely surfed because of access. Permission is needed to get there and it's a long hike. It favours a medium E swell and there's decent beachbreaks if the points are not cooking. If the swell is big, then check **Tolaga Point**, a right point on low to mid tide. **Loisells** at Waihau Bay has exposed beachbreaks with the odd rocky patch. It catches a lot of swell but is best with N-NW wind on a NE swell. There's also a rock and sand point within walking distance north. **Whangara**'s proximity to Gisborne means more surfers riding the consistent beachbreaks, especially in small conditions with W winds. If the swell picks up, check the island, there can be some excellent wedging peaks. **Pouawa**'s beachbreaks are a short walk across sand dunes and need similar conditions to Whangara but with NW winds. Makarori is a classic location with different peaks. **North Makarori** is home to Centers beachbreak but also holds consistent sand/reef peaks. Best with N winds, (SW winds are cross-shore) and big NE swells, but beware the jagged reef at low tide. It's a long paddle to **Makarori Point**'s long, cutback right, best on mid S-SE swells and low tide. Some say Wainui, not to be mistaken for Raglan's Wainui Beach, is New Zealand's most consistent beachbreak/reef with no less than five sections: Whales, Chalet, Pines, School and the primo spot **Stock Route**. Can get very heavy and hollow, supporting the theory that what east coast waves lack in consistency compared to the west coast, is more than made up for in sheer grunt. **Sponge Bay** despite its name, is not a bodyboarder heaven but a mediocre beach that wouldn't be mentioned if it were not the access to Gisborne's best

PAUL KENNEDY

wave: **Tuamotu Island**. Long hollow lefts produced by a medium SW swell with NE winds, require a very long paddle but when the Bowl is on, it's worth it! The **Gizzy Pipe** is another potential world-class barrelling beach sandbar but more often than not, it closes out. Waikanae and Midway Beach are ideal beginners' waves. On those rare big S swell or good NE swell days, carefully check the **Waipaoa River Bar** (aka Big River), a deceptive, long, sandy pointbreak with fun waves. Stay at least a month in the best period for a decent chance of scoring Pipe or the Big River with classic conditions.

New Zealand has multiple exposure to swell, with the west coast being more open to the regular SW-W groundswells. The east coast receives less swell as the southern lows are moving away but enjoys dominant offshores. Gisborne gets 3-10ft (1-3m) surf between April and October and this SW source rarely runs dry even in summer; check the Tatapouri buoy online for live data. Summer is the cyclone swell season (Jan-March) although the window for NE swells is narrow. Cyclone swells are rare but summer NE windswells are common, although not very good. Drive north to the Bay of Plenty in case of a significant NE swell. If it goes flat, the west coast is not more than 6h drive away. Dominant S-W winds are offshore and lighter than on the exposed west coast. Winds blow more N in summer and more S in winter. Tides are semi-diurnal and can reach 6ft (2m) on spring tides, this range affects beachbreaks and some sensitive reefbreaks.

**SPOT DESCRIPTION**

| Spot | Size | Btm | Type |
|---|---|---|---|
| ① | 8/2 | | |
| | 8/2 | | |
| ② | 10/2 | | |
| ③ | 6/1 | | |
| ④ | 10/2 | | |
| ⑤ | 8/2 | | |
| ⑥ | 6/1 | | |
| ⑦ | 6/1 | | |
| ⑧ | 6/1 | | |
| ⑨ | 8/1 | | |
| ⑩ | 10/3 | | |
| ⑪ | 10/2 | | |
| ⑫ | 12/2 | | |
| ⑬ | 8/3 | | |
| ⑭ | 6/2 | | |
| ⑮ | 10/3 | | |

| SURF STATISTICS | J F | M A | M J | J A | S O | N D |
|---|---|---|---|---|---|---|
| dominant swell | S-NE | S-E | S-E | S-E | S-E | S-NE |
| swell size (ft) | 3 | 4 | 4-5 | 5 | 4-5 | 2-3 |
| consistency (%) | 40 | 60 | 70 | 80 | 70 | 50 |
| dominant wind | S-W | NE-SW | S-W | S-W | SW-NW | SW-N |
| average force | F3-F4 | F4 | F4 | F4 | F4 | F4 |
| consistency (%) | 39 | 63 | 50 | 52 | 51 | 64 |
| water temp (°C/°F) | 19/66 | 18/64 | 16/61 | 14/57 | 14/57 | 16/61 |
| wetsuit | | | | | | |

Tuamotu Island

CORY SCOTT

# 121. New Georgia

## Summary
+ CLEAN, GLASSY SWELLS
+ QUALITY REEFBREAKS
+ CRYSTAL CLEAR WATER
+ NO CROWDS

− ERRATIC SEASONAL SWELLS
− SHALLOW REEFS
− VERY HOT AND HUMID
− REMOTE ACCESS

Composed of 992 rugged volcanic islands and tiny low-lying coral atolls, the Solomons are the third largest archipelago in the South Pacific. With soaring mountain peaks, dense tropical rainforest, cascading waterfalls, palm-fringed beaches and traditional villages, the Melanesian Islands are known for their unspoilt beauty and relaxed pace of life. The Solomons may not be in the best location to get swells but reports from divers and sailors have found that waves occur all over this area. Explorations in the easternmost islands; Nifiloli and Santa Cruz islands have revealed Byron and Kala Bay on the north coast as well as Nemba Bay on the west coast;

on Makira's eastern tip there's Tawarogha; Malaita hides Manu Point and Maluíu; Poro breaks on Santa Isabel. The north and east facing islands have more consistency during the austral winter, but the main problem is access

## TRAVEL INFORMATION

**Population:** 4,000 Gizo
**Coastline:** 370km (230mi)
New Georgia Is
**Contests:** None
**Other Resources:**
surftheeearth.com.au/Surf
%20Gizo.html
solomons.com

**Getting There** – No visa necessary but pay the $8.50 airport tax. Solomon Airlines flies direct to Honiara (HIR) from Oz. Air Vanuatu operates from Efate. There are 2 daily flights to Gizo (GZO), for $100r/t with a Twin-Otter (board restrictions apply). Land at Nusa Tupe, which is a 10min boat ride to Gizo. Munda should become Solomon's 2nd airport. Dep tax: $4

**Getting Around** – Renting a car is pointless; good fibreglass boats, with fast outboards are essential. Check Surf The Earth's packages: Gizo-7 nights include 5 surf trips by 4WD (Pailongge) or boat, while Zipolo Habu Resort has a 2h surf session daily to Skull Island. For extras, it cost $3 per person per hour to hire a full boat (up to 6 surfers). Rates are negotiable.

**Lodging and Food** – Surf The Earth has the best deals. The Gizo Hotel has a/c, pool view rooms. 7 nights full board package + air (Brisbane) +

boat is $920. Zapolo Habolo Resort costs for a tropical bungalow (4-share) are the same but flying to Munda (MUA) is easier, allowing bigger boards. Full meal package includes BBQ tuna, chilli mud crab and lobster.

**Weather** – The climate can be largely explained by the seasonal movement and development of the equatorial trough: Dec-April is the period of thunderstorms and thus the heaviest rainfall occurs at this time. With temps between 28°C (85°F) and 32°C (88°F), it can be unbearably hot and sticky, so A/C is essential to get a good night's sleep. Thunderstorms are relatively frequent over the large and more mountainous islands, building up inland on many afternoons and, if winds are favourable, drifting towards coastal areas. Over the ocean, storms are likely to occur in the night or early morning. On average, cyclones hit the Solomons once or twice a year, although this decreases in the Western Province. Tikopia, in the east however, was hit by 40ft (13m) waves generated by Cyclone Zoe in January 2003. The best time for travelling is between July and December but remember it's extremely wet with an average of 3600mm (142in) per year in

Munda. Water temps are ideal; use a long sleeve rashie to protect against the fierce sun.

**Nature and Culture** – Gizo's dive attraction is the WWII sunken battleship and other military relics. Several eco-lodges are scattered throughout world-famous Marovo lagoon with Uepi Island Resort a major dive destination. Climb 4956ft (1770m) high Kolombangara Volcano, and don't miss the Megapode skull shrines, or the crocodile farm and custom dances at Mbangopingo (Rendova).

**Hazards and Hassles** – Take anti-malarial medication, but the best defence is the prevention of mosquito bites. Water purity cannot be relied on, so drink bottled water. Be ready to face long boat rides in full sun exposure. Take reefboots.

**Handy Hints** – Take all gear including two favourite boards, lots of tropical wax and sunblock. It's possible to catch a last minute flight out of Brisbane when the swell is on. Use the sea kayaks to access the surf to nearby breaks. Local costs are relatively inexpensive. 95% of the population are Christian.

| WEATHER STATISTICS | J/F | M/A | M/J | J/A | S/O | N/D |
|---|---|---|---|---|---|---|
| total rainfall (mm) | 380 | 330 | 250 | 310 | 240 | 260 |
| consistency (days/mth) | 17 | 12 | 14 | 15 | 14 | 14 |
| min temp (°C/°F) | 24/75 | 23/74 | 23/74 | 23/74 | 23/74 | 23/74 |
| max temp (°C/°F) | 30/86 | 30/86 | 30/86 | 29/84 | 29/84 | 30/86 |

in this undeveloped region. The majority of discoveries have turned up on the SW facing coasts, when the Coral Sea cyclones kick in. The group's capital, Honiara, on Guadalcanal is the gateway to the Solomons and under the right conditions, there's surf at Beaufort Bay. Next to it, Russel Island is known to get some waves near Yandina but it is the Western Province where surfing has expanded, on the back of the diving resorts infrastructure.

Gizo is the capital of the Western Province and boasts the world's largest lagoon – Marovo. The coastline of Gizo Island (pronounced differently) is dotted with shipwrecks from World War II like the *Tao Maru*, which just failed to make it to port after being torpedoed. Overlooked by majestic Kolombangra, the tallest volcano in the region, Gizo is the first accommodation option with surf in the locality. The main break is **Pailongge**, where long rights pick up any swell in front of the namesake village. On large swells, the two hollow sections will merge to become a long, perfect wave over the coral reef. Next to it is **Titiana**, a powerful left when it's on. These two are within walking and paddling distance from accommodation in Gizo. An hour's boat ride away, another short, shallow left zips across the reef on **Makuti** Island. The second option is to stay on Lola Island at Zipolo Habu Resort, in order to shred **Skull Island** (1h30 boat trip from Gizo) when a mid to large swell hits. Possibly the longest rights in the Solomons, Skull is best at 3-6ft (1-2m) with NE-E wind. If the swell is too small, try **Despretes** further out; these peaky rights break close to shore with a great take-off that barrels down the line. Enter the beautiful lagoon through the reef pass. Not far eastward are two lefts and one right reef. **Mbirimbiri**'s wrapping rights are super shallow so avoid low tides and wait for NE winds. **Lavata** works on rare NW swell, produced by windswell in the Solomon Sea, and **Kundu Kundu** is a deep water left, 150m (450ft) away from the island. It picks up all available swell, W being best, works all tides, especially at mid and holds up to 10ft (3m), making it very long. There's a good chance of seeing fins but remember no diver has ever been attacked! New discoveries are being made on Rendova, 45 minutes boat ride from Lola, where many exposed left reefbreaks go unridden. **Coves** is a real swell-magnet and breaks off a reef near a tiny beach. Best at 3-6ft (1-2m), it's sheltered by high cliffs from any wind apart from W and the set-up is breathtaking. Check three other lefts nearby...

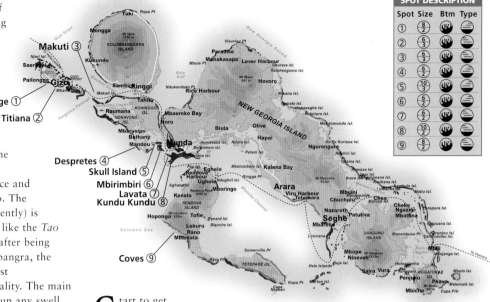

Marovo Lagoon

**SPOT DESCRIPTION**

| Spot | Size | Btm | Type |
|---|---|---|---|
| ① | 8/3 | | |
| ② | 6/3 | | |
| ③ | 6/3 | | |
| ④ | 6/2 | | |
| ⑤ | 10/3 | | |
| ⑥ | 6/2 | | |
| ⑦ | 6/2 | | |
| ⑧ | 10/3 | | |
| ⑨ | 8/2 | | |

Start to get excited when a tropical low develops east of far northern Queensland. The best time for swells is between December and April, when cyclones and lows build up, moving slowly south. When these

| SURF STATISTICS | J F | M A | M J | J A | S O | N D |
|---|---|---|---|---|---|---|
| dominant swell | S-SW | S-SW | SE-S | SE-S | SE-S | S-SW |
| swell size (ft) | 3-4 | 3 | 2 | 2-3 | 1-2 | 2-3 |
| consistency (%) | 60 | 50 | 40 | 50 | 20 | 40 |
| dominant wind | SW-NW | W-N | E-SE | E-S | E-S | E-S |
| average force | F3 | F2-F3 | F2-F3 | F3 | F3 | F2-F3 |
| consistency (%) | 55 | 42 | 65 | 85 | 76 | 49 |
| water temp (°C/°F) | 29/84 | 29/84 | 29/84 | 28/82 | 28/82 | 29/84 |
| wetsuit | | | | | | |

swells hit they can last for more than a week at a time giving excellent, clean, good sized swells. The Solomons also gets a consistent smaller winter swell May to August with lows travelling up from the Tasman Sea, hitting the east side of New Georgia Islands. The equatorial trough is an area of W-NW monsoonal winds, found close to, or south of the Solomons. NW windswells occur out of the Solomon Sea and E-NE are the most favourable winds, although winds often change and glassy days are not uncommon. May to November is the main season for the N-E facing Pacific Coast. SE trades become stronger, with more persistent winds blowing out of the sub-tropical ridge towards the equatorial trough. Trades are moisture bearing, so rainfall also occurs at that time. The transitional months are marked by less wind. Tides change from diurnal to semi-diurnal with diurnal inequality (different daily ranges), just remember they will not exceed 2ft (0.6m) and full moon phases don't necessarily result in the biggest tides.

# 122. Efate

SHANE MCINTYRE

## Summary
+ QUALITY CORAL REEFBREAKS
+ YACHTING AND SAILING STOP-OVER
+ WARM AND EMPTY LINE-UPS
+ GOOD TOURISM FACILITIES

− S-SW SWELL SHADOW
− LACK OF CONSISTENT SPOTS
− SE SWELL/WIND EXPOSURE
− HIGH FLIGHT AND LOCAL EXPENSES

Vanuatu, the "Timeless Islands" is a group of 83 islands, spanning 900km (563mi) on a north/south axis east of the Solomon's. Formerly known as the New Hebrides, there are many islands from the Torres & Banks islands in the north to Aneytium, Matthew and Hunter to the south, which remain unexplored by wave-riders. Situated 2,250km (1400mi) north-east of Sydney, and 800km (480mi) west of Fiji, Vanuatu would be an idyllic surf island if New Caledonia was not acting as a perfect swell warp against the main South Pacific swells. Vanuatu is the emerged part of an island arc, with a narrow rim delineated by a 2,000m (6000ft) isobath. Hence, when there is swell, it hits the coast with full strength. There are no lagoons or barrier reefs: there are only fringing reefs. This area is generally not more than 100m

SHANE MCINTYRE

CHRIS MCLENNAN/ALAMY

(300ft) wide and the reef is only a few metres thick. However, at some points, like Erakor Island on Efate, the fringing reef can be up to 2km (1.25mi) wide. Capital city Port-Vila sits on Efate, pretty much in the middle of

## TRAVEL INFORMATION

**Population:** 193,000
**Coastline:** 190km (118mi)
**Contests:** None
**Other Resources:**
vanuatuatoz.com
vanuatutourism.com

**Getting There** – No Visa for stays under 30 days. Air Vanuatu flies a B-737 to Port-Vila (VLI) from Auckland, Brisbane, Melbourne, Sydney, Nadi and Noumea. Air Calin flies from Noumea, Air Pacific from Nadi, Solomon Airlines from Honiara and Port Moresby. Domestic: Vanair services all major islands with 20 seat Twin Otter with 7ft board capacity. Dept Tax: $20.

**Getting Around** – There is no public transport. Privately owned mini buses and taxis are plentiful and relatively cheap. Small cars are fine for getting around Vila but a 4WD is recommended in north Efate, depending on rain. It takes 3 to 4 hours to drive around Efate. Rent a car at Discount Rentals for 7 days from $250/wk with 100km (60mi) free daily.

**Lodging and Food** – Pango Paradise Cove Resort has 10 self contained units and 6 deluxe studios: $845 for 3 nights and 3 people. Or Erakor Island Resort: 18 superb waterfront bungalows ($95/dble). For a cheaper stay, try Kaiviti Hotel and Guest Houses like basic Tafea ($20/dble). Expect to pay $10 for a cheap meal.

**Weather** – Vanuatu spans 900km (560mi) latitudinally, thus explaining the marked north-south thermal differences. There are even more striking latitudinal variations in annual precipitation levels, with 4000mm (158"in) rainfall around Banks and Torres islands but less than half that in southern Vanuatu. Rainfall in Efate is 2350mm (93"in) annually. Sheltered coasts are also much less humid than those swept by prevailing SE winds. The best time for good weather is April/May to October when temps range from 18-28°C (64-82°F). January to March is hot (26-34°C/79-94°F), often wet and prone to cyclones, but being low season it's a good time of year to take advantage of travel deals. Water remains tropical year round but if surfing in July-August, anticipate the windchill with a shorty.

**Nature and Culture** – Like most South Pacific islands, it's heaven for diving, fishing and golf courses. Numerous kava 'nakamals' are found around Port Vila, Mele Cascades are only a 12km (7mi) drive. On Tanna is Yasur, cited as the most accessible active volcano in the world. Witness the primitive origins of bungee jumping on Pentecost islands.

**Hazards and Hassles** – Beware shallow, razor-sharp reefs with no channels. Reef-cuts and snapped boards are frequent. There is one hospital in Vila with limited resources. Malaria is endemic in the outer islands, but Efate is relatively free. Tap water in urban areas is safe but not in rural areas. Nov 26, 1999, a 7.3 earthquake was reported NW of Ambrym.

**Handy Hints** – Take everything; a gun is not needed. Don't forget reefboots, sunblock and alarm clocks. The Vanuatu are strongly linked with France, expect French ex-pats and Australian and Japanese tourists. Ni-Vans are the islanders.

| WEATHER STATISTICS | J/F | M/A | M/J | J/A | S/O | N/D |
|---|---|---|---|---|---|---|
| total rainfall (mm) | 300 | 290 | 130 | 110 | 110 | 180 |
| consistency (days/mth) | 18 | 19 | 14 | 12 | 12 | 14 |
| min temp (°C/°F) | 23/74 | 23/74 | 21/70 | 19/66 | 20/68 | 22/72 |
| max temp (°C/°F) | 30/86 | 29/84 | 27/80 | 26/79 | 27/80 | 29/84 |

the Vanuatu archipelago. Free of skyscraper office blocks, this sleepy capital is set within a magnificent natural harbour inside Mélé Bay.

To the west of Mele is **Devil's Point**, a scary scene for radical lefts, offshore with the trades! On rare big swells, mediocre waves break inside Mélé Bay at **Black Sand Beach**. Many of the resorts are close to quality reefbreaks, which makes checking conditions easy. At **Pango Point**, Efate's number one spot, the entrance fee to this live coral reefbreak is less than a dollar and the point favours lefts and high tide for safer rides. If Pango Point feels kind of sketchy, check several reefs nearby. **British Beach** is quite deep, rideable on any tide, and is usually better than it looks. **Pounders** can be described as a tube orgy when it is on, but the barrelling lefts need high tide and no trades. **Erakor Island** is a well-known private resort island with many water activities but few surfers to ride the exposed, high tide lefts next to the island. Wind is a problem and glassy days are rare so be prepared to wake up before dawn and get there for the two to three hours of daylight before the trades pick up. **Tapi Point** has probably the longest waves on Efate, albeit quite sectiney. **Teouma Bay**'s protected beachies break very softly, perfect for beginners, although its pseudonym Shark Bay reveals the main danger. Further away is **Soumabal Point**, a potential left reefbreak but again trade wind exposure is maximum, so it's likely to be disorganised. **Forari Bay** has an interesting set-up, well protected from the SE trades on the inside lefts. There's a rare outside section and a right on the south side of the bay and despite its remoteness, is definitely worth a regular check. Drive to the north coast at least once to have a go at **Epao** and Takara's **Mangea Reefs**, next to

the Beachcomber. These spots have been rumoured to produce good surf but again, be ready for disappointment and patience. Another option is to fly to the southern islands, especially Port Resolution on Tanna and Aneityum where Anelgo could be Vanuatu's most promising left pointbreak.

Like Fiji, the main swell source should be the lows lashing the Tasman Sea with SW groundswells but there is a problem. 400km (250mi) long New Caledonia blocks 100% of the SW swells. Then New Zealand makes it hard for straight S swells to make it up there. However, SE groundswells from systems travelling east to South America or windswells from the trades, hit Vanuatu with some strength and consistency. However, the most exposed spots will be blown out by mid-morning, i.e. 9am, so wake up at dawn. Surf is rarely big, 2-8ft (0.6-2.5m) being the normal range. Coral Sea cyclones produce occasional NW-W swells, the best waves around Port-Vila, with many calm days and ideal NE-E conditions. From 1940 to 1985, 58 severe tropical storms and cyclones affected Vanuatu, 65% of which occurred in January and February. The trade winds are easterly in southern and central Vanuatu, and southerly in the far north where there is a clear equatorial climatic influence. Tidal range can reach 1.6m (5ft) on spring tides, averaging out at 1-1.2m (3-4ft) but is enough to change the surf conditions on high tide only surf spots. Get a tide table on Flinders; tides are semi-diurnal with diurnal inequality.

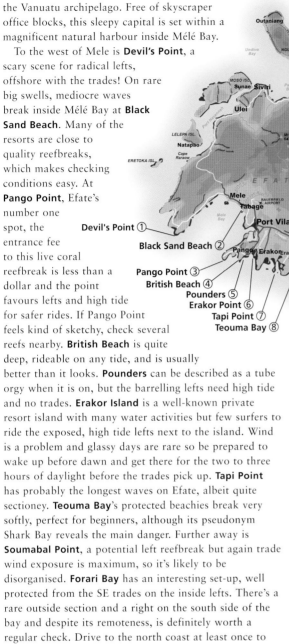

**Reef pass between Peli and Nguna Islands**

| SPOT DESCRIPTION | | | |
|---|---|---|---|
| Spot | Size | Btm | Type |
| ① | 10/3 | | |
| ② | 6/2 | | |
| ③ | 12/2 | | |
| ④ | 8/2 | | |
| ⑤ | 10/2 | | |
| ⑥ | 8/3 | | |
| ⑦ | 10/2 | | |
| ⑧ | 6/2 | | |
| ⑨ | • | | |
| ⑩ | • | | |
| ⑪ | • | | |
| ⑫ | • | | |

| SURF STATISTICS | J F | M A | M J | J A | S O | N D |
|---|---|---|---|---|---|---|
| dominant swell | W-NW | W-NW | S-SE | S-SE | S-SE | W-NW |
| swell size (ft) | 2-3 | 3 | 3-4 | 4-5 | 3-4 | 2 |
| consistency (%) | 60 | 50 | 60 | 40 | 30 | 20 |
| dominant wind | NE-SE | NE-SE | E-SE | E-SE | E-SE | E-SE |
| average force | F3 | F3 | F3-F4 | F3-F4 | F3 | F3 |
| consistency (%) | 62 | 62 | 63 | 69 | 72 | 59 |
| water temp (°C/°F) | 28/82 | 28/82 | 26/79 | 25/77 | 26/79 | 27/80 |
| wetsuit | | | | | | |

Frigates

**Summary**
+ POWERFUL, CONSISTENT SWELLS
+ QUALITY TUBULAR LEFTS
+ WARM BULA SPIRIT
+ RESORT CROWD – NO LOCALS
+ DIVING HEAVEN

– BIG AND WINDY IN WINTER
– RARE SUMMER RIGHTHANDERS
– COSTLY DEALS
– HEAVY RAIN
– OUTBOARD ACCESS ONLY

Until Cloudbreak made magazine cover shots, Fiji had been missing from the surfing map. Unlike French Polynesia, surfing wasn't traditional amongst fishermen. Surfing started in Suva in the early '80s, then ex pats searched an archipelago of 322 islands, starting in the Mamanucas with Tavarua/Namotu. The great distance to the breaks means spending more time in an outboard powered dingy than in a car. The Cloudbreak Syndrome refers to the way that waves appear as tiny smudges of whitewater on the horizon, making assessment difficult from the land and if it is visible, then it's probably too big. Powerful waves surging in from deep water, hitting shallow reef ledges that are very exposed to the main local problem – the wind. Being balanced between charter boats and surf camps,

outboards in Fiji matter a lot. Departure times, rotation, schedules, carrying capacity, engine power, safety equipment, comfort factor and the number of boats in operation are all important factors. Since most anticipate a rising wind, many surf in the morning, leaving the afternoon boats gambling on empty but rideable waves.

## TRAVEL INFORMATION

**Population:** 7,800 Kadavu
**Coastline:** 237km (148mi)
**Contests:** National – Lighthouse
**Other Resources:**
fijisurf.com
vitisurflegend.com
bulafiji.com
fijiguide.com

**Getting There** – Int'l flights (Air New Zealand, Qantas and nat'l South Pacific) get to Nadi, Suva being the nat'l hub. Get a taxi or an express bus down to Hideaway (1h), Waidroka (2h) or Pacific Harbour (3h). Daily flights with Sun Air from Nadi to Kadavu ($145r/t). Boards cost $60r/t. Vunisea runway got longer and tar-sealed in March 2003.

**Getting Around** – Don't rent a car ($50/d). Devote your budget to boat transfers. Durations depend on sea conditions. Frigates is 45min from Waidroka ($22), 30min from Yanutha (1h from P/H). The Suva/Kadavu freighter is cheap ($22 for a "saloon" bed) but be flexible. The crossing can be long (10h) and rough.

**Lodging and Food** – Penais is the most basic but the cheapest ($32/d) while at Batiluva there's a choice between a Love Shack and an 18 people

dorm ($50/d all inclusive with great food and 1 daily trip to Frigates with Bula). Jungle hotel (Waidroka: $50), beach resort (Nagigia: $120/night but as low as $47 in group) or deluxe resort (Marlin Bay: $190). Dorms are $10/night while doubles in 'bures' average $50. A meal plan, accommodation and transport to the surf will be between $50 and $100/day.

**Weather** – Fiji has a tropical climate, tempered by the ocean and trade winds. The leeward or western side of Viti Levu where most resorts are located averages an annual rainfall of 1700mm (71in), while windward Suva gets 300mm (12in) in Jan alone. Down by the coast and by islands like Beqa or Kadavu, rains are slightly thinner but expect lots of humidity and nebulosity. The cool and relatively dry months from May to October provide the best weather but swells and winds are the wildest. In July and August, temps may drop to 18°C (64°F). Spells of cloudy, cool weather with occasional rains alternate with warm, sunny days, sometimes of high humidity. The hot, wet season starts in November, but the stifling days are Jan-March. In winter, you need a bit of neoprene for the windchill.

**Nature and Culture** – Diving ($30 for a tank, relatively cheap), snorkelling, fishing and island hopping are the main extras. Beqa is Fiji diving spot #1 for pelagics and Kadavu Astrolabe Reef and Nagigia Island is world-class. Kava ceremonies with music and Meke dance are a must. Fijian people are amazingly friendly. Don't miss the fire walkers.

**Hazards and Hassles** – Surf conditions can be sketchy, watch out for power, rips and suck-outs on dry reefs. Injury is probable, be prepared. Crowds only occur at Frigates when several boats overpopulate the break. Waterproof bags and adequate clothing are a must as getting wet is a major factor. The 'Coup' in May 2001 only affected racial problems between Indians and Natives.

**Handy Hints** – Besides Viti Surf Legend in Nadi, there is the Waitui surf shop in Suva. Waidroka Resort has about 30 boards for rent, Nagigia about 15. Pure Blue is the only Fijian shaper working on bamboo boards and fixing damaged boards. Bring a full quiver! Phone numbers changed from 6 to 7 digits early 2002.

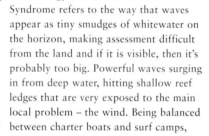

| WEATHER STATISTICS | J/F | M/A | M/J | J/A | S/O | N/D |
|---|---|---|---|---|---|---|
| total rainfall (mm) | 300 | 350 | 210 | 160 | 210 | 280 |
| consistency (days/mth) | 18 | 20 | 15 | 15 | 16 | 17 |
| min temp (°C/°F) | 23/74 | 23/74 | 22/72 | 20/68 | 21/70 | 22/72 |
| max temp (°C/°F) | 30/86 | 29/84 | 28/82 | 26/79 | 27/80 | 29/84 |

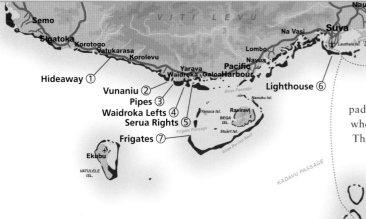

| Spot | Size | Btm | Type |
|---|---|---|---|
| ① | 6/2 | 🌀 | ◐ |
| ② | 8/2 | 🌀 | ◐ |
| ③ | 8/2 | 🌀 | ◐ |
| ④ | 6/2 | 🌀 | ◐ |
| ⑤ | 4/3 | ● | ◐ |
| ⑥ | 8/2 | 🌀 | ◐ |
| ⑦ | 18/2 | 🌀 | ◑ |
| ⑧ | 10/2 | 🌀 | ◐ |
| ⑨ | 12/3 | 🌀 | ◐ |
| ⑩ | 6/2 | ● | ◐ |
| ⑪ | 8/2 | 🌀 | ◐ |
| ⑫ | 8/2 | 🌀 | ◐ |
| ⑬ | 8/2 | 🌀 | ◐ |

Sunday was only allowed by the village leadership in December 2002. There are several spots within a 5min boat ride. **King Kong Left** is consistent, sheltered and within paddling distance of land, holding great shape when small and wild tubes over 6-8ft (2-2.5m). The gnarly **King Kong Right**s pick up a lot of swell but are usually blown out and for those who need a beginner wave, **Daku** reefs will provide fun walls. If there is a N wind, take the 1h trip to **Uatotoka**, a splendid right with easy barrels. On the Great Astrolabe Reef, three main passes including **Vesi** and **Typhoon Alley** host occasional, if sharky, classic waves when the wind comes from the N to W quadrant.

**Hideaway**'s rights are the only waves within paddling distance from land but as with all the rights in this region, it rarely works and dangerous rips scour the narrow channel. Rights only work on rare N winds but lefts usually handle the E trades, while most nearby spots require higher tides and a medium-to-big swell. **Pipes**' spitting tubes are more consistent than **Vunaniu** or **Serua**. Favour **Waidroka**, a remote jungle resort with access to nearby spots including Frigates. Ray Guinn and his family are serious about surfing, fishing and diving, operating three surfing boats from a shallow shelter. It's a "pay to play" system with extras for boats and food. If going to Suva, ask at the Trade Winds Motel or the yacht club for directions to the **Lighthouse** but it's inconsistent and polluted. Pacific Harbour (PH), Fiji's adventure capital, is the departure point for Yanutha, a tiny island off Frigates hosting two surf camps. Like Cloudbreak, **Frigates** boasts an impressive size range from small to huge. Up to 6ft (2m), it's not too radical with wrapping hollow walls, very sensitive to swell direction. At size, truly frightening barrels can be had. It can host up to 15 waveriders, which does not happen that often. Kadavu requires an extra flight, adding to an already costly bill but provides crowd-free line-ups and amazing flights in light aircraft. The 45min flight goes over Frigates and lands on a narrow mud airstrip, then, it's a 45min boat ride from Vunisea to Nagigia Island. Nagigia sports amazing underwater scenery and high speed satellite system internet facilities! Surfing on

Fiji is blessed by one of the greatest swell exposures on earth. The major source is SW from low pressures in the Tasman Sea. Although New Zealand blocks and bends some swell, the storms continue their way east providing lesser S-SE swells. Swell heights vary from 3-15ft (1-4.5m), March-November being the outstanding season. Being in the SE tradewind belt, Fiji favours lefts as the occasional rights get fully blown out by the trades, which average 15-25kph (9-16mph). Summer (Dec-March) is the main season for glassy days and north winds favouring rights but is disregarded for "lack" of swell. Most beginner to intermediate surfers should consider summer, especially on the south coast, as a reliable season despite the wet and hot climate. Southern seas are very active and summer gets a lot of head high to overhead days. In winter, the surf can get pretty intimidating at exposed surf spots. One of the surprising factors at this latitude happens to be the tides, reaching 8ft (2.5m) at spring tides, not only affecting reef shallows but also boat movements.

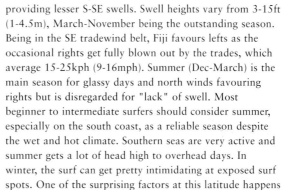
FIJISURF.COM/NAGIGA
**King Kong Left**

| SURF STATISTICS | J F | M A | M J | J A | S O | N D |
|---|---|---|---|---|---|---|
| dominant swell | S-SW | S-SW | SE-SW | SE-SW | SE-SW | S-SW |
| swell size (ft) | 3 | 5-6 | 6 | 7-8 | 7 | 2-3 |
| consistency (%) | 60 | 80 | 70 | 50 | 70 | 60 |
| dominant wind | NE-SE | NE-SE | E-SE | E-SE | E-SE | E-SE |
| average force | F4 | F3-F4 | F4 | F4 | F4 | F4 |
| consistency (%) | 63 | 72 | 64 | 62 | 73 | 67 |
| water temp (°C/°F) | 28/82 | 27/80 | 26/79 | 25/77 | 25/77 | 26/79 |
| wetsuit | 🧍 | 🧍 | 🧍 | 🧍 | 🧍 | 🧍 |

JOLI
**King Kong Lefts**

AMERICAN
SAMOA

WESTERN
SAMOA

COOK
ISLANDS

TONGA

# 124. Tutuila

GILLES CALVET

## Summary

+ RELIABLE SOUTH PACIFIC SWELLS
+ UNCROWDED POWERFUL
  REEFBREAKS
+ SOUTH COAST SPOT DENSITY
+ TROPICAL WARM WATERS

– LACK OF NORTH COAST SPOTS
– SUPER SHALLOW REEFS
– EXPOSED TO SE TRADES
– EXPENSIVE ACCESS
– INTENSE HEAT AND RAINFALL
  IN SUMMER

The only American land below the Equator, the territory of American Samoa consists of seven beautiful, tropical, volcanic islands, two of which are uninhabited coral atolls (Rose and Swains). Ta'u, Olosega and Ofu, known as the Manu'a group, are volcanic and dominated by high peaks. Tutuila is the largest island and also has the biggest population. Its nearest neighbour is Western Samoa, only 25 minutes away by plane. The surf in Savaii and Upolu is now well documented in the surf media, but Tutuila has mysteriously remained in the shadows for decades, despite being surfed by Americans since the early '60s. In terms of scope little has changed; the surfing population is still ex pat, no locals surf, and no surf

**Sliding Rock**

BRYAN JACKSON

**Pago Pago Harbour**

GILLES CALVET

camp has been erected. The waves are powerful reefbreaks with world-class potential, but the reality is that surf conditions are pretty fickle and surf spots dangerously shallow. Most breaks are located on the

## TRAVEL INFORMATION

**Population:** 60,000
**Coastline:** 102km (64mi)
**Contests:** None
**Other Resources:**
amsamoa.net/tourism/
    index1.html
slidingrockresort.com

**Getting There** – Tourist visa is $45 but most nationalities don't need it. Hawaiian Air flies direct from Pago Pago (PPG) to Honolulu. Polynesian Airlines, Air New Zealand and Air Pacific provide costly flights to New Zealand, Australia, Fiji, Tahiti... Samoa Air flies to Tonga and Western Samoa and provides inter-island services. No dept tax.

**Getting Around** – From $0.50 to $1 for longer rides, Aiga (pronounced Eye-Ing-a), local family coloured buses, run unscheduled services. The main road from Fagamalo to Onenoa is 50km (32mi). Rental cars cost $85 /day! Drive on the right. Taxis: Pago-Pago to Leone is $15. Say a nice "Talofa" to avoid being overcharged!

**Lodging and Food** – Unlike many South Pacific islands, there are no waterfront resorts, but a few small hotels around Pago Pago. The public Rainmaker Hotel is a joke. The Pago Airport Inn is $95/dble, Barry B&B in Leone costs $40/dble. Local BBQ and stone baked breadfruit, pork, chicken and bananas are the local dish; expect $6 for a meal.

**Weather** – Tutuila is tropical, wet, hot and very humid year round. Despite small temperature variations, Tutuila's climate is usually divided into two seasons. During the hot and rainy season from December to April, temps go up to 30°C (86°F) and 3cm of rain may fall on a typical day. The Pioa Mountain overlooking Pago Pago is called Rainmaker Mountain! However, the heat is tempered by the cooling effect of afternoon downpours and trade winds. The rainy season is also the cyclone season; Hurricane Val devastated Tutuila in 1991, killing 4 people, injuring 200 and leaving 4,000 people homeless. May to November is cooler and drier, with less humidity and pleasantly cool evenings. Water temps are among the warmest on earth – lycra for the sun or a shorty for windchill and razor sharp coral.

**Nature and Culture** – Climb lofty Mount Alava to view Pago Pago's natural harbour. Tutuila is covered in dense tropical rainforest, home to unique animals like the Flying Fox or the Pacific Boa, much of it protected by National Parks. The 'turtle and shark' legend is performed in Vaitogi. Check Tisa's Barefoot Beach & Bar in Alega. Golfing is cheap.

**Hazards and Hassles** – Be ready to airdrop into some shallow, square bowls: reef cuts are a given. There is a good hospital in town. Much of the coast around Pago Pago is quite developed with harbour facilities, marring slightly the 'untouched' feel to the place. No malaria or disease but it is steaming hot in summer. Religious beliefs dictate no surfing on Sunday apart from Sliding Rock.

**Handy Hints** – Bring at least 2 boards including a strong semi-gun. Contact The Dive Shop in Vaitogi for tips and board repair. 90% of the population are native Samoans, they wear a 'lava lava' (cloth wraparound) and dig Faia Samoa – the Samoan way. The int'l dateline passes west of Samoa; it's a day behind the rest of the world.

| WEATHER STATISTICS | J/F | M/A | M/J | J/A | S/O | N/D |
|---|---|---|---|---|---|---|
| total rainfall (mm) | 330 | 300 | 300 | 170 | 220 | 320 |
| consistency (days/mth) | 24 | 23 | 20 | 19 | 20 | 21 |
| min temp (°C/°F) | 24/75 | 24/75 | 24/75 | 23/74 | 24/75 | 24/75 |
| max temp (°C/°F) | 30/86 | 30/86 | 29/84 | 28/82 | 29/84 | 30/86 |

south coast, way too exposed to prevailing SE trades and the north coast of Tutuila is mostly sheer, black lava cliffs. Fortunately, the south coast has a relatively flat volcanic platform with fringing reefs and submerged coral banks, producing many surfable breaks.

The west end of Tutuila is the best surfing area with a superb coastal road skirting several quality surf spots. On occasional N swells, **Poloa** could be a blast but be very careful with low tide close-outs. **Amanave Bay** is one of those archetypal South Pacific scenic bays, where waves

Fatuuli Rock

have been surfed but not consistently. **Nua** is the most likely venue to find classic lefts with the dominant combo of SW swells and SE winds. **Asili Point** may reveal its fun side with N winds, along with the most user-friendly break in the area, **Sliding Rock**. Rides are pretty long compared to the majority of short sucky ledges but favour high tides. Close by is Fagatele Bay Sanctuary Marine Reserve, a hotspot for divers and all nature lovers. Going eastward, the cliffs become sheer and Vaitogi stands as the only entry point to this area. From the airport, the good potential reefs start again and can easily be checked from the road. **Nu'uuli** mushes out after take-off, **Faganeanea**'s sectioney lefts get good with rare NW winds, Matu'u is little more then an indicator and the **Fatuuli Rock** offers long rights with a barrelling bowl on the inside. **Coral Heads** is a small wave spot only. Pago Pago Bay is exposed to the trades and swell shadowed by the Taema offshore bank. The best bet is **Lauli'ituai** with awesome lefts and rights under the right conditions, ideal for square barrel experts rather than the average surfer. Further east, the bowling lefts at **Liea Point** are also known as Gas Stations and **Amouli** entertains a long, high tide, lefthand pointbreak, plus some rights on the other side. Both are easy to check, unlike Aunu'u Island that requires a 15min ferry ride from Auíasi. The lefts on **Aunu'u** can be world

class with the last section well sheltered from the trades. On W-NW wind, check **Aloa** or **Tula**; traditional American Samoan villages, which can be quite consistent and pleasant surf by Tutuilan standards.

Samoa has great swell exposure, catching all the SE-SW pulses that the South Pacific has to offer. Varying year round from 3-15ft (1-5m), conditions are often too messy on the open south coast. Only huge North Pacific NW swells make it down with any reasonable size, generally during Nov-Feb, but don't rely on these swells. Being right in the SE trade belt, Rarotonga is plagued (like Fiji and Tonga) by strong prevailing 20-30km/h (12-19mph) SE winds. The best conditions occur with the combination of clean S swells and rare N winds. NE winds favour lefts while NW favour rights. Summer (Dec-March) is the season for clean conditions but swell is not that plentiful and it frequently rains. Tidal range never goes over 5ft (1.5m), even on spring tides, but is still crucial over those shallow, low tide coral heads. Surfing bigger tides is preferable; choose your week so those high tides happen in the morning. Best are the incoming tides when high tide floods the reef; 2-3 hours before high tide is good and safe. Check with Flinders National Tidal Utility for monthly tide tables or contact John at the Tutuila Dive shop.

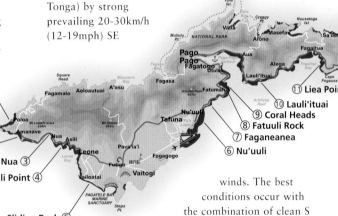

Poloa Bay ①
Amanave Bay ②
Nua ③
Asili Point ④
Sliding Rock ⑤

⑥ Nu'uuli
⑦ Faganeanea
⑧ Fatuuli Rock
⑨ Coral Heads
⑩ Lauli'ituai
⑪ Liea Point
⑫ Amouli
⑬ Aunu'u
⑭ Alao
⑮ Tula

| SPOT DESCRIPTION | | |
|---|---|---|
| Spot | Size | Btm Type |
| ① | • | |
| ② | • | |
| ③ | • | |
| ④ | • | |
| ⑤ | • | |
| ⑥ | • | |
| ⑦ | • | |
| ⑧ | • | |
| ⑨ | • | |
| ⑩ | • | |
| ⑪ | • | |
| ⑫ | • | |
| ⑬ | • | |
| ⑭ | • | |
| ⑮ | • | |

Oti Point

| SURF STATISTICS | J F | M A | M J | J A | S O | N D |
|---|---|---|---|---|---|---|
| dominant swell | N-NW | S-SW | SE-SW | SE-SW | S-SW | N-NW |
| swell size (ft) | 4-5 | 5 | 6-7 | 7 | 5-6 | 4-5 |
| consistency (%) | 70 | 60 | 40 | 30 | 40 | 70 |
| dominant wind | NE-SE | NE-SE | E-SE | E-SE | E-SE | NE-SE |
| average force | F3 | F3 | F3-F4 | F4 | F3-F4 | F3-F4 |
| consistency (%) | 56 | 68 | 72 | 82 | 76 | 60 |
| water temp (°C/°F) | 28/82 | 28/82 | 29/84 | 27/80 | 28/82 | 28/82 |
| wetsuit | | | | | | |

# 125. Rarotonga

**Summary**

+ NORTH AND SOUTH SWELLS
+ UNCROWDED REEF PASSES
+ EASY PADDLES FROM SHORE
+ OUTER ISLAND POTENTIAL

– LIMITED REEF PASS SET-UPS
– SHALLOW, HIGH TIDE REEFS
– TROPICAL DOWNPOURS
– EXPENSIVE LOCAL COSTS

ALL PHOTOS MICHAEL KEW

Many a round-the-world ticket includes the option of stopping in the Cook Islands, evoking thoughts of Pacific perfection. Considering these 15 islands sit in between world-class locations like Fiji, Tonga, Samoa and Tahiti, you would be forgiven for thinking that they must have awesome waves somewhere. The fact that they bear the name of the ultimate surf discoverer, James Cook, is not a guarantee of good surf and like Tubuai or Niue, the underwater topography doesn't suit epic surf requirements. However, devoting a few weeks should ensure sampling some decent and definitely uncrowded high tide waves. The Cook Islands, spreading over a staggering 2.2 million km² (1.4 million mi²) of ocean, consists of two groupings

with 1500km (940mi) between the two most remote islands. The southern group includes nine volcanic islands, although some are virtually atolls: Aitutaki, Atiu, Mangaia, Manuae, Mauke, Mitiaro, Palmerston, Rarotonga and Takutea. The northern group comprises of six low coral atolls: Manihiki, Nassau, Tongareva (or

## TRAVEL INFORMATION

**Population:** 10,000
**Coastline:** 33km (20mi)
**Contests:** None
**Other Resources:**
*Video:* Fu Man Chu
cookislandsurf.co.ck

**Getting There** – 30 day visitors permit issued on arrival. Air New Zealand is the main airline offering flights to Rarotonga (RAR) with direct flights from LAX, Auckland, Fiji and Tahiti. Aloha Airlines has 1 or 2 weekly flights from Vancouver via Hawaii. Most flights arrive and depart in the early hours of the morning. Dep tax is NZ$25 per person

**Getting Around** – Air Rarotonga operates flights to 8 islands. Aitutaki is $192r/t. Rarotonga's coastal road is 32km (20mi) long: cycling takes 2h. All drivers need a local driver's license, available from Avarua Police Station, with your own license ($6). Motorbike License test is $3. Car hire is $28 /day, while moped hire for only $30/4 days. Drive on the left.

**Lodging and Food** – Muri Beach is the main lodging area. Prices are on the high side for the South Pacific. Luxury self contained beach bungalow (from $165 / day), resort room (from $110), an economy bungalow (from $66), a budget room for $28. Palm Grove is $90/140$ per night while Tiare village is a cheap $10 per night. Expect $10 for a meal.

**Weather** – With 2116h of sunshine and 2087mm (82in) of rainfall annually, the climate is tropical. Rarotonga is almost opposite Honolulu in latitude and unlike the wet and dry extremes experienced by most equatorial nations, Rarotonga enjoys a pleasant climate year round with relatively minor fluctuations. The surfing season, May-Sept, has the 'cooler' months, with average daily temps around 25°C (77°F), down to 19°C (66°F) at night. The summer rainy season, Dec-April, can be hot and humid 29°C (84°F) by day with bright sunny mornings and late afternoon downpours. As the heat accumulates over the Pacific Ocean, lows bring torrential rains, strong winds and the occasional tropical cyclone, which means high humidity, sticky nights and more mosquitoes. Bring a shorty for windy winter days when water gets down around 22-23°C (72-74°F).

**Nature and Culture** – Rarotonga is a lush, beautiful place, enjoy its peace. Go to Saturday morning's Punanga-nui Market. Fishing is world-class! Common catches include bonefish, trevally, mahimahi, paara, marlin, snapper and tuna. The local record for marlin is 277kg (610lbs) or do Captain Tama's glass-bottom boat tour of the lagoon. Visit the other Cook islands!

**Hazards and Hassles** – While most of the surf is not treacherous, with easy paddle outs from shore, conditions are very iffy and surfing over shallow reef usually means reef cuts. Most local riders are cool bodyboarders! There is no malaria but occasional outbreaks of dengue. Locals call the scrape marks on tourists from motorcycle mishaps the Honda Rash or Rarotongan tattoo.

**Handy Hints** – Bring 2 boards for mid-size surf, contact Big Dave at Niki's Surf Shop in Tupapa (East Avarua) near Paradise Inn. It is a small shop with second-hand boards. High season is December to February. The Cook Islands are located across the dateline from New Zealand and Australia, so it's a day behind! Check the Surf The Earth deal.

| WEATHER STATISTICS | J/F | M/A | M/J | J/A | S/O | N/D |
|---|---|---|---|---|---|---|
| total rainfall (mm) | 238 | 226 | 170 | 109 | 114 | 187 |
| consistency (days/mth) | 15 | 14 | 12 | 10 | 9 | 11 |
| min temp (°C/°F) | 23/74 | 22/72 | 20/68 | 18/64 | 19/66 | 21/70 |
| max temp (°C/°F) | 29/84 | 28/82 | 26/79 | 25/77 | 26/79 | 27/80 |

Penrhyn), Pukapuka, Rakahanga and Suwarro. The majority of the population lives in the southern group. The capital Rarotonga is volcanic with a rugged, eroded centre of peaks and ridges, surrounded by flat lowlands about 1km wide. Since Rarotonga is the youngest island, it is physically unlike its other volcanic neighbours where erosion and periodic submersions have reduced mountains to gentle hills. Compared with other atolls, the lagoon surrounding Rarotonga is quite small, covering only 8km² (5mi²) and is relatively shallow. The fringing reef defines the lagoon, which is broad and sandy to the south, and narrow and rocky on the north and east. Most of the reef passes are too narrow, preventing waves from wrapping properly and explains why there is only a handful of surf spots in the Cook Islands. The waves break over shallow reef, so it's usually safest to surf at high tide and a decent size swell will also help the waves to break in deeper water. All the reefbreaks are easily accessible by paddling out one of the passages or directly over the reef.

Despite being on the windward side, one of the most surfed spots is **Avana**, helpfully located close to the popular accommodation at Muri Beach. The break is

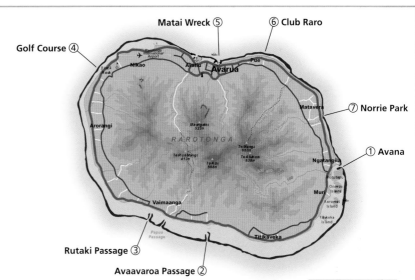

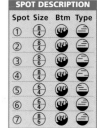

quite short and requires patience in selecting waves. The surf is neither that reliable nor challenging, even though it breaks over shallow reef, making it a bit too dangerous for beginners. Opposite the passage is a smaller right which is popular with bodyboarders. On moderate SW swells and summer NE winds, check **Rutaki Passage**, facing the Rarotongan Resort, or the thick, ferocious rights off the **Avaavaroa Passage** opposite the Palm Grove Resort. These passages are very narrow and usually close out in overhead conditions, requiring clean, organised swell to break properly. Check Papua passage nearby as well. On the leeward side, the best spot is undoubtedly **Golf Course** by Black Rock, next to the airport. The lefts get real good but beware the coral heads and pitching lips. This wave exudes true Polynesian power and

although it is uncrowded, negotiating its imperfections requires skill and guts. The **Matai Wreck** off Avarua has long been surfed and can offer hollow lefts on major N swells. For righthanders, head to the reef off **Club Raro** or **Norrie Park** which regularly produce some good waves. Rumours from other islands like Aitutaki, suggest their reef passes are as narrow as Rarotonga's, but there could be a gem somewhere in the other 13 Cook Islands...

The Cook Islands are blessed by one of the greatest swell exposures on earth but the coastline sucks. The South Pacific provides most of the swell in the shape of 3-15ft (1-5m) SE-SW swells, from March-November. Only huge North Pacific NW swells will make it so far south with reasonable size making the summer months very unreliable. Being below the SE trade belt, Rarotonga enjoys slightly less wind exposure than Fiji or Tonga. The prevailing SE wind favours lefts while the rights get blown out by the trades, which average 15-25 km/h (9-16mph). Summer (Dec-March) is the season for glassy days on the windward, east coast spots like Avana and then the N winds blow into the rights. Mid-sized, winter swells create the best chance of quality waves, breaking a bit further off the reef. Tidal range never goes over 3ft (1m), even on spring tides but remains a crucial factor. Since high tides are best for surfing it is advisable to check the tide tables for morning high tides with as much range as possible. Check with Flinders National Tidal Utility for monthly tide tables or ask Niki's shop in Rarotonga.

| SURF STATISTICS | J F | M A | M J | J A | S O | N D |
|---|---|---|---|---|---|---|
| dominant swell | N-NW | S-SW | SE-SW | SE-SW | S-SW | N-NW |
| swell size (ft) | 4-5 | 5 | 6-7 | 7 | 5-6 | 4-5 |
| consistency (%) | 40 | 50 | 60 | 60 | 50 | 40 |
| dominant wind | NE-SE | E-SE | E-SE | E-SE | E-SE | E-SE |
| average force | F4 | F4 | F4 | F4 | F4 | F4 |
| consistency (%) | 71 | 54 | 58 | 49 | 60 | 66 |
| water temp (°C/°F) | 26/79 | 26/79 | 25/77 | 23/74 | 23/74 | 25/77 |
| wetsuit | | | | | | |

# 126. Huahiné and Raiatea

KIRIBATI
Marquesas Islands
Tuamotu Archipelago
Society Islands
FRENCH
POLYNESIA
Tubuai Islands

## Summary
+ YEAR ROUND SWELL
+ POWERFUL REEF PASSES
+ POSTCARD SCENERY
+ ALL TYPES OF ACCOMODATION

− FIERCE LOCALISM
− REEF PASS DANGERS
− DIFFICULT ACCESS
− VERY EXPENSIVE TRIP

Faré Right

JOLI

Faré Left

SYLVAIN CAZENAVE

VALÉRY JONCHERAY

Tahiti is the crossroads of French Polynesia's 118 small islands, shared between 5 archipelagos (Society, Marquises, Tuamotu, Gambier and Australes) spread over a surface as large as Europe. Best known are the Society Islands consisting of the Windward Group (Tahiti, Moorea, Tetiaroa) and the Leeward Group (Huahiné, Raiatea/Tahaa, Maupiti and Bora Bora). Being only 200km (125mi) west of Tahiti, the Leeward Islands get pounded by the same swells; reef passes being the only surf spots. Most local waveriders have escaped the Tahitian crowds to enjoy a privileged environment of idyllic tubular waves with a handful of close friends. Because these islands are so remote, with a long history of resistance against the official government, a strong feeling of ownership of the spots, namely localism, has developed. The "Black Shorts" on Huahine and Raiatea will only let outsiders surf with them once they have proved themselves to be their friends and loyal to the surf. This involves a long process

## TRAVEL INFORMATION

**Population:** 30,000 (leeward islands)
**Coastline:**
62 & 82km (39 & 51mi)
**Contests:** None
**Other Resources:**
huahine.com/todo/
    watersports.html
bodyboardingtahiti.com
gotahiti.com
tahiti-tourisme.com

**Getting There** – Fly to Papeete (PPT) with Air New Zealand, Air France, Corsair from Paris/LAX, Hawaiian from Honolulu or Qantas from Oz. When in Faaa Airport, buy a pass with Air Tahiti or pay PPT-Huahinè: $108 (o/w); PPT-Raiatea: $124o/w, Huahiné-Raiatea: $54 (o/w). ATR 42 or 72 have a 6/7ft limit. Ferries are cheap (8h)! No dep tax

**Getting Around** – A rental car is expensive ($50/day) and not much help for remote reef passes. In Faré, rent a boat from JC Eychenne or get a 2-seater kayak ($15/4h) for close spots. Rent a jetski with Safari: $165 daily. Renting a 15Hp boat (4pax) from Europcar in Uturoa costs $72 for 8h + gas ($42). Raiatea has a public transport system (le Truck) to/from Uturoa.

**Lodging and Food** – You can stay in Faré at low costs. A cabin at Pension Poetaina is $20/day;

Pension Chez Guinette costs $40/single, Motel Vanille start from $45/pax. Sofitel Heiva Coralia is $210/dble. In Uturoa, Hinano Hotel ($80/day a/c room for 2) well located if you rent a boat. Expect $10 eating local food in 'Roulottes' or $20 in restaurants.

**Weather** – The Leeward Islands of the Society group enjoy warm, tropical weather year round. Cooled by the gentle breezes of the Pacific, the climate of these islands is sunny and pleasant – the year round lowest temp is 21°C (70°F). Seasons are the reverse of those in the Northern Hemisphere. From November through May the climate is warmer and very humid, with daily temperatures of about 29°C (84°F) and from June through October, the climate is cooler and drier with daily temperatures of 27°C (80°F). Most of the rain falls during the warmer season, but there are also many lovely sunny days with refreshing trade winds during these months. Water temps are just ideal around 27°C (80°F) and a bit of neoprene would only be useful to protect against coral cuts or gusty trades.

**Nature and Culture** – Faré comes to life on shipping day, Huahine's people travel to town by le truck to sell their pigs, copra and melons and buy goods from the incoming supply ships. Tourist attractions include buying pearls, shark feeding, big game fishing or sailing cruises. In Raiatea, visit Taputapuatea, the largest marae (religious monument) in Polynesia or vanilla plantations...

**Hazards and Hassles** – Localism is the main issue – face it. Prepare for Polynesian power and take a first-aid kit for reef cuts. Passe rips can be intense, beware if paddling across the lagoon and wear sun-cream. When it rains for days, streams wash out a lot of trash and the channel gets brown with worrying debris. On Motus, mind the pigs!

**Handy Hints** – Although some beat-up boards are for rent in Faré, take 2 boards (with a small gun for 6ft days) and trying to trade one with a local could be a way to negotiate some surfing rights. There are many surf tour operators, STC New Zealand have a 7 nights in Faré (Chez Guynette) from $910 with flights.

| | | | | | | |
|---|---|---|---|---|---|---|
| total rainfall (mm) | 310 | 170 | 100 | 50 | 65 | 230 |
| consistency (days/mth) | 17 | 13 | 10 | 7 | 7 | 15 |
| min temp (°C/°F) | 22/72 | 22/72 | 21/70 | 20/68 | 21/70 | 22/72 |
| max temp (°C/°F) | 31/88 | 31/88 | 30/86 | 30/86 | 30/86 | 31/88 |

of copious drinking at the local bars with them and much banter, handshaking, chest pounding and talking surf. Not everyone can do this so a cool attitude, a very low profile and a willingness to leave the surf if harassed are all essential ingredients.

The main feature of the surf is the proximity of the reef passes to the 'motus' or islets that lie inside the fringing barrier reef, making it possible to paddle from land. Another difference from Tahiti is the

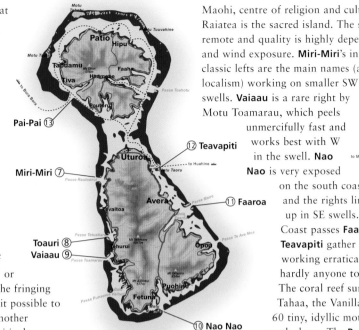

Maohi, centre of religion and culture 1000 years ago, Raiatea is the sacred island. The surf spots are more remote and quality is highly dependant on swell direction and wind exposure. **Miri-Miri**'s intense rights or **Toauri**'s classic lefts are the main names (again with some localism) working on smaller SW swells. **Vaiaau** is a rare right by Motu Toamarau, which peels unmercifully fast and works best with W in the swell. **Nao Nao** is very exposed on the south coast and the rights line up in SE swells. East Coast passes **Faaroa** and **Teavapiti** gather windswells, working erratically with hardly anyone to surf them. The coral reef surrounding Tahaa, the Vanilla Island, is crowned with 60 tiny, idyllic motus perched above the north shore. The **Pai-Pai** pass where major boats get in and out is too large for reliable surf but some days, it gets good and is unlikely to have angry locals.

It's a year round destination, favouring north winds for the epic rights. The northeasters blow from November-April, while swells are generated by massive low pressure systems in the North Pacific, getting there 3-5 days later than Hawaii. Despite large distances travelled, there's no shadowing en route and they arrive out of deep water with surprising ferocity and consistency, delivering anything from 3-10ft (1-3m) reef perfection. Swell duration usually lasts 2-3 days. The S swell season lasts the majority of the year, with the peak months being May-September, but it is not uncommon to have classic south swells before or after winter. They enter through a broad swell window spanning from SW to SE (reef passes are very sensitive to swell direction), can last for many days on end and produce similar sized swells as during the northerly season although the occasional larger swells (up to 20ft/6m) have occurred in past seasons. Like any South Pacific island, the surf can vary erratically from dead flat to 10ft (3m), with many 3-6ft (1-2m) days in between. Dominant winds are E-SE trades shifting NE and calming down in summer, Jan-March are the quietest and July-Sept the windiest. As for tides, it can be 2ft (0.6m) max but incoming or outgoing current will alter water heights.

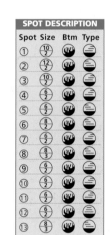

| SPOT DESCRIPTION | | | |
|---|---|---|---|
| Spot | Size | Btm | Type |
| ① | 10/2 | | |
| ② | 12/2 | | |
| ③ | 10/2 | | |
| ④ | 6/2 | | |
| ⑤ | 6/2 | | |
| ⑥ | 8/2 | | |
| ⑦ | 6/2 | | |
| ⑧ | 8/3 | | |
| ⑨ | 6/2 | | |
| ⑩ | 6/2 | | |
| ⑪ | 6/2 | | |
| ⑫ | 6/2 | | |
| ⑬ | 8/3 | | |

predominance of rights, especially on Huahinè, making the Leeward Group a reliable summer bet when NE winds blow. Huahiné is the best-known island since the Faré backpacker village sits within paddling distance of the break formerly called Bali Hai. **Faré Rights** are long, sectioney walls and plenty of short barrel opportunities in front of the once famous hotel that no longer operates. Paddle out from the jetty, just south of the hotel, where kids learn on a tiny reform. The **Faré Lefts** take about 20 min to paddle to but are classic Polynesian surf: long powerful walls wrap into the 'passe' but unfortunately are prone to localism. Out of the three classic spots here, **Fitii** probably has the best world-class potential with amazing rights providing open barrels and ideal launching pads for aerialists. A boat is advised to reach this localised break. Check the exposed southern pass of **Parea** on a flat windless day or on N wind, quality could be there with low crowd pressure. Stay at the Huahiné Beach Club for proximity. Another less surfed passe is **Motu Mahara** by the Sofitel Heiva where lefts offer fast walls in summer conditions. A scenic road, mostly non-paved, winds through green canopies and beautiful vistas for 32km (20mi) around the two islands, passing through small villages where 5,000 inhabitants live in colourful, modest homes. Located 220km (138mi) NW of Tahiti, Raiatea is the largest and the administrative centre of the Leeward Islands. In the past named Havaii, original land of the

**Faré Right**

**Pai-Pai**

| SURF STATISTICS | J F | M A | M J | J A | S O | N D |
|---|---|---|---|---|---|---|
| dominant swell | N-NW | S-SW | SE-SW | SE-SW | S-SW | N-NW |
| swell size (ft) | 4-5 | 5 | 6-7 | 7 | 5-6 | 4-5 |
| consistency (%) | 80 | 70 | 80 | 90 | 70 | 80 |
| dominant wind | NE-SE | NE-SE | E-SE | S-SE | E-SE | NE-SE |
| average force | F3-F4 | F3 | F3-F4 | F4 | F4 | F3-F4 |
| consistency (%) | 71 | 77 | 62 | 62 | 75 | 73 |
| water temp (°C/°F) | 28/82 | 28/82 | 27/80 | 26/79 | 26/79 | 27/80 |
| wetsuit | | | | | | |

KIRIBATI
Marquesas
Tuamotu
Society Islands
Australs    FRENCH
            POLYNESIA

# 127. Tuamotu

MICHAEL KEW

## Summary

+ YEAR ROUND SWELLS
+ JUICY REEF PASSES
+ WORLD CLASS FISHING AND DIVING
+ LUXURY BOAT TRAVEL

− OCCASIONAL FLAT SPELLS
− NO SHELTER FROM TRADE WINDS
− LARGE DISTANCES
   BETWEEN BREAKS
− EXTREMELY EXPENSIVE SURF TRIP.

MICHAEL KEW

If the word atoll conjures up images of the Maldives, it may come as a surprise to find that the vast majority of the world's 400 atolls are located in the Pacific. The Tuamotu, which cover a territory as vast as western Europe, 1800km (1125mi) long, 600km (375mi) wide, are undoubtedly the main group with 78 islands, 77 of them being atolls, the exception being Makatea, a raised coral island whose phosphate pits have been mined to exhaustion. This dusting of islands is also called The Labyrinth, or the Archipelago of the Rough Sea and has remained essentially uncharted due to the difficulty of navigating the local waters. The exotic appearance of these atolls are linked to the palm trees which have only been growing since 1860. Until then, the eroded peaks of the 6100-9100ft (2000-3000m) underwater mountains were merely flat barren patches of dead coral and white

BILL MORRIS

sands with no fresh water or soil to grow anything. In addition, the earlier natives, the Paumotus, were aggressive towards visitors, indulging in tribal wars and cannibalism until it was annexed to French Polynesia in 1880. In 1842, Darwin wrote that these atolls were the tops of old volcanoes and his theory was confirmed decades later. Mururoa and Fangataufa was the site for the now infamous nuclear testing programme run by the French Government in the SE corner of the Tuamotu's.

## TRAVEL INFORMATION

**Population:** 18,000
**Coastline:** 225km (140mi)
**Contests:** None
**Other Resources:**
Video: Quiksilver 2000
wavehunters.com/
   tuamotus/tuamotus.asp
manihi.com

**Getting There** – Book flights to Papeete (PPT) with Air New Zealand, Air Tahiti Nui from LAX or Hawaiian from Honolulu, or Air France, Corsair from Paris. Then, fly Air Tahiti but ATR 42 or 72 have a 6/7′ limit while Dornier planes can't take boards. It is 200 nm (20h min) sailing with the *Cascade* boats or much longer with goléttes (freighters).

**Getting Around** – DIY transport is not an option as most reef passes are not close to airports & docks. Book the trip of a lifetime aboard the *Cascade* (11-17 knots). A 13d trip costs $3,250 with 10 people. Travelling fast between spots is crucial

**Lodging and Food** – Rangiroa is by far the most visited atoll, followed by Manihi, Tikehau and Fakarava. Land-based accommodation would be useless. A stay on *Cascade* is like a 4 star hotel with all modern facilities, 3 meals a day and free Hinano Beer. Expect lots of fish and French cuisine. *Cascade* has a 14ft dory with 25hp and a jetski.

**Weather** – There is less difference between wet and dry seasons than Tahiti because there are no mountains to gather clouds and mists. There is more rain in the austral summer, which produces short and heavy thunderstorms that decrease through the winter. It's warm year round, but the period between May and October is the coolest (21°C/70°F min in August) and driest. There is more than 3000h of yearly sunshine. Statistically, there is only a serious cyclone every 25 years but there were 6 between Dec '82 and April '83: Lisa, Nano, Orama, Reeva, Veena and William! As there is no phreatic layer, the Tuamotu rely on rain for their water supply, so don't waste it.

Water temps are just ideal around 27°C (80°F) and a bit of neoprene would only be useful cover against coral cuts or gusty trades.

**Nature and Culture** – This is the middle of an immense ocean. Fishing rods and sea kayaks on board *Cascade*. Pearl farms (black pearls) and fish traps/farming provide the main economy.

**Hazards and Hassles** – Dogs chase small black tip sharks in 1ft of water: maos (sharks) are just about everywhere but attacks unlikely. Apart from reef cuts, sunburn and rough seas, the only worries are if anything went wrong in such an environment. Communication is possible via satellite phone but it will cost $5 a minute.

**Handy Hints** – Recommended quiver should contain 4 boards, from 6′5″ to 7′4″ incorporating pin tails or gunny shapes with 2 double swivel leashes (6ft to 9ft). Accomplished longboarders should survive. Bring reef booties, board shorts, rashies, helmet, ding repair and tropical wax.

| WEATHER STATISTICS | J/F | M/A | M/J | J/A | S/O | N/D |
|---|---|---|---|---|---|---|
| total rainfall (mm) | 200 | 130 | 95 | 70 | 110 | 170 |
| consistency (days/mth) | 17 | 14 | 12 | 11 | 14 | 18 |
| min temp (°C/°F) | 25/77 | 26/79 | 25/77 | 24/75 | 25/77 | 25/77 |
| max temp (°C/°F) | 23/74 | 23/74 | 22/72 | 21/70 | 22/72 | 23/74 |

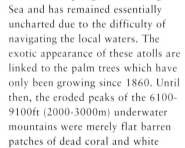

MICHAEL KEW

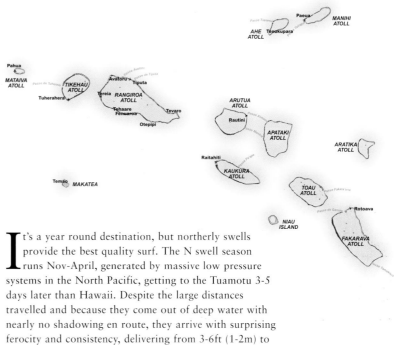

To the east are the younger atolls but it's the older atolls that are most likely to contain a reef pass, cut through the fringing reef to the inner lagoon. Out of 77 atolls, only 32 have at least one pass (only 10 have several); and most of these are found in the NW corner of the territory. The main atoll is Rangiroa, 75km (47mi) long, making it the world's second largest atoll after Kwajalein in Micronesia. The pass is a crucial resource for transport, fishing and now, surfing. It's likely that the first surfers came on sailing boats from Tahiti in the '80s. Compared to the major boat trip areas like the Mentawai or the Maldives, the Tuamotu experience rougher seas and the distance between breaks is higher so a fast and luxury boat is essential to cruise from one spot to another in a quick and comfortable way. Although the majority of the reef passes rely on north swells, there are also some SW exposed spots that are pretty consistent. The majority of North swells are clean, mid-size rights while South swells generally produce punchier lefts. Some waves are hollower on the outside reef and then actually back off into a mushier bowl as they wrap into the deeper passes, where water is flowing out from the lagoons. This makes some of the breaks in the Tuamotu okay for less experienced waveriders who can line up further inside and take off on the mushier bowl while the hardcore tube charger takes off deeper, further up the reef. It should be noted that in Rangiroa, the rip in the pass averages at 5km/h (3mph) and flows into the lagoon 35% of the time, while outgoing flow is 55%. While reef passes are the main spots, it's also possible to surf on fake passes, corners in the fringing reef, which offer less exposure to the gusty SE trades. This is probably the last major surfing frontier for boat trips; let's hope boat operators in the area will help preserve this unique ocean environment. The *Crossing* first showed up in 1999 scoring epic swells, then in January 2002, the top pros hit Tuamotu and the Super Trip was published in *Surfing* in June 2002. In terms of operation, *Archipels* from Moorea did the first commercial surf boat in the '90s with long time US ex pat Woody Ho. Wavehunters launched the *Cascade* in 2002, along with the Tahitian *Bluewater Dream* involving Aussie Chris O'Callaghan, who's also the contest director for the Teahupoo Pro and Moana David, Veteas brother and Moana Surf Tours boss.

It's a year round destination, but northerly swells provide the best quality surf. The N swell season runs Nov-April, generated by massive low pressure systems in the North Pacific, getting to the Tuamotu 3-5 days later than Hawaii. Despite the large distances travelled and because they come out of deep water with nearly no shadowing en route, they arrive with surprising ferocity and consistency, delivering from 3-6ft (1-2m) to 8-10ft (2.5-3m) island perfection. These swells last about 2-3 days. The S swell season lasts the majority of the year, with the peak months being May-September, but it is not uncommon to have classic S swells just before or after the

MICHAEL KEW

N season. They enter through a broad swell window spanning from SW to SE, they can last for many days on end. 3-6ft (1-2m) swells are common, as are 8-10ft (2.5-3m) swells. Larger swells up to 20ft (6m)

| SURF STATISTICS | J F | M A | M J | J A | S O | N D |
|---|---|---|---|---|---|---|
| dominant swell | N-NW | S-SW | SE-SW | SE-SW | S-SW | N-NW |
| swell size (ft) | 4-5 | 5 | 6-7 | 7 | 5-6 | 4-5 |
| consistency (%) | 70 | 60 | 70 | 80 | 60 | 70 |
| dominant wind | NE-SE | NE-SE | E-SE | E-SE | E-SE | NE-F4 |
| average force | F4 | F4 | F4 | F4 | F4 | F4 |
| consistency (%) | 75 | 78 | 60 | 62 | 70 | 72 |
| water temp (°C/°F) | 27/80 | 28/82 | 27/80 | 26/79 | 27/80 | 27/80 |
| wetsuit | | | | | | |

have occurred in past seasons with great infrequency. Like any South Pacific island, the surf can be very erratic.

Because the islands are flat and located right above the anticyclonic belt, E-SE trades can be damn strong, Jan-March being the weakest and July-Sept the windiest. As for tides, it's not even 1ft (0.3m) max but incoming or outgoing currents can alter water heights.

MICHAEL KEW

PITCAIRN

FRENCH POLYNESIA

□ Rapa Nui

# 128. Rapa Nui

Mata Veri

PAUL KENNEDY

**Summary**
+ YEAR ROUND SWELLS
+ POWERFUL LAVA REEFBREAKS
+ UNCROWDED SOUTH SHORE
+ UNREAL HISTORY AND LOCATION
+ GOOD WEATHER, CLEAR WATER.

– BIG, WILD WAVES
– NO QUALITY BEACHBREAKS
– SLEEPY HANGA ROA
– TRICKY EXIT/ENTRY POINTS
– EXPENSIVE AND REMOTE

JOLI

Known as Rapa Nui by its inhabitants, Easter Island is the most remote, inhabited place on earth. The nearest large landmasses are Chile 3,850km (2406mi) away and Tahiti 3,610km (2256mi) although Gambier and Pitcairn, about 1500km (938mi) away are actually the closest inhabited islands. "Te-Pito-O-Te-Henua" (the navel of the world) is one large open-air museum; a UN designated archaeological site of 'humankind treasure'. Its world-famous statues, the Moais, are 3-21m (10-66ft ) tall, made of volcanic basaltic rock, weigh between 20-300 tonnes and are thought to represent the faces of the royalty who ruled each of the 33 original tribes that lived on the island until the 16th century. These Moais

JOLI

are the largest monolithic expression in the entire Polynesian culture and amazingly, were moved as much as 18km (11mi) without mechanical help – legend has it they were moved by Mana, spiritual power. The island was formed by an eruption 3 million years ago from a single

## TRAVEL INFORMATION

**Population:** 3,000
**Coastline:** 64km (40mi)
**Contests:** Local
**Other Resources:**
*Video:* Step into liquid
Uma tahu
surfchile.cl
http://tackers1.tripod.com /easterisland/id2.html
iorana.net

**Getting There** – Visa: Chilean rules, no visa apart from US ($20). LanChile flies four times a week: two from Santiago and two from Tahiti (from $800r/t), travel int'l with LAN Chile for bargains. High season in summer gets busy, book early. A cargo ship comes to Hanga Piko port from Valparaiso in Chile 4 times a year. Dep tax: $18.

**Getting Around** – No public transport so walk or ride horses ($15/day), a great way to get around Hanga Roa. Most roads are unsealed dirt tracks but in good condition. Motorcycles cost from $25/day. Rental cars cost $45 to $90/day with agencies. A taxi company can take you anywhere for a better rate.

**Lodging and Food** – There are two main hotels (Hanga Roa and Iorana): $90 to $120/night full board. Backpackers have been opened recently ($12 to $20). Try "O'tama-Te-Ra'a" family

lodge or 'Chez Oscar' (US$12/night). Pea, facing Papa, is the best place to have lunch or dinner. Nightlife at Aloha Pub-Bar & Grill. Owner, Cesar Lagos is a pioneer surfer.

**Weather** – Easter Island is within the sub-tropical weather zone, which means a good balance of hot and humid tropical weather and the cold and windy weather, reminiscent of central Chile. The air temp is never below 17°C (63°F) and never above 28°C (82°F), with an annual rainfall of 1300mm (51in). There are two well-marked seasons: winter (wet) and summer (drier). Fed by the ocean, humidity is an ever-present factor, especially after quick, short rains. Fog never happens for the lack of a high altitude mountain barrier and electric storms are very unusual. The island is located outside the cyclone path along the South Pacific. Clear skies without clouds are very rare. Despite sub-tropical water temps from 19-24°C (66-75°F), the usual windy factor (10-30 knots) makes a lycra/rubber vest handy in summer and a 2mm springy or steamer in winter.

**Nature and Culture** – Enjoy open air, archaeological sites (don't miss Sebastian

Englert Museum), dive (with Orcas), trek (despite the lack of trees) or fish. Experience the word "isolation" watching the sunrise/sunset from the volcanoes. The coastline is filled with natural caves containing many religious petroglyphs based on sea life. Tapati Polynesian heritage festival is late January.

**Hazards and Hassles** – No disease: tap water is clean, mosquitoes are malaria free. Most of the lava reefs are flat with rare exposed rocks. South coast spots get very big but break in deep water. Take reef boots for the black sea urchins and a fast exit over the rocks. The hospital is modern but major surgery must be done in Chile.

**Handy Hints** – Take many boards including a thick 7'6 for medium size, south coast waves. Chargers need the full rhino-chasers to handle the big stuff. Big wave leashes are essential. No surf shops yet but boards can be fixed. Change your dollars in Santiago before arriving to get a better rate. Credit cards and travellers cheques are not widely accepted. Islanders show their hospitality with alcohol, mostly beers and Pisco.

| WEATHER STATISTICS | J/F | M/A | M/J | J/A | S/O | N/D |
|---|---|---|---|---|---|---|
| total rainfall (mm) | 110 | 110 | 110 | 80 | 80 | 120 |
| consistency (days/mth) | 11 | 11 | 12 | 8 | 8 | 12 |
| min temp (°C/°F) | 21/70 | 19/66 | 16/61 | 13/56 | 15/59 | 17/63 |
| max temp (°C/°F) | 29/84 | 29/84 | 27/80 | 25/77 | 26/79 | 29/84 |

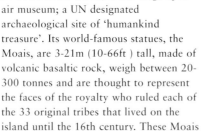

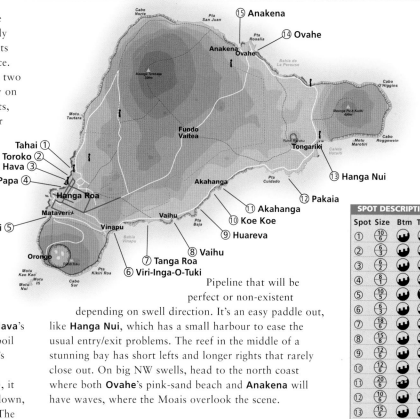

volcano in the bottom of the ocean. Geologically, the coastline is too young to have developed proper sandy beaches and consists of rugged lava cliffs, with heights between 2-7m (6-23ft) making entry/exit points scarce. Most spots are along the west and south coasts, plus two average quality beachbreaks with remarkable scenery on the north coast. There are no protected bays or points, but south coast exploration will reveal a safe bend or natural pool on the coastline to get in and out. Local surfers are friendly and open, showing typical Polynesian pride in their island and culture that demands respect. Despite having links to the ancient Tortoro reed boards, used as bellyboards, stand-up surfing is relatively new.

In Hanga Roa, both **Tahai** and **Toroko** reefbreaks are quite inconsistent. While Toroko breaks more frequently with short rights and longer lefts Tahai needs a massive NW swell to break, but when it does it has to be seen to be believed. The next two breaks along this coast are quite consistent. Facing the fishermen's inlet, **Motu Hava**'s lefts and rights give short rides before inside rocks spoil this fun, hot-dog reef. **Papas** will break even when it's onshore, providing lefts and rights ideal for the longboarder although in summer, at under 4ft (1.3m), it might be rammed with local bodyboarders. Further down, fickle **Mata Veri** has the longest wave on the island. The take-offs are easy on this fast and tubular wave which breaks in two sections, but it requires good timing to get in and out of the water. Conditions on the south coast can be deceptive, so have a good look before committing. Just beyond the oil terminal is **Viri-Inga-O-Tuki**, a less critical wave, suitable for longboards or thicker guns. It can have more than a couple of peaks depending on swell size, with both lefts and rights that break on the full side, but still have plenty of push. **Tanga Roa** was made famous most recently by Laird et al's second trip to the island in 2001, when they upped the ante by surfing insane tow-ins on heavy barrels over the reef. SE swells will make the entry/exit treacherous and avoid being caught inside the impact zone. **Vaihu**'s impressive but deceptive lefts break over uneven reef and unless it is over 10ft (3m), the ride will be short as it fades into deep water after take-off. The perfectly shaped, mini-pipe wave of **Huareva** provides a vert take-off on a short and intense lefthander. At 6ft (2m), both **Koe Koe** and **Akahanga** will start to break and the pointbreak at Akahanga will continue to break up to 20ft (6m), when it becomes the longest, big wave on the island. Heading east along this south coast, **Pakaia** is another short, intense, lava reef left, resembling a mutant

Pipeline that will be perfect or non-existent depending on swell direction. It's an easy paddle out, like **Hanga Nui**, which has a small harbour to ease the usual entry/exit problems. The reef in the middle of a stunning bay has short lefts and longer rights that rarely close out. On big NW swells, head to the north coast where both **Ovahe**'s pink-sand beach and **Anakena** will have waves, where the Moais overlook the scene.

Most of the swells come from the SE, S, and SW in winter (April-September) and W-NW in summer (October-March). The only east swell in living memory was, unfortunately, a giant tidal wave (the 2nd largest in history after Java's volcanic eruption) in 1960. Flat days are unusual because "the rock" picks up every ripple on the ocean. The most usual wave size is from head high – spring and summer time – to triple overhead during the rough winter storms. Rapa Nui waves are powerful and all surfable waves break over a lava reef bottom. This mixture should make every experienced, double overhead, maniac surfer happy. The prevailing wind is SE (spring and summer) and NW (autumn and winter). Both winds work offshore either way on the west or south coast. Worst case is a straight southerly which is onshore on both sides. "Glassy" for the locals sometimes means a rare 1 to 2 knots dawn patrol wind. Tides are not a problem. The difference is 40-65cm (16-26in) during half-moon periods, 10-90cm (4-36in) around the full and new moon periods.

Hanga Nui

Tanga Roa

### SPOT DESCRIPTION

| Spot | Size | Btm | Type |
|---|---|---|---|
| ① | 10/6 | rock | reef |
| ② | 6/3 | rock | reef |
| ③ | 6/2 | rock | reef |
| ④ | 8/1 | rock | reef |
| ⑤ | 10/6 | rock | point |
| ⑥ | 6/3 | rock | reef |
| ⑦ | 18/6 | rock | reef |
| ⑧ | 15/6 | rock | reef |
| ⑨ | 12/6 | rock | reef |
| ⑩ | 12/6 | rock | reef |
| ⑪ | 20/6 | rock | point |
| ⑫ | 10/6 | rock | reef |
| ⑬ | 15/6 | rock | reef |
| ⑭ | 6/3 | sand | beach |
| ⑮ | 6/3 | sand | beach |

### SURF STATISTICS

| | J F | M A | M J | J A | S O | N D |
|---|---|---|---|---|---|---|
| dominant swell | W-NW | SE-SW | SE-SW | SE-SW | SE-SW | W-NW |
| swell size (ft) | 3-4 | 4-5 | 6-7 | 7-8 | 6 | 3-4 |
| consistency (%) | 70 | 80 | 90 | 90 | 80 | 70 |
| dominant wind | NE-SE | N-E | E-SE | NW-NE | E-SE | N-SE |
| average force | F3-F4 | F3-F4 | F4 | F4 | F4 | F3-F4 |
| consistency (%) | 71 | 64 | 39 | 48 | 56 | 84 |
| water temp (°C/°F) | 24/75 | 23/74 | 21/70 | 20/68 | 20/68 | 22/72 |
| wetsuit | | | | | | |

Kauai

HAWAII

# 129. Kauai

Lalalau Lookout, Na Pali Coast

## Summary

+ Year round swells
+ Hawaiian power and quality
+ Super-scenic island
+ Variety of coastline
+ Hawaiian surf culture

– Mostly "experts only" surf
– Protective locals
– High local prices
– Rainy and windy
– Sharks

Hanalei Bay

KIRK LEE AEDER

K nown as the "The Garden Island", Kauai is an ancient and deeply eroded extinct volcano, rising 15,250ft (5000m) above the sea floor. Separated from Oahu by the angry, open ocean of the Kauai Channel, it was the only island that repelled King Kamehameha's efforts to unite Hawaii and remained self-governing until the 1820s. Kauai regulations state that no building may exceed the height of a coconut tree, preventing development from scarring the breathtaking scenery. There are more sandy beaches than many other islands and nearly 45% of its coastline is virtually deserted. Despite having over 300 surf spots, underwater topography is, allegedly, not as ideal as Oahu. The North

West Coast beachbreak

DON BALCH

Shore high volcanic cliffs hold few spots and the inaccessibility of the Na Pali coast makes it very dangerous to find and ride the few spots that face the brunt of the winter swells.

## TRAVEL INFORMATION

**Population:** 58,000
**Coastline:** 150km (94mi)
**Contests:** Pine Trees Longboard Classic, Roxy Jam, Vans Kauai Classic
**Other Resources:**
*Video:* Kauai Boys Runmental films
hanaleisurf.com
wavehunters.com/hawaii/ kauai/ktg.asp
http://kauai-kauai.com/

**Getting There** – Visa: 90days upon entry. United offers daily direct flights from LAX. Pleasant Hawaiian Holidays, low-cost airfare and package deals, has two weekly non-stop flights from LAX or SF. Alternatively, land in Honolulu, connect to a 30min flight with Aloha or Hawaiian Airlines (Board tax: $25). Landing on Lihue is dramatic, sit on the left side. Dep tax: $6

**Getting Around** – Since the coastal road is not circular, location is crucial to avoid undesired driving. It takes 2h to drive from Lihue to Kekaha. Lihue to Kapaa gets rush hours with slow traffic. Local rental car rates in low season (Jan, Apr. 16-to June, Aug 21-Dec 18) are $135/week ($150 high season). Private land restricts access on the north shore

**Lodging and Food** – First timers may prefer package deals. The Marriott at Kalapaki starts at $299/dble and the prestigious Princeville Resort in Hanalei also costs as much as a

surfboard per night. On the North Shore, try Hale Ho'o Maha in Kalihiwai: from $65/dble. Sheraton is great in Poipu or rent the condos: from $80/bedroom. Expect $20 for a meal. Princeville is reportedly the most expensive supermarket in the USA.

**Weather** – Though Kauai's climate is tropical, it consists of seven micro-climates ranging from dry, desert, sunny areas, lush river valleys, balmy foothills and high mountain rain forests. Temps range in 20-25°C (68-77°F), with winter night lows above 15°C (59°F). Summer brings day temps in the 25-30°C (77-86°F) and night lows above 20°C (68°F). The North Shore is 3-4°C (6-8°F) cooler than other parts. Cooler temps in the mountain areas such as Kokee offer a pleasant contrast. Besides creating a cooling effect, trade winds bring clouds and rain to the eastern slopes, with the rain increasing dramatically at higher altitude. The west side is dry while the Waialeale summit is the wettest spot in the world, with a record of 11680mm (467"in) in the '60s but it usually evens out at 10m/33ft a year. While Lihue gets 1000mm (39"in) of rain per year, Poipu with 860mm/33"in is semi-arid to tropical since the nearby Haupu Mountain range blocks most prevailing showers. Boardies year round!

**Nature and Culture** – The Point, on the water, is the Poipu hot spot and Hanalei Bay Resort is a music lover's gem. While the nightlife can't rival Honolulu's, the natural beauty is unbeatable. Visit Waimea Canyon or Kokee State Park, kayak along the Wailua River, take a Na Pali Cruise or walk the Kalalau trail, fly in a helicopter above Niihau or Na Pali cliffs.

**Hazards and Hassles** – Any bad attitude in the surf will not be tolerated by the locals. Be ready to surf at dawn, under heavy showers or in the trades. The North Shore can be really heavy with powerful sucky waves being more suited for bodyboarders. Shark sightings are backed up by regular attacks- a teenage girl lost her arm in Nov 03. Rains can be intense on the N-E sides, avoid river run-offs in the surf.

**Handy Hints** – Poipu hosts numerous surf schools like Kauai Surf School, or Margo Oberg's at the Nukumoi Surf Shop, at Brennecke's Beach. Check Hanalei Surf Company on the north shore. The cheapest place to rent a board is Activity Warehouse in Kapaa ($10/day). Shapers: Hamilton, Brewer, Wellman. Surf Forecast: 808/245-3564.

| WEATHER STATISTICS | J/F | M/A | M/J | J/A | S/O | N/D |
|---|---|---|---|---|---|---|
| total rainfall (mm) | 75 | 50 | 15 | 65 | 35 | 65 |
| consistency (days/mth) | 6 | 5 | 2 | 5 | 3 | 5 |
| min temp (°C/°F) | 16/61 | 17/63 | 18/64 | 20/68 | 20/68 | 17/63 |
| max temp (°C/°F) | 26/79 | 27/80 | 29/84 | 31/88 | 30/86 | 27/80 |

Just before the Prince Kuhio Hwy ends abruptly at the beginning of the Na Pali Coast, is **Tunnels**. Typically North Shore, it's wild, localised and sharky rights can be totally epic, breaking over sharp, live coral a long way from shore. This wave (and others in the area) are experts only if the locals are in a tolerant mood. **Hanalei Bay** is the focus of Kauai surfing, providing a range of waves in a small area. Below deluxe Princeville Resort is the righthand pointbreak that everyone wants to ride, crowding the sections of Impossible, Flat Rock and The Bowl on all sizes of board. Well protected from the wind it handles size but it's a very long paddle and of course, the locals are aggressive. Further round the bay there's average beachbreaks and some good reefs like Waikoko, Middles and Chicken Wing, or **Hideaways** further out in Princeville. The latter sits at the base of high cliffs and holds fun, scattered reefbreaks when small and not windy but has had a shark attack. Nestled beneath impressive cliffs is **Kalihiwai**, a featured wave in the

North Shore
DON BALCH

*Kauai Boyz* video, where even the best surfers can get thrashed by misjudging the elevator drop take-off or the intense, disproportionately massive barrels. Few people are permitted to partake. The Kilauea lighthouse marks entry to the rainy, onshore east coast, with low cliffs and extended valleys, aka the Coconut Coast. Rarely clean in the teeth of the easterlies, there are some fun reefs to ride in the headhigh range and some spots have a rideable wave 365 days of the year. **Unreals** at Anahola is a right pointbreak working consistently on the regular E windswells and Kona winds blow offshore. **Kealia**'s small, powerful (but predominantly onshore) waves can be a fun session and check **Horners** in Wailua, a traditional surfing locale for centuries. Wealthy beginners or longboarders might enjoy **Kalapaki**'s gentle reefbreak whilst staying at the Marriott right on the beach. For a life-threatening ledge, cross Nawiliwili Bay and surf Ammonia's sick rights off the concrete jetty. Poipu is the best place to stay with lots of cheap condos and close to several always offshore breaks. It's bodyboarding only at **Brenneckes**, but **PK**'s lefts, **Acid Drop**'s short barrelling rights and Center's treacherous righthand reefbreak are for experts only. The SW corner cloaks a few secrets plus the long perfect lefts of **Infinities** at Pakala. Will handle the bigger summer S swells while sharks, locals and sharp reef help regulate the crowd. Various quality reefs straddle the coast near Kekaha like **Davidson Point** near Ole Kamaole's Beach House. The Pacific Missile Range Base dominates the long and empty west coast beaches through Barking Sands up to **Majors Bay** and beyond to **Polihale**. Incredibly powerful

beachbreaks with terrifying rips to match where one ride can equate to a long walk down the beach. On the horizon is Niihau, where only full-blooded Hawaiians are permitted to live a traditional existence. This private island has been off limits (kapu) to everyone until recent years. Now only very limited non-intrusive helicopter tours are allowed. This virtually untouched island has no electricity, no phones, no cars, no roads, no hotels...but there is surf!

Born in the Aleutian Islands, the 3-30ft (1-9m) W to N swells generated between October to March, hit Kauai before the rest of Hawaii. These are the most powerful swells on earth with periods around 15-20 seconds! Overall, there are good conditions on the North Shore but they are less consistent than Oahu. From April to September, the North Shore is mostly flat but the South Shore gets long distance 2-8ft (0.6-2.5m) SW groundswell from the South Pacific. Year round, 3-8ft (1-2.5m) constant NE windswell can be ridden on the windward side. Because the island is round, many swells sweep up and down the coast. Trade winds are very stable. Easterly winds dominance varies from 27% (Dec) to 58% (Aug), with NE-E being the year round predominant direction. During the winter swell season, the winds turn SE more often, January being the best month for overall S winds. Occasionally Kona S/SW winds happen providing perfect conditions for the Coconut Coast and North Shore. Tide ranges are slight but spot quality relies a lot on combinations of swell, winds and tides plus the coral reefs are particularly sharp.

| SURF STATISTICS | J F M | A M J | J A S | O N D |
|---|---|---|---|---|
| dominant swell | NW-NE | NW-NE | SE-NE | SE-NE | NW-NE | NW-NE |
| swell size (ft) | 7-8 | 6-7 | 3-4 | 4 | 5-6 | 7-8 |
| consistency (%) | 90 | 80 | 60 | 70 | 80 | 90 |
| dominant wind | NE-SE | NE-E | NE-E | NE-E | NE-E | NE-SE |
| average force | F4 | F4 | F4 | F4 | F4 | F4 |
| consistency (%) | 63 | 66 | 76 | 88 | 77 | 77 |
| water temp (°C/°F) | 24/75 | 24/75 | 25/77 | 26/79 | 27/80 | 25/77 |
| wetsuit | | | | | | |

Map labels:
Hideaways 3, Kalihiwai 4, Hanalei Bay 2, Tunnels 1, Unreals 5, Kealia 6, Horners 7, Kalapaki 8, Brenneckes 9, PK 10, Acid Drop 11, Infinities 12, Davidson Point 13, Majors Bay 14, Polihale 15

| SPOT DESCRIPTION | | | |
|---|---|---|---|
| Spot | Size | Btm | Type |
| 1 | 10/3 | | |
| 2 | 15/2 | | |
| 3 | 6/2 | | |
| 4 | 15/2 | | |
| 5 | 6/2 | | |
| 6 | 6/2 | | |
| 7 | 6/2 | | |
| 8 | 4/1 | | |
| 9 | 6/2 | | |
| 10 | 8/2 | | |
| 11 | 12/3 | | |
| 12 | 10/2 | | |
| 13 | 8/2 | | |
| 14 | 10/2 | | |
| 15 | 8/2 | | |

HAWAII

# 130. Big Island

**Waipio Valley**

## Summary
+ EXPOSED TO MOST SWELLS
+ KONA SPOT DENSITY
+ REMOTE, UNCROWDED WAVES
+ VOLCANOES AND LAVA FLOWS
+ TROPICAL SNOW SPORTS

− NW SWELL SHADOW
− YOUNG COAST, STEEP CLIFFS
− SUPER-RAINY EAST COAST
− LOCALISED URBAN SPOTS
− 4WD REQUIRED FOR REMOTE SPOTS

While Oahu and Kauai are known for their north/south shore divide, the Big Island is an east/west side story. The youngest island in the chain, Hawaii is known as the Big.Island, due to its size, which is nearly double that of the others combined and, being a live volcano, continues to grow. Lava flowing from Kilauea is continually shaping a new landscape on its way to the sea where it can both create future surf breaks or destroy existing ones. Whilst Oahu usually grabs the surf history limelight, Polynesian immigrants probably initiated surfing at Kealakekua Bay centuries ago, making the Big Island the birthplace of surfing and the aloha spirit. Crowds and localism

**Secret Spot**

do exist but remote spots requiring long hikes or 4WD access will be empty and conditions will be less competitive than most Hawaiian line-ups.

**Kohala Lighthouse** is a good example of a secluded, localised hotspot. This classic left reefbreak is somewhat sheltered from NE trades despite its eastern location. Be

## TRAVEL INFORMATION

**Population:** 150,000
**Coastline:** 430km (270mi)
**Contests:**
Big Island Pro-Am
Kawaihae Longboard
**Other Resources:**
surfolhawaii.com
surfline.com
konaweb.com
gohawaii.com/
  vacationplanninghawaii

**Getting There** – Visa: 90 days upon entry. Fly through Honolulu (HNL) airport and use Aloha or Hawaiian Airlines. Most o/w inter-island flights are $93 full price (Board tax: $25). Note that Big Island has 2 int'l airports: Kona and Hilo. Kona gets flights from Japan (JAL) and LAX/SFO on United and LAX on American. Dep tax: $6

**Getting Around** – The Hawaii Belt Road circles the island. The Saddle Road (Hwy 200) linking E-W is not a shortcut from Kona to Hilo, but is rough, narrow and plagued by bad weather; most rental car agencies ban it. Local rental car rates in low season (Jan, Apr 16 to June, Aug 21-Dec 18) are $135/week ($150 high season). 4WD are $300.

**Lodging and Food** – Stay on Alii Drive for choice and mobility. Most of Kona's condos are well furnished with complete kitchens. The

weekly rate is 6x daily rate and the monthly is 3x weekly rate. Hale Kona Kai is $95/2p. A studio at Kona Bali Kai close to Banyans costs $195/2p (check Wavehunter's accomodation list on Nth Kona). Expect $20 for a meal.

**Weather** – Hawaii is full of microclimates, thanks to its high mountain peaks. Summer (May-Oct) temps are warmer, peaking in August and drier than the winter months. February and March are the coolest months. At the beach, the daytime high in summer is 29°C (84°F), while in winter it's 25°C (77°F), while night lows drop down by 10°C (18°F). During summer, the NE trades are more persistent and clear blue skies can last for weeks. In the winter, trades are frequently interrupted by fronts bringing SW-NW winds and intervals of widespread cloud and rain. During heavy winter storms, brought on by the onset of Kona winds from the SW, 10cm of rain can fall in an hour. Hilo is the USA's wettest city, with 4500mm (180in) a year, while at Kawaihae, it's a mere 150mm (6in). In the mountains, the higher the altitude, the colder the climate, dropping 1°C (3°F) every 150m, and snow is likely above 10,660ft (3500m). Water is tropical-warm; bring a shorty for windy winter days.

**Nature and Culture** – Climb to Observatory Hill, Mauna Kea's summit, 10km (6.5mi) distance and 1.5km (1mi) up. Snowboard up there or slide the Kapoho crater. Don't miss Hawaii Volcanoes National Park when Kilauea is pumping red lava, Kohala Coast petroglyphs and visit the Pacific Tsunami Museum in Hilo.

**Hazards and Hassles** – Don't enter the water with attitude – it will only bring trouble from the locals. Avoid Hilo and Kailua crowds. Beware while parking at remote spots; don't leave anything in the car. Reef cuts, rips and sunburn always a threat. Allow for long driving times. Hilo has been hit by two tsunamis in 1960 and 1946, the latter causing 156 deaths.

**Handy Hints** – As some airlines cost plenty to transport gear, it may be cheaper to buy there. Stop at Big Island Surf Company or Pacific Vibrations in Kailua or order from Orchidland Surfboards in Hilo. Girls only Big Island Surfcamp is based in Hilo. Learners should try Hawaii Lifeguards Surf Lessons in Keauhou or Ocean Ecotours in Honokohau.

| WEATHER STATISTICS | J/F | M/A | M/J | J/A | S/O | N/D |
|---|---|---|---|---|---|---|
| total rainfall (mm) | 55 | 45 | 50 | 60 | 40 | 40 |
| consistency (days/mth) | 5 | 5 | 5 | 4 | 3 | 4 |
| min temp (°C/°F) | 18/64 | 18/64 | 20/68 | 21/70 | 20/68 | 19/66 |
| max temp (°C/°F) | 27/80 | 27/80 | 28/82 | 29/84 | 29/84 | 28/82 |

very careful while parking there and keep a low profile. Several spots work nearby like Halelua where according to legend, centuries ago, chief Nu'uanupa'ahu was lured to his sharky death, by Chief Kalaniopu'u. The leeward Kohala Coast is fairly poor surf wise whereas the Kona Coast boasts the best conditions with offshore trades and a S to N swell window. **Kawaihae** Harbor is the island's official tidal measurement location and hosts several beginner-friendly reefs next to the breakwater. Plenty of rights in WNW swells, spied by a web cam. Most beaches are steep, narrow and strewn with grey to black sand like **Hapuna**, the island's largest. Ideal for bodysurfing or bodyboarding in the hollow dumpers plus a reef peak down the beach at this heavy, localised spot. The Kona

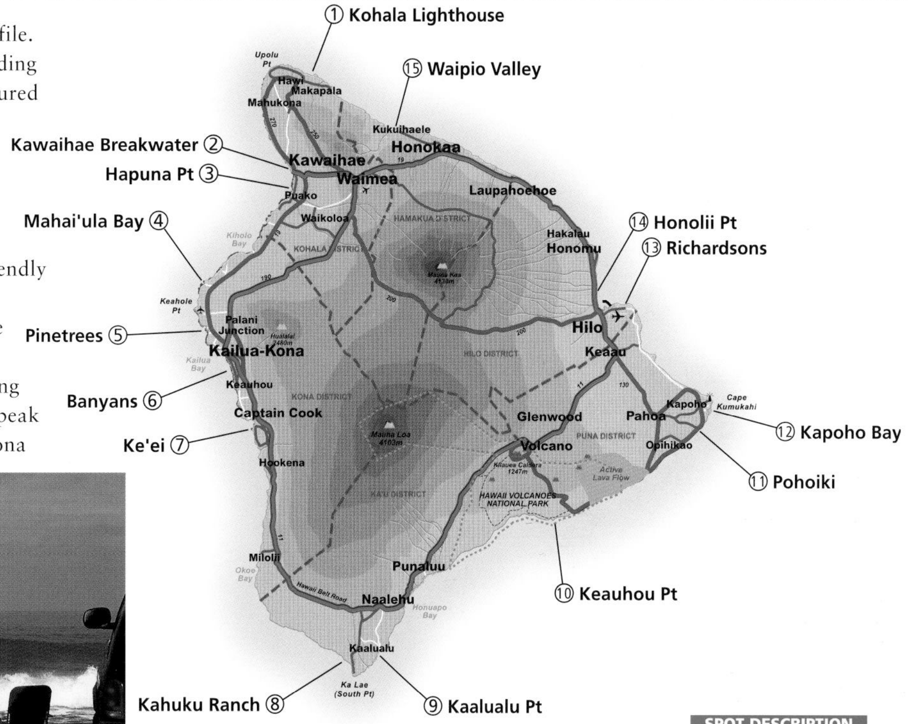

① Kohala Lighthouse
⑮ Waipio Valley
Kawaihae Breakwater ②
Hapuna Pt ③
Mahai'ula Bay ④
Pinetrees ⑤
Banyans ⑥
Ke'ei ⑦
Kahuku Ranch ⑧
⑨ Kaalualu Pt
⑩ Keauhou Pt
⑪ Pohoiki
⑫ Kapoho Bay
⑬ Richardsons
⑭ Honolii Pt
Upolu Pt
Hawi
Makapala
Mahukona
Kukuihaele
Honokaa
Kawaihae
Waimea
Puako
Laupahoehoe
Waikoloa
Kiholo Bay
Hakalau
Honomu
Keahole Pt
Palani Junction
Kailua-Kona
Kailua Bay
Hilo
Keaau
Keauhou
Captain Cook
Glenwood
Pahoa
Kapoho
Cape Kumukahi
Volcano
Opihikao
Hookena
Milolii
Okoe Bay
Punaluu
Naalehu
Honuapo Bay
Kaalualu
Ka Lae (South Pt)


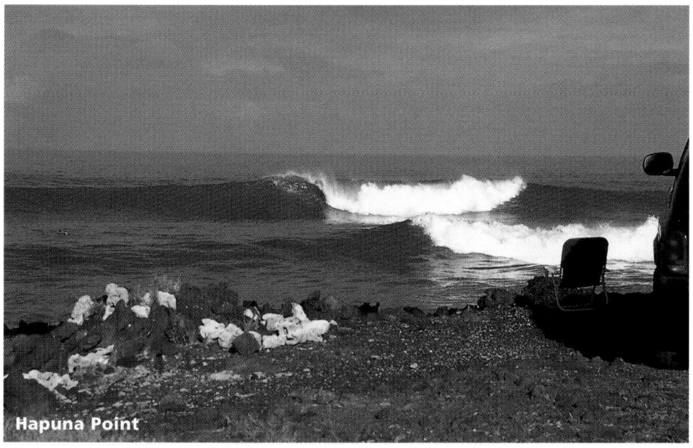

Hapuna Point

Coast State Park opened recently, allowing those ready to risk their rental car (and then hike) to powerful, long, coral reefbreaks at **Maha'ilua** or Makalawena, further along. **Pinetrees** is a quality wave-magnet, favouring lefts on any small to medium swell. Most contests on the Kona Coast are organised around Kailua reefbreaks, easily checked along Alii Drive, the Big Island's Kam Highway equivalent. **Banyans** is the locals' favourite, shaping hollow rights in winter NW'ers and shorter lefts in summer souths. Kealakekua Bay is Hawaii's first surf beach, where competent surfers find a way to **Ke'ei**'s small-size, perfect lefts, aka Shark Point. Remotely located to the south, it's a long paddle to reach these fast waves breaking over shallow coral. On S swells, drive down to the Kau coast, checking spots around South Point. On the west side is **Kahuku Ranch**; big, hairy peaks in anything S and it's offshore in NE trades. Don't miss the green sand beach and find a way to surf the long left pointbreak, sheltered from the trades by **Kaalualu Point**, when big S swells are running. To hike the Puna Coast trail, first register with the Kilauea Visitor Center, in the Hawaii Volcanoes National Park. On big S or SE swells, **Keauhou Point** holds long, walled-up lefts, or other peaks like Halape and Apua might work if it's big enough. **Pohoiki**'s three bays support some shallow lava reef rights and a left in bigger swells, but like **Kapoho Bay** further north, it's onshore in the trades. Hilo's strong wave-riding community remain cool at spots like **Richardsons**, where the mellow reefbreaks provide a good learning forum. At **Honolii** fast, consistent lefts and rights break into a rivermouth that has been saved from industrial projects to tame the river flow. Check **Waipio Valley**'s black sand beachbreaks for quiet peaks but the hellish access road is 4WD material or an hour's walk.

The Big Island's situation is tricky because of the Hawaiian chain's swell shadow to the north. Hawaii's winter swell supply is generally from the W-NW, but it should be noted that most NNW swells from 305° to 350° will suffer a serious filtering on their way to Big Island shores. Only expect 3-12ft (1-4m) from October to March, NNE being the best directions for Hilo, Hamakua, or W swells for Kohala and Kona. NE-E trades bring a nearly constant supply of NE-E 1-5ft (0.3-1.6m) windswells, best surfed during SW kona winds. From April to September, South Pacific SW swells bring a regular supply of 2-8ft (0.6-2.5m) waves to the Kona, Kau and Puna areas. July to October is the hot period for East Pacific hurricanes pushing 3-8ft (1-2.5m) E-SE swells to Puna and Hilo, but there are also rare SW winter swells from SW Pacific cyclones. Because of the high mountains, it's offshore on both sides in the morning then Hamakua and Hilo get most of the onshore NE trades. Those trades fade a bit in winter when glassy days occur and Kona south to westerly winds arrive courtesy of rogue low pressure cells known locally as Kona storms. Tide times are different around the island, although tidal range never exceeds 3ft (1m), be aware of the tide for some shallow spots. Surf News Network: 808-596-7873

**SPOT DESCRIPTION**

| Spot | Size | Btm | Type |
|---|---|---|---|
| ① | 10/3 | | |
| ② | 6/2 | | |
| ③ | 8/2 | | |
| ④ | 10/2 | | |
| ⑤ | 6/2 | | |
| ⑥ | 12/4 | | |
| ⑦ | 6/2 | | |
| ⑧ | 6/2 | | |
| ⑨ | 8/3 | | |
| ⑩ | 8/3 | | |
| ⑪ | 6/2 | | |
| ⑫ | 6/2 | | |
| ⑬ | 6/2 | | |
| ⑭ | 12/2 | | |
| ⑮ | 6/2 | | |

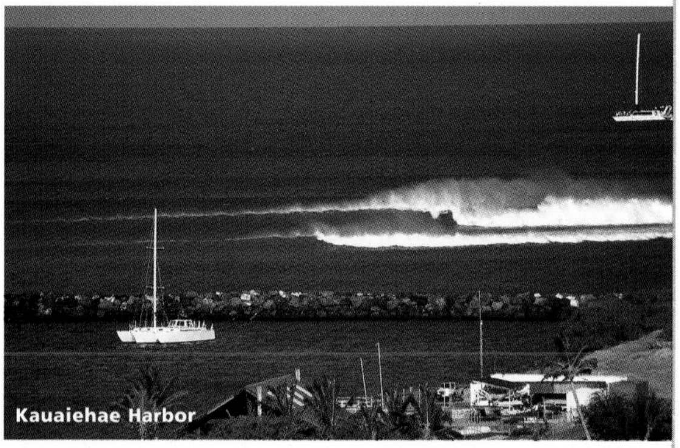

Kauaiehae Harbor

| SURF STATISTICS | J F | M A | M J | J A | S O | N D |
|---|---|---|---|---|---|---|
| dominant swell | W-NE | W-NE | NE-SW | NE-SW | NE-SW | W-NE |
| swell size (ft) | 5-6 | 4 | 3-4 | 4 | 4-5 | 5-6 |
| consistency (%) | 70 | 70 | 60 | 70 | 80 | 70 |
| dominant wind | NE-E | NE-E | NE-E | NE-E | NE-E | NE-E |
| average force | F4 | F4 | F4 | F4 | F4 | F4 |
| consistency (%) | 61 | 75 | 82 | 84 | 78 | 74 |
| water temp (°C/°F) | 24/75 | 23/74 | 25/77 | 26/79 | 27/80 | 25/77 |
| wetsuit | | | | | | |

# O'NEILL

ONEILLEUROPE.COM

CORY LOPEZ

"Everything is bigger and better in America!", including the beachbreaks at Ocean Beach, San Francisco. Unfortunately, America also experiences bigger polluted runoff, coastal hardening, access issues and hazards aplenty.

# North America

ROB GILLEY

# The Ocean Environment

Surfing is enjoyed by approximately three million people on the North American continent, and it is estimated that in the USA alone, 110 million people are squeezed into a coastal strip, which comprises only 12% of the country's total landmass. The mighty Pacific and the Gulf Stream blessed Atlantic meet vast urbanisations hugging a hardened coastline that is often inaccessible to the public, creating environmental issues

## Pollution

North America has the most urbanised coastline on the planet adding dramatically to ocean pollution as natural filters such as forests and wetlands are effectively removed. This is not an issue in the northwest but Alaska has some established environmental problems. A legacy of oil spills (*Exxon Valdez*) have damaged large stretches of coastline and the military have used coastal areas as weapons dumps, most notably for surfers on the Yakutat Peninsula. Of most concern to the coastal environment is the possible opening up of one of the last great wilderness areas to oil exploration. The coasts of British Columbia, Washington and Oregon can be pristine ocean

**SoCal from the air reveals many of the burning issues affecting the ocean environment.**

DAVID PU'U

on a scale found "only in America". Home to the largest surf-related environmental group on the planet, The Surfrider Foundation champions many projects, including grass roots education programmes, so future beach-goers have a better understanding of the dynamics of the coastal environment. The annual "State of the Beach" report updates the health of the beaches, while the "Beachscape Programme" surveys and maps the continents coastal environmental resources so that they may be protected.

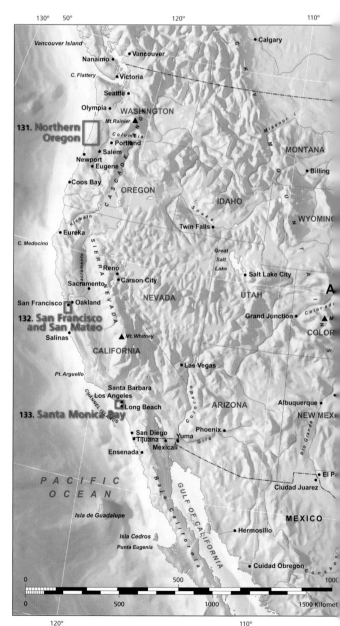

BILL TOVER

system, but local Surfrider Chapters do have limited schemes, leaving vast stretches of coastline where water quality is simply unknown. Northern California reflects the problems of the Pacific Northwest, while Central Cal is the beginning of the big urban sprawls like San Francisco where steep topography and a large, busy harbour bring plenty of unwanted elements to the ocean. The stretches of coast between cities are much cleaner, yet deforestation, agricultural effluent in rivers, oil spills, and the use of wave-runners in national parks are all issues. Statistics show that an urban block creates nine times more run-off than the same area of woodland. Mix this stormwater with standard city litter, butts, plastics, oil and detergents to mention but a few and then discharge into the sea. Southern California suffers the most from this polluted runoff and the stretch of coastline from Santa Barbara to San Diego is basically one big urban sprawl. Wetlands, open areas and woodland have all been urbanised, plus all rivers have been turned into concrete

environments in the many National Parks, Wildlife Refuges and Marine Sanctuaries, but they are not without problems. Local pollution exists from sawmill and wood pulping activities fouling rivermouths along with some local sewage or stormwater outflows. Neither Washington or Oregon has implemented a state-wide water monitoring

Some oil pollution on Southern Californian beaches arrives via the stormwater system, but busy ports and offshore drilling rigs are contributing in the background. Federal and state governments continue to tussle over offshore drilling rights to exploit oil and natural gas reserves.

drains, resulting in rapid runoff and coastal water quality not meeting bathing water regulations. For surfers it meant 6500 beach closures in 2001 and although there were fewer closures in 2002, this was thanks to a drought, resulting in less runoff and not tighter pollution controls. With ten million residents in the LA basin alone, the challenge is huge, as existing environmental legislation is either inadequate or impossible to enforce. Southern California's heavily surfed coastline is also blighted by an antiquated sewage system with rotting pipes, which have caused as many as 1500 leaks since 1995. Every year, 240 million gallons of poorly treated human waste continues to be discharged just 7km (4.5 mi) off the Orange County coastline. Further south and San Diego has similar sewage disposal problems, compounded by effluent drifting north from Tijuana, Mexico. Numerous cruise liners use the busy port, complete with major naval base, so pollution associated with discharging of ballast tanks, oil and fuel all add up to make water quality in the San Diego area pretty poor.

The Gulf of Mexico coast from Florida to Texas is cleaner than one would expect. Texas lacks cohesive,

is good, but Florida is blessed by the scouring force of the Gulf Stream, which deals with effluent and urban run-off issues. Inlet mouths are noisy with the huge numbers of commercial and private pleasure vessels that all add to the oil discharge problems around major ports. The Carolinas have better water quality than further north although a lack of monitoring means the whole picture is not available. Rivers bring agricultural effluent to the Intracoastal Waterway and septic systems are the norm on the coast. The Mid Atlantic states are home to every conceivable sort of pollution problem and a long history of offshore toxic dumping in the waters off New York and New Jersey. Recent improvements in inshore water quality have been achieved through advanced treatment processes for residential waste, plus tighter legislation for commercial waste management. Polluted run off from the metropolis of New York and the surrounding industrialised zone is a continual problem and hundreds of millions of gallons of untreated sewage get discharged into the Hudson when treatment plants break down. Outside the major conurbations, on rural Long Island, there's some affluent effluent being

The proposed ban on the use of PWCs (personal watercraft) in the Monterey Bay National Marine Sanctuary will have implications on tow-surfing at Mavericks.

ROB GILLEY

state-wide water monitoring so Surfrider Foundation chapters continue to test samples independently. Petrochemical plants line the Gulf, a major oil producing area, so spills are common and have decimated parts of the coastline in the past. The Mississippi delta is a huge dead zone, thanks to years of upriver agricultural pollution being deposited into the Gulf. Inland pollution is cited as contributing to Florida's coral reef destruction.

The eastern seaboard of North America is more heavily populated than the west coast, so pollution problems abound. Florida has implemented the most thorough and accessible beach testing system in the US. This is hardly surprising as its economy relies on the tourist dollars attracted to its beaches. This does not mean water quality

discharged by smaller coastal communities with poor treatment infrastructure. Mid Atlantic Surfrider chapters are extremely pro-active and government water quality testing is carried out on a regular basis leading to beach closures when necessary. New England's coastal waters have a legacy of pollution including poorly treated sewage and oil spills. Boston's upgraded sewage treatment system has not prevented primary treated sewage returning to the beaches in onshore winds. Plastic, fishing industry debris and other slowly degrading waste, regularly accumulate along the beaches. Nova Scotia has problems with poor sewage treatment and heavy marine traffic in Halifax harbour but in general, coastal conditions are good.

## Erosion

The huge scale of USA's coastal population has directly resulted in an enormous amount of coastal modifications being built over the last century. The Pacific Northwest remains largely in a state of natural flux, aside from the odd harbour wall and jetty to protect sheltered anchorages, although the Army Corp of Engineers have employed some reactionary schemes that caused more problems than they remedied. The mapping of all erosion control features is ongoing in Oregon and statistics are available from some government websites. Deforestation and over grazing are contributing to silting up of some lagoons, which then fail to replenish the beach with sediment. California is synonymous with beach houses, so it is no surprise that the state has some 160km (100mi) of armoured shoreline, while a further 1520km (950mi) of its coast is eroding (86%). Sea defences are built to protect private and public property built too close to the dynamic foreshore. Inappropriate seawalls and rock revetments attempt to halt the natural erosion along San Francisco's open beaches, while Santa Cruz residents try to stabilize cliffs in order to save their valuable sea views. In Ventura County, large stretches of the Pacific Coast Highway skirt the shoreline, underpinned by seawalls that have caused beach erosion, bringing the construction under constant wave attack. Large urban areas reduce sediment delivered to the ocean, vital for beach building. Concrete over an area the size of metropolitan LA, including all the river beds, build large dams to store water in an arid, low rainfall basin and sediment delivery falls to a trickle. With less sediment coming into the system, beaches narrow, heightening wave action erosion, threatening property, resulting in shoreline armouring. The sea defences exacerbate sand depletion, a valuable beach resource is lost and the viscous cycle continues. Alternatives to coastal armouring are at last being seriously considered, as setback lines are being drawn up preventing any new development within these lines, which may require future protection. Unfortunately, the astronomical value of coastal land ensures developers find ways around laws and controversial developments are still in the pipeline. Most notable is the Headlands development in Dana Point, California, threatening 123 acres of undeveloped land, harbouring many endangered species of plant and animal and a heavily surfed stretch of beachbreak running down to Salt Creek. The $500 million project would see construction of over a hundred homes, hotels, parks and a dreaded mall flanked by a 2.1km (1.3mi) seawall to protect it from erosion. This seawall is sure to affect the dynamics of the immediate coastline. Down the coast and the world-famous wave of Trestles is under a threat from reduced sediment inputs via the San Mateo Creek. The creek drains miles of un-developed hinterland, earmarked for a mall, 14,000 homes and a new toll road. If the proposal goes ahead then the reef at Trestles will no longer receive a supply of sediment but will get polluted runoff instead and over time the reef will erode.

The Gulf of Mexico is fringed by migrating barrier islands and erosion in Texas can reach 30ft+ (9m+). Private structures are no longer permitted on the beach and inlet jetties and piers provide the best wave forums in an ever-changing sandy environment, a situation

BILL TOVER

echoed all the way up the east Coast to New England. Florida has already armed 235km (147mi) of coastline and restrictions on further construction have recently been relaxed. New hard structures are forbidden in the Carolinas (and Maine) but many exist along with the ubiquitous fishing piers. Managed retreat is the only real way to deal with such a mobile stretch of coast like North Carolina's Outer Banks. The Cape Hatteras lighthouse found itself 430m (1400ft) closer to the high tide mark in just 65 years. Recently, road re-routing has reduced some access but it is the only option as it is futile trying to protect a coastline in motion. The Mid Atlantic states positively bristle with jetties, groynes, piers and seawalls, between which, constant re-nourishing and sand pumping programmes redistribute the wealth. A proposed beach nourishment plan to expand shoreline property at Long Beach, New York, involves the use of contaminated, dredged sand, to widen the beach. The sand would come from the current surfbreak and it is well known that a legacy of ocean dumping in the area means the sand probably contains toxins. Beach nourishment along other parts of Long Island has destroyed a dune system, to regain beach width. The beaches and crumbling sedimentary cliffs of Cape Cod are New England's erosion hotspot.

Top – **Sandspit is another example of a bungled Army Corps of Engineers' project. Instead of protecting the entrance to the Santa Barbara Harbor, they created a foil for growling righthand tubes and acute, angular backwash.**

Bottom – **Over 160km (100mi) of California's coast is armoured, leaving 10 times that amount to naturally erode. Sea views in Santa Cruz are a valuable commodity, so cliff-top home-owners are unlikely to agree with proposals to set-back all new construction.**

BOOTS MCGEE

## Access

Almost 70% of continental USA's coastline is privately owned. US federal law attempts to preserve public access below the high tide mark but state laws and private individuals often conspire to prevent people getting to the wet sand. The Alaskan and Canadian coastlines have extremely difficult access, befitting a surfing wilderness, so a good boat or seaplane are the best options, away from the few populated zones. Getting around in Washington is complicated by large tracts of private land, Native American reservations where a permit is needed and no coastal highway means hiking into a lot of spots. Oregon benefits from a coast hugging highway and plenty of access points. The state of California passed a motion in 1972, decreeing the creation of a public access, coastal trail. The modern day reality to accomplish this would involve purchasing rights of way costing $322 million and so it is unlikely to ever be completed. Northern and Central California have some issues with military reservations and the odd private ranch but access to most popular spots is straightforward. Southern California coastal inaccessibility is personified by the Bixby and Hollister ranches in Santa Barbara County, a 22km (14mi) stretch of private coastline littered with points and reefs from Point Conception to Gaviota. The only way in is by a good boat or knowing someone who owns a piece of the expensive, élitist real estate. Private gated communities cause intermittent problems, as do some military reservations where surfing is no longer allowed (Vandenberg), or permits are required to surf (Point Magu).

Texas Open Beaches Act guarantees public access to 587km (367mi) of beach, although a 4WD is essential to get to many of them, while swamps keep extensive stretches of Florida's Gulf Coast inaccessible.

On the East Coast, private land separates the public beach from the public road system and there simply are not enough access points. In Florida for example, the state provides an average of only 1 access point every 8km (5mi), which equates to 1 access point for every 10,000 local residents, not including tourists.

The Carolinas have excellent accessibility but in New Jersey, you must pay for 'beach tags' in order to get sand between your toes in the summer months. Further north and New Yorkers have the problem of large tracts of beach in areas like the Hamptons being totally private and restricted access to community beaches due to limited parking. Tagging, extortionate or non-existent parking, private beach clubs and no public access points can all spoil a session in New England.

Right – **Winter on the East Coast brings arctic temperatures and occasionally slushing seas. Extreme weather variations mean dry suits are often donned in New England, but six months later it could be almost warm enough for boardshorts. Narragansett, Rhode Island.**

Bottom – **Intermittant military installations can create public no-surf zones and private line-ups for surfing privates.**

## Hazards

North American waters have the highest incidence of unprovoked shark attacks in the seven seas. The West Coast has one of the largest populations of great whites, especially from Oregon down to Central California, often referred to as the Red Triangle. Surfers have been bitten, usually around rivermouths and/or seal colonies, but statistics suggest that these attacks are often mistaken identity. A very low fatality rate supports the theory that fibreglass and rubber don't taste so good. Surprisingly, San Diego has seen the most Californian attacks, but no fatality for almost 50 years. The state of Florida is the shark attack capital of the world, with a table topping count of over 500 attacks but only a dozen deaths. Smaller sharks from the requiem family infest the nutrient rich waters of the Gulf Stream and are a regular component of a Florida line-up. The threat greatly diminishes north of the Outer Banks and is non-existent in Maine.

Swarms of jellyfish can invade in summer and red tide is always a possibility in the Gulf and lower East Coast states.

In Washington, Oregon and Northern California, limited top quality breaks and an inbred paranoia that the whole of Southern California will soon move up north, means that many locals are unwelcoming should travellers stumble across their local reef. In the Point Conception to San Diego stretch, there are well over one million surfers squeezed into only 400km (250mi) of coastline. Add to this a pleasant Mediterranean climate, consistent, not too challenging, year round swells, hitting a limited number of quality spots, and the result is some serious crowd issues. Suffice to say, localism sits firmly at home in Southern California, varying from a bit of stink eye, right through to severe violence, aimed at both surfers and their vehicles. Recent landmark court cases have resulted in jail sentences for persistent, violent offenders.

# Surf Travel Resources

**COUNTRY INFORMATION**

| | USA | CANADA |
|---|---|---|
| Area (sq km/mi): | 9,169,000/3,540,000 | 9,970,610/3,849,674 |
| Population: | 280M | 32M |
| Waveriders: | 800,000 | 2,000 |
| Tourists (per yr): | 51M | 21M |
| Language: | English, Spanish | English, French |
| Currency: | US Dollar | Canadian Dollar |
| Exchange: | $1 = 1 USD | $1 = 1.55 CAD |
| GDP ($ per yr): | $36,200 | $24,800 |
| Inflation (%): | 3% | 3% |

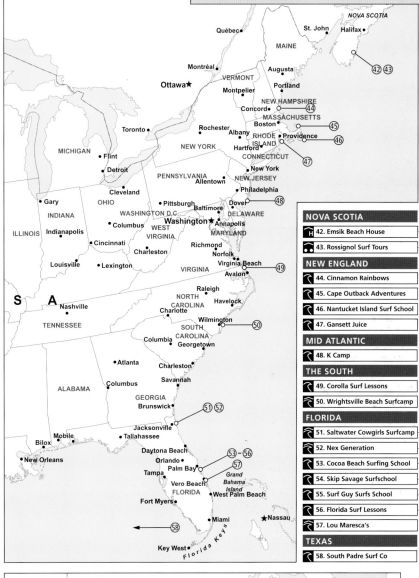

**NOVA SCOTIA**
- 42. Emsik Beach House
- 43. Rossignol Surf Tours

**NEW ENGLAND**
- 44. Cinnamon Rainbows
- 45. Cape Outback Adventures
- 46. Nantucket Island Surf School
- 47. Gansett Juice

**MID ATLANTIC**
- 48. K Camp

**THE SOUTH**
- 49. Corolla Surf Lessons
- 50. Wrightsville Beach Surfcamp

**FLORIDA**
- 51. Saltwater Cowgirls Surfcamp
- 52. Nex Generation
- 53. Cocoa Beach Surfing School
- 54. Skip Savage Surfschool
- 55. Surf Guy Surfs School
- 56. Florida Surf Lessons
- 57. Lou Maresca's

**TEXAS**
- 58. South Padre Surf Co

**BRITISH COLUMBIA**
- 1. Pacific Surf School
- 2. Bruhwiler Surf Camp
- 3. Inner Rythmn Surfcamp
- 4. Surf Sister
- 5. Tatchu Surf Adventures
- 6. Deep Snow & Surf

**WASHINGTON & OREGON**
- 7. Washington State Surf Camp
- 8. Adventure Surf Unlimited

**CENTRAL CALIFORNIA**
- 9. Girls Adventure Out
- 10. Surf Camp Pacifica
- 11. Bolinas Surf Lessons
- 12. Club ED Surfcamp
- 13. Richard Schmidt
- 14. Santa Cruz Surf School

**SOUTHERN CALIFORNIA**
- 15. No Limits Sports
- 16. Paddy Bex Surfschool
- 17. Surf Class.com
- 18. Davey Smith Surf Academy
- 19. Ventura Surf School
- 20. California Surfing School
- 21. Surfing L.A.
- 22. Malibu Makos
- 23. Malibu Surfing Lessons
- 24. Kanoa
- 25. Campsurf.com
- 26. Danger Woman
- 27. Corky Carroll's
- 28. Endless Summer Surfcamp
- 29. HB wahine
- 30. Paskowitz Surfcamp
- 31. Surf Academy
- 32. Groundswell surf Camp
- 33. San Diego Surfing Academy
- 34. Willy's Bros
- 35. Surf Sessions
- 36. Kahuna Bob's
- 37. Surfari Surf Camp
- 38. Pacific Surf
- 39. Executive Surfing Club
- 40. Surf Diva
- 41. Walking on Water

US moored buoys

CA moored buoys

# 131. Northern Oregon

Seaside Point

## Summary

+ POWERFUL, CONSISTENT SWELLS
+ SEASIDE POINT
+ BEAUTIFUL SCENERY
+ SPOT VARIETY

+ SWELLS OFTEN TOO BIG
+ STORMY CLIMATE
+ COLD WATER
+ LOCALISM & SHARKS

North Oregon gets great surf when the conditions align, which unfortunately isn't very often. It is a rugged land of natural wonder with a decent variety of surf spots, each requiring specific conditions to turn on. Lack of swell is never a problem, though it can be an issue during the wintertime, when every spot is maxed out. Wind is the critical factor for finding good waves in Oregon and fortunately, the north coast provides some protection either side of the major protruding points, capes and headlands. Some spots are crowded and well known, while others are empty and rarely spoken of. Wetsuit technology has increased the surfing population, most of whom are friendly. Surfing in Oregon has been happening for decades, despite the frigid water and sharks. The city of Seaside, Oregon's first coastal resort, is home to the famous Seaside Point, reputed to be the best wave in the Pacific Northwest and the best lefthand pointbreak in North America.

**Seaside Cove** is where the beach meets the rocks at the southern end of Oregon's premiere

Pacific City

MICHAEL KEW

seaside resort. At high tide, a left breaks into a strong rip that makes the paddle out easy, so expect mushy, sectiony walls with lots of longboarders on them. These lefts close out at low tide; when the sandbar peaks up the beach come alive especially in a NW swell.

**Seaside Point** consists of First and Second Point which both serve up long, cylindrical, sling-shot lefts up to triple overhead plus. Second point is shorter, heavier, and a little more exposed to the wind. Located along Tillamook

## TRAVEL INFORMATION

**Population:** 3.5M
**Coastline:** 476km (297mi)
**Contests:** Local
**Other Resources:**
*Video:* Finally the
Endless winter
oregonsurfpage.com
northwestwaves.com
oregon-coast.org

**Getting There** – No visa. Most international flights land in Portland, 112km (70mi) by road from Seaside. From Portland, Highway 6 leads to Highway 101 at Tillamook, while Highway 26 hits Highway 101 between Cannon Beach and Seaside.

**Getting Around** – Some public transport exists, but is definitely not the way to go. Renting a car (approx. $30/day) is the only workable option. Highway 101 is the main road. Fuel costs about $1.70/gallon. Road navigation and finding the surf spots is easy with a good map.

**Lodging and Food** – Camping is the ideal cheap option during the drier months. There is ample accommodation in all price ranges in Seaside, Cannon Beach, Tillamook and Pacific City. Good food can be found in all towns. Try the Pelican Pub & Brewery on the beach in Pacific City.

**Weather** – Oregon is very stormy from November to April; foggy in the summer; windy in the spring and variable in the autumn. Autumn is the best time for this area when the summer fog leaves, the wind is lighter, and clean NW swells begin. Winter is far too big of a gamble for the visiting surfer – more often than not, it'll be endlessly pounding rain with 35-knot SE winds, giant seas and few (if any) options for surfing. The water is always cold, requiring a 5/4mm hooded steamer, thick booties and gloves.

**Nature and Culture** – North Oregon is rugged, beautiful and easily viewed from Highway 101. There are many places for hiking and general nature enjoyment. Not much nightlife to speak of unless you're a local.

**Hazards and Hassles** – Besides localism at the pointbreaks, the surf gets big and heavy. There are many bad currents. Hypothermia is a real possibility. White sharks are everywhere.

**Handy Hints** – Maintain a low profile and respect the locals and the area. Don't go expecting epic conditions. The Pacific Northwest surf mantra is "We shall suffer". Bring plenty of warm clothing and a big board. Check out Cleanline and Seaside Surf Shops on Hwy 101 in Seaside or South County Surf in Pacific City.

| WEATHER STATISTICS | J/F | M/A | M/J | J/A | S/O | N/D |
|---|---|---|---|---|---|---|
| total rainfall (mm) | 220 | 150 | 65 | 25 | 110 | 260 |
| consistency (days/mth) | 21 | 19 | 14 | 8 | 13 | 21 |
| min temp (°C/°F) | 2/35 | 4/39 | 9/48 | 11/52 | 8/46 | 3/37 |
| max temp (°C/°F) | 9/48 | 12/54 | 16/61 | 20/68 | 18/64 | 10/50 |

Cape Lookout

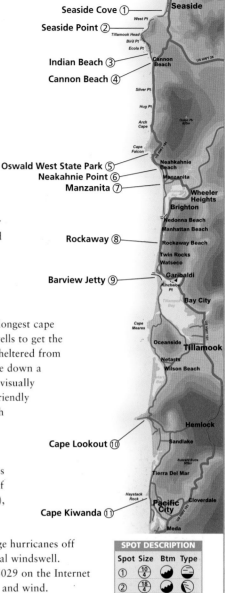

Gearhart
Seaside Cove ①
Seaside
Seaside Point ② — West Pt
Tillamook Head
Bird Pt
Ecola Pt
Indian Beach ③ — Cannon Beach
Cannon Beach ④
US HWY 26
Silver Pt
Hug Pt
Arch Cape
Onion Pk 227m
Cape Falcon
Oswald West State Park ⑤ — Neahkahnie Beach
Neakahnie Point ⑥ — Manzanita
Manzanita ⑦
Wheeler Heights
Brighton
Nedonna Beach
Manhattan Beach
Rockaway ⑧ — Rockaway Beach
Twin Rocks
Watseco
Garibaldi
Barview Jetty ⑨ — Kincheloe Pt
Tillamook Bay
Bay City
Cape Meares
Oceanside
Tillamook
Netarts
Wilson Beach
Cape Lookout ⑩
Sandlake
Blizzard Butte 503m
Hemlock
Tierra Del Mar
Haystack Rock
Cape Kiwanda ⑪ — Pacific City — Cloverdale
US HWY 101
Meda

Head, southerly storm winds are blocked, thus creating incredible midwinter sessions with big, glassy, spitting grinders along the boulders at all tides. Locals revere Seaside and have perpetuated a reputation for violent localism towards strange faces and out of state vehicles. Surviving the gnarly locals, the gnarlier lefts, the gnarliest sharks and the treacherous, ding-producing, boulder hopping, water entry and exit is what Seaside is all about. **Indian Beach** can be worth checking; the mouth of Ecola Creek occasionally has a good bar sheltered from the NW winds. **Cannon Beach** is basically all beachbreak, only surfable when small and clean. Just south of Cape Falcon, most North Coast denizens choose **Oswald West State Pk**, aka Short Sands Beach, as their premier spot due to its wind protection and sand bottom. The beautiful horseshoe cove is safe from all but W winds and entails a 20-minute stroll through old-growth forest to access the white sand, driftwood-strewn beach. The surf can either be peaky and hollow or soft and mushy, depending on the tide and swell factor. **Neakahnie Point** righthanders only break when it

Manzanita

gets big on the beachbreaks. **Manzanita** and **Rockaway Beach** punctuate miles of typical, flat-bottomed beachbreak, backed by grassy dunes and wide open to much wind and swell. The area is good during the summer with small, clean swells and east wind. **Barview Jetty** on the south entrance of Tillamook Bay offers organised jetty surf with fun, bowling waves. Magnificent **Cape Lookout**, the longest cape on the West Coast, needs straight W swells to get the best out of the quality righthand reef, sheltered from the prevailing NW wind. It's a long hike down a mountain and extremely fickle, but the visually stunning backdrop compensates. User-friendly beachbreak at **Cape Kiwanda** runs south to Pacific City and is at its best when small and glassy.

The primary source of swell comes from the NW lows in the Gulf of Alaska during winter (Nov-Mar), ranging in size from 3-30ft (1-9m). Summer (June-Sept) surf can originate from either big SW groundswells or huge hurricanes off Mexico, but summer is generally all local windswell. Check the Columbia River Bar Buoy 46029 on the Internet or weather radio for swell size, interval and wind. Dominant winds are NW year round, blowing cold and hard during spring (Mar-June) and bringing the fog during summer (June-Sept). A few spots like Cape Lookout and Oswald West State Park are protected from the NW wind. Winter storm SE winds blow offshore at Seaside Point. Tides are a major factor at all spots; local tide tables are available at any surf shop or sporting goods store.

| SPOT DESCRIPTION | | | |
|---|---|---|---|
| **Spot** | **Size** | **Btm** | **Type** |
| ① | 10/4 | | |
| ② | 18/4 | | |
| ③ | 8/2 | | |
| ④ | 8/2 | | |
| ⑤ | 8/2 | | |
| ⑥ | 8/2 | | |
| ⑦ | 6/2 | | |
| ⑧ | 8/2 | | |
| ⑨ | 8/2 | | |
| ⑩ | 15/2 | | |
| ⑪ | 6/2 | | |

| SURF STATISTICS | J F | M A M | J J A | S O N | D |
|---|---|---|---|---|---|
| dominant swell | W-NW | W-NW | S-SW | S-SW | W-NW | W-NW |
| swell size (ft) | 6-7 | 5 | 3-4 | 4 | 5-6 | 6-7 |
| consistency (%) | 80 | 70 | 60 | 60 | 70 | 80 |
| dominant wind | SE-SW | S-W | W-N | W-N | S-SW | SE-SW |
| average force | F4 | F4 | F3 | F3 | F3-F4 | F4 |
| consistency (%) | 45 | 48 | 51 | 56 | 29 | 48 |
| water temp (ºC/ºF) | 9/48 | 10/50 | 12/54 | 13/55 | 12/54 | 11/52 |
| wetsuit | | | | | | |

# 132. San Francisco and San Mateo

Mavericks

PATRICK TREFZ

## Summary
+ HIGH SWELL CONSISTENCY
+ BIG WAVE SPOTS
+ GREAT CITY ATTRACTIONS
+ ENTERTAINMENT & NIGHTLIFE

− COLD WATER
− URBAN CROWDS
− SHARK FACTOR
− LACK OF SUNSHINE

Ocean Beach

ROB GILLEY

Fort Point

DON BALCH

Despite being one of the world's best-loved tourist destinations, San Francisco is often overlooked by travelling surfers, who focus on the warmer water of Southern California or the numerous pointbreaks of "Surf City USA", namely Santa Cruz. The city breaks are regularly ignored by the surfing media, although this is definitely not the case with Mavericks, North America's prime big wave arena. Every winter, paddle-in or tow-in acts of bravado remind us that one of the heaviest breaks on the planet lies less than 48km (30mi) away from San Francisco's rolling hills, cable cars and famous bridge. Many surfers looking to escape city crowds will cross the Golden Gate Bridge and scout the Marin County coast, but for such a large metropolis, there is still room to move in the wide open spaces of Ocean Beach. Environmental problems centre on access and pollution at a handful of populated hotspots, plus there are always the white sharks to think about even though fatalities have been few in the last 75 years.

## TRAVEL INFORMATION

**Population:** 820,000
**Coastline:** 1,802km (1,126mi)
**Contests:** Local
**Other Resources:**
*Video:* Return of the Drag-In
pacificwaverider.com
mavsurfer.com
sfgate.com/traveler/guide/
sfvisitor.org
surfvid.com

**Getting There** – Coming from abroad, most flights land in San Francisco international airport (SFO). Airport shuttles cost $10 to reach the centre, 22km (14mi) away. It's a 10h drive from Los Angeles ($35 with Greyhound buses).

**Getting Around** – Within SF a car is not ideal mainly because it's so hard to park, but is necessary to reach other spots in the Bay Area. Rentals start around 160$/w and gas is cheap. Young drivers are charged extras. Although cable cars are a must for SF tourists, public transport is not an easy option for the surfer.

**Lodging and Food** – Most lodging options are concentrated in downtown SF. To be closer to the surf try the Ocean View Motel next to Ocean Beach ($70/dble), Best Western Lighthouse Hotel in Rockaway ($80/dble) or San Benito House in Half Moon Bay ($90/dble). One budget option is Marin Headlands Youth Hostel near Fort Cronkite ($18/p).

**Weather** – San Francisco has a temperate marine climate and enjoys mild weather year round. Cool summers and mild winters seem to blend into one. Temperatures seldom rise above 21°C (70°F) or fall below 5°C (40°F). Morning and evening fogs roll in during the summer months. Unlike SoCal, days warm enough for boardies are few and far between. These patches of fog also make for fast temperature changes. Anytime is good to visit, although the warm and dry months between September and November are considered the best.

**Nature and Culture** – Tourist highlights include Fisherman's Wharf, Golden Gate Bridge, Chinatown, Alcatraz... It's simple to see a bit of everything following the well indicated scenic drive. SF nightlife is great with many bars running concerts with acts such as the Mermen, a local surf-music band.

**Hazards and Hassles** – Part of the "Red Triangle" which counts 3 shark attacks per year. Pollution risks are obvious around the city breaks. Stay out of the water on the day following heavy rain, when bacteria levels hit record highs. Localism gets serious at Fort Point and a couple of other spots. Don't even think about riding big Mavs.

**Handy Hints** – A full quiver should include big guns for out of control Ocean Beach and Mavericks (of course). Good news is that there are plenty of surf shops (SF Surf Shop, Big Yank, Bob Wise) around Ocean Beach, and Mavs pioneer Jeff Clark shapes boards in HMB. Surfcamp Pacifica organises lessons.

| WEATHER STATISTICS | J/F | M/A | M/J | J/A | S/O | N/D |
|---|---|---|---|---|---|---|
| total rainfall (mm) | 95 | 55 | 10 | 0 | 15 | 70 |
| consistency (days/mth) | 8 | 6 | 2 | 0 | 2 | 7 |
| min temp (°C/°F) | 6/43 | 8/46 | 11/52 | 12/54 | 11/52 | 7/45 |
| max temp (°C/°F) | 14/57 | 17/63 | 20/68 | 22/72 | 22/72 | 16/61 |

Mavericks

ROB GILLEY

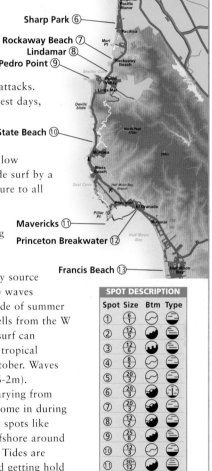

Fort Cronkhite ①
Fort Point ②
Deadmans ③
Kelly's Cove ④
Ocean Beach ⑤
Sharp Park ⑥
Rockaway Beach ⑦
Lindamar ⑧
Pedro Point ⑨
Montara State Beach ⑩
Mavericks ⑪
Princeton Breakwater ⑫
Francis Beach ⑬

As the first break north of the city, **Fort Cronkhite**'s beachbreak is still way too close to dodge the crowds, but can be a good summer surf option thanks to some protection from northerly winds. On the south side of the Golden Gate Bridge, and breaking right below it, **Fort Point** is an exceptional left with an exceptional view. It will stay clean during large winter swells and onshore winds, but suffers from strong currents, rocks in the line-ups, and serious localism. **Deadmans** is the city's other lefthand reef, it's a bit more consistent but apart from the sharks, the same hazards apply. **Kelly's Cove** distinguishes itself from other Ocean Beach peaks with a SW orientation that offers some protection from NW winds while helping to catch S swells. Easy access via the large, beachfront parking lots guarantees a high concentration of surfers. Some of the peaks along **Ocean Beach** have their own name (Sloat, South Windmill, VFW's or Noriega) but they all blend into a 5km (3mi) long beachbreak ranking among the best and heaviest on the planet. Although it's easily messed up by the wind, the strength of The Beach is its ability to hold any size without closing out. The biggest hurdle is paddling out through the thumping lines of whitewash. **Sharp Park** in Pacifica is basically a continuation of Ocean Beach, plus a few rocks and a pier to help hold the sand in place. Holds huge crowds when it's small and no crowds when it's huge. **Rockaway Beach** can produce clean peaks during storms since S winds blow offshore. This also applies to **Lindamar**, a mushier break popular with longboarders and intermediates. As a rule, Lindamar enjoys a higher tide than Rockaway. Fully exposed to large NW swells, **Pedro Point** is a good Mavericks

alternative for goofy-footers. Starts breaking at double overhead and does not stop. Has been surfed since the 1930s and always has a dedicated crew of local chargers on it. Clean, small W swells fire up the beachbreaks at **Montara State Beach**, but strong rips and the occasional crowd can ruin a session. Considering paddling out at **Mavericks** implies expertise in the field of big wave riding. Only a legitimate charger with specific training can expect to be able to ride one of the scariest waves in the world. It gets huge, is incredibly hollow with a jacking take-off, leading into a long fast wall to the channel. House sized boulders on the inside, angry currents and freezing water are just some of the challenges. Legendary big wave surfer Mark Foo met his death at this break, plus there have been two non-fatal shark attacks. Towing-in is the only way to ride the biggest days, but its impact on the environment may force an imminent ban on jetskis. **Princeton Breakwater** is an accessible, hollow beachbreak sheltered from the huge outside surf by a long jetty. **Francis Beach** has a total exposure to all swell and winds, making it a good bet on clean, smaller days. It's located within Half Moon Bay city limits but pay parking usually keeps the crowds down.

In winter, Aleutian lows are the primary source of NW swell. They push 3-15ft (1-5m) waves between October and March. Either side of summer sees frequent 2-6ft (0.6-2m) W groundswells from the W Pacific or near-shore windswell. Summer surf can originate from either SW groundswells or tropical cyclones off Mexico between July and October. Waves can reach 10ft (3m) but average 2-6ft (0.6-2m). Dominant winds year round are NW-N varying from 40% (Jan) to 70% (June); more S winds come in during the winter, and these can blow offshore at spots like Pedro Point. Only rare E winds will be offshore around Ocean Beach. Tides are significant and getting hold of a table is easy. These tides push big currents; they are strong at Ocean Beach and get huge around Fort Point, posing a serious risk to water-users.

| SPOT DESCRIPTION | | | |
|---|---|---|---|
| Spot | Size | Btm | Type |
| ① | 6/1 | | |
| ② | 12/5 | | |
| ③ | 12/6 | | |
| ④ | 8/2 | | |
| ⑤ | 20/3 | | |
| ⑥ | 20/3 | | |
| ⑦ | 20/3 | | |
| ⑧ | 12/3 | | |
| ⑨ | 25/8 | | |
| ⑩ | 12/3 | | |
| ⑪ | 30/12 | | |
| ⑫ | 8/3 | | |
| ⑬ | 8/2 | | |

Ocean Beach

ROB GILLEY

| SURF STATISTICS | J F | M A | M J | J A | S O | N D |
|---|---|---|---|---|---|---|
| dominant swell | W-NW | W-NW | S-SW | S-SW | W-NW | W-NW |
| swell size (ft) | 6 | 4-5 | 4 | 4-5 | 5 | 6 |
| consistency (%) | 80 | 75 | 60 | 60 | 70 | 80 |
| dominant wind | NW-N | NW-N | NW-N | NW-N | NW-N | NW-N |
| average force | F4 | F4 | F5 | F4-F5 | F4 | F4 |
| consistency (%) | 44 | 57 | 69 | 66 | 62 | 47 |
| water temp (°C/°F) | 12/54 | 13/55 | 13/56 | 14/57 | 14/58 | 13/55 |
| wetsuit | 🧍 | 🧍 | 🧍 | 🧍 | 🧍 | 🧍 |

# 133. Santa Monica Bay

Malibu

DON BALCH

## Summary
+ Consistent, diverse surf spots
+ Legendary Malibu
+ Entertainment LA style
+ Great weather

– Mainly beachbreak
– Uber crowds
– Bacterial pollution
– Hell-A traffic

Malibu

DAVID PU'U

A sprawling metropolis with a population of approximately 10 million people, Los Angeles is home to movie stars, extravagant homes, 12-lane freeways and nearly 96km (60mi) of Pacific Coast beaches. Among the surf spots of California's largest city, none can claim to be as famous as Malibu with its long righthanders breaking beside the coastal Highway 1. Tom Blake pioneered the break in 1926, but Malibu's fame really took off in the late '50s and early '60s. Along with a host of other surf legends, Miki Dora's stylish riding prowess exposed the wave to the surf world, while a movie based on a Malibu surfer girl, *Gidget*, was presenting surfing to the mainstream. With the exception of the area north of Santa Monica and the Palos Verdes peninsula, LA County is all beachbreak, but man-made structures like piers and jetties provide some good

Hermosa Beach

DON BALCH

sandbars. Over development of the LA basin has resulted in huge volumes of urban runoff from the coastal concrete jungle, causing regular beach closures from high bacteria counts and other toxic pollutants.

**Malibu** breaks best with S swells, thus making it a great summer spot. The omnipotent crowd spreads

## TRAVEL INFORMATION

**Population:** 35M
**Coastline:** 1,802km (1,126mi)
**Contests:** Local
**Other Resources:**
*Videos:* Malibu Madness;
Multiple Personalities;
Surfers Journal Vol 5
elporto.com
malibusurfing.com
digitalcity.com/losangeles/
 visitorsguide/

**Getting There** – Los Angeles International Airport (LAX) is one of the cheapest places worldwide to fly to. Shuttle vans take people downtown, 45mn away for around $15, which is half the cost of a taxi. LAX is not too far from El Segundo's spots.

**Getting Around** – Los Angeles has built an impressive system of broad streets and avenues including freeways up to 14 lanes wide. They allow movement quickly across the vast metropolitan complex except during the main commuting hours (7/9 AM and 4/6 PM). Rental cars start around $160/w but go as low as $50 for a local rent-a-wreck. Public transport sucks for a surfer with board.

**Lodging and Food** – The Malibu Beach Inn is right on the beach south of the pier ($170/dble), Casa Malibu Inn is a bit cheaper, starting at $100. Malibu Creek State Park Campground is open year round and affordable. Other options include the Hotel California in Santa Monica ($160) or Cadillac Hotel in Venice ($80).

**Weather** – Southern California is famous for its reliably sunny weather. It hardly ever rains especially from spring to fall, but there are many morning fogs, which dissipate by noon, unlike the constant LA smog. The sun shines, perpetuating light onshore sea breezes. The driest, sunniest time occurs with late summer Santa Ana conditions, when winds blow in from the desert. Nov to Feb brings mild winter weather with a few rainy days. Water temp is the warmest in California but still requires a steamer most of the time. Water is warmer in Santa Monica Bay than San Diego because there is no upwelling. El Niño years have warmer water temps, lots of swells and flooding rains.

**Nature and Culture** – Cruising on Coastal Highway 1 means checking the surf and the rich and famous' houses perched on the hillsides. Body-builders, posers, jugglers and activists: Venice boardwalk's characters' gallery is a must see. Of course LA offers endless entertainment possibilities.

**Hazards and Hassles** – Fires, floods and earthquakes have taken their toll on the Los Angeles area. In the water crowds and pollution are the main issues. There are no secret spots around here but the less accessible spots are definitely emptier. Many workers go for the dawn patrol; there may be fewer crowds during the day than early mornings.

**Handy Hints** – Only Redondo Beach Breakwater requires a gun, other breaks are best surfed on a regular shortboard or a longboard. Surf shops are numerous and a board costs around $400. Zuma Jay rents surfboards in Malibu ($20/d). Schools include Makos in Malibu, Pure Surfing Experience in Manhattan Beach and Surf Academy in Hermosa.

| WEATHER STATISTICS | J/F | M/A | M/J | J/A | S/O | N/D |
|---|---|---|---|---|---|---|
| total rainfall (mm) | 75 | 50 | 5 | 0 | 10 | 50 |
| consistency (days/mth) | 6 | 5 | 2 | 0 | 1 | 5 |
| min temp (°C/°F) | 8/46 | 9/48 | 13/55 | 16/61 | 13/55 | 9/48 |
| max temp (°C/°F) | 19/66 | 20/68 | 22/72 | 28/82 | 26/79 | 21/70 |

between three different take-off zones that will only connect with the largest, lined-up swells. Ranging from fast and hollow outside at Third Point to perfectly shaped, multi-functional First Point, Malibu breaks on all tides and supports an incredibly large and diverse crowd of surfers and surfcraft. Heavy rains cause the Malibu Lagoon to overflow into the line-up, usually resulting in beach closures due to bacterial pollution. **Topanga** State Beach has another long right pointbreak, less perfect and crowded than Malibu. **Chart House** rights offer a more intense ride as it breaks at high speed over shallow reef. Beware of rocks, currents and a packed line-up. A more user-friendly righthand pointbreak is **Sunset Boulevard**. On a large W swell, it offers mushy, sectiony walls and room for everyone. **Santa Monica** offers good jetty surf to those not afraid to face some of the highest pollution levels in California. There are good tubes to be found on a solid S-SW swell and the

break on a sandbar south of this jetty. The north side will pick-up winter's NW swells. **El Porto** Beach is always bigger than surrounding beaches, can hold size and gets quite hollow. Downside is that it's always crowded and really wind sensitive. Good peaky waves can break on either side of **Manhattan Beach** Municipal Pier, attracting many surfers to the beach that Dale Velzy first rode in 1951. **Hermosa Beach** is another popular beachbreak, best with small, broken up swells, since it tends to close out over 6ft (2m). **Redondo Beach Breakwater** is a serious, wedge of a lefthander, needing proper equipment and skills as it can hold up to triple overhead. More beachbreaks extend southwards to the Palos Verdes Peninsula. **Topaz Street** and neighbouring Sapphire Street provide jetty surf while **Burn Out** is one of Torrance's peaky beachbreaks.

El Porto

ROB GILLEY

Municipal Pier provides another surf option. For small beachbreak waves, the eternally popular **Bay Street** likes peaky windswells and low tides. Better known for outdoors gyms and basketball courts, **Venice Beach** holds some powerful winter peaks around the breakwater and jetty. With summer SW swells, Ballona Creek can have small, hollow rights at a spot called **Toes Over**, off the south jetty. The lefts south of there are better suited to longboarding and both spots suffer from high pollution levels. El Segundo was supposed to receive a new break in the form of Pratte's artificial reef, but the project was a failure and the sandbags dumped there are only appreciated by the fish, while surfers keep hanging out at **New Jetty**. With W or SW swells, short, hollow waves

The primary source of swell comes from the SW groundswells April to September or tropical cyclones off Mexico between July and October. Waves can reach 12ft (3.6m) but average 3-8ft (1-2.5m) as Santa Catalina Island can block some of the swell. Aleutian lows in winter (Oct-March), bring waves 2-8ft (0.6-2.5m) waves to the beaches but it won't get in between Malibu and Santa Monica. Before and after summer, frequent 2-6ft (0.6-2m) W swells appear from distant West Pacific groundswell or near-shore windswell. Calm days and offshore days are more common in winter even though the magical E Santa Ana winds tend to blow in late summer. Dominant winds are NW-W. NW sea breeze usually chops things up from noon until dusk. Winds are rarely strong and glassy days are a SoCal feature. Tides vary from 4-7ft (1.2-2.1m): getting a tide table is easy.

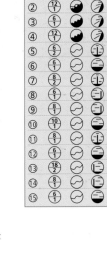

**SPOT DESCRIPTION**

| Spot | Size | Btm | Type |
|------|------|-----|------|
| ① | 12/3 | | |
| ② | 12/1 | | |
| ③ | 6/1 | | |
| ④ | 12/3 | | |
| ⑤ | 6/1 | | |
| ⑥ | 6/1 | | |
| ⑦ | 8/2 | | |
| ⑧ | 6/1 | | |
| ⑨ | 8/1 | | |
| ⑩ | 10/2 | | |
| ⑪ | 8/1 | | |
| ⑫ | 6/1 | | |
| ⑬ | 18/2 | | |
| ⑭ | 6/1 | | |
| ⑮ | 6/1 | | |

JOHN CALLAHAN

Topanga State Beach

| SURF STATISTICS | J F | M A | M J | J A | S O | N D |
|-----------------|-----|-----|-----|-----|-----|-----|
| dominant swell | W-NW | W-NW | S-SW | S-SW | W-NW | W-NW |
| swell size (ft) | 4-5 | 4 | 2-3 | 4 | 5 | 4-5 |
| consistency (%) | 70 | 60 | 50 | 50 | 70 | 70 |
| dominant wind | W-N | W-NW | W-NW | W-NW | W-NW | W-N |
| average force | F3 | F4 | F4 | F4 | F4 | F3 |
| consistency (%) | 63 | 60 | 65 | 66 | 66 | 66 |
| water temp (°C/°F) | 14/57 | 15/59 | 16/61 | 19/66 | 19/66 | 16/61 |
| wetsuit | | | | | | |

# 134. Texas

## Summary
+ WARM WATER
+ SOME UNCROWDED BREAKS
+ FRIENDLY LOCALS
+ NICE CLIMATE

− SMALL, SHORT-LIVED SWELLS
− RARE OFFSHORE WINDS
− DIFFICULT BARRIER ISLAND ACCESS
− SPRING BREAK CROWDS

Bob Hall Pier

STEELE

The Texas coastline accounts for a good proportion of the USA's beaches on the massive Gulf of Mexico, referred to by surfers as the Third Coast. The state may not be first choice when planning a USA surf trip, but should not be overlooked altogether. Its 600km (375mi) of low-lying coastline are all beaches with a continuous string of barrier islands receiving regular windswell and occasional hurricane swell from the Gulf. There are numerous passes, inlets, piers and jetties, providing the focus for waves along the endless, featureless strands. The intracoastal waterway creates access difficulties away from the

South Padre Island

STEELE

JP Luby Surf Park

STEELE

bridges and ferries, but 4WDs are permitted on many of the beaches, which all belong to the public. Galveston is Texas' original surfing hub, where it all began in the early 1930s despite the realisation that there is much better potential further south.

## TRAVEL INFORMATION

**Population:** 22M
**Coastline:** 590km (368mi)
**Contests:** Regional (Sept)
**Other Resources:**
*Video:* The Exposure; Step Into Liquid
thirdcoastsurf.com
coastalbendsurf.com
sopadre.com
traveltex.com

**Getting There** – Regular flights head to Brownsville/South Padre Island Airport 50km (30mi) W of South Padre. International flights will land in San Antonio. From there, head south on Interstate Hwy 37, then US Hwy 77, then Texas 100. South Padre is 190km (120mi) south of Corpus Christi.

**Getting Around** – Renting a car is necessary to reach all the remote spots. Gas is super-cheap. Driving on the barrier island beach roads is not possible without a 4x4. Renting a sand rail or dune buggy is an option to reach Port Mansfield. South Padre Island public transport is called "the wave".

**Lodging and Food** – A huge spring break hotel capacity ensures good deals the rest of the year. The Brown Pelican Inn is a comfortable bed & breakfast in SPI ($130/dble). Tiki

Condominiums have a Polynesian look ($120/dble). In Galveston, the Flagship gave its name to one of the best breaks ($150/dble). Eat at the Surf Club in Corpus Christi or the pier house next to Horace Caldwell Pier.

**Weather** – Influenced by continental systems and the warm Gulf of Mexico Texas is constantly switching between periods of settled and unstable weather. South Padre Island enjoys a sub-tropical environment with mild dry winters, and warm breezy summers. Temperatures average 18°C (65°F) in winter and 28°C (82°F) in summer. North winds blowing in the winter months will cool the atmosphere, but will be offshore at many spots. Winters are usually mild with daytime temperatures ranging between 10-21°C (50-70°F). Night temperatures are usually much cooler, but very rarely does the temperature drop to freezing. Galveston Island is one of the only locations where the summer daytime temperatures normally fail to rise above 27°C (80°F). Hurricanes threaten the whole coastline and strike Texas once every 3 years on average. Water is warm enough to trunk it all summer long, but winter requires a 3/2 full suit.

**Nature and Culture** – Beach is the big attraction here, but a variety of parks, museums and other types of entertainment exist. Schlitterbahn Water Park already has a standing wave you can bodyboard on, but James Fulbright has plans for a "Surf City Texas" that would use wave cannon technology to produce 8ft (2.6m) barrels.

**Hazards and Hassles** – Shark attacks have been recorded off Galveston and Padre Island, usually on swimmers. Except for Bob Hall Pier, which has a real competitive scene, most breaks have waves for everyone and the locals are friendly. Hurricane surf is dangerous because of the strong currents it generates, especially around passes.

**Handy Hints** – Waves generally lack power, so big floaty boards tend to work best. There are many fully stocked surf shops in Texas like Wind and Wave Water Sports in Corpus Christi or Beach Break conveniently located across from the Flagship hotel in Galveston. Pick-up a copy of *Gulf Coast Surf Magazine*.

| WEATHER STATISTICS | J/F | M/A | M/J | J/A | S/O | N/D |
|---|---|---|---|---|---|---|
| total rainfall (mm) | 40 | 40 | 80 | 60 | 110 | 40 |
| consistency (days/mth) | 8 | 5 | 7 | 6 | 7 | 7 |
| min temp (°C/°F) | 8/46 | 15/59 | 22/72 | 23/74 | 20/68 | 11/52 |
| max temp (°C/°F) | 19/66 | 25/77 | 31/88 | 33/92 | 30/86 | 22/72 |

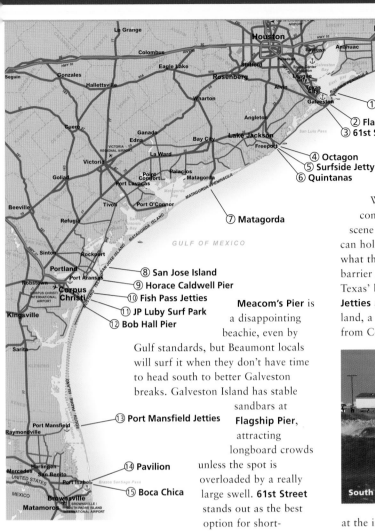

*GULF OF MEXICO*

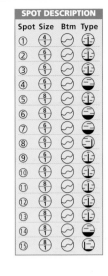

| SPOT DESCRIPTION | | | |
|---|---|---|---|
| Spot | Size | Btm | Type |
| ① | 4/1 | | |
| ② | 6/1 | | |
| ③ | 6/1 | | |
| ④ | 6/1 | | |
| ⑤ | 8/1 | | |
| ⑥ | 8/1 | | |
| ⑦ | 6/1 | | |
| ⑧ | 6/1 | | |
| ⑨ | 6/1 | | |
| ⑩ | 6/1 | | |
| ⑪ | 8/1 | | |
| ⑫ | 8/1 | | |
| ⑬ | 8/1 | | |
| ⑭ | 8/1 | | |
| ⑮ | 8/1 | | |

**Meacom's Pier** is a disappointing beachie, even by Gulf standards, but Beaumont locals will surf it when they don't have time to head south to better Galveston breaks. Galveston Island has stable sandbars at **Flagship Pier**, attracting longboard crowds unless the spot is overloaded by a really large swell. **61st Street** stands out as the best option for short-boarders since good sandbanks usually form north of the jetty. With the right conditions, peaks appear anywhere along the extensive seawall spreading the crowds. Heading south, **Octagon** is a bit more consistent than Galveston, and the beachbreaks to the north, may yield a faster, hollower wave. On large S, even SW swells, **Surfside Jetty** is the place to be since it's possible to jump from the end of the jetty into longer cleaner lines as they wrap in. With a large E swell, action shifts to **Quintana**, an otherwise mushy break that finds power at size. Halfway between Galveston and Port Aransas, the **Matagorda** peninsula produces the best barrel in northern Texas. This wave is made possible by the deeper waters of the Colorado River inlet channel, focusing the swell onto shallow sandbars. Corpus Christi/Port Aransas is the modern hub of Gulf Coast surfing. Getting to **San Jose Island** requires a quick boat or ferry ride, but the rewards can be clean peaks, provided the wind is offshore and the SE swell strong enough. In Port Aransas, the **Horace Caldwell Pier**

peaks up on either side depending on swell direction, sandbanks and tide levels. Heading south, **Fish Pass Jetties** provides good wind protection and long but usually mushy waves, making it a longboarder's favourite. The wide open beach of **JP Luby Surf Park** has its days alongside the old broken pier, but is better known as party central during the crowded college spring break. With direct access from Corpus Christi and consistent waves, **Bob Hall Pier** is the number one scene of the "coastal bend" area. It gets real good and can hold some size, but crowds are a given, no matter what the conditions are like. South Padre Island is a long barrier island, barely half a mile wide and is probably Texas' best surfing destination. Because **Port Mansfield Jetties** are isolated in the middle of this narrow strip of land, a 4WD is required to drive the sandy 80km (50mi) from Corpus Christi. This means that crowds are minimal

**South Padre Island**

at the inlet jetties that help to focus any swell direction into some of the longest, lined-up waves in the state. More accessible are the Brazos Santiago Pass breaks located close to Port Isabel. **Pavilion** beachbreak gets classic, as powerful, hollow walls hold shape on the north side of the jetty. Best on SE to E swells, while the south side at **Boca Chica** prefers some N to get the lefts running down the beach. As with most Texan passes, in-between the two jetties there are a couple of quality waves that only break on the biggest swells when the beaches are closed out.

Most of the swell comes from the prevailing onshore NE-SE winds blowing across the Gulf of Mexico as fronts approach. Several days of strong wind can build surf up to the 4-6ft (1.2-2m) range, but as the front brings in W to N offshore winds, the size diminishes quickly. In spring, fall and winter, fronts cycle on a weekly basis providing regular surf, while summer is usually flat unless a tropical system develops in the gulf. The hurricane season stretches from June to November but September and October are more likely to produce storms that cross into the Gulf from the Caribbean. Tidal range is minimal but can affect the strength of the currents at inlets and passes.

| SURF STATISTICS | J F | M A | M J | J A | S O | N D |
|---|---|---|---|---|---|---|
| dominant swell | S | S-SE | S-SE | S-SE | S-SE | S |
| swell size (ft) | 3 | 2-3 | 2 | 1-2 | 3 | 3-4 |
| consistency (%) | 40 | 35 | 30 | 20 | 50 | 40 |
| dominant wind | N-S | N-S | E-S | E-S | NE-SE | N-S |
| average force | F4 | F4 | F4 | F3-F4 | F4 | F4 |
| consistency (%) | 84 | 81 | 84 | 80 | 67 | 86 |
| water temp (°C/°F) | 18/64 | 19/66 | 24/75 | 27/80 | 26/79 | 21/70 |
| wetsuit | | | | | | |

**South Padre Island**

# 135. Rhode Island

Ruggles

STEVE FITZPATRICK

## Summary
+ CONSISTENT WINTER SWELLS
+ FALL HURRICANE SURF
+ SPOT DIVERSITY
+ SCENIC NEW ENGLAND

– COLD WATER
– WINDY
– SUMMER FLAT SPELLS
– SOME CROWDS

R hode Island may well be the smallest state in the USA, but over 640km (400mi) of coastline and 100+ beaches have earned it the nickname "the Ocean State". Narragansett Bay, a 48km (30mi) long arm of the Atlantic Ocean splits the state in two parts. To the west are sand spits, barrier beaches, lagoons and salt ponds, while low rounded hills compose the landscape to the east. There's a good concentration of surf spots with cobblestone reefs helping to groom the lines of swell into nice defined peaks. Famous for grandiose houses belonging to luminary families like the Kennedys, Newport is also a centre for yachting, giving it an air of exclusivity.

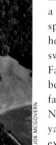

JOE MCGOVERN

JOE MCGOVERN

South of Westerly city, **Masquamicut** State Beach is an average beachbreak, usually on its best with a combination of S swell, N wind and low tide. **Breachway** offers jetty surf at low tide, allowing for longer rides than the surrounding beachbreaks, but doesn't handle much size. **Matunuck** is the centre of Rhode Island surfing because there are three top quality peaks. Furthest west, the bowly rights and longer, walled lefts of The Point,

## TRAVEL INFORMATION

**Population:** 1M
**Coastline:** 724km (452mi)
**Contests:** Local
**Other Resources:**
narragansettri.com
visitrhodeisland.com

**Getting There** – 1/2h from Narragansett, TF Green Airport (PVD) is the most convenient, but most people commute from Boston or NY. Travelling by ground, Boston is 90mn away; NY 3h thanks to the I-95, a major highway running along the whole US East Coast. There are also ferries from Long Island. Amtrak's Acela train service is fast and reliable.

**Getting Around** – Driving is the best way to go around Rhode Island. Most major car rental companies have offices at TF Green Airport and in Providence and Newport. Rates average $180/week. Interstate routes 95 and 195 offer access to most of Rhode Island's major cities. From Galilee it can be worth riding the ferry to the well-exposed Block Island.

**Lodging and Food** – The Sea Gull Guest House ($80/dble) is very close to Narragansett Pier while The Lighthouse Inn of Galilee is located next to Pt Judith breaks ($120). In between stands the Dunmere Gatehouse ($150), ideal for those who fancy castle life. Traditional local dishes are quahog clams, clam cakes, doughboys and johnnycakes.

**Weather** – Rhode Island has a humid, continental climate, but somewhat milder than the rest of New England thanks to the warm winds from Narragansett Bay. For the same reason temperatures are usually cooler along the coast than in the interior. The warmest months of the year are April through October with highs averaging 21°C (70°F), with a few days, usually in July and August, reaching 32°C (90°F). Winter temperatures along the coast average –1°C (30°F) and freezing temperatures occur on a daily basis between December and March. The climate is relatively wet with precipitation falling evenly throughout the year and snowfalls starting towards end November. Hurricane damage occurs every 10 to 15 years. Water temps get down to 3°C (36°F), making

the drysuit popular with some of the local crew. By stark contrast, springsuit/boardshort days are common in July/August.

**Nature and Culture** – Tourism is Rhode Island's second largest industry and Narragansett Bay stands as its central resource. Newport is an historic city from the early colonial era. Southern Rhode Island Green Trail offers parks, beaches, farmland, bird sanctuaries and wildlife refuges.

**Hazards and Hassles** – Crowds are an issue in summer and around major spots like Ruggles. A long history of environmental pollution peaked in January 1996 with the spill of 1M gallons of heating oil on beaches west of Point Judith; it will take years to assess the consequences.

**Handy Hints** – There are several well-stuffed surf shops around Narragansett with Warm Winds and Gansett Juice being the big names in town. The latter has a surf school and rents boards. Valuable possessions include a longer board for the go-big days and any cold-fighting item for the freezing midwinter sessions.

| WEATHER STATISTICS | J/F | M/A | M/J | J/A | S/O | N/D |
|---|---|---|---|---|---|---|
| total rainfall (mm) | 90 | 110 | 80 | 75 | 85 | 110 |
| consistency (days/mth) | 11 | 12 | 11 | 9 | 9 | 12 |
| min temp (°C/°F) | -5/23 | 1/34 | 11/52 | 17/63 | 11/52 | 1/34 |
| max temp (°C/°F) | 3/37 | 10/50 | 20/68 | 26/79 | 20/68 | 8/46 |

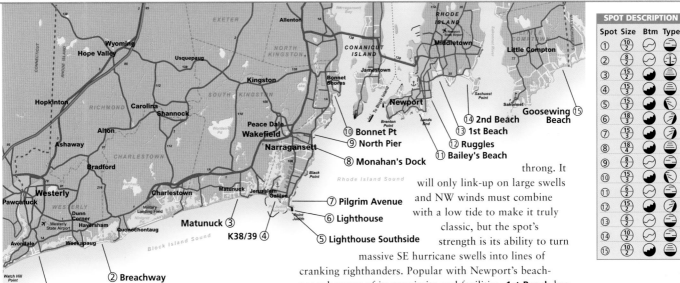

Photo credit: JOE McGOVERN

trundle towards the inside section known as The Bar, which is overlooked by a real bar, usually full of surfers and fishermen. The central peak is Trestles, showing some form similar to its Californian namesake, hollower on the rights and faster on the lefts. Deep Hole is essentially a low tide left, breaking over the multi-coloured cobblestones that underpin all these peaks. All can handle some size and picking the right spot depends mainly on swell orientation. Inside the large Point Judith Harbor, **K38** and **K39** (the Ks) are two peaks that will offer the longest lefts on the East Coast with good S/SE swells. A long wall but never hollow enough to get barrelled, they're longboarders' favourites. Point Judith's lighthouse is blessed with two pointbreaks breaking either side of it. **Southside** is the left, with three sections combining into one long ride as the swell gets bigger. The same happens at **Lighthouse**, a lengthy righthand point that can peel all the way to **Pilgrim Avenue** on a strong S swell. Steep, fast sections are followed by cutback sections and it can get up to triple overhead. Heading north from Point Judith, spots are named after the streets that lead to them. Pilgrim Avenue, the best among them, is a righthand point, which, although mushy, can handle size and strong SW winds. The peak at **Monahan's Dock** breaks both ways but the good stuff is only found on the rights. Thick, top-to-bottom barrels are on offer for those that can handle low tides' critical take-off right in front of the dock. The wave gets easier as the tide comes in, but such a tight take-off zone insures instant crowds. There are several consistent peaks around Narragansett's beach and **North Pier**. Small summer swells combining with offshore westerly winds always attract a glut of people. Its opposite number in terms of consistency, **Bonnet Point**'s lefthand break only lights up with a large S swell. Tube opportunities occur, but the walls are more adapted to linking turns to each other. Scoring a session at **Bailey's Beach** could mean hollow little peaks away from the mob, but the place seriously lacks consistency and parking spots. With several righthand reefs lining a point, **Ruggles** probably has the best reputation in Rhode Island and its allure entices a

throng. It will only link-up on large swells and NW winds must combine with a low tide to make it truly classic, but the spot's strength is its ability to turn massive SE hurricane swells into lines of cranking righthanders. Popular with Newport's beach-goers because of its proximity and facilities, **1st Beach** has little interest for surfers having passed the beginner stage. The gentle slope of the beach makes for small, soft-breaking waves that close-out over 6ft (2m). **2nd Beach** has more appeal since it's usually bigger and better shaped with the extra treat of a protected left pointbreak cranking-up as the swell rises. The large bay surrounding **Goosewing Beach** offers a mixture of beach, reef and pointbreaks, breaking on all tides and up to 10ft (3m). There are many other spots around this peninsula but access is minimal. Offshore, Block Island presents some excellent surfing in hurricane and winter swells.

Rhode Island's south facing coastline is ideally exposed to south and southeast hurricane swells. Between August and October these can pump overhead waves for several days in a row. Regular North Atlantic swells coming from the NE have a long way to wrap around Cape Cod but some slow moving lows will hang-out long enough in the middle of the Atlantic to send several days of good surf. Summer is usually small with more action on the beachbreaks. Such an indented coastline offers many options in terms of swell and wind combos, which is a good thing because winter storms are usually accompanied by high winds. S to W winds dominate in the summertime while the offshore N wind tends to occur more often in winter. Not exceeding 5ft (1.6m), the tidal range is not quite as important here as it is in northern New England or Nova Scotia, but will affect the pointbreaks, particularly on smaller swells.

| SURF STATISTICS | J F | M A | M J | J A | S O | N D |
|---|---|---|---|---|---|---|
| dominant swell | S-SE | S-SE | S-SE | SE | SE | S-SE |
| swell size (ft) | 4 | 3-4 | 2-3 | 2 | 3-4 | 4 |
| consistency (%) | 70 | 60 | 50 | 30 | 55 | 70 |
| dominant wind | SW-N | SW-NW | S-W | S-W | S-NW | SW-N |
| average force | F4-F5 | F4 | F4 | F3 | F3-F4 | F4-F5 |
| consistency (%) | 71 | 49 | 55 | 57 | 53 | 70 |
| water temp (°C/°F) | 4/39 | 5/41 | 13/55 | 20/68 | 17/63 | 9/48 |
| wetsuit | | | | | | |

# 136. Nova Scotia

ALL PHOTOS YASSINE OUHILAL

**Summary**
+ GREAT HURRICANE SWELLS
+ BREAK QUALITY AND DIVERSITY
+ MINIMUM CROWDS
+ UNSPOILT COASTLINE

− ICY WATER TEMPS
− HARSH WEATHER
− INCONSISTENT SUMMER
− RISING LOCALISM

A long with New Brunswick and Prince Edward Island, Nova Scotia belongs to the Maritime Provinces of Canada, where it is impossible to be more than 56km (35mi) away from the sea. While most towns are located along the coast, the province's interior is pitted with thousands of lakes scattered among forests and rocky hills. Only a narrow isthmus connects Nova Scotia to mainland Canada and the Atlantic Ocean surrounds 10,500km (6,500mi) of coastline ranging from bays, inlets and cliffs to gravel or sand beaches. This rugged shoreline provides a wealth of pointbreaks, offshore reefs and plenty of beachbreaks, with a huge variety of wind and swell combinations.

Minutes

Near the town of Musquodoboit Harbour, **Martinique** is Nova Scotia's longest sandy beach. A summer swell magnet, it is protected from SW winds and is more consistent and less crowded than nearby Lawrencetown. It's also a wild bird sanctuary, with piping plover nesting on the sand dunes. The popular Lawrencetown Beach is

## TRAVEL INFORMATION

**Population:** 950,000
**Coastline:** 7,400km (4,625mi)
**Contests:**
Lawrencetown Classic
Red Bull Icebreaker
**Other Resources:**
*Video:* True North;
5mm Canada
hurricanesurf.com
http://explore.gov.ns.ca/
destination-ns.com

**Getting There** – Halifax airport (YHZ) is the Atlantic Canadian flight hub. Most flights come from Boston, Newark, and London. US and Canadian highways join the Trans Canada Highway from New Brunswick into Nova Scotia. Greyhound buses connect with Acadian Lines in Nova Scotia. Lawrencetown is a 20min drive from Halifax.

**Getting Around** – Renting a car in Halifax cost under $300/week for over 25's. Highways numbered from 100 to 199 are efficient but provincial roads can be narrow. Nova Scotia has 10 "Scenic Travelways" including the Lighthouse Route going along the south shore from Halifax, and the Marine Drive along the eastern shore.

**Lodging and Food** – Out of Halifax, try the Moonlight Beach Inn in Lawrencetown ($100/dble) or Grants by the Sea Guesthouse in Eastern Passage (close to Cow Bay, $125/dble). In Port Joli, check the T.H. Raddall Park campground or the Emsik Beach House ($1000/wk). Whitepoint beach resort is $120/dble. Try the famous lobster.

**Weather** – Although mainland Canadians find Nova Scotia's oceanic winters mild, temps rarely rise above freezing. Spring remains cool before summer highs average 15°C (59°F). Precipitation peaks in late fall and early winter when storms are more frequent and it snows regularly in winter. Fog is also a common occurrence, especially in spring and early summer. If the Gulf Stream helps the water to reach 20°C (68°F) on the warmest day of late summer, it then drops radically to become the coldest ocean water in North America. With consistent sub zero air temperatures and tenacious NW winds coming straight from polar bear territory, winter water temps rarely break the 4°C (39°F) barrier. This means 6/5 suits, hoods, gloves, booties... and empty line-ups.

**Nature and Culture** – Nature enthusiasts will spot whales, seabirds and other marine creatures from the scenic, coastal routes. Kejimkujik National Park is home to a plethora of lakes. Fishing villages like Lunenburg and Lockeport are real standouts. Halifax is a lively city with top restaurants and good nightlife. Check the Bay of Fundy's tidal bore.

**Hazards and Hassles** – Some locals are a bit fed up with the influx of Americans each hurricane season, but with so many potential spots, only the pointbreaks of the Lawrencetown-Cow Bay area actually suffer from localism. Water quality is good at most of the surfbreaks due to the lack of coastal development. Booties are essential protection from rocks and cold.

**Handy Hints** – Longer, floatier boards help carry the necessary extra thick rubber. Several surfshops like Dacane Sports in Halifax, Rossignol in Port Joli and Happy Dude's in Seaforth. The first two offer lessons and rentals. There are thousands of other spots to be found away from the main coastal towns.

| WEATHER STATISTICS | J/F | M/A | M/J | J/A | S/O | N/D |
|---|---|---|---|---|---|---|
| total rainfall (mm) | 120 | 120 | 100 | 105 | 120 | 140 |
| consistency (days/mth) | 16 | 15 | 14 | 13 | 12 | 15 |
| min temp (°C/°F) | -9/16 | -3/27 | 7/45 | 13/55 | 7/45 | -3/27 |
| max temp (°C/°F) | 0/32 | 6/43 | 17/63 | 23/74 | 7/45 | 5/41 |

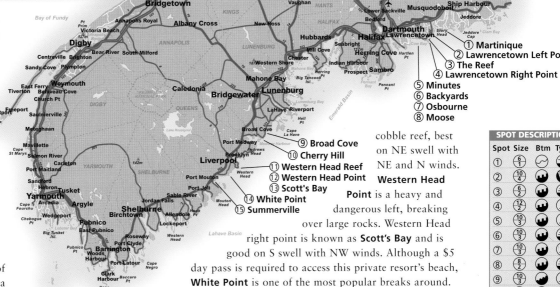

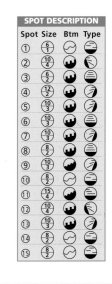

① Martinique
② Lawrencetown Left Point
③ The Reef
④ Lawrencetown Right Point
⑤ Minutes
⑥ Backyards
⑦ Osbourne
⑧ Moose

⑨ Broad Cove
⑩ Cherry Hill
⑪ Western Head Reef
⑫ Western Head Point
⑬ Scott's Bay
⑭ White Point
⑮ Summerville

one mile in length and faces south, producing uninspiring beach peaks up to 5ft (1.5m).
**Lawrencetown Left Point** only breaks well 5-10 days/year, when winter or spring swells combine with W to NE winds. Really tubular and breaking close to the rocks, it has to be one of the heaviest spots around. Located at the centre of the beach, **The Reef** is a small swell peak ideal for longboards or beginners, and is a favorite hang-out for a few locals and old-timers. Surfed since the early 1960s, **Lawrencetown Right Point**, at the western end of the beach, can break on either small swells or anything up to 12ft (4m). Good shape and length of ride coincides with a straight S swell, NW winds and mid tide. Cow Bay is another local's favourite, featuring numerous reefs including **Minutes**, named after timing rides that travel well over 500m (1500ft). Very fast peelers, best on E-SE groundswells, it's slightly sheltered from W-NW winds and coveted by the locals. Just around the corner is **Backyards**, a sometimes wedgy reef peak with a hollower left, which is good on a higher tide and is well sheltered from winter NW winds. **Osbourne** is a right pointbreak sheltered from all W winds and the long walk down the point can be worthwhile as it can offer very long rides around mid tide. The rocky beachbreak peak of **Moose** is one of the closest and easily accessible spots to Halifax, so it's often crowded. Gets good on higher tides, S-SE swells and NW winds, creating hollow but manageable lefts in front of the giant moose statue. South of the Halifax area, another bunch of popular breaks lie within striking distance of Liverpool. **Broad Cove** counts three pointbreaks with a cobble bottom. The main break is a long right, wrapping from the point into the bay. It works well on S swell with SW to NW winds. **Cherry Hill** is a long, white sand beach with a good left at one end, best checked on NE swell and NW winds. With three easily accessed breaks, Western Head is the best place to score large waves. **Western Head Reef** is a long left that can hold more than 15ft (5m), breaking over deep water

cobble reef, best on NE swell with NE and N winds. **Western Head Point** is a heavy and dangerous left, breaking over large rocks. Western Head right point is known as **Scott's Bay** and is good on S swell with NW winds. Although a $5 day pass is required to access this private resort's beach, **White Point** is one of the most popular breaks around. While white sand and crystal clear water convince most beachgoers to fork out the cash, surfers are more interested in the left and right sandbar that picks up any swell direction. **Summerville**'s long white sand beach offers good breaks at both ends, with the south end's rivermouth regularly producing the best sand bars.

| SPOT DESCRIPTION | | | |
|---|---|---|---|
| Spot | Size | Btm | Type |
| ① | 6/1 | | |
| ② | 10/1 | | |
| ③ | 6/2 | | |
| ④ | 12/1 | | |
| ⑤ | 10/1 | | |
| ⑥ | 10/3 | | |
| ⑦ | 10/3 | | |
| ⑧ | 8/1 | | |
| ⑨ | 10/3 | | |
| ⑩ | 8/2 | | |
| ⑪ | 15/4 | | |
| ⑫ | 10/4 | | |
| ⑬ | 10/3 | | |
| ⑭ | 8/2 | | |
| ⑮ | 8/2 | | |

The hurricane season offers the best potential for a much sought-after combination of bearable water temps and quality surf. Between August and November hurricanes will send overhead surf with good power, while North Atlantic storms start winding up, bringing consistent surf to the East coast. These nor'easters and deep North Atlantic low pressure systems send regular 12-15ft swells in winter, but those come with storm force winds, heavy snowfall and water temps almost reaching the freezing point. Buoys go over 100ft (33m) almost every year! Spring is generally overlooked as water temps remain super cold while the surf starts decreasing. Summer surf consists of small locally-generated NE to SW windswells of 1-1.5m (1m-1.5m). NW offshores are common in winter while onshore SW winds prevail in summer. Tides in the Bay of Fundy, west of Nova Scotia are the highest in the world, reaching 16m (48ft). Even on average days, the water levels rise or drop by over 0.3m (1ft) every 12 minutes! Tides on the east side of the province are comparatively small, with an 2.5m (8ft) range that affects most breaks.

| SURF STATISTICS | J F | M A | M J | J A | S O | N D |
|---|---|---|---|---|---|---|
| dominant swell | NE-SE | NE-SE | NE-SW | NE-SW | NE-S | NE-SE |
| swell size (ft) | 5-6 | 4-5 | 3-4 | 2-3 | 5 | 5-6 |
| consistency (%) | 70 | 60 | 50 | 40 | 60 | 70 |
| dominant wind | W-N | W-N | S-W | S-W | SW-N | W-N |
| average force | F5-F6 | F5 | F4 | F4 | F4-F5 | F5 |
| consistency (%) | 62 | 55 | 54 | 61 | 61 | 57 |
| water temp (°C/°F) | 1/34 | 3/37 | 9/48 | 15/59 | 12/54 | 4/39 |
| wetsuit | | | | | | |

# 'Green' Surf Magazine

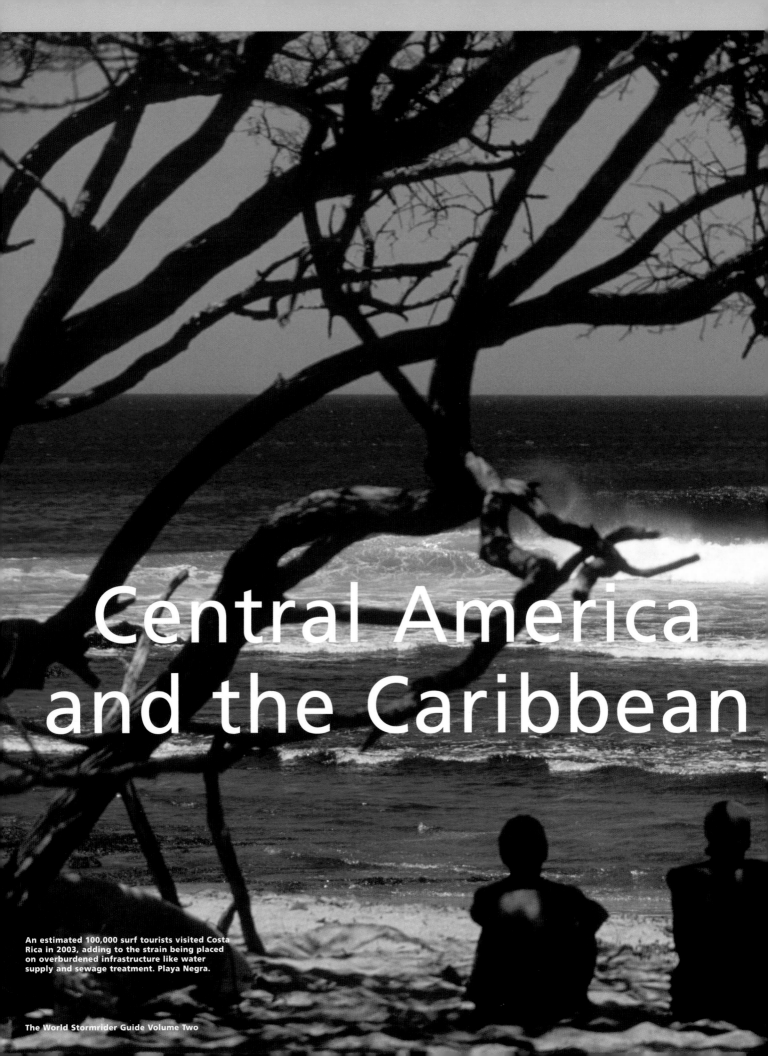

# Central America
# and the Caribbean

An estimated 100,000 surf tourists visited Costa
Rica in 2003, adding to the strain being placed
on overburdened infrastructure like water
supply and sewage treatment. Playa Negra.

# The Ocean Environment

Central America and the Caribbean is a continental conduit displaying features from both North and South America, plus a diverse range of unique environs. Many Central American countries have experienced recent civil war or social unrest, leaving their economies on the brink of poverty and environmental issues low on the list of priorities. Vast natural gas and oil reserves remain untapped, awaiting exploitation and the accompanying potential for environmental disaster. It is an area under enormous pressure as the USA taps into its cheap labour force and unregulated industries that allow commercial gain at the expense of the environment. The Panama Canal is one of the busiest shipping lanes on earth, directing traffic through the Caribbean, which happens to be one of the busiest tourist destinations on earth.

### Pollution

The coral reefs of Central America and The Caribbean are under serious threat from coastal development. The destruction of the widespread mangrove swamps and loss of sea grass beds has removed the coastal runoff filter that sieves solid particles and absorbs toxic elements. Without the mangroves, sediment smothers the reefs, cutting out the essential sunlight. Excessive nutrients from sewage or agriculture cause algal blooms, resulting in death by eutrophication and the subsequent loss of bio-diversity is causing increasing concern. Developing nations pollution control is notoriously poor, which is graphically illustrated across Central America. Industrial and domestic waste is often untreated and discharged raw into rivers or directly into the ocean. Cancun in Mexico has evolved from a fishing town population of 200 into a 21km (13mi) strip of high-rise hotels attracting 3 million visitors a year. The environmental price has been the loss of 60,000 hectares (148,000 acres) of rainforest, degradation of lagoon and coral reef habitat, devastated fish stocks and half a million workers living in near poverty adding to the huge sewage and solid waste treatment problems. Developments such as the string of marinas proposed for the Baja Peninsula will bring pollution to harbours that don't exist yet, and tourists

to a region devoid of any basic infrastructure. Similar, ill-conceived coastal development and rapid deforestation is responsible for reef degradation, highlighted by the clearing of native rainforest for agricultural land use. Reefs are being smothered and poisoned by runoff, particularly on the Caribbean coast, affecting waters off Mexico, Belize, Guatemala, Honduras, Nicaragua, Costa Rica and Panama.

Tourism is the main stress on the Caribbean ecosystem, exerting a greater strain on available resources, since it is estimated that the average tourist uses ten times as much water and electricity than a local. Across the Leeward and Windward Islands, rapid tourist development means local sewage systems simply cannot cope and in much of the Caribbean, 90% of domestic waste enters the ocean untreated. Away from the over-developed tourist destinations and conditions can still live up to the pristine Caribbean vision, but the threats of agricultural, oil and tourist related pollution are growing throughout the region.

**Mangroves are a crucial coastal barrier, designed to hold the ground together, prevent erosion, provide a hatchery habitat for countless species and filter pollutants in the airless mud.**

BRUCE SUTHERLAND

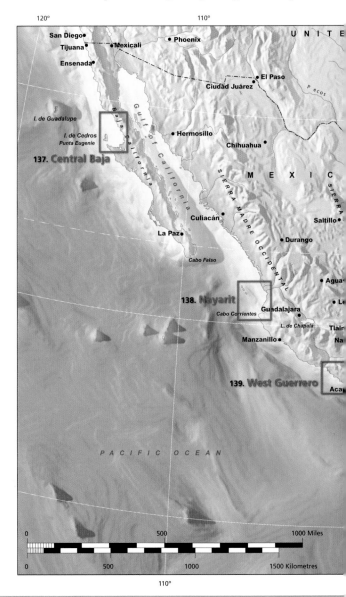

## Erosion

Mangroves and sea grass play a major role in pollution control, but they are also an essential part of the coastal sea defences. A stabilizing force in the battle against severe erosion, they bind the mobile coastline together, holding a line in the face of strong hurricanes, which regularly funnel through these regions. These hurricanes can do massive damage to fringing reefs, already weakened due to pollution, plus uprooting trees, destruction of habitats and storm surges are all part of this regular, natural phenomenon.

Mexico has already lost one of the best waves in the world at Petacalco due to a combination of a new harbour for a steel works, followed by a huge hurricane robbing it of its Escondido style sandbanks. Of far greater current concern is the Escalera Nautica (nautical ladder), proposed for the Baja Peninsula. Mexico's tourist board plan is to construct a marina every 160km (100mi) along the Pacific and Gulf of California coasts of Baja, enticing North American sailors to new, undeveloped areas. Hotels and golf courses are part of the huge building program, designed to attract the affluent tourist dollar. Escalera Nautica obviously has serious environmental repercussions and five marinas would be

Surfrider Foundation involvement in marine reserve designation of Tres Palmas, Puerto Rico has undoubtedly helped preserve dwindling populations of specific corals such as elkhorn.

built across world-class points, including Punta Abreojos, Santa Rosalillita and Scorpion Bay. Fortunately for surfers, a flotilla of environmental campaigners have raised intelligent objections and exposed flaws in the $1.6 billion "ecocidal" project, forcing a temporary stay of execution.

Tourism has also had a major affect on Caribbean coastal erosion, perpetrating mass mangrove destruction for beach resorts, while coral sand is regularly used as a building material. Tres Palmas in Rincon, Puerto Rico has been declared a marine reserve after Surfrider

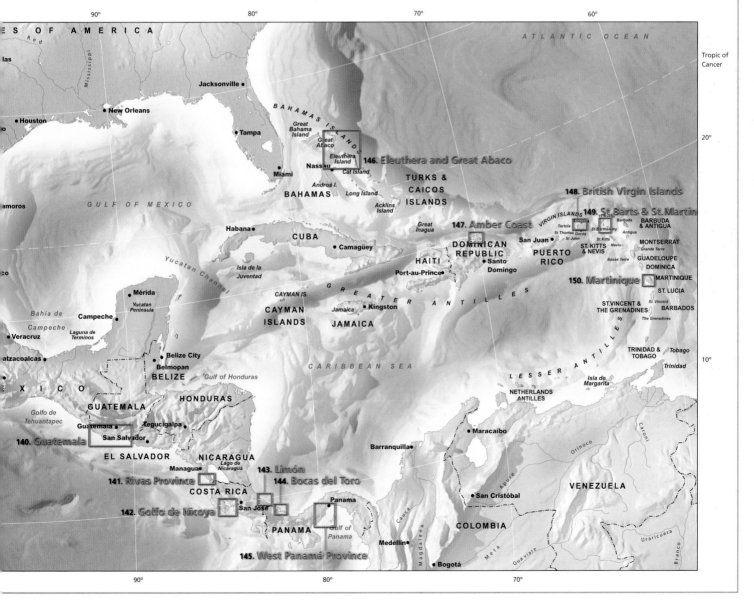

Foundation lobbying thwarted a proposed hotel and condominium project. The great waves and small, country town environment will be preserved, along with one of the last strongholds for elkhorn coral.

The US Virgin Islands banned cruise ships from anchoring in their water as they were destroying the reefs with heavy anchors. The British Virgin Islands saw this as an opportunity to gain some tourist dollars and the same ships are now destroying their reefs instead. Marina development in the Caribbean has been rampant, but as of yet few surf spots have been lost as a result.

# Surf Travel Resources

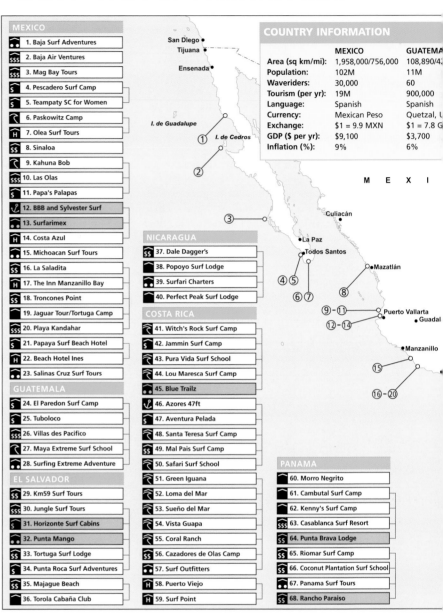

**MEXICO**
- 1. Baja Surf Adventures
- 2. Baja Air Ventures
- 3. Mag Bay Tours
- 4. Pescadero Surf Camp
- 5. Teampaty SC for Women
- 6. Paskowitz Camp
- 7. Olea Surf Tours
- 8. Sinaloa
- 9. Kahuna Bob
- 10. Las Olas
- 11. Papa's Palapas
- 12. BBB and Sylvester Surf
- 13. Surfarimex
- 14. Costa Azul
- 15. Michoacan Surf Tours
- 16. La Saladita
- 17. The Inn Manzanillo Bay
- 18. Troncones Point
- 19. Jaguar Tour/Tortuga Camp
- 20. Playa Kandahar
- 21. Papaya Surf Beach Hotel
- 22. Beach Hotel Ines
- 23. Salinas Cruz Surf Tours

**GUATEMALA**
- 24. El Paredon Surf Camp
- 25. Tuboloco
- 26. Villas des Pacifico
- 27. Maya Extreme Surf School
- 28. Surfing Extreme Adventure

**EL SALVADOR**
- 29. Km59 Surf Tours
- 30. Jungle Surf Tours
- 31. Horizonte Surf Cabins
- 32. Punta Mango
- 33. Tortuga Surf Lodge
- 34. Punta Roca Surf Adventures
- 35. Majague Beach
- 36. Torola Cabaña Club

**NICARAGUA**
- 37. Dale Dagger's
- 38. Popoyo Surf Lodge
- 39. Surfari Charters
- 40. Perfect Peak Surf Lodge

**COSTA RICA**
- 41. Witch's Rock Surf Camp
- 42. Jammin Surf Camp
- 43. Pura Vida Surf School
- 44. Lou Maresca Surf Camp
- 45. Blue Trailz
- 46. Azores 47ft
- 47. Aventura Pelada
- 48. Santa Teresa Surf Camp
- 49. Mal Pais Surf Camp
- 50. Safari Surf School
- 51. Green Iguana
- 52. Loma del Mar
- 53. Sueño del Mar
- 54. Vista Guapa
- 55. Coral Ranch
- 56. Cazadores de Olas Camp
- 57. Surf Outfitters
- 58. Puerto Viejo
- 59. Surf Point

**PANAMA**
- 60. Morro Negrito
- 61. Cambutal Surf Camp
- 62. Kenny's Surf Camp
- 63. Casablanca Surf Resort
- 64. Punta Brava Lodge
- 65. Riomar Surf Camp
- 66. Coconut Plantation Surf School
- 67. Panama Surf Tours
- 68. Rancho Paraiso

**COUNTRY INFORMATION**

| | MEXICO | GUATEMA |
| --- | --- | --- |
| Area (sq km/mi): | 1,958,000/756,000 | 108,890/4... |
| Population: | 102M | 11M |
| Waveriders: | 30,000 | 60 |
| Tourism (per yr): | 19M | 900,000 |
| Language: | Spanish | Spanish |
| Currency: | Mexican Peso | Quetzal, U |
| Exchange: | $1 = 9.9 MXN | $1 = 7.8 G |
| GDP ($ per yr): | $9,100 | $3,700 |
| Inflation (%): | 9% | 6% |

Map labels: San Diego, Tijuana, Ensenada, I. de Guadalupe, I. de Cedros, M E X I, Culiacán, La Paz, Todos Santos, Mazatlán, Puerto Vallarta, Guadal, Manzanillo

Above – **Rainy season turns roads to porridge, drastically cutting access to many Central American coastlines. A capable 4WD is indispensible.**

Right – **Cheap and dependable. Buses ponderously ply the highways between major centers.**

CHRISSY DOLLIMORE

## Access

Central America is renowned for having an unreliable transport system, poor roads and regular diversions down dried up riverbeds. In reality, Mexico's primary public transport, the bus, runs to a strict timetable, and bus travel throughout the region is dependable, albeit slow.

In the more isolated areas, roads deteriorate into ungraded tracks, becoming impassable in the wet season for all but the best 4x4's, plus the threat of side road banditry prevents most travel at night.

Cheap and reliable buses work well between major centres of population, but a lack of coastal roads means only a 4WD, hiking or a boat enables further progress to more remote breaks. Offshore Panama and El Salvador are probably best accessed with the aid of guides and organised trips with local surf camps.

Caribbean Islands generally have a reasonable road network, allowing a person with a rental car access to much of the coastline. Hiking into the more inaccessible spots may be possible, but private property is an issue, often belonging to exclusive resorts. Getting to some of

AMEZAGA

the outer islands or reefs via rental boats is generally expensive and whilst inter-island ferries exist, transport networks to and on the smaller islands are generally pretty poor.

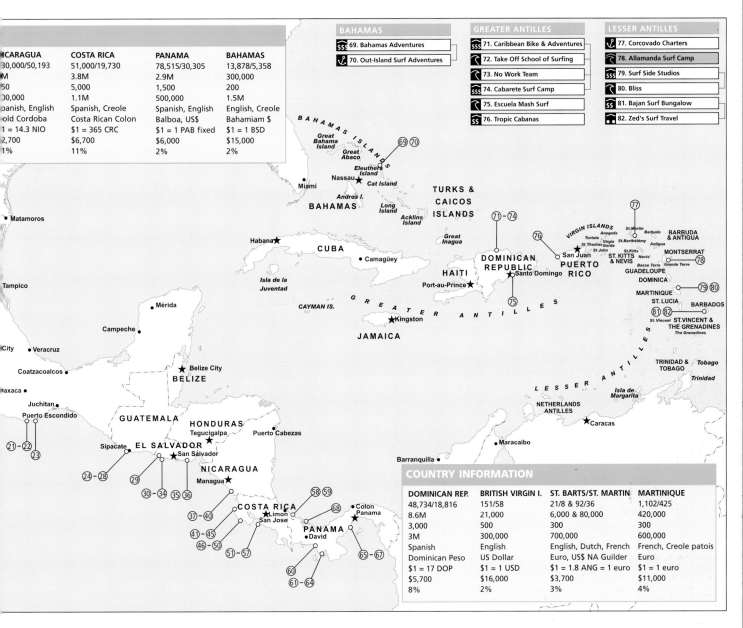

| CARAGUA | COSTA RICA | PANAMA | BAHAMAS |
|---|---|---|---|
| 30,000/50,193 | 51,000/19,730 | 78,515/30,305 | 13,878/5,358 |
| M | 3.8M | 2.9M | 300,000 |
| 50 | 5,000 | 1,500 | 200 |
| 00,000 | 1.1M | 500,000 | 1.5M |
| panish, English | Spanish, Creole | Spanish, English | English, Creole |
| old Cordoba | Costa Rican Colon | Balboa, US$ | Bahamiam $ |
| 1 = 14.3 NIO | $1 = 365 CRC | $1 = 1 PAB fixed | $1 = 1 BSD |
| 2,700 | $6,700 | $6,000 | $15,000 |
| 1% | 11% | 2% | 2% |

**BAHAMAS**
- 69. Bahamas Adventures
- 70. Out-Island Surf Adventures

**GREATER ANTILLES**
- 71. Caribbean Bike & Adventures
- 72. Take Off School of Surfing
- 73. No Work Team
- 74. Cabarete Surf Camp
- 75. Escuela Mash Surf
- 76. Tropic Cabanas

**LESSER ANTILLES**
- 77. Corcovado Charters
- 78. Allamanda Surf Camp
- 79. Surf Side Studios
- 80. Bliss
- 81. Bajan Surf Bungalow
- 82. Zed's Surf Travel

**COUNTRY INFORMATION**

| | DOMINICAN REP. | BRITISH VIRGIN I. | ST. BARTS/ST. MARTIN | MARTINIQUE |
|---|---|---|---|---|
| | 48,734/18,816 | 151/58 | 21/8 & 92/36 | 1,102/425 |
| | 8.6M | 21,000 | 6,000 & 80,000 | 420,000 |
| | 3,000 | 500 | 300 | 300 |
| | 3M | 300,000 | 700,000 | 600,000 |
| | Spanish | English | English, Dutch, French | French, Creole patois |
| | Dominican Peso | US Dollar | Euro, US$ NA Guilder | Euro |
| | $1 = 17 DOP | $1 = 1 USD | $1 = 1.8 ANG = 1 euro | $1 = 1 euro |
| | $5,700 | $16,000 | $3,700 | $11,000 |
| | 8% | 2% | 3% | 4% |

## Hazards

Sharks are common across Central America and The Caribbean, however attacks are rare. Mexico has the highest figures, including a 100% fatality rate in the eastern state of Quintana Roo, while Panama comes a clear second in total incidences. The Bahamas follows the Florida trend of a high number of attacks but only one fatality, and the Greater Antilles figures report more deaths but not in the last 60 years. For such a vast ocean playground, the Lesser Antilles shark attack figures are virtually negligible. Coral is prevalent and an issue with regards to infection, especially if you have the misfortune to land on some fire coral. Getting caught in the path of a major hurricane could be the biggest hazard of the region, often accompanied by floods and mudslides. In Central America, armed robbery and occasional politically motivated kidnappings should not be discounted. Officials are often corrupt and bribes are commonly accepted in many countries.

Central America has some well-established surfing communities where localism exists in isolated pockets. Often initiated by ex pat Americans, it should be taken into consideration that violence is often tolerated by the authorities in these semi lawless states. In more popular areas and well-known breaks, like Puerto Escondido in Mexico, a hardcore local community enforce line-up etiquette and punish any lack of respect with blatant drop ins! Puerto Rico is a renowned surf zone and acts of localism can include theft from cars. Across the Windward and Leeward Islands, localism is sporadic, with isolated, classy spots like Cane Garden Bay on Tortola, prone to some hassle when swell tracking, mainland Americans fly in to compete with the local islanders. Guadeloupe and Barbados are the most consistent islands in this chain and have the biggest surfing populations, leading to pressure at the banner spots.

UNITED STATES OF AMERICA

MEXICO
NORTH

BAJA CALIFORNIA

# 137. Central Baja

**Open Doors**

JOHN CALLAHAN

**Summary**

+ QUALITY RIGHT POINTBREAKS
+ NATIVIDAD TUBING WAVES
+ MILES OF UNCROWDED SURF
+ OFFSHORE TRADEWINDS ON
  S FACING SPOTS

− LACK OF LEFTS
− SURPRISINGLY COLD WATER
− BAD ROADS AND REMOTE
  NATIVIDAD
− BASIC ACCOMMODATION

GILLES CALVET

**B**aja California is a long, narrow peninsula extending south of San Diego, barely linked to the Mexican mainland by a thin strip of land. Dominated by a spine of mountains, this unique region separates the Pacific Ocean and the Gulf of California (aka Sea of Cortez), resulting in one of the most interesting and diverse geographical areas of the world. This arid, rocky finger has long been a playground for surfers from "Upper California" seeking righthand pointbreak perfection, without the urban crowds that dominate the USA line-ups. With a sub-tropical climate and 4,800km (3000mi) of relatively untouched beaches and coastline, Baja has been the cause of wars and disputes over the centuries. Long frequented by pirates, Baja California is today a favourite destination for adventurous surfers looking for the treasure chest of waves that adorn the Pacific Coast. Recent development plans to

**Natividad**

HUMP

build a string of harbours, marinas and tourist resorts not more than a day's sail apart, along both coasts of the peninsula have foundered (but not sunk) under a withering environmentalist backlash.

While Northern Baja picks up both N and S swell, Punta Eugenia and Cedros Island conspire to block southerly swells from much of Bahia Sebastian Vizcaino. **Punta Canoas** is one of the last spots able to pick up SW

## TRAVEL INFORMATION

**Population:** 3.1M (Baja)
**Coastline:** 4800km (3000mi)
**Contests:** None
**Other Resources:** Video: Just Surfing
bajaairventures.com
bajasurfadventures.com
bajaquest.com
baja.com

**Getting There** – Get a tourist card ($20 fee) and have it validated after entering Mexico. Drive down from San Diego (10h) or fly to Guerrero Negro (GUB). Fly to Natividad from San Diego with Baja Air Ventures ($945/4 days all-inclusive) or boat from Punta Eugenia. Fly to Cedros from Guerrero Negro.

**Getting Around** – The Trans-Peninsula Highway is Baja California's lifeline, linking the tracks that lead to the coast. Punta Rosalillita can be reached with a standard car, but a high-clearance vehicle and/or 4WD is essential for many other spots. Rental cars are only available in major cities (Tijuana, Loreto, La Paz) usually from $40/d.

**Lodging and Food** – Camping is the only type of accommodation available close to the breaks. If you're willing to drive for an hour's , there's several more comfortable places to stay for around $25 in Guerrero Negro (El Morro) or try the hotels in Bahia Tortuga. Fresh Lobster & ice-cold Pacificos make a stylin' surf meal.

**Weather** – The climate of Baja California is generally hot and dry, but since it lies north of the Tropic of Cancer, it also has a cold season. The weather in the central area is characteristically cool and damp being a coastal desert climate, with the Pacific Ocean largely controlling the temperature. The winter is cold, with periodic rains, and the summer is long and cool. The hurricane season, stretching from June to October, may bring in some rain. If it gets really hot inland, the nights will get chilly on the coast (10°C/50°F). The cool ocean waters of the area limit summer hurricanes' northward trajectories.

**Nature and Culture** – Besides fishing, main visitor attractions are the whale-watching tours to the nearby lagoons (Laguana Ojo de Liebre ) between January and April, exploring nearby Sierras for Indian art, and checking out Exportadora de Sal, the largest salt-producing plant in the world. Nothing to do but surf on Natividad.

**Hazards and Hassles** – Roads are bad, gas stations are rare you may get stuck or lost for a while. Federales will stop cars for any reason and suggest paying a fine directly to them. It might be advantageous to suggest paying at the station.

**Handy Hints** – Take all equipment including 4/3 wetsuits in winter. Spanish is the official language in Mexico, however, English is widely spoken on the Baja peninsula. US dollars are accepted everywhere. Local fishermen know the ocean better than anyone, ask them for tips.

| WEATHER STATISTICS | J/F | M/A | M/J | J/A | S/O | N/D |
|---|---|---|---|---|---|---|
| total rainfall (mm) | 35 | 15 | 5 | 15 | 75 | 30 |
| consistency (days/mth) | 4 | 3 | 1 | 2 | 4 | 4 |
| min temp (°C/°F) | 10/50 | 12/54 | 16/61 | 20/68 | 20/68 | 17/63 |
| max temp (°C/°F) | 21/70 | 24/75 | 27/80 | 30/86 | 28/82 | 24/75 |

Open Doors

JOHN MATTHEWS

**SPOT DESCRIPTION**

| Spot | Size | Btm | Type |
|---|---|---|---|
| ① | 8/2 | ● | ◨ |
| ② | 8/2 | ● | ◨ |
| ③ | 8/2 | ● | ◨ |
| ④ | 8/2 | ● | ◨ |
| ⑤ | 8/2 | ◐ | ◨ |
| ⑥ | 6/2 | ● | ◨ |
| ⑦ | 8/2 | ● | ◨ |
| ⑧ | 8/2 | ● | ◨ |
| ⑨ | 6/2 | ● | ◨ |
| ⑩ | 10/2 | ● | ◨ |
| ⑪ | 8/2 | ● | ◨ |
| ⑫ | 8/2 | ◐ | ▭ |
| ⑬ | 10/2 | ◐ | ▭ |
| ⑭ | 8/2 | ● | ▭ |

option head to Isla Natividad. Located on the east side of the island, the dredging barrels of **Open Doors** are offshore every afternoon, but be prepared for powerful, board-snapping lefts. Other breaks include Siren Bay's big wave option, Old Mans and Frijole. Back on the mainland, **Bahia Tortuga** is a seldom surfed area with numerous breaks. From there, air and water get warmer as you enter Baja California Sur.

swells, and enjoys consistent, clean surf, thanks to high cliffs offering good wind protection. **Punta Blanca** is one of the series of seven major points known as the Seven Sisters. It's a fine right pointbreak, working best on a W swell and is definitely among those requiring a 4WD. Starting from the rights of **Punta Cono**, only W to NW winter swells are reliable. **Punta Maria** is a class act; a long wrapping right, which can only be seen on major W swells that usually coincide with winter's offshore winds. **El Cardon** point may be one of the smaller points in the area, but rides are actually really long and sand dunes provide protection from the afternoon winds. Next door, **Punta Lobos** looks like an elongated version of **El Cordon**, complete with wind protection and an even sandier bottom. Sharks have been spotted among the guaranteed numbers of surfers in the line-up. Yet another good right pointbreak, **Punta Negra** enjoys offshore winds early and late in the day during the winter months. Just up the (bad) road from Punta Rosalillita, **Puerto San Andrés** receives strong offshores that attract a few windsurfers and surfers looking for real hollow waves. Whenever a

P unta Eugenia and Cedros Island make the most of the southerly swells to hit this central area. Only spots above Punta Blanca or below Natividad can rely on the consistent, long-travelled, clean S-SW swells coming from the South Pacific. The seven sisters only wake up when winter's North Pacific W-NW swells hit their shores. Winds blow from the NW all year long,

| SURF STATISTICS | J F | M A | M J | J A | S O | N D |
|---|---|---|---|---|---|---|
| dominant swell | W-NW | W-NW | SW-W | SW-W | W-NW | W-NW |
| swell size (ft) | 4 | 3-4 | 2-3 | 3 | 3-4 | 4 |
| consistency (%) | 80 | 75 | 55 | 55 | 65 | 70 |
| dominant wind | NW-N | W-NW | NW | W-NW | W-N | NW-N |
| average force | F4 | F4 | F4 | F3-F4 | F3-F4 | F4 |
| consistency (%) | 74 | 80 | 72 | 76 | 85 | 72 |
| water temp (°C/°F) | 11/52 | 13/55 | 16/61 | 20/68 | 20/68 | 17/63 |
| wetsuit | 🧍 | 🧍 | 🧍 | 🧍 | 🧍 | 🧍 |

veering more N between November and February with the strongest winds blowing during spring. The strong winds cause upwelling, which makes for surprisingly cold water considering the latitude. Tide range reaches 2m (6ft); get a tide table before leaving.

Natividad

GILLES CALVET

really big W swell comes in, **Punta Santa Rosalillita** is an obvious choice with the point situated to the north of the bay delivering truly classic, extra-long rides and providing several other breaks along the bay. A traveller's favourite, this small fishing village is earmarked for both marina development (construction of breakwalls in the surf zone has already begun) and as an entry point for a road connection to the Sea of Cortez. Punta Rosarito is so consistent, it has earned the nickname of **The Wall**, but winds, even if offshore, can get too strong to surf. Cruise around El Tomatal fish camp in the area known as **Miller's Landing** to find the nice cobblestone right point and a neighbouring left. A big island like Isla Cedros seems attractive but it's really windy and breaks like **Playa Elefante** are only of medium quality. If flying is an

Chapala

BAJA CALIFORNIA

Punta Canoas ①

Parador Punta Prieta

Bahia Blanca

Punta Blanca ①

Punta Prieta

El Cardon

Bahia Falsa

Punta Cono ③
Punta Maria ④

El Maron

El Cardón ⑤
Punta Lobos ⑥

Pta Rocosa

Punta Negra ⑦

Rosarito

Puerto San Andrés ⑧

Pta Rosarito

Punta Sta Rosalillita ⑨

The Wall ⑩

El Tomatal

Miller's Landing ⑪

Ejido Morelos

ISLAS SAN BENITO

Morro Sto Domingo

Playa Elefante ⑫

ISLA CEDROS

Car Vargas 1135m

Cedros

BAHIA SEBASTIAN VIZCAINO

Canal de Keller

Guerrero Negro

ISLA NATIVIDAD

Pta Eugenio

BAJA CALIFORNIA SUR

Open Doors ⑬

Pta Rompiente

Pta Malarrimo

Laguna Ojo de Liebre

Bahia Tortugas ⑭

Bahia Tortugas

Cabo Tortolo

MEXICO
SOUTH

• Acapulco

# 138. Nayarit

TOM KÖRBER

## Summary

+ SURFABLE YEAR ROUND
+ TOP LONGBOARD SPOTS
+ SURF SCHOOLS, CAMPS & BOATS
+ RESORTS OPTION
+ RELATIVELY SAFE

− LACK OF "MEXICAN JUICE"
− RESTRICTED ACCESS SPOTS
− SOME SHARKY LOCATIONS
− BUGS FROM HELL IN SAN BLAS
− RAINY PEAK SURF SEASON

Sayulita

TOM KÖRBER

Located in western Mexico on the Pacific Ocean, the State of Nayarit is an extremely scenic area, with lush tropical jungles, mangroves and deciduous forests lining the coast. To the east and south lie high volcanic mountains, from which several rivers flow to the ocean, cutting the landscape into valleys and deep gorges along the way. Mostly undeveloped, the coastline of Nayarit has attracted hardcore surfers since the mid '60s. For those pioneers, the chance of scoring an epic session at San Blas' Matanchen Bay, known as the longest right in the world, was

TOM KÖRBER

worth the suffering inflicted by the "jejenes" (local sand flies) and mosquitoes. But things have changed with the fast rise of Puerto Vallarta, once a tiny fishing village in the neighbouring state of Jalisco, now attracting 500,000 tourists each year.

## TRAVEL INFORMATION

**Population:** 930,000
**Coastline:** 289km (180mi)
**Contests:** Sayulita (Oct)
**Other Resources:**
Video: Cosmic Children
amigosurfmexico.com
surflasolas.com
visitnayarit.com
sayulita.com

**Getting There** – A $20 tourist card is required on arrival. Over 450 flights a week serve Gustavo Diaz Ordaz International Airport (PVR). From Mexico City, fly with Aeromexico or Mexicana Airlines ($250r/t, $90/boardbag should only apply for int'l flights) or a 13hrs bus ride ($80o/w). It's a challenging 2-3 days drive from the USA.

**Getting Around** – Sayulita is a good 1h drive north of Puerto Vallarta on Highway 200; ride the bus ($4) or rent a car in PV ($55/d). Regular local buses cover the whole Bahia de Banderas area and accept surfboards. Punta de Mita is 45min from Puerto Vallarta. Bahia de Banderas' northern spots are accessed from Destiladeras or Corral del Risco for boat-ins.

**Lodging and Food** – Resorts are plentiful in San Blas and PV. In Sayulita try Bungalows Las Gaviotas ($25/dble) or Las Olas all women

surfcamp ($2000/week). Viva Vallarta resort faces Punta del Burro, Punta de Mita's Meson de Mita is $40/dble and Surfamigo's Yacht Sylvester is $1,500/wk all inc. A dinner of tasty specialties costs $10.

**Weather** – Located right under the Tropic of Cancer, Nayarit is blessed with warm temperatures year round. Abundant rains in the summer, mixed with intense sunshine, regularly take temperatures beyond 30°C (86°F). The mountains generate cooler breezes at night, making the climate more bearable than further south. The tropical rainy season starts mid-June and stretches to the end of October bringing heavy rain and humidity, particularly in August and September. Winter sees daytime temperatures around 27°C (80°F), but nights get cooler, down to 15°C (59°F). Hurricane Kenna's ravages in October 2002 showed that this stretch of coast is vulnerable despite having been spared for the previous 74 years. Most of the time, hurricanes stay out at sea or track northwest towards Baja California, or west towards Hawaii. With water temps of 28°C (82°F), in the summer all that is needed are boardshorts but it gets down to 22°C (73°F) in the winter, and a spring suit is advisable.

**Nature and Culture** – Sayulita is a laid-back city. San Blas is Nayarit's tourism centre and starting point for jungle river boating to La Tovara springs. Check out remote beaches, or snorkel/dive around Islas Marietas. Along the Malecón (downtown PV), a strip of restaurants, bars and clubs will provide all night entertainment.

**Hazards and Hassles** – Unlike other Mexican breaks of bone-crushing fame, these are more adapted to intermediate level surfers. Locals don't always see the influx of surfers positively, but crowd levels are low on spots requiring a boat. San Blas surroundings are infested with jejenes (tiny sand gnats) that come out at night and provoke intense itching.

**Handy Hints** – Avoid Puerto Vallarta's polluted waters. Recommended quiver includes a longboard or fish rather than a gun. Equipment and rentals are available at Coral Reef Surf Shop in Bucerias or Acción Tropical Surf Shop in La Cruz de Huanacaxtle. Puerto Vallarta (Jalisco State) is 1h ahead of Sayulita and Punta de Mita (Nayarit).

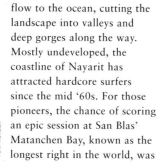

| WEATHER STATISTICS | J/F | M/A | M/J | J/A | S/O | N/D |
|---|---|---|---|---|---|---|
| total rainfall (mm) | 25 | 40 | 100 | 160 | 230 | 75 |
| consistency (days/mth) | 2 | 4 | 8 | 12 | 14 | 5 |
| min temp (°C/°F) | 16/61 | 18/64 | 23/74 | 24/75 | 24/75 | 19/66 |
| max temp (°C/°F) | 26/79 | 27/80 | 30/86 | 32/90 | 32/90 | 28/82 |

Surf camps and schools have proliferated in the last ten years and even a remote offshore island surfbreak like **Hammerhead** can be surfed from surf charters leaving from Nuevo Vallarta. Unlike the benchmark Mexican beachbreak of Puerto Escondido, the banks of **Los Corchos** are powerless, but the 'playa' still gets good occasionally. After passing the resort town of San Blas and its poor beachbreak, **Stoner's Point** is the first classic pointbreak, memorably ridden on a perfect day by Jeff Hakman and Jock Sutherland in the film *Cosmic Children*. *The Guinness Book of Records* certifies **Las Islitas** as the longest wave in the world, covering 5,700ft (2250m), as it wraps into Matanchen Bay. It's a mellow wall with occasional tubing sections and if still able to feel the legs at the end of a ride, make the long walk back to the point. Unfortunately new constructions mean it hardly ever breaks and only a huge S swell will do, along with a very long board. The lefts of **Aticama**'s pointbreak are much more consistent and of excellent quality, but being so close to a fishery there's plenty of sharks drawn to the area. Just as good but a little less sharky, despite its rivermouth, the **Santa Cruz** left pointbreak peels perfectly along a cliff, with rides over 600ft (200m). The point needs some swell, so check the rivermouth if it's too small. The breaks around Chacala are best reached by boat, and finding the way to the lefts of Caleta or **Lolas** is usually rewarding. After Santa Cruz comes San Francisco, or **San Pancho** as the locals call it. Close to the huge Costa Azul resort sits a fast lefthand reefbreak that can hold some size and gets hollow around low tide. **Ostiones** is accessible by sea or land (long walk) and the lefts are worth checking on a big swell. **Punta Sayulita**'s good wave reputation has lead to the place turning into a mini surf city. The reefs are mellow and ideally suited to beginners and longboarders. With three quality breaks including Anclote and the long workable rights of **El Faro**, Punta de Mita would be a great hub, but since the point was purchased to build the luxurious Four Seasons Resort, access is thoroughly guarded and requires a long paddle or a boat. Corral del Risco's beach, El Anclote, is the place to go to hire a "panga" (local 23ft/7m fishing boat) at the small harbour's Fishermen Cooperative. As the swell wraps into the Bahia de Banderas, Mexico's largest bay, it hits a series of reefs producing clean, smaller waves on a 9.5km (6mi) long stretch of coast called **Costa Banderas**. This set-up favours rights and la Lancha, Punta Burros, Pools and Destiladeras are all worthy spots. Boat access only except for Destiladeras. Puerto Vallarta is too deep in the bay to receive much swell, except on big days when the beaches at El Tizate and the Holiday Inn in the hotel zone are pumping. The beachbreak at the rivermouth south of town is also worth checking. Having arrived at Boca de Tomatlan, on the south shore, a panga water taxi can be taken to **Quimixto**, a popular local beachbreak. The **Islas Marietas** are a longer boat ride 8km (5mi) away from Punta de Mita where the surf seldom breaks but fortunately great snorkelling, diving and whale watching make up for the lack of waves.

The state of Nayarit receives consistent, reliable swells most of the year. Winter (November-March) is the best season for Banderas Bay, when W and NW Aleutian swells will wrap into the bay, losing some size but cleaning-up with the northerly offshores. Occasional W swells will provide the biggest conditions on most spots. The summer surf season will start after the transition months of March and April, which are usually windier than the rest of the year. South Pacific activity and seasonal hurricanes push-in long period swells from SW to S directions, although Nayarit seems to lack a bit of size and power compared to southern Mexican states. For northern breaks, summer is a more consistent time than winter, with regular swell in the 4-8ft (1.2-2.5m) range and excellent direction for the lefthand breaks north of Punta de Mita. Northerly winds prevail in the winter season before progressively shifting to a W-NW direction that will continue all summer. The tidal range hovers around 3ft (1m) and there are usually 2 tides daily.

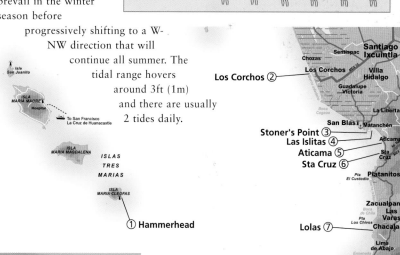

| SURF STATISTICS | J F | M A | M J | J A | S O | N D |
|---|---|---|---|---|---|---|
| dominant swell | NW | S-SW | S-SW | S-W | S-W | NW |
| swell size (ft) | 3 | 3-4 | 4 | 5 | 4-5 | 3-4 |
| consistency (%) | 65 | 75 | 80 | 80 | 80 | 65 |
| dominant wind | NW-N | W-N | W-NW | W-NW | W-N | NW-NE |
| average force | F3-F4 | F3 | F3-F4 | F3 | F3 | F3 |
| consistency (%) | 71 | 86 | 73 | 49 | 60 | 82 |
| water temp (°C/°F) | 23/74 | 23/74 | 25/77 | 28/82 | 28/82 | 26/79 |
| wetsuit | | | | | | |

| SPOT DESCRIPTION | | | |
|---|---|---|---|
| Spot | Size | Btm | Type |
| ① | • | | • |
| ② | 8/2 | | |
| ③ | 10/3 | | |
| ④ | 10/2 | | |
| ⑤ | 10/2 | | |
| ⑥ | 10/3 | | |
| ⑦ | 10/2 | | |
| ⑧ | 10/2 | | |
| ⑨ | 10/4 | | |
| ⑩ | 8/2 | | |
| ⑪ | 10/2 | | |
| ⑫ | 10/2 | | |
| ⑬ | 8/2 | | |
| ⑭ | 8/2 | | |

Map labels: Santiago Ixcuintla, Sentipac, Chozas, Los Corchos, Villa Hidalgo, Guadalupe Victoria, Isla San Juanito, ISLA MARIA MADRE, Hospital, To San Francisco La Cruz de Huanacaxtle, Boca Cegada, La Libertad, San Blas, Matanchén, Los Corchos ②, Stoner's Point ③, Las Islitas ④, Aticama ⑤, Aticama, Sta Cruz, Sta Cruz ⑥, ISLA MARIA MAGDALENA, ISLAS TRES MARIAS, Pta El Custodio, Platanitos, Zacualpan, Las Varas, Boca de Chila, Pta Los Chivos, Chacala, ISLA MARIA CLEOFAS, Lolas ⑦, ① Hammerhead, Lima de Abajo, Pta Raza, Ensenada El Tecuan, Los Ayala, San Pancho ⑧, Lo de Marcos, To Isla Maria Madre, Ostiones ⑨, San Francisco, Sayulita, Punta Sayulita ⑩, NAYARIT, San Juan de Abajo, Ensenada Litigu, Pta De Mita, La Cruz de Huanacaxtle, Bucerías, El Faro ⑪, Nuevo Vallarta, Ixtapa, Islas Marietas ⑭, Pta Las Cargaderas, To Isla Maria Madre, Las Juntas, Costa Banderas ⑫, Bahia De Banderas, Puerto Vallarta, Quimixto ⑬, Mismaloya, Pta La Iglesia, Chimo, Yelapa, Cabo Corrientes, JALISCO, El Tuito

Las Islitas

JOHN CALLAHAN

MEXICO
SOUTH

Acapulco

# 139. West Guerrero

PAUL FARRARIS

**Summary**

+ LONG SURF SEASON
+ SALADITA LONGBOARD HEAVEN
+ SURFBREAKS GALORE
+ GOOD WEATHER

− NO STANDOUT SHORTBOARD WAVE
− EXPENSIVE RESORTS
− BANDIDOS AT WORK
− RAINY SEASON, HURRICANE RISK
− BAD WATER QUALITY

The state of Guerrero is still haunted by the ghost of Petacalco, an insane, world-class right, in a land of mellow lefts. It's southern neighbour Oaxaca, is home of the most famous Mexican wave, Puerto Escondido, but it was Guerrero that catapulted Mexico onto the world tourism stage. The state became increasingly popular in the 1940s with the development of Acapulco, still the #1 tourist destination in the country today. In the 1970s the federal government tried to repeat Acapulco's rapid growth, and promoted Ixtapa Zihuatanejo as the place to go. Surfing began in the extremely mountainous state in the 1960s, with exploration

JOHN CALLAHAN

based along a narrow, 500km (312mi) long, coastal strip. In the '70s surf explorers Naughton and Peterson unveiled Petacalco perfection to the world.

The long, intense righthand barrels could be counted among the planet's best surf, but expansion of the neighbouring port of Lázaro Cárdenas turned the wave into an ugly close-out. **Petacalco** has recently risen from the ashes and is now rideable on huge swells but has not yet reclaimed its legendary shape and speed. The industrial city of Lázaro Cárdenas receives some thumping surf along a dozen jetties and **El Faro** is the most commonly surfed spot. With no accommodation available in El Capire, **The Ranch** remained a secret for many years. Today surfers staying in nearby resorts regularly drive or boat up here to enjoy very consistent rights and lefts that hold up to double overhead. Longboarders will prefer **La Saladita**, half an hour south.

## TRAVEL INFORMATION

**Population:** 3.1M
**Coastline:** 9,330km (5,800mi)
**Contests:** Escolleras, P.Linda, Loma Bonita
**Other Resources:**
*Video:* Siestas & Olas, The Far Shore
surf-mexico.com/surfing/ Guerrero
zihua-ixtapa.com/

**Getting There** – An $18 tourist card is required upon entering the country. Aeromexico and Mexicana fly to Zihua (ZIH) and Acapulco (ACA) from Mexico City, Alaska Airlines has a direct flight from Los Angeles to Zihua. Buses link Mexico City to Zihua (11h, $50) and Acapulco (7h, $30). Acapulco is 5h drive from Zihua ($15). Dep tax $17.

**Getting Around** – Booking a car in advance may end up being cheaper than picking one up upon arrival ($60/d). A 4WD isn't necessary for most beaches. Bring portable surf racks. Driving at night isn't safe, but during daylight hours, the Green Angels are there to assist motorists. Taxi fares are fixed within cities. Buses are dirt cheap.

**Lodging and Food** – Winter is peak season with top prices. Itxapa is packed with luxury resorts;

Zihuatanejo is more accessible with doubles around $30. Troncones area offers plenty of surf facing accommodations. Try Troncones SC, Casa Delfin Sonriente or the Saladita SC (all around $65). Enjoy shrimp and fish tacos or tiritas (fish & onions).

**Weather** – Guerrero enjoys a semi-tropical climate year round with an average of 300 sunny days a year. In the winter months, between December and April the daytime temperature hovers around 31°C (88°F) with the nights going down 22°C (72°F). During this time there is little to no rainfall. The rainy season stretches through summer, between late June and mid-October. Precipitation usually occurs in the evenings or nights except during peak hurricane season, in August and September. Hurricane Pauline, the most destructive hurricane to strike the Pacific Coast of Mexico in the past 50 years, ripped through Acapulco in 1997. Zihuatanejo has been relatively spared since Madeline brought 230km/h (145mph) winds in 1976. The annual water temperature averages 26°C (79°F), so no neoprene required.

**Nature and Culture** – Explore the cave in Troncones. Fishing and hiking is available in the surrounding area. In Zihuatanejo check out the central market and walk over to the lighthouse (El Faro) from Las Gatas. Ixtapa is a modern resort with many nightclubs (Christine Club). Take a trip to the colonial town of Petatlán.

**Hazards and Hassles** – The mellow waves of Guerrero area should bring less damage to body and quiver than those of Puerto Escondido, but big days happen. Bandidos are known to work the Highway 200 at night; also be careful if camping. Take hurricane warnings seriously, winds over 200km/h (120mph) are no laughing matter.

**Handy Hints** – Take regular shortboard and a slightly longer board for bigger days. A longboard is the perfect tool on many waves in the area. Gear can be found at Catcha L'Ola Surf Shop in Ixtapa or Anfibios in Zihuatanejo. Rent boards at Jaguar Tours or The Inn at Manzanillo Bay. Jaguar Tours can organise surf lessons in Troncones.

| WEATHER STATISTICS | J/F | M/A | M/J | J/A | S/O | N/D |
|---|---|---|---|---|---|---|
| total rainfall (mm) | 5 | 0 | 160 | 250 | 270 | 25 |
| consistency (days/mth) | 0 | 0 | 6 | 11 | 11 | 1 |
| min temp (°C/°F) | 22/72 | 23/74 | 25/77 | 25/77 | 25/77 | 24/75 |
| max temp (°C/°F) | 31/88 | 31/88 | 32/90 | 33/92 | 32/90 | 32/90 |

A soft-breaking lefthand pointbreak nicknamed Ubilam as it breaks like a reverse Malibu. It's a long paddle to the point, but rides over a minute long are the usual reward. The left pointbreak at **Manzanillo** packs much more power, with steep drops and large barrels. Overhead days are safer as the wave breaks further away from the urchin-covered rocks. This is a surf rich area, with other points and a rivermouth as you head

PAUL FARRARIS

north. Just south of Manzanillo, **Troncones** is a 5km (3mi) long stretch of beach marked with rock outcrops that encourage sandbars. These bars create consistent peaks in the same spots. In Ixtapa, **Playa Linda** is usually mushy but the rivermouth can produce long left walls as the wave reels into a sandy lagoon. There's a ferry to Ixtapa Island, where there's rumours of a zipping right. **Escolleras** at Playa del Palmar benefits from currents running along the marina, which sometimes shape a tubular right, but it gets busy. **Playa las Gatas** was the cradle of Zihua's surfing. This tiny beach is reached after a long walk or paddle, the best option being to get a boat from the municipal pier. The left there needs a good amount of swell to break over a man-made reef, but there doesn't seem to be an upper size limit. There are more chances for a solitary surf at **Barra de Potosí**, but the break only goes off once or twice a year. There's a left and a right pointbreak but neither is really breathtaking. Less than 1h south of Zihua, **Loma Bonita** is usually a good

beachbreak with powerful waves, plus the option of La Barrita 2km (1.25mi) south. Many peaks line the coastal highway through Joluchuca, including **Playa Icacos** and Punta Japutica further south. **Papanoa** is an average beachbreak with fast walls, but tends to close-out. The set-ups are usually better around Tenexpa and Tetitlan. **Playa Boca Chica** is a consistent beachbreak surfable year round, and probably the last option before reaching Acapulco. Caca's Point is the only surfable spot within the Bay of Acapulco, otherwise there's more surf at Copa Cabana. At the northern end of **Revolcadero** beach is a big wave spot, rideable when the nearby beachbreaks of Punto Muerto and Playa Princess are closing out. Playa Bonfil's consistent beachbreak is directly in front of Acapulco Airport.

Guerrero can be considered a year round surfing destination. Southern Hemisphere weather systems and hurricanes provide the biggest swells between April and October. Offshore hurricanes will produce two days of pounding surf up to 10ft (3m), or messy, huge and rainy conditions if it gets too close. Unlike in neighbouring Oaxaca, huge rideable surf is not a common occurrence. Between November and March wave heights drop a notch – usually waist to head high. W-NW winds prevail all year, only July to September sees SE winds on a regular basis. Calms occur 10% of the time and in general, count on offshore/calm wind in the morning before an afternoon seabreeze comes in. Tidal range hardly ever goes over 2ft (0.6m).

JOHN CALLAHAN

| SURF STATISTICS | J F | M A | M J | J A | S O | N D |
|---|---|---|---|---|---|---|
| dominant swell | NW | S-SW | S-SW | S-W | S-W | NW |
| swell size (ft) | 3 | 4 | 5 | 6 | 5 | 4 |
| consistency (%) | 65 | 80 | 85 | 85 | 85 | 65 |
| dominant wind | W-NW | W-NW | W-NW | W-NW | W-NW | W-NW |
| average force | F3 | F3 | F3 | F3 | F3 | F3 |
| consistency (%) | 54 | 66 | 57 | 37 | 41 | 48 |
| water temp (°C/°F) | 26/79 | 25/77 | 26/79 | 27/80 | 27/80 | 26/79 |
| wetsuit | | | | | | |

**SPOT DESCRIPTION**

| Spot | Size | Btm | Type |
|---|---|---|---|
| ① | 12/3 | | |
| ② | 12/4 | | |
| ③ | 8/3 | | |
| ④ | 10/2 | | |
| ⑤ | 10/4 | | |
| ⑥ | 10/3 | | |
| ⑦ | 10/2 | | |
| ⑧ | 8/2 | | |
| ⑨ | 15/3 | | |
| ⑩ | 10/2 | | |
| ⑪ | 8/2 | | |
| ⑫ | 8/2 | | |
| ⑬ | 8/3 | | |
| ⑭ | 8/2 | | |
| ⑮ | 15/6 | | |

# 140. Guatemala

La Barra

ALL PHOTOS JAVIER AMEZAGA

**Summary**
+ HARDLY EVER FLAT
+ DRY SEASON OFFSHORE WINDS
+ COMPLETELY UNCROWDED
+ CHEAP LODGING & FOOD
+ AMAZING CULTURE AND PEOPLE

− BEACHBREAKS ONLY
− NO COASTAL ROAD
− LACK OF TOURISM INFRASTRUCTURE
− ONSHORE & RAINY SUMMER
− OCCASIONAL PETTY CRIME

Guatemala is a small country with striking contrasts between its topographic features. The Sierra Madre mountain range runs parallel to the Pacific with over thirty volcanoes and many peaks rising above 13,100ft (4,000m). But despite two-thirds of the country being mountainous and volcanic, not a single rock can be spotted along the 250km (156mi) coastline, making for a continuous stretch of mostly black sand beachbreaks, only interrupted by the occasional rivermouth. This is the main reason why travelling surfers predominantly consider Guatemala as a transit zone between the more challenging breaks of Mexico to the north and the clean pointbreaks of El Salvador to the south. The lack of coast roads means long drives between breaks, but few crowds to share the punchy beach and rivermouth peaks with. Guatemala was first surfed in the 1960s but it wasn't until 1984 that the first surfing contest was organised in Puerto San José. The last decade saw a steady group of some 100 local surfers

San Jose

hit the water on a regular basis and the birth of the first surf school, Maya Extreme.

Less than 10km (6mi) away from the Mexican border, **Ocos** provides the first surf opportunity where the rivermouth builds occasionally good sandbars. The beachbreak at **Tilapa** is easily accessed and is complimented by a rivermouth peak and an estuary.

## TRAVEL INFORMATION

**Population:** 790,000
**Coastline:** 400km (250mi) (Pacific Coast)
**Contests:** Puerto & Sipacate (Sept & Feb)
**Other Resources:**
elparedonsurfcamp. tripod.com
mayaextreme.com
virtualguatemala.com

**Getting There** – No visa required for most nationalities. Fly to Guatemala City (GUA). Grupo Taca is the national airline. Direct buses run to Puerto San José (2h) Iztapa (3h) and Monterrico (4h). Sipacate is a 2h drive from Guatemala City, or 3h by public transport with a connection in Escuintla. Dep tax is $30

**Getting Around** – The Carretera al Pacifico (CA-2) is a fast highway running parallel to the coast about 50km (31mi) inland. There's no proper coastal road, except for the Chulamar-Monterrico stretch. Rent a car ($370/week) to avoid the overcrowded "Chicken Bus".

**Lodging and Food** – The tourism infrastructure isn't fully developed on the coast and low-

standard hotels are the rule except in Chulamar, Iztapa and Monterrico. Check out the new Tuboloco surfcamp in Likin. El Parédon surfcamp ($5/d) offers basic accommodation in the village while its beachfront camp is being built. Complete meal=$10.

**Weather** – Guatemala is known as "The land of eternal spring" for the mild temperatures that bless the highlands all year long. Like the rest of the lowlands or "tierras calientes" (hot lands), the Pacific Coast swelters in tropical temperatures, often hovering above 35°C (95°F). The difference between the two seasons is dramatic. The rainy months run from May to October with maximum rainfalls in July and September (over 400mm/34in). The constant high humidity diminishes a little in the dry season from November to April. In 1998, Hurricane Mitch caused relatively little damage to Guatemala compared to its neighbours but the risk exists nevertheless. Water temperatures range between 27-29°C (80-84°C) year round.

**Nature and Culture** – The Mayan ruins of Tikal are at the other end of the country. The beautiful Lake Atitlán isn't that far, but favour San Pedro over Panajachel. In Monterrico, check out the Biotopo Monterrico-Hawaii nature reserve. Around Sipacate, bird watching, canoeing and fishing will fill a flat day.

**Hazards and Hassles** – No rocks to hit, but beware of the strong currents around rivermouths. Tourists are commonly targeted for robbery, bus and car-jackings. Travelling after sunset should be avoided. Malaria risk exists but dengue fever is the main concern in coastal areas.

**Handy Hints** – Take everything including favourite beachbreak board. Extra bars of warm water wax will befriend the locals. Maya Extreme Surf School gives surfing and bodyboarding lessons. The majority of Guatemalans are descendents of the ancient Maya culture and hold onto their traditions and native languages.

| WEATHER STATISTICS | J/F | M/A | M/J | J/A | S/O | N/D |
|---|---|---|---|---|---|---|
| total rainfall (mm) | 5 | 50 | 280 | 310 | 350 | 35 |
| consistency (days/mth) | 1 | 3 | 14 | 15 | 15 | 3 |
| min temp (°C/°F) | 19/66 | 21/70 | 22/72 | 22/72 | 22/72 | 20/68 |
| max temp (°C/°F) | 31/88 | 32/90 | 31/88 | 31/88 | 30/86 | 31/88 |

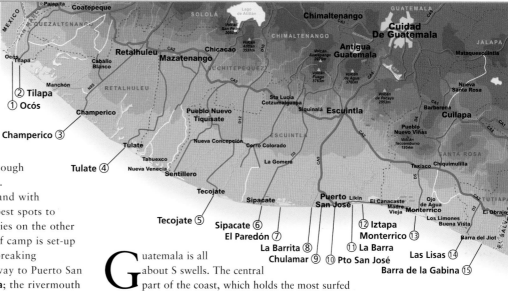

Despite being an unattractive coastal city, **Champerico** should not be overlooked by surfers. On a clean SW swell, the pier may go off with overhead, barrelling waves. Several cheap hotels make it possible to wait for those occasional days. **Tulate** is a nicer beach but the estuary break is also a bit hit or miss. The Rio Coyolate comes all the way from the central highlands, sometimes bringing enough sand to form a good sandbar in **Tecojate**. **Sipacate** is all about beachbreak peaks, and with miles of beach available, it's one of the best spots to catch quick, powerful rides. **El Parédon** lies on the other side of the Canal de Chiquimulilla; a surf camp is set-up in this fishing community, facing a fast breaking beachbreak best on a high tide. On the way to Puerto San José, it may be worth checking **La Barrita**; the rivermouth comes alive late spring and develops nice peaks throughout summer. Next, is Marina del Sur, a coastal resort beachie that gets classic with an incoming tide and the right swell. The beach of **Chulamar** isn't as steep as neighbouring ones and on a small swell there's well-organised waves. Rapidly accessed from Guatemala City, **Puerto San José** is Guatemala's most important seaside resort and as such, is the most surfed beach in the country. Take the boat across the Canal de Chiquimulilla to reach the grubby beach where good surf can be found around the pier. From Puerto San José to Monterrico lies the longest stretch of coastal road in Guatemala, allowing multiple beaches to be checked out without really leaving the highway. 5km (3mi) after Puerto San José is Balneario Likin, one of the country's only high-end coastal resorts. The surf also ranks among the best in the country, with hollow rivermouth and jetty waves at **La Barra**, rideable to slightly overhead. Another 7km (4.5mi) east is the fishing port of **Iztapa**, where the rivermouth usually offers good surf on small days. If a big swell hits with the right angle, it's rideable up to the 10ft (3m). A new jetty is currently under construction, bringing unknown effects to Guatemala's big wave spot. **Monterrico** is a beautiful

Guatemala is all about S swells. The central part of the coast, which holds the most surfed spots between Tecotaje and Monterrico, faces due south, while the western part of the country is a bit more open to the swells coming from the west. Southern hemisphere winters bring consistent swell in the 3-12ft (1-3.5m) range that coincides with Guatemala's rainy season, between June and October. Unlike its Mexican and Salvadorian neighbours, the country is plagued with a lack of both rocky points, capable of handling size, or large bays that provide sheltered spots. Swells coming with an angle are less likely to close-out, which explains why many spots favour SW swells or occasional SE swells. South Pacific activity is reduced the rest of the year, but the smaller conditions are perfect for the beachbreaks and since the off-season is blessed by E-NE winds, offshores will be a regular occurrence. During the rainy period, winds will be offshore in the morning, then switch sideshore/onshore around 11am. Tidal range can reach 8ft (2.5m), affecting the beachbreaks as much as the rivermouths, where the currents can be horrendous on the push and drop.

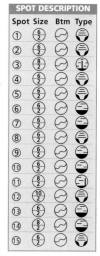

| SPOT DESCRIPTION | | | |
|---|---|---|---|
| Spot | Size | Btm | Type |
| ① | 6/2 | ◔ | ⬤ |
| ② | 6/2 | ◔ | ⬤ |
| ③ | 8/2 | ◔ | ⬤ |
| ④ | 6/2 | ◔ | ⬤ |
| ⑤ | 6/2 | ◔ | ⬤ |
| ⑥ | 6/2 | ◔ | ◒ |
| ⑦ | 6/2 | ◔ | ◒ |
| ⑧ | 6/2 | ◔ | ◒ |
| ⑨ | 6/2 | ◔ | ◒ |
| ⑩ | 6/2 | ◔ | ◒ |
| ⑪ | 8/2 | ◔ | ◒ |
| ⑫ | 10/2 | ◔ | ◒ |
| ⑬ | 6/2 | ◔ | ◒ |
| ⑭ | 6/2 | ◔ | ◒ |
| ⑮ | 6/2 | ◔ | ⬤ |

| SURF STATISTICS | J F | M A | M J | J A | S O | N D |
|---|---|---|---|---|---|---|
| dominant swell | S-SW | S-SW | S-SW | S-SW | S-SW | S-SW |
| swell size (ft) | 2 | 3 | 4-5 | 5 | 4-5 | 2 |
| consistency (%) | 65 | 75 | 80 | 75 | 70 | 65 |
| dominant wind | NW-E | NW-E | NE-SE | NE-SE | SW-N | NW-E |
| average force | F3 | F3 | F3 | F3 | F3-F4 | F3-F4 |
| consistency (%) | 78 | 62 | 42 | 56 | 50 | 75 |
| water temp (°C/°F) | 27/80 | 28/82 | 29/84 | 28/82 | 28/82 | 27/80 |
| wetsuit | 🩳 | 🩳 | 🩳 | 🩳 | 🩳 | 🩳 |

La Barra

tourist town, with thatched roof houses bordered by black sand beach and volcanoes. The surf is less photogenic; basic beachbreak close-outs best for bodyboarders. **Las Lisas**, via the inland freeway, avoids the usual shorebreak set-up and allows some bigger waves to be ridden. From there to **Barra de la Gabina** and the border with El Salvador, several secluded beaches offer as many options again to get wet, with rivermouths providing the best odds for scoring some waves.

El Paredon

HONDURAS

NICARAGUA

COSTA RICA

# 141. Rivas Province

ALL PHOTOS STEVE FITZPATRICK

## Summary
+ Long swell season
+ Dominant offshore winds
+ Low crowd levels
+ Quickly developing country

− Hard-access to surf spots
− No standout righthanders
− Natural disasters threat
− Lacks tourist infrastructure

The bulk of Nicaragua's coastline makes up the Mosquito Coast on the Caribbean side, where an extensive, shallow shelf drains what meagre swells are available. Most of Nicaragua's known surf spots are concentrated in the developed southwest corner where a narrow stretch of coastline separates Lake Nicaragua (the largest lake in Central America) from the Pacific. This huge body of water creates the perfect atmospheric conditions, causing winds to blow offshore for most of the year, around the San Juan Del Sur area. Surfing in Nicaragua started to grow a decade ago as the newly established democracy allowed the return of a bunch of self-exiled locals that had discovered surfing in Florida. They

then started tapping into their own country's wealth of excellent beachbreaks and left points.

**El Tránsito** is one of the remote, central coast fishing villages where half decent waves can go unridden for weeks. Try the long, easy, left pointbreak, or the

## TRAVEL INFORMATION

**Population:** 180,000
**Coastline:** 305km (190mi) (Pacific Coast)
**Contests:**
Playa Madera (Mar)
**Other Resources:**
*Video:* Circle One
nicasurf.com
surfnicaragua.com
surfaricharters.com
sanjuandelsur.org.ni
intur.gob.ni

**Getting There** – Most nationalities obtain a Tourist Card upon arrival. Many companies fly to Managua (MGA) including national airline Nica. Ride the afternoon express bus to San Juan Del Sur from the Mercado Huembes terminal (2 1/2h) to avoid connecting in Ricas (3h+1h). Driving takes 1h to Las Salinas, 3h to SJDS. Dep tax $20.

**Getting Around** – The Pan-American Highway runs inland, there's no coastal highway and sometimes no road at all. Dale Dagger's Masayita is available for boat access only spots ($160/d). Surfari Charters runs all-inclusive 4x4 trips ($510/w). Over-crowded buses are a pickpocket's heaven, but are otherwise reliable. Car rental is in Managua ($280/w inc. insurance).

**Lodging and Food** – Spared by Hurricane Mitch, San Juan del Sur is Nicaragua's #1

coastal resort with many budget places to stay. Dale Dagger offers upscale accommodation + boat trips for $160/d. In Las Salinas check out the Popoyo Surf Lodge ($24/dble). Try "Gallo Pinto" the local rice and bean combo. Beer and rum are second to none in Central America.

**Weather** – The Pacific lowlands of Nicaragua are always extremely hot, but the air feels fresher during the rainy season (May to November). Torrential downpours and flooding can be expected around October. In November 1998, Hurricane Mitch devastated the country with a year's worth of rain falling in a week. The dry season (December to April) brings winds that send clouds of brown dust across the plains, especially in the last months (mid-April to mid-May). The early dry season is generally considered as the most pleasant time to visit, but is not the optimum swell season. The constant offshore winds present throughout the year on the Pacific Coast can get very strong and make the water temperatures drop quickly. Some neoprene may be necessary despite the average water temp staying around a very comfortable 26°C (79°F).

**Nature and Culture** – Around San Juan del Sur go to the refuge at La Flor beach, where thousands of turtles lay their eggs between July and January. Walk to the lighthouse or the "antennas" for stunning views of neighbouring Costa Rica. Take the trip to 'Isla de Ometepe' on Lake Nicaragua, which is inhabited by freshwater sharks.

**Hazards and Hassles** – After over 40 years of dictatorship and 11 years of Sandinista rebel's power, Nicaragua shifted to a democracy in 1990. The country has also had its share of natural disasters with Hurricane Mitch and the 1972 earthquake that destroyed a large part of Managua. Like all Central American countries, use caution and avoid travelling at night.

**Handy Hints** – Don't count on the surf shops in Managua and SJDS (Action) to carry much choice, come equipped with a regular shortboard and semi-gun. Rental boards are available in Mundo skate'n'surf and Majagual. In San Juan, drop by Ricardo's bar for food and good advice. Expect all rooms to be sold out for Semana Santa.

| WEATHER STATISTICS | J/F | M/A | M/J | J/A | S/O | N/D |
|---|---|---|---|---|---|---|
| total rainfall (mm) | 10 | 5 | 200 | 170 | 300 | 50 |
| consistency (days/mth) | 1 | 1 | 14 | 19 | 20 | 6 |
| min temp (°C/°F) | 21/70 | 23/74 | 24/75 | 23/74 | 22/72 | 21/70 |
| max temp (°C/°F) | 33/92 | 35/95 | 34/94 | 31/88 | 31/88 | 31/88 |

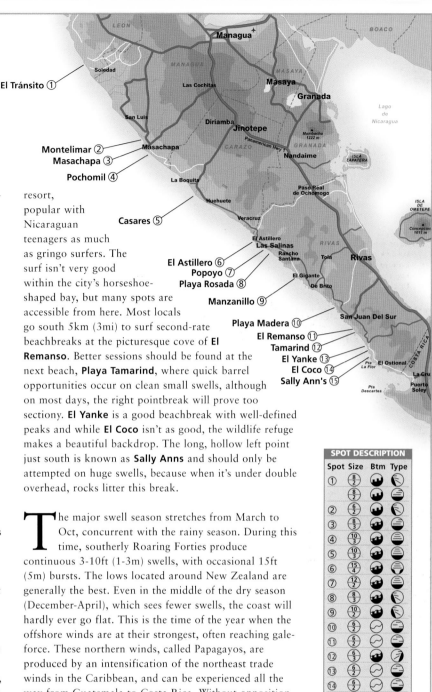

hollower right on the other side of town. The private, all-inclusive beach resort of **Montelimar** is certainly of higher standard than the sluggish left pointbreak out front best ridden on a pushing tide, but the odd inside tube section can spice up a session. **Masachapa**'s rights will only go off on a rare combination of big swell and low tide on a windless day. Also check out the nearby pier. **Pochomil** is a popular vacation spot only 1h drive from Managua. The main bay is beautiful, but the best peak, a slow, rolling A-frame, is to be found south of town. **Casares** is a small fishing village with friendly locals; if a good swell is running, several peaks will appear in the area. Head to **El Astillero** where the spot facing the Escalante River has been surfed up to triple overhead. The reef mainly produces long, walling lefts that get hollow and pack plenty of punch. The break known as **Popoyo** is actually located in Playa Sardinas, north of Playa Popoyo. The wave is an A-frame that breaks hollower and faster on low, then fatter and more makeable on high tide. Go right for a tube or left for a longer ride. Outside is the break known as The Outer Reef, a super heavy, bombora style, lefthand reefbreak that can get double overhead. It's ultra shallow, very hollow and suffers from vicious rips, suitable for chargers only. Rancho Santana is a gated community with 3km (1.5mi) of coastline. Fortunate owners enjoy access to three private beaches, including **Playa Rosada** where a fast wedging left breaks in shallow water. The classic, but fickle left of **Manzanillo** put Nicaragua under the spotlight when it appeared in *Surfer Magazine* under the false name of Punta Reloj. The swell needs to be big enough and south enough to wrap into the bay and ignite this outstanding pointbreak replete with tubular inside section. Since the point is surrounded by private property, a boat is essential for access, but worth the expense when everything aligns. Best at mid tide. The beachbreak of **Playa Madera** is probably the best around San Juan. Very consistent, sometimes hollow, it hosted the first national contest in May 2002. Over the years, the fishing village of San Juan del Sur has become a cruise port and seaside

resort, popular with Nicaraguan teenagers as much as gringo surfers. The surf isn't very good within the city's horseshoe-shaped bay, but many spots are accessible from here. Most locals go south 5km (3mi) to surf second-rate beachbreaks at the picturesque cove of **El Remanso**. Better sessions should be found at the next beach, **Playa Tamarind**, where quick barrel opportunities occur on clean small swells, although on most days, the right pointbreak will prove too sectiony. **El Yanke** is a good beachbreak with well-defined peaks and while **El Coco** isn't as good, the wildlife refuge makes a beautiful backdrop. The long, hollow left point just south is known as **Sally Anns** and should only be attempted on huge swells, because when it's under double overhead, rocks litter this break.

The major swell season stretches from March to Oct, concurrent with the rainy season. During this time, southerly Roaring Forties produce continuous 3-10ft (1-3m) swells, with occasional 15ft (5m) bursts. The lows located around New Zealand are generally the best. Even in the middle of the dry season (December-April), which sees fewer swells, the coast will hardly ever go flat. This is the time of the year when the offshore winds are at their strongest, often reaching gale-force. These northern winds, called Papagayos, are produced by an intensification of the northeast trade winds in the Caribbean, and can be experienced all the way from Guatemala to Costa Rica. Without opposition, they shriek over Nicaragua's large lakes, producing a continuous jet of offshore wind from November through to September. Only October seems to suffer from regular SW-W onshore winds. The tidal range reaches 2.5m (8ft) but tides are still a crucial element at many of the rocky spots. Tide tables are extremely useful but in short supply.

| SPOT DESCRIPTION | | |
|---|---|---|
| Spot | Size | Btm | Type |
| ① | 8/2 | | |
| ② | 8/2 | | |
| ③ | 6/2 | | |
| ④ | 10/3 | | |
| ⑤ | 10/2 | | |
| ⑥ | 15/2 | | |
| ⑦ | 12/2 | | |
| ⑧ | 8/3 | | |
| ⑨ | 10/2 | | |
| ⑩ | 6/2 | | |
| ⑪ | 6/2 | | |
| ⑫ | 6/3 | | |
| ⑬ | 6/2 | | |
| ⑭ | 6/2 | | |
| ⑮ | 10/4 | | |

| SURF STATISTICS | J F | M A | M J | J A | S O | N D |
|---|---|---|---|---|---|---|
| dominant swell | S-SW | S-SW | S-SW | S-SW | S-SW | S-SW |
| swell size (ft) | 2-3 | 3-4 | 5 | 5-6 | 4-5 | 2-3 |
| consistency (%) | 70 | 80 | 90 | 90 | 80 | 70 |
| dominant wind | N-E | NE-E | NE-E | NE-E | SW-W | N-E |
| average force | F4 | F4 | F3-F4 | F4 | F3-F4 | F3-F4 |
| consistency (%) | 86 | 64 | 41 | 58 | 32 | 77 |
| water temp (°C/°F) | 26/79 | 27/80 | 28/82 | 28/82 | 27/80 | 26/79 |
| wetsuit | | | | | | |

HONDURAS
EL SALVADOR
NICARAGUA
COSTA RICA
PANAMA

# 142. Golfo de Nicoya

Boca Barranca

JOHN CALLAHAN

**Summary**
+ GREAT LEFT POINTBREAKS
+ CONSISTENT, POWERFUL BEACHES
+ BOTH SOUTH AND NORTH SWELLS
+ EXOTIC, WARM AND FRIENDLY

− BEST SWELLS IN RAINY SEASON
− BEACHES CLOSE-OUT EASILY
− CROWDED BREAKS, BUSY RESORTS
− SOME BAD ROADS AND PETTY CRIME

In the '70s, Central America began to attract US surfers, looking for exotic waves close to home. Costa Rica was a major draw, where it was possible to be surfing an endless, peeling pointbreak, within an hour's drive of the airport and with a choice of two very different coastlines. Political stability, high degree of education and an absence of civil war, so popular in neighbouring countries, has earned it the reputation of being a 'Latin Switzerland'. Compared to its population, Costa Rica has an incredible number of surfing expats and travellers, representing 10% of all tourists, which translates to 100,000 surfers. Areas such as Guanacaste, became a victim of its own success, so new waves were sought around the Nicoya Gulf, opening up places like Mal Pais. Despite the shocking access roads

LEE ROBERTSON

Playa Hermosa

JAVIER AMEZAGA

requiring 4WD in the wet season, this wild area became a surf-school heaven, trading on idyllic tropical scenery, incredible national park wildlife and mellow beachbreaks.

The northern limit of the surf schools and camps terrain is around **Playa Coyote**, where the long beach boasts a short but sweet righthand pointbreak, near to

---

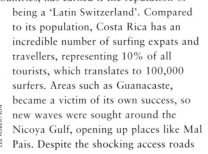

## TRAVEL INFORMATION

**Population:** 380,000 (Puntarenas)
**Coastline:** 1200km (750mi)
**Contests:** Rabbit Kekai Classic (Oct)
**Other Resources:**
*Video:* Lost in Costa Rica, Trippin' in Costa Rica
surf-costarica.com
costaricasurfing
 travelguide.com
guiascostarica.com
costarica.net

**Getting There** – No visa but 30d limit for many countries. Int'l arrivals are in Juan Santamaria (SJO) in Alajuela only 10K from San José. Nat'l airline: Lacsa (lowest board charge: $25). For Mal Pais, use the new Tempisque Bridge north of Puntarenas, way up in the Nicoya Gulf. It takes 5-6h. Jaco is only 2h max. Dep tax: $17.

**Getting Around** – Rental cars start from $300/w, read the Tico Times for bargains. Roads around Jaco are okay but some spot access is by boat/walk. New Tempisque Bridge saves ferry hassle. 4WD is essential in winter around Playa Coyote. Don't drive at night: wildlife and crazy drivers abound! Fan or A/C is crucial.

**Lodging and Food** – Plenty of choices to stay in Jaco (Vista Guapa) but favour Playa Hermosa

for its proximity to quality surf: Las Olas ($50/night/2pp), Terraza del Pacifico ($85/night/2pp): prices have risen over the years. Ask for winter or long stay discounts! The Mal Pais Surf Camp is $50/day full board. A typical food bill would be $8-10.

**Weather** – The Nicoya Peninsula is located in the central Pacific region, found between the tropical dry zone farther north known as Guanacaste and the tropical wet zone to the south. There are distinct dry (Dec-April) and wet (May-Nov) seasons. Dec-April is called summer despite Costa Rica being in the Northern Hemisphere. This is the peak tourist season and year round high humidity is more noticeable away from the coastal sea breezes. Rain comes evenings and nights. Temps average about 29°C (84°F) in dry season and a little less during the wet season. This is boardshort weather year round; take booties for the few sharp rock spots at low tide.

**Nature and Culture** – Lots of outdoor activities like horseriding, kayaking or river rafting. In Jaco/Hermosa area try the Waterfalls and Canopy Tour in the jungle forest, or fly tandem paragliding! Nightlife in Jaco is heavy; check Disco La Central or Papagayo. In Mal Pais, it's quieter with plenty of wildlife. Don't miss Cabo Blanco National Park.

**Hazards and Hassles** – Walking on black sand at noon can burn feet; prepare to sprint! Crowds can be dense with experienced expats, hot ticos and plenty of surf schools. People have drowned in Playa Hermosa's heavy waves, competent swimming ability is necessary when double overhead. Bugs, caterpillars and mosquitoes can be pretty bad in the wet season. Sea-lice!

**Handy Hints** – Because of heavy airlines tax, it may be cheaper to rent or buy boards in Jaco/Hermosa. A custom (Fry or Pico Surfboards) shortboard costs $380, longboards are $520. Lots of ding repairers. Plenty of surf shops in Jaco like Paradise, Jass Jaco, Kimoís or Pacific Surf. Travel off-season (Sept-Oct) and save up to 25%.

| WEATHER STATISTICS | J/F | M/A | M/J | J/A | S/O | N/D |
|---|---|---|---|---|---|---|
| total rainfall (mm) | 5 | 20 | 200 | 200 | 270 | 75 |
| consistency (days/mth) | 1 | 3 | 16 | 18 | 21 | 8 |
| min temp (°C/°F) | 23/74 | 23/74 | 23/74 | 23/74 | 23/74 | 22/72 |
| max temp (°C/°F) | 35/95 | 35/95 | 33/92 | 32/90 | 32/90 | 32/90 |

the Hotel Arca de Noe. Further north, up to Playa Carillo, there are good beachbreaks and reefs but 4WD is a must due to the rivers and heavy mud. Experienced surfers will probably prefer **Playa Caletas** with its different reefbreaks, the best being a high tide right on the north side. The north end reefs on **Manzanillo** beach need strong swells to show some potential plus there are a few other isolated spots nearby. **Playa Santa Teresa** has quickly become a mainstream spot because this white sand beachbreak is hollow and consistent, especially at lower tides. Stay at Cabinas Sta Teresa to be right in front of the surf and beat the Mal Pais crowds. Often referred to as Mal

Map labels:
- Playa Coyote ①
- Playa Caletas ②
- Playa Manzanillo ③
- Playa Sta Teresa ④
- Playa Carmen ⑤
- Punta Barigona ⑥
- Boca Barranca ⑦
- Puerto Caldera ⑧
- Tivives ⑨
- Playa Escondida ⑩
- Playa Jacó ⑪
- Roca Loca ⑫
- Playa Hermosa ⑬
- Boca Tusubres ⑭
- Esterillos Oeste ⑮

Mal Pais
LEE ROBERTSON

Pais, **Playa Carmen** is where most of the action happens, right where the Cobano Road meets the beach. A decent-size SW swell will awaken the lefts of **Punta Barigona** next to the Mar Azul Cabinas, down towards the Cabo Blanco Reserve. Since April 2003, the Tempisque Bridge, (780m/2,340ft long), one of the longest in Central America, is an alternative to the Naranjo ferry for crossing this stretch of water. On a major swell, **Boca Barranca** is an endless peeling left second only to Pavones in terms of length which is why it gets chosen as a longboard competition site but beware the river pollution. Close by, other quality lefts can be ridden like **Puerto Caldera**, a full-on harbour spot with jetty, boats and the pervasive smell of fish. **Titives'** surprisingly polluted, various peaks are not easy to find, but occasionally there's a barrelling rivermouth left. The reliable reef peaks at **Playa Escondida** (Hidden Beach) are private and access is by boat rented out at Playa Herradura. **Jacó** is Costa Rica's main surf town with

plenty of hotels, surf shops, bars and discos but the beachbreak is a joke compared to its southerly neighbour. **Roca Loca** is a great right with occasional lefts on a good swell, but it's a hike to get there. Take heed of the barely submerged rocks at low to mid tide. The 7km (4.5mi) long black sand, zooed-out beachbreak at **Hermosa** is another version of Mexico's Puerto Escondido with less shorebreak drama but enough power and rips to scare on double overhead days when close-outs rule. Ultra reliable, favours high tides and is less crowded further south towards Tulin's. The walk down to **Boca Tusubres** reveals virgin peaks on lower tides and bigger, punchier waves! South facing **Esterillos Oeste**, consists of a long sandy stretch with some lava reefs outside. Even further east, there's more empty waves at Esterillos Centro and Este plus plenty of places to stay.

The major swell season is April to Oct, with exposure to all S-SW swells. The southern latitudes produce numerous 3-10ft (1-3m) swells, the lows located around New Zealand being the best providers. The combination of beach and pointbreaks make all swells rideable somewhere, but wet season roads can be seriously washed out from Mal Pais to Playa Carillo/Samara. Dec-April gets a fair share of WNW Arctic swells, combined with frequent offshores and no rain, resulting in clean 3-4ft (1-1.2m) waves on the Mal Pais/Playa Coyote stretch, but very little for the eastern side of the Nicoya Gulf. As for winds, the main feature is the lack of them. There is a gentle SW-W period from May to November (wet). Typically, mornings are offshore before a sea breeze picks up. Then, the winter dry period has a lot of low wind days with variable directions but with a NW-NE dominance. Tides can reach 10ft and change the reefbreak and rivermouth profiles, so get a chart in one of the many Jaco/Hermosa surfshops or on www.crsurf.com.

**SPOT DESCRIPTION**

| Spot | Size | Btm | Type |
|---|---|---|---|
| ① | 6/1 | | |
| ② | 6/1 | | |
| ③ | 6/2 | | |
| ④ | 8/1 | | |
| ⑤ | 6/1 | | |
| ⑥ | 8/2 | | |
| ⑦ | 10/3 | | |
| ⑧ | 8/2 | | |
| ⑨ | 6/2 | | |
| ⑩ | 8/2 | | |
| ⑪ | 6/1 | | |
| ⑫ | 10/2 | | |
| ⑬ | 10/1 | | |
| ⑭ | 8/1 | | |
| ⑮ | 8/1 | | |

| SURF STATISTICS | J F | M A | M J | J A | S O | N D |
|---|---|---|---|---|---|---|
| dominant swell | S-SW | S-SW | S-SW | S-SW | S-SW | S-SW |
| swell size (ft) | 3-4 | 5 | 6 | 5-6 | 5 | 4 |
| consistency (%) | 70 | 80 | 90 | 90 | 80 | 70 |
| dominant wind | W-NE | W-NE | SW-W | SW-W | SW-W | SW-W |
| average force | F3 | F3 | F3 | F3 | F3 | F3 |
| consistency (%) | 67 | 49 | 49 | 57 | 65 | 56 |
| water temp (°C/°F) | 26/79 | 27/80 | 28/82 | 27/80 | 27/80 | 26/79 |
| wetsuit | | | | | | |

PEDRO SALINAS

# 143. Limón

Salsa Brava

STEVE FITZPATRICK

## Summary
+ Consistent, seasonal swell
+ Powerful reefbreaks
+ Insignificant tidal range
+ Laid back Caribbean style

– Flat between seasons
– Lack of good beachbreaks
– Extremely wet
– Petty crime

JOHN CALLAHAN

Costa Rica is a member of that privileged club which receives swell from two very different suppliers on its schizoid coastline. The Pacific Ocean delivers year round long distance swells from both the north and south, producing the perfect small to medium, west coast waves that Costa Rica is famed for. Not so well known is the fact that the Caribbean side receives fairly big and wild waves from short lived, seasonal storms, mainly centred off Colombia. It's truly amazing how much power is contained in the short fetch Caribbean swells, which break in the 2-12ft (0.6-4m) range. It is possible to cross from Puntarenas on the west coast to Puerto Limón in 5-6hrs, meaning both coasts can be surfed in the same day. The Caribbean coastline is short (212km/133mi), the majority being within the Tortuguero National Park, a long sandy line backed by huge waterways with countless

Near Westfalia

STEVE FITZPATRICK

beachbreaks and potential rivermouths but with no access and brimming with sea-life.

A boat from Puerto Moin is best for accessing the northern breaks of Parismina, **Tortuguero** or Barra Colorado. The remaining stretch from Limón to the Panamanian border, features endless black sand beaches

## TRAVEL INFORMATION

**Population:**
360,000 (Limón)
**Coastline:** 212km (132mi)
**Contests:** Op Latin Pro – Uvita (July)
**Other Resources:**
*Video:* Lost in Costa Rica, Trippin' in Costa Rica
surf-costarica.com
costaricasurfing
  travelguide.com
greencoast.com
guiascostarica.com

**Getting There** – No visa but a 30d limit for many countries. International arrivals are in Juan Santamaria (SJO) in Alajuela, 10K from San José. National airlines: Lacsa (usually charge for boards). Puerto Viejo is 4h drive from San José so it's better to take the bus or a rent a car than fly to Limon (LIO) with Sansa or Travel Air. Dep tax: $17

**Getting Around** – No main bus terminal in San José but there is a new Caribe terminal. Rental cars cost at least $300/w, read the *Tico Times* for bargains. The paved coastal road enables many views of the surf. Roads around Puerto Viejo are dirt tracks and heavy rains tend to produce deep muddy patches, drive very slowly.

**Lodging and Food** – For nice hotels, avoid Limón (apart from Park Hotel) and head to Playa Bonita (Matama ($60/dble) or Cocori ($30/dble). In Puerto Viejo, go to Kurt Van Dyke's major hotel ($16/dble or $5 /basic room) or Surf Point at Punta Cocles (25$/dble). A good meal with seafood at Stanford's costs $12, beware the spices!

**Weather** – The Talamanca coastal region is affected by an extremely wet climate. Rainfall averages 2400mm (95in), which is close to rainforest weather. Unfortunately, the rainiest months (Dec/Jan, July/Aug) correspond with the swell; it can rain for days on end, but the sun usually comes out a bit every day. Rain can come in heavy downpours, often at night, followed by clearing skies. Temps are similar throughout the year. Typically the lows will be above 21°C (70°F) and the highs below 30°C (86°F). Expect high humidity and cooling breezes. Go to San José, the City of 'eternal spring' for some light relief. Water temps are very stable in the 26°C (29°F) range; boardies all the time.

**Nature and Culture** – Cahuita National Park swarms with wildlife like howler monkeys, sloths, iguanas, parrots, hummingbirds and toucans. Diving can be good when surf is flat. The Caribbean side means serious nightlife, especially in Limón (Springfield) and PV (Crucial Bar or Sunset Reggae). Have a look at Bri-Bri handicrafts.

**Hazards and Hassles** – Be prepared to face intense downpours. These waves have power and intensity and can be dangerous especially at Salsa Brava, the most crowded spot. Jellyfish appear in the murky water at certain times of year. Things to avoid: Rasta wannabees selling drugs, street crime, bugs and mosquitoes!

**Handy Hints** – Take a semi-gun for Salsa/Limon spots. There are several shops in San José (Mango, Shaka Bra) and gear to rent in Puerto Viejo as well as Dan Garcia, a reliable shaper. Bring wet weather clothing! The Black and Creole population make up an interesting cultural diversity: enjoy the pura vida!

| WEATHER STATISTICS | J/F | M/A | M/J | J/A | S/O | N/D |
|---|---|---|---|---|---|---|
| total rainfall (mm) | 260 | 240 | 280 | 350 | 180 | 390 |
| consistency (days/mth) | 18 | 14 | 16 | 21 | 14 | 21 |
| min temp (°C/°F) | 20/68 | 21/70 | 22/72 | 22/72 | 22/72 | 21/70 |
| max temp (°C/°F) | 30/86 | 30/86 | 31/88 | 30/86 | 30/86 | 30/86 |

and occasional white sand coves, fringed with small coral reefs. In April 1991, a 7.4 earthquake raised the coral reefs by 2-3ft (0.6-1m) and early locals claimed that all the spots were gone. This is not quite true; the main area where the reef setup has been affected is Limón, where spots like Playa Bonita in the Portete area used to break with better shape. **Playa Bonita** is the main beach in the area and is an easy base for checking the variety of local breaks between Portete and Piuta like the rare rights of **Cocaine Point**, or the serious ledges of **Roca Alta** and Bonita itself. **Isla Uvita**, where Columbus landed in 1502, is a good place to stay as the left off the island is consistent and well-shaped. If there aren't any boats for hire in Limón, the paddle from the mainland takes about 20mins; jellyfish rather than sharks are the major cause for concern. En route to Cahuita there is 60km of average but consistent beachbreaks like **Westfalia**, where sandbanks are deserted but close-out when over 4ft (1.2m). Check the **Barco Quebrado** at the Rio del Banano rivermouth where better shaped banks are often seen. Don't expect crowds until close to Cahuita, whose national park attracts more trekkers and divers than surfers and remains uncrowded. The main beachbreak, **Playa Negra**, occasionally gets good. The road gets rough to Puerto Viejo but is worth the hassle as it is home to the notorious **Salsa Brava**, a righthand reefbreak that can hold 12ft+ (4m). This fairly short but barrelling wave with two distinct sections is consistent, heavy and crowds are the rule. Surfing during heavy rain helps dilute the line-up. The outer reef, Long Shoal, is another daredevil area, without the crowd. To the NW of the beachbreaks of **Playa Cocles**, a short left breaks beside an island until the swell gets overhead. **Little Shoal** has steep, short and fast waves like the other local breaks of **Punta Uva** or **Manzanillo**, which rattles off some high speed rights.

Salsa Brava

GILLES LECLAIRE

Playa Bonita

JOHN CALLAHAN

The Caribbean Sea spawns some of the strongest windswells on earth, producing clean and very consistent, 2-12ft (0.6-4m) surf, during two distinct seasons. The main season is winter from Dec to March with many storms churning off Cartagena in Columbia. The main ENE direction aims directly at Costa Rica. This brings stormy weather to the coast but the Talamanca coastal range helps to calm down local squalls and induces offshore winds. There is also a June-August season, July being the safer bet. Caribbean tropical cyclones and hurricanes from August to October usually track north of Costa Rica and are more likely to spray the Greater West Indies and US East Coast. Due to its swell window Costa Rica is fortunate not to be plagued by strong and consistent onshores but it's still necessary to wake up early for calm winds. Although tidal phases can reach 1m (3ft), it won't be as significant as on the Pacific side and it's not necessary to get a tide table.

| SURF STATISTICS | J F | M A | M J | J A | S O | N D |
|---|---|---|---|---|---|---|
| dominant swell | NE-E | NE-E | NE-E | NE-E | NE-E | NE |
| Eswell size (ft) | 3-4 | 3 | 1-2 | 3 | 1 | 3 |
| consistency (%) | 80 | 60 | 30 | 60 | 10 | 70 |
| dominant wind | N-E | NE-E | NE-E | NE-E | NE-E | N-E |
| average force | F4 | F4 | F4 | F4 | F3 | F4 |
| consistency (%) | 95 | 84 | 78 | 85 | 61 | 91 |
| water temp (°C/°F) | 26/79 | 26/79 | 27/80 | 27/80 | 27/80 | 27/80 |
| wetsuit | | | | | | |

① Tortuguero Beach
② Cocaïne Point
③ Playa Bonita
④ Roca Alta
⑤ Isla Uvita
⑥ Westfalia
⑦ Barco Quebrado
⑧ Playa Negra
⑨ Salsa Brava
⑩ Playa Cocles
⑪ Little Shoal
⑫ Punta Uva
⑬ Manzanillo

**SPOT DESCRIPTION**

| Spot | Size | Btm | Type |
|---|---|---|---|
| ① | 6/2 | | |
| ② | 6/1 | | |
| ③ | 10/2 | | |
| ④ | 8/2 | | |
| ⑤ | 10/2 | | |
| ⑥ | 6/1 | | |
| ⑦ | 6/1 | | |
| ⑧ | 6/1 | | |
| ⑨ | 12/4 | | |
| ⑩ | 6/3 | | |
| ⑪ | 6/1 | | |
| ⑫ | 6/1 | | |
| ⑬ | 6/1 | | |

# 144. Bocas del Toro

Paunch

CLEMENTE COUTINHO

## Summary
+ SEASONAL CONSISTENT SWELL
+ QUALITY ON ALL TIDES
+ NATURAL BEAUTY AND ECO-ACTIVITIES
+ CHEAP AND SAFE AREA
+ LESS CROWDED THAN COSTA RICA

− FLAT BETWEEN SEASONS
− LACK OF RIGHTS
− WET AND WINDY AFTERNOONS
− TIME-CONSUMING TRIPS TO SPOTS

Christopher Columbus landed in Bocas del Toro in October 1502, unaware that if he had arrived a few months later, his crew would have had to fight through some decent surf to get to terra firma. Columbus left his name to the main island of this archipelago consisting of nine major islands, 59 smaller islands and a myriad of mangrove cays. Located off Panama's Caribbean coast, these islands are only 32km (20mi) south of the Costa Rican border and slightly over 100km (60mi) away from the surf rich Pacific Coast. Modern travellers will find much of the medieval natural environment that greeted the explorers, remains intact, however the inexorable march of progress and expansion is becoming more apparent. The city of Bocas del Toro exudes a

Bluff

WILLY URIBE

WILLY URIBE

decidedly Caribbean style and flavour and is notable as Panama's only city built exclusively using wood. A building boom and accelerating growth are exposing many of the beautiful, virtually deserted beaches to more people than ever before. There are some remarkable surfspots in this zone but the two windows of surf throughout the year are slender.

## TRAVEL INFORMATION

**Population:** 10,000
**Coastline:** 1000km (625mi)
**Contests:** None
**Other Resources:** purosurf.com bocasdeltoro.com

**Getting There** – Some visitors need a tourist card sold for $5 upon arrival. Fly to Panama City (PTY), ride a bus to Almirante from the Albrook terminal (10h, $23) then catch a water taxi, or fly directly for $50. Both options are difficult with boards, buses lack space and airlines may refuse boards over 6'. From CR go though Sixaola or Changinola. $20 dep tax.

**Getting Around** – There's no need for your own means of transportation. Share taxis to Isla Colon's breaks ($3 to Paunch, $5 to Bluff) and small boats to other islands ($3 to Careñeros, $5 to Bastimientos). Ask the driver to pay on the return journey to avoid walking back. The city is conveniently small and you can walk around it easily.

**Lodging and Food** – Share a basic room at the well located Bocas Caribe ($6) or the nicer Mondo Taitu ($8), a bit further away. $15 will get a nice double in town, Las Brisas has a private boat deck. Eat like the locals at Don Chicho's cafeteria ($3 plate) or have some fine cuisine of El Pecado ($10). Don't miss the local beer (Balboa).

**Weather** – Being less than 10° from the Equator, Bocas del Toro would get real hot if it wasn't for the cooling breeze. Temps are similar throughout the year. Typically the lows will be above 21°C (70°F) and the highs below 30°C (86°F). It's a wet climate and the rainiest months (Dec/Jan, July/Aug) unfortunately correspond to the swell season, but precipitations are still lower than around Puerto Viejo, Costa Rica. Water temps are very stable in the 26°C (79°F) range, boardies time, any time. The city of Bocas itself is sheltered from the tradewinds by the outlying islands.

**Nature and Culture** – Try to spot the red frogs at the similarly named beach on Bastimientos, trek through the rainforest, or enjoy the coral reefs and clear waters while diving or snorkelling ($15 day trip). Best nightlife spots are the Barco Hundido (a.k.a. the wreck deck) and the Loop.

**Hazards and Hassles** – Getting in and out at Paunch and Dumpers will require reef boots. Don't forget mosquito repellent, although there's hasn't been malaria in Bocas for years. Sessions may turn into missions: no drivers around, truck stuck in the sand, boat running out of gas... Generally speaking, the city feels safe in the current stable political situation.

**Handy Hints** – Bring your equipment, there's no surfshop in Bocas although visitors sell boards before leaving. A gun will be required for Silverbacks. There are 2 surfshops in Panama City (Rio Surf Shop), but their board selection is minimal and prices rather high. National currency, the Balboa is equivalent to the American dollar, use whichever.

| WEATHER STATISTICS | J/F | M/A | M/J | J/A | S/O | N/D |
|---|---|---|---|---|---|---|
| total rainfall (mm) | 200 | 170 | 215 | 250 | 120 | 300 |
| consistency (days/mth) | 18 | 14 | 16 | 21 | 14 | 21 |
| min temp (°C/°F) | 20/68 | 21/70 | 22/72 | 22/72 | 22/72 | 21/70 |
| max temp (°C/°F) | 30/86 | 30/86 | 31/88 | 30/86 | 30/86 | 30/86 |

Silverback

Silverback

Furthest north from Bocas del Toro, is the consistent stretch of beach known as **Bluff**. Hollow and powerful waves break super-close to the shore, plenty of which close-out. Pick the right ones for a quick barrel at this spot that is ideally suited to bodyboards. **Dumpers** gets its name from the garbage dump across the road, an unsightly blemish in such beautiful surroundings. The wave is short and super-hollow, only suited to experienced surfers as it ends on a ledge of dry reef. On big days, an inside wave breaks and offers longer, mellower rides. A 10-15min drive from town is the quality reefbreak of **Paunch**. The lefts start with a tubular section, before wrapping into a more workable wall. A fun wave when small, it gets real sucky with a bigger swell. There is also the option of a few rights off the peak when everybody focuses on the lefts but they are a shadow of the main wave. Sharp reef at Paunch and Dumpers make reef boots a necessity. The boat option is best used to navigate around the slim island of **Careñeros** to check the surf at its northern tip. This left pointbreak peels down the east coast of the island, for a ride that can top 200m (600ft). It's usually a mellow wave, but it holds size and can have some long tubing sections. The more adventurous (and budget conscious) can paddle to Careñeros from Bocas, then walk around the island. Bastimientos is home to two radically different breaks. **Silverbacks** is Bocas' big wave spot and it's the only right reefbreak in the zone. The ride is short, but the drops are long as the wave ledges up into a large barrel. Boards over 7' are recommended to surf this spot. It needs a good size swell to start breaking and will hold over 20ft (6m). On the other hand, First Beach, sometimes referred to as Wizard Beach, is a basic beachbreak with patches of reef, whose main attribute is to pick up more swell

than any other spot. Accessed via boat to the south side of the island, leaving a good 20min walk across fields, more when the trail gets muddy. It's definitely not the best surf around but will be the only option if it's flat everywhere else, and the beauty of the beach makes up for the poor quality of the surf. The rest of the archipelago is open to exploration if you can find a boat driver willing to venture across the strong currents flowing between the open sea and the lagoon of Chiriqui. Isla Popa's swell window is reduced by surrounding islands and the Zapatillas Keys, two islands located on a coral platform. Cayo de Agua's NE shore could be a better bet with a series of points (Nispero and Tiburon) surrounded by coral. The Valiente Peninsula principally attracts biologists and geologists, but a wave search along its coast should be rewarding. The area has great swell exposure and points are plentiful.

Believe it or not, the Caribbean Sea produces some of the strongest windswells on earth, creating clean and very consistent 2-12ft (0.6-4m) surf. Wave height typically hovers around 4-6ft (1.2-2m) during the two extremely distinct seasons. The main season is winter, from December to March, with many storms churning off Cartagena in Columbia. There is also a June-August season, July being the safest bet. The main ENE direction aims perfectly at this corner of Panama, while the area is away enough from the centre of the storms to let the swell cleanup and avoid constant onshore winds. Caribbean tropical cyclones and hurricanes from August to October usually track north of Costa Rica and are more likely to spray the Greater West Indies and US East Coast. Tides only fluctuate about 3ft (1m) so spots will be breaking all day, but favour mornings for windless sessions.

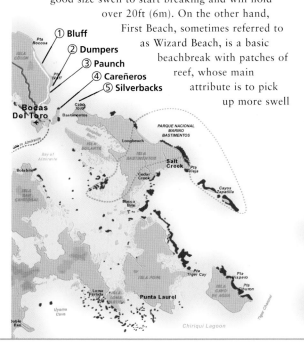

① Bluff
② Dumpers
③ Paunch
④ Careñeros
⑤ Silverbacks

Bocas Del Toro

| SPOT DESCRIPTION | | | |
|---|---|---|---|
| Spot | Size | Btm | Type |
| ① | 6/1 | | |
| ② | 10/2 | | |
| ③ | 8/2 | | |
| ④ | 10/2 | | |
| ⑤ | 15/8 | | |

| SURF STATISTICS | J F | M A | M J | J A | S O | N D |
|---|---|---|---|---|---|---|
| dominant swell | NE-E | NE-E | NE-E | NE-E | NE-E | NE-E |
| swell size (ft) | 3-4 | 3 | 1-2 | 3 | 1 | 3 |
| consistency (%) | 80 | 60 | 30 | 60 | 10 | 70 |
| dominant wind | N-E | NE-E | NE-E | NE-E | NE-E | N-E |
| average force | F4 | F4 | F4 | F4 | F3 | F4 |
| consistency (%) | 95 | 84 | 78 | 85 | 61 | 91 |
| water temp (°C/°F) | 26/79 | 26/79 | 27/80 | 27/80 | 27/80 | 27/80 |
| wetsuit | | | | | | |

# 145. West Panamá Province

Madroño

PATRICK CASTAGNET

**Summary**
+ GOOD WAVE DENSITY
+ EASY, FUN WAVES
+ SIMPLE ACCESS & GETTING AROUND
+ SAFE FOR CENTRAL AMERICA
+ PANAMA CITY ENTERTAINMENT

– NARROW SWELL WINDOW
– FLAT IN OFFSHORE SEASON
– FICKLE QUALITY SPOTS
– POLLUTED & CROWDED CITY BREAKS

Panama deserves its nickname of "The crossroads of the World". This narrow strip of land not only makes the link between Central and South America, but also joins the mighty Pacific and Atlantic oceans via the 80km (50mi) long Panama Canal. The cosmopolitan metropolis of Panama City hugs the eastern bank of the Pacific entrance to the Canal, deep in the sheltered Golfo de Panama, where only the strongest south swells can penetrate. However, an hour's drive west on the Pan-American Highway leads to another string of sandy beaches with better surf and much cleaner waters.

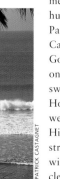

Rio Mar

PATRICK CASTAGNET

Playa Malibu

PATRICK CASTAGNET

**Rio Mar** is one of the last beaches before entering the province of Coclé. It's a long walk to reach the extensive rock ledge where a fun right breaks down the point at low tide. If the tide is too high, give the adjacent beachbreaks a try. Bigger swells light up **Punta Palmar**'s fast powerful righthanders at high tide. The misleadingly named peaks of **Hawaiisito** (Little Hawaii) favour lefts,

## TRAVEL INFORMATION

**Population:**
Panama City 1.4M
**Coastline:** 1500km
(937mi) (Pacific Coast)
**Contests:** Malibu (Feb),
Rio Mar (Aug)
**Other Resources:**
riomarsurfcamp.com
purosurf.com
panamainfo.com
visitpanama.com

**Getting There** – Some visitors need a tourist card costing $5 upon arrival. Most flights to Panama City (PTY) go through Miami. Crossing the border from Costa Rica is another option. Copa is the national airline. Buses to San Carlos leave from the Albrook terminal every 45mn ($6, 1 1/2h) or drive 90km (55mi) on the Pan American Highway. Dep tax: $20.

**Getting Around** – Panama's road system is among the best in Central America, and the 4 lanes Pan-American Highway follows the coast till Rio Hato. Public transport is generally efficient with inexpensive buses and taxis allowing you to cruise between Rio Mar and Gorgona. Rent a car ($250/week) for faster, independent travel.

**Lodging and Food** – Accommodation is affordable but not dirt cheap as in other Central Am countries. The Rio Mar Surf Camp has rooms from $12. Their $400/week deal includes airport transfers and 4x4 transport to neighbouring breaks. More hotels are available in Coronado and Gorgona. $10 gets you a great meal, try Patacones (plantains).

**Weather** – Expect a wet tropical climate with high temperatures year round. There is a prolonged rainy season between May and November with oppressive heat and intense downpours especially in the afternoons. The short dry season occurs when the winds turn northerly between Dec and April and coincides with Panama's tourist season. Rainfall rather than temperature changes determines the seasons, so June to October is called winter, which is odd since Panama is located in the Northern Hemisphere. Water temps remain very warm year round; boardshorts and a long sleeve lycra rashvest is enough.

**Nature and Culture** – A tour of Panama City should include the ruins of the 16th Century original city, Casco Viejo – the colonial city, and the modern skyscraper city. See ships passing through the Panama Canal at the Miraflores locks. Taboga is an attractive island with nature and wildlife. Panama City nightlife has something for everybody.

**Hazards and Hassles** – All city breaks suffer from pollution and some are localised, so surf the SW part of the province. Compared to other countries in Central America, Panama feels richer and safer but some areas of the capital are best avoided at night. The risk of malaria is really low in this part of the country and it's safe to drink the water.

**Handy Hints** – There are two surf shops in Panama City (Rio Surf Shop), but their board selection is minimal. Boa surfboards are made locally. Rio Mar Surf Camp rents boards ($15/day) and can arrange lessons ($20/h). National currency, the Balboa is equivalent to the American dollar, use whichever.

| WEATHER STATISTICS | J/F | M/A | M/J | J/A | S/O | N/D |
|---|---|---|---|---|---|---|
| total rainfall (mm) | 30 | 45 | 200 | 190 | 225 | 190 |
| consistency (days/mth) | 3 | 3 | 12 | 11 | 13 | 11 |
| min temp (°C/°F) | 22/72 | 23/74 | 23/74 | 23/74 | 23/74 | 23/74 |
| max temp (°C/°F) | 32/90 | 32/90 | 31/88 | 31/88 | 30/86 | 30/86 |

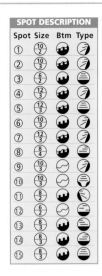

- ⑮ Mojon Beach
- ⑭ Nuevo Loco
- ⑬ La Zurda
- ⑫ Panamá La Vieja
- ⑪ Las Bóvedas

- ⑩ Playa Malibú
- ⑨ Playa Serena
- ⑧ Rocky Pt
- ⑦ Pta Teta
- ⑥ Rinconsito
- ⑤ Esmeralda
- ④ San Carlos Pt
- ③ Pta Palmar
- ② Hawaiisito
- ① Rio Mar

**SPOT DESCRIPTION**

| Spot | Size | Btm | Type |
|---|---|---|---|
| ① | 10/2 | | |
| ② | 10/3 | | |
| ③ | 6/2 | | |
| ④ | 12/3 | | |
| ⑤ | 12/3 | | |
| ⑥ | 10/3 | | |
| ⑦ | 12/2 | | |
| ⑧ | 8/3 | | |
| ⑨ | 10/3 | | |
| ⑩ | 10/3 | | |
| ⑪ | 8/2 | | |
| ⑫ | 6/2 | | |
| ⑬ | 8/3 | | |
| ⑭ | 8/3 | | |
| ⑮ | 8/3 | | |

**Las Bóvedas** is a rock-bottomed pointbreak with good lefts ending on a large rock. Such a location insures maximum crowds and minimum safety (pollution and thievery). **Panamá la Vieja** is a rare case of "mudbreak" since most of the sand previously there was used for construction. Highway pilings block the swell and even on the biggest days with the biggest tide, it's nothing but a mushy wave. The two breaks in Boca la Caja pack more punch and are popular with bodyboarders. **La Zurda** is a large, ledgy, barrelling lefthander breaking only on the highest tides, while **Nuevo Loco** is a fickle right breaking next to a large protruding rock. Be aware of localism and general insecurity in this neighbourhood. **Mojon Beach** offers a choice of three peaks, with Las Piedras and Nuevo Ride breaking around high tide, while La Lama is a low tide break. These are OK breaks if confined to the city, but none are really worth facing the crowd and pollution.

PATRICK CASTAGNET

are readily accessible, but will not handle swell above head high. There's also a popular beachbreak between both points, which serves as a contest site, despite most waves tendency to close-out. The fishing town of **San Carlos** also has a right pointbreak, locally known as Jeffreys, where long, fast rides can be had down the rock and sand point. For a choice of rights and lefts, check out the namesake reef peaks in Costa **Esmeralda** around high tide. The wave can be mushy, dependant on sand distribution, and never contains the emerald green water that the name implies. **Rinconsito** (Little Rincon) is reminiscent of the famous Californian pointbreak, but it requires some sizeable swell and is generally inconsistent. The rights at **Punta Teta** lead into some decent beachbreaks, shaped by the outflow of the Teta River. Various good rights, some fast lefts and an A-frame peak a bit further along, breaking over a mix of rock and sand. This is one of the locals' favourite breaks.

Between Teta and Coronado at Punta Barco, **Rocky Point** needs just the right size swell to be breaking without closing out. It's predominantly rights but there are a few lefts too. Coronado Beach may not be the nicest in the area, but the righthand pointbreak of **Playa Serena** peels hard and hollow from the take-off, before turning into a long and easy wall ideal for longboarding. Unfortunately, it's dependant on sand distribution, so it's quite fickle. **Playa Malibú** is located near the small oceanside community of Gorgona. This rivermouth break always picks up a little more swell than other spots in the area and is surfable at all tides. Count on fast tubular waves when the Chame River and tidal action combine to shape the black sand. Underwater trees are just one of the rivermouth's hazards. Between Punta Chame and Panama City, the swell is blocked by Punta Chame itself and a few offshore islands, while Bahia Chorrera is simply too shallow for the surf to reach the coast. The next spots lie within the city itself and will break on very large swells, but be aware that water quality is appalling. Right in the middle of the Casco Viejo (Old Quarter),

The major swells come in the southerly swell season – between April and October aka the green season. At that time, the Roaring Forties produce numerous 3-12ft (1-4m) swells and the best New Zealand lows produce a SSW angle, which equates to an optimum swell direction around 210°. Compared to Santa Catalina or the best breaks on the Peninsula de Azuero, the swell here is generally about half the size, but it is usually clean. The NW swells coming from cyclonic activity off Mexico can't reach inside the Gulf of Panama. During the winter dry period, between December and May, offshore northerly winds are the rule; unfortunately you can't count on regular swells this time of the year. Then comes a time of rather quiet winds, typically with offshore mornings before a sea breeze picks up. Finally between September and November, onshore south westerly winds tend to dominate. Tides can reach 17ft (5.5m), which is insane; get a chart in Panama City.

| SURF STATISTICS | J F | M A | M J | J A | S O | N D |
|---|---|---|---|---|---|---|
| dominant swell | S-SW | S-SW | S-SW | S-SW | S-SW | S-SW |
| swell size (ft) | 1-2 | 2-3 | 3-4 | 4 | 3-4 | 1-2 |
| consistency (%) | 30 | 60 | 80 | 60 | 60 | 30 |
| dominant wind | NW-NE | NW-NE | NW-NE | NW-N | S-W | NW-NE |
| average force | F3-F4 | F3-F4 | F3 | F3 | F3 | F3-F4 |
| consistency (%) | 90 | 82 | 44 | 61 | 58 | 60 |
| water temp (°C/°F) | 26/79 | 26/79 | 27/80 | 27/80 | 27/80 | 26/79 |
| wetsuit | | | | | | |

# 146. Eleuthera and Great Abaco

ALL PHOTOS ALEX WILLIAMS

## Summary
+ GOOD, VARIED REEFBREAKS
+ LOW CROWD PRESSURE
+ INCREDIBLY CLEAR WATER
+ GREAT WEATHER
+ CLOSE TO FLORIDA

− FLAT SUMMERS
− UNRELIABLE HURRICANE SWELLS
− UNPREDICTABLE WINDS
− QUITE EXPENSIVE
− CLOSE TO FLORIDA

Seen from the air, the Bahamas is a swirling mass of deep blue ocean, dotted with patches of turquoise water and a strip of islands rimmed in white sand. These 700 low-lying islands, along with over 2,400 islets called cays, are surface projections of two oceanic banks composed of coral with a limestone base. Around the islands is found approximately 5% of the world's coral, an amount surpassing even Australia's Great Barrier Reef. Extending from 80km (50mi) east of Florida to 80km (50mi) northeast of Cuba and crossing the Tropic of Cancer, technically speaking, the archipelago is not a part of the Caribbean. All the eastern "out islands" have good surfing potential but only Abaco and Eleuthera receive traveling surfers on a regular basis. During the '70s, Puerto Rican surfers expanded their horizons and the Bahamas became a hot surfing destination but during the '80s its popularity began to fade as places such as Costa Rica became known for being cheaper and more consistent.

The northernmost "out island" in the Bahamas, Abaco is actually a collection of islands but the 10km (6.5mi) long Elbow Cay seems to hold all the popular spots. A way to escape the Elbow Cay 'scene' is to rent a boat to reach **Willawahs** on the north tip of Manjack Cay, a virtually uninhabited island where a right pointbreak

## TRAVEL INFORMATION

**Population:** 300,000
**Coastline:** 3,542km (2,210mi)
**Contests:** Local
**Other Resources:**
*Video:* Surf NRG 2000
Atlantic Crossing
bahamasadventures.com
out-island-surf-
adventures.com
bahama-out-islands.com
abacos.com

**Getting There** – No visa required for most nationals. Flights from Florida (Miami, Fort Lauderdale) are common and cheap. For Abaco, fly to Marsh Harbour (MHH) then ride the ferry to Elbow Cay ($12r/t, 40mn). For Eleuthera, fly to Governors Harbour (GHB), 30km (20mi) south of Gregory Town. Bahamasair is the national airline, dep tax $15.

**Getting Around** – Go through Nassau to hop between Abaco & Eleuthera and 'mailboats' are quite slow. Car rentals average $60/d; a 4x4 is required to reach James Point. A golf cart ($35/d) or bike ($10/d) will do for Elbow Cay. Don't count on public transport. Small boat rentals start at $100/d. Out Island Surf Adventures boat trips focus on islands below Eleuthera ($850/p/7d).

**Lodging and Food** – The Bahamas is not a budget destination, winter is peak tourism season and camping is not allowed. On Elbow Cay, the Abaco Inn is the place to be ($140 /dbl cabin). Bahamas Out-Island Adventures offers guided camping surfaris on Eleuthera. Other lodging options include The Cove Eleuthera in Gregory Town ($120/dble).

**Weather** – Cooled by the prevailing southeasterly trade winds in the summer and warmed by the surrounding waters and the Gulf Stream in the cooler months, the Bahamas have a warm, pleasant climate, which varies little year round. Despite Elbow Cay's slightly higher latitude than Palm Beach, the winter temperatures are commonly 5°C (9°F) warmer than Florida and the summer highs are generally lower due to the moderating effects of the surrounding waters. Rainfalls are low during the winter surf season but heavy squalls or thundershowers occur during the hurricane months of June through October. Water temps stay well above 20°C (68°F) year round but a neoprene vest will protect against winter windchill.

**Nature and Culture** – Fishing, snorkelling and diving are great, live coral, tropical fish and dolphins are abundant. The Abacos are known as the 'Sailing Capital of the World'. In Hopetown, take photos of the lighthouse and from the lighthouse. Check out the handsome and hip Harbour Island.

**Hazards and Hassles** – The Bahamas have to be one of the rare spots in the world where crowd levels are lower than 30 years ago. Live coral heads lurk but most spots are deep enough – take reef boots to get in and out. There are sharks around the Bahamas, but they don't seem to be interested in humans. The burning sun is much more of a threat; use plenty of sunscreen.

**Handy Hints** – Take regular shortboard plus a longer one for those steep waves on Eleuthera. Rebecca's beach shop in Gregory Town, serves as Eleuthera's surf shop. Boards can be rented for $15/d and Rebecca's husband, Peter, is a great source of information. There are many more islands with good surf in the Bahamas.

| WEATHER STATISTICS | J/F | M/A | M/J | J/A | S/O | N/D |
|---|---|---|---|---|---|---|
| total rainfall (mm) | 40 | 60 | 130 | 130 | 170 | 50 |
| consistency (days/mth) | 5 | 5 | 11 | 13 | 14 | 7 |
| min temp (°C/°F) | 18/64 | 20/68 | 22/72 | 24/75 | 23/72 | 20/68 |
| max temp (°C/°F) | 24/75 | 26/79 | 29/84 | 31/88 | 30/86 | 26/79 |

reels into a small bay. It needs a bit of size to break safely and not too much NE wind. Elbow Cay's largest settlement is Hopetown, a little village with only two roads. The "Down Along" road runs along the water, leading to **Four Rocks**, a rare beachbreak in a sea of coral reefs. **Indicas** may well be the best barrel in the Bahamas, forming stand-up tubes over a shallow, live coral reef. It's a great left up to 6ft (2m), before turning into the area's proving grounds, holding up to double overhead. **Rush Reef** may be a better option on a large swell as the rights break way offshore, in deep water. The long paddle allows time to study the shifting line-up. For quieter rides, the fun peaks at the Abaco Inn Pools will do the job. Along with Indicas, **Garbanzo** is also a highly regarded break. Consistent, long lefts and occasional rights break along the reef, which is deep enough that urchins and fire coral aren't a big worry while surfing, but getting in and out of the water around low tide requires some serious reef dancing. There are more breaks on the way to **Tilloo Cut** that receive consistent surf on the remote, southern tip of the cay, which is boat access only. Long and thin, Eleuthera is under 2km (1.2mi) wide for 160km (100mi) of shoreline with pink and white beaches, sheltered coves and dramatic cliffs. The deep water, bowling A-frame on the west side of **Egg Island** takes a good N swell to work, but is usually clean since the trades will blow offshore there. Ride a boat from Spanish Wells to check it out. On dropping tides good waves can wrap on each side of the cut between Eleuthera and Harbour Island and **Whale Point. Holiday Beach** is Eleuthera's most radical wave. Steep and hollow, the left is usually the wave of choice. Overhead waves and mid tide are optimal conditions. Down the road from Gregory Town's pineapple farm and small tourism hub, lies the 3km (2mi) long **Surfer's Beach**. The long lefts that drew heaps of surfers to the area in the '70s will take any swell and some steep rights appear once in a while. It's a fast wave with an intense inside section breaking over a sand bottom. Next comes Hatchet Bay with the long, fat, workable left known as **Ledges** on the northern side and a good right known as The Dump on the

Pools

southern side. Ledges will work best on a northern swell while The Dump enjoys a more southerly direction. Since closing the neighbouring chicken processing factory shark sightings have diminished. Rainbow Bay area catches lots of swell but will be only heavy beachbreak unless it's big enough for **Hidden Beach**'s point to reveal itself. On an E to SE wind, **James Point** will probably be the only offshore spot working. Combine that with a N swell and it becomes the place to be for clean, hollow peaks. Unfortunately, there are no good roads leading there and only a 4x4 will avoid getting buried in the sand. Both **North Palmetto Point** and **Rock Sound** can occasionally fire, with perfect, powerful peaks on a S swell, but few surfers bother going down there.

| SPOT DESCRIPTION | | | |
|---|---|---|---|
| Spot | Size | Btm | Type |
| ① | 8/4 | | |
| ② | 8/2 | | |
| ③ | 12/4 | | |
| ④ | 15/4 | | |
| ⑤ | 12/2 | | |
| ⑥ | 8/3 | | |
| ⑦ | 10/4 | | |
| ⑧ | 8/4 | | |
| ⑨ | 10/4 | | |
| ⑩ | 10/2 | | |
| ⑪ | 8/2 | | |
| ⑫ | 8/3 | | |
| ⑬ | 6/3 | | |
| ⑭ | 8/4 | | |
| ⑮ | 6/3 | | |

① Willawahs
② Four Rocks
③ Indicas
④ Rush Reef
⑤ Garbanzo
⑥ Tilloo Cut

⑧ Whale Point Cut
⑨ Holiday Beach
⑩ Surfer's Beach
⑪ Ledges
⑫ Hidden Beach
⑬ James Pt.
⑭ North Palmetto Point
Egg Island ⑦
⑮ Rock Sound

Winter is the prime surfing season when a great number of swells arrive from the North Atlantic lows between October and April. These NE swells vary from 3-10ft (1-3m), with rare and short 12ft+ (4m) bursts. Summer is flat most of the time before August to October brings the possibility of small but clean hurricane swells. Eleuthera's boomerang shape maximizes the swell window and offers more swell/wind combination than Abaco. The swell window is close to 180° with northern spots picking up the northern swells (N-NE) while southern breaks enjoy more E-SE. Winds are predominantly onshore easterlies throughout the year but tend to blow more from the NE between October and April and from the SE between May and September. These winds are seldom strong, except during hurricane season, but remain quite unpredictable. The wind should shift offshore as soon as a cold front leaves the US East Coast, but two weeks of nor'easters could ruin any plans. Tidal range can reach 5ft (1.5m), which is enough to affect the shallower spots.

| SURF STATISTICS | J F | M A | M J | J A | S O | N D |
|---|---|---|---|---|---|---|
| dominant swell | N-NE | N-NE | N-NE | E-SE | E-SE | N-NE |
| swell size (ft) | 4-5 | 4 | 2-3 | 1-2 | 3 | 4 |
| consistency (%) | 80 | 60 | 40 | 20 | 50 | 60 |
| dominant wind | NW-E | E-S | E-S | E-SW | NE-E | N-E |
| average force | F4-F5 | F4 | F3-F4 | F3 | F4 | F4 |
| consistency (%) | 57 | 49 | 57 | 74 | 49 | 55 |
| water temp (°C/°F) | 22/72 | 23/74 | 25/77 | 27/80 | 26/79 | 24/75 |
| wetsuit | | | | | | |

# 147. Amber Coast

## Summary

+ INDENTED COASTLINE WITH GOOD REEFS
+ GREAT SURF/WIND/KITE COMBO
+ ALL-INCLUSIVE, COMFORTABLE RESORTS
+ CHEAP FOR THE CARIBBEAN

− SHORT SWELL SEASON
− UNFAVOURABLE TRADE WINDS
− NO REAL SURF SHOPS
− SHALLOW, URCHIN INFESTED REEFS

Secret Spot

ALL PHOTOS THIERRY GIBAUD

Encuentro

The Dominican Republic is the second largest and most populous country in the Caribbean, occupying the eastern two thirds of the island of Hispaniola, adjacent to Haiti. To the east of the Dominican Republic is the Mona Passage, which separates it from Puerto Rico. Both the Atlantic Ocean to the north and the Caribbean Sea to the south produce rideable surf on an ideally indented coastline. While the Dominican Republic is a mountainous country, golden sandy beaches remain the main tourist attraction, which explains the high concentration of hotels and resorts on the Amber Coast, especially the 65km (41mi) zone between Puerto Plata and Cabarete.

Next to the colonial fort in the tourist hub of Puerto Plata, a channel splits the reefs of **La Puntilla**, offering intense rights and lefts on a head high northerly swell. The city's other option, **Coffee Break** is a reef peak worth checking when it's too small for La Puntilla.

## TRAVEL INFORMATION

**Population:** 320,000 (Puerto Plata)
**Coastline:** 1,288km (805mi)
**Contests:** Encuentro (Dec)
**Other Resources:**
surfingdr.com
fedosurf.tripod.com.ar
hispaniola.com
sosua.com

**Getting There** – Most visitors are required to purchase a tourist card ($10). It's best to fly directly into Puerto Plata's International Airport (POP), only 6km (4mi) away from Sosua by minibus. Santo Domingo airport (SDQ) is 4h away by bus (Caribe Tours, $6). An all-inclusive package tour may be the cheapest way to get there. Departure tax is $10.

**Getting Around** – The main roads are in good condition and a well-maintained, two-lane highway follows the north coast. Rent a car for $50/d or a motorbike for $15/day. Be aware that reckless driving is the norm and that traffic police may be open to corruption. Public transportation system is extensive with long distance bus operators and cheap "publicós" bus as well as "moto conchos" bikes within cities.

**Lodging and Food** – There are various resorts scattered along the north coast. Sosua packs plenty of hotels, like the Waterfront ($40/dble). Several breaks are within walking distance of the LTI-Sol de Plata Resort ($70/p/dble). Cabarete Surfcamp has something for every budget, from campground to apartments ($20/p cottage room). Dominican dishes come with brown beans (habichuelas) and rice. Presidente is the local beer.

**Weather** – The Dominican Republic has a semi-tropical climate, tempered by prevailing easterly winds. The so-called "cool" season (November to April) is pleasantly warm with low humidity and precipitation. On the coast, the temperature hovers fairly constantly around 29°C (84°F) during the day and drops to around a comfortable 20°C (68°F) at night. During the summer months, temperatures range between 28°C-35°C (60-95°F). The highlands are considerably cooler. The wet season stretching from June to November sees short tropical showers. June to September is also the hurricane season, but chances of seeing one blowing through are minimal.

**Nature and Culture** – Sosua and Cabarete are busy little towns with bars, restaurants food and clubs spinning Caribbean and American music. Around Rio San Juan take a boat ride through the thick, dark mangroves of Gri Gri Lagoon. Visit the beautiful island of Cayo Lavandado, in the Bay of Samana or travel through the highest mountain chain in the Caribbean. Windsurfing conditions are world-class in Cabarete.

**Hazards and Hassles** – Most locals are friendly bodyboarders. Urchins cover many reefs, so bring booties. Most areas are quite safe, with the exception of some slum areas, such as the back streets of Los Charamicos in Sosua, particularly at night. Malarial precautions may be necessary, check before arrival.

**Handy Hints** – Surf equipment is rare; take boards and leashes. No Work Team, located in the centre of Cabarete organises transfers to Encuentro, board rentals and surf lessons. Take Off School of Surfing also has board rentals ($20/d) and lessons ($25). The peso is the national currency, but many businesses prefer US$.

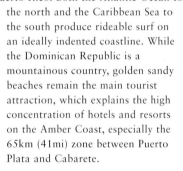

| WEATHER STATISTICS | J/F | M/A | M/J | J/A | S/O | N/D |
|---|---|---|---|---|---|---|
| total rainfall (mm) | 170 | 140 | 90 | 75 | 110 | 280 |
| consistency (days/mth) | 11 | 10 | 8 | 7 | 9 | 14 |
| min temp (°C/°F) | 21/70 | 22/72 | 24/75 | 25/77 | 24/75 | 22/72 |
| max temp (°C/°F) | 27/80 | 27/80 | 29/84 | 30/86 | 30/86 | 28/82 |

Compared to the developed Puerto Plata, Sosua is a real jewel of a beach town with coconut trees lining idyllic beaches. On the biggest northern swells, impressive lefts will break in **La Bahia**, groomed by the offshore trades, creating clean, powerful walls. Conversely, **La Boca** is fully exposed to the predominately easterly trade winds and needs calm conditions for the rights at this consistent beachbreak to work. **El Canal** is only surfed by experts on big days when neighbouring **Encuentro** starts closing out. Holds double overhead plus walling lefts and there is also a short right over a rocky bottom. Encuentro is the Dominican Republic's showcase break and the locals' favourite. The Encuentro Eco-Surf International competition takes place every year on this consistent, quality break. Take-off is quite easy before the rights zip through the inside sandbar. The lefts are more challenging, pitching a heavy barrel over a shallow, uneven reef. They also need more swell to really work. The treacherous peak at **Coco Pipe** is always less crowded for the simple reason that it ledges dangerously. The large **Yucca Bay** hosts several breaks including a right pointbreak. Next come the small but fast lefts of **Yellow Rock Reef** and the larger **Gun Point** rights, which are best on an overhead swell. There's also a beachbreak between these two spots. Like Yucca Bay, **Playa Goleta** is home to several breaks and lots of urchins. The main peak boasts a long right and shorter left. 12km (8mi) east of Sosua, the large bay of **Cabarete** is known as one of the best windsurf destinations in the world and is an official stop on the world tour. Wind and kite-surfers proliferate along

La Preciosa

Brandon Samford

this 6km (4mi) stretch of beaches. The strong winds will blow out any surf, but glassy early morning sessions are common. Note that an outer reef prevents the surf from reaching downtown beaches. 15 minutes past the town of

Rio San Juan, long rights peel down a reef in front of the main entrance to the **Playa Grande** beach. Best on N swell, this wave speeds-up as it goes down the line. Rarely crowded due to the variety of peaks available, including the inside shorebreak known as La Punta. Just down the road, **La Preciosa** is one of the most consistent breaks in the area and the A-frame peak is known to get picture perfect.

The north shore, referred to as "La Costa" by the locals, receives consistent North Atlantic swells between November and March. N swells are perfect for the Amber Coast, arriving from lows located off Florida, usually tracking NE towards Europe. These 2-15ft (0.6-5m) waves hit the exposed northern coastline and the major breaks receive up to 15ft (5m) a couple of times a year. Early winter (November and December) is usually good despite rain making surfing less pleasant. Then the rains diminish, but the trade winds will pick-up from mid-January. Prevailing winds are of E/NE all year round and will get super strong in winter; fortunately a few spots around Sosua/Cabarete will remain offshore under the trades. It's generally a good idea to surf early in the morning before the trades kick in. The Caribbean cyclonic swells don't produce waves on that side of the Dominican Republic, summer is the time to head to the south of the islands where many spots will fire under such conditions. Tidal range remains under 0.6m (2ft).

| SURF STATISTICS | J F | M A | M J | J A | S O | N D |
|---|---|---|---|---|---|---|
| dominant swell | N-NE | N-NE | N-NE | N-NE | N-NE | N-NE |
| swell size (ft) | 3-4 | 3 | 1-2 | 1 | 3 | 3-4 |
| consistency (%) | 80 | 65 | 30 | 30 | 60 | 75 |
| dominant wind | NE-E | NE-E | NE-SE | NE-E | NE-SE | NE-E |
| average force | F4 | F4 | F4 | F4 | F4 | F4 |
| consistency (%) | 79 | 76 | 89 | 81 | 84 | 79 |
| water temp (°C/°F) | 25/77 | 26/79 | 27/80 | 28/82 | 28/82 | 27/80 |
| wetsuit | | | | | | |

**SPOT DESCRIPTION**

| Spot | Size | Btm | Type |
|---|---|---|---|
| ① | 8/4 | | |
| ② | 4/2 | | |
| ③ | 10/4 | | |
| ④ | 6/2 | | |
| ⑤ | 15/8 | | |
| ⑥ | 10/4 | | |
| ⑦ | 10/3 | | |
| ⑧ | 10/3 | | |
| ⑨ | 4/2 | | |
| ⑩ | 10/4 | | |
| ⑪ | 10/3 | | |
| ⑫ | 8/3 | | |
| ⑬ | 10/3 | | |
| ⑭ | 10/2 | | |

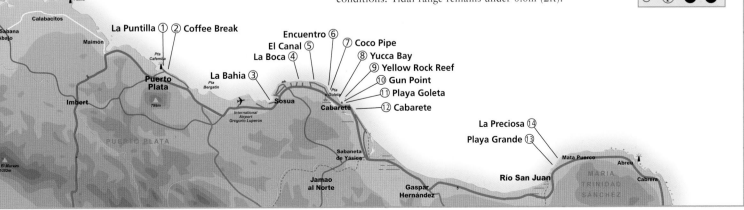

La Puntilla ① ② Coffee Break
Calabacitos
Pta Patilla
Sabana Abajo
Maimón
Pta Cafemba
Puerto Plata
La Bahia ③
Pta Bergatin
Imbert
799m
International Airport Gregorio Luperón
El Murazo 1083m
PUERTO PLATA
Sosua
Encuentro ⑥
El Canal ⑤ ⑦ Coco Pipe
La Boca ④ ⑧ Yucca Bay
⑨ Yellow Rock Reef
Pta Goleta
⑩ Gun Point
Cabarete ⑪ Playa Goleta
⑫ Cabarete
Sabaneta de Yásica
Jamao al Norte
Gaspar Hernández
La Preciosa ⑭
Playa Grande ⑬
Mata Puerco
Abreu
Rio San Juan
MARIA TRINIDAD SANCHEZ
Cabrera

# 148. British Virgin Islands

Capoon's Bay
JAKE FITZJONES

## Summary

+ WORLD-CLASS CANE GARDEN BAY
+ CONSISTENT BEACHBREAKS
+ SAFE TROPICAL DESTINATION

− SHORT SWELL SEASON
− LACK OF CONSISTENT REEFS
− BOAT ACCESS ONLY BREAKS
− EXPENSIVE

Tortola is the largest of these islands and the BVI capital, thanks to an important yacht harbour in Road Town. The north shore of the island is dotted with a series of bays and beaches offering a good diversity of surfing locations. **Capoon's Bay**, aka Little Apple Bay, holds a perfectly symmetrical A-frame reef that should provide a buzz, as does the mushroom tea sometimes served at Bomba Shack, just in front of the break. While getting high is not everyone's cup of tea, a user-friendly, walling wave that can handle big swells and remain unaffected by the trades, most definitely is! As good as Capoon's Reef may be, the title of 'world-class wave' in this area goes to **Cane Garden Bay**. The west facing, right pointbreak will only fire on the biggest swells of the year, but when it's on, tubular walls will peel against

Bomba Shack
JAKE FITZJONES

Capoon's Bay
STEVE FITZPATRICK

the hill for rides reaching several hundred metres. It would have been hard to keep such a wave a secret, especially knowing that the beach facing the break is one of the most popular on Tortola. A surf magazine cover shot a few years back drew international surfers to the place and many US East Coasters and Puerto Ricans now have the place dialled and will plan short hops to Tortola

## TRAVEL INFORMATION

**Population:** 21,000
**Coastline:** 80km (50mi)
**Contests:** Josiah's Bay & Apple bay (Dec-Feb)
**Other Resources:**
hiho-bvi.com
ultimatebvi.com

**Getting There** – Most nationals do not require a visa. There are no direct flights from either North America or Europe, fly through Puerto Rico (SJU) or the US Virgin Islands (STT). From there take an inter-island flight to Tortola (EIS) or use the ferry service from San Juan, PR (1h, $44 r/t). There's a $10 air tax and $5 sea dep tax.

**Getting Around** – Tortola's bus service is unpredictable and taxis are expensive. Rent a little 4x4 ($50/d), Dede's car rental is a favourite among surfers. Fly BVI has flights to Virgin Gorda & Anegada ($60r/t). Ferries island hop to Virgin Gorda ($15) and Jost Van Dyke. If it's within budget, the best way to get around remains a chartered sailboat.

**Lodging and Food** – The BVI are not a cheap getaway destination: food is pricey and accommodation's in short supply. Most visitors sleep on their chartered yachts. On land the only budget option is Brewer's Bay campground at $10/night. Starting at $135/dble in season, Sebastian's is a middle price hotel and is right on the beach in Little Apple Bay.

**Weather** – Because of their position within the trade wind belt, the islands have a balmy, sub-tropical climate. The blazing sun is continuously tempered by the constant ocean breezes. Summer is humid with temperatures over 30°C (86°F), winter is slightly cooler. The temperatures drop by 5°C (9°F) at night. Average water temperatures remain around 26°C (79°F) year round. The total rainfall is quite low and even in the rainy season, starting in late summer and ending just before Christmas, the islands receive less than 5 rainy days a month. Like most semi-tropical and tropical locations, the BVI is in a hurricane zone; watch out between June and November.

For all these reasons, the surf season is also the ideal time to visit, especially after Christmas.

**Nature and Culture** – Cruise the islands on a yacht or on a kayak depending on your budget. Top diving spots include the sunken *HMS Rhone*, off Salt Island and Horseshoe Reef (Anegada). Good Snorkelling in Smugglers Cove. Check out the Baths on Virgin Gorda, a series of very large boulders located along the seashore.

**Hazards and Hassles** – Skin threats include sunburn, fire coral, urchins and jellyfish. Sharks abound but risks are low. Locals are friendly but should be respected. Weird things happen during the (in)famous Bomba Shack "full moon parties" in Apple Bay.

**Handy Hints** – Take usual shortboard or longboard plus a semi-gun for big Cane days. HIHO is a ex-pro run surf/windsurf shop where all kinds of rental boards are available from $20/d. The Red Stripe Surf Series contests alternate between Josiahs and Apple Bay.

| WEATHER STATISTICS | J/F | M/A | M/J | J/A | S/O | N/D |
|---|---|---|---|---|---|---|
| total rainfall (mm) | 40 | 60 | 85 | 85 | 110 | 100 |
| consistency (days/mth) | 4 | 3 | 4 | 5 | 5 | 6 |
| min temp (°C/°F) | 22/72 | 23/74 | 25/77 | 25/77 | 24/75 | 23/74 |
| max temp (°C/°F) | 28/82 | 29/84 | 30/86 | 31/88 | 30/86 | 29/84 |

Cane Garden Bay

STEVE FITZPATRICK

rideable waves from the occasional summer hurricane swells. Anegada is completely different from all the other British Virgin Islands in that this coral island's highest point is only 10m (30ft) above sea level, in fact the whole island looks just like a giant beach. The surrounding reef is a popular diving area and wide exposure to the wind probably makes it better for sailboarding. **West End** is actually a great windsurf spot, but if the wind drops or goes south, a long righthand pointbreak will reveal itself. It can either be a mellow, cruisey wave or turn heavy with huge rips. Another option on the island is **Loblolly Bay**, which is usually onshore since it faces east, but it picks up a maximum of swell. This spot is very remote and it's a long paddle to the peak. On a windless day, there will be a long, relaxed left and a much more intense and hollow right.

as soon as they see a major swell on the way. It will occasionally get big, and some sections break in just a couple of feet of water over a particularly hungry reef. **Josiah's Bay** is the most consistent beachbreak and unlike Cane Garden, this beach is slightly off the beaten track, attracting more cows than sunbathers. The quality of the wave depends on the shape of the sandbanks, but there's always something to ride on a small day, including a long right, ideally suited for longboarding. Another advantage is that it can hold loads of surfers but unfortunately it stinks when the swell gets overhead. There are more

waves on the island, including powerful beachies in remote, roadless locations. Finding them would require boating along the coast or making friends in the small, local surfing community. There are a couple of surf spots on mountainous Virgin Gorda, the island known for its massive boulders. **Yacht Harbors** reef is worth checking on a large NW swell, it's a tubular A-frame with longer rides to be had on the rights. Other islands and islets have surfing potential, but just aren't reliable enough to be considered proper spots. The east facing shores of the islands SW of Virgin Gorda are known to receive

Surf season in the British Virgin Islands is roughly between November and March when winter lows leave the US East Coast before tracking NE towards Europe. They send 2-10ft (0.6-3m) surf on the exposed shores with occasional 12ft+ (4m+) faces at Cane Garden. The season may go on till May but the frequency of swells is then considerably reduced. The E windswell and the occasional hurricane swells will provide summertime surf on the SE exposed shores, but long flat spells are way too common to plan a surf trip at this time of the year. The wind dominance is E year round with more NE winds between November and March. Surf early or right after storms. The tidal range is minimal, hovering around 30cm.

| SURF STATISTICS | J F | M A | M J | J A | S O | N D |
|---|---|---|---|---|---|---|
| dominant swell | N-E | N-E | NE-SE | NE-SE | N-E | N-E |
| swell size (ft) | 4 | 3 | 1-2 | 2 | 3-4 | 4 |
| consistency (%) | 80 | 60 | 30 | 30 | 60 | 70 |
| dominant wind | NE-E | NE-E | NE-SE | NE-SE | NE-SE | NE-E |
| average force | F4 | F4 | F4 | F4 | F4 | F4 |
| consistency (%) | 80 | 77 | 85 | 97 | 89 | 76 |
| water temp (°C/°F) | 25/77 | 25/77 | 26/79 | 27/80 | 28/82 | 26/79 |
| wetsuit | | | | | | |

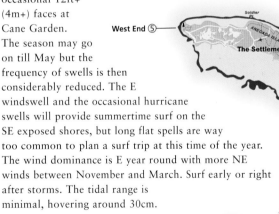

West End ⑤   ⑥ Loblolly Bay
Soldier Pt.
ANEGADA ISLAND
The Settlement
East Pt.

Josiah's Bay ③

Cane Garden Bay ②

Capoon's Bay ①

Yacht Harbor ④

SpanishTown
Roadtown

| SPOT DESCRIPTION | | | |
|---|---|---|---|
| Spot | Size | Btm | Type |
| ① | 12/2 | | |
| ② | 15/5 | | |
| ③ | 6/1 | | |
| ④ | 10/3 | | |
| ⑤ | 10/3 | | |
| ⑥ | 10/3 | | |

# 149. St Martin and St Barthélémy

THIERRY GIBAUD

## Summary

+ GOOD REEFS AND POINTBREAKS
+ MULTIPLE SWELL AND WIND COMBOS
+ SMALL SIZED ISLANDS
+ UNCROWDED & FRIENDLY LOCALS

– SHORT GROUNDSWELL SEASON
– WIND SENSITIVE BREAKS
– FICKLE BEST BREAKS
– VERY EXPENSIVE

TIKI YATES

Together with Anguilla, St Martin and St Barthélémy are the northernmost eastern Caribbean islands. The hilly interior is hemmed by 36 white sandy beaches, which fill a 60km (40mi) long strip of bays and coves. Good exposure to northern swells and a mixture of sand, rock and coral breaks make these islands a quality Caribbean surf trip, if you can afford it. St Martin is the smallest island in the world to be shared by two sovereign governments, with French Saint Martin taking-up about two-thirds of the landmass to the north and Dutch Sint Maarten to the south. The border is almost imperceptible but each side has managed to retain much of the distinctiveness of its own national culture. St. Maarten is more commercially developed with the

ANNABEL YATES

major airport, a busy port and the largest resorts on the island. St. Martin has smaller hotels, more beaches and a general emphasis on comfort and elegance.

Just north of Marigot, the small mellow waves of **Friar's Bay** make it an ideal longboard spot. It breaks on

## TRAVEL INFORMATION

**Population:** 68,000
**Coastline:** 59km (37mi)
**Contests:** None
**Other Resources:**
surfingcharters.com
sxm-info.com
st-barths.com

**Getting There** – Citizens of most countries do not need a visa for their entry to St Maarten. St Martin and St Barths are subject to French immigration. St Maarten is the main gateway to St Barths through Juliana Airport (SXM). From Europe, Guadeloupe is another option (45 min connecting flight). Departure tax costs $20US.

**Getting Around** – From St Maarten, 10mn flights land on the tiny airstrip of St Barths. Powerboats get there in 1h30 and cost $50 r/t. Motorcycles are popular on St Barths. Rates are about $30/d while a car is $50. St Martin has a well-developed network of mini-buses with marked stops along the roadside. The *Corcovado*, a 40ft (13m) sailing vessel based in St Barths runs surfing trips throughout the French West Indies.

**Lodging and Food** – St Martin is about big resorts and hotels while half the beds in St Barths are in privately owned villas and apartments. Options range from moderate to very expensive – forget about budget travel. In St Barths, the surf season is tourist season with top rates. Try La Plantation in St Martin (Orient Bay, $120/dble studio), Maho Beach hotel in St Maarten ($245/dble) or Les Mouettes in St Barths ($150 Dble)

**Weather** – The climate in St Barths and St Martin is tropical and dry. The temperature is nearly constant at 28°C (82°F) in winter and 30°C (86°F) in summer. Moist, Atlantic trade winds bring orographic rainfall to the lush eastern coast, leaving the western side of the islands with far less rain and wind. The only deviation is in hurricane season, between July and November. In September 1995 Hurricane Luis caused great damage to the vegetation and buildings. Some beaches lost sand, while others were enlarged. Marine weather information is available at every marina's harbourmaster's office. The water temperature will range from 26°C (79°F) in the winter and 30°C (86°F) in the summer.

**Nature and Culture** – The four streets wide city of Marigot, on St Martin is one of the most French in spirit of all the Caribbean, with colonial houses, cafés, pastry shops and luxury boutiques. Naturalists will enjoy Eden Park and the Butter Fly Farm, naturists Orient Beach. There's great diving & fishing in St. Barths, but the accent is on civilised living like shopping and eating.

**Hazards and Hassles** – Some reefs are shallow and the coral is sharp, reef booties are worth packing. There aren't too many locals on either island but give respect to both them and the strong sunshine.

**Handy Hints** – Surfboards and bodyboards can be rented at Hookipa Surf Shop in Saint Jean, St Martin ($15) or Totem Surf, which is run by surfers in Gustavia, St Barths ($18). Other shops on St Martin include Beach Stuff Surf Shop in Marigot and West Indian Surf Shop in Saint Jean. Each island has their own currency but US$ are accepted everywhere.

| | | | | | | |
|---|---|---|---|---|---|---|
| total rainfall (mm) | 50 | 50 | 75 | 90 | 110 | 95 |
| consistency (days/mth) | 12 | 9 | 11 | 12 | 14 | 13 |
| min temp (°C/°F) | 23/74 | 24/75 | 25/77 | 25/77 | 25/77 | 24/75 |
| max temp (°C/°F) | 28/82 | 29/84 | 30/86 | 30/86 | 31/88 | 29/84 |

a large flat shallow reef and will be best on N-NW swells. At the northern tip of the island, **Wilderness** is a classy right pointbreak that goes off with an overhead N swell and S to E winds. It takes a long walk to get to this remote beach, with its inspiring mountainous jungle backdrop. The popular Orient Beach is protected from the swell by a coral ridge, but jetskis can take you to surrounding breaks on the islands outside the bay. **Le Gallion** is easily accessed, but the waves will usually be blown out by the trade winds. Off the small island on the other side of the Baie de l'Embouchure, **The Bowl** is a right pointbreak that can handle size. Getting in and out is quite tricky and booties are required, but this reefbreak will be the premium wave with an eastern hurricane swell. **Guana Bay** is a mediocre beachbreak, but an extra wide swell window makes it the most consistent spot around. Another beachbreak, **Mullet Bay** packs more punch and should be checked out on a NW swell. The lefts are usually best but close-out on a big swell, which is when the rights reveal themselves. Another serious righthand reefbreak is **Cupecoy**; if it's big and coming from the NW, the wave will pitch a couple of barrelling sections before ending right on a cliff. 32km (20mi) to the south of St Martin lies the French island of St Barths. It is hard to overstate the differences between the two islands, weird given their geographical proximity. St Martin is in many ways a typical Caribbean island, whereas St Barths oozes class, catering to expensive tastes in shopping, yachts, hotels and restaurants. With virtually no crime and intensely beautiful scenery, it is also blessed with some great waves for the fortunate few. Its coastline is irregular and has many coves and bays mostly protected by coral reefs. **Anse des Lézards** is a small swell, consistent reefbreak with very accessible lefts and the odd right on a N/NE swell. A mellow and occasionally very long left can be found at **Anse des Cayes**. There is also a hollow right with a sketchy, super shallow coral reef ending. The decent rights and lefts in **St-Jean** suffer from both wind exposure and some badly placed coral heads. The cross/onshores attract windsurfers, who shred underneath the small planes that land at the adjacent airstrip. Orient is St Barths' surfing hub, where members of the Reefer's Surf Club meet before or after a session at **The Ledge**, a shallow A-frame reef. Hot locals will also tackle the

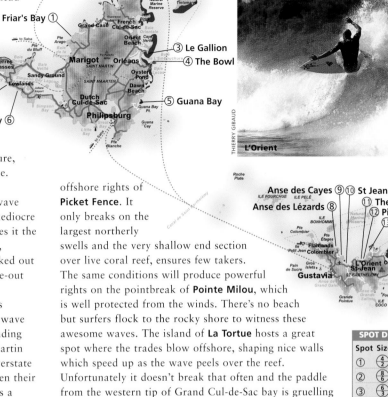

THIERRY GIBAUD

L'Orient

offshore rights of **Picket Fence**. It only breaks on the largest northerly swells and the very shallow end section over live coral reef, ensures few takers. The same conditions will produce powerful rights on the pointbreak of **Pointe Milou**, which is well protected from the winds. There's no beach but surfers flock to the rocky shore to witness these awesome waves. The island of **La Tortue** hosts a great spot where the trades blow offshore, shaping nice walls which speed up as the wave peels over the reef. Unfortunately it doesn't break that often and the paddle from the western tip of Grand Cul-de-Sac bay is gruelling against the prevailing strong currents. Find a boat! **Toiny** is on the southern side of the island, which means it will break with southern swells sent by summer/autumn hurricanes or on big wrap-around swells from the NE. When it's on, it's a fast barrel going both ways, a short gnarly right and a long, glorious walling left. There are further reefs and peaks west of the main wave at Toiny, but they are hollow and shallow, so take care.

The main surf season stretches from late November until early April, when winter lows leave the US East Coast before tracking NE towards Europe. They send 2-10ft (0.6-3m) surf on the exposed shores with occasional 12ft (4m) faces at L'Orient. When there's no storm the choppy windswell is all there is to ride on east facing shores, but the reefs make the most of it. Occasional hurricane swells will provide summertime surf on the SE exposed shores, but long flat spells are a certainty. The wind is predominantly easterly year round with more N winds between November and March. Surf early or right after a storm for glassy conditions. The tidal range is minimal, hovering around 0.3m (1ft).

| SPOT DESCRIPTION | | | |
|---|---|---|---|
| Spot | Size | Btm | Type |
| ① | 4/2 | 🌀 | ⬱ |
| ② | 8/6 | 🪨 | 🞃 |
| ③ | 5/3 | 🪨 | ⬱ |
| ④ | 10/4 | 🪨 | 🞃 |
| ⑤ | 6/2 | 🌀 | ⬱ |
| ⑥ | 5/2 | 🌀 | ⬱ |
| ⑦ | 8/3 | 🪨 | ⬱ |
| ⑧ | 6/2 | 🪨 | ⬱ |
| ⑨ | 6/2 | 🪨 | ⬱ |
| ⑩ | 6/2 | 🪨 | ⬱ |
| ⑪ | 6/3 | 🪨 | ⬱ |
| ⑫ | 10/4 | 🌀 | ⬱ |
| ⑬ | 10/4 | 🪨 | ⬱ |
| ⑭ | 8/4 | 🪨 | ⬱ |
| ⑮ | 10/3 | 🪨 | ⬱ |

Toiny

THIERRY GIBAUD

| SURF STATISTICS | J F | M A | M J | J A | S O | N D |
|---|---|---|---|---|---|---|
| dominant swell | N-E | N-E | NE-SE | NE-SE | N-E | N-E |
| swell size (ft) | 4 | 3 | 1-2 | 2 | 3-4 | 4 |
| consistency (%) | 80 | 60 | 30 | 30 | 60 | 70 |
| dominant wind | NE-E | NE-E | NE-SE | NE-SE | NE-SE | NE-E |
| average force | F4 | F4 | F4 | F4 | F4 | F4 |
| consistency (%) | 80 | 77 | 85 | 97 | 89 | 76 |
| water temp (°C/°F) | 25/77 | 25/77 | 26/79 | 28/82 | 28/82 | 26/79 |
| wetsuit | 🏄 | 🏄 | 🏄 | 🏄 | 🏄 | 🏄 |

# 150. Martinique

ALL PHOTOS NICOLAS LABAT

## Summary

+ GOOD RIGHTHAND REEF SET-UPS
+ CONSISTENT TARTANE BREAKS
+ SAFE TOURIST HAVEN

− SEASONAL NORTH SWELLS
− ONSHORE TRADE WINDS
− SOME CROWDED SPOTS

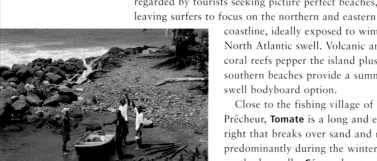

Martinique lies in the heart of the Caribbean Archipelago as one of the many islands making up the group of Lesser Antilles, or "Breezy Islands." The land rises gradually from the coast towards the centre and northern parts of the island, where the peaks of the Carbet and the Mont Pelée dormant volcanoes can be found. The southern shores are highly regarded by tourists seeking picture perfect beaches, leaving surfers to focus on the northern and eastern coastline, ideally exposed to winter's North Atlantic swell. Volcanic and coral reefs pepper the island plus the southern beaches provide a summer swell bodyboard option.

Close to the fishing village of Le Prêcheur, **Tomate** is a long and easy right that breaks over sand and reef, predominantly during the winter northerly swells. **Céron** also needs a sizeable N swell, is a bit shorter but packs more punch as it ends in a shorebreak on a beautiful black sand beach. Whilst being good waves, they are but mere shadows of neighboring **Anse Couleuvre**, possibly the best wave on the island. These long, tubular rights start with an easy take-off, but the walls are fast and powerful, before the wave ends over coral and urchins. Skills are required to ride this inconsistent, wind-protected beauty. Located at the

## TRAVEL INFORMATION

**Population:**
87,000 (La Trinite)
**Coastline:** 350km (220mi)
**Contests:**
Regional (Sept-Feb)
**Other Resources:**
surfmartinique.com
perso.wanadoo.fr/
 body972/
martinique.org
la-martinique.net

**Getting There** – This is French territory; visas are required for Japanese, Brazilians and South-African citizens. Lamentin Airport (FDF) has regular flights from the US, Europe and other Caribbean islands. Martinique can also be reached from Guadeloupe by catamaran ($80r/t, 31/2h). Tartane is 30min away from Fort de France, 20min from the airport.

**Getting Around** – Rent a car in Fort-de-France, rates begin at $40/d, including taxes, insurance and unlimited mileage. While public buses are inexpensive, much public transport is by collective taxis, 8-passenger limousines bearing the sign TC. Traffic jams are common and can happen any time of the day.

**Lodging and Food** – Scattered all over the island accommodation options range from large hotel to family-run establishments called "Relais Créoles," to "Gîtes de France", usually studios in private homes. Around Tartane, try Résidence Océane ($89ₐ/dble) or L'hôtel La Caravelle ($60/dble). Sample Martinique's culinary magic, a marriage of French and Creole cuisines.

**Weather** – Martinique has a tropical climate with relative humidity ranging from 77-85% all year. The two main seasons are "carême" with cooler and drier months from January to June, and a wet season called "hivernage" from July to December. The southern area of the island tends to be drier. The island is warm year round, with temperatures reaching 30°C (86°F) in the daytime. There is only about a 5°C (9°F) difference between summer and winter temperatures. Two regular, alternating wind currents (east and northeast).

**Nature and Culture** – While keeping a Caribbean cachet, Martinique exudes a distinctly French feeling. Hiking, diving and mountain biking are great. There's a wealth of sightseeing: white sand beaches, tropical rainforest, floral gardens and the majestic Mount Pelee. Visit rum distilleries for a sampling of their product before dancing to Biguine and Zouk.

**Hazards and Hassles** – Spots around Tartane can get crowded, but it's easy to move to less popular spots. Stay clear of the poisonous manchineel trees that border some beaches; they are sometimes marked with red paint. Martinique has the best medical care in the Eastern Caribbean.

**Handy Hints** – Surfing equipment at Familee surfshop or X-trème Pro Shop. A regular shortboard is all that is needed most of the times, but reef boots are a valuable possession. Bliss surf school located on the "Plage des Surfeurs" offers surf lessons ($19/h) and board rentals ($23/d).

| WEATHER STATISTICS | J/F | M/A | M/J | J/A | S/O | N/D |
|---|---|---|---|---|---|---|
| total rainfall (mm) | 95 | 80 | 160 | 240 | 240 | 170 |
| consistency (days/mth) | 15 | 13 | 17 | 22 | 19 | 18 |
| min temp (°C/°F) | 21/70 | 22/72 | 23/74 | 24/75 | 24/75 | 23/74 |
| max temp (°C/°F) | 27/80 | 28/82 | 29/84 | 29/84 | 30/86 | 29/84 |

northern tip of the island, Grand-Rivière hosts 2 quality breaks. **Bagasse**'s powerful, barrelling rights and lefts will attract tube seekers while **Charlot** reefbreaks will cater to those looking for longer rides. The rights of **Basse-Pointe** break right into the port and getting in is tricky. The lefts breaking on the other side

**Plage des Surfeurs**

are equally impressive, as they get seriously hollow. **Le Lorrain** is more advisable for beginning surfers; it's a mellow beachbreak away from any crowds. **Charpencaye** is Anse Charpentier's right reefbreak. The take-off is straight into a tube section, followed by a fast, peeling wall that ends on a reef ledge. Be warned that getting in and out requires a bit of reef dancing and that the strong currents have led to a complete ban on swimming here. There's also a beachbreak on the other side of the wild bay. The best concentration of consistent spots is then found on the Caravelle peninsula, a 10km (6mi) long arm of land jutting into the Atlantic near the town of La Trinité. Facing the VVF (camping) in Anse l'Etang, **Cocoa** is a technically challenging fast and powerful left. 2km (1.2mi) from the centre of the fishing port of Tartane, Anse Bonneville hosts the **Plage des Surfeurs**, the most consistent (although often messy) and best known spot on the island. After paddling around a large coral patch, mellow rights and lefts can be surfed, with some longer rides possible on the rights. A surf school takes advantage of the smaller inside wave. **Pelle à Tarte** is a short walk or a 15min paddle from there. This wave is much more shallow and powerful with a hollow but makeable right and a death defying left that only a few bodyboarders dare tackling. On the south shore of the island, the reefbreaks give way to a string of beachbreaks that tend to close-out quickly and therefore only attract bodyboarders looking for launch ramps. The road to **Anse Trabaud** crosses private property and the owner charges $2.50 for the privilege. The wave is a shorebreak on the left side of the beach. There's also a reef outside,

but it's an exhausting paddle and rarely worth it. Around Le Diamant a few regulars take on violent shorebreaks such as **Diams** or **Banzaï**. **Anse Cafard** is just more of the same stuff and should only appeal to bodyboarders.

The main swell season is from November to March, with 3-10ft (1-3m) N-NE ground-swells, sent down the North Atlantic by storms and cold fronts off the east coast of North America. Constant 2-5ft (0.6-1.6m) E windswells occurs year round, so surfing small sloppy waves is always an option around

the Caravelle peninsula. The hurricane season can bring some of the largest swell of the year between July and September but they're highly unpredictable and may well wreak havoc on the island if they get too close. Dominant E trade winds vary from 44% (Nov) to 70% (Jul). It blows NE more than SE except May-June and Sept-Oct. Spots located on the northwest tip of the island will see perfect glassy days with a straight North swell and SE winds. Don't worry about tides.

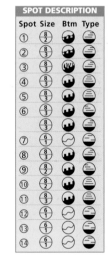

**SPOT DESCRIPTION**

| Spot | Size | Btm | Type |
|---|---|---|---|
| ① | 8/3 | | |
| ② | 8/3 | | |
| ③ | 8/3 | | |
| ④ | 8/3 | | |
| ⑤ | 8/3 | | |
| ⑥ | 8/3 | | |
| ⑦ | 6/1 | | |
| ⑧ | 8/3 | | |
| ⑨ | 8/2 | | |
| ⑩ | 8/2 | | |
| ⑪ | 8/3 | | |
| ⑫ | 6/1 | | |
| ⑬ | 6/1 | | |
| ⑭ | 6/1 | | |

**SURF STATISTICS**

| | J F | M A | M J | J A | S O | N D |
|---|---|---|---|---|---|---|
| dominant swell | N-E | N-E | NE-SE | NE-SE | N-E | N-E |
| swell size (ft) | 4 | 3 | 1-2 | 2 | 3-4 | 4 |
| consistency (%) | 70 | 60 | 40 | 40 | 60 | 70 |
| dominant wind | NE-E | NE-E | NE-SE | NE-SE | NE-SE | NE-E |
| average force | F4 | F4 | F4 | F4 | F4 | F4 |
| consistency (%) | 80 | 77 | 85 | 97 | 89 | 76 |
| water temp (°C/°F) | 25/77 | 25/77 | 26/79 | 28/82 | 28/82 | 26/79 |
| wetsuit | | | | | | |

surfing evolve

Menber of the S-CORE Project

Premier Peruvian pointbreak Herradurra has a long and distinguished history written by a procession of talented Lima locals. Often targetted for potential developments of various wave destroying description, it remains a valuable surf resource.

boz

# South America

G BARANDIARAN

# The Ocean Environment

South America is a continent of significant environmental importance, nurturing some vast swathes of true wilderness on both the Pacific and Atlantic coasts. Paradoxically, these areas exist alongside intensely crowded coastal metropolises, expelling vast quantities of concentrated industrial pollution and the population's barely treated sewage. South America's economic frailties play a large part in the environmental issues that are only slowly being addressed by governments and citizens that would prefer more affluence to less effluent.

## Pollution

The cold Humboldt Current scours the Pacific Coast of South America, constantly replenishing the area's nutrient rich water from deep ocean supplies. The Galapagos are a protected national park, showcasing the diverse wildlife that led Darwin to his theory of evolution. Part of modern evolution are cruise liners and commercial shipping, leading to the 1999 grounding of a vessel on Isla Santa Cruz, which leaked large quantities of poisonous fuel oil. Serious environmental disaster was averted by a swift response and calm ocean conditions, but the fragile eco-system is put under threat with every visitor. Predictably, major cities are the big problem in South America, and while Quito in Ecuador is deep inland, lack of residential waste-water treatment means 70% of river pollutants are directly attributed to sewage. In neighbouring Colombia, only 6% of all effluent receives even the most basic treatment. Lima is the most densely populated region on the west coast and its suburban line-ups suffer from chronic pollution since untreated industrial and domestic effluent is released into the major rivers that flow directly to the sea. Incredibly, the same polluted river water is used to irrigate vegetable growing farmland, resulting in dangerous bacteria entering the human food chain. Hundreds of millions of

FRANCISCO CHAGAS

dollars are earmarked for upgrading the cities old system but it will take years to come on line. The rest of the Peruvian coast experiences localised problems from domestic waste, the odd fish factory, and after heavy rains flush out dried up rivers and drains. Recent El Niño events brought floods to normally arid areas and coastal waters were seriously polluted as a result. Chile's dynamic coastal environment rapidly disperses pollutants plus the country is aiming for 100% city sewage infrastructure and treatment by 2005. Waste management has been privatised but billions of dollars of investment is needed to improve river systems that have been used as open sewers. Typhoid, hepatitis and polluted irrigation supplies for the commercial fruit growers are some of the side effects. Hazardous mining wastes containing high levels of arsenic are produced in central and northern regions and are often discharged directly into the sea. In Antofagasta, some of the city's effluent receives tertiary treatment and is pumped 40km (25mi) to desert copper mining operations, but the bulk is released through a long ocean outfall. The point at Topocalma has been the scene of a battle to halt marina development, which in turn has raised the profile and popularity of the spot, leading to an increase in surfer numbers crossing private ranchland to camp on the point. With no sanitary facilities, unthinking surfers have rapidly defiled the woods to such an extent that the once potable water of the stream now carries potential disease directly into the line-up. Save The Waves, instrumental in saving the point are now coordinating the clean up. In Argentina, over 95% of Buenos Aires sewage continues to be dumped directly into the Rio del Plata or into makeshift septic tanks, cesspools or directly onto streets and open fields. Argentina's coast around Mar del Plata and Miramar is lightly populated, until holiday season when many seaside towns' antiquated and rudimentary sewage systems are unable to cope with the influx of summer visitors and water-borne diseases are a constant concern. Brazil has a densely populated coast where the great urban sprawls of Recife and Rio de Janeiro combine with the heavy industrial complexes of São Paulo to darken the Atlantic. Coastal water quality, especially after rain, can be horrendous, especially around Rio. Guandara Bay, inside the harbour, but only a couple of coastal miles

Top – **Most South American cities are awash with sewage problems and adequate treatment facilities remain years away.**

Bottom – **While rivermouths sculpt some nice sandbanks, many act as open sewers for inland cities.**

TOM KORBER

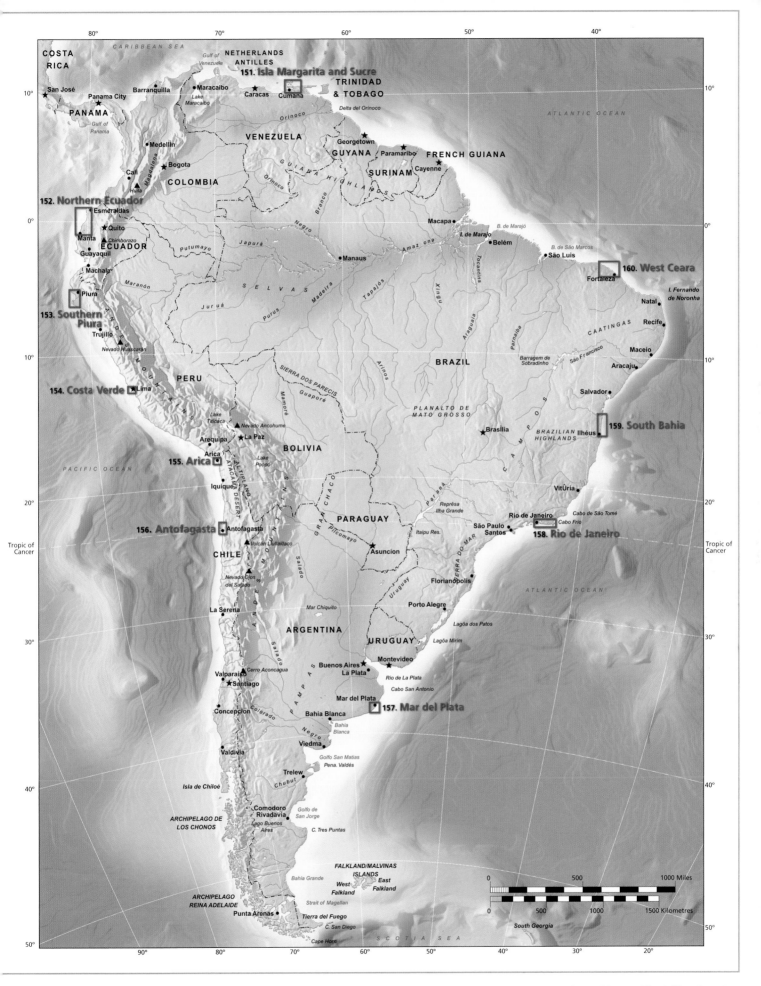

CARIBBEAN SEA

COSTA RICA
San José
Panama City
PANAMA
Gulf of Panama

Barranquilla
Maracaibo
Lake Maracaibo
Medellín
Cali
Huila
Bogota
COLOMBIA

Gulf of Venezuela
NETHERLANDS ANTILLES
Caracas
Cumana
**151. Isla Margarita and Sucre**
TRINIDAD & TOBAGO
Delta del Orinoco

VENEZUELA
Orinoco
Orinoco
Branco
GUIANA HIGHLANDS
Georgetown
GUYANA
Paramaribo
SURINAM
Cayenne
FRENCH GUIANA

ATLANTIC OCEAN

**152. Northern Ecuador**
Esmeraldas
Quito
Manta
Chimborazo
ECUADOR
Guayaquil
Machala
Piura
**153. Southern Piura**
Trujillo

Putumayo
Japurá
Negro
Amazona
Macapa
I. de Marajo
B. de Marajó
Belém
B. de São Marcos
São Luis

**160. West Ceara**
Fortaleza
I. Fernando de Noronha
Natal

Marañon
SELVAS
Manaus
Juruá
Purus
Madeira
Tapajós
Xingu
Tocantins
Araguaia

Recife
CAATINGAS
Maceio
Aracaju
Salvador

Nevado Huascaran
ANDES MOUNTAINS
PERU

SIERRA DOS PARECIS
Mamoré
Guaporé
Alinos
Parnaiba
São Francisco
Barragem de Sobradinho

BRAZIL

**154. Costa Verde**
Lima
Lake Titicaca
Nevado Ancohume
Arequipa
La Paz
**155. Arica**
Arica
Iquique
ALTIPLANO
ATACAMA DESERT

BOLIVIA
Lake Poopó
GRAN CHACO
PARAGUAY
Itaipu Res.
Asuncion

PLANALTO DE MATO GROSSO
Brasilia
CAMPOS
BRAZILIAN HIGHLANDS
Ilhéus
**159. South Bahia**
Vitúria

**156. Antofagasta**
Antofagasta
Volcán Llullaillaco
CHILE
Nevado Ojos del Salado

SERRA DO MAR
Parana
Reprêsa Ilha Grande
São Paulo
Santos
Rio de Janeiro
Cabo Frio
**158. Rio de Janeiro**
Cabo de São Tomé

Tropic of Cancer

PACIFIC OCEAN

La Serena
Valparaiso
Cerro Aconcagua
Santiago
Concepcion
Valdivia
Isla de Chiloé

Mar Chiquito
Salado
ARGENTINA
PAMPAS
Buenos Aires
La Plata
Colorado
Negro
Bahia Blanca
Viedma
Golfo San Matias
Pena. Valdés
Trelew
Chubut

URUGUAY
Montevideo
Rio de La Plata
Cabo San Antonio
Mar del Plata
**157. Mar del Plata**

Florianópolis
Porto Alegre
Lagôa dos Patos
Lagôa Mirim

ATLANTIC OCEAN

Tropic of Cancer

ARCHIPELAGO DE LOS CHONOS
Comodoro Rivadavia
Lago Buenos Aires
Golfo de San Jorge
C. Tres Puntas

ARCHIPELAGO REINA ADELAIDE
Punta Arenas
Bahia Grande
Strait of Magellan
Tierra del Fuego
C. San Diego
Cape Horn
SCOTIA SEA

FALKLAND/MALVINAS ISLANDS
West Falkland
East Falkland

South Georgia

0    500    1000 Miles

0    500    1000    1500 Kilometres

from Copacabana and Ipanema beaches has been a dumping ground for every conceivable form of man-made pollution. Since 2000, three major tanker or pipeline oil spills have occurred, the biggest being 340,000 ton of heavy fuel oil, alongside a continual discharge of raw sewage into a bay with a history of illegally dumped, highly toxic, industrial waste. Across South America, poorly enforced environmental laws are no deterrent for industries that profit heavily from not having to dispose of waste properly, while clean up operations struggle to deal with the worst incidences. By 2005, Brazil will be implementing contracts for 3,700 towns and cities to construct or renovate sanitation services.

Above – **This unusual protrusion on Chile's coast was an island before being reconnected to the coast. Flanked by a large man-made port to the north the Alacran Peninsula represents one of the engineered attempts to provide safe anchorages along the Pacific coast.**

Top – **Arid, desert landscapes shadow the Humbolt Current, presenting some challenging territory to traverse before hitting the water.**

Bottom – **Brazil's urban line-ups are frenetic and hyper competitive.**

## Erosion

Harbour and marina construction threaten waves around South America's coastline and beach stabilisation exists around many cities. Some Peruvian line-ups suffer from ill-placed fishing piers, including Cabo Blanco, where the end section of the wave is bisected. Originally planned to extend out through the peak, the revised structure is too short and big north swell sets engulf the pier. Three left points in the Pichilemu area of Chile are under threat from a development proposal for 50,000 houses, golf courses, amenities and three marinas along a stretch of virgin coastline. Local surfers and pressure group Save The Waves lobbied planning authorities and the development company has revised the proposal to exclude all the marinas. Suspicions remain that the pointbreaks will be affected by altered sand flow and that marina approval will follow once the land-based development has been completed. Brazilian surfers have suffered due to a large harbour development in Recife that has had a profound effect on the surrounding eco-system. Construction diminished fish stocks and the local sharks were forced to include surfers amongst their new diet, resulting in the subsequent closure of 60km (37mi) of surfing beaches. In Rio de Janeiro, seawall construction on the famous Copacabana Beach has completely altered the beach profile. The expansion of the promenade wall seawards to allow for prime real estate to be developed, led to beach steepening, transforming a classic, swell holding beachbreak into a rarely breaking mush-burger.

## Access

The Galapagos Islands are a strictly controlled nature reserve and hence access is restricted to the smaller islands. Surfing is not permitted on some islands and even main area access is difficult, relying on hiking or a boat trip. Peru's main coastal highway is good but roads leading down to coastal villages are poorly maintained and can be impassable during rains. Chile's northern surfing zone has easy access around the towns of Arica and Iquique, but the southern surf zone is a lot trickier. Large areas of coast are huge private ranches and permits need to be obtained before entering by 4WD. The swell increases further south and so does the effort required to reach the coast. The Brazilian love for the beach and beach culture assures good access in urban areas, but it deteriorates as much as the roads in rural regions where rainfall is high. The ban on surfing any of the beaches from Recife to Porto de Suape remains in force, although some locals take their chances with the sharks. Fernando de Noronha is a nature reserve and visitor numbers are carefully controlled.

## Hazards

Sharks do patrol in South American waters, particularly on the east coast, but attacks are rare. The main exception is Brazil where a quarter of the 80 reported shark attacks have been fatal. The northern city of Recife saw an increase in fatalities shortly after the aforementioned harbour development and six surfers lost their lives. Strong currents, sharp rocks and cold water are all regular features of Peruvian and Chilean surf, plus El Nino years bring floods and mud slides to the west coast. With some densely populated surf zones and a Latin culture, local surfers are highly competitive especially at city breaks or class reefs. Intensity varies with locals ruling by skill and knowledge of the break although rigorously policed hierarchical line-ups do exist. Intimidation and violence are rare, but expect to be regularly dropped in on.

# Surf Travel Resources

**ECUADOR**
- H 1. Mompiche Beach Lodge
- H 2. La Posada de Daniel
- 3. Canoas Surf Explorer
- H 4. Hotel Bambu
- S 5. Casa del Sol
- H 6. Finca Punta Ayampe

**PERU**
- SS 7. Bungalows Playa Blanca
- SS 8. Mancora Beach Bungalows
- 9. Las Olas
- 10. Hostal Los Delfines
- H 11. Huanchaco Int'l Hotel
- H 12. Hostal Chicama
- S 13. Santa Rosa Surf Camp
- 14. Surf-peru.com
- H 15. Hamacas
- S 16. Casa Resort Peñascal
- 17. Surfinperu
- 18. Escuela De Tabla
- 19. Rocio Surf School
- 20. Peru Surf Dreams
- 21. Escola Gaucha de Surf
- SS 22. Pico Alto Int'l Surf Camp
- 23. Luisfer Surf Camp
- H 24. Kahunas Surf Host
- 25. Señoritas Surf Camp
- 26. Olas Peru
- 27. Casa Barco
- 28. Surfs Charter Eco Tours

**CHILE**
- H 29. Hotel Sainte-Georgette
- 30. Las Rocas Surf Camp
- SS 31. Desierto Surfero
- SS 32. Tio Peco
- H 33. Quiksilver Surf Camp
- S 34. Cabañas Waitara
- H 35. Hotel Chile España
- 36. Lobos del Pacifico

**ARGENTINA**
- S 37. Conosur Surfcamp

**URUGUAY**
- 38. Sunvalley surfschool

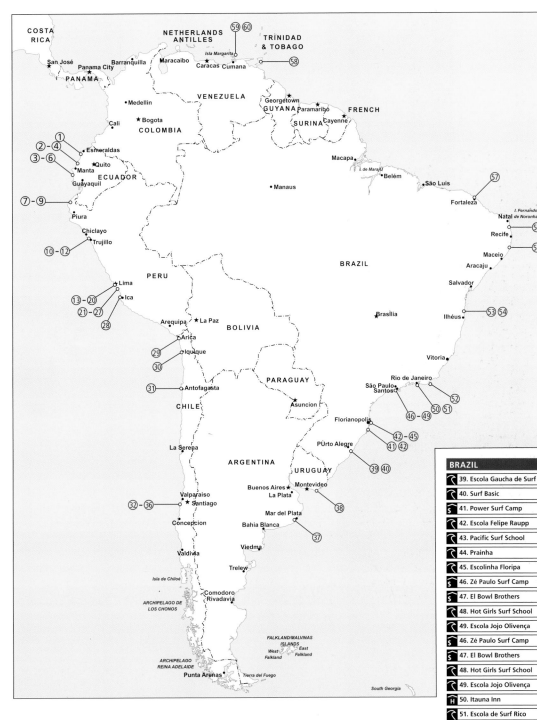

**BRAZIL**
- 39. Escola Gaucha de Surf
- 40. Surf Basic
- S 41. Power Surf Camp
- 42. Escola Felipe Raupp
- 43. Pacific Surf School
- 44. Prainha
- 45. Escolinha Floripa
- S 46. Zé Paulo Surf Camp
- S 47. El Bowl Brothers
- 48. Hot Girls Surf School
- 49. Escola Jojo Olivença
- S 46. Zé Paulo Surf Camp
- S 47. El Bowl Brothers
- 48. Hot Girls Surf School
- 49. Escola Jojo Olivença
- H 50. Itauna Inn
- 51. Escola de Surf Rico
- SS 52. Sossego Surf Camp
- S 53. Easydrop
- S 54. Lawrence's Surf House
- H 55. Pousada dos Coqueiros
- H 56. Casablanca Resort
- 57. Chandler Surf

**VENEZUELA**
- SS 58. Paradise Found Villa
- H 59. Casa Viento B&B
- 60. Water Extasis

## COUNTRY INFORMATION

| | VENEZUELA | ECUADOR | PERU | CHILE | ARGENTINA | BRAZIL |
|---|---|---|---|---|---|---|
| Area (sq km/mi): | 912,050/352,145 | 283,000/109,000 | 1,285,000/496,000 | 756,000/292,000 | 2,780,400/1,073,518 | 8,500,000/3,267,000 |
| Population: | 24M | 13M | 27M | 15M | 37M | 175M |
| Waveriders: | 20,000 | 3,000 | 20,000 | 8,000 | 30,000 | 500,000 |
| Tourists (per yr): | 600,000 | 500,000 | 1M | 1.7M | 3M | 5.4M |
| Language: | Spanish | Spanish, Quechua | Spanish, Quechua | Spanish | Spanish, English | Portuguese |
| Currency: | Bolivar | US Dollar | Nuevo Sol | Chilean Peso | Argentine Peso | Real |
| Exchange: | $1 = 1,400 VEB | $1 = 1 USD | $1 = 3.6 PEN | $1 = 690 CLP | $1 = 3.6 ARS | $1=3 BRL |
| GDP ($ per yr): | $6,200 | $2,900 | $4,550 | $10,000 | $12,900 | $6,500 |
| Inflation (%): | 13% | 96% | 4% | 5% | 4% | 6% |

# 151. Isla Margarita and Sucre

ALL PHOTOS THIERRY GIBAUD

### Summary
+ ISLAND AND MAINLAND SURF
+ BEAUTIFUL WHITE SAND BEACHES
+ TOURIST HEAVEN, GREAT NIGHTLIFE
+ PERFECT WEATHER

– ALWAYS SMALL
– WINDY AND CHOPPY CONDITIONS
– UNSTABLE POLITICAL SITUATION
– NOT SO CHEAP

Just 40km (25mi) off mainland Venezuela, Margarita Island emerges out of the warm water of the Caribbean Sea, showcasing beautiful beaches, majestic mountains and verdant valleys. Rather than attracting eco-tourists, this rich natural backdrop overlooks a hedonistic, beach-going, tax-free shopping, party-orientated crowd. While the social life is hardcore, the surfing is not, but provides a small wave, warm water option for those looking for good times under the sun. With a swell window reduced by the Caribbean islands, Venezuela has to rely on easterly windswells and long distance North Atlantic swells wrapping around the West Indies. These swells come with regular onshore winds on the exposed coast but if it picks-

up enough, the northwest tip of the island will receive clean surf. Heading west, away from the festive side of Margarita, a causeway crosses the marshes and lagoons of a national park before reaching the Macanao Peninsula. Here the lush vegetation disappears to leave deserted landscapes that end in steep cliffs or isolated beaches.

## TRAVEL INFORMATION

**Population:** 375,000 Nueva Esparta
**Coastline:** 160km (100mi)
**Contests:** National
**Other Resources:**
surfreport.com.ve
surfreportvenezuela.com
surfschoolmargarita.
 4mg.com
veweb.com
margaritaonline.com

**Getting There** – Most nationalities don't need a visa. Fly direct to the Santiago Mariño International Caribbean Airport (PMV), 20min away from Porlamar or go through Caracas (CCS, $50, 35mn). Aeropostal is the domestic airline. Playa Parguito is 40min away from the airport by taxi ($13). The international departure tax is US$22.

**Getting Around** – Rent a car for around $350/w. Taxi cabs are identified by yellow tags, most lines have fixed rates and are usually fairly priced. Ride the really inexpensive buses if on a budget and in no hurry. To reach the mainland, ride the ferry from Punta de Piedras to Carúpano (4h).

**Lodging and Food** – The Bolivar lost about 40% of its value in 2002, resulting in better prices for visitors, but Margarita still isn't a budget destination. Stay at the Hosteria el Agua ($35 dble), at the Posada Casa Blanca In Playa Copey ($25 dble). A meal is around $15; try the local Catalana fish and arepanas (stuffed pancakes).

**Weather** – In contrast to the rest of the country, weather in Margarita changes little between seasons and the warm tropical sun shines throughout the year. The dry season that stretches between mid-December and mid-April matches with the surf season and proves to be the best time to visit. At that time, it seldom rains and the temperatures remain just under 30°C (86°F). The island is out of the hurricane belt. The temperatures may reach 37°C (100°F) in the summer months but cooling breezes help to make it liveable. January is the coldest month, September the warmest. Rains occur mostly at night, in strong and heavy showers. Sun radiation is extremely strong; don't forget sunscreen.

**Nature and Culture** – Windsurfers will head to famous El Yaque. Take a boat tour on the Lagoon of the Restinga national park or hike to the Castle of Santa Rosa from which the whole island can be seen. Go to Porlamar on a shopping mission (Margarita is tax-free) or for raging nightlife (Senor Frog's...)

**Hazards and Hassles** – Some sharks cruise Venezuelan water but present no threat around Margarita. Locals are keen surfers and usually friendly. In July 1997, Venezuela's worst earthquake in decades hit Cumana and Cariaco. Registering 6.9 on the Richter Scale, it killed 59 people and injured about 320. Hangovers are probably the worst thing that can happen.

**Handy Hints** – Take a fish or a longboard for the numerous small, mushy days. A few shops carry surf equipment (Kasual Surf Shop in Porlamar). A new board costs around $300. Water temps remain around 27°C (80°F), so bring boardies. The oil strike that started in December 2002 sent the whole country into a crisis state.

| WEATHER STATISTICS | J/F | M/A | M/J | J/A | S/O | N/D |
|---|---|---|---|---|---|---|
| total rainfall (mm) | 10 | 10 | 75 | 120 | 70 | 40 |
| consistency (days/mth) | 6 | 2 | 5 | 7 | 5 | 9 |
| min temp (°C/°F) | 24/75 | 25/77 | 25/77 | 26/79 | 26/79 | 25/77 |
| max temp (°C/°F) | 28/82 | 29/84 | 30/86 | 30/86 | 31/88 | 29/84 |

The fishermen's huts of **Punta Arena** extend along a beach that can produce hollow waves provided the surf is big enough to get there; locals swear it only happens a couple of times a year. **Funeral Point** is definitely off the beaten track for tourists but surfers should check it out. Back on the main island, facing north, the white sand beach of **Playa Caribe** receives a bit more swell than **Puerto Cruz**, but the latter is located between two rocky hills providing shelter from virtually any wind. This right pointbreak reels over a rocky bottom and the long rides it offers are worth waiting for. The northeast coast of Margarita is perfectly orientated to receive any available swell and has become the surf hub of the island. Among Margarita's 27 beaches, covering 53km (33mi) of its 160km (100mi) shoreline, **Playa el Agua** is one of the longest and widest, and definitely the busiest. Venezuelans like to come here to exhibit their tanned bodies while drinking cocktails on the water's edge. The Miragua Restaurant is actually a good lookout spot since the best peaks regularly break out front. It's even possible

to rent a microlight to fly out over the neighbouring spots and maybe even locate some semi secret spots. Taking its name from the red snapper fish, **Parguito** is the island's primo surf spot. Its extra consistency makes it a regular pick for surf contests and national championships are regularly organised here. It was also home to the Pan American Surfing Games in February 2002, which saw the local team take victory ahead of Guadeloupe and Peru. Parguito can get hollow despite the regular onshore winds. Down south, **Guacuco** offers small, empty peaks at this 5km (3mi) long beach A more radical way to get away from Margarita's hype is to cruise the mainland. Stretching for 70km (45mi) under Margarita, the Peninsula de Araya is sheltered from the swell by the Isla Coche, itself sitting in water too deep for waves to break. However el Morro de **Chacopata** is fully exposed, and the reefbreak represents the closest reliable spot for Cumana's surfing community. On the way to Carupano, check out **La Esmeralda** and **Punta de Guiria** which should pick-up more swell than most of the coast. **Playa Copey**'s righthand pointbreak and other peaks, 7km (4mi) before Carúpano, have been the site of

national surfing championships. There are good waves in **Carúpano** itself, but be prepared to surf in troubled water around the rivermouth. Further east, there are more breaks on the way to Rio Caribe, which could serve as a base for expeditions to the Peninsula de Paria. A 4WD is advised to access most of these beaches. The uncrowded rights and left reefs of **Chaguarama** are only 10 minutes away from Rio Caribe and an extra 20mn will take you to **Pui Puy**, a consistent, uncrowded, long stretch of beachbreaks where several peaks can be found. Further investigation of the Peninsula de Paria should bring some rewards.

The premium season for waves is December to April, when North Atlantic groundswells wrap around the West Indies island chain and hit the NE facing coasts. The biggest ones will wrap around the island to produce cleaner surf on the other side. Expect year round knee high windswell. Venezuela is too far south for cyclone swells in the rainy season. The strong trade winds give El Yaque a worldwide reputation among windsurfers. They're lighter up north but will still mess up the surf. Wind direction doesn't vary much; E trade winds blow all year round, but summertime's straight E winds give way to stronger N-NE winds between December and March. Mornings can have calm conditions. The tide range is minimal and shouldn't be a concern.

| SPOT DESCRIPTION | | | |
|---|---|---|---|
| Spot | Size | Btm | Type |
| ① | 6/1 | | |
| ② | 6/1 | | |
| ③ | 6/1 | | |
| ④ | 8/2 | | |
| ⑤ | 6/1 | | |
| ⑥ | 6/1 | | |
| ⑦ | 6/1 | | |
| ⑧ | 8/2 | | |
| ⑨ | 8/2 | | |
| ⑩ | 6/1 | | |
| ⑪ | 8/2 | | |
| ⑫ | 6/1 | | |
| ⑬ | 8/2 | | |
| ⑭ | 6/1 | | |

| SURF STATISTICS | J F | M A M | J J A | S O | N D |
|---|---|---|---|---|---|
| dominant swell | NE-E | NE-E | NE-E | NE-E | NE-E | NE-E |
| swell size (ft) | 3 | 2-3 | 1 | 1 | 1-2 | 2-3 |
| consistency (%) | 60 | 50 | 30 | 20 | 30 | 45 |
| dominant wind | NE-E | NE-E | NE-SE | NE-SE | NE-SE | NE-E |
| average force | F4 | F4 | F4 | F3-F4 | F3 | F3-F4 |
| consistency (%) | 88 | 86 | 96 | 91 | 90 | 84 |
| water temp (°C/°F) | 26/79 | 26/79 | 27/80 | 28/82 | 28/82 | 27/80 |
| wetsuit | | | | | | |

Map labels:
5 Playa El Agua
Puerto Cruz ④
Playa Caribe ③
6 Playa Parguito
Funeral Point ②
⑦ Guacuco
Punta Arena ①
La Asunción
Carúpano ⑫
Playa Copey ⑪
Chaguarama ⑬
⑭ Pui Puy
8 Chacopata
Punta de Guiria ⑩
La Esmeralda ⑨
ISLA MARGARITA
Porlamar
Punta de Piedras
El Yaque
ISLA CUBAGUA
ISLA COCHE
San Pedro
Morro de Chacopata
Cumaná
PENINSULA DE ARAYA
Araya
GOLFO DE CARIACO
Cariaco
SUCRE
Carúpano
Rio Caribe

# 152. Northern Ecuador

COLOMBIA

ECUADOR

PERU
NORTH

Mompiche

PAUL KENNEDY

**Summary**

+ N & S SWELL EXPOSURE
+ EXPLORATION POTENTIAL
+ LESS CROWDS THAN S ECUADOR
+ BEAUTIFUL NATURAL AREA
+ CHEAP LODGING AND TRANSPORT

– SHORT N SWELL SEASON
– FLAT SPELLS
– HARD TO REACH MOMPICHE
– RAINY SURF SEASON
– SECURITY ISSUES

Ecuador has long been popular with surfers looking for a warm water fix after enduring the cold Humboldt Current that pervades the South American Pacific Coast. Travellers concentrated on the Montañita area in the south but rumours of a perfect left set-up in Mompiche have attracted the more adventurous to the "green province" of Esmeraldas. The northernmost coastal province enjoys lush vegetation, from tropical rainforest to mangroves while estuaries cut the land into remote territories only accessible by boat. Esmeraldas itself is best avoided as its reputation stands as one of the most dangerous cities around, with only a murky, mushy beachbreak for desperadoes.

Secret Garden

TOM KÖRBER

TOM KÖRBER

**Atacames** is much more tourist-orientated but some caution is still needed. Facing lively beach bars, the beachbreak ranks highly on the fun scale with barrels at low tide and long rides at high tide. It needs a NW or strong W swell to function. Solitude-seekers may feel

## TRAVEL INFORMATION

**Population:** 430,000
**Coastline:** 2,237km (1,400mi)
**Contests:** Local (Canoa)
**Other Resources:**
canoasurfexplorer.com
fesurf.org
ecuadorexplorer.com
thebestofecuador.com

**Getting There** – No Visa. Fly to Quito then go to Esmeraldas by plane (1/2h, $90r/t) or bus (6h, $8), then bus to Muisne (3h, $4). Or bus from Quito to Santo Domingo (2h, $2) then bus to Muisne (4h, $5). Mompiche is a short boat ride from Muisne ($10, 1h). If you come from the south ride a boat from Cojimies.

**Getting Around** – A paved highway now links Pedernales to Atacames but runs 9km (5.5mi) inland of Mompiche. Tropical rainstorms may close local roads from December to June. Renting a car is quite expensive ($60/day). Plenty of cheap, crowded, uncomfortable, and slow buses. Canoa Surf Explorer offers 4WD package tours with expert local guides. (11d, $700).

**Lodging and Food** – Budget hotels are $5 a night. Same, Atacames and Esmeraldas have high-end resorts. Mompiche beach's Casablanca resort is $45/d w/meals; Hotel Gabeal is $15/d w/breakfast. In Canoas, head to La Posada de Daniel (from $6/d). Try 'Sancocho Esmeraldeño' (fish soup) and 'mariscos encocada', seafood prepared in a savory coconut sauce.

**Weather** – As the country's name suggests, equatorial climate can be expected, but climate throughout the country ranges from tropical equatorial rainy weather to perpetual snow on the top of the mountains due to the influence of the Andean mountain range in the highlands. Esmeraldas is the wettest coastal province and the surf season matches the rainy season, between January and March. Surprisingly, January and February are also the months receiving the most sun, making it one of the best times to visit. Days typically awaken to bright sunshine before tropical showers start pouring in the afternoon and continue at night. Temperatures are stable year round with 23°C/74°F minimum and 27°C/80°F maximum.

**Nature and Culture** – The coast is quite nice around Caraquez or Atacames. Check out mangrove forests and abundant fauna in the Manglares Mataje/Cayapas Ecological Reserve. Wild partying in Atacames' beach bars and discos. Sua is a fishing village with pretty beaches and a quieter atmosphere. Enjoy the relaxed atmosphere of the island of Muisne.

**Hazards and Hassles** – Dysentery, hepatitis A and cholera are the main concerns: drink only agua purificada and be careful with ceviches (raw fish dishes). Mosquitoes love the rainy season and malaria could be a problem in Esmeraldas, check with your doctor. Be careful in the city of Esmeraldas as well as on Atacames beach after dark – muggings occur. Drugs are cheap, jail terms are long.

**Handy Hints** – There are no surf shops near the spots except in Manta and they don't carry much. Bring regular boards and lycra sun protection. Crowds are rarely a problem. Ecuador is a very cheap visit.

| WEATHER STATISTICS | J/F | M/A | M/J | J/A | S/O | N/D |
|---|---|---|---|---|---|---|
| total rainfall (mm) | 100 | 110 | 40 | 15 | 10 | 15 |
| consistency (days/mth) | 4 | 4 | 1 | 1 | 1 | 1 |
| min temp (°C/°F) | 23/74 | 24/75 | 23/74 | 23/74 | 23/74 | 23/74 |
| max temp (°C/°F) | 27/80 | 28/82 | 27/80 | 27/80 | 27/80 | 27/80 |

better in the fishing village of **Tonchigue**, but the local left pointbreak is usually quite section. Same for the élite resort of the Esmeraldas province and, while the beachbreaks here are short of spectacular, **Casa Blanca** will pick-up any swell but is best when it's from the SW. **Punta Galera** is like a slow copy of Suspiro and Mompiche. It's usually worth checking in the mornings when a NW or strong W swell shows up. The tedious access keeps the crowd levels down. Just as hard to reach, **Estero del Plátano** has a good reputation among surfers of northern Ecuador. What appears to be a beachbreak ultimately breaks over reef since the sand is covering a good rock set-up. Waves regularly barrel thanks to typically offshore winds in the morning. It needs NW, or very strong W swells. One of Ecuador's best waves, **Mompiche** is all about long tubular rides in perfect scenery. This left pointbreak starts with a barrelling first section before reeling over a sharp rock ledge and is well protected from the wind. Despite the long walk the wave is popular with surfers from Bahía de Caráquez and Atacames. These locals are usually friendly, but be respectful. NW and W swells work best but it has been surfed on strong SW swells. A few clicks south, **Punta Suspiro** is an underrated wave needing the same conditions, used as a crowd escape from Mompiche. It's another left pointbreak with long, classy rides. **Portete** is a powerful righthander just on the other side of Suspiro, it will break with any swell direction but doesn't offer the same wind protection and therefore gets blown out very easily. This spot is quite dangerous at low tide. There's no surf right in **Cojimies**, the first stop in Manabí Province, but with the help of a boat, hardcore explorers will reach the outer sandbanks (a couple of km offshore) where a bunch of beachbreaks can prove worth the effort. On the way down to **Perdernales** are more beachbreaks that sometimes get epic. NW or W swells, morning offshores and a 4WD to access the beach are vital. Predominantly a major hub for the shrimp industry, Pedernales also has a stretch of fun beachbreaks, which occasionally get heavy and square. Over the Equator, the long rides of **Punta Ballena** would be a longboard paradise if it wasn't so fickle. Sometimes the lines do connect for long rides, other times it gets crumbly, un-makeable sections. It needs NW, W swells and wind can be an issue. **Cabo Pasado** is a reefbreak only accessible by boat from Canoa, which explains why it's only a recent discovery. With NW to W swells it can provide perfect,

crystal water barrels. 16kms (10mi) of beach stretch around **Canoa**; the beachbreaks are top quality, with long rides or tubes depending on what the tide is doing. It will take any swell direction but again, NW and W are best. Individual spot names include The Bridge, The Lab and Briceño. There's no surf within Bahía de Caráquez's peaceful eco-city but the fickle pointbreak of **Punta Bellaca** will fire occasionally. When on (with good SW-W swells), a bunch of locals will be there to enjoy powerful waves around the low tide. If the swell comes from the NW it's best to go down to **La Mesita**, a remote left pointbreak offering long rides away from any crowd.

| SURF STATISTICS | J F | M A | M J | J A | S O | N D |
|---|---|---|---|---|---|---|
| dominant swell | NW | NW | S-SW | S-SW | S-SW | NW |
| swell size (ft) | 4 | 3 | 2-3 | 4 | 2-3 | 2-3 |
| consistency (%) | 70 | 60 | 40 | 40 | 40 | 60 |
| dominant wind | S-SW | S-SW | S-SW | S-SW | S-SW | S-SW |
| average force | F3 | F2-F3 | F3 | F3-F4 | F4 | F3-F4 |
| consistency (%) | 43 | 41 | 84 | 90 | 89 | 85 |
| water temp (°C/°F) | 25/77 | 25/77 | 23/74 | 22/72 | 21/70 | 22/72 |
| wetsuit | | | | | | |

**E**cuador is one of those rare countries to be exposed to both N and S swells. Although N swells will decay over the 8-10 days they take to reach the Equator and arrive during the wet season, they determine the prime surf season because of regular glassy conditions or light onshore sea breezes. Between December and April, there are many days in the 2-6ft (0.6-2m) range with occasional 8-10ft (2.5m-3m) 'oleajes' that activate many good breaks. SW swells in the austral winter are more consistent but the Esmeraldas region is not well exposed to receive them. In addition their core season (April-August) matches with the trade winds that mess up the surf and bring colder temps. S-SW winds dominate up to 90% of the time but much less during the rainy season when the winds are lighter and blow from the N-NE on a regular basis. Overall wind trends are good for the N swells. Despite noticeable exceptions, waves are not that tide-sensitive and tide tables are non-existent.

**SPOT DESCRIPTION**

| Spot | Size | Btm | Type |
|---|---|---|---|
| ① | 6/2 | | |
| ② | 6/2 | | |
| ③ | 6/1 | | |
| ④ | 8/3 | | |
| ⑤ | 8/3 | | |
| ⑥ | 8/3 | | |
| ⑦ | 8/4 | | |
| ⑧ | 8/3 | | |
| ⑨ | 6/2 | | |
| ⑩ | 6/2 | | |
| ⑪ | 8/3 | | |
| ⑫ | 8/3 | | |
| ⑬ | 6/2 | | |
| ⑭ | 8/4 | | |
| ⑮ | 6/3 | | |

Map labels:
Atacames ①
Pta Tonchigue ②
Casa Blanca ③
Pta Galera ④
Estero del Plátano ⑤
Mompiche ⑥
Pta Suspiro ⑦
Portete ⑧
Bocana del Cojimies ⑨
Pta Pedernales ⑩
Pta Ballena ⑪
Cabo Pasado ⑫
Canoa ⑬
Punta Bellaca ⑭
La Mesita ⑮

Esmeraldas, Arrecife de Atacames, Atacames, Súa, Tonchigue, Galera, Macara, Quingüe, Cabo de Francisco, San Francisco, Salto, Muisne, ESMERALDAS, Ensenada de Mompiche, Pta Bolívar, San Gregorio, Bolívar, Daule, Cojim o Cojimies, RESERVA BIOLOGICA MACHE CHINDUL, Salima, San José de Chamanga, Mache, Cañaveral, Pedernales, EQUATOR, Cabuyal, Los Camarones, Don Juan, MANABÍ, Jama, Pta Cabuyal, Cabo Pasado, to Quito, El Rosario, San Isidro, Flavio Alfaro, Limón, Canoa, Boyacá, San Vicente, Bahía de Caráquez, Chávez, Chone, Pta Charapotó, San Jacinto, Tosagua, Cálceta, Bahía de Manta, Cañitas, Crucita, Cabo San Mateo, Rocafuerte, Junín, Manta, Jaramijó, to Portoviejo, GUAYAS

PAUL KENNEDY

# 153. South Piura

THIERRY GIBAUD

## Summary

+ WORLD-CLASS LEFTS
+ COMPLETELY UNCROWDED
+ ALWAYS OFFSHORE
+ PRISTINE NATURAL AREA

– 4WD ACCESS ONLY
– HEAVY LINE-UPS AND RIPS
– ZERO FACILITIES
– "EL NIÑO" RISK

In a country boasting over 2,400km (1500mi) of surf pounded coastline with only 12,000 surfers, it's not too much of a hassle finding quality, uncrowded surf. Heading towards remote Bayovar seems unnecessary when the ultra long rides of Chicama are just a few hours south and the deep tubes of Cabo Blanco a few hours north. However, persistent rumours of 10ft (3m) barrels reeling forever are enough to lure the intrepid to this vast desert region of sand dunes and granite cliffs. Conditions are extremely harsh and for the most part, untouched by tourists (there isn't even a hotel) leaving daily activity to the companies that operate a pipeline bringing petroleum from the Amazon basin or tapping into one of the largest phosphate deposits in the world. Paita is the only real "coastal resort" in the area as it provides a port and accessible beaches for Piura, the fifth largest city in the country, 50km (30mi) inland.

GONZALO BARANDIARAN

Nonura

GONZALO BARANDIARAN

The 20km (12mi) long beach of **Colán** is very popular for its warm waters and gorgeous sunsets but has little value for surfers. **Punta Negra**, 17km (10mi) south of Paita, provides the best chance of a decent beachbreak in proximity to the city. The small beach of **Yacila** is protected from the strong winds by a large rock, attracting local bodyboarders to the mediocre, beachbreak close-outs in summertime. **La Islilla** is a

## TRAVEL INFORMATION

**Population:** 1.7M
**Coastline:** 384km (240mi)
**Contests:** None
**Other Resources:**
peruazul.com
olasperu.com
piuravirtual.com/
piuranet.com

**Getting There** – After reaching Lima (LIM) embark on one of the regular domestic flights to Piura (Aerocontinente, 1h30, $150r/t) or drive 15h (1000km/600mi) along the recently repaired Pan American Highway. Bayovar is 120km (75mi) from Piura by road, part of which is hardtop and part unpaved. Getting into Bayovar requires a permit from Petroperú in Piura.

**Getting Around** – Renting a 4x4 in Piura ($90/d) is essential to negotiate the trails that lead to Punta Nonura and the other beaches around Bayovar. Bayovar is three hours from the city of Paita. A bus service links Bayovar and Sechura.

**Lodging and Food** – There is not a single hotel around Bayovar; bring camping equipment, and get supplies in Piura before heading there. In Paita try Hostal Las Brisas ($17/p) or rent a bungalow in Playa Colán Lodge ($55 triple). Gustatory delights include baby goat and rice, and seco de chevalo (pork, rice and plantains).

**Weather** – Like the rest of the South American Pacific coastline, this area has an unusual desert and semi-desert climate, caused by the cold waters of the Humboldt Current flowing northwards. Rain is scarce, even during the rainy season running from January through March, but when the El Niño phenomenon arises, the water temps rise, and the skies open, causing flooding with widespread damage to roads, bridges and towns. Nights are colder with mild mornings in the Andean region. The differences in water temps are radical from the north to the south of the zone, ranging from boardies/springy to a light steamer.

**Nature and Culture** – There's great diving in places like Colán, Punta Bapo and Isla lobos de Tierra. Yacila and Colán are beautiful beaches in Paita. Witness archaeological remains of the Vicús Culture, masters of ceramics and goldsmithing, in Catacaos. The Virrilá estuary is a bird (watching) paradise.

**Hazards and Hassles** – Crowds or localism definitely won't be a problem, but being absolutely alone is much less enjoyable when out of fresh water or food, lost, or stuck in the sand. Driving skills on unpaved or sand roads is recommended. Wild animals may steal food.

**Handy Hints** – Be environmentally aware – recent complaints about surfers leaving litter and not using adequate latrines could jeopardise the issuing of permits, which are required for some of the distant and virgin beaches. Before driving on sand, deflate tyres to avoid getting stuck. Try to go with someone that already has good knowledge of the area.

| WEATHER STATISTICS | J/F | M/A | M/J | J/A | S/O | N/D |
|---|---|---|---|---|---|---|
| total rainfall (mm) | 10 | 10 | 0 | 0 | 0 | 0 |
| consistency (days/mth) | 0 | 0 | 0 | 0 | 0 | 0 |
| min temp (°C/°F) | 23/74 | 22/72 | 19/66 | 17/63 | 17/63 | 19/66 |
| max temp (°C/°F) | 32/90 | 31/88 | 28/82 | 26/79 | 28/82 | 30/86 |

Nonura

GONZALO BARANDIARAN

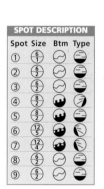

Colán ①
Pta Negra ②
Palta
Yacila ③
Yacila
Isla Foca · La Islilla
La Islilla ④
El Lobo
Piura
Catacaos
Dunes
La Unión
San Pedro
Sechura
Matacaballo
Punta Aguja ⑤
Ensenada de Sechura
Pta Bapo
Nonura ⑥
Pta Nonura
Bayóvar
Puerto Rico · Vichayo
Punta Tur ⑦
Pta La Negra
Reventazón ⑧
PIURA / LAMBAYEQUE
Cabo Verde ⑨
ISLA LOBOS DE TIERRA

fishing village where local kids like to ride the waves on wooden boards fashioned from the decks of decommissioned fishing boats. The righthand pointbreak on the right side of this little bay can get really hollow. The bay of Sechura, the largest in the country, hosts a string of beautiful warm water beaches but receives little swell. The beaches of Bayovar, 150km (94mi) SW of Piura are arguably the last pristine beaches in Peru. Consisting of wide bays, fringed by white granite rocky formations and dunes, these beaches are washed by crystal-clear waters filled with dolphins, turtles and flocks of seabirds. **Punta Aguja** marks the spot where the Humboldt Current converges with the Equatorial Counter Current, meaning the water gets radically colder south of these rocky peaks. Bayovar's world-class spot, **Nonura** is only accessible by 4WD and camping is the only accommodation option. A long, tough paddle-out against strong currents, leads to the classic tubular pointbreak lefts. Nonura will take any swell from the SW to the NW but it needs to be big enough as the wave only really reveals itself over 5ft (1.8m) and maxes out around 10-12ft (3-4m). This wave is to be taken seriously. A bit further along the Bayovar headland lays **Punta Tur** another great lefthander. It breaks further away from the shore than Nonura, resulting in really long waves, although it peels so fast that the ride is usually split into different sections. Punta Tur also suffers from really strong currents making jetskis a highly desirable tool. Located on the south side of the headland **Reventazón** picks up plenty of swell but is more exposed to the winds. There's another average beachbreak in **Cabo Verde**, at the Piura/Lambayeque border but the swell window can be blocked by Lobos de Tierra island.

The Bayovar area relies on two sources of swell coming at different times of the year. April-October is the best season for regular 3-12ft (1-4m) S-SW swells coming from lows down in the southern latitudes, with a minimum of 2-3ft (0.6-1m) swell produced by the southerly winds accompanying the cold Humboldt Current. The winter months from May to August typically see the largest swells. Between November and February, NW swells will come down from the North Pacific 5-6 days after pounding the Hawaiian shores. Because of the constant temp difference between dry land and relatively cold water, prevailing S winds are perfect and regular. The direction is direct southerly 40-55% of the time and SE 30-45%, which is offshore on NW exposed bays like Nonura. Usually, SE morning winds turn to the S after noon. The tidal range doesn't exceed 5ft (1.6m) but that's enough to affect the pointbreaks.

| SURF STATISTICS | J | F | M | A | M | J | J | A | S | O | N | D |
|---|---|---|---|---|---|---|---|---|---|---|---|---|
| dominant swell | | NW | | S-SW | | S-SW | | S-SW | | S-SW | | NW |
| swell size (ft) | | 4 | | 3 | | 4 | | 4-5 | | 4 | | 3-4 |
| consistency (%) | | 70 | | 70 | | 80 | | 80 | | 70 | | 60 |
| dominant wind | | SE-E | | SE-E | | SE-E | | SE-E | | SE-E | | SE-E |
| average force | | F3 | | F3 | | F3-F4 | | F3-F4 | | F3 | | F3 |
| consistency (%) | | 81 | | 86 | | 88 | | 90 | | 91 | | 85 |
| water temp (°C/°F) | | 22/72 | | 22/72 | | 19/66 | | 18/64 | | 17/63 | | 19/66 |
| wetsuit | | | | | | | | | | | | |

| SPOT DESCRIPTION | | | |
|---|---|---|---|
| Spot | Size | Btm | Type |
| ① | 6/1 | | |
| ② | 6/2 | | |
| ③ | 6/2 | | |
| ④ | 8/2 | | |
| ⑤ | 8/2 | | |
| ⑥ | 12/5 | | |
| ⑦ | 12/4 | | |
| ⑧ | 6/2 | | |
| ⑨ | 6/2 | | |

T-Land

BARANDIARAN

# 154. Costa Verde

Herradura

GONZALO BARANDARIÁN

## Summary
+ HIGHLY CONSISTENT SWELL
+ GREAT SPOT DENSITY
+ EASY ACCESS AND CHEAP
+ LIMA ENTERTAINMENT
+ PERUVIAN CULTURE

− NOT PERU'S BEST SURF
− COLD WATER
− COASTAL WINTER FOG
− CITY CROWDS AND POLLUTION

STEVE FITZPATRICK

El Cabezo

GONZALO BARANDARIÁN

Peru's surf culture goes way back to the Totora reed horses ridden since 1000BC, and more recently, Felipe Pomar's world title victory ahead of Nat Young in 1965. A true surf city, Lima was first surfed in the mid 1920s, as a dedicated group of riders formed the Waikiki Club in Miraflores, one of the first three surf clubs in the world. Peru's capital is constantly outgrowing its boundaries, accommodating one third of the population so crowds, noise and pollution are serious issues. Most surfers prefer to head to the quieter Punta Hermosa area, half an hour south, but surfing the city remains a viable option.

Isla San Lorenzo is Peru's largest island, lying 4km (2.5mi) offshore from the city shores. A left will break at **El Cabezo** on the largest NW/SW swells, but is little documented since the island is deserted with no regularly scheduled trips. **El Camotal** is another 'secret island' and it's possible, although not recommended, to paddle from la Punta. The wave breaks both ways and gets occasionally hollow, but wind exposure usually makes the wave face choppy. The Costa Verde is a string of beaches located at the foot of the cliffs that plunge down from the Miraflores district of Lima. Unchallenging, consistent lefts and rights break at **Punta Roquitas**, where boulders roll around in the shorebreak. **Pampilla** looks just the same with small conditions but the shifty peaks develop into a better right in larger swells. The Jose

## TRAVEL INFORMATION

**Population:**
8.6M (Lima & Callao)
**Coastline:**
2,414km (1,509mi)
**Contests:** National
**Other Resources:**
peruazul.com
olasperu.com
enjoyperu.com
playasperu.com

**Getting There** – Most travellers do not need visas. Jorge Chávez International Airport (LIM), 30mn from Lima's historic centre, is the main point of entry to Peru's capital. From there good bartering can get a cab to the centre for under $10. Departure tax $25.

**Getting Around** – With so much traffic and so little parking spots, a rental car would be more a hindrance than a help. Public transport is the way to go, the packed buses are dirt-cheap and taxis are everywhere as many car owners drive people around as an extra source of revenue.

**Lodging and Food** – Lima is among the most expensive places in the country but there is a wide range of accommodation options. Miraflores is a safer, expensive neighborhood; try the Imperial Inn ($12/p) or the trendier Hostal Lucerna ($55/dble). Both are a short cab ride to Costa Verde. Backpackers should head to Mochilero's in Barranco ($8/p).

**Weather** – Lima's climate is temperate with any equatorial heat moderated by the Pacific Ocean, which sweeps cold Antarctic currents northward along the coast. It hardly ever rains, daily variations are minimal, temps are never too hot or too cold (maybe in the deepest winter) but that does not mean straight sunshine everyday. Actually, the land/sea temperature difference brings a constant fog, called Garua, except Dec-March. It is a type of very light rain with very small, almost invisible particles of water. Water requires a light fullsuit May-Nov and a springsuit the rest of the time. Even if the water gets much warmer, avoid the disastrous el Niño years.

**Nature and Culture** – Explore the city's colonial past or witness the Inca's wealth and culture in the city museums. Pachacamac ruins are among the largest pre-Columbian settlement on the Peruvian coast but can't compare with Macchu Picchu; save time and budget for a short hop to the Andes.

**Hazards and Hassles** – Crowds are common especially at La Herradura. Rolling boulders in the shorebreak may result in sprained ankles. Shining Path stories are a thing of the past, but razorblade maestros (pickpockets) operate in buses and all the main tourist areas. Eat only cooked & boiled food to avoid cholera.

**Handy Hints** – Surfing equipment can be found at competitive prices in the city's surf shops. Lima has very good shapers, like Wayo Whilar. A new board costs $200 and a gun is $250. Take booties for urchins & rocks and a light fullsuit (Boz is a good local brand). Punta Hermosa breaks are only 1/2h away.

| WEATHER STATISTICS | J/F | M/A | M/J | J/A | S/O | N/D |
|---|---|---|---|---|---|---|
| total rainfall (mm) | 1 | 1 | 1 | 2 | 1 | 1 |
| consistency (days/mth) | 0 | 0 | 0 | 1 | 0 | 0 |
| min temp (°C/°F) | 19/66 | 18/64 | 16/61 | 14/57 | 15/59 | 17/63 |
| max temp (°C/°F) | 26/79 | 25/77 | 21/70 | 18/64 | 20/68 | 23/74 |

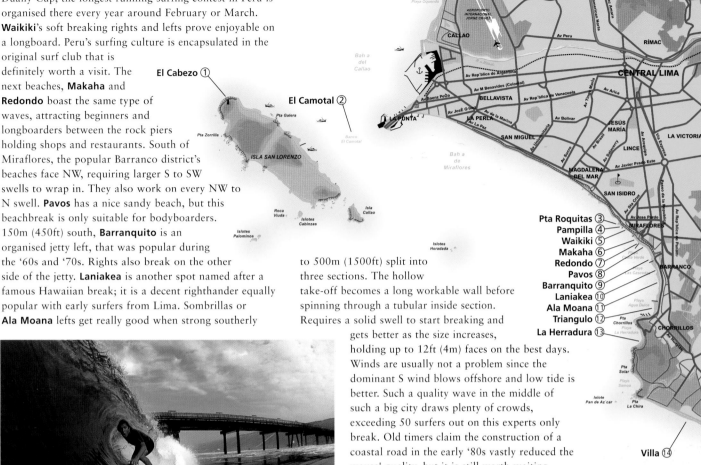

Duany Cup, the longest running surfing contest in Peru is organised there every year around February or March. **Waikiki**'s soft breaking rights and lefts prove enjoyable on a longboard. Peru's surfing culture is encapsulated in the original surf club that is definitely worth a visit. The next beaches, **Makaha** and **Redondo** boast the same type of waves, attracting beginners and longboarders between the rock piers holding shops and restaurants. South of Miraflores, the popular Barranco district's beaches face NW, requiring larger S to SW swells to wrap in. They also work on every NW to N swell. **Pavos** has a nice sandy beach, but this beachbreak is only suitable for bodyboarders. 150m (450ft) south, **Barranquito** is an organised jetty left, that was popular during the '60s and '70s. Rights also break on the other side of the jetty. **Laniakea** is another spot named after a famous Hawaiian break; it is a decent righthander equally popular with early surfers from Lima. Sombrillas or **Ala Moana** lefts get really good when strong southerly

El Cabezo ①
El Camotal ②

Pta Roquitas ③
Pampilla ④
Waikiki ⑤
Makaha ⑥
Redondo ⑦
Pavos ⑧
Barranquito ⑨
Laniakea ⑩
Ala Moana ⑪
Triangulo ⑫
La Herradura ⑬

Villa ⑭

to 500m (1500ft) split into three sections. The hollow take-off becomes a long workable wall before spinning through a tubular inside section. Requires a solid swell to start breaking and gets better as the size increases, holding up to 12ft (4m) faces on the best days. Winds are usually not a problem since the dominant S wind blows offshore and low tide is better. Such a quality wave in the middle of such a big city draws plenty of crowds, exceeding 50 surfers out on this experts only break. Old timers claim the construction of a coastal road in the early '80s vastly reduced the waves' quality, but it is still worth waiting around for. South of Lima, **Villa** is a small swell beach where hollow, punchy peaks need slack wind conditions. A good option when other breaks are struggling but can get heavy close-outs and strong longshore currents.

Conchan, near Villa

GONZALO BAVANDIAVAN

swells hit the area. It has an easy paddling channel and winds are offshore most of the time. There are more boulder beaches in the Agua Dulce area and **Triangulo** is the one when all the other beaches are closed out. It's very protected from both swell and wind, creating mellow, rolling peaks that don't break well very often. **La Herradura** is the best pointbreak in Lima, isolated in a relatively deserted, horseshoe bay in the Chorrillos district. This powerful left breaks along a high cliff for up

Regular 4-15ft (1.2-5m) S-SW swells come from the lows down in the southern latitudes, along with a minimum of 2-3ft (0.6-1m) swell produced by constant S winds associated with the cold Humboldt Current. The constant temperature difference between the hot, dry land and the relatively cold water drives the prevailing S-SE winds. The straight S side-shore sea breeze blows 30-40% of the time while it's SE 35-55%, which is offshore at the NW facing spots and southern corners. Usually, SE morning winds turn to S after noon. Tides don't matter much and tide tables can be obtained at the better surf shops in Lima.

| SPOT DESCRIPTION | | |
|---|---|---|
| Spot Size | Btm | Type |
| ① ⑥/④ | | |
| ② ⑥/④ | | |
| ③ ⑥/② | | |
| ④ ⑧/③ | | |
| ⑤ ⑧/② | | |
| ⑥ ⑥/② | | |
| ⑦ ⑥/② | | |
| ⑧ ⑥/① | | |
| ⑨ ⑧/① | | |
| ⑩ ⑧/② | | |
| ⑪ ⑧/② | | |
| ⑫ ⑥/② | | |
| ⑬ ⑫/⑥ | | |
| ⑭ ⑧/② | | |

Lima's Beaches

JUAN FERNANDEZ

| SURF STATISTICS | J F | M A | M J | J A | S O | N D |
|---|---|---|---|---|---|---|
| dominant swell | S-SW | S-SW | S-SW | S-SW | S-SW | S-SW |
| swell size (ft) | 3 | 3-4 | 4-5 | 5-6 | 4-5 | 3 |
| consistency (%) | 65 | 80 | 85 | 90 | 80 | 70 |
| dominant wind | SE-S | SE-S | SE-S | SE-S | SE-S | SE-S |
| average force | F3 | F3 | F3 | F3-F4 | F3-F4 | F3 |
| consistency (%) | 81 | 87 | 83 | 85 | 88 | 85 |
| water temp (°C/°F) | 20/68 | 21/70 | 19/66 | 17/63 | 18/64 | 19/66 |
| wetsuit | | | | | | |

# 155. Arica

The Alacrán Peninsula

FREDERIC LE LEANNEC

## Summary
+ ULTRA CONSISTENT SWELL
+ POWERFUL REEFBREAKS
+ MAGIC ALACRÁN PENINSULA
+ BIG WAVE RIDING OPTIONS
+ DRY, WARM CLIMATE

− SHALLOW REEFS AND URCHINS
− BOARD-BREAKING CONDITIONS
− FAR FROM INTERNATIONAL HUBS
− INCREASING CROWDS
− WETSUITS NECESSARY

The extreme north of Chile conceals a string of perfect reefs in the driest desert in the world, the Atacama. Unlike the long points of the southern Pichilemu area, most northern breaks are gnarly reefbreaks, breaking close to the shore. 400km (250mi) from Iquique and its North Shore-style concentration of reefs, Arica's fame comes from the magic Alacrán Peninsula, circled by four potential spots. An oasis in the Atacama Desert, Arica has been inhabited since at least 6000BC, well before the lure of its golden sand dunes, miles of seashore, duty-free shopping and lively nightlife helped it transform into an increasingly popular seaside resort. Only 20km (12.5mi) from the Peruvian border, Arica

Las Machas

ALFREDO ESCOBAR

El Gringo

ALFREDO ESCOBAR

has been a trade city for centuries and only developed as a surf city when groups of Peruvian and southern Chilean surfers discovered the potential in the late '70s. Skills and equipment prevented the pioneers from tackling the reefbreaks, so the surfing scene was focused on the beachbreaks north of town.

In the summer of 1983, the first Arica surf championship, maybe the first in the country, was held in

## TRAVEL INFORMATION

**Population:** 420,000
**Coastline:** 330km (206mi)
**Contests:** National (Aug)
**Other Resources:**
*Video:* Perro En Bote
aricasurf.cl
nortextremo.cl
muniarica.cl
arica.cl

**Getting There** – No visa required. LanChile flies daily to Chacalluta Airport from Santiago (31/2h, $140r/t) with two stopovers. Overland, Arica is 2000km (1250mi) away from Santiago de Chile (bus: $50, 26h) and 20km (12mi) from the Peruvian border, via the Pan American Highway.

**Getting Around** – Renting a car ($300/w) is not crucial unless you plan to explore the area between Arica & Iquique. The collectivos bus service is cheap and reliable and many spots lie within walking distance. A collectivo to Iquique only costs $10 (4h). Bike rentals are available for $12/d. Lan-Chile passes are good value.

**Lodging and Food** – There are many budget hotels in town and $25 will get a nice double. Try Hostal Chez Charlie ($14/dble), Hotel Lynch ($37/dble) or Hotel San Marcos ($15/dble). $10 gets an excellent seafood meal, which can be accompanied by Chilean wine or Pisco Sour.

**Weather** – Nicknamed "ciudad de la eterna primavera" (city of eternal spring) Arica benefits from mild temperatures year round thanks to the rivermouth that brings a constant supply of fresh water to the city. The lows go to 13°C (56°F) in winter, which is quite good for Chile. It never, ever rains; the world record of less than 1mm of precipitation per year makes it the driest spot on Earth. The coastal fog, known as Camanchaca doesn't stick around as long as the Peruvian Garua.

**Nature and Culture** – Arica is the gateway to the Altiplano, check out geoglyphs (pictures

drawn on the hillsides) and pukaras (Indian fortresses). El Morro Hill is a national historic monument, offering great panoramic views. The San Marcos de Arica church was designed by Gustav Eiffel. People meet around El Alacrán at night time.

**Hazards and Hassles** – Wave dangers are obvious – big peaks, powerful lips, shallow, sharp reefs and urchins. Crowds are mostly bodyboards and foreigners, peaks are not real crowded but 10 guys are enough to fill the take-off zone. No land dangers.

**Handy Hints** – Arica has several surf shops (Huntington, Solari) but bring a quiver, with real guns if big waves tempt. Booties are essential. A surf school called Swells was started in the year 2000; it already has close to 100 students. Most men work in mines in the desert and the city is filled with good-looking Chilean girls.

| WEATHER STATISTICS | J/F | M/A | M/J | J/A | S/O | N/D |
|---|---|---|---|---|---|---|
| total rainfall (mm) | 0 | 0 | 0 | 0 | 0 | 0 |
| consistency (days/mth) | 0 | 0 | 0 | 0 | 0 | 0 |
| min temp (°C/°F) | 18/64 | 17/63 | 14/57 | 13/55 | 14/57 | 16/61 |
| max temp (°C/°F) | 27/80 | 25/77 | 21/70 | 19/66 | 21/70 | 24/75 |

El Buey

*PAUL KENNEDY*

can break both ways, the left remains the better option, as it's always hollower than the right. The spot can hold 20ft (6m), but is quite wind sensitive. There's another similar big wave spot called La Capilla, 4km (1.2mi) south of town on the way to which the road passes **Playa Brava** and **Arenillas Negras**, two beachbreaks favouring rights.

S-SW swells from the Antarctic's lows are super-consistent and send plenty of large swells in winter and a reasonable amount in the summer. It's advantageous to be located in the north of the country to avoid being pounded by constant storms. Breaking waves vary between 3-15ft (1-5m) year round. Some of the spots will break even better with the occasional summer NW swells between November and March. S-SE wind dominance remains around 65% year round, with more SE except between Oct-Nov. Annually, 10-12% of the time it is calm. Mornings are typically windless, then light offshores pick up till noon when gentle S sea breezes create a little chop on the wave face. Some spots are really wind sensitive and are only surfed in the morning. Tidal range never exceeds 6ft (2m) but is relevant for shallow reefs.

El Buey

*ALFREDO ESCOBAR*

playa **Las Machas**. This long stretch of beach is super-consistent and peaks abound. The waves are usually better around high tide and although the sandbanks shift a lot, it's usually worth checking the Rio Lluta mouth which marks the end of the beach. Many Ariqueños and tourists will set up their tents here in the summertime. Playa Chinchorro is the natural southerly extension of Las Machas. **El Tubo** is a right breaking next to the pier, but despite its name is more of a beginner-friendly break. **La Puntilla** is a rare left breaking at the mouth of the San José river. Due to its location, only the largest swell will produce rideable waves. The rights breaking south of **El Puerto** (the port) are seldom ridden as most of the action occurs around Alacrán. The Alacrán Peninsula used to be an island before being connected to the land when the port of Arica was built in the '60s. **El Brazo**'s sand-covered reef breaks at the northern tip of the island but requires a large swell and SW winds. When on, it's a large tubular A-frame. **La Isla** is one of the most highly regarded breaks around, especially on summer northerly swell days where the lefthander forms a hollow wall with tubing sections. It breaks really close to the rocks and needs a medium-size swell to be at its best. With a larger swell, those willing to spice things up may want to measure themselves by the treacherous **El Tojo Viejo**, an intense left breaking on the west side of the peninsula. It's only ridden when over 6ft (2m) with a south swell direction and good days are rare. Sometimes nicknamed the Chilean Pipeline, **El Gringo** is another tubular A-frame crashing close to the shore with serious power. It's a fast wave too, pushing surfers to go for broke and score a great barrel or get slammed on the reef. **El Buey** is a big wave arena, 700m (2100ft) offshore from the modern beach scene of playa El Laucho. Even though it

| SURF STATISTICS | J F | M A | M J | J A | S O | N D |
|---|---|---|---|---|---|---|
| dominant swell | S-SW | S-SW | S-SW | S-SW | S-SW | S-SW |
| swell size (ft) | 4 | 4-5 | 5-6 | 6-7 | 5-6 | 4 |
| consistency (%) | 70 | 75 | 80 | 90 | 80 | 60 |
| dominant wind | S-SE | S-SE | S-SE | S-SE | S-SE | S-SE |
| average force | F2 | F2-F3 | F2-F3 | F3 | F3 | F2-F3 |
| consistency (%) | 65 | 66 | 60 | 62 | 67 | 65 |
| water temp (°C/°F) | 20/68 | 19/66 | 18/64 | 16/61 | 17/63 | 18/64 |
| wetsuit | | | | | | |

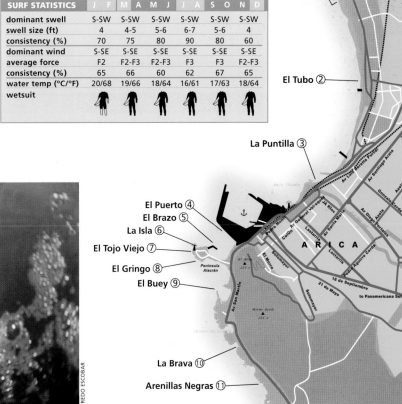

El Gringo

Las Machas ①
El Tubo ②
La Puntilla ③
El Puerto ④
El Brazo ⑤
La Isla ⑥
El Tojo Viejo ⑦
El Gringo ⑧
El Buey ⑨
La Brava ⑩
Arenillas Negras ⑪

*ALFREDO ESCOBAR*

# 156. Antofagasta

PERU
BOLIVIA
CHILE
ARGENTINA
Santiago

Cúpula

ALL PHOTOS ALFREDO ESCOBAR

## Summary
+ GREAT LEFT POINTBREAKS
+ CONSISTENT SWELL
+ SPOT DIVERSITY
+ NEVER RAINS

– FEW RIGHTS
– COOL WATER
– DESERT AREA
– LACK OF TOURIST INTEREST

Much like Chile itself, the city of Antofagasta is long and narrow, sandwiched between the mighty Pacific Ocean and the lofty Andes mountains. The largest city of the Norte Grande region, Antofagasta lays just 10km (6mi) south of the Tropic of Capricorn. With 20km (12mi) of sandy beaches scattered among rocky coves, this port town is increasingly turning into a beach resort, but still lacks attractiveness for the tourist masses. It's also off the beaten path for surfers, who tend to congregate at the northern cities of Arica and Iquique. Things may change with the completion of the Ruta 1 coastal highway which makes the 400km (250mi) long Iquique-Antofagasta stretch of coastline much more accessible.

Some 80km (50mi) north of Antofagasta, the small bay of **Pozo Verde** has surf on both sides, with both left and right points that get perfect

Cúpula

around 6ft (2m). The popular coastal resort of **Hornitos** has a long beach with good short rides, provided the wind is not too strong, nor the tide too high. The beach is known to be the warmest place around which attracts beach-goers year round. A hammer-shaped headland sticks out of the coast after Mejillones, the last town of

## TRAVEL INFORMATION

**Population:** 480,000
**Coastline:** 510km (319mi)
**Contests:** National
**Other Resources:**
*Video:* Perro en bote
http://groups.msn.com/
surfantofagasta
antofasurf.tk
antofagastavirtual.cl
puntoantofagasta.cl
desiertosurfero.com

**Getting There** – No visa required. LanChile flies daily to Cerro Moreno airport, 25km (16mi) north of the city. Flights are around $150 and the ride to town costs $6. Buses from Santiago costs under $40 but it's a 1,350km (845mi), 18h ride along the Pan American Highway. From Iquique $20/6h buses are available.

**Getting Around** – Antofagasta's location on the Pan-American Hwy, eases transportation to the rest of the country. Rent a car ($35/d) to cruise the 20km (12mi) long coastal road facing the Pacific Ocean or follow the impressive Ruta 1 coastal highway all the way to Iquique. It's possible to rely on public transport with collectivos to Portada and Mejillones ($2) or Hornitos ($4) running in the summertime.

**Lodging and Food** – Budget rooms under $15 are widely available. Comfort options include the beach facing Hotel Tatio ($80/dble) and Hotel Antofagasta ($120/dble). Hotel Capitania in Mejillones is the base for Janosurf's Desierto Surfero; they know the area perfectly. Excellent seafood is available around the Terminal Pesquero.

**Weather** – Antofagasta has an excellent coastal desert climate with little change between summer and winter. Cool sea breezes prevent the area from getting too hot in summer 24°C (75°F) and maximums remain around 17°C (63°F) in winter. Being the driest region in the world, this part of the Atacama Desert never sees a drop of rain. The skies are also the clearest in the world with clouds appearing only 20 days per year. This fact led to the construction of the world's largest telescope on Mount Paranal, 200km (125mi) south of Antofagasta. Because the city is located on a large peninsula the cold Humboldt Current passes away from the coast which makes for water temps a little higher than in surrounding spots. A 3/2 steamer will be necessary for most of the year.

**Nature and Culture** – A modern city with good restaurants and entertainment spots, yet Antofagasta remains an unlikely tourist destination. The city's architecture has a European feel with a clock tower replica of Big Ben. La Portada is a natural arch shaped by erosion into a giant rock while the Mano Del Desierto (Hand of the Desert) is a large sculpture 50km (31mi) south of Antofagasta.

**Hazards and Hassles** – With surfing and bodyboarding becoming increasingly popular among young Chileans, crowds are developing and vibes are not always positive. Sharp reefs and urchins are often lurking under the water, so bring reef boots. Don't mess with the araña del rincón; these reclusive Chilean spiders are extremely venomous.

**Handy Hints** – Limited choice of surf equipment is available at the DMG and 5ªAvda Surf. It's best to bring over a quiver or a good all-around board. Most shops are closed in the afternoon till 5pm. Desierto Surfero runs 2 days all-inclusive surf schools.

| WEATHER STATISTICS | J/F | M/A | M/J | J/A | S/O | N/D |
|---|---|---|---|---|---|---|
| total rainfall (mm) | 0 | 0 | 1 | 2 | 1 | 0 |
| consistency (days/mth) | 0 | 0 | 0 | 0 | 0 | 0 |
| min temp (°C/°F) | 16/61 | 14/57 | 12/54 | 10/50 | 12/54 | 14/57 |
| max temp (°C/°F) | 24/75 | 21/70 | 19/66 | 16/61 | 18/64 | 21/70 |

any size north of Antofagasta. On the southern part of the desert headland, **Choralillo** is a fun, left point and a good playground for practising radical manoeuvers. **Isla Santa Maria**, a desert island 1.6km (1mi) offshore, hosts three distinct breaks. One is a giant, deep-water A-frame, while the other two reefbreaks are left points best surfed around 6ft (2m). **Peñarol** is another mysterious and secluded desert break; the rights there are quite long but sectiony. In the Bahia Moreno, **Cordeles** is a very consistent beachbreak, near the famous natural arch of **La Portada**, off which reels a long left with three sections. The natural environment is impressive but unfortunately the point is extremely wind sensitive. Just north of Antofagasta, **Budeo** is an excellent right break, powerful and tubular. It's regularly crowded with bodyboarders looking for small but clean tubes. The W-NW orientation of the coast between Antofagasta and Cabo Jara makes for some good lefthand set-ups. The first wave in Antofagasta, **Piedra del Lobo** is a classic left holding up to 9ft (2.8m) with rides 100m long. Heavy wipe-outs are not uncommon but rocks are no threat at this spot. Another wave worth searching for is the hollow and powerful right called **Andrómeda**; it holds up to 9ft (2.8m) and is never too crowded. Breaking next to an artificial sand beach, **La Puntilla**'s left pointbreak is Antofagasta's most central and famous wave. With lots of sections it can accommodate city crowds. **Ram5** is a very powerful left breaking very close to the rocks, making entry and exit quite difficult. The piece of land facing it is owned by the military but surfers always find their way in. Regularly picked as a national contest site, **Cúpula** is regarded as the best wave in the zone. It breaks best at 6-12ft (2-4m) and locals compare it to Tavarua. Exaggeration or not, the wave is indeed a long left with several tubular sections, breaking over magma rock reef. The occasional shorter right can be ridden as well. Friendly locals may give tips on how to handle the rocks sticking out in front of the wave and the urchins and seashells covering the seafloor. 12km (8mi) south of the city centre, in the discotheque sector, **Huáscar** is yet another left point, but this one breaks better in the summertime, when the largest northern swells roll in between 6-15ft (2-5m). **Nuluhaga** stands as the most

Cúpula

impressive wave around showing some Teahupoo characteristics. Heavy drops are followed by stratospheric tubes with little water over the reef. Since it only breaks over 9ft (2.8m) scoring the tube of a lifetime...or just a radically shortened lifetime are both on the cards.

| SURF STATISTICS | J F | M A | M J | J A | S O | N D |
|---|---|---|---|---|---|---|
| dominant swell | S-SW | S-SW | S-SW | S-SW | S-SW | S-SW |
| swell size (ft) | 4 | 4-5 | 5-6 | 7 | 5-6 | 4 |
| consistency (%) | 70 | 75 | 80 | 90 | 80 | 60 |
| dominant wind | SE-SW | SE-SW | SE-SW | SE-SW | SE-SW | SE-SW |
| average force | F2-F3 | F3 | F3 | F3 | F2-F3 | F2-F3 |
| consistency (%) | 83 | 81 | 74 | 75 | 81 | 85 |
| water temp (°C/°F) | 18/64 | 17/63 | 16/61 | 15/59 | 16/61 | 17/63 |
| wetsuit | | | | | | |

S-SW swells from Antarctic lows are super consistent and the powerful Humboldt Current helps bring plenty of large swells in winter and a fair amount in the summer. Summertime surf is smaller but usually cleaner as well. It's a good thing to be located in the north of the country to avoid being pounded by constant storms. Breaking waves vary between 3-15ft (1-5m) and surf can is consistent year round. Southerly winds prevail year round but winds are calm 10% of the time. Mornings are typically windless, then light offshores pick up until noon when gentle S sea breezes create a little chop on the wave face. Some spots are really wind sensitive and are only surfed in the morning. Tidal range never exceeds 2m (6ft) but tides are relevant on the shallow reefs.

**SPOT DESCRIPTION**

| Spot | Size | Btm | Type |
|---|---|---|---|
| ① | 8/3 | | |
| | 8/4 | | |
| ② | 8/3 | | |
| ③ | 8/4 | | |
| ④ | 8/4 | | |
| | 12/4 | | |
| ⑤ | 8/3 | | |
| ⑥ | 8/2 | | |
| ⑦ | 8/3 | | |
| ⑧ | 6/3 | | |
| ⑨ | 10/4 | | |
| ⑩ | 10/6 | | |
| ⑪ | 8/4 | | |
| ⑫ | 8/4 | | |
| ⑬ | 12/4 | | |
| ⑭ | 15/6 | | |
| ⑮ | 15/8 | | |

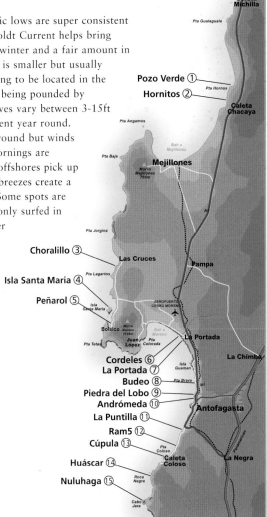

Pozo Verde ①
Hornitos ②
Choralillo ③
Isla Santa Maria ④
Peñarol ⑤
Cordeles ⑥
La Portada ⑦
Budeo ⑧
Piedra del Lobo ⑨
Andrómeda ⑩
La Puntilla ⑪
Ram5 ⑫
Cúpula ⑬
Huáscar ⑭
Nuluhaga ⑮

La Portada

# 157. Mar del Plata

PEDRO SALINAS

**Summary**

+ SPOT CONCENTRATION
+ BREAK DIVERSITY
+ MANY WIND AND SWELL OPTIONS
+ WIDE RANGE OF ACCOMMODATION

− CROWDED URBAN SPOTS
− SUMMER SURFING BANS
− FREEZING WINTERS
− BUILT UP AND POLLUTED
− RECENT ECONOMIC CRISIS

Second largest country on the South American continent, Argentina counts around 300km (186mi) of surfable beaches, most of them located in Buenos Aires Province. The east side of the country called Pampas, consists mainly of grassy plains while the country's western regions climb into the vertiginous Andes. Argentina recently celebrated 40 years of surfing at a variety of breaks ranging from natural pointbreaks to man-made jetties. Mar del Plata stands as the main summer getaway for "Porteños" escaping their Buenos Aires lives. The city beaches stretch over 8km (5mi), but dozens of piers and jetties bisect the coastline into many surf spots.

PEDRO SALINAS

**Necocha**

JAVIER AMEZAGA

The highest concentration of these man-made wave-breakers is on the north side of town and the best break in this area is certainly **La Pepita**. It's a wide beach south of the main bay, where tubular righthanders will line-up

---

## TRAVEL INFORMATION

**Population:**
14M Buenos Aires
**Coastline:** 47km (30mi)
Pueyrredon Region
**Contests:** None
**Other Resources:**
*Video:* Marpla XXI
elsurfero.com
portalsurfer.com.ar
mardelplata.com
mardelplataonline.com

**Getting There** – No visa, 90-day tourist cards distributed on arrival. Aeropuerto Internacional Ezeiza, 35km (22mi) outside Buenos Aires is Argentina's main hub. Bus to MDP costs $20 for a 5 1/2h ride from the large Retiro terminal. Flights are $60 and up (Aerolinas Argentinas). If planning to rent a car, do so in Buenos Aires and drive the 400km (250mi) down to MDP. $30 dep tax.

**Getting Around** – Car rentals are rather expensive averaging $45/day with limited mileage, but offer the flexibility to find the best spot on any given day. It's possible to move around MDP by bus, they run regularly and go pretty much everywhere. Surfboards may not be accepted during summer peak season. Buses run between MDP and Miramar (1h, $3).

**Lodging and Food** – Among 700 lodging options in MDP, Hotel Electra ($15/p), Hosteria

San Valentin ($25/dble) and Hotel Traful ($75/dble) are all close to the central beaches and La Pepita. The classier Gran Hotel Iruña has rooms with views to the beaches next to La Popular for $120/dble. Argentina's beef is the best in the world.

**Weather** – Stretching as far north as the Tropic of Capricorn all the way to the Cape Horn, Argentina knows a wide diversity of climate. The coastal central area is relatively humid with great variations in temperatures. The winter is dry and cold with temperatures remaining between 5-13°C (41-56°F) in July/August. It's possible to go snowboarding between July and September. Rainfalls are more pronounced in the east of the country than in the west and shallow summer flooding is not uncommon in the flat Pampas areas. The bay of Miramar enjoys a great climate, as it seems to receive fewer storms than MDP. The water gets real cold in the peak wave season. Between June and August a 5/4/3 fullsuit complete with booties, gloves and hood is what it takes to avoid freezing in 9°C (48°F) waters. 3/2 fullsuits are good between seasons before summer (December/February) allows springsuits and maybe even quick dips wearing only boardshorts.

**Nature and Culture** – MDP in summer is as packed as a city can be and everything revolves around hanging-out at the beach, bar-hopping around Plaza Mitre and dancing the rest of the night. Hang out around the port or visit the Museo del Mar, which displays over 30,000 shells. Juan Manuel Fangio has his own museum in Balcarce.

**Hazards and Hassles** – Most of the crowds happen in the summer when the city is assaulted by Porteños and free surf schools give everyone a chance to hit the waves. Local surfers remain friendly towards foreigners. Economic crisis exploded in late 2001, leaving the country with high unemployment and poverty levels. No mad cow disease in the local beef.

**Handy Hints** – A regular shortboard is all that is needed around summer but a small gun can come in handy for serious winter swells. The Crow is the main surf shop in Miramar, and more are found in MDP. Hola Surf gives daily surf reports. Recent devaluation makes the country much cheaper to visit. Some of the country's best spots are actually located in Necochea, 80km (50mi) south of Miramar.

| WEATHER STATISTICS | J/F | M/A | M/J | J/A | S/O | N/D |
|---|---|---|---|---|---|---|
| total rainfall (mm) | 70 | 70 | 60 | 50 | 55 | 65 |
| consistency (days/mth) | 7 | 8 | 7 | 7 | 8 | 8 |
| min temp (°C/°F) | 15/59 | 12/54 | 6/43 | 5/41 | 7/45 | 12/54 |
| max temp (°C/°F) | 25/77 | 22/72 | 15/59 | 13/56 | 17/63 | 22/72 |

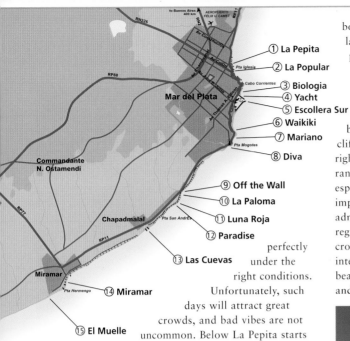

① La Pepita
② La Popular
③ Biologia
④ Yacht
⑤ Escollera Sur
⑥ Waikiki
⑦ Mariano
⑧ Diva
⑨ Off the Wall
⑩ La Paloma
⑪ Luna Roja
⑫ Paradise
⑬ Las Cuevas
⑭ Miramar
⑮ El Muelle

perfectly under the right conditions. Unfortunately, such days will attract great crowds, and bad vibes are not uncommon. Below La Pepita starts another bay where jetties mark the spots' limits. The most famous one is aptly named **La Popular** and local bodyboarders are all over these little hollow peaks. The next bay used to host the "Rincon-esque" Cabo Corrientes pointbreak, remembered as the best wave in Argentina, but one too many jetties have made it a thing of the past. North of the city's port, Playa Grande is renowned for its consistency and has several breaks where contests are regularly organised. Next to the northern pier, a regular current takes you to **Biologia**'s line-up. This left pointbreak works particularly well with a NE swell and will be offshore with summertime's frequent W/NW winds. Across the bay, **Yacht** is protected from winter's southern winds, which makes it possible to ride this long, classic right when most of the other spots are blown out. A sandbank regularly forms at the entrance of the port, creating a wave going right from the **Escollera Sur** (south breakwater). Because swells hit there with full force, it's one of the best spots to ride big waves in the country. Seals hang out around here and like to follow surfers as they ride. Sitting south of the port, **Waikiki** deserves to be mentioned as it hosted the first Argentinean surf session back in 1963. The place was known as Kikiway back then and the surf club bearing that name still exists today. It's not an impressive wave, but is still the best place for beginners or longboarders looking for a small but fun right. On the other side of Punta Cantera, **Mariano** is quite the opposite, a powerful and barrelling reefbreak only tackled by expert surfers and

La Popular

bodyboarders. Just as tubular and only ridden with the largest swell, **Diva** is a queen of the coast when it reels perfectly in front of the lighthouse. The sections, named Maquinita and Horizonte, can be considered waves of their own and served as the contest site for the 1999 Pan-American games. South of Mar del Plata the coast bends to face the SE and therefore has better exposure to S swells. Requiring a walk down the cliff and a long paddle, **Off the Wall** is a treacherous right breaking over a flat rock. These super-fast barrels ranging between 6-12ft (2-4m) usually find few takers, especially as the high tide makes entry and exit virtually impossible. **La Paloma**, the next break south, is equally admirable and excellent, where tubing rights break on a regular basis but more challenging access keeps the crowds down. Comparatively the next spots lack intensity, but **Luna Roja** is a consistent lefthander beside a beautiful beach and **Paradise**'s pointbreak rights are long and hollow. Both spots break over rock bottoms and will

Playa Grande

have tubing waves with NW winds. The only city of any size between Mar de Plata and Miramar, Chapadmalal, is home to **Las Cuevas**, which includes a decent left reef, a nice but shallow right and good beachbreak peaks in between. Like Mar del Plata, **Miramar** has been inundated with jetties, resulting in plenty of beachbreak options. It also has a proper pier, which accounts for the long rights of **El Muelle**. This wave will accommodate large S swells without closing out.

Most of the swell comes from Roaring Forties wintertime depressions that send 3-12ft (1-4m) of swell before tracking east towards Africa. In the summer, constant NE winds will send smaller and inconsistent windswells between November and February. Summer dominant NE winds typically blow offshore in the morning before shifting onshore between 12-5pm. NW winds dominate in autumn before SE takes over in September/October. The indented shape of the coast and the numerous jetties help shelter from strong winds, but as a rule the best sessions occur when the winds go back to blowing offshore after the howling SE'er that sent the swell. Tides should be watched closely as they can make quite a difference on certain breaks.

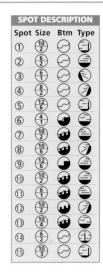

| SPOT DESCRIPTION | | | |
|---|---|---|---|
| Spot | Size | Btm | Type |
| ① | 10/2 | | |
| ② | 6/2 | | |
| ③ | 6/1 | | |
| ④ | 8/2 | | |
| ⑤ | 12/2 | | |
| ⑥ | 4/1 | | |
| ⑦ | 10/2 | | |
| ⑧ | 10/6 | | |
| ⑨ | 12/4 | | |
| ⑩ | 10/2 | | |
| ⑪ | 6/1 | | |
| ⑫ | 10/2 | | |
| ⑬ | 10/4 | | |
| ⑭ | 6/2 | | |
| ⑮ | 10/3 | | |

| SURF STATISTICS | J F | M A | M J | J A | S O | N D |
|---|---|---|---|---|---|---|
| dominant swell | SE-S | S-E | S-E | S-E | S-E | SE-S |
| swell size (ft) | 2-3 | 3 | 4 | 4-5 | 4 | 2-3 |
| consistency (%) | 50 | 60 | 70 | 75 | 70 | 60 |
| dominant wind | N-NE | SE-NE | W-N | SW-N | NE-S | N-E |
| average force | F4 | F3-F4 | F4 | F4 | F4 | F4 |
| consistency (%) | 38 | 43 | 50 | 58 | 56 | 48 |
| water temp (°C/°F) | 18/64 | 17/63 | 12/54 | 9/48 | 10/50 | 15/59 |
| wetsuit | | | | | | |

# 158. Rio de Janeiro

Barra de Tijuca

JOHN CALLAHAN

### Summary

+ BRAZIL'S BEST BEACHBREAKS
+ CONSISTENT YEAR-ROUND
+ DRIER WINTER TIME
+ BUZIOS/CABO FRIO OPTIONS
+ RIO ACCESS AND SERVICES

– LACK OF POINTS AND REEFS
– RARE EPIC CONDITIONS
– ULTRA-CROWDED MAIN SPOTS
– HIGH STREET CRIME RATE

Rio's physical features are dominated by the Sierra do Mar mountain range, which is cloaked by the Mata Atlantica forest. Mountains plunge into the sea, forests meet the beaches and cliff faces rise abruptly from the extended lowlands. This combination forms the landscape of rare beauty that has made Rio famous as the Wonderful City – 'Cidade Maravilhosa'. It's one of the most densely populated places on earth, with seven million "Cariocas" indulging in dancing, drinking, beach-going and sunbathing. The low coastline has been deeply altered by years of earthwork and has several offshore islands in the background.

Ipanema Beach

DON BALCH

Saquarema

FÁBIO MINDUIM

To the west of Rio is a region with a concentration of high-class hotels and condos and from **Barra da Tijuca**, a magnificent beach extends along Avenida Semambetiba up to Recreio. Further west is the cove at Prainha, which has epitomised the Brazilian surf experience for decades

## TRAVEL INFORMATION

**Population:** 15M
**Coastline:** 636km (397mi)
**Contests:** WCT Itauna (Oct)
**Other Resources:**
waves.terra.com.br
surfreporter.
  cidadeinternet.com.br
riodejaneiro-
turismo.com.br/pt
riodejaneiroturismo.tur.br/
  english/index.htm

**Getting There** – No visa up to 90 days. Most int'l flights hit Rio's Galeão airport (GIG) or São Paulo, 6h drive. Shuttle flights to São Paulo leave from Santos Dumont airport. National Varig/Vasp usually charge ±$30 for boards. Domestic flights are expensive, better use 'leite' (deluxe bus) for long distance. Buzios is only 3h away by road. Dep tax: $7.

**Getting Around** – Rent a car from Locabarra in Tijuca and pay $135/week. Driving in Rio is a hassle and dangerous; in some areas, car doors should be kept locked. Head for the 'Rodoviaria' and use 'leite', comfortable executive buses, which leave late at night for long destinations. Boards are free. Saquarema: 2h ($5), Buzios: 3h ($9). Good road network.

**Lodging and Food** – Be like Lola and spend a while around Copacabana where most int'l hotels are located, like Edificio Jucati ($30/dble). Try Pousada Barra Sol for $20/25 in Tijuca. In Saquarema, Itauna Inn 'Casal' (double) for $22/27 with ideal surf views. Plenty of Pousadas in Buzios, try Sossego surf camp ($15-20). Expect tasty Prato do dia to cost ±$3.

**Weather** – Rio is tropical, warm and humid, with local variations due to differences in altitude, vegetation and proximity to the ocean, the average annual temp is 22°C (72°F), with daily averages higher in summer from 30-32°C (86-90°F); rains vary from an annual 1,200 to 2,800mm (48-110in). It can also be dreadfully humid; there are more showers in summer than at other times, but they rarely last long. From December to March, the high summer season, very hot days are followed by luminous evenings when heavy and rapid rains usually bring relief and starlit nights. Most surfers tend to come in winter; take a shorty for the morning windy days but boardshorts rule this coast!

**Nature and Culture** – The beach in Rio is the main place to go for action, sport, parties, shows...Futvolei is big! Don't miss Pão de Azucar (1120ft/400m) or Corcovado Cristo Redentor (1988ft/710m) for sunset views of the city from a cable car. Pillion flights with a pilot hang/para-gliding off the 510m Pedra Bonita can be arranged. Excellent hiking and climbing.

**Hazards and Hassles** – Surfing is popular around Rio so expect thick crowds at any urban spot any time, look for long beaches with hiking access for hassle-free line-ups. Other sea hazards are rare, aside from pollution. Drug abuse and violence litter the streets and crime rate is very high. Avoid strolling in favelas (shantytowns), Rocinha, being the largest one.

**Handy Hints** – Get boards in Rio. They are cheap ($150-200, shortboard) and good quality. Shapers: Lelot, André Cebola, Akio. Shops: Mercomundi in Gavea, Gaya Surf or Stomp. Gun use is unlikely, hire one if need be. Few surf schools: Escola de Surf Rico (Ipanema, Barra) or ES Paulo Dolabella (Ipanema). Avoid Carnival time!

| WEATHER STATISTICS | J/F | M/A | M/J | J/A | S/O | N/D |
|---|---|---|---|---|---|---|
| total rainfall (mm) | 110 | 120 | 85 | 55 | 90 | 130 |
| consistency (days/mth) | 11 | 12 | 9 | 7 | 10 | 13 |
| min temp (°C/°F) | 23/74 | 22/72 | 20/68 | 19/66 | 20/68 | 22/72 |
| max temp (°C/°F) | 30/86 | 29/84 | 26/79 | 26/79 | 26/79 | 28/82 |

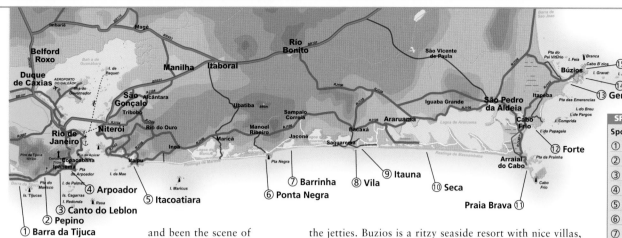

**SPOT DESCRIPTION**

| Spot | Size | Btm | Type |
|------|------|-----|------|
| ① | 6/1 | | |
| ② | 10/4 | | |
| ③ | 12/2 | | |
| ④ | 10/4 | | |
| ⑤ | 8/1 | | |
| ⑥ | 6/1 | | |
| ⑦ | 6/1 | | |
| ⑧ | 8/1 | | |
| ⑨ | 12/4 | | |
| ⑩ | 6/1 | | |
| ⑪ | 6/1 | | |
| ⑫ | 8/1 | | |
| ⑬ | 6/1 | | |
| ⑭ | 6/1 | | |
| ⑮ | 8/3 | | |

and been the scene of many contests. Restinga de Marambaia represents 40kms (25mi) of mostly off-limits beachbreaks because of military restrictions followed by Rio's westernmost surf located on Ilha Grande. One of Rio's great spots is **Pepino** where lefts can be tubular but frequently zooed out by bodyboarders in the water and lots of hang-gliders circling above. **Arpoador** is Brazil's surfing birthplace and usually entertains the best surf of the Zona Sul (South Side), easily recognised by its giant rock lookout. On medium to big E swells, lefts can reach 10ft (3m) and the best way to avoid thick crowds is to come surfing at night since the beach is lit. When the proper SW wind blows though, there's good surfing all the way from Ipanema to Leblon where the seaside strip is even more densely populated. **Canto do Leblon** is Rio's best wave, attracting big wave/tow-in riders when conditions allow, as beefy rights up to 12ft (4m) are sheltered from the W/SW winds at the pointbreak and there are beach peaks as well. The 4km (2.5mi) of Copacabana beach are known worldwide and although the surf is not all that good, boogies have found a square, Shark Island type right reef named Shorey or Expresso Escorpiao. Take the 14km (9mi) Niteroi bridge to cross the Bahia de Guanabara and reach **Itacoatiara** (Costão) where local hot surfers are all over the amazingly reliable beachbreaks including Meio and Pampo. Many travellers opt to head for Saquarema, stopping en route at **Ponta Negra**'s powerful beachbreak, best with easterly swell. If the swell increases and shifts to the SW, check nearby Jaconé's sheltered waves. Next along is **Barrinha**, polluted but consistent especially with a SW swell. Many Cariocas consider Saquarema to have the most consistent, quality waves in Brazil, with **Itauna** at the heart of it all. 10-12ft (3-4m) and clean is not that rare an occurrence. Overlooked by the Nazaré Church, built in 1630, the outside lefts can be reached through a channel. Inside rights sometimes referred to as the Expresso hold up to 6ft (2m) surf. **Vila**, aka Praia do Canto, on other side of Nazaré Hill is more urban and can also hold some size. Then, the Massambada Restinga stands out as another endless beach with myriads of potential peaks, best on S to E mid-size swells and N winds. Check as many access points as possible, like **Seca** about halfway down. **Praia Brava** sometimes holds long, perfect lefts in Arraial do Cabo, when NE winds clean an E swell. It's necessary to hike on the other side of Itajaru Canal and nudists pepper the wild beach. Cabo Frio, the 'cold cape', gets consistent surf by a 1616 built fort, thus called **Forte**. It's pretty urban so expect competitive crowds, especially by the jetties. Buzios is a ritzy seaside resort with nice villas, friendly pousadas and beautiful people. In the '70s, hippies would escape there from the military dictatorship. **Geriba** is Buzios' most consistent beachbreak, best on NE wind and S to E swell, but it gets super-crowded on weekends. Scenic **Brava** gets punchy on big E swell; beware the Laje do Criminoso currents. The outside reefbreaks of **Laje Rasa** are rare but the waves are quality on both sides. Be ready for a 30min paddle or get a boat out there.

The littoral 'carioca' is well exposed to the frequent S-SE Antarctica swells (April-Oct), providing 2-10ft (0.6-3m) conditions most of the time. Expect unusual late-winter E swells produced by lows tracking way off the coast or by major highs blowing strong E winds which send short ENE groundswells. Swells rarely get big which is convenient because few spots seem to hold size. Dominant wind comes from the E varying from 16% (June) to 32% (Oct); NE-SE is the usual direction while winters seem to produce more SW-S winds when cold fronts move towards the coast. Offshores only occur on calm mornings before 10am when the E seabreeze picks up or on SW spots with NE winds. The good news is that tidal range is really low and doesn't matter most of the time. Grab a 'tabua de mares' for better understanding.

**Nazaré Church, Saquarema**

TONY FLEURY

| SURF STATISTICS | J F | M A | M J | J A | S O | N D |
|-----------------|-----|-----|-----|-----|-----|-----|
| dominant swell | S-SE | S-SE | S-SE | S-SE | S-SE | S-SE |
| swell size (ft) | 2 | 2-3 | 3-4 | 4 | 3-4 | 2 |
| consistency (%) | 50 | 60 | 80 | 90 | 80 | 50 |
| dominant wind | N-E | NE-E | NE-E | NE-E | NE-E | NE-SE |
| average force | F3-F4 | F3-F4 | F3-F4 | F3-F4 | F4 | F3-F4 |
| consistency (%) | 67 | 46 | 39 | 48 | 47 | 60 |
| water temp (°C/°F) | 24/75 | 25/77 | 22/72 | 20/68 | 20/68 | 23/74 |
| wetsuit | | | | | | |

# 159. South Bahia

Jeribucacu

## Summary

+ CONSISTENT WINDSWELLS
+ EASY BEGINNER'S WAVES
+ BOCA DA BARRA LONG RIDES
+ LESS CROWDED HIKING SPOTS
+ ECO-FRIENDLY BRAZIL

− RARELY EPIC
− CROWDED MAIN BREAKS
− RAINY AUTUMN/WINTER
− DISTANT AIRPORTS
− LONG HIKES

Capoeira

The overwhelming image of Brazil is Carnival and Salvador de Bahia undoubtedly hosts the most intense one. Surfers in the mid '70s searching the coast from Salvador found out about Itacaré, lying 300km (188mi) south. It's the Bahia State capital, set amidst the Atlantic rainforest, where an abundance of juicy, warm water beachbreaks, reefbreaks and an amazingly long rivermouth right. Early travellers would have come across the surfing godfather "Old Joaquim", who befriended every surfer and told many tales under moonlight before Itacaré became a renowned backpacker town.

The highlight of Itacaré surf is **Boca da Barra**, a super-long, fun righthander that peels across a sandbank at the mouth of the River Contas. On a really big S swell, the first section 'Boca' links with **Pontal**'s hollow walls, resulting in a two minute

Corais

ride! Across the river are 6km (4mi) of exposed, deserted beachbreaks on fine sand backed by coconut trees, although Praia da Coroia suffers from pollution. Whilst Boca is a longboard paradise, hardcore shortboarders should head to the lighthouse next to **Corais**. These are

## TRAVEL INFORMATION

**Population:** 7,000 Itacaré
**Coastline:** 670km (419mi) South Bahia
**Contests:** Supersurf (Sept)
**Other Resources:**
Itacaresurf.com.br
easydrop.com
itacare.com
ilheusamado.com

**Getting There** – No visa. The closest airport is Ilhéus (IOS) only 70km (44mi) or 2h by bus from Itacaré. Most int'l flights hit Rio (GIG), São Paulo (GRU), or Salvador da Bahia (SSA). A r/t GIG - IOS starts at $250, if bought in Brazil. By bus, it takes 23h ($65). From SSA, it's 7h by 'nibus' Leito Executivo (bus) and costs $18. Even from SSA, it is necessary to go to IOS first.

**Getting Around** – A rental car isn't strictly necessary; use buses for long distance and local taxis. To get to the beaches, ask a 'pousada' for transport, rides cost $3-5. Easydrop, Lawrence's and Hawaii Aqui have 4WD jeeps. Walking through jungle to breaks means hiking shoes and backpacks are vital.

**Lodging and Food** – Three lodging areas: Tiririca, Caminho da Praia (Beachway) or in town. Easydrop (2 weeks package: $859) is the

main operator for beginners who stay in Pousada Belfort or Pousada Ilha Verde. Try Lawrence's Surf House, Hawaii Aqui or Sao José Eco resort ($120). Lots of natural food, a hot meat with beans, rice and salad is ±$4.

**Weather** – Bahia coastal weather is hot and humid, without a real dry season. The annual rainfall is over 1,500mm (63in), which is why rainforest (Mata Atlantica) is found on the coast. Despite regular rainfall, sunshine is plentiful varying from 12 days a month in July-August to 29 days in Dec-Jan. Air temps can reach 40°C (104°F) from December to March, but normally range from 32-38°C (90-101°F). Irregular heavy rain periods with temps between 25-30°C (77-86°F) characterise autumn from April to June. In winter, from June to September, Itacaré has temps around 26°C (79°F) and lots of rainfall, but even with windy days and rainfall, temperatures never fall below 15°C (59°F). Oct-Nov are the calmest months and the best period for uncrowded sessions. The water temp is warm varying between 23-30°C (74-86°F), but usually hovers around 25°C (77°F). Only take a shorty or vest for the coldest spells.

**Nature and Culture** – The Contas River is great for rafting. Outdoor sports like canoeing, ecobike, rappel or trekking are easy to do with specialised guides. Capoeira is big! September 9th-29th St Michael's Festivity is good. During New Year and Carnival, streets are filled with axl and beer, bands play all night long, while people dance and party hard.

**Hazards and Hassles** – While mosquitoes don't transmit malaria, there have been some dengue fever related cases. Beware the "beach-rats" – keep valuables hidden. Don't walk at night in cities like Ilheus or Bahia. Crowds occur at Tiririca and Corails but this shore is one of the less disputed in Brazil. High summer season is super-busy; avoid it.

**Handy Hints** – A longboard would be great for Boca da Barra and a gun unnecessary. Since boards in Brazil are cheap and good quality, buy one there. Kalay, Easydrop shaper, sells shortboards for $250 and longboards for $380. Boards, leash, wax and lycra shirts can be hired for $5/day. If not included, transfer services from the Ilheus to Itacaré cost $20.

| WEATHER STATISTICS | J/F | M/A | M/J | J/A | S/O | N/D |
|---|---|---|---|---|---|---|
| total rainfall (mm) | 160 | 270 | 190 | 150 | 110 | 170 |
| consistency (days/mth) | 9 | 14 | 11 | 10 | 6 | 9 |
| min temp (°C/°F) | 22/72 | 21/70 | 19/66 | 19/66 | 21/70 | 21/70 |
| max temp (°C/°F) | 30/86 | 29/84 | 28/82 | 26/79 | 28/82 | 29/84 |

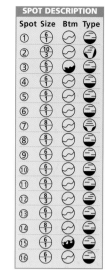

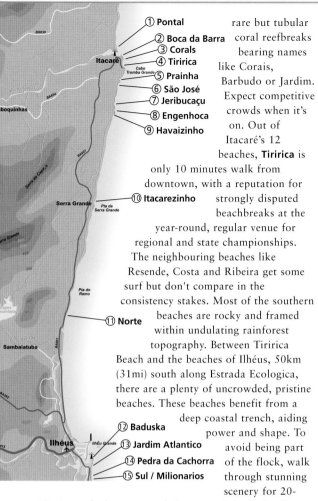

① Pontal
② Boca da Barra
③ Corals
④ Tiririca
⑤ Prainha
⑥ São José
⑦ Jeribuçacu
⑧ Engenhoca
⑨ Havaizinho
⑩ Itacarezinho
⑪ Norte
⑫ Baduska
⑬ Jardim Atlantico
⑭ Pedra da Cachorra
⑮ Sul / Milionarios

Tiririca

Engenhoca

| SPOT DESCRIPTION | | | |
|---|---|---|---|
| Spot | Size | Btm | Type |
| ① | 6/1 | | |
| ② | 10/3 | | |
| ③ | 6/3 | | |
| ④ | 6/1 | | |
| ⑤ | 6/1 | | |
| ⑥ | 6/1 | | |
| ⑦ | 6/1 | | |
| ⑧ | 6/1 | | |
| ⑨ | 6/1 | | |
| ⑩ | 6/1 | | |
| ⑪ | 6/1 | | |
| ⑫ | 6/3 | | |
| ⑬ | 6/1 | | |
| ⑭ | 6/1 | | |
| ⑮ | 6/1 | | |
| ⑯ | 6/1 | | |

rare but tubular coral reefbreaks bearing names like Corais, Barbudo or Jardim. Expect competitive crowds when it's on. Out of Itacaré's 12 beaches, **Tiririca** is only 10 minutes walk from downtown, with a reputation for strongly disputed beachbreaks at the year-round, regular venue for regional and state championships. The neighbouring beaches like Resende, Costa and Ribeira get some surf but don't compare in the consistency stakes. Most of the southern beaches are rocky and framed within undulating rainforest topography. Between Tiririca Beach and the beaches of Ilhéus, 50km (31mi) south along Estrada Ecologica, there are a plenty of uncrowded, pristine beaches. These beaches benefit from a deep coastal trench, aiding power and shape. To avoid being part of the flock, walk through stunning scenery for 20-40mins to find an uncrowded spot. **Prainha** is the closest example to Itacaré, a quality beachbreak plus a potential left pointbreak on the northern headland. Neighbouring **São José** is a slightly smaller beach, a further 10min walk away, keeping crowds lower. The beautiful **Jeribuçacu** rivermouth holds good left and right beachbreak peaks, but it's a 9km (6mi) drive followed by a 40min walk! It's a shorter walk to **Engenhoca**'s horseshoe-shaped beach, holding mainly lefts plus a rare pointbreak with a paddling channel whatever the swell size. **Havaizinho** has a set of 3 beaches, which are inconsistent but reveal some power amongst the many scattered rocks. Good lefts on low tide! Further south is **Itacarezinho**, a long beach with trenches inside and some coral reefs outside, which creates currents aplenty. A summertime longboard wave, it can be reached by 4WD. Ilheus' most consistent beach

is **Norte** stretching for 50km (30mi) of low tide barrels. There are several access points to the green waves as the road parallels the Rio Almada. With an 8ft (2.5m) plus swell, **Baduska** in town is one of the longest rights in Brazil. If the sections Baduska, Concha and Boca de Barra link, 1km rides are do-able. **Jardim Atlantico** hotel looks out over a hollow beachbreak. **Pedra da Cachorra** claims to be the most consistent beach in downtown Ilheus. Bigger swells create lefts that break behind the 'pedra' (rock). **Sul**, hosting contests at times, occasionally has powerful reefbreaks, but needs to be glassy. Check out **Milionarios Beach** luxury villas and beautiful people! Remember Olivenia down south is another great surfing hub with reefs and beaches!

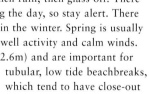

During the winter rainy season, it is rarely flat because of a constant windswell pushed by the E-SE trade winds. Most waves hover in the 2-6ft (0.6-2m) range, with better shape and power on the beachbreaks than most east facing states, thanks to deep trenches by the beach. The 6-8ft (2-2.6m) swells, which are necessary for the rivermouth rights, are pretty rare. Because most beaches are well sheltered by headlands, S-SE winds must be really strong to ruin the surf. In winter, rainy storms bring wind, then rain, then glass off. There can be several cycles during the day, so stay alert. There are more SE winds than E in the winter. Spring is usually the best time with decent swell activity and calm winds. Tidal range can reach 8ft (2.6m) and are important for tubular, low tide beachbreaks, which tend to have close-out sections. Get a tidal chart on the internet before going.

Cidade

| SURF STATISTICS | J F | M A | M J | J A | S O | N D |
|---|---|---|---|---|---|---|
| dominant swell | E-SE | E-SE | E-SE | E-SE | E-SE | E-SE |
| swell size (ft) | 1-2 | 2-3 | 3-4 | 4 | 3 | 1-2 |
| consistency (%) | 40 | 60 | 70 | 80 | 70 | 50 |
| dominant wind | NE-SE | NE-SE | E-SE | E-SE | NE-SE | NE-SE |
| average force | F3 | F3 | F3-F4 | F4 | F3-F4 | F3-F4 |
| consistency (%) | 94 | 92 | 82 | 86 | 93 | 92 |
| water temp (°C/°F) | 27/80 | 27/80 | 27/80 | 26/79 | 25/77 | 26/79 |
| wetsuit | | | | | | |

# 160. West Ceara

Icarai Point

FRANCIS CHAGAS

Titanzinho

CHAGAS

## Summary

+ TWO SOURCES OF SWELL
+ QUALITY HOLLOW WAVES
+ PUNCHY BEACHIES & RIGHT POINTS
+ EASY ACCESS, FORTALEZA FACILITIES
+ SUPERB BEACHES

– MOSTLY BLOWN-OUT IN SUMMER
– LACK OF SIZE
– INTENSE HEAT
– CROWDS AND POLLUTION
– BIG TIDAL VARIATION

The powerful waves discovered in Fernando do Noronha, show that Brazil also relies on a significant supply of North Atlantic winter swells, allowing a separate surf season on this north facing coast. Centred around Natal and Fortaleza, this coast also boasts the 'pororoca' on the river Amazon, regarded as the best tidal bore waves in the world. One of the most interesting aspects of the Ceara coast is its regularity, only broken by calm bays and narrow rivermouths. At the seashore, long sand dunes, coconut palms and shrubs litter the landscape. Fortaleza is known for having the wildest Monday nights in the world at the bars and restaurants of Praia Iracema, after spotting dolphins and watching the sunset from Ponte dos Ingleses. Further NW is Paracuru, a proper surf town with four main righthand pointbreaks that fire from

Paracura

TONY FLEURY

## TRAVEL INFORMATION

**Population:** 25,000 Paracura
**Coastline:** 573km (358mi)
**Contests:** Icarai (CBS) Junior (Apr)
**Other Resources:** surfreporter. cidadeinternet.com.br turismo.cegov.br ceara.com.br

**Getting There** – No Visa. Lots of direct flights to Fortaleza's (FOR) new airport from Europe (Tap, Alitalia) and Miami (AA). Most likely to land in Rio or São Paulo first. Domestic flights are expensive; Vasp or Nordeste is cheaper than Varig. Expect $350r/t. A leite bus is cheaper ($112o/w but 45h!). Dep tax: $36 (check if inc. in ticket).

**Getting Around** – There are many buses going to/from Paracuru ($2o/w), it takes 2h. Buggies can be rented in Paracuru to avoid sinking in sand dunes; $30/d. Some highways, at night, are dangerous: there are risks of assault but Fortaleza is way less dangerous than Rio.

**Lodging and Food** – Surf and high tourist season coincide. Favour pousadas for budget quality

lodges, prices have gone down thanks to the low Real exchange rates. In Fortaleza, try hotel Praia e Sol by Futuro or America do Sol ($22). In Icaraí, pousada Baiano, or Planalto Hotel. In Paracuru, try Pousada Villa Verde ($20) or Club Tropical hotel ($22). Expect $5 for a meal.

**Weather** – Ceara has a warm and relatively wet climate with a mean temp of 27°C (80°F), 77% humidity, and 1380mm (55in) of rain. The rest of Nordeste (NE Brazil) is composed of semi-arid regions with 500-800mm/year (20-32in). In the interior like Sobral, the rainy season occurs between January and June, but the main rainfall is March-April. Some years, rainfall is low causing drought and desertification in most semi-arid areas, the result of a vicious circle of overpopulation, poverty and exploitation of the natural resources. The Mata Atlantica (forest) of Ceara is shattered into relatively small 'islands' deep inland. During the surf season, it's hot and the sun is fierce. No need for a wetsuit but a rashie is essential for sun protection.

**Nature and Culture** – Paracuru 'Cidade alegre' is similar to Buzios, being a pleasant resort for wealthy Cearense & Brazilians. Carnival gets pretty big there, including Corridas de Buggy and sand surfing. Hit Jericoacoara if windsurfing and Quixad for hang-gliding. Carnauba Wax is exuded by the leaves of the Brazilian "Tree of Life".

**Hazards and Hassles** – Ceara is on the Equator; the sun is cruel. Bring high SPF sunblocks, the sun can be deceiving due to the cool ocean breezes. Street crime is much lower than the major urban parts of Brazil. Crowds and pollution can be appalling around Fortaleza but getting up early is often a safe bet.

**Handy Hints** – Boards in Brazil are super-cheap but light: FeC, Super Série, World Boards (shortboard for $250). Try the Bagus Board shop, Ocean Drive, Prancho, Bichinho, or World. Bodyboarding is big and longboarding's popularity is increasing. A board for hollow waves is required but not a gun. Chandler Surf runs a surf school.

| WEATHER STATISTICS | J/F | M/A | M/J | J/A | S/O | N/D |
|---|---|---|---|---|---|---|
| total rainfall (mm) | 160 | 330 | 160 | 30 | 10 | 25 |
| consistency (days/mth) | 7 | 12 | 5 | 1 | 1 | 1 |
| min temp (°C/°F) | 25/77 | 23/74 | 23/74 | 22/72 | 24/75 | 25/77 |
| max temp (°C/°F) | 31/88 | 30/86 | 30/86 | 30/86 | 31/88 | 31/88 |

**Icarai Point**

November to February. Jericoacoara, aka Jeri, 300kms (180mi) west of Fortaleza is an established stop for the travelling surfing community and remember Malhada beach has good waves as well!

Potentially the best right point on a northerly swell, **Boca Do Poço** offers very long rides on a pushing tide, when crowds are guaranteed. Right in town, **Ronco do Mar**'s hard breaking rights are dangerous when low tide exposes the rocky reef but it's consistent from mid tide up. Suited to longboarders, **Curral**, works on any tide and has long, fun walls. Last option for a right point is **Pedra do Meio**, only a few kms west, identified by big boulder rocks next to the take-off and it's somewhat sheltered position from E winds. If not much is happening on the points, try **Hawaiizinho**, which can fire on high tides, offering barrels similar to the Noronha beaches. **Outside**'s coral reef lefts near Petrobras Pier are shallow and shape up best with a N swell. **Tabinha** is a real swell magnet beachbreak, best on mid tide, and spreads out the crowds of Paracuru surfers who go there when it's on. There is major working harbour in **Pecém**, where the surf is notoriously inconsistent, even in a decent swell, leaving the outside lefts to the windsurfers. From Caucaia, hit the coast at **Icarai** for a taste of Ceara's most consistent and strongest beachbreaks. It's a regular WQS contest site and attracts intense crowds. Check by Casa Amarela Restaurant or at Cata-Vento. Fortaleza has many breaks but most of them are badly polluted and crowded, especially with bodyboards. **Barra do Ceara**'s polluted peaks are where Portuguese sailors first landed here in 1603.

**Leste Oeste**'s urban beachbreaks offer shelter from the pervading E winds and prefer low water. Jump from the old steel pier to ride **Ponte Metalica**'s quality reefbreak peaks. They're best with N swell and low tides; the E winds aren't a problem but the crowds and pollution are. The same detractors are found at **Portão**, the most reliable spot around. Along the bustling **Volta da Jurema** there are many beachbreaks like Praia do Nautico, Jacqueline, Apito, Icarema, Meireles and Diarios, all favouring lower tides. **Titanzinho**, next to the Muricipe terminal, is Fortaleza's most consistent right reefbreak. Currently under threat from harbour development, this spot sits in front of a huge favela and has crowds and localism. If not blown-out, **Praia do Futuro** with 5kms (3mi) of exposed beachbreaks has fewer crowds than Fortaleza. Just check the webcams as most of main Ceara surf spots are online!

There are two sources of swell. The best hit during the North Atlantic winter from October to March but due to the distance travelled, about 5000km (3125mi), it's safer to focus on the heart of the season, Nov-Feb. Although the shore faces NE, the best spots are the north facing breaks, better exposed to those long distance quality swells. Size varies from 2-8ft (0.6-2.5m), producing 4-6ft (1.2-2m) quality lines on the right pointbreaks. Swells usually last 2-3 days, being quite consistent during the season. Then, the E-SE trades start kicking in and produce mushy 2-5ft (0.6-1.5m) swell with predominantly onshore conditions, favouring steep NE facing beachbreaks like Taibinha, Icarai or Futuro. July-August has the strongest wind, often preferred by the windsurfing community. Avoid transitional months like March-April or September. Funnily enough, the wind tends to back off around noon and be stronger morning and evenings. The further west, the more dramatic the tidal range, reaching up to 10ft (3m). Get a tidal chart at the Bagus Board shop or print one from a website before leaving.

| SPOT DESCRIPTION | | | |
|---|---|---|---|
| Spot | Size | Btm | Type |
| ① | 6/2 | | |
| ② | 6/1 | | |
| ③ | 6/1 | | |
| ④ | 6/1 | | |
| ⑤ | 6/1 | | |
| ⑥ | 6/2 | | |
| ⑦ | 8/1 | | |
| ⑧ | 6/2 | | |
| ⑨ | 6/1 | | |
| ⑩ | 6/1 | | |
| ⑪ | 6/2 | | |
| ⑫ | 6/2 | | |
| ⑬ | 6/2 | | |
| ⑭ | 6/2 | | |
| ⑮ | 6/2 | | |
| ⑯ | 6/1 | | |

| SURF STATISTICS | J F | M A | M J | J A | S O | N D |
|---|---|---|---|---|---|---|
| dominant swell | N-NE | E-SE | E-SE | E-SE | E-SE | N-NE |
| swell size (ft) | 3-4 | 2-3 | 2 | 2-3 | 1-2 | 2-3 |
| consistency (%) | 70 | 60 | 50 | 80 | 50 | 70 |
| dominant wind | NE-SE | NE-SE | E-SE | E-SE | E-SE | E-SE |
| average force | F3-F4 | F3-F4 | F4 | F4-F5 | F4 | F4 |
| consistency (%) | 96 | 86 | 83 | 89 | 96 | 94 |
| water temp (°C/°F) | 27/80 | 27/80 | 27/80 | 26/79 | 26/79 | 26/79 |
| wetsuit | | | | | | |

**Taiba Point**

Ronco do Mar ②
Boca do Poço ①
③ Curral
④ Pedra do Meio
⑤ Hawaiizinho
⑥ Outside

Pta Aguda
Lagoinha
Paraipaba
Pta Paracuru
**Paracuru**

⑦ Taibinha
⑧ Praia do Pecém

Pta Taiba
**Taiba**
Pta Pecém
**Pecém**

⑩ Barra do Ceara
⑪ Leste Oeste
⑫ Ponte Metalica
⑬ Portão
⑭ Volta da Jurema
⑮ Titanzinho

**São Gonçalo do Amarante**
Coité
Cumbuco
⑨ Icarai

Croatá
BR222
Serra do Camar 381m
Pana Icarai
Iparana
Pta de Mucuripe
⑮ Praia do Futuro

**Caucaia**
**Fortaleza**
Aeroporto
Pinto Martins
Serra do Ju
648m

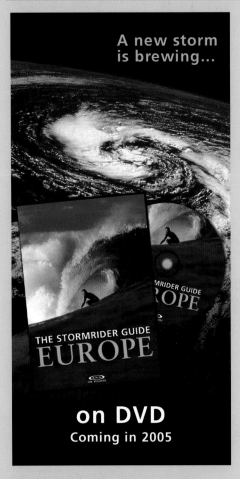

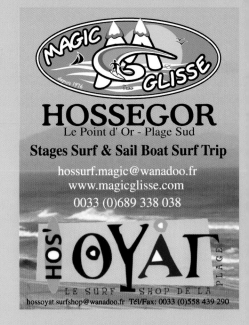
**ECOLE DE SURF DE GUÉTHARY – FRANCE**
Résidence Itsasoan, n° 11, 64210, Guéthary
Tel:  +33 (0)6 08 68 88 54      Fax: +33 (0) 559 54 81 78
surf.guethary@wanadoo.fr     http://surf.guethary.free.fr/

Surfcamp facing the famous spot of Parlementia in the village of Guéthary – Surfing lessons for all skill levels – Established 1996 Board & wetsuit rental – English spoken – Se habla espanol Accessories for sale – Open year round.

**GOOFYS' GUESTHOUSE – UK**
5 Headland Road, Newquay, Cornwall, TR7 1HW
Tel: +44 (0)1637 872684         Mobile: +44 (0)7968 293961
info@goofys.co.uk                www.goofys.co.uk

Warm, friendly guesthouse in the heart of Newquay. Secure board and wetsuit storage. Continental style breakfast eaten at your leisure. A perfect base to enjoy all Cornwall has to offer.

**ESCUELA CANTABRA DE SURF & BODYBOARD – SPAIN**
Surf School, Surf Shop, Surf Camp
Playa de Somo, Cantabria, SPAIN
Tel: +34 (942)510615         +34 609482823
ecsurf@escuelacantabradesurf.com
www.escuelacantabradesurf.com

The 1st surf school in Spain, born in 1991; considered as one of the most prestigious schools in Europe. Specialised teachers. Classes available for beginners and advanced surfers. Classes given in English. Surf Camp.

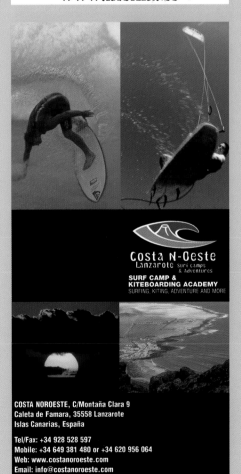

## DYNAMIC LOISIRS – MOROCCO

BP 6241 - Anza Agadir

Tel: + 212 48 31 46 55      Fax: + 212 48 31 46 54

dynamic10@iam.net.ma      www.surf-maroc.com

Surf camp / guest house with great food, surf school recognized by F.R.M.S.B., surf + wetsuit rental, surf training courses, private beach in Agadir, jet skis, quads, mountain bike rental, kite surf school, bivouac.

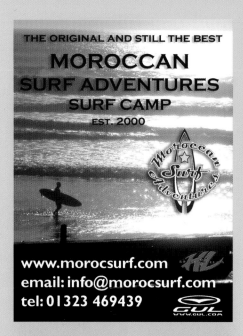

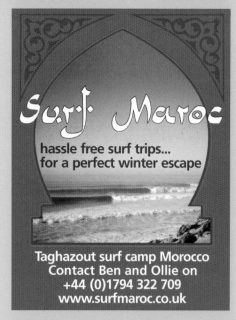

## DOLPHIN BAY SURF TOUR – SOUTH AFRICA

East London, SOUTH AFRICA

Tel: +27 (0)832934768

Fax: +27 43 7220592

stuart@sunshine-coast.co.za

www.sunshine-coast.co.za

Surf tours and accommodation. Stay at Blue Bend surf beach. Surf quality spots on the Sunshine Coast. Lessons available. Extension to J-Bay, Transkaii. Free East London airport pick-up. Two shapers next door. Check with Julie and Stuart. Group discounts.

## ISLAND VIBE BACKPACKERS – SOUTH AFRICA

10 Dageraad Street 6330, Jeffrey's Bay

Tel: +27 42 2931625      Fax: +27 42 2932586

Mobile: 27 83 4635922

ivibe@lantic.net      www.islandvibe.co.za

The ultimate surf side accommodation. Epic uncrowded surf on our doorstep, budget surfaris, board and wetsuit rentals. Camping, dorms and en-suite doubles. Swap surf stories and travel tales in our laid back bar.

## THE BEACH HOUSE – SOUTH AFRICA

Supertubes, Jeffrey's Bay

Tel/Fax: +27 42 293 1522      Mobile: +27 (0) 823 202 904

thebeachhouse@mweb.co.za

Live right on the line-up at Supertubes. Budget to upmarket catered for. All travel info on surfing. Tours. Game drives. Surf lessons and board hire. Contact Andrew Carter – Surfer/Owner.

## MADA SURFARI TRAVEL AND TOURS – MADAGASCAR

Fred Ralaimihoatra, PO Box 8323, 101 Antananarivo

T/F: +261 (0) 20 22 301 40    Mobile: +261 (0) 32 02 411 76

infos@mada-surfari.com      www.mada-surfari.com

Discover and surf Madagascar: East coast surf camp; surf charter boats; 4WD and desert truck rental; eco-tourism. International and domestic flights. We speak English, French, Malagasy. Talk to Fred.

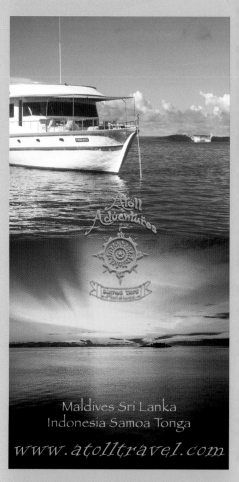

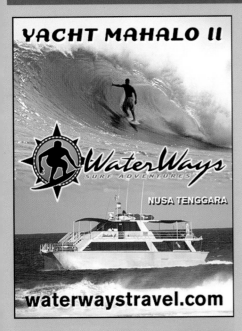

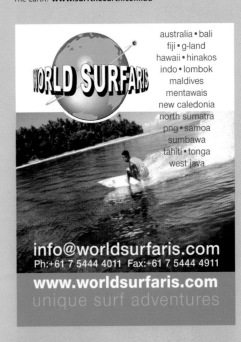

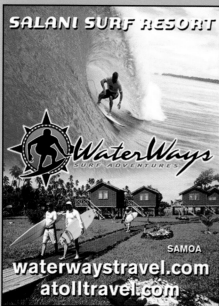
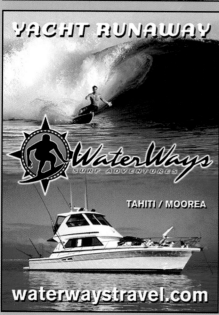
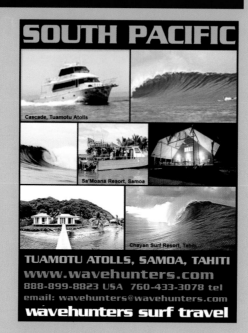
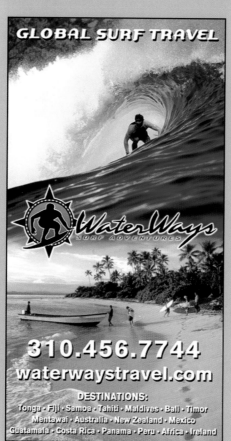

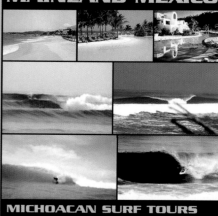

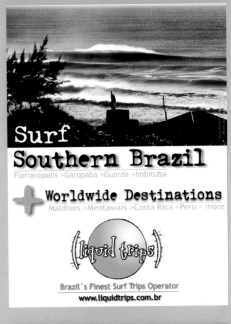
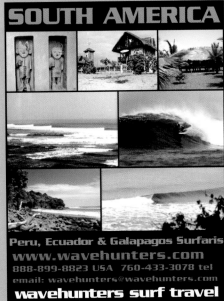

EUROPEAN
SURF IS
BOOMING

Aritz Aramburu
Hardcore surf
Hawaii

PUKAS

HEXCEL    The strength within™

# Spot Index with Zone Numbers

# World Guide series

## If you don't go,

# Continental Guide series

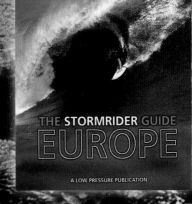